AMERICAN HISTORY

1600 TO THE PRESENT

SOURCE READINGS

AMERICAN HISTORY

1600 TO THE PRESENT

SOURCE READINGS

Edited by

NEIL HARRIS · DAVID J. ROTHMAN · STEPHAN THERNSTROM

Harvard University　　　*Columbia University*　　　*Brandeis University*

HOLT, RINEHART AND WINSTON, INC.

New York　Chicago　San Francisco　Atlanta　Dallas　Montreal　Toronto　London　Sydney

Design by Arthur D. Ritter

Preface

This collection is an instrument that will aid the user in understanding the history of the United States. It is designed to bring to life the people and events of the past. History should not be a dry chronicle of names and dates; it deals with characters as real as those of whom we read in the daily newspaper. The documents here assembled will bring the reader close to the figures of earlier eras and thus help explain the evolution of the American nation.

It takes an effort of the imagination to understand that the strange costumes of seventeenth- and eighteenth-century portraits clothed living human beings. Through the curious antique lanes of old towns and through the forest clearings of the wilderness, moved men and women whose emotions, ambitions, and ideas were not exactly the same as our own but also not entirely discontinuous with ours. The student of history must try to comprehend these people, different though they were. Fortunately he can do so through the written material they left behind. The collection that follows has arranged such materials so as to illuminate the development of the Americans through their whole history.

The aim of making these records of the past interesting and understandable dictated the standards of selection as well as the organization of this volume. The editors wished each document to speak directly to the students who will read it. Each selection treats an important subject in a way that will attract and hold the attention of twentieth-century young people who are not themselves historians. Furthermore each item drawn into the collection is long enough so that the student, once immersed in it, can learn something not only of the subject concerned, but also of the language and style and therefore of the way of thinking of the era represented.

The collection is unique in the range of materials represented. The selections touch on all the important aspects of the history of the United States, economic, social and intellectual, as well as political. Each document is presented in a form full enough to convey its own flavor; yet each also fits into a coherent pattern which, taken as a whole, provides a vivid introduction to the American past.

Historians refer to sources such as are here assembled as primary. By this they mean that the books or manuscripts from which the selections are drawn are first-hand or eyewitness accounts, printed or written at about the same time as the events with which they deal. Such material is always valuable as evidence of something. But these written survivals from the past fall into several categories, which the reader must understand if he is to make effective use of them.

Some primary sources are produced in the course of contemporary transactions. The people who wrote them intended such documents to serve only specific purpose. A bill of sale or a contract, for instance, completed a business deal, and no one considered the possibility that it might some day prove useful to a historian. Such records consequently are reliable; they are just what they say they are, although what they mean must be explained by interpretation. Among other sources of this sort on which historians depend are acts of legislation and decisions of courts, the journals of legislatures and conventions, and petitions to such bodies about important issues of the times.

Even more useful are materials produced without conscious guile in the normal course of some transaction. Farmers and businessmen keep records for their own use and therefore try to be as accurate as possible. These records are evidence of how such enterprises really operated. By the same token, letters written for a specific purpose reveal the political concerns of the writers or describe military or domestic events.

Still another kind of primary material is that recorded by participants and observers with some conscious purpose. The reasons why each document was written must therefore be understood, for that may have influenced its contents. Yet the account may nonetheless be valuable. Among such records are journals and diaries, set down from direct observation, as well as the narratives of settlers and travelers. Contemporary histories are usually even more interpretive, for their authors generally wish to make some point that will persuade future readers. More often than not, too, there is some purpose behind the writing of an autobiography. As a man looks back over his life, he wishes to set down the facts, but also to justify his past actions or to draw a moral from them; and he may not be able to separate the two aspects of his writing. The same caution applies to newspaper accounts. Reporters have a professional purpose in chronicling the news, yet their views may well color their stories.

Some contemporary documents, of course, are clearly and explicitly cases of argument or pleading. The authors intend to make a case and select and organize the facts accordingly. The value of these materials lies less in the facts they detail than in the ideas they express. American history is rich in tracts of this sort, whether published originally as pamphlets or as articles in periodicals. Whether the argument is presented with restraint or with fanatical zeal, its importance for the student lies in the view it offers of the thinking of its author.

Other forms of persuasion are also common. Newspaper editorials directly express opinions and thus reflect the ideas of their writers and of their readers. Orations and sermons were long the most familiar means of persuasion; they remain important because they often held the close attention of Americans.

In a quite different category are the unconscious expressions of attitudes and ideas that appear in popular and formal literature. A story, a poem, or a play often reveals the underlying beliefs of people, particularly when written without artifice. Satires and campaign songs thus convey a good deal of information about current political practices, for they show what symbols and concepts aroused popular enthusiasm or mockery.

In arranging their selections from the great variety of primary sources in American history, the editors have held in view the needs of the students who will use this collection. They have held to the highest standards of accurate scholarship. But in the interest of clarity and readability they have modernized antique spellings and punctuation, and they have omitted ellipses from certain passages. Without in the least altering the meaning of the originals, they have sought to make these documents completely accessible to the modern student. The result will enrich the understanding of the American past.

Cambridge, Massachusetts　　　　　　　　Oscar Handlin
February 1969

Contents

PART TWO
Independence, 1754–1820

Introduction

PART FIVE
The Quest for Order, 1890–1929

PART SIX
The World in Conflict, 1929–1968

AMERICAN HISTORY

1600 TO THE PRESENT
SOURCE READINGS

PART ONE

The Colonial Heritage, 1600–1754

The movement of Europeans to North America, which was merely a trickle in the sixteenth century, dramatically increased in the years following 1600. Many motives drove men to abandon their familiar surroundings and challenge an unknown wilderness. Desperation about the old order mingled with hope for the new. Economic dislocation, religious persecution, political uncertainty, and social confusion helped push many Englishmen away from their native country.

It would be wrong to see the great migration as evidence of weakness and instability alone. The men who provided leadership were often vigorous and optimistic entrepreneurs, able to construct dreams of success that dazzled their followers. Some of them claimed to have discovered an earthly paradise in America, where men could grow wealthy and secure with a minimum of hard work. If there was no gold or silver such as the Spanish found in Mexico and Peru, there was at least the promise of raising valuable commodities—silk, tropical fruits, tobacco, hemp—which would add to the wealth and glory of the mother country. Agriculture and commerce seemed destined to thrive.

Other leaders saw the promise not in natural resources but in emptiness, a spatial void that could be filled by religious and social experiments. Fulfillment would not come from material prosperity itself but through creation of a holy community that could carry out the cosmic work of redemption by establishing a model for the entire world to behold and imitate. A sense of urgency, of energetic and enthusiastic faith, pervaded the exhortations of religious independents who helped establish the New England colonies.

Whether it was economic desire or religious mission that inspired the early settlers, they faced taxing physical and social adjustments. No expectation adequately described the new reality. In Virginia the promised prosperity was slow in coming. Dangers of climate, of Indians, and of dissension threatened to destroy the community before it got under way, while constant supplies of new men and more money were necessary to keep life going until a staple crop could be discovered. It became necessary to tinker with old institutions, to attempt novel kinds of regulations, rewards, and punishments before an effective social order could be established. When tobacco appeared to be the path to riches, the population dispersed, seeking more of the apparently unlimited land on which to grow their crop. A system of administration and social differentiation not very unlike England's began to develop, but there were important differences. Virginia's scattered people lacked towns and easy methods of communication. On their borders were hostile Indians who resented the rapid spread of this new empire, and several times massacred the outnumbered settlers. The colony's great men were often new to their wealth and distinction, and had to learn all at once those methods of absorbing deference that English squires had been practicing for generations.

The New Englanders were better prepared to meet hardship. Not only were their migrations larger and better organized than those of the individual travelers who made their way to the Chesapeake area, but their theology helped make explicable the trials they faced. No calamity or disaster was allowed to pass unnoticed, and even the most casual events of daily life bore religious implications. As a result of New England's communal objectives, its population dispersal was different from the Chesapeake diffusion. Because of the need for church congregations to serve as the basis for social organization, New Englanders moved in groups, and received their land as townships, not as individuals. The town's control of land emphasized the power of local institutions in America. New England selectmen (like Virginia justices of the peace) were men of influence, their power resting not on the dignity and strength of colonial government, but on their status among their neighbors.

The success of English colonization contrasted with the attempts of other European states to settle portions of America. For a time groups of Swedes and Dutch gathered at the mouths of rivers along the Middle Atlantic coast. New Amsterdam particularly was an ambitious attempt by a Dutch trading company to establish a permanent outpost on the North American mainland. Because of inadequate support and overactive supervision, New Amsterdam's growth was slow, and the Dutch settlements were absorbed by the more active English.

The failure of the Dutch governing class pointed up the gifts of the English leaders. Survival in the wilderness rested on the ability to solve many kinds of problems quickly and equitably, and maintain, at the same time, the community's social unity. Puritan Massachusetts owed a great deal to its governor, John Winthrop, who faced political jealousies, religious schisms, Indian attacks, economic inflation, and social deviance, among other dilemmas. Winthrop's personal gifts, however, did

2

not produce undue dependence on one man. A number of other colonies also received enlightened leadership in their early years, but everywhere representative institutions were crucial. Under conditions of permanent emergency the English settlers did not yield to the efficiency of dictatorship in order to satisfy immediate wants as did some other European colonists. Local institutions—town meetings, church vestries—and provincial assemblies shared in the exercise of power, and thus involved large portions of the population in major decisions.

To a large extent, major decisions were made, not at the seat of empire, in Westminster, but in the small, scattered seaboard settlements. In the middle of the seventeenth century England was undergoing the agonies of civil war and regicide. Within the space of twenty years a monarch was executed, a commonwealth established, and another king crowned. It was impossible for civil servants and administrators to impose their concepts of order on their countrymen overseas, and what political turmoil helped establish, barriers of time and distance perpetuated. The ocean was wide; travel and communication were infrequent and unpredictable. The settlers were insulated and isolated by geography, and forced upon their own resources. It was not surprising then, that the steady growth of their settlements by midcentury produced some self-confidence in their political skills, and a feeling that God and historical necessity were uniting to make America a future seat of empire. When they compared their own situation with the lot of their countrymen in the Old World, the settlers felt pleased. Puritans beheld in Boston a bustling metropolis with churches, docks, schools, and commerce where three decades earlier had been only wilderness and savages. Virginia boosters did not have to look to the future as did the authors of promotional literature before the 1620s in order to demonstrate the country's bounty. In almost every material item—diet, dress, recreation, health—the common man of America seemed to hold the advantage over the farmers and workers of seventeenth-century England.

This prosperity, moreover, did not seem purchased at the cost of order and tradition. Though in retrospect the English colonies can be seen developing in novel directions, the early settlers still thought in European terms about the structure and safety of their communities. Hierarchy, rank, servitude, deference, obedience to authority, piety, and prayer were not discarded as unnecessary relics. The outposts of empire were not intended to refute or challenge social arrangements at home, but to purify and re-create them. Unhampered by corruption or tyrannical authority, undamaged by destitution and physical poverty, facing the opportunity to convert the heathen natives and increase and multiply according to the Biblical command, the colonists sought to imitate rather than to innovate. In family life, in education, in religion, in morals, their aims were conservative and traditional. That their effectiveness and appropriateness were lessening, went largely unnoticed before 1660. America was a new world, and they had succeeded in making a first, initial conquest. They had developed from company settlements to political societies. This was impressive enough for forty years. The deeper changes would become clear only afterward.

But over the next century something approaching a distinctive life style began to appear in America. There was no easy unity to this pattern, for the colonies

3

differed dramatically among themselves, and even within themselves. New England was becoming famous for its commerce and shipbuilding, its enterprising merchants seizing every opportunity to exploit new routes of trade, but concentrating particularly on the West Indies with their great sugar exports, and on Africa, whose human cargoes of Negro slaves were brought to work the Caribbean and Southern plantations. Cities like Newport and Boston began to acquire the urban character of cosmopolitan life, although the bulk of New England's population was engaged in agriculture, living in small towns and villages.

To the south of New England lay the middle colonies of New York, New Jersey, and Pennsylvania whose ethnic and religious heritage was quite different. Dutch influences survived in New York long after the weakened West Indies Company was forced to succumb to English expansion. New York City, still lagging in population growth, had nonetheless begun to exploit its superb harbor and its river passage to upper New York and the settlement at Albany. Its merchants, farmers, and fur traders were beginning to give the New Englanders lively competition.

In Pennsylvania, where trade and farming had at least equal opportunities, attention centered on the religious and political innovations of Quakerism. William Penn's colony was certainly the most benevolent proprietorship in North America, its founder insisting on standards of religious tolerance and compassion for the Indians, which were unprecedented in the New World. The city of Philadelphia, with its grid pattern lying between the waters of the Schuylkill and the Delaware, would develop into the most famous city in British North America, and one of the largest in the British Empire, by 1750. Its greatest figure, Benjamin Franklin, pioneered in the establishment of municipal conveniences like fire fighting and care for the sick, and his program of cooperative benevolence would attract interest and support from many other parts of the colonies.

Virginia, the Carolinas, and Georgia, which was founded by James Oglethorpe and his associates as a refuge for imprisoned debtors, possessed fewer towns of importance than their northern neighbors. Their populations had become divided into two distinct and contrasting portions: slave and free. Although many Southerners were suspicious about the legitimacy and future effects of Negro slavery, and some even tried to prohibit the institution by law, the economic advantages of involuntary labor on the growing tobacco, rice, and sugar plantations proved too attractive. The indentured servants, who at one time found the Chesapeake area hospitable to small farming and increasing incomes, were forced to compete with this new labor force, and many of the small farmers went northward to Pennsylvania.

America had begun to attract travelers. Roads were still very poor and communication difficult, but a network of transportation and information exchanges was developing. Wealth in planting or commerce allowed the construction of comfortable and fashionable houses in some parts of the colonies, while cities like Charleston, Boston, and Newport were centers of varied social entertainments. Travelers noted the differences among the various provinces, in religion, language, occupation, and politics, but they could have noted similarities as well.

Provincial Americans shared many experiences, not the least of which was their dependent status upon the British Government. With the Glorious Revolution of 1688, the Protestant succession ended the dangers of Catholic monarchy, and the government at home acquired new direction and vigor. But the instabilities and disorders of the 1670s and 1680s in England were matched by the series of conflicts and insurrections in America. New York, Massachusetts, and Virginia were plagued by the most memorable disorders. Although the issues were frequently confused and local, they all bore on the problem of administering political order while the real source of power was thousands of miles away. In the eighteenth century royal governors found their task increasingly difficult, as colonial assemblies gained assurance and political skill, and demanded more important roles for themselves. The colonies also began to discover special interests, particularly in trading and currency regulations, which put them in opposition to the needs of the home government. Administrators, even the most talented, were hard pressed to satisfy both British officials and powerful local magnates whose antagonism to government could paralyze the programs and shrink the patronage of the British ministers.

A more constructive bond of union was religion. Although the colonies contained a number of religious minorities, including some Catholics and Jews, the vast bulk of the population was Protestant, and often aggressively so. In the late seventeenth century vestiges of the faith in their religious destiny, which had inspired the first Pilgrims and Puritans, lingered on in New England. Theology still provided a filter through which experience could be drawn, and the Salem witch trials of 1691 were a revelation of just how deep and persistent were older ways of viewing reality.

But the witch trials were a late expression, perhaps even a final one, of the old world view. Several prominent Puritans involved repudiated their actions and made public confessions to atone for their guilt. More and more, in the early eighteenth century, the colonists turned their attention to economic matters. The growth of towns, the increase of shipping, and the development of small manufacturing presented fertile fields to imaginative speculators who could overcome religious scruples in pursuing economic goals, even to the point of practicing deceit. In the first years of the eighteenth century many bemoaned the lack of religious fervor in America as an indication of degeneration since the heroic days of the founders.

The religious impulse was far from dead, however; its focus merely shifted. Where once men had followed deferentially the teachings of their ministers and religious leaders, they now demanded more intense personal experiences. Instead of a highly intellectualized theological preaching, they began to respond to more emotional and even theatrical sermons, searching for salvation in an aggressive, occasionally violent, fashion. The revivals, which attracted some attention in the 1720s, spread gradually, until by the 1740s with the visit of the noted British evangelist, George Whitefield, they were surging through all the colonies. The issues of the Great Awakening—itinerant preaching, lay participation, emotional conversions—divided the older churches into battling sects and splintered established denominations into separate and antagonistic groups. By moving over so large an area, however, and involving so many groups of people, the Awakening established

5

new and less tangible bonds of union among the Protestants scattered along the seaboard and helped prepare them for the democratic nationalism just thirty years away.

Another factor emphasizing religious unity was the presence of French power, to the north and west of the English colonies. Until their defeat in the Seven Years' War, the French posed a threat to the physical and spiritual security of the colonists. Since the end of the seventeenth century a staple of colonial literature had been the captivity narrative, detailed and sometimes horrifying descriptions of life spent among the heathen Indians or the Papist French. The Indians practiced physical torture; the French inflicted religious torment. The presence of these perceived dangers made the colonists more aware of the power of British arms, and sustained their loyalties to the distant crown. But when the danger was diminished, after midcentury, there would come more severe tests of their loyalty.

A final bond of union was less physical or religious than intellectual. In communication with the European intellectual world, Americans had begun, by the middle of the eighteenth century, to receive some of the invigorating ideas which were part of the intellectual excitement known as the Enlightenment. Combining foreign inspiration with a native heritage, civic philosophers like Benjamin Franklin utilized the new newspapers and the growing printing industry to disseminate plans of benevolence throughout the distant colonies. With the immediate physical tasks apparently accomplished, there was time to consider the demands of mind and manners. Having conquered the wilderness, Americans were now searching for ways to express their position in the world. Aggressive merchants, ambitious lawyers and administrators, enterprising artisans, and industrious scholars were beginning to yearn for a larger theatre of action. By 1750, these outposts of empire had acquired distinctive economic goals and were beginning to discover the meaning of their colonizing experience. The era of the Revolution lay just ahead.

1

Daily Life in Massachusetts

John Winthrop (1588–1649) was the major figure among the first generation of New England Puritans. An attorney and country squire in England, Winthrop was elected Governor of the settlement in 1629, while still in England, and for many of the next twenty years he served as the chief executive of Massachusetts Bay. In a few famous speeches he evocatively presented some of the basic hopes and expectations of the founding Puritans, their ideas of order, of rank, of community, and of religious obligation. On board the *Arbella* just before beginning the great experiment, Winthrop sought to sketch his dream of a holy city, testimony to the glory of God, and a lesson to the world of man.

If *A Modell of Christian Charity* reveals something of Puritan theory, Winthrop's careful *Journal* tells us much about Puritan practice and daily experience. Details of religion, government, housing, warfare, criminal justice, and family life are mingled together, a picture of the frustrations and satisfactions yielded by existence in the Bay Colony, and a testament to Winthrop's gifts of mind and character.

A MODELL OF CHRISTIAN CHARITY
John Winthrop

Written on board the Arbella, *on the Atlantic Ocean*
Anno 1630

God almighty in his most holy and wise providence hath so disposed of the condition of mankind, as in all times some must be rich, some poor, some high and eminent in power and dignity, others mean and in subjection.

Reason: First, to hold conformity with the rest of his works, being delighted to show forth the glory of his wisdom in the variety and difference of the creatures and the glory of his power, in ordering all these differences for the preservation and good of the whole. And the glory of his greatness that as it is the glory of princes to have many officers, so this great King will have many stewards counting himself more

From John Winthrop, *A Modell of Christian Charity, Winthrop Papers* (Boston, 1931). II: 282–283, 294–295. Reprinted by permission of the Massachusetts Historical Society.

honored in dispensing his gifts to man by man, than if he did it by his own immediate hand.

Reason: Secondly, that he might have the more occasion to manifest the work of his spirit. First, upon the wicked in moderating and restraining them, so that the rich and mighty should not eat up the poor, nor the poor and despised rise up against their superiors and shake off their yoke. Secondly, in the regenerate in exercising his graces in them, as in the great ones, their love, mercy, gentleness, temperance, etc., in the poor and inferior sort, their faith, patience, obedience, etc.

Reason: Thirdly, that every man might have need of other, and from hence they might be all knit more nearly together in the bond of brotherly affection. From hence it appears plainly that no man is made more honorable than another, or more wealthy, etc., out of any particular and singular respect to himself, but for the glory of his creator and the common good of the creature, man.

Thus stands the cause between God and us. We are entered into covenant with him for this work, we have taken out a commission, the Lord hath given us leave to draw our own articles, we have professed to enterprise these actions upon these and these ends, we have hereupon besought him of favor and blessing. Now if the Lord shall please to hear us, and bring us in peace to the place we desire, then hath he ratified this covenant and sealed our commission, [and] will expect a strict performance of the articles contained in it, but if we shall neglect the observations of these articles which are the ends we have propounded, and dissembling with our God, shall fall to embrace this present world and prosecute our carnal intentions seeking great things for ourselves and our posterity, the Lord will surely break out in wrath against us, be revenged of such a perjured people, and make us know the price of the breach of such a covenant.

Now the only way to avoid this shipwreck and to provide for our posterity is to follow the counsel of Micah, to do justly, to love mercy, to walk humbly with our God. For this end we must be knit together in this work as one man, we must entertain each other in brotherly affection, we must be willing to abridge ourselves of our superfluities for the supply of others' necessities, we must uphold a familiar commerce together in all meekness, gentleness, patience, and liberality, we must delight in each other, make others' conditions our own, rejoice together, mourn together, labor, and suffer together, always having before our eyes our commission and community in the work, our community as members of the same body. So shall we keep the unity of the spirit in the bond of peace. The Lord will be our God and delight to dwell among us as his own people, and will command a blessing upon us in all our ways, so that we shall see much more of his wisdom, power, goodness and truth than formerly we have been acquainted with. We shall find that the God of Israel is among us, when ten of us shall be able to resist a thousand of our enemies, when he shall make us a praise and glory, that men shall say of succeeding plantations, the Lord make it like that of New England. For we must consider that we shall be as a city upon a hill, the eyes of all people are upon us. So that if we shall deal falsely with our God in this work we have undertaken and so cause him to withdraw his present help from us, we shall be made a story and a by-word through the world, we shall open the mouths of enemies to speak evil of the ways of God and all professors for God's sake, we shall shame the faces of many of God's worthy servants, and cause their prayers to be turned into curses upon us till we be consumed out of the good land whither we are going. And to shut up this discourse with that exhortation of Moses, that faithful servant of the Lord in his last farewell to Israel, Deut. 30., Beloved, there is now set before us life and good, death and evil, in that we are commanded this day to love the Lord our God, and to love one another, to walk in his ways and to keep his commandments and his ordinance, and his laws, and the articles of our covenant with him that we may live and be multiplied, and that the Lord our God may bless us in the land whither we go to possess it. But if our hearts shall turn away so that we will not obey, but shall be seduced and worship other Gods, our pleasures, our profits, and serve them, it is propounded unto us this day we shall surely perish out of the good land whither we pass over this vast sea to possess it. Therefore let us choose life, that we, and our seed, may live, and by obeying his voice, and cleaving to him, for he is our life, and our prosperity.

JOURNAL OF JOHN WINTHROP

May 8, 1632

A general court at Boston. Whereas it was (at our first coming) agreed, that the freemen should choose the assistants, and they the governor, the whole court agreed now that the governor and assistants should all be new chosen every year by the general court, the governor to be always chosen out of the assistants. And accordingly, the old governor, John Winthrop, was chosen.

A proposition was made by the people, that every company of trained men might choose their own captain and officers. But the governor giving them reasons to the contrary, they were satisfied without it.

Every town chose two men to be at the next court, to advise with the governor and assistants about the raising of a public stock, so as what they should agree upon should bind all, etc.

July

At Watertown there was (in the view of divers witnesses) a great combat between a mouse and a snake. And, after a long fight, the mouse prevailed and killed the snake. The pastor of Boston, Mr. Wilson, a very sincere, holy man, hearing of it gave this interpretation. That the snake was the devil; the mouse was a poor, contemptible people, which God had brought hither, which should overcome Satan here and dispossess him of his kingdom. Upon the same occasion he told the governor that, before he was resolved to come into this country, he dreamed he was here, and that he saw a church arise out of the earth, which grew up and became a marvelous goodly church.

February 26, 1633

Two little girls of the governor's family were sitting under a great heap of logs, plucking of birds, and the wind driving the feathers into the house, the governors'

Winthrop's Journal, 1630–1649, James K. Hosmer, ed., (New York, 1908), I: 79, 83–84, 99, 103–104, 111–113, 124–125, 132–134, 143–144, 235–238.

wife caused them to remove away. They were no sooner gone but the whole heap of logs fell down in the place, and had crushed them to death if the Lord, in his special providence, had not delivered them.

August 6, 1633

Two men, servants to one Moody, of Roxbury, returning in a boat from the windmill, struck upon the oyster bank. They went out to gather oysters and, not making fast their boat, when the flood came it floated away and they were both drowned, although they might have waded out on either side. But it was an evident judgment of God upon them, for they were wicked persons. One of them, a little before, being reproved for his lewdness and put in mind of hell, answered that if hell were ten times hotter he had rather be there than he would serve his master, etc. The occasion was because he had bound himself for divers years, and saw that if he had been at liberty he might have had greater wages, though otherwise his master used him very well.

October 11, 1633

The scarcity of workmen had caused them to raise their wages to an excessive rate, so as a carpenter would have three shillings the day, a laborer two shillings and sixpence, etc. And accordingly, those who had commodities to sell advanced their prices sometimes double to that they cost in England, so as it grew to a general complaint, which the court, taking knowledge of, as also of some further evils which were springing out of the excessive rates of wages, they made an order that carpenters, masons, etc., should take but two shillings the day, and laborers but eighteen pence, and that no commodity should be sold at above four pence in the shilling more than it cost for ready money in England, oil, wine, and cheese, in regard of the hazard of bringing, excepted. The evils which were springing were: 1. Many spent much time idly, etc., because they could get as much in four days as would keep them a week. 2. They spent much in tobacco and strong waters, etc., which was a great waste to the commonwealth which, by reason of so many foreign commodities expended, could not have subsisted to this time, but that it was supplied by the cattle and corn which were sold to newcomers at very dear rates.

The ministers in the bay and Saugus did meet, once a fortnight, at one of their houses by course, where some question of moment was debated. Mr. Skelton, the pastor of Salem, and Mr. Williams, who was removed from Plymouth thither, took some exception against it, as fearing it might grow in time to a presbytery or superintendency, to the prejudice of the churches' liberties. But this fear was without cause; for they were all clear in that point, that no church or person can have power over another church. Neither did they in their meetings exercise any such jurisdiction, etc.

May 14, 1634

At the general court Mr. Cotton preached, and delivered this doctrine, that a magistrate ought not to be turned into the condition of a private man without just cause, and to be publicly convict, no more than the magistrates may not turn a private man out of his freehold, etc., without like public trial, etc. This falling in question in the court, and the opinion of the rest of the ministers being asked, it was referred to further consideration.

The court chose a new governor, viz., Thomas Dudley, Esq., the former deputy; and Mr. Ludlow was chosen deputy; and John Haines, Esq., as assistant, and all the rest of the assistants chosen again.

At this court it was ordered that four general courts should be kept every year, and that the whole body of the freemen should be present only at the court of election of magistrates, etc., and that, at the other three, every town should send their deputies, who should assist in making laws, disposing lands, etc. Many good things were made this court. It held three days, and all things were carried very peaceably, notwithstanding that some of the assistants were questioned by the freemen for some errors in their government, and some fines imposed, but remitted again before the court brake up. The court was kept in the meeting-house at Boston, and the new governor and the assistants were together entertained at the house of the old governor, as before.

September 4, 1634

The general court began at Newtown, and continued a week, and then was adjourned fourteen days. Many things were there agitated and concluded, as fortifying Castle Island, Dorchester, and Charlestown. Also against tobacco, and costly apparel, and immodest fashions. And committees appointed for setting out the bounds of towns, with divers other matters which do appear upon record. But the main business, which spent the most time and caused the adjourning of the court, was about the removal of Newtown. They had leave, the last general court, to look out some place for enlargement or removal, with promise of having it confirmed to them if it were not prejudicial to any other plantation. And now they moved that they might have leave to remove to Connecticut. The matter was debated divers days, and many reasons alleged pro and con. The principal reasons for their removal were,

1. Their want of accomodation for their cattle, so as they were not able to maintain their ministers, nor could receive any more of their friends to help them. And here it was alleged by Mr. Hooker, as a fundamental error, that towns were set so near each to other.

2. The fruitfulness and commodiousness of Connecticut, and the danger of having it possessed by others, Dutch or English.

3. The strong bent of their spirits to remove thither.

Against these it was said,

1. That in point of conscience, they ought not to depart from us, being knit to us in one body, and bound by oath to seek the welfare of this commonwealth.

2. That in point of state and civil policy, we ought not to give them leave to depart. 1. Being we were now weak and in danger to be assailed. 2. The departure of Mr. Hooker would not only draw many from us, but also divert other friends that would come to us. 3. We should expose them to evident peril, both from the Dutch (who made claim to the same river, and had already built a fort there) and from the Indians, and also from our own state at home, who would not endure they should sit down without a patent in any place which our king lays claim to.

3. They might be accomodated at home by some enlargement which other towns offered.

4. They might remove to Merrimack, or any other place within our patent.

11

5. The removing of a candlestick is a great judgment, which is to be avoided.

Upon these and other arguments the court being divided, it was put to vote, and of the deputies, fifteen were for their departure, and ten against it. The governor and two assistants were against it (except the secretary, who gave not vote); whereupon no record was entered, because there were not six assistants in the vote, as the patent requires. Upon this grew a great difference between the governor and assistants, and the deputies. They would not yield the assistants a negative voice, and the others (considering how dangerous it might be to the commonwealth, if they should not keep that strength to balance the greater number of the deputies) thought it safe to stand upon it. So, when they could proceed no farther, the whole court agreed to keep a day of humiliation to seek the Lord, which accordingly was done in all the congregations, the 18th day of this month. And the 24th, the court met again. Before they began Mr. Cotton preached (being desired by all the court, upon Mr. Hooker's instant excuse of his unfitness for that occasion). He took his text out of Hag. ii, 4, etc., out of which he laid down the nature or strength (as he termed it) of the magistracy, ministry, and people, viz.,—the strength of the magistracy to be their authority; of the people, their liberty; and of the ministry, their purity. And showed how all of these had a negative voice, etc., and that yet the ultimate resolution, etc., ought to be in the whole body of the people, etc., with answer to all objections, and a declaration of the people's duty and right to maintain their true liberties against any unjust violence, etc., which gave great satisfaction to the company. And it pleased the Lord so to assist him, and to bless his own ordinance, that the affairs of the court went on cheerfully. And although all were not satisfied about the negative voice to be left to the magistrates, yet no man moved aught about it, and the congregation of Newtown came and accepted of such enlargement as had formerly been offered them (by Boston and Watertown). And so the fear of their removal to Connecticut was removed.

At this court Mr. Goodwin, a very reverend and godly man, being the elder of the congregation of Newtown, having, in heat of argument, used some unreverend speech to one of the assistants, and being reproved for the same in the open court, did gravely and humbly acknowledge his fault, etc.

Dec. 11, 1634

This day, after the lecture, the inhabitants of Boston met to choose seven men who should divide the town lands among them. They chose by papers [ballots], and in their choice left out Mr. Winthrop, Coddington, and others of the chief men. Only they chose one of the elders and a deacon, and the rest of the inferior sort, and Mr. Winthrop had the greater number before one of them by a voice or two. This they did, as fearing that the richer men would give the poorer sort no great proportions of land, but would rather leave a great part at liberty for newcomers and for common, which Mr. Winthrop had oft persuaded them unto, as best for the town, etc. Mr. Cotton and divers others were offended at this choice, because they declined the magistrates. And Mr. Winthrop refused to be one upon such an election as was carried by a voice or two, telling them, that though, for his part, he did not apprehend any personal injury nor did doubt of their good affection towards him, yet he was much grieved that Boston should be the first who should shake off their magistrates, especially Mr. Coddington, who had been always so forward for their enlargement, adding further reason of declining this choice, to blot out so bad a precedent. Whereupon, at the motion of Mr. Cotton, who showed them that it was the Lord's order among the Israelites to have all such businesses committed to the elders, and that it had been nearer the rule to have chosen some of each sort, etc., they all agreed to go to a new election, which was referred to the next lecture day.

The reason why some were not willing that the people should have more land in the bay than they might be likely to use in some reasonable time, was partly to prevent the neglect of trades, and other more necessary employments, and partly that there might be place to receive such as should come after, seeing it would be very prejudicial to the commonwealth if men should be forced to go far off for land, while others had much and could make no use of it more than to please their eye with it.

September 22, 1637

Two men were hanged at Boston for several murders. The one, John Williams, a ship carpenter who, being lately come into the country and put in prison for theft, brake out of prison with one John Hoddy whom, near the great pond in the way to Ipswich, beyond Salem, he murdered, and took away his clothes and what else he had, and went in them to Ipswich (where he had been sent to prison), and was there again apprehended. And though his clothes were all bloody, yet he would confess nothing, till about a week after that the body of Hoddy was found by the kine, who, smelling the blood, made such a roaring as the cow-keeper, looking about, found the dead body covered with a heap of stones.

The other, William Schooler, was a vintner in London, and had been a common adulterer (as himself did confess), and had wounded a man in a duel, for which he fled in the Low Country, and from thence he fled from his captain and came into this country, leaving his wife (a handsome, neat woman) in England. He lived with another fellow at Merrimack, and there being a poor maid at Newbury, one Mary Sholy, who had desired a guide to go with her to her master, who dwelt at Pascataquack, he inquired her out and agreed, for fifteen shillings, to conduct her thither. But two days after, he returned, and being asked why he returned so soon, he answered that he had carried her within two or three miles of the place, and then she would go no farther. Being examined for this by the magistrates at Ipswich, and no proof founded against him he was let go. But about a year after, being impressed to go against the Pequods, he gave ill speeches, for which the governor sent warrant for him, and being apprehended (and supposed it had been for the death of the maid, some spake what they had heard, which might occasion suspicion), he was again examined, and divers witnesses produced about it. Whereupon he was committed, arraigned, and condemned, by due proceeding. The effect of the evidence was this:—

1. He had lived a vicious life, and now lived like an atheist.

2. He had sought out the maid, and undertook to carry her to a place where he had never been.

3. When he crossed Merrimack, he landed in a place three miles from the usual path, from whence it was scarce possible she should get into the path.

4. He said he went by Winicowett house, which he said stood on the contrary side of the way.

13

5. Being, as he said, within two or three miles of Swanscote, where he left her, he went not thither to tell them of her, nor stayed by her that night, nor, at his return home, did tell anybody of her, till he was demanded of her.

6. When he came back he had above ten shillings in his purse, and yet he said she would give him but seven shillings, and he carried no money with him.

7. At his return he had some blood upon his hat, and on his skirts before, which he said was with a pigeon which he killed.

8. He had a scratch on the left side of his nose, and being asked by a neighbor how it came, he said it was with a bramble, which could not be, it being of the breadth of a small nail. And being asked after by the magistrate, he said it was with his piece [gun], but that could not be on the left side.

9. The body of the maid was found by an Indian, about half a year after, in the midst of thick swamp, ten miles short of the place he said he left her in, and about three miles from the place where he landed by Merrimack, and (it was after seen, by the English), the flesh being rotted off it, and the clothes laid all on an heap by the body.

10. He said, that soon after he left her, he met with a bear and he thought that bear might kill her, yet he would not go back to save her.

11. He brake prison and fled as far as Powder Horn Hill, and there hid himself out of the way, for fear of pursuit, and after, when he arose to go forward he could not, but (as himself confessed), was forced to return back to prison again.

At his death he confessed he had made many lies to excuse himself, but denied that he had killed or ravished her. He was very loath to die, and had hope he should be reprived. But the court held him worthy of death, in undertaking the charge of a shiftless maid, and leaving her (when he might have done otherwise) in such a place as he knew she must needs perish, if not preserved by means unknown. Yet there were some ministers and others, who thought the evidence not sufficient to take away his life.

2

The Decline of New Netherland

For more than forty years the United Netherlands maintained colonies on the mainland of North America. For much of the first half of the seventeenth century, the Netherlands was a major cultural and commercial center, its bankers, merchants, artists, and scientists attracting the respect and admiration of other Europeans.

The Dutch West India Company, however, owner of the North American grants, was unable to maintain its government, or to get enough settlers for the safety and economic health of its colonies. Despite its magnificent geographical setting, New Netherland lagged far behind the English settlements to the North and South. The following document, signed by eleven opponents of Governor Peter Stuyvesant, reveals some of the reasons why. Angered by a series of grievances, these New Netherlanders sought greater economic freedom, the encouragement of emigration to their province, and a settlement of foreign-boundary disputes. Though the signers, some of whom went to the Netherlands personally to press their case, received a few concessions, no major alterations in the form of government were made; in 1664 the colony fell easily into the hands of the English.

THE REPRESENTATION
OF NEW NETHERLAND

Among all the people in the world, industrious in seeking out foreign lands, navigable waters and trade, those who bear the name of Netherlanders, will very easily hold their place with the first, as is sufficiently known to all those who have in any wise saluted the threshold of history, and as will also be confirmed by the following relation. The country of which we propose to speak, was first discovered in the year of our Lord 1609, by the ship *Half Moon,* of which Hendrik Hudson was master and supercargo—at the expense of the chartered East India Company, though in search of a different object. It was subsequently called New Netherland by our people, and very justly, as it was first discovered and possessed by Netherlanders, and at their cost; so that even at the present day, those natives of the country who

From *The Representation of New Netherland, 1650, Narratives of New Netherland, 1609–1664,* J. Franklin Jameson, ed. (New York 1909), 293–296, 300–306, 319–322, 324, 327, 333–341, 346–347, 352–354.

are so old as to recollect when the Dutch ships first came here, declare that when they saw them, they did not know what to make of them, and could not comprehend whether they came down from Heaven, or were of the Devil. Some among them, when the first one arrived, even imagined it to be a fish, or some monster of the sea, and accordingly a strange report of it spread over the whole land. We have also heard the savages frequently say, that they knew nothing of any other part of the world, or any other people than their own, before the arrival of the Netherlanders. For these reasons, therefore, and on account of the similarity of climate, situation and fertility, this place is rightly called New Netherland.

The land is naturally fruitful, and capable of supporting a large population, if it were judiciously allotted according to location. The air is pleasant here, and more temperate than in the Netherlands. The winds are changeable, and blow from all points, but generally from the southwest and northwest; the former prevailing in summer, and the latter in winter, at times very sharply, but constituting, nevertheless, the greatest blessing to the country as regards the health of the people, for being very strong and pure, it drives far inland or consumes all damps and superfluous moisture.

The land is adapted to the production of all kinds of winter and summer fruits, and with less trouble and tilling than in the Netherlands. It produces different kinds of wood, suitable for building houses and ships, whether large or small, consisting of oaks of various kinds, as post-oak, white smooth bark, white rough bark, gray bark, black bark, and still another kind which they call, from its softness, butter oak, the poorest of all, and not very valuable; the others, if cultivated as in the Netherlands, would be equal to any Flemish or Brabant oaks. It also yields several species of nut wood, such as oil-nuts, large and small; walnut of different sizes, in great abundance, and good for fuel, for which it is much used, and chestnut, the same as in the Netherlands, growing in the woods without order.

The indigenous fruits consist principally of acorns, some of which are very sweet; nuts of different kinds, chestnuts, beechnuts, but not many mulberries, plums, medlars, wild cherries, black currants, gooseberries, hazel nuts in great quantities, small apples, abundant strawberries throughout the country, with many other fruits and roots which the savages use. There is also plenty of bilberries or blueberries, together with ground-nuts and artichokes, which grow under ground. Almost the whole land is full of vines, in the wild woods as well as on the maize lands and flats; but they grow principally near to and upon the banks of the brooks, streams and rivers, which are numerous, and run conveniently and pleasantly everywhere, as if they were planted there. The grapes comprise many varieties, some white, some blue, some very fleshy, and only fit to make raisins of, others on the contrary juicy; some are very large and others small.

The tame cattle are in size and other respects about the same as in the Netherlands, but the English cattle and swine thrive and grow best, appearing to be better suited to the country than those from Holland. They require, too, less trouble, expense and attention; for it is not necessary in winter to look after such as are dry, or the swine, except that in the time of a deep snow they should have some attention. Milch cows also are much less trouble than they are in Holland, as most of the time, if any care be requisite, it is only for the purpose of giving them occasionally a little hay.

The natives are generally well set in their limbs, slender round the waist, broad across the shoulders, and have black hair and dark eyes. They are very nimble and fleet, well adapted to travel on foot and to carry heavy burdens. They are foul and slovenly in their actions, and make little of all kinds of hardships; to which indeed they are by nature and from their youth accustomed. They are like the Brazilians in color, or as yellow as the people who sometimes pass through the Netherlands and are called Gypsies. The men generally have no beard, or very little, which some even pull out. They use very few words, which they first consider well. Naturally they are very modest, simple and inexperienced; though in their actions high-minded enough, vigorous and quick to comprehend or learn, be it right or wrong, whenever they are so inclined. They are not straightforward as soldiers but perfidious, accomplishing all their enterprises by treachery, using many stratagems to deceive their enemies, and usually ordering all their plans, involving any danger, by night. The desire of revenge appears to be born in them. They are very obstinate in defending themselves when they cannot run, which however they do when they can; and they make little of death when it is inevitable, and despise all tortures which can be inflicted upon them while dying, manifesting no sorrow, but usually singing until they are dead. They understand how to cure wounds and hurts, or inveterate sores and injuries, by means of herbs and roots, which grow in the country, and which are known to them. Their clothing, both for men and women, is a piece of duffels or leather in front, with a deer skin or elk's hide over the body. Some have bears' hides of which they make doublets; others have coats made of the skins of raccoons, wild-cats, wolves, dogs, otters, squirrels, beavers and the like, and also of turkey's feathers. At present they use for the most part duffels cloth, which they obtain in barter from the Christians. They make their stockings and shoes of deer skins or elk's hide, and some have shoes made of corn-husks, of which they also make sacks. Their money consists of white and black *zeewant,* which they themselves make. Their measure and valuation is by the hand or by the fathom; but their corn is measured by *denotas,* which are bags they make themselves. Ornamenting themselves consists in cutting their bodies, or painting them with various colors, sometimes even all black, if they are in mourning, yet generally in the face. They hang *zeewant,* both white and black, about their heads, which they otherwise are not wont to cover, but on which they are now beginning to wear hats and caps bought of the Christians. They also put it in their ears, and around their necks and bodies, wherewith after their manner they appear very fine. They have long deer's hair which is dyed red, and of which they make rings for the head, and other fine hair of the same color, to hang from the neck like tresses, of which they are very proud. They frequently smear their skin and hair with different kinds of grease. They can almost all swim. They themselves make the boats they use, which are of two kinds, some of entire trees, which they hollow out with fire, hatchets and adzes, and which the Christians call canoes; others are made of bark, which they manage very skilfully, and which are also called canoes.

Traces of the institution of marriage can just be perceived among them, and nothing more. A man and woman join themselves together without any particular

17

ceremony other than that the man by previous agreement with the woman gives her some *zeewant* or cloth, which on their separation, if it happens soon, he often takes again. Both men and women are utterly unchaste and shamelessly promiscuous in their intercourse, which is the cause of the men so often changing their wives and the women their husbands. Ordinarily they have but one wife, sometimes two or three, but this is generally among the chiefs. They have also among them different conditions of persons, such as noble and ignoble. The men are generally lazy, and do nothing until they become old and unesteemed, when they make spoons, wooden bowls, bags, nets and other similar articles; beyond this the men do nothing except fish, hunt and go to war. The women are compelled to do the rest of the work, such as planting corn, cutting and drawing fire-wood, cooking, taking care of the children and whatever else there is to be done. Their dwellings consist of hickory saplings, placed upright in the ground and bent arch-wise; the tops are covered with barks of trees, which they cut for this purpose in great quantities. Some even have within them rough carvings of faces and images, but these are generally in the houses of the chiefs. In the fishing and hunting seasons, they lie under the open sky or little better. They do not live long in one place, but move about several times in a year, at such times and to such places as it appears best and easiest for them to obtain subsistence.

They are divided into different tribes and languages, each tribe living generally by itself and having one of its number as a chief, though he has not much power or distinction except in their dances or in time of war. Among some there is not the least knowledge of God, and among others very little, though they relate many strange fables concerning Him.

They are in general much afraid of the Devil, who torments them greatly; and some give themselves up to him, and hold the strangest notions about him. But their devils, they say, will have nothing to do with the Dutch. No haunting of spirits and the like are heard of among them. They make offerings to the Devil sometimes, but with few solemnities. They believe in the immortality of the soul. They have some knowledge of the sun, moon and stars, of which they are able to name many, and they judge tolerably well about the weather. There is hardly any law or justice among them, except sometimes in war matters, and then very little. The nearest of blood is the avenger. The youngest are the most courageous, and do for the most part what they please. Their weapons formerly were the bow and arrow, which they employ with wonderful skill, and the cudgel, but they now, that is, those who live near the Christians or have many dealings with them, generally use firelocks and hatchets, which they obtain in trade. They are exceedingly fond of guns, sparing no expense for them; and are so skilful in the use of them that they surpass many Christians. Their food is coarse and simple, drinking water as their only beverage, and eating the flesh of all kinds of animals which the country affords, cooked without being cleansed or dressed. They eat even badgers, dogs, eagles and such like trash, upon which Christians place no value. They use all kinds of fish, which they commonly cook without removing the entrails, and snakes, frogs and the like. They know how to preserve fish and meat until winter, and to cook them with corn-meal. They make their bread of maize, but it is very plain, and cook it either whole or broken in a pestle block.

After Their High Mightinesses, the Lords States General, were pleased, in the year of our Lord 1622, to include this province in their grant to the Honorable West India Company, their Honors deemed it necessary to take into possession so naturally beautiful and noble a province, which was immediately done, as opportunity offered, the same as in all similar beginnings. Since the year of our Lord 1623, four forts have been built there by order of the Lords Directors.

These forts, both to the south and north, are so situated as not only to close and control the said rivers, but also to command the plantations between them, as well as those round about them, and on the other side of the river as far as the ownership by occupation extends. These the Honorable Company declared they owned and would maintain against all foreign or domestic powers who should attempt to seize them against their consent. Yet, especially on the northeast side of New Netherland this has been not at all regarded or observed by the English living to the eastward; for notwithstanding possession was already fully taken by the building and occupation of Fort Good Hope, and there was no neglect from time to time in warning them, in making known our rights, and in protesting against their usurpation and violence, they have disregarded all these things and have seized and possessed, and still hold, the largest and best part of New Netherland, that is, on the east side of the North River, from Cape Cod to within six leagues of the North River, where the English have now a village called Stamford, from whence one could travel in a summer's day to the North River and back again, if one knows the Indian path.

This and similar difficulties these people now wish to lay to our charge, all under the pretence of a very clear conscience, notwithstanding King James, of most glorious memory, chartered the Virginia Companies upon condition that they should remain an hundred miles from each other, according to our reckoning. They are willing to avail themselves of this grant, but by no means to comply with the terms stipulated in it.

In short, it is just this with the English, they are willing to know the Netherlanders, and to use them as a protection in time of need, but when that is past, they no longer regard them, but play the fool with them. This happens so only because we have neglected to populate the land; or, to speak more plainly and truly, because we have, out of regard for our own profit, wished to scrape all the fat into one or more pots, and thus secure the trade and neglect population.

We cannot sufficiently thank the Fountain of all Goodness for His having led us into such a fruitful and healthful land, which we, with our numerous sins, still heaped up here daily, beyond measure, have not deserved. We are also in the highest degree beholden to the Indians, who not only have given up to us this good and fruitful country, and for a trifle yielded us the ownership, but also enrich us with their good and reciprocal trade, so that there is no one in New Netherland or who trades to New Netherland without obligation to them. Great is our disgrace now, and happy should we have been, had we acknowledged these benefits as we ought, and had we striven to impart the Eternal Good to the Indians, as much as was in our power, in return for what they divided with us. It is to be feared that at the Last Day they will stand up against us for this injury. Lord of Hosts forgive us for not having conducted therein more according to our reason; give us also the means and so direct our hearts that we in future may acquit ourselves as we ought for the salvation of our own souls and of theirs, and for the magnifying of thy Holy Name, for the sake of Christ. Amen.

As we shall speak of the reasons and causes which have brought New Netherland into the ruinous condition in which it is now found to be, we deem it necessary to state first the difficulties. We represent it as we see and find it, in our daily experience. To describe it in one word, (and none better presents itself,) it is *bad government,* with its attendants and consequences, that is, to the best of our knowledge, the true and only foundation stone of the decay and ruin of New Netherland. This government from which so much abuse proceeds, is twofold, that is; in the Fatherland by the Managers, and in this country. We shall first briefly point out some orders and mistakes issuing from the Fatherland, and afterwards proceed to show how abuses have grown up and obtained strength here.

The Managers of the Company adopted a wrong course at first, and as we think had more regard for their own interest than for the welfare of the country, trusting rather to flattering than true counsels. This is proven by the unnecessary expenses incurred from time to time, the heavy accounts of New Netherland, the registering of colonies—in which business most of the Managers themselves engaged, and in reference to which they have regulated the trade—and finally the not peopling the country. It seems as if from the first, the Company have sought to stock this land with their own employees, which was a great mistake, for when their time was out they returned home, taking nothing with them, except a little in their purses and a bad name for the country, in regard to its lack of sustenance and in other respects. In the meantime there was no profit, but on the contrary heavy monthly salaries, as the accounts of New Netherland will show.

Had the Honorable West India Company, in the beginning, sought population instead of running to great expense for unnecessary things, which under more favorable circumstances might have been suitable and very proper, the account of New Netherland would not have been so large as it now is, caused by building the ship *New Netherland* at an excessive outlay, by erecting three expensive mills, by brick-making, by tar-burning, by ash-burning, by salt-making and like operations, which through bad management and calculation have all gone to nought, or come to little; but which nevertheless have cost much. Had the same money been used in bringing people and importing cattle, the country would now have been of great value.

The land itself is much better and it is more conveniently situated than that which the English possess, and if there were not constant seeking of individual gain and private trade, there would be no danger that misfortunes would press us as far as they do.

It is impossible for us to rehearse and to state in detail wherein and how often the Company have acted injuriously to this country. They have not approved of our own countrymen settling the land, as is shown in the case of Jacob Walingen and his people at the Fresh River, and quite recently in the cases at the South River; while foreigners were permitted to take land there without other opposition than orders and protests. It could hardly be otherwise, for the garrisons are not kept complete conformably to the Exemptions, and thus the cause of New Netherland's bad condition lurks as well in the Netherlands as here. Yea, the seeds of war, according to the declaration of Director Kieft, were first sown by the Fatherland; for he said he had express orders to exact the contribution from the Indians; which would have been very well if the land had been peopled, but as it was, it was premature.

Trade, without which, when it is legitimate, no country is prosperous, is by their acts so decayed, that it amounts to nothing. It is more suited for slaves than freemen, in consequence of the restrictions upon it and the annoyances which accompany the exercise of the right of inspection. We approve of inspection, however, so far as relates to contraband.

The Directors here, though far from their masters, were close by their profit. They have always known how to manage their own matters very properly and with little loss, yet under pretext of the public business. They have also conducted themselves just as if they were the sovereigns of the country. As they desired to have it, so it always had to be; and as they willed so was it done. "The Managers," they say, "are masters in Fatherland, but we are masters in this land." As they understand it it will go, there is no appeal. And it has not been difficult for them hitherto to maintain this doctrine in practice; for the people were few and for the most part very simple and uninformed, and besides, they needed the Directors every day. And if perchance there were some intelligent men among them, who could go upon their own feet, them it was sought to oblige.

The bowl has been going round a long time for the purpose of erecting a common school and it has been built with words, but as yet the first stone is not laid. Some materials only are provided. The money nevertheless, given for the purpose, has already found its way out and is mostly spent; or may even fall short, and for this purpose also no fund invested in real estate has ever been built up.

The poor fund, though the largest, contains nothing except the alms collected among the people, and some fines and donations of the inhabitants. A considerable portion of this money is in the possession of the Company, who have borrowed it from time to time, and kept it. They have promised, for years, to pay interest. But in spite of all endeavor neither principal nor interest can be obtained from them.

Flying reports about asylums for orphans, for the sick and aged, and the like have occasionally been heard, but as yet we can not see that any attempt, order or direction has been made in relation to them. From all these facts, then, it sufficiently appears that scarcely any proper care or diligence has been used by the Company or its officers for any ecclesiastical property whatever—at least, nothing as far as is known—from the beginning to this time.

The Administration of Director Stuyvesant in Particular

We wish much we were already through with this administration, for it has grieved us, and we know ourselves powerless; nevertheless we will begin, and as we have already spoken of the public property, ecclesiastical and civil, we will consider how it is in regard to the administration of justice, and giving decisions between man and man. And first, to point as with a finger at the manners of the Director and council. As regards the Director, from his first arrival to this time, his manner in court has been to treat with violence, dispute with or harass one of the two parties, not as becomes a judge, but as a zealous advocate, which has given great discontent to every one, and with some it has gone so far and has effected so much, that many of them dare bring no matter before the court, if they do not stand well or tolerably so with the Director. For whoever has him opposed, has as much as the sun and moon against him. Though he has himself appointed many of the councillors, and placed them under obligation to him, and some pretend that he can overpower the rest by plurality of votes, he frequently puts his opinion in writing, and that so fully that it covers several pages, and then he adds verbally, "Monsieur, this is my advice, if any one has aught to say against it, let him speak." If then any one rises to make objection, which is not easily done, though it be well grounded, His Honor bursts out immediately in fury and makes such gestures, that it is frightful; yea, he rails out frequently at the councillors for this thing and the other, with ugly words which would better suit the fish-market than the council chamber; and if this be all endured, His Honor will not rest yet unless he has his will. To demonstrate this by examples and proof, though easily done, would nevertheless detain us too long; but we all say and affirm that this has been his common practice from the first and still daily continues. And this is the condition and nature of things in the council on the part of the Director, who is its head and president. Let us now briefly speak of the councillors individually. The Vice Director, Lubbert van Dincklagen, has for a long time on various occasions shown great dissatisfaction about many different matters, and has protested against the Director and his appointed councillors, but only lately, and after some others made resistance. He was, before this, so influenced by fear, that he durst venture to take no chances against the Director, but had to let many things pass by and to submit to them. He declared afterwards that he had great objections to them, because they were not just, but he saw no other way to have peace. This man then is overruled. Let us proceed farther. Monsieur la Montagne had been in the council in Kieft's time, and was then very much suspected by many. He had no commission from the Fatherland, was driven by the war from his farm, is also very much indebted to the Company, and therefore is compelled to dissemble. But it is sufficiently known from himself that he is not pleased, and is opposed to the administration. Brian Newton, lieutenant of the soldiers, is the next. This man is afraid of the Director, and regards him as his benefactor. Besides being very simple and inexperienced in law, he does not understand our Dutch language, so that he is scarcely capable of refuting the long written opinions, but must and will say *yes*. Sometimes the commissary, Adrian Keyser, is admitted into the council, who came here as secretary. This man has not forgotten much law, but says that he *lets God's water run over God's field*. He cannot and dares not say anything, for so much can be said against him that it is best that he should be silent. The captains of the ships, when they are ashore, have a vote in the Council; as Ielmer Thomassen, and Paulus Lenaertson, who was made equipment-master upon his first arrival, and who has always had a seat in the council, but is still a free man. What knowledge these people, who all their lives sail on the sea, and are brought up to ship-work, have of law matters and of farmers' disputes any intelligent man can imagine. Besides, the

Director himself considers them so guilty that they dare not accuse others, as will appear from this passage at Curacao, before the Director ever saw New Netherland. As they were discoursing about the price of carracks, the Director said to the minister and others, "Domine Jóhannes, I thought that I had brought honest ship-masters with me, but I find that I have brought a set of thieves"; and this was repeated to these councillors, especially to the equipment-master, for Captain Ielmer was most of the time at sea. They have let it pass unnoticed—a proof that they were guilty. But they have not fared badly; for though Paulus Lenaertssen has small wages, he has built a better dwellinghouse here then anybody else. How this has happened is mysterious to us; for though the Director has knowledge of these matters, he nevertheless keeps quiet when Paulus Lenaertssen begins to make objections, which he does not easily do for any one else, which causes suspicion in the minds of many. There remains to complete this court-bench, the secretary and the *fiscaal,* Hendrick van Dyck, who had previously been an ensign-bearer. Director Stuyvesant has kept him twenty-nine months out of the meetings of the council, for the reason among others which His Honor assigned, that he cannot keep secret but will make public, what is there resolved. He also frequently declared that he was a villain, a scoundrel, a thief and the like. All this is well known to the *fiscaal,* who dares not against him take the right course, and in our judgment it is not advisable for him to do so; for the Director is utterly insufferable in word and deed. What shall we say of a man whose head is troubled, and has a screw loose, especially when, as often happens, he has been drinking. To conclude, there is the secretary, Cornelius van Tienhoven. Of this man very much could be said, and more than we are able, but we shall select here and there a little for the sake of brevity. He is cautious, subtle, intelligent and sharp-witted—good gifts when they are well used. He is one of those who have been longest in the country, and every circumstance is well known to him, in regard both to the Christians and the Indians. With the Indians, moreover, he has run about the same as an Indian, with a little covering and a small patch in front, from lust after the prostitutes to whom he has always been mightily inclined, and with whom he has had so much to do that no punishment or threats of the Director can drive him from them. He is extremely expert in dissimulation. He pretends himself that he bites when asleep, and that he shows externally the most friendship towards those whom he most hates. He gives every one who has any business with him—which scarcely any one can avoid—good answers and promises of assistance, yet rarely helps anybody but his friends; but twists continually and shuffles from one side to the other. In his words and conduct he is shrewd, false, deceitful and given to lying, promising every one, and when it comes to perform, at home to no one.

Great distrust has also been created among the inhabitants on account of Heer Stuyvesant being so ready to confiscate. There scarcely comes a ship in or near here, which, if it do not belong to friends, is not regarded as a prize by him. Though little comes of it, great claims are made to come from these matters, about which we will not dispute; but confiscating has come to such repute in New Netherland, that nobody anywise conspicuous considers his property to be really safe. It were well if the report of this thing were confined to this country; but it has spread among the neighboring English—north and south—and in the West Indies and Caribbee Islands. Everywhere there, the report is so bad, that not a ship dare come hither from those places; and good credible people who come from thence, by the way of Boston, and others here trading at Boston, assure us that more than twenty-five ships would come here from those islands every year if the owners were not fearful of confiscation. It is true of these places only and the report of it flies everywhere, and produces like fear, so that this vulture is destroying the prosperity of New Netherland, diverting its trade, and making the people discouraged, for other places not so well situated as this, have more shipping. All the permanent inhabitants, the merchant, the burgher and peasant, the planter, the laboring man, and also the man in service, suffer great injury in consequence; for if the shipping were abundant, everything would be sold cheaper, and necessaries be more easily obtained then they are now, whether they be such as the people themselves, by God's blessing, get out of the earth, or those they otherwise procure, and be sold better and with more profit; and people and freedom would bring trade. New England is a clear example that this policy succeeds well, and so especially is Virginia.

Besides this, the country of the Company is so taxed, and is burdened and kept down in such a manner, that the inhabitants are not able to appear beside their neighbors of Virginia or New England, or to undertake any enterprise. It seems—and so far as is known by us all the inhabitants of New Netherland declare—that the Managers have scarce any care or regard for New Netherland, except when there is something to receive, for which reason, however, they receive less.

Although we are well assured and know, in regard to the mode of redress of the country, we are only children, and Their High Mightinesses are entirely competent, we nevertheless pray that they overlook our presumption and pardon us if we make some suggestions according to our slight understanding thereof, in addition to what we have considered necessary in our petition to Their High Mightinesses.

In our opinion this country will never flourish under the government of the Honorable Company, but will pass away and come to an end of itself without benefiting thereby the Honorable Company, so that it would be better and more profitable for them, and better for the country, that they should divest themselves of it and transfer their interests.

To speak specifically. Provision ought to be made for public buildings, as well ecclesiastical as civil, which, in beginnings, can be ill dispensed with. It is doubtful whether divine worship will not have to cease altogether in consequence of the departure of the minister, and the inability of the Company. There should be a public school, provided with at least two good masters, so that first of all in so wild a country, where there are many loose people, the youth be well taught and brought up, not only in reading and writing, but also in the knowledge and fear of the Lord. As it is now, the school is kept very irregularly, one and another keeping it according to his pleasure and as long as he thinks proper. There ought also to be an almshouse and an orphan asylum, and other similar institutions.

The country must also be provided with godly, honorable and intelligent rulers who are not too indigent, or indeed are not too covetous. A covetous chief makes poor subjects. The manner the country is now governed falls severely upon it, and is intolerable, for nobody is unmolested or secure in his property longer than the Director pleases, who is generally strongly inclined to confiscating; and although one does well, and gives the Heer what is due to him, one must still study always to please him if he would have quiet. A large population would be the consequence of a good government, as we have shown according to our knowledge in our petition; and although to give free passage and equip ships, if it be necessary, would be expensive at first, yet if the result be considered, it would be an exceedingly wise measure, if by that means farmers and laborers together with other needy people were brought into the country, with the little property which they have; as also the Fatherland has enough of such people to spare. We hope it would then prosper, especially as good privileges and exemptions, which we regard as the mother of population, would encourage the inhabitants to carry on commerce and lawful trade. Every one would be allured hither by the pleasantness, situation, salubrity and fruitfulness of the country, if protection were secured within the already established boundaries. It would all, with God's assistance, then, according to human judgment, go well, and New Netherland would in a few years be a worthy place and be able to do service to the Netherland nation, to repay richly the cost, and to thank its benefactors.

3

The Good Life
in the Chesapeake

Little is known about the author of the following pamphlet. Hammond claimed to have spent more than twenty years in America participating in the disorders that occurred in Maryland in 1652. He supported the positions of Governor Stone and the Proprietor, Lord Baltimore. For this, he was placed under sentence of death by parliamentary commissioners sent out from England, but he managed to escape.

Much of Hammond's analysis is reminiscent of the promotional literature published some forty years earlier. Like the writers commissioned by the Virginia Company, he insists on the benevolence of the climate, the fertility of the soil, and the possibilities for personal advancement. But emphases have changed somewhat during the four decades of Virginia's history, and Hammond's discussion was meant to appeal to settlers whose values, backgrounds, and purposes varied from the hopes of the early founders.

THE TWO FRUITFULL SISTERS
VIRGINIA AND MARY-LAND
John Hammond

It is the glory of every nation to enlarge themselves, to encourage their own foreign attempts, and to be able to have of their own, within their own territories, as many several commodities as they can attain to, that so others may rather be beholding to them, then they to others; and to this purpose have encouragements, privileges and immunities been given to any discoveries or adventurers into remote colonies, by all politic commonwealths in the world.

But alas, we Englishmen (in all things else famous, and to other countries terrible) do not only fail in this, but villify, scandalize and cry down such parts of the unknown world, as have been found out, settled and made flourishing, by the charge, hazard and diligence of their own brethren, as if because removed from us, we either account them people of another world or enemies.

This is too truly made good in the odiums and cruel slanders cast on those two famous countries of Virginia and Maryland, whereby those countries, not only are many times at a stand, but are in danger to molder away, and come in time to

From John Hammond, *Leah and Rachel, or the Two Fruitfull Sisters Virginia and Mary-Land, Narratives of Early Maryland, 1633–1684,* Clayton C. Hall, ed. (New York, 1910), 283–300.

nothing; nor is there anything but the fertility and natural gratefulness of them left a remedy to prevent it.

To let our own nation (whose common good I covet, and whose commonwealth's servant I am, as born to no other use) be made sensible of these injuries, I have undertaken in this book to give the true state of those places, according to the condition they are now in; and to declare either to distressed or discontented, that they need not doubt because of any rumor detracting from their goodness, to remove and cast themselves and fortunes upon those countries.

In respect these two sister countries (though distinct governments) are much of one nature, both for produce and manner of living; I shall only at present treat of the elder sister Virginia, and in speaking of that include both.

The country is reported to be an unhealthy place, a nest of rogues, whores, dissolute and rooking persons; a place of intolerable labor, bad usage and hard diet, etc.

To answer these several calumnies, I shall first show what it was. Next, what it is.

At the first settling and many years after it deserved most of those aspersions (nor were they then aspersions but truths). It was not settled at the public charge, but when found out, challenged and maintained by adventurers, whose avarice and inhumanity brought in these inconveniences, which to this day brands Virginia.

Then were jails emptied, youth seduced, infamous women drilled in, the provisions all brought out of England, and that embezzled by the trustees (for they durst neither hunt, fowl, nor fish, for fear of the Indian, which they stood in awe of), their labor was almost perpetual, their allowance of victuals small, few or no cattle, no use of horses nor oxen to draw or carry (which labors men supplied themselves), all which caused a mortality; no civil courts of justice but under a martial law, no redress of grievances, complaints were repaid with stripes, moneys with scoffs, tortures made delights, and in a word all and the worst that tyranny could inflict or act. Which when complained of in England (but so were they kept under that it was long ere they would suffer complaints to come home), the bondage was taken off, the people set free, and had lands assigned to each of them to live of themselves and enjoy the benefit of their own industry. Men then began to call what they labored for their own, they fell to making themselves convenient housing to dwell in, to plant corn for their food, to range the woods for flesh, the rivers for fowl and fish, to find out somewhat staple for supply of clothing, to continue a commerce, to purchase and breed cattle, etc. But the bud of this growing happiness was again nipped by a cruel massacre committed by the natives, which again pulled them back and kept them under, enforcing them to get into forts (such as the infancy of those times afforded). They were taken off from planting, their provisions destroyed, their cattle, hogs, horses, etc., killed up, and brought to such want and penury, that diseases grew rife, mortality exceeded. But receiving a supply of men, ammunition and victuals out of England, they again gathered heart, pursued their enemies, and so often worsted them, that the Indians were glad to sue for peace, and they, desirous of a cessation, consented to it.

They again began to bud forth, to spread further, to gather wealth, which they rather profusely spent (as gotten with ease) than providently husbanded or aimed at any public good, or to make a country for posterity. But from hand to mouth, neglecting discoveries, planting of orchards, providing for the winter preservation of their stocks, or thinking of anything staple or firm. And while tobacco, the only commodity they had to subsist on, bore a price, they wholly and eagerly followed that, neglecting their very planting of corn, and much relied on England for the chiefest part of their provisions; so that being not always amply supplied, they were often in such want, that their case and condition being related in England, it hindered and kept off many from going thither, who rather cast their eyes on the barren and freezing soil of New England, than to join with such an indigent and sottish people as were reported to be in Virginia.

Yet was not Virginia all this while without divers honest and virtuous inhabitants, who observing the general neglect and licentiousness there, caused assemblies to be called and laws to be made tending to the glory of God, the severe suppression of vices, and the compelling them not to neglect (upon strict punishments) planting and tending such quantities of corn, as would not only serve themselves, their cattle and hogs plentifully, but to be enabled to supply New England (then in want) with such proportions, as were extreme reliefs to them in their necessities.

From this industry of theirs and great plenty of corn (the main staff of life), proceeded that great plenty of cattle and hogs (now innumerable) and out of which not only New England hath been stocked and relieved, but all other parts of the Indies inhabited by Englishmen.

The inhabitants now finding the benefit of their industries, began to look with delight on their increasing stocks (as nothing more pleasurable than profit), to take pride in their plentifully furnished tables, to grow not only civil but great observers of the Sabbath, to stand upon their reputations, and to be ashamed of that notorious manner of life they had formerly lived and wallowed in.

They then began to provide and send home for gospel ministers, and largely contributed for their maintenance; but Virginia savoring not handsomely in England, very few of good conversation would adventure thither, (as thinking it a place wherein surely the fear of God was not), yet many came, such as wore black coats, and could babble in a pulpit, roar in a tavern, exact from their parishioners, and rather by their dissoluteness destroy than feed their flocks.

Loath was the country to be wholly without teachers, and therefore rather retain these than to be destitute; yet still endeavors for better in their places, which were obtained, and these wolves in sheep's clothing, by their assemblies questioned, silenced, and some forced to depart the country.

Then began the gospel to flourish; civil, honorable, and men of great estates flocked in; famous buildings went forward, orchards innumerable were planted and preserved; tradesmen set on work and encouraged, staple commodities, as silk, flax, potash, etc. of which I shall speak further hereafter, attempted on, and with good success brought to perfection; so that this country which had a mean beginning, many back friends, two ruinous and bloody massacres, hath by God's grace outgrown all, and is become a place of pleasure and plenty.

And having briefly laid down the former state of Virginia, in its infancy, and filth, and the occasion of its scandalous aspersions, I come to my main subject, its present condition and happiness (if anything can be justly called happy in this transitory life otherwise than as blessings which in the well using whereof, a future happiness may be expected).

I affirm the country to be wholesome, healthy, and fruitful; and a model on which industry may as much improve itself in, as in any habitable part of the world; yet not such a lubberland as the fiction of the land of ease is reported to be.

In the country's minority, and before they had well cleared the ground to let in air (which now is otherwise), many imputed the stifling of the woods to be cause of such sickness, but I rather think the contrary. For divers new rivers lately settled, were at their first coming upon them as woody as James River, the first place they settled in, and yet those rivers are as healthy as any former settled place in Virginia or England itself. I believe (and that not without reason) it was only want of such diet, good drinks, and wholesome lodgings as best agreed with our English natures, which were the cause of so much sickness as were formerly frequent, which we have now amended and therefore enjoy better health. To which I add, and that by experience since my coming into England (and many if not all Virginians can do the like), that change of air does much alter the state of our bodies, by which many travelers thither may expect some sickness, yet little danger of mortality.

If any are minded to repair thither, if they are not in a capacity to defray their own charges let them not be seduced by those mercenary spirits that know little of the place, nor aim at any good of theirs, but only by foisting and flattering them to gain a reward of those they procure them for. Beware them.

Let such as are so minded not rashly throw themselves upon the voyage, but observe the nature, and enquire the qualities of the persons with whom they engage to transport themselves, or if (as not acquainted with such as inhabit there, but go with merchants and mariners, who transport them to others), let their convenant be such, that after their arrival they have a fortnight's time assigned them to enquire of their master, and make choice of such as they intend to expire their time with, nor let that brand of selling of servants be any discouragement to deter any from going, for if a time must be served, it is all one with whom it be served, provided they be people of honest repute, with which the country is well replenished.

And be sure to have your contract in writing and under hand and seal, for if you go over upon promise made to do this or that, or to be free or your own men, it signifies nothing, for by a law of the country (waiving all promises) any one coming in, and not paying their own passages, must serve if men or women four years, if younger according to their years, but where an indenture is, that is binding and observing.

The usual allowance for servants is (besides their charge of passage defrayed) at their expiration, a year's provision of corn, double apparel, tools necessary, and land according to the custom of the country, which is an old delusion, for there is no land customary due to the servant, but to the master, and therefore that servant is unwise that will not dash out that custom in his covenant, and make that due land absolutely his own, which although at the present not of so great consequence, yet will be of much worth, as I shall hereafter make manifest.

When you go aboard, expect the ship somewhat troubled and in a hurliburly, until you clear the land's end, and that the ship is rummaged, and things put to rights, which many times discourages the passengers, and makes them wish the voyage unattempted; but this is but for a short season, and washes off when at sea, where the time is pleasantly passed away, though not with such choice plenty as the shore affords.

But when you arrive and are settled, you will find a strange alteration, an abused country giving the lie in your own approbations to those that have calumniated it. And these infallible arguments may convince all incredible and obstinate opinions, concerning the goodness and delightfulness of the country: that never any servants of late times have gone thither, but in their letters to their friends commend and approve of the place, and rather invite than dissuade their acquaintance from coming thither. Another is this, that seldom (if ever) any that hath continued in Virginia any time, will or do desire to live in England, but post back with what expedition they can; although many are landed men in England, and have good estates here, and divers ways of preferments propounded to them, to entice and persuade their continuance.

The labor servants are put to is not so hard nor of such continuance as husbandmen nor handicraftmen are kept at in England. As I said, little or nothing is done in winter time, none ever work before sun rising nor after sun set. In the summer they rest, sleep, or exercise themselves five hours in the heat of the day. Saturday afternoon is always their own, the old holidays are observed and the Sabbath spent in good exercise.

The women are not (as is reported) put into the ground to work, but occupy such domestic employments and housewifery as in England, that is dressing victuals, righting up the house, milking, employed about dairies, washing, sewing, etc., and both men and women have times of recreation, as much or more than in any part of the world besides. Yet some wenches that are nasty, beastly and not fit to be so employed are put into the ground, for reason tells us, they must not at charge be transported and then maintained for nothing, but those that prove so awkward are rather burdensome than servants desirable or useful.

The country is fruitful, apt for all and more than England can or does produce. The usual diet is such as in England, for the rivers afford innumerable sorts of choice fish (if they will take the pains to make wires or hire the natives, who for a small matter will undertake it), winter and summer, and that in many places sufficient to serve the use of man, and to fatten hogs. Water-fowl of all sorts are (with admiration to be spoken of) plentiful and easy to be killed, yet by many degrees more plentiful in some places than in othersome. Deer all over the country, and in many places so many that venison is accounted a tiresome meat; wild turkeys are frequent, and so large that I have seen some weigh near threescore pounds; other beasts there are whose flesh is wholesome and savory, such are unknown to us; and therefore I will not stuff my book with superfluous relation of their names; huge oysters and plenty of them in all parts where the salt water comes.

The country is exceedingly replenished with neat cattle, hogs, goats and tame fowl, but not many sheep; so that mutton is somewhat scarce, but that defect is supplied with store of venison, other flesh and fowl. The country is full of gallant orchards, and the fruit generally more luscious and delightful than here, witness the peach and quince. The latter may be eaten raw savorily, the former differs and as much exceeds ours as the best relished apple we have doth the crab, and of both most excellent and comfortable drinks are made. Grapes in infinite manners grow wild, so do walnuts, chestnuts, and abundance of excellent fruits, plums and berries, not growing or known in England; grain we have, both English and Indian for bread and beer, and peas besides English of ten several sorts, all exceeding ours in England; the gallant root of potatoes are common, and so are all sorts of roots, herbs and garden stuff.

It must needs follow then that diet cannot be scarce, since both rivers and woods afford it, and that such plenty of cattle and hogs are everywhere, which yield beef, veal, milk, butter, cheese and other made dishes, pork, bacon, and pigs, and that as sweet and savory meat as the world affords; these with the help of orchards and gardens, oysters, fish, fowl and venison, certainly cannot but be sufficient for a good diet and wholesome accomodation, considering how plentifully they are, and how easy with industry to be had.

Those servants that will be industrious may in their time of service gain a competent estate before their freedoms, which is usually done by many, and they gain esteem and assistance that appear so industrious. There is no master almost but will allow his servant a parcel of clear ground to plant some tobacco in for himself, which he may husband at those many idle times he hath allowed him and not prejudice but rejoice his master to see it, which in time of shipping he may lay out for commodities, and in summer sell them again with advantage, and get a sow-pig or two, which anybody almost will give him, and his master suffer him to keep them with his own. By that time he is for himself, he may have cattle, hogs and tobacco of his own, and come to live gallantly; but this must be gained (as I said) by industry and affability, not by sloth nor churlish behavior.

And whereas it is rumored that servants have no lodging other than on boards, by the fireside, it is contrary to reason to believe it: first, as we are Christians; next as people living under a law, which compels as well the master as the servant to perform his duty; nor can true labor be either expected or exacted without sufficient clothing, diet, and lodging; all which both their indentures (which must inviolably be observed) and the justice of the country requires.

But if any go thither, not in a condition of a servant, but pay his or her passage, which is some six pounds, let them not doubt but it is money well laid out; yet however let them not fail, although they carry little else, to take a bed along with them, and then few houses but will give them entertainment, either out of courtesy, or on reasonable terms; and I think it better for any that goes over free, and but in a mean condition, to hire himself for reasonable wages of tobacco and provision the first year, provided he happen in an honest house, and where the mistress is noted for a good housewife, of which there are very many (notwithstanding the cry to the contrary) for by that means he will live free of disbursement, have something to help him the next year, and be carefully looked to in his sickness (if he chance to fall sick). And let him so covenant that exceptions may be made, that he work not much in the hot weather, a course we always take with our new hands (as they call them) the first year they come in.

If they are women that go after this manner, that is paying their own passages, I advise them to sojourn in a house of honest repute, for by their good carriage they may advance themselves in marriage, by their ill, overthrow their fortunes. And although loose persons seldom live long unmarried if free, yet they match with as dissolute as themselves, and never live handsomely or are ever respected.

Now for those that carry over families and estates with a determination to inhabit, my advice is that they neither sojourn, for that will be chargeable; nor on the sudden purchase, for that may prove unfortunate; but that they for the first year hire a house (for seats are always to be hired), and by that means they will not only find content and live at a cheap rate, but be acquainted in the country and learn the worth and goodness of the plantation they mean to purchase; and so not rashly entangle themselves in an ill bargain, or find where a convenient parcel of land is for their turns to be taken up.

Yet are the inhabitants generally affable, courteous and very assistant to strangers (for what but plenty makes hospitality and good neighborhood) and no sooner are they settled, but they will be visiting, presenting and advising the stranger how to improve what they have, how to better their way of livelihood.

Justice is there duly and daily administered; hardly can any travel two miles together, but they will find a justice which hath power of himself to hear and determine mean differences, to secure and bind over notorious offenders, of which very few are in the country.

In every county are courts kept, every two months, and oftener if occasion require, in which courts all things are determined without exceptions; and if any dislike the proceedings of those courts, they have liberty to appeal to the Quarter Court, which is four times a year; and from thence to the Assembly, which is once or oftener every year; so that I am confident, more speedy justice and with smaller charge is not in any place to be found.

Theft is seldom punished, as being seldom or never committed; for as the proverb is, where there are no receivers, there are no thieves; and although doors are nightly left open (especially in the summer time), hedges hanging full of clothes, plate frequently used amongst all comers and goers (and there is good store of plate in many houses), yet I never heard of any loss ever received either in plate, linen, or anything else out of their houses all the time I inhabited there.

Indeed I have known some suffer for stealing of hogs, (but not since they have been plentiful) and whereas hogstealing was once punished with death, it is now made penal, and restitution given very amply to the owner thereof.

Cases of murder are punished as in England, and juries allowed, as well in criminal causes, as in all other differences between party and party, if they desire it.

Servants' complaints are freely harkened to, and (if not causelessly made), their masters are compelled either speedily to amend, or they are removed upon second complaint to another service; and oftentimes not only set free (if the abuse merit it), but ordered to give reparation and damage to their servant.

The country is very full of sober, modest persons, both men and women, and many that truly fear God and follow that perfect rule of our blessed Savior, to do as they would be done by; and of such a happy inclination is the country, that many who in England have been lewd and idle, there in emulation or imitation (for example moves more than precept) of the industry of those they find there, not only grow ashamed of their former courses, but abhor to hear of them, and in small time wipe off those stains they have formerly been tainted with. Yet I cannot but confess, there are people wicked enough (as what country is free) for we know some natures will never be reformed, but these must follow the Friar's Rule, *Si non caste, tamen caute* [If not chastely, then at any rate, cautiously]. For if any be known, either to profane the Lord's day, or his name, be found drunk, commit whoredom, scandalize or disturb his neighbor, or give offense to the world by living suspiciously in any bad courses, there are for each of these, severe and wholesome laws and remedies made, provided and duly put in execution. I can confidently affirm, that since my being in England, which is not yet four months, I have been an eye and ear witness of more deceits and villainies (and such as modesty forbids me to utter) than I either ever saw or heard mention made of in Virginia, in my one and twenty years abroad in those parts.

And therefore those that shall blemish Virginia any more, do but like the dog bark against the moon, until they be blind and weary; and Virginia is now in that secure growing condition, that like the moon so barked at, she will pass on her course, maugre [in spite of] all detractors, and a few years will bring it to that glorious happiness, that many of her calumniators will intercede to procure admittance thither, when it will be hard to be attained to. For in small time, little land will be to be taken up; and after a while none at all; and as the mulberry trees grow up, which are by everyone planted, tobacco will be laid by, and we shall wholly fall to making of silk (a sample of 400 lb. hath already been sent for England, and approved of) which will require little labor; and therefore shall have little use of servants. Besides children increase and thrive so well there, that they themselves will sufficiently supply the defect of servants, and in small time become a nation of themselves sufficient to people the country. And few there are but are able to give some portions with their daughters, more or less, according to their abilities; so that many coming out of England have raised themselves good fortunes there merely by matching with maidens born in the country.

And therefore I cannot but admire, and indeed much pity the dull stupidity of people necessitated in England, who rather than they will remove themselves, live here a base, slavish, penurious life; as if there were a necessity to live and to live so, choosing rather than they will forsake England to stuff Newgate, Bridewell and other jails with their carcasses, nay cleave to Tyburn itself, and so bring confusion to their souls, horror and infamy to their kindred or posterity. Others itch out their wearisome lives in reliance of other men's charities, an uncertain and unmanly expectation; some more abhorring such courses betake themselves to almost perpetual and restless toil and drudgeries out of which (while their strength lasts) they (observing hard diets, early and late hours) make hard shift to subsist from hand to mouth, until age or sickness takes them off from labor and directs them the way to beggery, and such indeed are to be pitied, relieved, and provided for.

The country is not only plentiful but pleasant and profitable, pleasant in regard of the brightness of the weather, the many delightful rivers on which the inhabitants are settled (every man almost living in sight of a lovely river), the abundance of game, the extraordinary good neighborhood and loving conversation they have one with the other.

Pleasant in their buildings, which although for most part they are but one story besides the loft, and built of wood, yet contrived so delightful, that your ordinary houses in England are not so handsome, for usually the rooms are large, daubed and whitelimed, glazed and flowered, and if not glazed windows, shutters which are made very pretty and convenient.

Pleasant in observing their stocks and flocks of cattle, hogs, and poultry, grazing, whisking and skipping in their sights, pleasant in having all things of their own, growing or breeding without drawing the penny to send for this and that, without which in England they cannot be supplied.

The manner living and trading there is thus: each man almost lives a freeholder, nothing but the value of 12 d. a year to be paid as rent, for every 50 acres of land; firing cost nothing; every man plants his own corn and need take no care for bread; if anything be bought, it is for convenience, exchanged presently, or for a day; payment is usually made but once a year.

In summer when fresh meat will not keep, seeing every man kills of his own, and quantities are inconvenient, they lend from one to another such portions of flesh as they can spare, which is repaid again when the borrower kills his.

If any fall sick, and cannot compass to follow his crop, which if not followed, will soon be lost, the adjoining neighbors will either voluntarily or upon a request join together, and work in it by spells, until the owner recovers, and that gratis, so that no man by sickness lose any part of his year's work.

Let any travel, it is without charge, and at every house is entertainment as in a hostery, and with it hearty welcome are strangers entertained.

In a word, Virginia wants no good victuals, wants not good dispositions, and as God hath freely bestowed it, they as freely impart with it, yet are there as well bad natures as good.

The profit of the country is either by their labor, their stock, or their trade.

By their labors is produced corn and tobacco, and all other growing provisions, and this tobacco however now low-rated, yet a good maintenance may be had out of it (for they have nothing of necessity but clothing to purchase), or can this mean price of tobacco long hold, for these reasons: first that in England it is prohibited, next that they have attained of late those sorts equal with the best Spanish, thirdly that the sickness in Holland is decreasing, which hath been a great obstruction to the sale of tobacco.

And lastly, that as the mulberry tree grows up, tobacco will be neglected and silk, flax, two staple commodities generally fallen upon.

Of the increase of cattle and hogs, which advantage is made, by selling beef, pork, and bacon, and butter etc. either to shipping, or to send to the Barbados, and other islands, and he is a very poor man that hath not sometimes provision to put off.

By trading with Indians for skins, beaver, furs, and other commodities, oftentimes good profits are raised. The Indians are in absolute subjection to the English, so that they both pay tribute to them and receive all their several kings from them, and as one dies they repair to the English for a successor, so that none need doubt it a place of security.

Several ways of advancement there are and employments both for the learned and laborer, recreation for the gentry, traffic for the adventurer, congregations for the ministry (and oh that God would stir up the hearts of more to go over, such as would teach good doctrine, and not paddle in faction, or state matters; they could not want maintenance, they would find an assisting, an embracing, a conforming people).

It is known (such preferment hath this country rewarded the industrious with) that some from being wool-hoppers and of as mean and meaner employment in England have there grown great merchants, and attained to the most eminent advancements the country afforded. If men cannot gain by diligence states in those parts (I speak not only mine own opinion, but divers others, and something by experience) it will hardly be done, unless by mere luck as gamesters thrive, and other accidentals.

Now having briefly set down the present state of Virginia not in fiction, but in reality, I wish the judicious reader to consider what dislike can be had to the country, or upon what grounds it is so infamously injured. I only therein covet to stop those blackmouthed babblers, that not only have and do abuse so noble a plantation, but abuse God's great blessing in adding to England so flourishing a branch, in persuading many souls rather to follow desperate and miserable courses in England, than to engage in so honorable an undertaking as to travel and inhabit there. To those I shall (if admonition will not work on their recreant spirits) only say, "Let him that is filthy be filthy still."

4

The Presence of Witches

Cotton Mather (1663–1728) was one of the most prolific and illustrious ornaments of the Puritan ministry, the son of another famous minister and a president of Harvard College, Increase Mather. The author of innumerable sermons, tracts, histories, and collections of interesting data, Cotton Mather assiduously gathered material to demonstrate the constant interventions of the devil in the affairs of mankind, particularly in New England, which was founded as a holy commonwealth, and therefore, a natural target for evil spirits.

In his zeal to expose the forces of darkness, Mather, like many of his contemporaries, believed implicitly in the existence of witches, men and women who were in the power of the devil and given the ability to torment their fellow human beings. *The Wonders of the Invisible World* was published in Boston in 1692 to defend this belief and the proceedings that had recently occurred in Salem. Although a number of New Englanders later pronounced the witchcraft trials a delusion and repudiated their roles in them, Cotton Mather believed in their justice to the end of his life. He never gave up his belief in witches or in the special providence of the New England settlements.

THE WONDERS
OF THE INVISIBLE WORLD
Cotton Mather

It was as long ago as the year 1637, that a faithful minister of the Church of England whose name was Mr. Edward Symons, did in a sermon afterwards printed, thus express himself: "At New England now the sun of comfort begins to appear, and the glorious day-star to show itself. There will come times in after ages, when the clouds will over-shadow and darken the sky there. Many now promise to themselves nothing but successive happiness there, which for a time through God's mercy they may enjoy, and I pray God, they may a long time, but in this world there is no happiness perpetual." An observation, or I had almost said, an inspiration, very dismally now verified upon us! It has been affirmed by some who best know New England, that the world will do New England a great piece of injustice, if it acknowledge not a measure of religion, loyalty, honesty, and industry,

From Cotton Mather, *The Wonders of the Invisible World* (London, 1862), 9–17, 120–129.

in the people there, beyond what is to be found with any other people for the number of them. We are still so happy, that I suppose there is no land in the universe more free from the debauching and debasing vices of ungodliness. The body of the people are hitherto so disposed, that swearing, Sabbath-breaking, whoring, drunkenness, and the like, do not make a gentleman but a monster, or a goblin, in the vulgar estimation. All this notwithstanding, we must humbly confess to our God that we are miserably degenerated from the first love of our predecessors. The first planters of these colonies were a chosen generation of men, who were first so pure, as to disrelish many things which they thought wanted reformation elsewhere; and yet withal so peaceable, that they embraced a voluntary exile in a squalid, horrid, American desert, rather than to live in contentions with their brethren. Those good men imagined that they would leave their posterity in a place where they should never see the inroads of profanity or superstition. And a famous person returning hence, could in a sermon before the Parliament, profess, "I have now been seven years in a country, where I never saw one man drunk, or heard one oath sworn, or beheld one beggar in the streets all the while." New England was a true Utopia. But in short, those interests of the Gospel, which were the errand of our fathers into these ends of the earth, have been too much neglected and postponed, and the attainments of a handsome education have been too much undervalued, by multitudes that have not fallen into exorbitances of wickedness; and some, especially of our young ones, when they have got abroad from under the restraints here laid upon them, have become extravagantly and abominably vicious. Hence 'tis, that the happiness of New England has been but for a time, as it was foretold, and not for a long time, as has been desired for us. A variety of calamity has long followed this plantation; and we have all the reason imaginable to ascribe it unto the rebuke of heaven upon us for our manifold apostasies; we make no right use of our disasters. If we do not, "Remember whence we are fallen, and repent, and do the first works." But yet our afflictions may come under a further consideration with us. There is a further cause of our afflictions, whose due must be given him.

The New Englanders are a people of God settled in those which were once the devil's territories; and it may easily be supposed that the devil was exceedingly disturbed, when he perceived such a people here accomplishing the promise of old made unto our blessed Jesus, "That he should have the utmost parts of the earth for his possession." I believe that never were more satanical devices used for the unsettling of any people under the sun, than what have been employed for the extirpation of the vine which God has here planted. But, all those attempts of hell have hitherto been abortive. Wherefore the devil is now making one attempt more upon us, an attempt more difficult, more surprising, more snarled with unintelligible circumstances than any that we have hitherto encountered. We have been advised by some credible Christians yet alive, that a malefactor accused of witchcraft as well as murder, and executed in this place more than forty years ago, did then give notice of a horrible plot against the country by witchcraft and a foundation of witchcraft then laid, which if it were not seasonably discovered, would probably blow up and pull down all the churches in the country. And we have now with horror seen the discovery of such a witchcraft! An army of devils is horribly broke in upon the place which is the center, and after a sort, the first-born of our English settlements. And the houses of the good people there are filled with the doleful shrieks of their children and servants, tormented by invisible hands with tortures altogether preternatural. After the mischiefs there endeavored, and since in part conquered, the terrible plague of evil angels hath made its progress into some other places, where other persons have been in like manner diabolically handled. These our poor afflicted neighbors, quickly after they became infected and infested with these demons, arrive to a capacity of discerning those which they conceive the shapes of their troublers; and notwithstanding the great and just suspicion that the demons might impose the shapes of innocent persons in their spectral exhibitions upon the sufferers (which may perhaps prove no small part of the witch-plot in the issue), yet many of the persons thus represented, being examined, several of them have been convicted of a very damnable witchcraft. Yea, more than one twenty have confessed, that they have signed unto a book which the devil showed them, and engaged in his hellish design of bewitching and ruining our land. We know not, at least I know not, how far the delusions of Satan may be interwoven into some circumstances of the confessions; but one would think all the rules of understanding human affairs are at an end, if after so many most voluntary harmonious confessions, made by intelligent persons of all ages, in sundry towns, at several times, we must not believe the main strokes wherein those confessions all agree; especially when we have a thousand preternatural things every day before our eyes, wherein the confessors do acknowledge their concernment, and give demonstration of their being so concerned. If the devils now can strike the minds of men with any poisons of so fine a composition and operation, that scores of innocent people shall unite, in confessions of a crime which we see actually committed, it is a thing prodigious, beyond the wonders of the former ages, and it threatens no less than a sort of a dissolution upon the world.

Doubtless, the thoughts of many will receive great scandal against New England from the number of persons that have been accused, or suspected, for witchcraft, in this country. But it were easy to offer many things that may answer and abate the scandal. The kingdoms of Sweden, Denmark, Scotland, yea and England itself, as well as the province of New England, have had their storms of witchcraft breaking upon them, which have made most lamentable devastations, which also, I wish, may be the last. And it is not uneasy to be imagined, that God has not brought out all the witchcraft in many other lands with such a speedy, dreadful, destroying jealousy, as burns forth upon such high treasons, committed here in a land of uprightness. Transgressors may more quickly here than elsewhere become a prey to the vengeance of Him "Who has eyes like a flame of fire, and, who walks in the midst of the golden candlesticks." Moreover, there are many parts of the world, who if they do upon this occasion insult over this people of God, need only to be told the story of what happened at Loim, in the Duchy of Gulic, where a popish curate having ineffectually tried many charms to eject the devil out of a damsel there possessed, he passionately bid the devil come out of her into himself; but the devil answered, "What need I meddle with one whom I am sure to have, and hold at the last day as my own for ever!"

The Trial of G.B. at a Court of Oyer
and Terminer Held in Salem, 1692

Glad should I have been, if I had never known the name of this man, or never had this occasion to mention so much as the first letters of his name. But the government requiring some account of his trial to be inserted in this book, it becomes me with all obedience to submit unto the order.

This G. B. was indicted for witchcraft, and in the prosecution of the charge against him, he was accused by five or six of the bewitched, as the author of their miseries; he was accused by eight of the confession witches as being a head actor at some of their hellish rendezvouzes, and one who had the promise of being a king in Satan's kingdom, now going to be erected. He was accused by nine persons for extraordinary lifting, and such feats of strength, as could not be done without a diabolical assistance. And for other such things he was accused, until about thirty testimonies were brought in against him; nor were these judged the half of what might have been considered for his conviction. However they were enough to fix the character of a witch upon him according to the rules of reasoning by the judicious Gaule in that case directed.

The court being sensible that the testimonies of the parties bewitched used to have a room among the suspicions or presumptions brought in against one indicted for witchcraft, there were now heard the testimonies of several persons who were most notoriously bewitched and every day tortured by invisible hands, and these now all charged the spectres of G. B. to have a share in their torments. At the examination of this G. B. the bewitched people were grievously harassed with preternatural mischiefs, which could not possibly be dissembled; and they still ascribed it unto the endeavors of G. B. to kill them. And now upon the trial of one of the bewitched persons, testified, that in her agonies, a little black haired man came to her, saying his name was B. and bidding her set her hand to a book which he showed unto her; and bragging that he was a conjurer, above the ordinary rank of witches, that he often persecuted her with the offer of that book, saying, "She should be well, and need fear nobody, if she would but sign it." But he inflicted cruel pains and hurts upon her, because of her denying so to do. The testimonies of the other sufferers concurred with these. And it was remarkable, that whereas biting was one of the ways which the witches used for the vexing of the sufferers, when they cried out of G. B. biting them, the print of the teeth would be seen on the flesh of the complainers, and just such a set of teeth as G. B.'s would then appear upon them, which could be distinguished from those of some other men. Others of them testified, that in their torments, G. B. tempted them to go unto a sacrament, unto which they perceived him with a sound of trumpet, summoning of other witches, who quickly after the sound, would come from all quarters unto the rendezvouz. One of them falling into a kind of trance, affirmed, that G. B. had carried her away into a very high mountain, where he showed her mighty and glorious kingdoms, and said, "he would give them all to her, if she would write in his book," but she told him, "They were none of his to give," and refused the motions, enduring of much misery for the refusal.

It cost the court a wonderful deal of trouble, to hear the testimonies of the sufferers; for when they were going to give in their depositions, they would for a long time be taken with fits, that made them uncapable of saying anything. The Chief Judge asked the prisoner who he thought hindered these witnesses from giving their testimonial. And he answered, "He supposed it was the devil." That honorable person replied, "How comes the devil then to be so loath to have any testimony born against you?" Which cast him into very great confusion.

It has been a frequent thing for the bewitched people to be entertained with apparitions of ghosts of murdered people, at the same time that the spectres of the witches trouble them. These ghosts do always afright the beholders more than all the other spectral representations; and when they exhibit themselves, they cry out of being murdered by the witchcrafts or other violences of the persons who are then in spectre present. It is further considered, that once or twice these apparitions have been seen by others, at the very same time they have shown themselves to the bewitched; and seldom have there been these apparitions, but when something unusual or suspected have attended the death of the party thus appearing. Some that have been accused by these apparitions accosting of the bewitched people, who had never heard a word of any such persons ever being in the world, have upon a fair examination, freely and fully confessed the murders of those very persons, although these also did not know how the apparitions had complained of them. Accordingly several of the bewitched had given in their testimony, that they had been troubled with the apparitions of two women, who said, that they were G. B.'s two wives, and that he had been the death of them; and that the magistrates must be told of it, before whom if B. upon his trial denied it, they did not know but that they should appear again in court. Now, G. B. had been infamous for the barbarous usage of his two late wives, all the country over. Moreover, it was testified, the spectre of G. B. threatening of the sufferers, told them, he had killed (besides others) Mrs. Lawson and her daughter, Ann. And it was noted, that these were the virtuous wife and daughter of one at whom this G. B. might have a prejudice for his being serviceable at Salem village, from whence himself had in ill terms removed some years before. And that when they died, which was long since, there were some odd circumstances about them, which made some of the attendants there suspect something of witchcraft, tho none imagined from what quarter it should come.

Well, G. B. being now upon his trial, one of the bewitched persons was cast into horror at the ghost of B.'s two deceased wives then appearing before him, and crying for vengeance against him. Hereupon several of the bewitched persons were successively called in, who all not knowing what the former had seen and said, concurred in their horror of the apparition, which they affirmed that he had before him. But he, tho much appalled, utterly denied that he discerned anything of it; nor was it any part of his conviction.

Judicious writers have assigned it a great place in the conviction of witches, when persons are impeached by other notorious witches to be as ill as themselves, especially if the persons have been much noted for neglecting the worship of God. Now, as there might have been testimonies enough of G. B.'s antipathy to prayer, and the other ordinances of God, tho by his profession singularly obliged thereunto; so, there now came in against the prisoner, the testimonies of several persons who confessed their own having been horrible witches, and ever since their confessions, had been themselves terribly tortured by the devils and other witches, even like the other sufferers; and therein undergone the pains of many deaths for their confessions.

These now testified that G. B. had been at witch-meetings with them; and that he was the person who had seduced and compelled them into the snares of witchcraft. That he promised them fine clothes for doing it; that he brought poppets to them, and thorns to stick into these poppets, for the afflicting of other people; and that he exhorted them with the rest of the crew, to bewitch all Salem Village, but be sure to do it gradually if they would prevail in what they did.

When the Lancashire witches were condemned I don't remember that there was any considerable further evidence, than that of the bewitched, and than that of some that confessed. We see so much already against G. B. But this being indeed not enough, there were other things to render what had been already produced credible.

A famous divine recites this among the convictions of a witch, "The testimony of the party bewitched, whether pining or dying; together with the joint oaths of sufficient persons that have seen certain prodigious pranks or feats wrought by the party accused." Now, God had been pleased so to leave this G. B. that he had ensnared himself by several instances which he had formerly given for a preternatural strength, and which were now produced against him. He was a very puny man, yet he had often done things beyond the strength of a giant. A gun of about seven foot barrel, and so heavy that strong men could not steadily hold it out with both hands; there were several testimonies, given in by persons of credit and honor, that he made nothing of taking up such a gun behind the lock, with but one hand, and holding it like a pistol, at arms-end. G. B. in his vindication, was so foolish as to say, that an Indian "was there, and held it out at the same time." Whereas none of the spectators ever saw any such Indian; but they supposed, the Black Man (as the witches call the devil; and they generally say he resembles an Indian), might give him that assistance. There was evidence likewise brought in, that he made nothing of taking up whole barrels filled with molasses or cider, in very disadvantageous postures, and carrying of them through the difficultest places out of a canoe to the shore.

Yea, there were two testimonies that G. B. with only putting a forefinger of his right hand into the muzzle of an heavy gun, a fowling-piece of about six or seven foot barrel, did lift up the gun and hold it out at arms-end, a gun which the deponents thought strong men could not with both hands lift up, and hold out at the butt end as usual. Indeed, one of these witnesses was over-persuaded by some

41

persons, to be out of the way upon G. B.'s trial; but he came afterwards with sorrow for his withdrawal, and gave in his testimony. Nor were either of these witnesses made use of as evidences in the trial.

There came in several testimonies relating to the domestic affairs of G. B. which had a very hard aspect upon him; and not only proved him a very ill man, but also confirmed the belief of the character which had been already fastened on him.

'Twas testified, that keeping his two successive wives in a strange kind of slavery, he would when he came home from abroad, pretend to tell the talk which any had with them; that he has brought them to the point of death by his harsh dealings with his wives, and then made the people about him to promise that in case death should happen, they would say nothing of it; that his wives had privately complained unto the neighbors about frightful apparitions of evil spirits with which their house was sometimes infested; and that many such things have been whispered among the neighborhood. There were also some other testimonies relating to the death of people whereby the consciences of an impartial jury were convinced that G. B. had bewitched the persons mentioned in the complaints. But I am forced to omit several passages, in this, as well as in all the succeeding trials, because the scribes who took notice of them, have not supplied me.

One Mr. Ruck, brother-in-law to this G. B. testified, that G. B. and himself, and his sister, who was G. B.'s wife, going out for two or three miles to gather strawberries, Ruck and his sister, the wife of G. B., rode home very softly with G. B. on foot in their company. G. B. stepped aside a little into the bushes, whereupon they halted and helloed for him. He not answering, they went away homewards with a quickened pace, without expectation of seeing him in a considerable while. And yet when they were got near home, to their astonishment they found him on foot with them, having a basket of strawberries. G. B. immediately then fell to chiding his wife, on the account of what she had been speaking to her brother, of him, on the road; which when they wondered at, he said, "He knew their thoughts." Ruck being startled at that, made some reply, intimating, that the devil himself did not know so far; but G. B. answered, "My God makes known your thoughts unto me." The prisoner now at the bar had nothing to answer unto what was thus witnessed against him that was worth considering. Only he said, "Ruck and his wife left a man with him, when they left him." Which Ruck now affirmed to be false; and when the court asked G. B. "What the man's name was?" his countenance was much altered; nor could he say, who 'twas. But the court began to think, that he then stepped aside, only that by the assistance of the Black Man he might put on his invisibility, and in that fascinating mist, gratify his own jealous humor, to hear what they said of him. Which trick of rendering themselves invisible, our witches do in their confessions pretend, that they sometimes are masters of; and it is the more credible because there is demonstration that they often render many other things utterly invisible.

Faltering, faulty, unconstant, and contrary answers upon judicial and deliberate examination, are counted some unlucky symptoms of guilt in all crimes, especially in witchcraft. Now there never was a prisoner more eminent for them than G. B., both at his examination and on his trial. His tergiversations, contradictions,

42

and falsehoods, were very sensible; he had little to say, but that he had heard some things that he could not prove, reflecting upon the reputation of some of the witnesses. Only he gave in a paper to the jury, wherein, altho he had many times before granted, not only that there are witches, but also, that the present sufferings of the country are the effects of horrible witchcraft, yet he now goes to evince it, "that there neither are, nor ever were witches, that having made a compact with the devil, can send a devil to torment other people at a distance." This paper was transcribed out of Ady; which the court presently knew, as soon as they heard it. But he said, he had taken none of it out of any book; for which, his evasion afterwards, was, that a gentleman gave him the discourse in a manuscript, from whence he transcribed it.

The jury brought him in guilty; but when he came to die, he utterly denied the fact, whereof he had been thus convicted.

The Pious in Captivity

In the late seventeenth and early eighteenth centuries the inland portions of the British colonies remained sparsely populated and subject to all the dangers of the frontier. Connecticut river towns were particularly vulnerable to marauding Indians and a number of towns, like Deerfield, were burned and sacked.

The Reverend John Williams (1664–1729) was a minister in Deerfield when the Indians attacked in the winter of 1703/4; he was taken prisoner along with many others. Colonists who survived such experiences often wrote them up in the form of captivity narratives, and Williams was no exception. This genre frightened and thrilled most Americans, none of whom lived very far from the threat of Indian or French enemies. Despite the torture of their captors, the hardships of forced marches, and the poison of forced conversions, redeemed captives like Williams indulged in little public bitterness or recrimination. For the devout such experiences were tests of faith, and their eventual release evidence of divine mercy. Williams himself was returned to Boston in 1706, and the following year produced his masterful narrative. He remarried in 1707, fathered five more children, and spent his last years preaching to a rebuilt Deerfield.

THE REDEEMED CAPTIVE RETURNING TO ZION
Reverend John Williams

On Tuesday, the 29th of February, 1703/4, not long before break of day, the enemy came in like a flood upon us; our watch being unfaithful;—an evil, the awful effects of which, in the surprisal of our fort, should bespeak all watchmen to avoid, as they would not bring the charge of blood upon themselves. They came to my house in the beginning of the onset, and by their violent endeavors to break open doors and windows, with axes and hatchets, awaked me out of sleep; on which I leaped out of bed, and, running towards the door, perceived the enemy making their entrance into the house. I called to awaken two soldiers in the chamber, and returning toward my bedside for my arms, the enemy immediately broke into the

From John Williams, *The Redeemed Captive Returning to Zion* (Northampton, 1835), 10–21, 29–32.

room, I judge to the number of twenty, with painted faces, and hideous acclamations. I reached up my hands to the bed-tester for my pistol, uttering a short petition to God, for everlasting mercies for me and mine, on account of the merits of our glorified Redeemer; expecting a present passage through the valley of the shadow of death; saying in myself, as Isa. xxxviii. 10, 11, "I said, in the cutting off of my days, I shall go to the gates of the grave: I am deprived of the residue of my years. I said, I shall not see the Lord, even the Lord, in the land of the living: I shall behold man no more with the inhabitants of the world." Taking down my pistol, I cocked it, and put it to the breast of the first Indian that came up; but my pistol missing fire, I was seized by three Indians, who disarmed me, and bound me naked, as I was in my shirt, and so I stood for near the space of an hour. Binding me, they told me they would carry me to Quebec. My pistol missing fire was an occasion of my life's being preserved; since which I have also found it profitable to be crossed in my own will. The judgment of God did not long slumber against one of the three which took me, who was a captain, for by sunrising he received a mortal shot from my next neighbor's house; who opposed so great a number of French and Indians as three hundred, and yet were no more than seven men in an ungarrisoned house.

I cannot relate the distressing care I had for my dear wife, who had lain in but a few weeks before; and for my poor children, family, and Christian neighbors. The enemy fell to rifling the house, and entered in great numbers into every room. I begged to God to remember mercy in the midst of judgment; that he would so far restrain their wrath, as to prevent their murdering of us; that we might have grace to glorify his name, whether in life or death; and, as I was able, committed our state to God. The enemies who entered the house, were all of them Indians and Macquas, insulted over me awhile, holding up hatchets over my head, threatening to burn all I had; but yet God, beyond expectation, made us in a great measure to be pitied; for though some were so cruel and barbarous as to take and carry to the door two of my children and murder them, as also a negro woman; yet they gave me liberty to put on my clothes, keeping me bound with a cord on one arm, till I put on my clothes to the other; and then changing my cord, they let me dress myself, and then pinioned me again. Gave liberty to my dear wife to dress herself and our remaining children. About sun an hour high, we were all carried out of the house, for a march, and saw many of the houses of my neighbors in flames, perceiving the whole fort, one house excepted, to be taken. Who can tell what sorrows pierced our souls, when we saw ourselves carried away from God's sanctuary, to go into a strange land, exposed to so many trials; the journey being at least three hundred miles we were to travel; the snow up to the knees, and we never inured to such hardships and fatigues; the place we were to be carried to, a Popish country. Upon my parting from the town, they fired my house and barn. We were carried over the river, to the foot of the mountain, about a mile from my house, where we found a great number of our Christian neighbors, men, women, and children, to the number of an hundred, nineteen of which were afterward murdered by the way, and two starved to death, near Cowass, in a time of great scarcity, or famine, the savages underwent there. When we came to the foot of the mountain,

45

they took away our shoes, and gave us in the room of them Indian shoes, to prepare us for our travel.

After this, we went up the mountain, and saw the smoke of the fires in the town, and beheld the awful desolations of Deerfield. And before we marched any farther, they killed a sucking child belonging to one of the English. There were slain by the enemy of the inhabitants of Deerfield, to the number of thirty-eight, besides nine of the neighboring towns. We travelled not far the first day; God made the heathen so to pity our children, that though they had several wounded persons of their own to carry upon their shoulders, for thirty miles, before they came to the river, yet they carried our children, incapable of travelling, in their arms, and upon their shoulders. When we came to our lodging place, the first night, they dug away the snow, and made some wigwams, cut down some small branches of the spruce-tree to lie down on, and gave the prisoners somewhat to eat; but we had but little appetite. I was pinioned and bound down that night, and so I was every night whilst I was with the army. Some of the enemy who brought drink with them from the town fell to drinking, and in their drunken fit they killed my negro man, the only dead person I either saw at the town, or in the way.

In the night an Englishman made his escape; in the morning (March 1), I was called for, and ordered by the general to tell the English, that if any more made their escape, they would burn the rest of the prisoners. He that took me was unwilling to let me speak with any of the prisoners, as we marched; but on the morning of the second day, he being appointed to guard the rear, I was put into the hands of my other master, who permitted me to speak to my wife, when I overtook her, and to walk with her to help her in her journey. On the way, we discoursed of the happiness of those who had a right to an house not made with hands, eternal in the heavens; and God for a father and friend; as also, that it was our reasonable duty quietly to submit to the will of God, and to say, "The will of the Lord be done." My wife told me her strength of body began to fail, and that I must expect to part with her; saying, she hoped God would preserve my life, and the life of some, if not of all our children with us; and commended to me, under God, the care of them. She never spake any discontented word as to what had befallen us, but with suitable expressions justified God in what had happened. We soon made a halt, in which time my chief surviving master came up, upon which I was put upon marching with the foremost, and so made my last farewell of my dear wife, the desire of my eyes, and companion in many mercies and afflictions. Upon our separation from each other, we asked for each other grace sufficient for what God should call us to. After our being parted from one another, she spent the few remaining minutes of her stay in reading the Holy Scriptures; which she was wont personally every day to delight her soul in reading, praying, meditating on, by herself, in her closet, over and above what she heard out of them in our family worship. I was made to wade over a small river, and so were all the English, the water above knee deep, the stream very swift; and after that to travel up a small mountain; my strength was almost spent, before I came to the top of it. No sooner had I overcome the difficulty of that ascent, but I was permitted to sit down, and be unburdened of my pack. I sat pitying those who were behind, and entreated my master to let me go down and help my wife; but he refused, and would not let me stir from him. I asked each of the prisoners (as they passed by me) after her, and heard that, passing through the above-said river, she fell down, and was plunged over head and ears in the water; after which she travelled not far, for at the foot of that mountain, the cruel and bloodthirsty savage who took her slew her with his hatchet at one stroke, the tidings of which were very awful. And yet such was the hard-heartedness of the adversary, that my tears were reckoned to me as a reproach. My loss and the loss of my children was great; our hearts were so filled with sorrow, that nothing but the comfortable hopes of her being taken away, in mercy to herself, from the evils we were to see, feel, and suffer under (and joined to the assembly of the spirits of just men made perfect, to rest in peace, and joy unspeakable and full of glory, and the good pleasure of God thus to exercise us), could have kept us from sinking under, at that time. That Scripture, Job 1.21, "Naked came I out of my mother's womb, and naked shall I return thither: the Lord gave, and the Lord hath taken away; blessed be the name of the Lord,"—was brought to my mind, and from it, that an afflicting God was to be glorified; with some other places of Scripture, to persuade to a patient bearing my afflictions.

We were again called upon to march, with a far heavier burden on my spirits than on my back. I begged of God to overrule, in his providence, that the corpse of one so dear to me, and of one whose spirit he had taken to dwell with him in glory, might meet with a Christian burial, and not be left for meat to the fowls of the air and beasts of the earth; a mercy that God graciously vouchsafed to grant. For God put it into the hearts of my neighbors, to come out as far as she lay, to take up her corpse, carry it to the town, and decently to bury it soon after. In our march they killed a sucking infant of one of my neighbors; and before night a girl of about eleven years of age. I was made to mourn, at the consideration of my flock being, so far, a flock of slaughter, many being slain in the town, and so many murdered in so few miles from the town; and from fears what we must yet expect, from such who delightfully imbrued their hands in the blood of so many of His people. When we came to our lodging place, an Indian captain from the eastward spake to my master about killing me, and taking off my scalp. I lifted up my heart to God, to implore his grace and mercy in such a time of need; and afterwards I told my master, if he intended to kill me, I desired he would let me know of it; assuring him that my death, after a promise of quarter, would bring the guilt of blood upon him. He told me he would not kill me. We laid down and slept, for God sustained and kept us.

On the Sabbath day (March 5), we rested, and I was permitted to pray, and preach to the captives. When we arrived at New France, we were forbidden praying one with another, or joining together in the service of God.

Tuesday, March 7, in the morning, before we travelled, one Mary Brooks, a pious young woman, came to the wigwam where I was, and told me she desired to bless God, who had inclined the heart of her master to let her come and take her farewell of me. Said she, "By my falls on the ice yesterday, I injured myself, causing a miscarriage this night, so that I am not able to travel far; I know they will kill me today; but," says she, "God has (praised be his name!) by his spirit, with his word, strengthened me to my last encounter with death;" and so mentioned to me some places of Scripture seasonably sent in for her support. "And," says she, "I am not afraid of death; I can, through the grace of God, cheerfully submit to his will. Pray for me," said she, at parting, "that God would take me to himself." Accordingly, she was killed that day. I mention it, to the end I may stir up all, in their young days, to improve the death of Christ by faith, to a giving them an holy boldness in the day of death.

The next day (Wednesday, March 8), we were made to scatter one from another into smaller companies; and one of my children was carried away with Indians belonging to the eastern parts. At night my master came to me, with my pistol in his hand, and put it to my breast, and said, "Now I will kill you, for," he said, "you would have killed me with it if you could." But by the grace of God, I was not much daunted, and whatever his intention might be, God prevented my death.

The next day (Thursday, March 9), I was again permitted to pray with that company of captives with me, and we were allowed to sing a psalm together. After which, I was taken from all the company of the English, excepting two children of my neighbors, one of which, a girl of four years of age, was killed by her Macqua master the next morning (Friday, March 10); the snow being so deep when we left the river, that he could not carry the child and his pack too.

[At Shamblee] The next morning the bell rang for mass. My master bid me go to church; I refused; he threatened me, and went away in a rage. At noon the Jesuits sent for me to dine with them, for I ate at their table all the time I was at the fort; and after dinner they told me the Indians would not allow of any of their captives staying in their wigwams whilst they were at church, and were resolved by force and violence to bring us all to church if we would not go without. I told them it was highly unreasonable so to impose upon those who were of a contrary religion, and to force us to be present at such a service as we abhorred, was nothing becoming Christianity. They replied, they were savages, and would not hearken to reason, but would have their wills. Said also, if they were in New England themselves, they would go into their churches and see their ways of worship. I answered, the case was far different, for there was nothing (themselves being judges) as to matter or manner of worship but what was according to the word of God in our churches, and therefore it could not be an offence to any man's conscience. But among them there were idolatrous superstitions in worship. They said, "Come and see, and offer us conviction of what is superstitious in worship." To which I answered, that I was not to do evil that good might come of it, and that forcing in matters of religion was hateful. They answered, "The Indians are resolved to have it so, and they could not pacify them without my coming; and they would engage they should offer no force or violence to cause any compliance with their ceremonies." The next mass, my master bid me go to church. I objected; he rose and forcibly pulled me by my head and shoulders out of the wigwam to the church, which was nigh the door. So I went in and sat down behind the door: and there saw a great confusion, instead of any Gospel order; for one of the Jesuits was at the altar saying mass in a tongue unknown to the savages, and the other, between the altar and the door, saying and singing prayers among the Indians at the same time; and many others were at the same time saying over their Pater-nosters and Ave Mary by tale from their chapelit, or beads on a string. At our going out we smiled at their devotion so managed, which was offensive to them, for they said we made a derision of their worship. When I was here a certain savagess died. One of the Jesuits told me she was a very holy woman, who had not committed one sin in twelve years. After a day or two the Jesuits asked me what I thought of their way now I saw it. I told them I thought Christ said of it, as Mark vii. 7, 8, 9, "Howbeit, in vain do they worship me, teaching for doctrines the commandments of men. For laying aside the commandment of God, ye hold the tradition of men, as the washing of pots and cups; and many other such like things ye do. And he said unto them, Full well ye reject the commandment of God, that ye may keep your own tradition." They told me they were not the commandments of men, but apostolical traditions, of equal authority with the Holy Scriptures; and that after my death I would bewail my not praying to the Virgin Mary, and that I should find the want of her intercession for me with her Son; judging me to hell for asserting the Scriptures to be a perfect rule of faith; and said I abounded in my own sense, entertaining explications contrary to the sense of the Pope, regularly sitting with a General Council, explaining Scripture and making articles of faith. I told them it was my comfort that Christ was to be my judge, and not they, at the great day; and as for their censuring and judging me, I was not moved with it.

One day a certain savagess taken prisoner in Philip's war, who had lived at Mr. Bulkley's at Weathersfield, called Ruth, who could speak English very well and who had been often at my house, being now proselyted to the Romish faith, came into the wigwam, and with her an English maid who was taken in the last war. She was dressed in Indian apparel, and was unable to speak one word of English. She could neither tell her own name nor the name of the place from whence she was taken. These two talked in the Indian dialect with my master a long time; after which my master bade me cross myself; I told him I would not; he commanded me several times, and I as often refused. Ruth said, "Mr. Williams, you know the Scripture, and therefore act against your own light; for you know the Scripture saith, 'Servants, obey your masters'; he is your master and you his servant." I told her she was ignorant and knew not the meaning of the Scripture; telling her I was not to disobey the great God to obey my master, and that I was ready to die and suffer for God if called thereto. On which she talked with my master: I suppose she interpreted what I said. My master took hold of my hand to force me to cross myself, but I struggled with him, and would not suffer him to guide my hand. Upon this he pulled off a crucifix from off his own neck, and bade me kiss it; but I refused once and again. He told me he would dash out my brains with his hatchet if I refused. I told him I should sooner choose death than to sin against God. Then he ran and took up his hatchet and acted as though he would have dashed out my brains. Seeing I was not moved, he threw down his hatchet, saying he would bite off all my nails if I still refused. I gave him my hand and told him I was ready to suffer: he set his teeth in my thumb-nail and gave a gripe, and then said, "No good minister, no love God, as bad as the Devil," and so left off. I have reason to bless God, who strengthened me to withstand. By this he was so discouraged, as never more to meddle with me about my religion. I asked leave of the Jesuits to pray with those English of our town that were with me; but they absolutely refused to give us any permission to pray one with another, and did what they could to prevent our having any discourse together.

6

Religion and the Profit Motive

In the early years of the eighteenth century provincial economies grew more complex, and enterprising Americans became more venturesome. Shrewd minds could detect great profits in commerce and even in manufacturing, and some of them were not averse to using sharp and unethical business practices, if these would aid their quest for money.

For some businessmen, however, brought up holding rigorous religious values, their commercial dealings produced guilt feelings along with the profits. Josiah Quinby, the author of the following pamphlet, which was published by John Peter Zenger in 1740, was one of them. Imprisoned for debt after a long and checkered commercial career, Quinby reveals some of the conflicts that afflicted his generation of traders, and along with them some of the opportunities that lay open to a clever New Yorker.

A SHORT HISTORY
OF A LONG JOURNEY
Josiah Quinby

I was born at Westchester in the year 1693, of honest parents and good livers, according to the custom of that place. I being my father's eldest son, he wanted my help on his farm, and so brought me up to husbandry. I had very little schooling. I could read pretty well but was but a poor writer. As my father and mother were of those called Quakers, so they endeavored to bring me up in that way of religion. But I proved rude and very unlucky or mischievous amongst my companions, tho' at some times I was sober and religious.

When I was about 17 years old I grew more sober and religious, and before I was 19 was accounted a member of that church, and had so good an impression of virtue and religion on my mind, that those of that Society received me as such, and the eyes of many were on me for good, hoping that I would prove a good, religious, self-denying man.

I was very sincere and tender in those days, and really intended, through the help of grace that then seemed to rest in me, to have given up my mind to live answerable thereto. But yet at times I grew careless, and after that fell upon several projects and schemes of business.

From *A Short History of a Long Journey; It being some Account of the Life of Josiah Quinby, until he came to enter into the 48th Year of his Age* (New York, 1740), 11–36, 49–54, 56–61.

Some of my business was such that it did not become neither me nor any of that Society to which I belonged, nor indeed any religious Christian. And for these my proceedings, several members and elders of the Meeting that I belonged to, came to me and let me know they were concerned to forward me of the ill consequences of my following such a course of business as I had done. For by this time I had bought and sold many uncertainties, and got into the law, which I had no reason to have done. I was so forward an adventurer that not only many of this county sought to me, and I to them, but also several others from several parts of this government, and some from other adjacent governments, came to me to truck, traffic, buy and sell, in very uncertain affairs and business, some of which went hard on my side, I losing large sums of money. Yet for the most part I got the better of those with whom I ventured.

I got money by large sums, for my dealings were not much in trifles, but in houses, lands, mills, and chiefly things of great consequence. Tho' I also bought some tracts of land fairly, and, dividing them, sold them fairly and gained considerable money by such fair dealings, and I gained money by several projects and contrivances. I had a way to get money yet I had not a faculty to keep it. I got large sums from rich men that were more wise and honest than myself, and fools sometimes got it from me again. I sometimes thought there was a just judgment upon me for this business I followed, for tho' I got large sums of money and great bargains and had money very plenty at times, yet sometimes I wanted money very much, so that I hired 12 or 15 hundred pounds, and for several years I gained above 500 pounds a year, and one year I gained upwards of 900 pounds.

This my going on grieved many of my religious friends, who saw that I was grown more careless concerning religion and virtue than I had been. Whereupon several of the elders again dealt with me, by censoring me for my uncommon proceedings and running of ventures in hazards not much better than gaming. They read to me the advice and counsel of the yearly Meeting of London, and others of Friends' orders and discipline, wherein it is set forth and declared, "That those in unity with that church may not cheat the King by running of goods, nor act deceivably with any of his subjects." And they knowing I was got into a strange sort of juggling business, too much like that of the South Sea Stock, some of them were for denying me, except I would adhere to their counsel. Others advised to the contrary, for though some of my business was wrong, yet they said, "That I was a good commonwealth man, for I had bought and sold a great deal very fairly, and employed many men, whom I generally paid very punctually, so that my word would pass for hundreds of pounds at ready money." They therefore advised me to desist some part of my business, such as they thought unfair, and endeavored to enforce their arguments against me. I answered them with my reasons, and went on still with my notions and business according to my own humor. I undertook and employed many hands in building and rebuilding several stocks of mills, and for my projecting had several sums of money.

As I had made many uncertain bargains of many other kinds, so I have some uncertain bargains concerning mills, one of which I will relate something of in particular, by which you may partly judge of others. The case was this.

I met with some merchants at New York, solid, honest men, and they understanding I was reckoned somewhat acute or famous for projecting or building of mills, and knowing I had a stream which might serve to set a stock of mills on, they viewed the place, and found that at best it would afford but a low head of water. They wanted mills, and as there had been a mill built on the place before by a noted millwright, which mill could never grind so much as 5 bushels an hour of good meal, these merchants thought it impossible for me to build mills there to grind above 6 bushels an hour of good bolting meal, 6 hours in one tide. Yet I proposed to build mills on the said place to great perfection and performance. In the conclusion we agreed, and made the price according to what they should grind for 6 hours together, in an hour, for that was to be the trial. But tho' these men knew and did their common business well, yet they did not know nor believe that I was capable of making any great performance with mills in that place, but I knew it, and therefore I was the more guilty of overreaching them. However, we agreed and went on. I was to build the mills and they were to have them at a price according to the wheat they could grind in 6 hours, in one tide. I had a great mind to have got their consent to have made the said trial with the great pair of stones which was 5 feet broad, and the lesser but 4 feet and 7 inches, for after the mills were finished and both pairs of stones proved by grinding, I offered to drop 164 pounds the price of the mills if they would consent that the trial should be made with the great pair of stones, but they refused that. Now this trial was difficult because in this province of New York wheat and flour are supposed to be the greatest articles of produce we have, and mills being exceeding plenty and wanting custom a great deal of their time, so the millers or owners of mills have been very nice and careful to grind for the bolters in the exactest manner the very best of bolting meal to gain custom.

We then got ready for said trial, and after the stones had ground a little while and seemed to be well settled in their motion, and came to make good bolting meal to the unanimous satisfaction of said judges, then I began to grind measured wheat and went on the trial. The first hour I ground upwards of 16 bushels of wheat, and after that I ground near 18 bushels an hour, and so on until the mills were shut down, grinding as fast and well to the end as at any time at all. Indeed I had a mind to have brought the said little pair of stones to have ground 20 bushels an hour on the trial, but the judges persuaded me that I ground fast enough.

I would not have been so particular in relating this matter, but that several persons, some of whom saw this trial performed and are now living, have urged me to publish the said trial to the world as an advertisement to excite those that are concerned in mills, to endeavor to come to a greater perfection in grinding than is usually performed.

Yet they came to an unreasonable price, nigh two thousand pounds more than they were really worth. I was guilty of this imposition on these men, because I knew most concerning these affairs. For it was not under their notice what a performance I could make. I believe they wanted mills and were willing to give a good honest price for them, but I wanted an advantage. This I do declare to my own shame, and have sincerely thought that I have found as much guilt and

53

condemnation within myself for this thing as ever I found for any deed that ever I did in the course of all my life and business, because this was done with a premeditated design.

However these merchants, after they saw themselves caught, made a vigorous defense against paying so much money, and their lawyers found fault with our bonds and articles of agreement. I sued them, and tho' I seemed too hard for them in the law, yet they found means to avoid the payment of the money, until partly by arbitrations and partly by consent of parties, a great part or all of the extravagant price was dropped, and they finally paid me 975 pounds and court charges. As for their opposition and defense against my unreasonable demands, I think they were to be commended.

Now sometimes men have come to me with a design to overreach me in bargains, knowing that I was very bold and apt to venture, and if such should happen to be bit, as we call it, I did not pity them so much. Many such I have met with, some of which went away with loss, and others with gain and triumph, and thus I have stood many chances. But when I found I had overdone honest men it hath made me heartily sorry for them, and in such cases I have given back many hundreds of pounds.

I often had occasion to travel to New England, and by inquiring there amongst their traders I found by their invoices and bills of parcels made at Boston, that many sorts of goods, especially land goods, were considerably cheaper at New York than they were at Boston. I also observed that barreled pork, wheat and flax seed were much cheaper in Connecticut government than at New York, considering the difference of the moneys. And observing that some of the traders in New England sold many things to the inhabitants extreme dear, I thought some of them used great extortion in dealing so with the people, and that I could use them much better, and perhaps mend thereby my decaying circumstances. So I ventured to trade from New York to New England. I took some hundred pounds worth of goods in New York, and sold them in New England for advance, and I likewise got good returns for New York. I advanced on pork twelve shillings per barrel, on wheat, thirteen pence, and on flax seed, sixteen pence per bushel. And tho' then I sold goods cheap, the returns made out profit enough, and this success encouraged me to go largely the second year. Now the natural courage and boldness of my temper commonly used to lead me to extremes, and now I wanted money, so I ventured to set up several stores in New England, and when it came to be generally known in New York that I kept stores in New England, the merchants in New York were very fond of my custom. One would call me into this store and another into another, so that I have been called into 4 or 5 in going about 40 or 50 rods. Then they would show me their good pennyworths, some again would take me by the hand, others by the coat, some claiming old acquaintance and offering me credit, both Jews and Gentiles. And by such means I was prevailed on to take great quantities of goods where I intended to have taken less. There were several likewise in New England who encouraged me, telling me that they could by trading turn several thousand pounds worth of goods into profitable returns for New York in a year.

Now as I said, being got out of business and into debt, and being both ambitious and loath to break of business, and considering that several times by bold and uncommon enterprises (which I thought more unlikely to hit than this) and yet some of them had taken wonderful turns in my favor, to the amending my circumstances, I now concluded to go on with great business of this kind, and therefore set up stores in several places in New England, giving orders to my storekeepers to sell cheap, considerably cheaper than other traders did. Tho' to the best of my understanding, I ordered everything we sold to be sold for more than what they cost me. And I hoped to make some profit by returns to New York, and by my underselling others I thought to have drawn a vast custom in the several parts in which I traded. I was of opinion that very small gains in a large trade would have made all answer. For as I employed several factors in different towns and places, so I thought every one had his business in selling the goods and taking in suitable returns for New York. And I likewise concluded if a man could get profit by trading in one place or town, so I might get more profit by many factors in several towns.

But as I was much in debt before I entered into this precarious business of so large trading, several of those I owed money to began to think I was got into a more dangerous strain by trading in New England than the business I was in before. Some of them therefore pressed hard on me for their moneys, wherefore I was forced to pay moneys to some and to secure others. Yet still I encouraged myself I should do great matters by trading in very great quantities of goods, and by making profitable returns to New York. But in this I was deceived, for tho' some of my factors were careful, yet others got confused in their accounts and made great mistakes. I myself was but a poor writer, and did not understand such affairs. Neither was I so careful as I should have been, but trusted too much to others.

Towards the latter end of February, 1737/8, I being at New Haven, selling goods and taking in effects for New York, I was taken sick with a sort of a pleurisy, the news of which quickly got to New York amongst my creditors, and was as quickly followed by the news of my death.

The merchants, hearing I was dead, got into a great stir and care how they should get their money. And making inquiry one among another, they found my debts large and many. And altho' they were informed by my letters to them that I had been sick but was recovering, and intended to come home in a little time, yet they were got into such a stir and strife who should get their moneys first, that at my coming home I heard that several of them had ordered writs out against me, thinking (I suppose) I might lay down money or secure the first that arrested me. This I heard was their contrivance, tho' it was for money not then due by several months.

As I had been a man of much business, and had business with great numbers of people, so I had many hearty friends, and some back door friends (as we call them) for I have heard that some of them at that time went to my creditors and informed them that I had a large sea sloop right fitted for the sea, and that in all probability I would take my wife, child, goods, and money, and go off to some foreign part of the world. Some of my creditors were afraid that these reports were likely to be true. By this time I was come home to my house at Mamaroneck from New England, and then heard more of these tumults and discontents amongst the merchants, my creditors at New York, and that some of them had taken out writs against me for the monies as aforesaid. I therefore shut my doors and dispatched a messenger directly to my creditors, and thereby acquainted them that I had heard of their uneasiness concerning the goods I had had of them, and that I understood there were some writs out against me, that I had shut my doors against such writs, and could not stand such a storm as was risen against me. But since it had happened thus, I knew that I could not go on with business. If therefore they would choose a committee, I would deliver all I had into their hands for the use or security of my creditors in general, on a settlement, for that I intended to do them all the justice that was in my power.

We had much discourse and drinking tea together, they seemed very friendly, and in conclusion told me this: That what I offered them was all that my creditors could now expect of me. Tho' they were sorry that my lands were claimed by others and my circumstances so mean, but however they concluded to go to New York and inform my creditors of the state of things, and get power from them to make a settlement if they consented, as they doubted not but they would. And accordingly they went for New York to return within a few days, and accordingly returned. But they brought writs and took me prisoner about the beginning of April, Anno 1738. Others likewise by their orders brought more writs against me, until I was arrested for about eight thousand pounds New York currency. So they brought me to Westchester and delivered me to the high sheriff Isaac Willet, who, as some thought, would have me committed to close jail. I being now in his care, it may not be amiss to mention the usage that prisoners now have, and heretofore have had under the several preceding high sheriffs of this county, which hath been thus. When they have arrested such prisoners that could not get bail because of the largeness of their debts, yet if they were such as the sheriff dare to confide in, he let them have the liberty of the county, until the debt or debts have been ripened to execution. And then such trusty prisoners have come and delivered themselves to jail, and such have had the best of the rooms within the verge and court of the prison house, which is sufficiently commodious and comfortable for debtors, when at the same time those that cannot be trusted, are shut up in a close room, or rooms with bolts, bars and locks. But notwithstanding my debts were so very large and many, yet providence so ordered it that I have had the same favors with the said officer, as hath been usually granted to the most trusty prisoners.

The time passed until about the last of October, Anno 1738, and then I had an execution served on me, in consequence of which I came to this place, and so have continued under this roof from that time until this day, it being the 30th of April, Anno 1740, and I am now 47 years and one month old. As to my living here I have no reason to complain. As to my diet, I live temperately, eat sparingly. And since I have been here, and for many years before, have chiefly drank water, and at some times small beer. As to rum I want none, and as to wine I don't drink a pint in three months. I now generally work part of every day, following some small timber business, by which I earn some money, more than any ever earned here before. The other part of the day I can read, converse with my friends, and recollect the past times. Generally, ever since I came here, I have taken something of the care of the close prisoners, both of the debtors, criminals and condemned. As to those debtors that are kept close, I generally find them some work or employment whereby they can earn their provisions and live tolerable comfortable, without being chargeable either to me or the public. Whereas they used to live by begging, and sometimes almost starved, they now wish and pray that I may continue long here for their said help and comfort. But I wish I could do better for my creditors than I am able to do. I have let that company, viz. my creditors, have considerable money and effects since they have confined me, that I could have kept from them, for which some people blame me, because I have always stood ready and have offered my creditors to deliver all I had to them in the best manner I could, if they would have accepted of it on a settlement. But they have not accepted, and I am now ready to do the same, without the least deceit or evasion if they would, and more I cannot do. I have no blame to lay to their charge. I believe they proceeded against me as they did, believing that it would have proved most to their profit and safety, yet I conceive their so proceeding has made things abundantly more dark and difficult than they would have been, and it is not in my power now to mend it.

For my own part, I do not much regard all that hath or is like to fall on me, for I am fully persuaded that I never have received any wrong by any man, nor by any creature whatsoever, and am satisfied that that affliction, contradiction and punishments which I have met with, are all of them not only just, but more abundantly I have deserved.

And now, if any would inquire further how I can account for these miscarriages and miscomputations which I have made, and being brought up but a ploughman, how I came to run into such a multiplicity of business and inventions that did not properly belong to me, it being beyond my proper sphere, I answer and say, "It was of covetousness in a great measure that thus led me out of the way. For that I had a mind to get money, and then let my mind out to seek after many inventions to satisfy this my inordinate desire, some of which was commendable, and others not good. And so I entered into many undertakings, which in the end hath not only been a hurt to me, but to my said creditors also."

And now coming toward conclusion, I believe that there be many of my friends and acquaintance that would be glad to inquire of me whether I can be content in these times of my confinement. To which I answer, "there is several sorts of content. There is a content proper to beasts and birds, but that is a low and mean sort of content." For altho' they of them that are strong glory in their strength and delight to tear and devour the prey, yet the bear and lion may be bereaved of their whelps, and also miss of their desired prey, and meet with sickness and anguish. And then all their content is turned into bitter torments and strong pains. So also there is some sorts of contents amongst men of all ranks and stations, high and low, which is too much like that of the beasts, soon rushed into the utmost confusion. And so all content that is amongst mankind is low, mean, and to be despised as not

57

fit to be rested in, except it be only which proceeds from a resigned mind to the will of divine providence, and so far the minds of men are reconciled and united to whatever the great wise order of providence brings about. So far mankind may rest, in an undisturbed mind, and say from a true principle of obedience, "Thy will be done, thy Kingdom come."

But now I have been greatly affected and troubled that I should become an instrument to hurt others, either in their minds or estates. I have often most sincerely thought that I could and would willingly suffer the pains of many deaths, if it was possible thereby to take away the damages and offenses from those with whom I have been concerned. But I find that what I cannot possibly bring back must rest as it is.

But sure I am that I cannot rest nor be content in any other temper of mind, than that I stand ready in singleness of heart to do the best for them all for the future, that possible I can. And now I stand open and free to receive counsel from them, and from all others, that can advise me. And in this resolution and disposition of mind I find that content that will not be easily taken away.

But concerning true content and religious influences, I would in modesty and meekness have shut my mouth and held my pen, because of the folly that I have been guilty of. But it is thought a little of the power of resigned mind and warmth of love that makes me bold to declare what is truth. And whosoever he be that knows the power of a full resigned mind, well knows that it makes the spirit of a man bolder than a lion and stronger than the unicorn. The weights of the rocks and hills cannot bear it down, the flames of fire cannot consume it, nor the seas drown it. Its strength is only in the cross of Jesus, and in being resigned, it is found in the deep valley of humility. So this is a light in opposition to that darkness, and it never was nor can be rightly known, only but by being felt, and it is to be felt only in the inmost part. And whoever do so feel as to find it will see it to be that grace and truth that came by Jesus.

And it will float us above the troubles of this unquiet world, where there is felicity and an undisturbed content, and then if the sea should roar and tumults arise in the world, yet there remains a sanctuary to those of a resigned mind. May we all so resign our own wills to his will, who rules in wisdom now and ever more, is that which is heartily desired by,

Your Friend and Well Wisher,

Josiah Quinby

7

The Great Awakening

The series of religious revivals of the 1730s and 1740s, known collectively as the Great Awakening, was a bitterly divisive experience for eighteenth-century Americans. While many found the sudden conversions and energetic preaching of itinerant ministers to be an obvious work of God, others feared the excesses and enthusiasm, and doubted that the conversions were permanent. Schisms and disputes developed in Protestant churches as a result, and the religious unity of many communities was permanently shattered.

Thomas Prince (1687–1758), a Boston minister, supported the cause of the revivals and published his account of them in the 1740s. His was but one of many pamphlets debating the character and piety of evangelicals like George Whitefield and Gilbert Tennent, but Prince's prestige and learning added strength to the cause of the revivalists.

AN ACCOUNT OF THE REVIVAL OF RELIGION IN BOSTON
Thomas Prince

It is, I hope, for the glory of God and the public good, that I have drawn up the following narrative of the late revival of religion here, according to the best of my remembrance.

And that the grace and power of God may appear the more illustrious, it seems fit to give a brief and previous history of the general state of religion here, even from my returning hither in 1717, after above eight years travelling abroad, to the time of this revival at the end of 1740.

On my said return, there were five Congregational churches settled with pastors in this town; though now they are increased to five more. And this town and country were in great tranquility both civil and religious. But though there were many bright examples of piety in every seat and order, yet there was a general complaint among the pious and elderly persons, of the great decay of godliness in the lives and conversations of people both in the town and land, from what they had seen in the days of their fathers. There was scarce a prayer made in public by

From Thomas Prince, *An Account of the Revival of Religion in Boston, in the Years 1740, 1, 2, 3* (Boston, 1823), 3–10, 12–18.

the elder ministers without some heavy lamentation of this decay: in their sermons also they frequently mourned it: and the younger ministers commonly followed their example therein.

Soon after my arrival I was called to preach to the South Church: and in 1718, ordained their co-pastor.

In the spring of 1721, the eight ministers who carried on the public Lecture, taking into consideration the lamentable defect of piety among our young people, agreed to preach a Course of Sermons at the Lecture to them. The audiences were considerably crowded: and while the word of God was loudly sounding, He lifted up His awful rod, by sending the small-pox into the town, which began to spread to our general consternation: scarce a quarter of the people being thought to have had it; and none of the numerous youth under eighteen years of age; it being so many years since that fatal pestilence had prevailed among us. The sermons were quickly printed, with another added by the venerable Dr. Increase Mather, for further benefit. Many of the younger people especially were then greatly awakened: and many hundreds of them quickly after swept into eternity.

In the spring of 1722, the distemper left us: but so little reformed were the surviving youth, that at the end of the summer, the pastors agreed to move their churches to keep in each successively "a day of prayer and fasting, to ask of God the effusion of his Holy Spirit, particularly on the rising generation." And the churches readily received the motion.

But though a solemnity appeared on many, yet it pleased the holy God to humble us and sparingly to give the blessing.

And though in the spring of 1726, in an awakening view of the deplorable decay of family religion, as a principal source of all other decays, the pastors went into a course of Public Lectures on that important subject; yet they had the further sorrow to see those Lectures too thinly attended to expect much benefit from them.

But after all our endeavors, both our security and degeneracy seemed in general to grow, until the night after the Lord's Day, October 29, 1727, when the glorious God arose and fearfully shook the earth through all these countries. By terrible things in righteousness He began to answer us, as the God of our salvation.

On the next morning a very full assembly met at the North Church, for the proper exercises on so extraordinary an occasion. At five in the evening a crowded concourse assembled at the Old Church: and multitudes unable to get in, immediately flowed to the South, and in a few minutes filled that also.

The ministers endeavored to set in with this extraordinary and awakening work of God in nature, and to preach His word in the most awakening manner; to show the people the vast difference between conviction and conversion, between a forced reformation either in acts of piety, justice, charity, or sobriety, by the mere power of fear, and a genuine change of the very frame and relish of the heart by the supernatural efficacy of the Holy Spirit; to lead them on to true conversion and unfeigned faith in Christ, and to guard them against deceiving themselves.

In all our congregations, many seemed to be awakened and reformed: and professing repentance of their sins and faith in Christ, entered into solemn covenant with God, and came into full communion with our several churches. In ours, within eight months after, were about eighty added to our communicants. But then comparatively few of these applied to me to discourse about their souls until they came to offer themselves to the Communion, or afterwards: the most of those who came to me seemed to have passed through their convictions before their coming to converse with me about approaching to the Lord's Table: though I doubt not but considerable numbers were at that time savingly converted.

However the goodness of many seemed as the morning cloud and early dew which quickly passes away. A spiritual slumber seemed soon to seize the generality; even the wise as well as foolish virgins. And though in 1729, the small pox came into town and prevailed again; yet in a few months left us, both unawakened, ungrateful, unreformed. The Holy Spirit awfully withheld his influence in convincing and converting sinners, and enlivening others. In three or four years we rather grew to a greater declension than ever: and so alarmed were the pastors of the town with the dismal view, that in the summer of 1734, they agreed to propose another Course of Days of Prayer and Fasting among our several congregations: "To humble ourselves before God for our unfruitfulness under the means of grace, and to ask the effusion of his Spirit to revive the power of godliness among us," which our people readily complied with and observed.

And though the sovereign God was pleased to give us now and then a sprinkling, for which His name be praised; yet the parching drought continued, and He made us wait for a larger effusion.

In this year the terrible throat-distemper broke out and spread among the youth in the easterly parts of this country, and destroyed multitudes. In some towns it cut off almost all the children. The next year it came into Boston, and began to destroy and strike us with a general awe: but gently treated us, and the next year left us; to melt our hearts into a grateful repentance. And yet we generally seemed to grow more stupid and hard then ever.

About this time indeed, viz. 1735, there was a most remarkable revival of religion in the westerly parts of the country: not only at Northampton, but also in about twelve other congregations in the county of Hampshire, and in about fourteen others in the neighboring colony of Connecticut. And the solemn rumor of that surprising work of God resounding through the country, was a special means of exciting great thoughtfulness of heart in many irreligious people; and great joy in others, both in the view of what the mighty power and grace of God had wrought, and in the hopeful prospect that this blessed work begun would go on and spread throughout the land. And as this excited the extraordinary prayers of many, so it seemed to prepare the way in divers places for that more extensive revival of religion which in five years after followed. But, in the mean while, the general decay of piety seemed to increase among us in Boston. And for the congregation I preach to, though for several years some few offered themselves to our Communion, yet but few came to me in concern about their souls before. And so I perceive it was in others: and I remember some of the ministers were wont to express themselves as greatly discouraged with the growing declension both in principle and practice, especially among the rising generation. From the year 1738, we had received accounts of the Rev. Mr. Whitefield, as a very pious young minister of the

Church of England, rising up in the spirit of the Reformers, and preaching their doctrines first in England and then in America, with surprising power and success: which raised desires in great numbers among us to see and hear him. And having received invitations to come hither, he, from Georgia and South-Carolina, arrived at Rhode-Island, on Lord's Day, Sept. 14, 1740, and the Thursday evening after came to Boston.

He began with a short and fervent prayer: and after singing, took his text from John xvii, 2. Gave us a plain, weighty, regular discourse: representing that all our learning and morality will never save us; and without an experimental knowledge of God in Christ, we must perish in hell for ever. He spake as became the oracles of God in demonstration of the Spirit and of power. And especially when he came to his application, he addressed himself to the audience in such a tender, earnest and moving manner, exciting us to come and be acquainted with the dear Redeemer, as melted the assembly into tears.

Next morning, at Dr. Sewall's and my desire, he preached at the South Church, to further acceptance.

He spake with a mighty sense of God, eternity, the immortality and preciousness of the souls of his hearers, of their original corruption, and of the extreme danger the unregenerate are in; with the nature and absolute necessity of regeneration by the Holy Ghost; and of believing in Christ, in order to our pardon, justification, yielding an acceptable obedience, and obtaining salvation from hell, and an entrance into heaven. His doctrine was plainly that of the Reformers: declaring against putting our good works or morality in the room of Christ's righteousness, or their having any hand in our justification, or being indeed pleasing to God while we are totally unsanctified, acting from corrupt principles, and unreconciled enemies to him: which occasioned some to mistake him as if he opposed morality. But he insisted on it, that the tree of the heart is by original sin exceedingly corrupted, and must be made good by regeneration, that so the fruits proceeding from it may be good likewise: that where the heart is renewed, it ought and will be careful to maintain good works; that if any be not habitually so careful, who think themselves renewed, they deceive their own souls: and even the most improved in holiness, as well as others, must entirely depend on the righteousness of Christ for the acceptance of their persons and services. And though now and then he dropped some expressions that were not so accurate and guarded as we should expect from aged and long studied ministers; yet I had the satisfaction to observe his readiness with great modesty and thankfulness to receive correction as soon as offered.

In short, he was a most importunate wooer of souls to come to Christ for the enjoyment of him, and all his benefits. He distinctly applied his exhortations to the elderly people, the middle aged, the young, the Indians and negroes; and had a most winning way of addressing them. He affectionately prayed for our magistrates, ministers, colleges, candidates for the ministry, and churches, as well as people in general: and before he left us, he in a public and moving manner observed to the people, how sorry he was to hear that the religious assemblies, especially on lectures, had been so thin, exhorted them earnestly to a more general attendance on our public ministrations for the time to come, and told them how glad he should be to hear of the same.

Multitudes were greatly affected and many awakened with his lively ministry. Though he preached every day, the houses were exceedingly crowded: but when he preached in the common, a vaster number attended: and almost every evening the house where he lodged was thronged, to hear his prayers and counsels.

Upon invitation he also preached in several neighboring towns; travelled and preached as far as York, above seventy miles northeast of Boston; returned hither; gave us his farewell affectionate sermon, Lord's Day evening, October 12. Next morning left us; travelled westward to Northampton; thence through Connecticut, New York and New Jersey, to Philadelphia, and thence sailed to South Carolina. And as far as I could then see or learn, he parted in the general esteem and love both of ministers and people: and this seemed to continue until the Journal of his Travels in New England came abroad, wherein some passages offended many, and occasioned their reflections on him.

But upon Mr. Whitefield's leaving us, great numbers in this town were so happily concerned about their souls, as we had never seen any thing like it before, except at the time of the general earthquake: and their desires excited to hear their ministers more than ever: so that our assemblies both on Lectures and Sabbaths were surprisingly increased, and now the people wanted to hear us oftener. In consideration of which, a public Lecture was proposed to be set up at Dr. Colman's church, near the midst of the town, on every Tuesday evening.

Upon the Rev. Mr. Gilbert Tennent's coming and preaching here, the people appeared to be yet much more awakened about their souls than before. He came, I think, on Saturday, December 13, this year: preached at the New North on both the parts of the following day; as also on Monday in the afternoon, when I first heard him, and there was a great assembly.

He did not indeed at first come up to my expectation; but afterwards exceeded it. In private converse with him, I found him to be a man of considerable parts and learning; free, gentle, condescending: and from his own various experience, reading the most noted writers on experimental divinity, as well as the Scriptures, and conversing with many who had been awakened by his ministry in New Jersey, where he then lived; he seemed to have as deep an acquaintance with the experimental part of religion as any I have conversed with; and his preaching was as searching and rousing as ever I heard.

He seemed to have no regard to please the eyes of his hearers with agreeable gesture, nor their ears with delivery, nor their fancy with language; but to aim directly at their hearts and consciences, to lay open their ruinous delusions, show them their numerous, secret, hypocritical shifts in religion, and drive them out of every deceitful refuge wherein they made themselves easy, with the form of godliness without the power. And many who were pleased in a good conceit of themselves before, now found, to their great distress, they were only self-deceived hypocrites. And though while the discovery was making, some at first raged, as they

63

have owned to me and others; yet in the progress of the discovery many were forced to submit; and then the power of God so broke and humbled them, that they wanted a further and even a thorough discovery; they went to hear him, that the secret corruptions and delusions of their hearts might be more discovered; and the more searching the sermon, the more acceptable it was to their anxious minds.

From the terrible and deep convictions he had passed through in his own soul, he seemed to have such a lively view of the divine Majesty, the spirituality, purity, extensiveness, and strictness of his law; with his glorious holiness, and displeasure at sin, his justice, truth, and power in punishing the damned; that the very terrors of God seemed to rise in his mind afresh, when he displayed and brandished them in the eyes of unreconciled sinners. And though some could not bear the representation, and avoided his preaching; yet the arrows of conviction, by his ministry, seemed so deeply to pierce the hearts of others, and even some of the most stubborn sinners, as to make them fall down at the feet of Christ, and yield a lowly submission to him.

And here I cannot but observe, that those who call these convictions by the name of religious frights or fears, and then ascribe them to the mere natural or mechanical influence of terrible words, sounds and gestures, moving tones, or boisterous ways of speaking, appear to me to be not sufficiently acquainted with the subjects of this work, as carried on in the town in general, or with the nature of their convictions; or at least as carried on among the people I have conversed with. For I have had awakened people of every assembly of the Congregational and Presbyterian way in town, in considerable numbers repairing to me from time to time; and from their various and repeated narratives shall show the difference.

I don't remember any crying out, or falling down, or fainting, either under Mr. Whitefield's or Mr. Tennent's ministry all the while they were here; though many, both women and men, both those who had been vicious, and those who had been moral, yea, some religious and learned, as well as as unlearned, were in great concern of soul. But as Dr. Colman well expressed it in his Letter of November 23, 1741, "We have seen little of those extremes or supposed blemishes of this work in Boston, but much of the blessed fruits of it have fallen to our share. God has spoken to us in a more soft and calm wind; and we have neither had those outcries and faintings in our assemblies, which have disturbed the worship in many places; nor yet those manifestations of joy inexpressible, which now fill some of our eastern parts."

As to Mr. Whitefield's preaching—it was, in the manner, moving, earnest, winning, melting: but the mechanical influence of this, according to the usual operations of mechanical powers, in two or three days expired; with many, in two or three hours; and I believe with the most, as soon as the sound was over, or they got out of the house, or in the first conversation they fell into. But with the manner of his preaching, wherein he appeared to be in earnest, he delivered those vital truths which animated all our martyrs, made them triumph in flames; and led his hearers into the view of that vital, inward, active piety, which is the mere effect of the mighty and supernatural operation of a divine Power on the souls of men;

which only will support and carry through the sharpest trials, and make meet for the inheritance of the saints in light. His chief and earnest desires and labors appeared to be the same with the apostle Paul for the visible saints at Ephesus; viz. that they might know (i.e. by experience) what is the exceeding greatness of his power (i.e. the power of God) to us-ward who believe, according to the working of his mighty power which he wrought in Christ when he raised him from the dead.—Eph. 1. And they were these things, and this sort of preaching with surprising fervency, that the Holy Spirit was pleased to use as means to make many sensible they knew nothing of these mighty operations, nor of these vital principles within them; but that with Simon Magus, who was a visible believer and professor of Christ and his religion, they were in "the gall of bitterness and in the bonds of iniquity;" i.e. in the state, pollution, guilt and power of sin, which is inexpressibly more disagreeable to the holy God than the most bitter gall to men, and will be bitterness to them, without a mighty change, in the latter end.

It was by such means as these, that the Holy Spirit seized and awakened the consciences of many; and when the mechanical influence on the animal passions ceased, still continued these convictions, not only for many days, but weeks and months after the sound was over; yea, to this very day with some; while they excited others to an earnest and persevering application to Jesus for his Spirit to quicken them, till they came to an hopeful perception of his quickening influence in them; and while in others the sovereign and offended Spirit leaving off to strive, these convictions in their consciences, the effects thereof, have either sooner or later died away.

As to Mr. Tennent's preaching—It was frequently both terrible and searching. It was often for matter justly terrible, as he, according to the inspired oracles, exhibited the dreadful holiness, justice, law, threatenings, truth, power, majesty of God; and His anger with rebellious, impenitent, unbelieving and Christless sinners; the awful danger they were every moment in of being struck down to hell, and being damned for ever; with the amazing miseries of that place of torment. But his exhibitions, both for matter and manner, fell inconceivably below the reality: and though this terrible preaching may strongly work on the natural passions and frighten the hearers, rouse the soul, and prepare the way for terrible convictions; yet those mere natural terrors, and these convictions are quite different things.

Nothing is more obvious than for people to be greatly terrified with the apprehensions of God, enternity and hell, and yet have no convictions.

In Old England and New, where I have been a constant preacher and an observer of the religious state of those who heard me, for above thirty years, many have passed under scores of most dreadful tempests of thunder and lightning.

Yea, even since the Revival, viz. on Friday night, July 30, 1742, at the lecture in the South Church, near nine o'clock being very dark, there came on a very terrible storm of thunder and lightning: and just as the blessing was given, an amazing clap broke over the church with piercing repetitions, which set many a shrieking, and the whole assembly into great consternation for near two hours together. And yet in all these displays of the majesty of God, and terrifying apprehensions of danger of sudden destruction; neither in this surprising night, nor in all the course of thirty years have I scarce known any, by these kinds of terrors brought under genuine convictions. And what minister has a voice like God, and who can thunder like Him?

So on Lord's Day, June 3d last, in our time of public worship in the forenoon, when we had been about a quarter of an hour in prayer, the mighty power of God came on with a surprising roar and earthquake; which made the house with all the galleries to rock and tremble, with such a grating noise as if the bricks were moving out of their places to come down and bury us: which exceedingly disturbed the congregation, excited the shrieks of many, put many on flying out, and the generality in motion. But though many were greatly terrified, yet in a day or two their terrors seemed to vanish, and I know of but two or three seized by convictions on this awful occasion.

No! conviction is quite another sort of thing. It is the work of the Spirit of God, a sovereign, free and Almighty agent; wherein He gives the sinful soul such a clear and lively view of the glory of the Divine Sovereignty, omnipresence, holiness, justice, truth and power, the extensiveness, spirituality and strictness of His law; the binding nature, efficacy and dreadfulness of His curses; the multitude and heinousness of its sins both of commission and omission; the horrible vileness, wickedness, perverseness and hypocrisy of the heart, with its utter impotence either rightly to repent, or believe in Christ, or change itself: so that it sees itself in a lost, undone and perishing state; without the least degree of worthiness to recommend it to the holy and righteous God, and the least degree of strength to help itself out of this condition.

Such were the convictions wrought in many hundreds in this town by Mr. Tennent's searching ministry: and such was the case of those many scores of several other congregations as well as mine, who came to me and others for direction under them. And indeed by all their converse I found, it was not so much the terror, as the searching nature of his ministry, that was the principal means of their conviction. It was not merely, nor so much his laying open the terrors of the law and wrath of God, or damnation of hell (for this they could pretty well bear, as long as they hoped these belonged not to them, or they could easily avoid them); as his laying open their many vain and secret shifts and refuges, counterfeit resemblances of grace, delusive and damning hopes, their utter impotence, and impending danger of destruction: whereby they found all their hopes and refuges of lies to fail them, and themselves exposed to eternal ruin, unable to help themselves, and in a lost condition. This searching preaching was both the suitable and principal means of the conviction: though it is most evident, the most proper means are utterly insufficient; and wholly depend on the sovereign will of God, to put forth His power and apply them by this or that instrument, on this or that person, at this or that season, in this or that way or manner; with these or those permitted circumstances, infirmities, corruptions, errors, agencies, oppositions; and to what degree, duration and event He pleases.

A remarkable instance of conviction also, has been sometimes under the ministry of the Rev. Mr. Edwards of Northampton: a preacher of a low and moderate voice, a natural way of delivery; and without any agitation of body, or any thing else in the manner to excite attention; except his habitual and great solemnity, looking and speaking as in the presence of God, and with a weighty sense of the matter delivered. And on the other hand, I have known several very worthy ministers of loud and rousing voices; and yet to their great sorrow the generality of their people, for a long course of years asleep in deep security. It is just as the Holy Spirit pleases, to hide occasions of pride from man: and if Mr. Tennent was to come here again and preach more rousingly than ever, it may be, not one soul would come under conviction by him.

8

Proposals for Living

Benjamin Franklin (1706–1790) was perhaps the most extraordinary and versatile American of his century—printer, author, inventor, philanthropist, philosopher, diplomat, and statesman; any list of his accomplishments would take up immense space. Shortly after moving from Boston to Philadelphia in 1723, Franklin purchased *The Pennsylvania Gazette*, and was soon publishing his famous almanacs as well. His interest in civic improvement, ranging from philosophical societies and hospitals to fire prevention and insurance, reflected the benevolence of the man and the character of the American Enlightenment. Paralleling in time the proposals for human improvement being submitted in contemporary Europe, Franklin's plans were distinguished by their practicality, their simplicity, and, quite frequently, their wry sense of humor. The following selections merely hint at the range of Franklin's thought, and reveal how more secular and profit-oriented was the intellectual life of mid-century America. The "Rules" were drawn up in 1728 and helped form the basis for The Junto, a club of Franklin's acquaintances. *The Way to Wealth* was an assembly of many of the maxims Franklin had popularized in *Poor Richard's Almanac* between 1732, the year of his first Almanac, and 1757, when this compilation first appeared.

RULES FOR A CLUB
FOR MUTUAL IMPROVEMENT
Benjamin Franklin

**Previous Question, To Be Answered
at Every Meeting**

Have you read over these queries this morning, in order to consider what you might have to offer the Junto touching any one of them? viz.

1. Have you met with any thing in the author you last read, remarkable, or suitable to be communicated to the Junto? particularly in history, morality, poetry, physic, travels, mechanic arts, or other parts of knowledge.

From "Rules for a Club Established for Mutual Improvement," "The Way to Wealth," and "Self-denial Not the Essence of Virtue" in *The Works of Benjamin Franklin*, Jared Sparks, ed. (Boston, 1836), II: 9–12, 63–66, 94–103.

2. What new story have you lately heard agreeable for telling in conversation?

3. Hath any citizen in your knowledge failed in his business lately, and what have you heard of the cause?

4. Have you lately heard of any citizen's thriving well, and by what means?

5. Have you lately heard how any present rich man, here or elsewhere, got his estate?

6. Do you know of a fellow citizen, who has lately done a worthy action, deserving praise and imitation; or who has lately committed an error, proper for us to be warned against and avoid?

7. What unhappy effects of intemperance have you lately observed or heard; of imprudence, of passion, or of any other vice or folly?

8. What happy effects of temperance, of prudence, of moderation, or of any other virtue?

9. Have you or any of your acquaintance been lately sick or wounded? If so, what remedies were used, and what were their effects?

10. Whom do you know that are shortly going voyages or journeys, if one should have occasion to send by them?

11. Do you think of any thing at present, in which the Junto may be serviceable to *mankind,* to their country, to their friends, or to themselves?

12. Hath any deserving stranger arrived in town since last meeting, that you have heard of? And what have you heard or observed of his character or merits? And whether, think you, it lies in the power of the Junto to oblige him, or encourage him as he deserves?

13. Do you know of any deserving young beginner lately set up, whom it lies in the power of the Junto any way to encourage?

14. Have you lately observed any defect in the laws of your *country,* of which it would be proper to move the legislature for an amendment? Or do you know of any beneficial law that is wanting?

15. Have you lately observed any encroachment on the just liberties of the people?

16. Hath any body attacked your reputation lately? And what can the Junto do towards securing it?

17. Is there any man whose friendship you want, and which the Junto, or any of them, can procure for you?

18. Have you lately heard any member's character attacked, and how have you defended it?

19. Hath any man injured you, from whom it is in the power of the Junto to procure redress?

20. In what manner can the Junto, or any of them, assist you in any of your honorable designs?

21. Have you any weighty affair on hand, in which you think the advice of the Junto may be of service?

22. What benefits have you lately received from any man not present?

23. Is there any difficulty in matters of opinion, of justice, and injustice, which you would gladly have discussed at this time?

24. Do you see any thing amiss in the present customs or proceedings of the Junto, which might be amended?

Any person to be qualified [as a member of the JUNTO], to stand up, and lay his hand upon his breast, and be asked these questions, viz.

1. Have you any particular disrespect to any present members? *Answer.* I have not.

2. Do you sincerely declare, that you love mankind in general, of what profession or religion soever? *Answer.* I do.

3. Do you think any person ought to be harmed in his body, name, or goods, for mere speculative opinions, or his external way of worship? *Answer.* No.

4. Do you love truth for truth's sake, and will you endeavour impartially to find and receive it yourself, and communicate it to others? *Answer.* Yes.

SELF-DENIAL NOT
THE ESSENCE OF VIRTUE

It is commonly asserted, that without self-denial there is no virtue, and that the greater the self-denial the greater the virtue.

If it were said, that he who cannot deny himself any thing he inclines to, though he knows it will be to his hurt, has not the virtue of resolution or fortitude, it would be intelligible enough; but, as it stands, it seems obscure or erroneous.

Let us consider some of the virtues singly.

If a man has no inclination to wrong people in his dealings, if he feels no temptation to it, and therefore never does it, can it be said that he is not a just man? If he is a just man, has he not the virtue of justice?

If to a certain man idle diversions have nothing in them that is tempting, and therefore he never relaxes his application to business for their sake, is he not an industrious man? Or has he not the virtue of industry?

I might in like manner instance in all the rest of the virtues; but, to make the thing short, as it is certain that the more we strive against the temptations to any vice, and practise the contrary virtue, the weaker will that temptation be, and the stronger will be that habit, till at length the temptation has no force, or entirely vanishes; does it follow from thence, that in our endeavours to overcome vice we grow continually less and less virtuous, till at length we have no virtue at all?

If self-denial be the essence of virtue, then it follows that the man, who is naturally temperate, just, &c., is not virtuous; but that in order to be virtuous, he must, in spite of his natural inclination, wrong his neighbours, and eat, and drink, &c., to excess.

But perhaps it may be said, that by the word *virtue* in the above assertion, is meant merit; and so it should stand thus; Without self-denial there is no merit, and the greater the self-denial the greater the merit.

The self-denial here meant, must be when our inclinations are towards vice, or else it would still be nonsense.

By merit is understood desert; and, when we say a man merits, we mean that he deserves praise or reward.

We do not pretend to merit any thing of God, for he is above our services; and the benefits he confers on us are the effects of his goodness and bounty.

All our merit, then, is with regard to one another, and from one to another.

Taking, then, the assertion as it last stands,

If a man does me a service from a natural benevolent inclination, does he deserve less of me than another, who does me the like kindness against his inclination?

If I have two journeymen, one naturally industrious, the other idle, but both perform a day's work equally good, ought I to give the latter the most wages?

Indeed lazy workmen are commonly observed to be more extravagant in their demands than the industrious; for, if they have not more for their work, they cannot live as well. But though it be true to a proverb, that lazy folks take the most pains, does it follow that they deserve the most money?

If you were to employ servants in affairs of trust, would you not bid more for one you knew was naturally honest, than for one naturally roguish, but who has lately acted honestly? For currents whose natural channel is dammed up, till the new course is by time worn sufficiently deep, and become natural, are apt to break their banks. If one servant is more valuable than another, has he not more merit than the other? and yet this is not on account of superior self-denial.

Is a patriot not praiseworthy, if public spirit is natural to him?

Is a pacing-horse less valuable for being a natural pacer?

Nor, in my opinion, has any man less merit for having in general natural virtuous inclinations.

The truth is, that temperance, justice, charity, etc. are virtues, whether practised with, or against our inclinations, and the man, who practises them, merits our love and esteem; and self-denial is neither good nor bad, but as it is applied. He that denies a vicious inclination, is virtuous in proportion to his resolution; but the most perfect virtue is above all temptation; such as the virtue of the saints in heaven; and he, who does a foolish, indecent, or wicked thing, merely because it is contrary to his inclination (like some mad enthusiasts I have read of, who ran about naked, under the notion of taking up the cross), is not practising the reasonable science of virtue, but is a lunatic.

THE WAY TO WEALTH

Courteous Reader

I have heard, that nothing gives an author so great pleasure as to find his works respectfully quoted by others. Judge, then, how much I must have been gratified by an incident I am going to relate to you. I stopped my horse lately, where a great number of people were collected at an auction of merchants' goods. The hour of the sale not being come, they were conversing on the badness of the times; and one of the company called to a plain, clean, old man, with white locks, "Pray, Father Abraham, what think you of the times? Will not these heavy taxes quite ruin the country? How shall we ever be able to pay them? What would you advise us to?" Father Abraham stood up, and replied, "If you would have my advice, I will give it you in short; for *A word to the wise is enough,* as Poor Richard says." They joined in desiring him to speak his mind, and gathering round him, he proceeded as follows.

"Friends," said he, "the taxes are indeed very heavy, and, if those laid on by the government were the only ones we had to pay, we might more easily discharge them; but we have many others, and much more grievous to some of us. We are taxed twice as much by our idleness, three times as much by our pride, and four times as much by our folly; and from these taxes the commissioners cannot ease or deliver us, by allowing an abatement. However, let us hearken to good advice, and something may be done for us; *God helps them that help themselves,* as Poor Richard says.

"It would be thought a hard government, that should tax its people one-tenth part of their time, to be employed in its service; but idleness taxes many of us much more; sloth, by bringing on diseases, absolutely shortens life. *Sloth, like rust, consumes faster than labor wears; while the used key is always bright,* as Poor Richard says. *But dost thou love life, then do not squander time, for that is the stuff life is made of,* as Poor Richard says. How much more than is necessary do we spend in sleep, forgetting, that *The sleeping fox catches no poultry,* and that *There will be sleeping enough in the grave,* as Poor Richard says.

"*If time be of all things the most precious, wasting time must be,* as Poor Richard says, *the greatest prodigality;* since, as he elsewhere tells us, *Lost time is never found again; and what we call time enough, always proves little enough.* Let us then up and be doing, and doing to the purpose; so by diligence shall we do more with less perplexity. *Sloth makes all things difficult, but industry all easy;* and *He that riseth late must trot all day, and shall scarce overtake his business at night;* while *Laziness travels so slowly, that Poverty soon overtakes him. Drive thy business, let not that drive thee;* and *Early to bed, and early to rise, makes a man healthy, wealthy, and wise,* as Poor Richard says.

"So what signifies wishing and hoping for better times? We may make these times better, if we bestir ourselves. *Industry need not wish, and he that lives upon hopes will die fasting. There are no gains without pains; then help, hands, for I have no lands;* or, if I have, they are smartly taxed. *He that hath a trade hath an estate; and he that hath a calling, hath an office of profit and honor,* as Poor Richard says; but then the trade must be worked at, and the calling followed, or neither the estate nor the office will enable us to pay our taxes. If we are industrious, we shall never starve; for, *At the working man's house hunger looks in, but dares not enter.* Nor will the bailiff or the constable enter, for *Industry pays debts, while despair increaseth them.* What though you have found no treasure, nor has any rich relation left you a legacy, *Diligence is the mother of good luck, and God gives all things to industry. Then plough deep while sluggards sleep, and you shall have corn to sell and to keep.* Work while it is called to-day, for you know not how much you may be hindered to-morrow. *One to-day is worth two to-morrows,* as Poor Richard says; and further, *Never leave that till to-morrow, which you can do to-day.* If you were a servant, would you not be ashamed that a good master should catch you idle? Are you then your own master? Be ashamed to catch yourself idle, when there is so much to be done for yourself, your family, your country, and your king. Handle your tools without mittens; remember, that *The cat in gloves catches no mice,* as Poor Richard says. It is true there is much to be done, and perhaps you are weak-handed; but stick to it steadily, and you will see great effects; for *Constant dropping wears away stones; and By diligence and patience the mouse ate in two the cable; and Little strokes fell great oaks.*

"Methinks I hear some of you say, 'Must a man afford himself no leisure?' I will tell thee, my friend, what Poor Richard says, *Employ thy time well, if thou meanest to gain leisure; and, since thou art not sure of a minute, throw not away an hour.* Leisure is time for doing something useful; this leisure the diligent man will obtain, but the lazy man never; for *A life of leisure and a life of laziness are two things. Many, without labor, would live by their wits only, but they break for want of stock;* whereas industry gives comfort, and plenty, and respect. *Fly pleasures, and they will follow you. The diligent spinner has a large shift; and now I have a sheep and a cow, everybody bids me good morrow.*

"But with our industry we must likewise be steady, settled, and careful, and oversee our own affairs with our own eyes, and not trust too much to others; for, as Poor Richard says,

I never saw an oft-removed tree,
Nor yet an oft-removed family,
That throve so well as those that settled be.

And again, *Three removes are as bad as a fire;* and again, *Keep thy shop, and thy shop will keep thee;* and again, *If you would have your business done, go; if not, send.* And again,

He that by the plough would thrive,
Himself must either hold or drive.

And again, *The eye of a master will do more work than both his hands;* and again, *Want of care does us more damage than want of knowledge;* and again, *Not to oversee workmen, is to leave them your purse open.* Trusting too much to others' care is the ruin of many; for *In the affairs of this world men are saved, not by faith, but by the want of it;* but a man's own care is profitable; for, *If you would have a faithful servant, and one that you like, serve yourself. A little neglect may breed great mischief; for want of a nail the shoe was lost; for want of a shoe the horse was lost; and for want of a horse the rider was lost, being overtaken and slain by the enemy; all for want of a little care about a horse-shoe nail.*

"So much for industry, my friends, and attention to one's own business; but to these we must add frugality, if we would make our industry more certainly successful. A man may, if he knows not how to save as he gets, keep his nose all his life to the grindstone, and die not worth a groat at last. *A fat kitchen makes a lean will;* and

Many estates are spent in the getting,
Since women for tea forsook spinning and knitting,
And men for punch forsook hewing and splitting.

If you would be wealthy, think of saving as well as of getting. The Indies have not made Spain rich, because her outgoes are greater than her incomes.

73

"Away then with your expensive follies, and you will not then have so much cause to complain of hard times, heavy taxes, and chargeable families; for

Women and wine, game and deceit,
Make the wealth small and the want great.

And further, *"What maintains one vice would bring up two children.* You may think, perhaps, that a little tea, or a little punch now and then, diet a little more costly, clothes a little finer, and a little entertainment now and then, can be no great matter; but remember, *Many a little makes a mickle.* Beware of little expenses; *A small leak will sink a great ship,* as Poor Richard says; and again, *Who dainties love, shall beggars prove;* and moreover, *Fools make feasts, and wise men eat them.*

"Here you are all got together at this sale of fineries and knick-knacks. You call them *goods;* but, if you do not take care, they will prove *evils* to some of you. You expect they will be sold cheap, and perhaps they may for less then they cost; but, if you have no occasion for them, they must be dear to you. Remember what Poor Richard says; *Buy what thou hast no need of, and ere long thou shalt sell thy necessaries.* And again, *At a great pennyworth pause a while.* He means, that perhaps the cheapness is apparent only, and not real; or the bargain, by straitening thee in thy business, may do thee more harm than good. For in another place he says, *Many have been ruined by buying good pennyworths.* Again, *It is foolish to lay out money in a purchase of repentance;* and yet this folly is practised every day at auctions, for want of minding the Almanac. Many a one, for the sake of finery on the back, have gone with a hungry belly and half-starved their families. *Silks and satins, scarlet and velvets, put out the kitchen fire,* as Poor Richard says.

"These are not the necessaries of life; they can scarcely be called the conveniences; and yet, only because they look pretty, how many want to have them! By these, and other extravagances, the genteel are reduced to poverty, and forced to borrow of those whom they formerly despised, but who, through industry and frugality, have maintained their standing; in which case it appears plainly, that *A ploughman on his legs is higher than a gentleman on his knees,* as Poor Richard says. Perhaps they have had a small estate left them, which they knew not the getting of; they think, *It is day, and will never be night;* that a little to be spent out of so much is not worth minding; but *Always taking out of the meal-tub, and never putting in, soon comes to the bottom,* as Poor Richard says; and then, *When the well is dry, they know the worth of water.* But this they might have known before, if they had taken his advice. *If you would know the value of money, go and try to borrow some; for he that goes a borrowing goes a sorrowing,* as Poor Richard says; and indeed so does he that lends to such people, when he goes to get it in again. Poor Dick further advises, and says,

Fond pride of dress is sure a very curse;
Ere fancy you consult, consult your purse.

And again, *Pride is as loud a beggar as Want, and a great deal more saucy.* When you have bought one fine thing, you must buy ten more, that your appearance may be all of a piece; but Poor Dick says, *It is easier to suppress the first desire, than to satisfy all that follow it.* And it is as truly folly for the poor to ape the rich, as for the frog to swell in order to equal the ox.

Vessels large may venture more,
But little boats should keep near shore.

It is, however, a folly soon punished; for, as Poor Richard says, *Pride that dines on vanity, sups on contempt. Pride breakfasted with Plenty, dined with Poverty, and supped with Infamy.* And, after all, of what use is this pride of appearance, for which so much is risked, so much is suffered? It cannot promote health, nor ease pain; it makes no increase of merit in the person; it creates envy; it hastens misfortune.

"But what madness must it be to *run in debt* for these superfluities? We are offered by the terms of this sale, six months' credit; and that, perhaps, has induced some of us to attend it, because we cannot spare the ready money, and hope now to be fine without it. But, ah! think what you do when you run in debt; you give to another power over your liberty. If you cannot pay at the time, you will be ashamed to see your creditor; you will be in fear when you speak to him; you will make poor, pitiful, sneaking excuses, and, by degrees, come to lose your veracity, and sink into base, downright lying; for *The second vice is lying, the first is running in debt,* as Poor Richard says; and again, to the same purpose, *Lying rides upon Debt's back;* whereas a free-born Englishman ought not to be ashamed nor afraid to see or speak to any man living. But poverty often deprives a man of all spirit and virtue. *It is hard for an empty bag to stand upright.*

"What would you think of that prince, or of that government, who should issue an edict forbidding you to dress like a gentleman or gentlewoman, on pain of imprisonment or servitude? Would you not say that you were free, have a right to dress as you please, and that such an edict would be a breach of your privileges, and such a government tyrannical? And yet you are about to put yourself under such tyranny, when you run in debt for such dress! Your creditor has authority, at his pleasure, to deprive you of your liberty, by confining you in gaol till you shall be able to pay him. When you have got your bargain, you may, perhaps, think little of payment; but, as Poor Richard says, *Creditors have better memories than debtors; creditors are a superstitious sect, great observers of set days and times.* The day comes round before you are aware, and the demand is made before you are prepared to satisfy it; or, if you bear your debt in mind, the term, which at first seemed so long, will, as it lessens, appear extremely short. Time will seem to have added wings to his heels as well as his shoulders. *Those have a short Lent, who owe money to be paid at Easter.* At present, perhaps, you may think yourselves in thriving circumstances, and that you can bear a little extravagance without injury; but

For age and want save while you may:
No morning sun lasts a whole day.

Gain may be temporary and uncertain, but ever, while you live, expense is constant and certain; and *It is easier to build two chimneys, than to keep one in fuel,* as Poor Richard says; so, *Rather go to bed supperless, than rise in debt.*

Get what you can, and what you get hold;
'Tis the stone that will turn all your lead into gold.

And, when you have got the Philosopher's stone, sure you will no longer complain of bad times, or the difficulty of paying taxes.

"This doctrine, my friends, is reason and wisdom; but, after all, do not depend too much upon your own industry, and frugality, and prudence, though excellent things; for they may all be blasted, without the blessing of Heaven; and, therefore, ask that blessing humbly, and be not uncharitable to those that at present seem to want it, but comfort and help them. Remember, Job suffered, and was afterwards prosperous.

"And now, to conclude, *Experience keeps a dear school, but fools will learn in no other,* as Poor Richard says, and scarce in that; for, it is true, *We may give advice, but we cannot give conduct.* However, remember this, *They that will not be counselled, cannot be helped;* and further, that, *If you will not hear Reason, she will surely rap your knuckles,* as Poor Richard says."

Thus the old gentleman ended his harangue. The people heard it, and approved the doctrine; and immediately practised the contrary, just as if it had been a common sermon; for the auction opened, and they began to buy extravagantly. I found the good man had thoroughly studied my Almanacs, and digested all I had dropped on these topics during the course of twenty-five years. The frequent mention he made of me must have tired any one else; but my vanity was wonderfully delighted with it, though I was conscious that not a tenth part of the wisdom was my own, which he ascribed to me, but rather the gleanings that I had made of the sense of all ages and nations. However, I resolved to be the better for the echo of it; and, though I had at first determined to buy stuff for a new coat, I went away resolved to wear my old one a little longer. Reader, if thos wilt do the same, thy profit will be as great as mine. I am, as ever, thine to serve thee,

Richard Saunders

Independence, 1754–1820

To American colonists in the eighteenth century, revolution was a most dangerous act. It threatened, they believed, terrible consequences, upheaval, chaos, and bloodshed. They considered war to be far less dangerous; in an era of mercenaries when battles rarely occurred in towns or well-populated villages, armed conflict and even national defeat did not usually touch the day-to-day lives of the people. Revolution, by contrast, affected everybody. Men were forced to examine their most basic loyalties and often brother opposed brother. Uncertainty and confusion held sway, for when the pot boiled anything might come to the top. The colonists knew that, in 1688, England had undergone a bloodless revolution. But how could one be sure that this remarkable achievement would be repeated? Given the perils, one did not begin a revolution for light or transient causes.

And yet, in 1776, Americans chose to revolt. Only a few years before, the colonists had been not only at peace with the mother country but enthusiastic about their ties. In 1763, the Treaty of Paris ended the French and Indian War and the colonists appeared to appreciate, more keenly than ever, the advantages of imperial relations. After all, through English assistance the French had been driven from North America so that peaceful borders and untroubled expansion seemed to be ahead. Even the conduct of the war had brought benefits, as English gold flowed to America in unprecedented amounts to arm, feed, and clothe the troops. Content with the diplomatic settlement and basking in the glow of economic well-being, the colonists' loyalty appeared firm. Few anticipated that within thirteen years the Americans would be in revolt.

Between 1763 and 1776 the colonists came to believe that revolution was imperative and could be conducted without unduly upsetting the social order. During these years they became conscious of their own history and the unusual quality of their political and social life. Their understanding of their past development and present conditions fostered their conviction that revolution was imperative.

British legislation first prompted this introspection. In the aftermath of the French and Indian War, England was caught between heavy expenses and narrowing sources of revenue. It had chosen to take Canada rather than the small but rich Sugar Islands from the French, thereby increasing administrative costs without any prospect of immediate returns. Since it had to defend what it had won in conflict, the mother country turned to the colonies for financial assistance. From Parliament's perspective, the step was logical and appropriate. While England groaned under heavy land taxes, the colonists were practically free of such burdens. Yet the fruits of the war had gone to the Americans; British troops were to protect colonial welfare. Surely, Parliament thought it was right to call upon the colonies to contribute to the benefit of the realm. In 1764 it passed a Revenue Act, then a Stamp Act; upon the latter's repeal it enacted the Townsend Duties and, soon, a Tea Act. To enforce these regulations and collect the duties, Parliament created in America new administrative posts, sent over officials, and established courts. It was determined to compel the colonists to contribute to the costs of empire.

But the colonists did not share Parliament's attitude. The legislation came at a bad time economically, for the flow of funds and the expenditures of the army had stopped after the war and a severe recession set in. The Americans were also angry and insulted for not having been consulted in the making of these decisions. Parliament had acted brusquely and imprudently, without even meaningfully soliciting colonial opinion. Why had not the colonists been allowed to raise the necessary sums by their own methods? Why instead were they saddled with a stamp tax? But most important of all, the colonists believed that Parliament was guilty of more than poor timing and of a lack of political finesse and sensitivity. They saw in English actions nothing less than a basic threat to their way of life. Their lives and liberties were at stake in the confrontation with Parliament on the issue of taxation.

As the colonists read European history, surveyed contemporary governments, and considered their own brief past, they concluded that liberty—the opportunity to live free from arbitrary power—was a phenomena at once rare and temporary. The lesson was apparent in Roman history—a subject they read incessantly—and could be found repeated everywhere from Scandinavia to the Mediterranean: republics all too often degenerated into despotism. Those who did not diligently protect their liberties soon came under the yoke of unlimited power. The colonists believed that England itself was beginning to experience this transformation. Were there not men in England—John Wilkes undoubtedly the most prominent—who had good cause to claim from their imprisonment that Parliament was more intent on protecting its own prerogatives than defending the liberties of the people? Did a similar fate await the colonists? Americans now began to appreciate the self-government that had long been familiar to them. They were living in liberty. Through the power to control taxation, the assemblies, representing the people, had learned to keep the Royal Governor, appointed by the crown, well in check. By supervising his appropriations and controlling his salary, they had used control over the purse to keep power within limits. But did Parliament's intrusion into taxation signal a decline in colonial liberties?

The fears of 1764 became the confirmed beliefs of 1776. Over the course of these years Parliament paid little attention to colonial protests. Its official pronouncements were mostly concerned with reaffirming the supreme and sovereign powers of Parliament—a stance that gave little comfort to the Americans. At the same time, colonial attitudes became more refined and fixed as pamphlet followed pamphlet and the principles of government became a familiar subject of discussion. With logical arguments and vivid language, writers from Pennsylvania's John Dickinson to newcomer Thomas Paine alerted, coaxed, persuaded, and convinced their countrymen of the dangers they faced. Finally, successive British actions corroborated every colonial fear. The Americans watched Parliament continue to tax, to establish courts in the colonies without provision for trial by jury, and to send and quarter troops in peacetime against the inhabitants' will. As expected, the results were such crimes against them as the Boston Massacre of 1770. Surely the time had arrived for the colonists to act with vigilance, to protect their liberties by revolution.

But would the cure be worse than the disease? Would revolution promote more chaos, disorder, and arbitrary rule than even the acts of a stubborn and irresponsible Parliament? By 1776 the colonists confidently answered "no." The imperial crisis prompted them to examine their society as well as their polity, making them aware of their unusual attributes. They began to understand that the American society was not simply a transplanted European community in a different setting. Old World guidelines were not necessarily applicable to New World conditions. There was in America a cohesiveness and stability that was as vital as it was unique. Harmony, and not dissension, characterized the social order, making it unlikely for external conflict with the mother country to spark internal conflict at home. The most dramatic manifestation of this perspective came in the cooperation of all classes in the riots protesting British legislation. Riots were dangerous political weapons. They could begin with one goal and end with another; those who led the mob might find themselves its victim. Yet, wealthy merchants joined, and in fact often headed artisans and laborers in violent protest against various imperial policies, from the Stamp Act to the Tea Act. And their confidence, with only few exceptions, was usually justified. The mob turned on British officials not on the rich, on would-be stamp collectors not on leading citizens. Thus Americans could dare a revolution certain that their liberties would be safer in their own hands than in those of Parliament.

During the course and aftermath of the Revolution, the new nation struggled to fulfill its grandiose goals. Its confidence in the stability of American society was on the whole demonstrated by the events of these years; and through resourceful and imaginative innovations, new meanings and defenses enveloped and expanded traditional practices. The conduct of the war itself was an exceptionally demanding test, not only of courage and military skill but of the strength of the republican ideal. There was some treachery and greed and a good deal of inefficiency in the war effort; but most important, the military brought victory and support to the republican government. The virtue and integrity of George Washington was the outstanding example of a popular commitment. Soldiers and their leaders, for all the loss of pay and the hardships they had suffered, disbanded and went home at the close of hostilities; a few disgruntled officers vaguely considered political action but Washington forthrightly and without exceptional difficulty kept them in bounds. The republic weathered its first crisis handsomely—a battlefield victory by a loyal army.

Moreover, citizens at home also attempted to fulfill republican ideals. At a time when all traditional authority collapsed, when the Royal Governor fled the province and colonial assemblies were without legality, Americans quickly devised new rules and institutions for government. Townspeople gathered to elect representatives to constitutional conventions, which would offer proposals and pass on suggestions. Rather than flounder before the specter of anarchy, they created constitutions and state governments. Their work, in fact, showed surprisingly few signs of tension or haste. The constitutions were carefully composed and often remarkably long-lived, drawing on the colonial experience for lessons in protecting liberty. Thus, they typically weakened the office of Governor by not giving him a final veto on legislation or the exclusive right to make political appointments; they put the bulk of authority in the legislatures, but then created bicameral bodies to check abuses and called for frequent elections to insure responsibility. They banned plural officeholding so that no individual or clique could monopolize authority for its own account. To be sure, the constitutions did not escape older prejudices completely. There were still property requirements for voting and office-holding, and there was scant effort, insofar as slavery was concerned, to implement the idea that all men were created equal. Still the new documents established order and delegated power while protecting individual liberty.

Americans had more difficulty establishing a national government. Long familiar with the operations of local and provincial bodies, they were at once removed from and suspicious of national political institutions. They created, through the Articles of Confederation, a central government that presented no danger to state prerogatives but at the same time was too weak and ill-equipped to protect and promote the general welfare. To its credit, the Confederation government oversaw the military and diplomatic effort and made important starts in settling the question of distributing the western lands, paying the war debt, and regulating the currency; but it was helpless to operate without the goodwill and cheerful compliance of the states. It lacked coercive power—the ability to collect taxes, to enforce treaties, to smooth internal and external relations, to amend its articles without the unanimous approval of the states. These defects were soon apparent and in the summer of 1787 representatives from most of the states gathered at Philadelphia to design a more powerful central government.

The architects of the Constitution were not insensitive to the privileges of the states or the liberties of the citizens. Recognizing that a national government needed more power, they nevertheless tried to hedge and limit its exercise. Their unusual solutions are now familiar, most of them still in effect almost two hundred years later. They ranged from a federal system—with national and state governments each operating in its own sphere—to a bicameral Congress, where the House of Representatives and the Senate watched and checked each other, from an independent Supreme Court, appointed by the President with the approval of the Senate, to an executive who must ratify Congressional legislation but whose veto could be overridden. Would these schemes establish a government of sufficient power that would not trample the liberties of the people? In ratifying conventions, in newspapers, and in pamphlets, Americans debated the issue. Some found the safeguards inadequate; others believed they were more than equal to the task. Everyone recognized that the balance between power and liberty was exceptionally difficult to achieve, that nothing less than the future of republican government in the United States was at stake. One by one the states decided to accept the new Constitution; and in 1790 under the Presidency of George Washington, Americans began their experiment to see whether government power and individual liberty could coexist.

The adventure of constitutional government was novel and even frightening to many experienced American leaders. Having thrown off a king and the protections of a vast empire, they were about to embark on an unprecedented voyage. The new government rested solely upon the consent of its citizenry; none of the traditional sanctions of divine royalty, hereditary nobility, established church, or habits of obedience existed to guarantee its success. Major economic and political problems remained unsolved. At home, hostile Indians and European occupation loomed across national frontiers. Abroad, old enemies and even new allies competed for the foreign trade that was necessary for economic prosperity. Every major political decision involved perilous consequences, and there were few guiding lines. The history of the world presented many analogies, but few Americans were certain of their applications. No republic of this size had been attempted for almost eighteen hundred years, and history was strewn with the relics of earlier hopes.

In this atmosphere of crisis and self-consciousness, no problem was too small to deserve serious discussion. The simple question of what to entitle the President, and the etiquette of his congressional reception, plunged the Senate into prolonged debate. With few established conventions or the solace of unquestioned traditions, every phrase, gesture, and act of government acquired enormous emotional significance. Even the greatness of Washington and confidence in his personal character were not enough entirely to allay fears that the executive office might ultimately turn into an engine of repression, and return to America those evils which the Revolution was intended to destroy forever.

Washington's presidency did give vital stability to the new state, however, and his person provided a link with the revered Revolutionary past and even the older days of British administration. To gain still further security, some Americans sought inspiration from the past. The new federal buildings in Washington were based upon designs that Greeks and Romans had employed thousands of years earlier. Some hoped that the columns, domes, and friezes would ally the young government with the cause of beauty, and bestow upon it some of the legitimacy of the classical world.

In some areas, tradition seemed less important than innovation. The Revolutionary spirit was not confined to government. No aspect of human society was too trivial for reformers who wished the American state to signal a new era in the affairs of mankind. Schemes of reformation, from penal institutions to systems of spelling, were canvassed and debated. Having escaped some of the constraints of tryanny and superstition, Americans could now use a benevolent rationalism to devise institutions for the improvement of humanity. Moreover, these institutions of education and communication would help give a common identity to a people whose heterogeneous racial and religious origins were re-emphasized by their dispersion over an enormous tract of land.

Rationalism, however, was not the only means of unification. The great men of the Revolutionary era were frequently deists, who had little or no formal religious connections, and who considered themselves children of the Enlightenment in their devotion to general schemes of human improvement. But the alliance between evangelicals and deists against orthodox religious establishments came to an end in the 1790s. In the first decade of the new century a wave of revivalism swept over many of the frontier areas and included older settlements as well. Baptists and Methodists gathered in camp meetings in the territories of Kentucky and Tennessee, seeking an experience of grace and engaging often in violent and ecstatic behavior. Revivalism was seen by some as a means of providing unity in an atmosphere of sectarian dispute and of reawakening Protestant fervor in an age when unchurched citizens far outnumbered members of congregations.

Religious virture could also be promoted by encouraging the study of American history. Although George Washington was reviled by political opponents while in office, he was practically deified by this generation, and his death in 1799 touched off a stream of eulogistic biographies and sermons. A pantheon of heroes was one way of stimulating an attachment to American values, and Washington's disinterestedness, honesty, and strength of will were attractive qualities to celebrate. Some biographers, like Mason Weems, emphasized this hero's religious faith as an instrument to convince younger Americans that true glory and patriotism were impossible without religion.

Washington's death came only months before the momentous elections of 1800, which transferred power to another Revolutionary figure, Thomas Jefferson. Jefferson's election was in many ways a repudiation of the policies of his predecessor, John Adams, who failed to retain a wide support for his leadership. Adams' willingness to accept legislation curtailing civil liberties contributed to his downfall, but the ease of transition from a Federalist to a Democratic-Republican administration, testified to the success of constitutional government. After a decade of trial, the republic was strong enough to withstand a change of party without the destruction or subversion of any of its major political institutions.

Jefferson's Presidency began with high hopes and great enthusiasm. The simplicity of his famous inaugural testified to his commitment to agrarian virtues, and his belief that on the virtue of free, independent, yeomen farmers rested the future of the country. But however popular his domestic policies were, and however experienced and cosmopolitan Jefferson stood in European circles, he was helpless to avoid the effects of the great European war in progress. Believing that involvement in the conflict might cost the United States its independence, Jefferson adopted strenuous and aggressive policies to isolate the country from the din of battle. His embargo, however, increased domestic discord without solving foreign problems, and the cessation of foreign commerce only served to stimulate domestic manufacturing, which Jefferson feared so much.

His fellow Virginian, James Madison, was also unable to steer an independent course, and, by 1812, less than three decades after the Revolution was over, the United States was again at war with Great Britain. The optimism and expansionism with which Americans began the war was tempered by a succession of defeats, including the humiliating disaster of the burning of Washington. Although sea victories and some stalemated land battles indicated that resistance to Britain would be stiff, it was less military skill than the reluctance of the Liverpool government to pursue an American war at a time of domestic trouble, which led to the Peace of Ghent. The treaty was far better than many Americans had expected. Although it settled few of the issues which had led to the war in the first place, it did not penalize the United States, and indicated permanent British acceptance of an independent America, and the possibility of a rapprochement in the years ahead.

After the Treaty of Ghent, the bitter party feuding which had characterized the first administrations ended. James Monroe presided over an era that gave greater energy to economic development and geographical expansion than to political disputes. While the "Good Feelings" frequently disguised harsh political competition, no single issue divided the mass of the population. Beneath the surface, however, forces were building that would eventuate, forty years later, in bitter civil war.

To some, the symbol of these forces was the angry debate over the admission of Missouri in 1820, and the question of the expansion of slavery. To Jefferson the issue tolled like "a firebell in the night," warning of disaster to follow. Sensitive observers had begun to notice that national expansion had split the young republic into great sections, often holding incompatible goals and interests. The middle states and New England, traditionally the centers of international commerce, were nursing the first large-scale domestic industries and seeking a tariff on manufactured goods imported from abroad. The slaveholding South, centering more and more of its capital on the raising of cotton, found the tariff unnecessary and discriminatory to its economic position. And Western farmers, filling up the Mississippi and Ohio river valleys, spreading out into the territory purchased from France in 1807 by Jefferson, were demanding internal improvements to ease their problems of transportation and communication with coastal cities. Still muted as an issue, but on the minds of many, was the dilemma of slavery. In 1820 there were still Southerners ready to attack the institution as a denial of American principles, but they were growing fewer, and the attacks of Northerners were growing more angry. Economic disputes were still the most obvious source of sectional disagree-

83

ment, but the country was becoming more aware of the paradox of servitude in a nation of free men.

The first thirty years of constitutional government had witnessed remarkable political and economic growth. The number of states in the Union had almost doubled, the population had almost tripled to more than nine and one-half million, and the federal government was sovereign over a territory of more than two million square miles. Great innovations in transport would soon defy the tyranny of distance, and bring Western farmers and Southern planters in close connection with the burgeoning cities of the Northeast. Even more impressive was the obvious and satisfying stability of the Constitution itself. War, economic crisis, even threats of insurrection and secession had not seriously challenged its effectiveness. Still worried about the danger of Old World powers, Americans had accepted a new position of power in the Western Hemisphere, and in the Monroe Doctrine committed themselves to an energetic role in the defense of its independence from foreign colonialism. And artists, writers, and scholars had begun, at least tentatively, to shape the contours of a distinctive national culture. No longer an outpost of the European world, and not quite yet a distinctive and coherent civilization, the United States by 1820 had demonstrated the power of its republican ideology and had channeled the emotional fervor of its Revolutionary era into viable and stable political institutions.

9
The Revolutionary Mobs

Violence was a constant component of the political events that culminated in the outbreak of the American Revolution. From the riots that accompanied the introduction of the Stamp Act in the colonies in 1765, to the Boston Massacre in 1770, to the Boston Tea Party in 1773, Americans had frequent recourse to mob action. British officials and sympathizers found these outbursts brazen, malicious, and symptomatic of the most serious breakdown of the social order. But a surprising number of colonists themselves viewed these incidents with greater enthusiasm and satisfaction. The Boston Massacre—an incident considered by the British to be one in which no more than a handful of hoodlums received their due—was for the colonists an occasion for patriotic discourse by ministers and political leaders, a custom that they continued annually.

The colonial mob was of a very special sort. It is no easy matter to put together a list of people who joined it, or reconstruct with any precision its activities. But there are several valuable contemporary accounts of mob activity that help clarify its character. Three such narratives follow below. The first, written by New York's Lieutenant-Governor, Cadwallader Colden, describes the Stamp Act riot in New York City. The second is an account of the Boston Massacre. The third is a report to a former Governor of Massachusetts, Sir Francis Bernard, of the Boston Tea Party.

ACCOUNT
OF THE STAMP ACT RIOT
Cadwallader Colden

The People of New York are properly Distinguished into different Ranks.

1st The Proprietors of the large Tracts of Land, who include within their claims from 100,000 acres to above one Million of acres under one Grant. Some of these remain in one single Family. Others are, by Devises & Purchases claim'd in common by considerable numbers of Persons.

From "The Account of the Lieutenant-Governor of New York, Cadwallader Colden, of the Stamp Act Riot, Sent to the Secretary of State and the Board of Trade in England" in *The Colden Letter Books*, New York Historical Society, *Collections for the Year 1877* (New York, 1878), II: 68–71, 74–77.

2nd The Gentlemen of the Law make the second class in which properly are included both the Bench & the Bar. Both of them act on the same Principles, & are of the most distinguished Rank in the Policy of the Province.

3rd The Merchants make the third class. Many of them have rose suddenly from the lowest Rank of the People to considerable Fortunes,. & chiefly by illicit Trade in the last War. They abhor every limitation of Trade and Duty on it, & therefore gladly go into every Measure whereby they hope to have Trade free.

4thly—In the last Rank may be placed the Farmers and Mechanics. Tho' the Farmers hold their Lands in fee simple, they are as to condition of Life in no way superior to the common Farmers in England; and the Mechanics such only as are necessary in Domestic Life. This last Rank comprehends the bulk of the People, & in them consists the strength of the Province. They are the most usefull and the most Morall, but allwise made the Dupes of the former; and often are ignorantly made their Tools for the worst purposes.

The Gentlemen of the Law, both the Judges & principal Practitioners at the Bar, are either Owners Heirs or strongly connected in family Interest with the Proprietors. In general all the Lawyers unite in promoting Contention, prolonging Suits & encreasing the Expence of obtaining Justice. Every artifice & chicanery in the Law has been so much connived at, or rather encouraged that honest Men who are not of affluent fortunes are deterr'd from defending their Rights or seeking Justice.

People in general Complain of these Things & lament the state of Justice, but yet the power of the Lawyers is such that every Man is affraid of offending them and is deterr'd from makeing any public opposition to their power & the daily increase of it. The Lieut. Governor sensible that he could not do his Majesty or the People committed to his care more eminent piece of service than by reforming the abuses of the Law & the dangerous power of the Lawyers took every opportunity during his administration to promote a Work as necessary as Salutary—this drew upon him the most virulent & malicious Resentment of the Lawyers which they have pursued in a manner that shews they intend, that by the ruin of the only Man who has ventured publicly to oppose them, all others shall be deterred.

The Gentlemen of the Law some years since entered into an association with intention among other things to assume the direction of Government by the influence they had in the Assembly, gained by their family connections and by the profession of the Law, whereby they are unavoidably in the secrets of many Families—many Court their Friendship, & all dread their hatred. By these means, tho' few of them are Members, they rule the House of Assembly in all Matters of Importance. The greatest number of the Assembly being Common Farmers who know little either of Men or Things are easily deluded & seduced.

By this association, united in interest & family Connections with the proprietors of the great Tracts of Land, a Domination of Lawyers was formed in this Province, which for some years past has been too strong for the Executive powers of Government.—A Domination founded on the same Principles and carried on by the same wicked artifices that the Domination of Priests formerly was in the times of ignorance in the papeish Countries. Every Man's character who dares to discover his Sentiments in opposition to theirs is loaded with infamy by every falsehood which malice can invent, and thereby exposed to the brutal Rage of the Mob. Nothing is too wicked for them to attempt which serves their purposes—the Press is to them what the Pulpit was in times of Popery. No man who Reads the Papers publish'd in New York for some time past, & what has happen'd there in consequence of them, can doubt of what is now said, however improbable on first sight it may appear to be.

When the King's [Stamp Act] Order in his Privy Council, of the 26th of July arived in September last it revived all the Rage of the Profession of the Law, & they takeing the advantage of the Spirit of Sedition which was raised in all the Colonies against the act of Parliament for laying a stamp Duty in the Colonies, they turn'd the Rage of the Mob against the Person of the Lieut Governor, after all other methods which their Malice had invented for that purpose had failed. The Malice of the Faction against the Lieut. Governor is so evident that their inclination to expose every failing in his administration cannot be doubted, & when they have nothing to charge him with besides his supporting the Right of the Subject to Appeal to the King, it gives the strongest presumption in his favour that they cannot otherwise blame any part of his administration.

In the night of the 1st of November a great Mob came up to the Fort Gate with two Immages carried on a Scaffold: one representing their gray haired Governor, the other the Devil whispering him in the Ear. After Continuing thus at the Gate, with all the insulting Ribaldry that Malice could invent, they broke open the Lieut. Governor's Coach House which was without the walls of the Fort, carried his chariot round the streets of the Town in triumph with the Immages—returned a second time to the Fort Gate, and in an open place near the Fort, finished their Insult with all the Indignities that the Malice of their Leaders could invent. Their view certainly was to provoke the Garrison, then placed on the Ramparts, to some act which might be called a Commencement of Hostilities, in which case it cannot be said what was farther intended. Being disappointed in this the Mob expended their Rage by destroying everything they found in the House of Major James of the Royal Artillery, for which no reason can be assigned other than his putting the Fort in a proper state of Defence as his Duty in his Department required of him.

While the Lieut Governor was in the Country as usual during the heats of summer he received a Letter from General Gage informing him that the public Papers were crammed with Treason. The Minds of the People disturbed excited & encouraged to Revolt against the Government, to subvert the Constitution & trample on the Laws. That every falsehood that Malice can invent is propagated as Truth to sow dissention & create animosities between Great Britain & the Colonies concluding an offer of such military assistance as the Lieut Governor should think requisite in support of the Civil Authority. The Lieut. Governor immediately answered this Letter with his Opinion that one Battalion would be requisite with the Garrison of the Fort, but that he would immediately return to Town and take the advice of the Council on the subject of his Letter.

Tho' this advice was contrary to the Lieut Governor's private Sentiments he thought it most prudent to submit the matter to the General. The argument made use of by the Council that it would be more safe to shew confidence in the people than to discover a distrust of them by calling in any assistance to the civil power, in the Lt Governor's Opinion goes too far, as it discouraged every precaution. The event has shewn that it was not well judged, for it is most probable that had a Battalion of Regulars been brought to New York, all the Riots and Insults on Government had been prevented. The acting with vigour seemed the more necessary as the eyes of all the other Colonies were on New York where the King had a Fort allwise garrisoned with Regular Troops. The General kept his head Quarters there, and two Friggates and a sloop of War were in the Port. When the Lieut. Governor came to Town he found the General had ordered Major James to carry in such Artillery & Military Stores as he thought necessary for the Defence of the Fort; and two Companies of artillery having opportunely arrived at that time from England they had likewise been ordered into the Fort to strengthen the Garrison. Mr James is certainly a Benevolent Humane Man, & had distinguished himself on several occasions in the late War. No objection could be made to him, but his daring to put the King's Fort in a state of Defence, against the Sovereign Lords the People as they stiled themselves, for which offence they Resolved to make him an example of their Displeasure.

Before these additional Defences were made, & while the Garrison consisted only of 44 Privates & two subaltern officers, the Fort could not have been defended against 100 resolute Men, in which case the Govr must have submitted to every shamefull condition which the insolence of the Leaders of the Mob should think proper to impose upon him. They certainly had this in view while the Fort remained in its defenceless State. But after it was put in that state of offence as well as Defence, in which it was put after the 1st of November by the Engineers of the Army, the stile of the Leaders of the Mob was changed from Threatening to Deprecating, & they only wanted some Colour for desisting from their Designs to save their Credit with the deluded People. It became evident that the Fort could not be carried by assault, & that in the attempt the town would be exposed to Desolation. In the state the Fort then was, it was the Opinion of the Gentlemen of the army, that one Regiment in the city would have been sufficient to have subdued the Seditious Spirit which then prevailed.

The Authors of the Sedition place their Security in the number of offenders, and that no Jury in the Colonies will convict any of them. Were it possible that these men could succeed in their hope of Independency on a British Parliament, many judicious Persons think (tho' they dare not declare what they think) we shall become a most unhappy People. The obligation of Oaths daringly profaned—& every Bond of Society dissolved. The Liberty & Property of Individuals will become subject to the avarice & ambition of wicked Men who have art enough to keep the Colony in perpetual Factions, by deluding an ignorant Mob: and the Colonies must become thereby useless to Great Britain.

THE HORRID MASSACRE
IN BOSTON

Perpetrated in the evening of the fifth day of March, 1770, by soldiers of the Twenty-ninth Regiment, which with the Fourteenth Regiment were then quartered there; with some observations on the state of things prior to that catastrophe. Gathered and printed by the Town of Boston, 1770.

It may be a proper introduction to this narrative, briefly to represent the state of things for some time previous to the said Massacre; and this seems necessary in order to the forming a just idea of the causes of it.

At the end of the late war, in which this province bore so distinguished a part, a happy union subsisted between Great Britain and the colonies. This was unfortunately interrupted by the Stamp Act; but it was in some measure restored by the repeal of it. It was again interrupted by other acts of parliament for taxing America; and by the appointment of a Board of Commissioners, in pursuance of an act, which by the face of it was made for the relief and encouragement of commerce, but which in its operation, it was apprehended, would have, and it has in fact had, a contrary effect. By the said act the said Commissioners were "to be resident in some convenient part of his Majesty's dominions in America." This must be understood to be in some part convenient for the whole. But it does not appear that, in fixing the place of their residence, the convenience of the whole was at all consulted, for Boston, being very far from the centre of the colonies, could not be the place most convenient for the whole. Judging by the act, it may seem this town was intended to be favored, by the Commissioners being appointed to reside here; and that the consequence of that residence would be the relief and encouragement of commerce; but the reverse has been the constant and uniform effect of it; so that the commerce of the town, from the embarrassments in which it has been lately involved, is greatly reduced. For the particulars on this head, see the state of the trade not long since drawn up and transmitted to England by a committee of the merchants of Boston.

The residence of the Commissioners here has been detrimental, not only to the commerce, but to the political interests of the town and province; and not only so, but we can trace from it the causes of the late horrid massacre. Soon after their arrival here in November, 1767, instead of confining themselves to the proper business of their office, they became partizans of Governor Bernard in his political schemes; and had the weakness and temerity to infringe upon one of the most essential rights of the house of commons of this province—that of giving their votes with freedom, and not being accountable therefor but to their constituents. One of the members of that house, Capt. Timothy Folgier, having voted in some affair contrary to the mind of the said Commissioners, was for so doing dismissed from the office he held under them.

These proceedings of theirs, the difficulty of access to them on office-business, and a supercilious behavior, rendered them disgustful to people in general, who in

From *A Short Narrative of the Horrid Massacre in Boston* (Boston, 1770; reprinted, New York, 1849), 13–19, 21–22, 28–30.

consequence thereof treated them with neglect. This probably stimulated them to resent it; and to make their resentment felt, they and their coadjutor, Governor Bernard, made such representations to his Majesty's ministers as they thought best calculated to bring the displeasure of the nation upon the town and province; and in order that those representations might have the more weight, they are said to have contrived and executed plans for exciting disturbances and tumults, which otherwise would probably never have existed; and, when excited, to have transmitted to the ministry the most exaggerated accounts of them.

Unfortunately for us, they have been too successful in their said representations, which, in conjunction with Governor Bernard's, have occasioned his Majesty's faithful subjects of this town and province to be treated as enemies and rebels, by an invasion of the town by sea and land. While the town was surrounded by a considerable number of his Majesty's ships of war, two regiments landed and took possession of it; and to support these, two other regiments arrived some time after from Ireland; one of which landed at Castle Island, and the other in the town.

Thus were we, in aggravation of our other embarrassments, embarrassed with troops, forced upon us contrary to our inclination—contrary to the spirit of Magna Charta—contrary to the very letter of the Bill of Rights, in which it is declared, that the raising or keeping a standing army within the kingdom in time of peace, unless it be with the consent of parliament, is against law, and without the desire of the civil magistrates, to aid whom was the pretence for sending the troops hither; who were quartered in the town in direct violation of an act of parliament for quartering troops in America.

As they were the procuring cause of troops being sent hither, they must therefore be the remote and a blameable cause of all the disturbances and bloodshed that have taken place in consequence of that measure.

We shall next attend to the conduct of the troops, and to some circumstances relative to them.

The challenging the inhabitants by sentinels posted in all parts of the town before the lodgings of officers, which (for about six months, while it lasted), occasioned many quarrels and uneasiness.

Capt. Wilson, of the 59th, exciting the negroes of the town to take away their masters' lives and property, and repair to the army for protection, which was fully proved against him. The attack of a party of soldiers on some of the magistrates of the town—the repeated rescues of soldiers from peace officers—the firing of a loaded musket in a public street, to the endangering a great number of peaceable inhabitants—the frequent wounding of persons by their bayonets and cutlasses, and the numerous instances of bad behavior in the soldiery, made us early sensible that the troops were not sent here for any benefit to the town or province, and that we had no good to expect from such conservators of the peace.

It was not expected, however, that such an outrage and massacre, as happened here on the evening of the fifth instant, would have been perpetrated. There were then killed and wounded, by a discharge of musketry, eleven of his Majesty's subjects, viz.:

Mr. Samuel Gray, killed on the spot by a ball entering his head.

Crispus Attucks, a mulatto, killed on the spot, two balls entering his breast.

Mr. James Caldwell, killed on the spot, by two balls entering his back.

Mr. Samuel Maverick, a youth of seventeen years of age, mortally wounded; he died the next morning.

Mr. Patrick Carr mortally wounded; he died the 14th instant.

Christopher Monk and John Clark, youths about seventeen years of age, dangerously wounded. It is apprehended they will die.

Mr. Edward Payne, merchant, standing at his door; wounded.

Messrs. John Green, Robert Patterson, and David Parker; all dangerously wounded.

The actors in this dreadful tragedy were a party of soldiers commanded by Capt. Preston of the 29th regiment. This party, including the Captain, consisted of eight, who are all committed to jail.

What gave occasion to the melancholy event of that evening seems to have been this. A difference having happened near Mr. Gray's ropewalk, between a soldier and a man belonging to it, the soldier challenged the ropemakers to a boxing match. The challenge was accepted by one of them, and the soldier worsted. He ran to the barrack in the neighborhood, and returned with several of his companions. The fray was renewed, and the soldiers were driven off. They soon returned with recruits and were again worsted. This happened several times till at length a considerable body of soldiers was collected, and they also were driven off, the ropemakers having been joined by their brethren of the contiguous ropewalks. By this time Mr. Gray being alarmed interposed, and with the assistance of some gentlemen prevented any further disturbance. To satisfy the soldiers and punish the man who had been the occasion of the first difference, and as an example to the rest, he turned him out of his service; and waited on Col. Dalrymple, the commanding officer of the troops, and with him concerted measures for preventing further mischief. Though this affair ended thus, it made a strong impression on the minds of the soldiers in general, who thought the honor of the regiment concerned to revenge those repeated repulses. For this purpose they seem to have formed a combination to commit some outrage upon the inhabitants of the town indiscriminately; and this was to be done on the evening of the 5th instant or soon after.

Samuel Drowne [a witness] declares that, about nine o'clock of the evening of the fifth of March current, standing at his own door in Cornhill, he saw about fourteen or fifteen soldiers of the 29th regiment, who came from Murray's barracks, armed with naked cutlasses, swords, &c., and came upon the inhabitants of the town, then standing or walking in Cornhill, and abused some, and violently assaulted others as they met them; most of whom were without so much as a stick in their hand to defend themselves, as he very clearly could discern, it being moonlight, and himself being one of the assaulted persons. All or most of the said soldiers he saw go into King street (some of them through Royal Exchange lane), and there followed them, and soon discovered them to be quarrelling and fighting with the people whom they saw there, which he thinks were not more than a dozen, when the soldiers came first, armed as aforesaid. Of those dozen people, the most of them were gentlemen, standing together a little below the Town House, upon the Exchange. At the appearance of those soldiers so armed, the most of the twelve persons went off, some of them being first assaulted.

The violent proceedings of this party, and their going into King street, "quarrelling and fighting with the people whom they saw there" (mentioned in Mr. Drowne's deposition), was immediately introductory to the grand catastrophe.

These assailants, who issued from Murray's barracks (so called), after attacking and wounding divers persons in Cornhill, as above-mentioned, being armed, proceeded (most of them) up the Royal Exchange lane into·King street; where, making a short stop, and after assaulting and driving away the few they met there, they brandished their arms and cried out, "Where are the boogers! where are the cowards!" At this time there were very few persons in the street beside themselves. This party in proceeding from Exchange lane into King street, must pass the sentry posted at the westerly corner of the Custom House, which butts on that lane and fronts on that street. This is needful to be mentioned, as near that spot and in that street the bloody tragedy was acted, and the street actors in it were stationed: their station being but a few feet from the front side of the said Custom House. The outrageous behavior and the threats of the said party occasioned the ringing of the meeting-house bell near the head of King street, which bell ringing quick, as for fire, it presently brought out a number of the inhabitants, who being soon sensible of the occasion of it, were naturally led to King street, where the said party had made a stop but a little while before, and where their stopping had drawn together a number of boys, round the sentry at the Custom House. Whether the boys mistook the sentry for one of the said party, and thence took occasion to differ with him, or whether he first affronted them, which is affirmed in several depositions,—however that may be, there was much foul language between them, and some of them, in consequence of his pushing at them with his bayonet, threw snowballs at him, which occasioned him to knock hastily at the door of the Custom House. From hence two persons thereupon proceeded immediately to the main-guard, which was posted opposite to the State House, at a small distance, near the head of the said street. The officer on guard was Capt. Preston, who with seven or eight soldiers, with fire-arms and charged bayonets, issued from the guardhouse, and in great haste posted himself and his soldiers in front of the Custom House, near the corner aforesaid. In passing to this station the soldiers pushed several persons with their bayonets, driving through the people in so rough a manner that it appeared they intended to create a disturbance. This occasioned some snowballs to be thrown at them, which seems to have been the only provocation that was given. Mr. Knox (between whom and Capt. Preston there was some conversation on the spot) declares, that while he was talking with Capt. Preston, the soldiers of his detachment had attacked the people with their bayonets; and that there was not the least provocation given to Capt. Preston or his party; the backs of the people being toward them when the people were attacked. He also declares, that Capt. Preston seemed to be in great haste and much agitated, and that, according to his opinion, there were not then present in King street above seventy or eighty persons at the extent.

The said party was formed into a half circle; and within a short time after they had been posted at the Custom House, began to fire upon the people.

Captain Preston is said to have ordered them to fire, and to have repeated that order. One gun was fired first; then others in succession, and with deliberation, till ten or a dozen guns were fired; or till that number of discharges were made from the guns that were fired. By which means eleven persons were killed and wounded, as above represented.

A NARRATIVE
OF THE TEA ACT MOB

The Advices received from Boston, in Letters from Gov$_r$ Hutchinson, Admiral Montagu, and the Commandant of the Kings Troops at Castle William, and the Information taken here of Capt Scott, lately arrived from thence, contain the following Facts—

That, in the night between the 1st & 2^d of November, anonymous Letters were delivered at the Houses of the Persons Commissioned by the East India Company, for the Sale of Teas sent on their own Account to Boston, requiring them to appear next day at noon at Liberty Tree to make a Public Resignation of their Commission, and Printed notices were posted up in several parts of the Town of Boston desiring the Freemen to meet at Liberty Tree in order to receive such Resignation, and to oblige said Agents to swear they would reship any such Tea to London.

That on the 2^d of November, the *Select Men of Boston, the Town Clerk and three or four Members of the House* of Representatives,—accompanied by a number of Inhabitants, assembled at Liberty Tree for the purposes aforementioned, and that soon after Mr *Molineux*, attended by a number of other persons, calling themselves a Committee of the said Meeting, consisting among others of Mr Denny, Dr Warren, Dr Church, and Mr Johanat, repaired to the House of Mr Clark, one of the said Agents and being asked by Mr Clark what they expected of him, Mr Molineux read a paper, in which, among other things, it was demanded that the persons, to whom it was expected the Tea would be consigned, would engage not to receive it, but that it should be sent back to England, and that one of the Bills of Lading should be delivered to them that they might send it to their Agent in London.

That upon Mr Clarke and the other Agents who were present declaring they would not comply with this Demand, Mr Molineux declared that they either were or would be voted Enemies to their Country and must expect to be treated as such.

That after this the Committee with the Mob that attended them retired, and soon after returned, assaulted Mr Clarke's House, the Doors of which were Shut

From "The Papers of the Former Governor of Massachusetts, Sir Francis Bernard (1773)," *The Barrington-Bernard Correspondence, 1760–1770*, Edward Channing and Archibald Coolidge, eds. (Cambridge, Mass., 1912), 294–302.

from an apprehension of Violence, and having forced open the Doors attempted to make their way up Stairs, but meeting with Resistance they desisted.

That during the proceedings a Mr Hatch a Gentleman in the Commission of the Peace, required the Mob to disperse; but they hooted at him, and one of them having Struck him a blow, he retired.

That on the 5th of Novr a Town Metting was held at Faneuil Hall, at which it was voted that the Honble John Hancock Esqre, Mr John Pitt, Mr Samuel Adams, Mr Samuel Abbot, Dr Joseph Warren, Mr William Powell, and Mr Nathaniel Appleton, should be a Committee to wait on the Agents of the East India Company, and to request them from a regard to their own Character, and the Peace & good Order of the Town and Province, immediately to resign their Appointment, with this request the Agents refused to comply and signified their refusal in Letters to the Honble John Hancock who was Moderator of the Town Meeting.

That on the 12th of Novr Information was given to Mr Oliver the Lieut^t Governor, that an Attack would be made that Evening upon some of the Agents; Intimation of this being given to them they left their Houses, but no such attack was made.

That on the 17th in the Evening a Mob of between one and two hundred people, beset the House of Mr Hutchinson one of the said Agents, but finding that he was not at home, they went to the House of Mr Clarke, another of the said Agents, which they Attacked, and endeavoured to break open the Door, but meeting with resistance they contented themselves with breaking the Glass and Frame of the Window, and then dispersed.

That in consequence of the disturbance before mentioned, the Governor Assembled his Council, and laid before them the necessity of some Measures being taken for preserving the Peace, and supporting the Authority of Government.

That during their deliberations a Petition was delivered from the Agents stating the Insults they had received, and the danger to which they were exposed; and praying that they might be at liberty to resign themselves, and the Property committed to their care, to the Governor and Council, as the Guardians and Protectors of the People, but the Council broke up without coming to any Resolution.

That on the 23^d of Novr the Council met again without doing any thing but referring the Business to a further consideration on the 29th when they took into consideration a Report made by a Committee in which it is stated that the proceedings of Parliament had given just ground of discontent to the People, and those proceedings are assigned as the cause of the present Disturbances.—The Agents are referred to the Justices of the Peace for the protection they desire, and it is declared that the Council had no Authority to take charge of the Tea, and *that should they direct or advise any measure for Landing it, they would of course advise to a Measure for procuring Payment of the Duty, which being inconsistent with the declared Sentiments* of both Houses in the last Winter Sessions of the General Court, they apprehend to be altogether inexpedient and improper.—That with regard to the disturbances the Authors of them ought to be prosecuted, and they advise that the Governor should renew his Orders to the Justices, Sheriff and other Peace Officers, to exert them selves to the utmost for the Security of the Kings Subjects the preservation of Peace & good Order, and for preventing all Offences against the Laws.

That this Report was accordingly agreed to, whereupon the Governor demanded of the Council, whether they would not give him any Advice upon the Disorders then prevailing in the Town of Boston, and it was answered in general, That the Advice already given was intended for that purpose.

That on, or about the 26th of November the Ship Dartmouth [of] Captn Hall, arrived at Boston, having on board a Cargo of Tea consigned by the East India Company to their Agents there; in consequence of which Notifications were posted up, desiring the Inhabitants of the Town and Country to Assemble on the 29th—

That on the 29th the Inhabitants of the said Town & Country in number about five Thousand were accordingly Assembled; whereupon the Governor, (the Council having declined advising to any Measure respecting that unlawful Assembly in particular) Ordered the Sheriff to repair to the said Meeting with a Proclamation, Warning, Exhorting, and Requiring them forthwith to disperse, and to cease all further unlawful Proceedings.

That the Sheriff having been permitted to read this Proclamation, a Question was moved and put, Whether the Assembly should be dispersed in Consequence thereof; and it was unanimously Resolved that they should not.

That Jonathan Williams Esqre was chosen Moderator at this Meeting, and that the said Meeting came to the following Resolutions; amongst others Vizt That they were absolutely determined that the Tea arrived in Captn Hall, should be returned to the place from whence it came at all Events, in the same Ship.—That no Duty should be paid upon it, and that the Owner of the Ship be directed not to Enter the Tea at his Peril. That the Master of the Ship be informed, that he is not at his peril to suffer any of the Tea to be Landed. That a Military Watch should be Appointed for the Security of the Ship and Cargo, of which watch Mr Proctor was appointed Captain, and a List made of the names of the Persons who offered themselves as Volunteers for that purpose.

That the Conduct of the Governor in requiring the Justices of the Peace to meet, in order to suppress any Riot was a reflection on that Assembly and solely calculated to serve the Views of Administration.

That on Tuesday the 30 of November the Inhabitants were again Assembled, when a Letter from the Agents was read, declaring their Willingness to give satisfaction to the Town but as that could only be effected by sending back the Tea, they declared that it was not in their power so to do but that they were willing to Store the Tea until they could write to their Constituents and receive further Orders.

That upon reading this Letter it was moved whether if any of the Agents could be prevailed upon to come to the Meeting their persons might be safe until their Return to the place from whence they should come?—which question having been put it was carried in the Affirmative unanimously and that two Hours should be allowed them, whereupon the Meeting adjourned to the Afternoon.

That upon their Meeting in the Afternoon Report was made that the Agents thinking that nothing would be satisfactory, short of returning the Tea, which was out of their power, they thought it best not to appear, which Report having been voted to be in no degree satisfactory, an Order was made that the Owner & Master of the Ship Dartmouth should attend & it was again unanimously resolved that it should be required of them, that the Tea should be returned to England in the Bottom in which it came, and Capt. Hall was forbid to Assist in Unloading the Tea at his peril, and ordered that if he continued Master of the Vessel, he should carry the same back to London.

That after taking Measures for a Continuance of the Military Watch resolved to be Established on the preceding day, & directing that if they were insulted they should give alarm to the Inhabitants by ringing or tolling the Bells as the case should happen, it was resolved that if any person or persons shall here after Import Tea from Great Britain or if any Master or Masters of any Vessel or Vessels in Great Britain shall take the same on board to be Imported to this place until the unrighteous Act of Parliament laying a Duty upon it should be repealed, he or they should be deemed by this Body an Enemy to his Country and they would prevent the Landing and Sale of the same, and the payment of the Duty thereon and would effect the Return thereof to the place from whence they should come.

That it was further resolved at this Meeting that the foregoing Vote should be printed and sent to England, and all the Sea ports of the Province.

That Mr Saml Adams, the Honble John Hancock Esqre, Willm Philips Esqre John Rowe Esq, Jonathan Williams Esqre be a Committee to transmit fair Copies of the whole proceedings of the Meeting to New York and Philadelphia.

That it is the Determination of the Body to carry their Votes and Resolutions into Execution at the risk of their Lives and Fortunes.

That the Persons who principally proposed the questions on which the above Resolutions and proceedings were founded, were, Mr Adam's, Mr Molineux, Doctor Young & Doctor Warren, & that they used many Arguments to induce the People to concur in these Resolutions.

That after the Dissolution of this unlawful Assembly the Persons called the *Committee of Correspondence;* met from time to time called in the Committee's of other Towns to join with them, kept up a Military Watch on Guard, to prevent the Landing of the Tea, who were Armed with Muskets and Bayonets, and every half hour during the night, regularly passed the Word—*all is well*, like Centinels in a Garrison.

That Mr Hancock the Govrs Captn of his Cadet Company was one of the Guard on Board the Ships.

That the said Committee appeared to be the Executioners of the Resolves & Orders passed at the aforesaid Assembly.

That this Committee repeatedly sent for the Owner of the Ship Dartmouth requiring him to comply with the request of the Town and send his Ship with the Tea back to England—In excuse for his Refusal he said that he could not obtain a Clearance from the Custom House, wereupon Notifications were again posted upon the 14th of Decemr for another Meeting of the Inhabitants which was accordingly held in the Afternoon.

That at this Meeting it was determined that the Owner of the Ship Dartmouth should demand at the Custom House a Clearance of the Teas for England, which was accordingly done in the presence of twelve Persons appointed to see it done.

That upon the Refusal of the Custom House to grant such Clearance the Meeting was adjourned to the next day, in order to consider what was to be done, when the said Owner was required to demand a Permit from the Naval Officer to pass the Castle, which being also refused, he was ordered to apply to the Governor in person for such Permit; which being also refused he returned and made his Report to the Meeting; whereupon numbers of the people cried out a Mob, a Mob, & left the House, and immediately a body of Men disguised like Indians, & encouraged by Mr John Hancock, Saml Adams and others repaired to the Wharf, where three Vessels having Tea on board, lay aground, and took possession of the said Vessels, and in two hours the whole of the Tea was consumed.

10

The Rhetoric of Revolution

One of the most important effects of the new British imperial policy was in prompting many Americans to think for the first time about the most basic constitutional questions. The years after 1763 witnessed an incredible outpouring of pamphlets exploring the premises governing a tie between a mother country and her colony, the dangers of unlimited power, and the requirements for liberty. The Stamp Act, for example, provoked not only riots but the most strenuous efforts to define the proper limits of government in general, and its rights of taxation in particular; and since items of British legislation followed each other in rapid succession, the debate never let up.

All sorts of ingenious distinctions on the rights of Parliamentary taxation emerged from the pamphlet literature. Perhaps the vital result of these discussions was in elevating questions of politics to matters of principle. The pamphlets moved quickly from considerations of internal versus external taxes to the need for the colonists to protect their most vital heritage, liberty. John Dickinson, a leading Philadelphia lawyer, and member of the Pennsylvania legislature, was only one among many Americans who cautioned his countrymen to keep alert and to be prepared to defend their liberties. As the selection from Dickinson's *Letters from a Farmer in Pennsylvania* (1767) well illustrates, once the American-British debate became tied to principle, it would not be easily compromised by ordinary political adjustments.

LETTERS FROM A FARMER IN PENNSYLVANIA
John Dickinson

My dear Countrymen,

Some states have lost their liberty by *particular accidents:* But this calamity is generally owing to the *decay of virtue.* A *people* is travelling fast to destruction, when *individuals* consider *their* interests as distinct from *those of the public.* Such notions are fatal to their country, and to themselves. Yet how many are there, so

From *Letters from a Farmer in Pennsylvania* (reprinted, New York, 1903), Letter XII, 132–146.

weak and *sordid* as to *think* they perform *all the offices of life,* if they earnestly endeavor to increase their own *wealth, power,* and *credit,* without the least regard for the society, under the protection of which they live; who, if they can make an *immediate profit to themselves,* by lending their assistance to those, whose projects plainly tend to the injury of their country, rejoice in their *dexterity,* and believe themselves entitled to the character of *able politicians.* Miserable men! Of whom it is hard to say, whether they ought to be most the objects of *pity* or *contempt:* But whose opinions are certainly as *detestable,* as their practices are *destructive.*

Though I always reflect, with a high pleasure, on the integrity and understanding of my countrymen, which, joined with a pure and humble devotion to the great and gracious author of every blessing they enjoy, will, I hope, ensure to them, and their posterity, all temporal and eternal happiness; yet when I consider, that in every age and country there have been bad men, my heart, at this threatening period, is so full of apprehension, as not to permit me to believe, but that there may be some on this continent, *against whom you ought to be upon your guard* —Men, who either hold, or expect to hold certain advantages, by setting examples of servility to their countrymen.—Men, who trained to the employment, or self taught by a natural versatility of genius, serve as decoys for drawing the innocent and unwary into snares. It is not to be doubted but that such men will diligently bestir themselves on this and every like occasion, to spread the infection of their meanness as far as they can. On the plans *they* have adopted, this is *their* course. *This* is the method to recommend themselves to their *patrons.*

It is not intended, by these words, to throw any reflection upon gentlemen, because they are possessed of offices: For many of them are certainly men of virtue, and lovers of their country. But supposed obligations of *gratitude,* and *honor,* may induce them to be silent. Whether these obligations *ought to be* regarded or not, is not so much to be considered by others, in the judgment they form of these gentlemen, as whether they *think they* ought to be regarded. Perhaps, therefore, we shall act in the properest manner towards them, if we neither *reproach* nor *imitate* them. The persons meant in this letter, are the *base spirited wretches,* who may endeavor to *distinguish themselves,* by their sordid zeal in defending and promoting measures, which *they know, beyond all question,* to be *destructive* to the *just rights* and *true interests* of their country. It is scarcely possible to speak of *these men* with any degree of *patience*—It is scarcely possible to speak of them with any degree of *propriety*—For no words can truly describe their *guilt* and *meanness*—

From *them* we shall learn, how *pleasant* and *profitable* a thing it is, to be for our SUBMISSIVE behavior *well spoken of* at *St. James's,* or *St. Stephen's;* at *Guildhall,* or the *Royal Exchange.* Specious fallacies will be dressed up with all the arts of delusion, to persuade one colony to *distinguish herself from another,* by unbecoming condescensions, *which will serve the ambitious purposes of great men at home,* and therefore will be thought by them *to entitle their assistants in obtaining them* to considerable rewards.

Our fears will be excited. Our homes will be awakened. It will be insinuated to us, with a plausible affectation of *wisdom* and *concern,* how *prudent* it is to please the *powerful*—how *dangerous* to provoke them—and then comes in the perpetual incantation that freezes up every generous purpose of the soul in cold, inactive expectation—"that if there is any request to be made, compliance will obtain a favorable attention."

Our *vigilance* and our *union* are *success* and *safety*. Our *negligence* and our *division* are *distress* and *death*. They are *worse*—They are *shame* and *slavery*. Let us equally shun the benumbing stillness of *overweening sloth*, and the feverish activity of that *ill informed zeal*, which busies itself in maintaining *little, mean* and *narrow* opinions. Let us, with a truly wise *generosity* and *charity*, banish and discourage all *illiberal distinctions*, which may arise from differences in *situation*, forms of *government*, or modes of *religion*. Let us consider ourselves as MEN—FREEMEN—CHRISTIAN FREEMEN—*separated from the rest of the world, and firmly bound together by the same rights, interests* and *dangers*. Let *these* keep our attention inflexibly fixed on the GREAT OBJECTS, which we must CONTINUALLY REGARD, in order to *preserve those rights, to promote those interests*, and to *avert those dangers*.

Let these *truths* be indelibly impressed on our minds—*that* we *cannot be* HAPPY, *without being* FREE—that we cannot be free, *without being secure in our property*—that *we* cannot be secure in our property, *if, without our consent, others may, as by right, take it away*—that *taxes imposed on us by parliament*, do thus take it away—that *duties laid for the sole purpose of raising money*, are taxes—that *attempts* to lay such duties *should be instantly and firmly opposed*—that this opposition can never be effectual, *unless it is the united effort of these provinces*—that therefore BENEVOLENCE *of temper towards each other*, and UNANIMITY *of counsels*, are essential to the welfare of the whole—and lastly, that for this reason, every man among us, who in any manner would encourage either *dissension, dissidence*, or *indifference*, between these colonies, is an enemy to *himself*, and *to his country*.

The belief of these truths, I verily think, my countrymen, is indispensably necessary to your happiness. I beseech you, therefore, "teach them diligently unto your children, and talk of them when you sit in your houses, and when you walk by the way, and when you lie down, and when you rise up." [Deuteronomy 6:7.]

What have these colonies to *ask*, while they continue free? Or what have they to *dread*, but insidious attempts to subvert their freedom? *Their prosperity* does not depend on *ministerial favors doled* out to *particular* provinces. *They* form *one* political body, of which *each colony is a member. Their happiness* is founded on *their constitution*; and is to be promoted, by preserving that constitution in unabated vigor, *throughout every part*. A spot, a speck of decay, however small the limb on which it appears, and however remote it may seem from the vitals, should be alarming. We have *all the rights* requisite for our prosperity. The legal authority of *Great Britain* may indeed lay hard restrictions upon us; but, like the spear of *Telephus*, it will cure as well as wound. Her unkindness will instruct and compel us, after some time, to discover, in our *industry* and *frugality*, surprising remedies—*if our rights continue unviolated:* For as long as the *products* of our *labor*, and the *rewards* of our *care, can properly* be called *our own*, so long it will be worth our while to be *industrious* and *frugal*. But if when we plow—

sow—reap—gather—and thresh—we find, that we plow—sow—reap—gather—and thresh *for others,* whose PLEASURE is to be the SOLE LIMITATION *how much* they shall *take,* and *how much* they shall *leave,* WHY should we repeat the unprofitable toil? *Horses* and *oxen* are content with *that portion of the fruits of their work,* which their *owners* assign them, in order to keep them strong enough to raise successive crops; but even *these beasts* will not submit to draw for their *masters,* until they are *subdued* by *whips* and *goads.*

Let us take care of our *rights,* and we *therein* take care of *our prosperity.* "SLAVERY IS EVER PRECEDED BY SLEEP." *Individuals* may be *dependent* on ministers, if they please. STATES SHOULD SCORN IT;—and if *you* are not wanting *to yourselves,* you will have a *proper regard* paid *you* by *those,* to whom if you are not *respectable,* you will be *contemptible.* But—if *we have already forgot* the *reasons* that urged us with unexpanded unanimity, to exert ourselves two years ago—if *our zeal* for the public good is *worn out* before the *homespun cloths,* which it caused us to have made—if *our resolutions* are *so faint,* as by our present conduct to *condemn* our own late *successful* example—if *we are not affected* by any reverence for the memory of our ancestors, who transmitted to us that freedom in which they had been blessed—if *we are not animated* by any regard for posterity, to whom, by the most sacred obligations, we are bound to deliver down the invaluable inheritance—THEN, indeed, any *minister*—or any *tool* of a minister—or any *creature* of a tool of a minister—or any *lower instrument of administration,* if lower there be, is a *personage* whom it may be dangerous to offend.

If any person shall imagine that he discovers, in these letters, the least dislike of the dependence of these colonies on *Great Britain,* I beg that such person will not form any judgment on *particular expressions,* but will consider the *tenor of all the letters taken together.* In that case, I flatter myself, that every unprejudiced reader will be *convinced,* that the true interests of *Great Britain* are as dear to me, as they ought to be to every good subject.

If I am a *Enthusiast* in any thing, it is in my zeal for the *perpetual dependence* of these colonies on their mother country.—A dependence founded on *mutual benefits,* the continuance of which can be secured only by *mutual affections.* Therefore it is, that with extreme apprehension I view the smallest seeds of discontent, which are unwarily scattered abroad. *Fifty* or *Sixty* years will make astonishing alterations in these colonies; and this consideration should render it the business of *Great Britain* more and more to cultivate our good dispositions towards her: But the misfortune is, that those *great men,* who wrestling for power at home, think themselves very slightly interested in the prosperity of their country *Fifty or Sixty* years hence, but are deeply concerned in blowing up a popular clamor for supposed *immediate advantages.*

For my part, I regard *Great Britain* as a Bulwark, happily fixed between these colonies and the powerful nations of *Europe.* That kingdom remaining safe, we, under its protection, enjoying peace, may dissuse the blessings of religion, science, and liberty, through remote wilderness. It is therefore incontestably our *duty,* and our interest, to support the strength of *Great Britain.* When confiding in that strength, she begins to forget from whence it arose, it will be an easy thing to show

101

the source. She may readily be reminded of the loud alarm spread among her merchants and tradesmen, by the universal association of these colonies, at the time of the *Stamp Act,* not to import any of her MANUFACTURES.

I shall be extremely sorry, if any man mistakes my meaning in any thing I have said. Officers employed by the crown, are, while according to the laws they conduct themselves, entitled to legal obedience, and sincere respect. These it is a duty to render them; and these no good or prudent person will withhold. But when these officers, through rashness or design, desire to enlarge their authority beyond its due limits, and expect improper concessions to be made to them, from regard for the employments they bear, their attempts should be considered as equal injuries to the crown and people, and should be courageously and constantly opposed. To suffer our ideas to be confounded by *names* on such occasions, would certainly be an *inexcusable weakness,* and probably an *irremediable error.*

We have reason to believe, that several of his Majesty's present ministers are good men, and friends to our country; and it seems not unlikely, that by a particular concurrence of events, we have been treated a little more severely than they wished we should be. *They* might not think it prudent to stem a torrent. But what is the difference to *us,* whether arbitrary acts take their rise from ministers, or are permitted by them? Ought any point to be allowed to a good minister, that should be denied to a bad one? The mortality of ministers, is a very frail mortality. A——— may succeed a *Shelburne*——A ——— may succeed a *Conway.*

We find a new kind of minister lately spoken of at home—"THE MINISTER OF THE HOUSE OF COMMONS." The term seems to have peculiar propriety when referred to these colonies, *with a different meaning annexed* to it, from that in which it is taken there. By the word "minister" we may understand not only a *servant of the crown,* but a *man of influence* among the commons, who regard themselves as having a share in the *sovereignty* over us. The "minister of the house" may, in a point respecting the colonies, be so strong, that the minister of the crown *in* the house, if he is a distinct person, may not choose, even where his sentiments are favorable to us, to come to a pitched battle upon our account. For tho' I have the highest opinion of the deference of the house for the King's minister, yet he may be so good natured, as not to put it to the test, except it be for the mere and immediate profit of his master or himself.

But whatever kind of *minister* he is, that attempts to innovate *a single* iota in the privileges of these colonies, him I hope you will *undauntedly oppose;* and that you will never suffer yourselves to be either *cheated* or *frightened* into any *unworthy obsequiousness.* On such emergencies you may surely, without presumption, believe, that ALMIGHTY GOD himself will look down upon your righteous contest with gracious approbation. You will be a *"band of brothers,"* cemented by the dearest ties—and strengthened with inconceivable supplies of force and constancy, by that sympathetic ardor, which animates good men, confederated in a good cause. Your *honor* and *welfare* will be, as they now are, most intimately concerned; and besides—*you are assigned by divine providence,* in the appointed order of things, the *protectors of unborn ages,* whose *fate* depends upon your *virtue.* Whether *they* shall arise the *generous* and *indisputable heirs* of the noblest

102

patrimonies, or the *dastardly and hereditary drudges* of imperious task-masters, YOU MUST DETERMINE.

To discharge this double duty to *yourselves,* and to your *posterity,* you have nothing to do, but to call forth into use the *good sense* and *spirit* of which you are possessed. You have nothing to do, but to conduct your affairs *peaceably— prudently—firmly—jointly.* By *these means* you will support the character of *freemen,* without losing that of *faithful subjects*—a good character in any government—one of the best under a *British* government.—You will *prove,* that *Americans* have that true *magnanimity* of soul, that can resent injuries, without falling into rage; and that tho' your devotion to *Great Britain* is the most affectionate, yet you can make PROPER DISTINCTIONS, and know what you owe to *yourselves,* as well as *to her*—You will, at the same time that you advance your *interests,* advance your *reputation*—You will convince the world of the *justice of your demands,* and the *purity of your intentions.*—While all mankind must, with unceasing applauses, confess, that YOU indeed DESERVE liberty, who so *well understand* it, so *passionately love* it, so *temperately enjoy* it, and so *wisely, bravely,* and *virtuously assert, maintain,* and *defend* it.

"*Certe ego libertatem, quae mihi a parente meo tradita est, experiar: Verum id frustra an ob rem faciam, in vestra manu situm est, quirites.*"

For my part, I am resolved to contend for the liberty delivered down to me by my ancestors, but whether I shall do it effectually or not, depends on you, my countrymen. "How littlesoever one is able to write, yet when the liberties of one's country are threatened, it is still more difficult to be silent."

A Farmer

11

Common Sense
and Imperial Relations

Perhaps the most famous and widely read pamphlet to emerge from the Revolutionary crisis was Thomas Paine's, *Common Sense,* published in 1776. Paine was born in England in 1737 of a modest family, received a mediocre education, and came to the colonies in 1774. Upon introduction to some important colonial leaders, especially Benjamin Franklin, Paine immediately threw himself into the political events. By 1783, especially on the basis of *Common Sense,* he enjoyed a world-wide reputation as an American radical. Paine, true to his own notion of "brotherhood with every Christian European," did not limit his political activities to the United States. In 1789, while in England, he published an equally famous tract, *Rights of Man,* inspired by the French Revolution. Eventually Paine moved to Paris, was imprisoned when his faction lost power, and was freed through American intervention. His last years were spent in the United States in quiet obscurity.

Common Sense, written after the outbreak of hostilites in April 1775, at Lexington, is a masterpiece of political rhetoric, and justly famous as an extraordinarily moving and effective tract. Paine appealed both logically and passionately to the colonists to break the last cord tying them to the mother country and to strike out for independence. The modern reader of *Common Sense* gains insight into the arts of political persuasion and into the minds of the colonists as they wondered whether or not to take the irrevocable step.

THOUGHTS ON THE PRESENT STATE
OF AMERICAN AFFAIRS
Thomas Paine

In the following pages I offer nothing more than simple facts, plain arguments, and common sense; and have no other preliminaries to settle with the reader than that he will divest himself of prejudice and prepossession, and suffer his reason and his feelings to determine for themselves; that he will put on, or rather that he will not

From *Common Sense* (Philadelphia, 1776; reprinted, Indianapolis, 1953), 18–34.

put off, the true character of a man, and generously enlarge his views beyond the present day.

Volumes have been written on the subject of the struggle between England and America. Men of all ranks have embarked in the controversy, from different motives and with various designs; but all have been ineffectual, and the period of debate is closed. Arms as the last resource decide the contest; the appeal was the choice of the king, and the continent has accepted the challenge.

It has been reported of the late Mr. Pelham (who, though an able minister, was not without his faults) that, on his being attacked in the House of Commons on the score that his measures were only of a temporary kind, replied, "they will last my time." Should a thought so fatal and unmanly possess the colonies in the present contest, the name of ancestors will be remembered by future generations with detestation.

The sun never shined on a cause of greater worth. 'Tis not the affair of a city, a county, a province, or a kingdom, but of a continent—of at least one-eighth part of the habitable globe. 'Tis not the concern of a day, a year, or an age; posterity are virtually involved in the contest, and will be more or less affected even to the end of time by the proceedings now. Now is the seedtime of continental union, faith, and honor. The least fracture now will be like a name engraved with the point of a pin on the tender rind of a young oak; the wound would enlarge with the tree, and posterity read it in full-grown characters.

By referring the matter from argument to arms, a new era for politics is struck—a new method of thinking has arisen. All plans, proposals, etc., prior to the nineteenth of April, i.e., to the commencement of hostilities, [at Lexington] are like the almanacs of the last year, which, though proper then, are superseded and useless now. Whatever was advanced by the advocates on either side of the question then terminated in one and the same point, viz., a union with Great Britain; the only difference between the parties was the method of effecting it—the one proposing force, the other friendship; but it has so far happened that the first has failed, and the second has withdrawn her influence.

As much has been said of the advantages of reconciliation, which, like an agreeable dream, has passed away and left us as we were, it is but right that we should examine the contrary side of the argument and inquire into some of the many material injuries which these colonies sustain, and always will sustain, by being connected with and dependent on Great Britain. To examine that connection and dependence on the principles of nature and common sense; to see what we have to trust to, if separated, and what we are to expect, if dependent.

I have heard it asserted by some that, as America has flourished under her former connection with Great Britain, the same connection is necessary toward her future happiness and will always have the same effect. Nothing can be more fallacious than this kind of argument. We may as well assert that because a child has thrived upon milk that it is never to have meat, or that the first twenty years of our lives is to become a precedent for the next twenty. But even this is admitting more than is true; for I answer roundly that America would have flourished as much, and probably much more, had no European power had anything to do with her. The commerce by which she has enriched herself are the necessaries of life and will always have a market while eating is the custom of Europe.

But she has protected us, say some. That she has engrossed us is true, and defended the continent at our expense as well as her own is admitted; and she would have defended Turkey from the same motive, viz., for the sake of trade and dominion.

Alas! we have been long led away by ancient prejudices and made large sacrifices to superstition. We have boasted the protection of Great Britain without considering that her motive was *interest,* not *attachment;* and that she did not protect us from *our enemies* on *our account* but from *her enemies* on *her own account,* from those who had no quarrel with us on any *other account* and who will always be our enemies on the *same account.* Let Britain waive her pretensions to the continent or the continent throw off the dependence, and we should be at peace with France and Spain, were they at war with Britain.

It has lately been asserted in Parliament that the colonies have no relation to each other but through the parent country, i.e., that Pennsylvania and the Jerseys, and so on for the rest, are sister colonies by the way of England; this is certainly a very roundabout way of proving relationship, but it is the nearest and only true way of proving enemyship, if I may so call it. France and Spain never were, nor perhaps ever will be, our enemies as *Americans,* but as our being the *subjects of Great Britain.*

But Britain is the parent country, say some. Then the more shame upon her conduct. Even brutes do not devour their young nor savages make war upon their families; wherefore the assertion, if true, turns to her reproach; but it happens not to be true, or only partly so, and the phrase "parent" or "mother country" has been jesuitically adopted by the king and his parasites with a low papistical design of gaining an unfair bias on the credulous weakness of our minds. Europe, and not England, is the parent country of America. This New World has been the asylum for the persecuted lovers of civil and religious liberty from *every part* of Europe. Hither have they fled, not from the tender embraces of the mother, but from the cruelty of the monster; and it is so far true of England that the same tyranny which drove the first emigrants from home pursues their descendants still.

In this extensive quarter of the globe, we forget the narrow limits of three hundred and sixty miles (the extent of England) and carry our friendship on a larger scale; we claim brotherhood with every European Christian, and triumph in the generosity of the sentiment.

It is pleasant to observe by what regular gradations we surmount the force of local prejudices as we enlarge our acquaintance with the world. A man born in any town in England divided into parishes will naturally associate most with his fellow parishioners (because their interests in many cases will be common) and distinguish him by the name of "neighbor"; if he meet him but a few miles from home, he drops the narrow idea of a street and salutes him by the name of "townsman"; if he travel out of the county and meet him in any other, he forgets the minor divisions of street and town, and calls him "countryman," i.e., "countyman"; but if in their foreign excursions they should associate in France, or any other part of *Europe,* their local remembrance would be enlarged into that of "Englishmen." And by a just parity of reasoning, all Europeans meeting in America, or any other quarter of the globe, are "countrymen"; for England, Holland, Germany, or Sweden, when compared with the whole, stand in the same places on the larger scale which the divisions of street, town, and county do on the smaller ones—distinctions too limited for continental minds. Not one third of the inhabitants, even of this province [Pennsylvania], are of English descent. Wherefore I reprobate the phrase of parent or mother country applied to England only as being false, selfish, narrow, and ungenerous.

But, admitting that we were all of English descent, what does it amount to? Nothing. Britain, being now an open enemy, extinguishes every other name and title; and to say that reconciliation is our duty is truly farcical. The first king of England of the present line (William the Conqueror) was a Frenchman, and half the peers of England are descendants from the same country; wherefore, by the same method of reasoning, England ought to be governed by France.

Much has been said of the united strength of Britain and the colonies, that in conjunction they might bid defiance to the world. But this is mere presumption; the fate of war is uncertain, neither do the expressions mean anything; for this continent would never suffer itself to be drained of inhabitants to support the British arms in either Asia, Africa, or Europe.

Besides, what have we to do with setting the world at defiance? Our plan is commerce, and that, well attended to, will secure us the peace and friendship of all Europe; because it is the interest of all Europe to have America a free port. Her trade will always be a protection, and her barrenness of gold and silver secure her from invaders.

I challenge the warmest advocate for reconciliation to show a single advantage that this continent can reap by being connected with Great Britain. I repeat the challenge; not a single advantage is derived. Our corn will fetch its price in any market in Europe, and our imported goods must be paid for, buy them where we will.

But the injuries and disadvantages we sustain by that connection are without number, and our duty to mankind at large, as well as to ourselves, instruct us to renounce the alliance; because any submission to or dependence on Great Britain tends directly to involve this continent in European wars and quarrels and sets us at variance with nations who would otherwise seek our friendship and against whom we have neither anger nor complaint. As Europe is our market for trade, we ought to form no partial connection with any part of it. It is the true interest of America to steer clear of European contentions, which she never can do while, by her dependence on Britain, she is made the makeweight in the scale of British politics.

Europe is too thickly planted with kingdoms to be long at peace; and whenever a war breaks out between England and any foreign power, the trade of America goes to ruin *because of her connection with Britain.* The next war may not turn out like the last; and should it not, the advocates for reconciliation now will be wishing for separation then, because neutrality in that case would be a safer convoy than a man-of-war. Everything that is right or natural pleads for separation. The blood of the slain, the weeping voice of nature cries, " *'Tis time to part.*" Even the distance at which the Almighty has placed England and America is a strong and natural proof that the authority of the one over the other was never the design of heaven. The time likewise at which the continent was discovered adds weight to the argument, and the manner in which it was peopled increases the force of it. The Reformation was preceded by the discovery of America—as if the Almighty graciously meant to open a sanctuary to the persecuted in future years, when home should afford neither friendship nor safety.

The authority of Great Britain over this continent is a form of government which sooner or later must have an end. And a serious mind can draw no true pleasure by looking forward, under the painful and positive conviction that what he calls "the present constitution" is merely temporary. As parents, we can have no joy, knowing that this government is not sufficiently lasting to insure anything which we may bequeath to posterity. And by a plain method of argument, as we are running the next generation into debt, we ought to do the work of it; otherwise we use them meanly and pitifully. In order to discover the line of our duty rightly, we should take our children in our hand and fix our station a few years farther into life; that eminence will present a prospect which a few present fears and prejudices conceal from our sight.

Though I would carefully avoid giving unnecessary offense, yet I am inclined to believe that all those who espouse the doctrine of reconciliation may be included within the following descriptions. Interested men, who are not to be trusted, weak men who *cannot* see, prejudiced men who *will not* see, and a certain set of moderate men who think better of the European world than it deserves; and this last class, by an ill-judged deliberation, will be the cause of more calamities to this continent than all the other three.

It is the good fortune of many to live distant from the scene of sorrow; the evil is not sufficiently brought to *their* doors to make *them* feel the precariousness with which all American property is possessed. But let our imaginations transport us a few moments to Boston; that seat of wretchedness will teach us wisdom and instruct us forever to renounce a power in whom we can have no trust. The inhabitants of that unfortunate city who, but a few months ago, were in ease and affluence have now no other alternative than to stay and starve or turn out to beg. Endangered by the fire of their friends if they continue within the city, and plundered by the soldiery if they leave it. In their present condition they are prisoners without the hope of redemption; and in a general attack for their relief they would be exposed to the fury of both armies.

Men of passive tempers look somewhat lightly over the offenses of Great Britain and, still hoping for the best, are apt to call out, "Come, come, we shall be friends again for all this." But examine the passions and feelings of mankind, bring the doctrine of reconciliation to the touchstone of nature, and then tell me whether you can hereafter love, honor, and faithfully serve the power that has carried fire and sword into your land? If you cannot do all these, then are you only deceiving yourselves, and by your delay bringing ruin upon posterity. Your future connection with Britain, whom you can neither love nor honor, will be forced and unnatural, and being formed only on the plan of present convenience will, in a little time, fall into a relapse more wretched than the first. But if you say you still can pass the violations over, then I ask, has your house been burned? Has your property been destroyed before your face? Are your wife and children destitute of a bed to lie on or bread to live on? Have you lost a parent or a child by their hands, and yourself the ruined and wretched survivor? If you have not, then are you not a judge of those who have. But if you have and can still shake hands with the murderers, then are you unworthy the name of husband, father, friend, or lover; and whatever may be your rank or title in life, you have the heart of a coward and the spirit of a sycophant.

This is not inflaming or exaggerating matters, but trying them by those feelings and affections which nature justifies and without which we should be incapable of discharging the social duties of life or enjoying the felicities of it. I mean not to exhibit horror for the purpose of provoking revenge, but to awaken us from fatal and unmanly slumbers, that we may pursue determinately some fixed object. It is not in the power of Britain or Europe to conquer America, if she do not conquer herself by delay and timidity. The present winter is worth an age if rightly employed, but if lost or neglected the whole continent will partake of the misfortune; and there is no punishment which that man will not deserve, be he who or what or where he will, that may be the means of sacrificing a season so precious and useful.

It is repugnant to reason, to the universal order of things, to all examples from former ages, to suppose that this continent can longer remain subject to any external power. The most sanguine in Britain does not think so. The utmost stretch of human wisdom cannot, at this time, compass a plan, short of separation, which can promise the continent even a year's security. Reconciliation is *now* a fallacious dream. Nature has deserted the connection, and art cannot supply her place. For, as Milton wisely expresses, "never can true reconcilement grow where wounds of deadly hate have pierced so deep."

Every quiet method for peace has been ineffectual. Our prayers have been rejected with disdain, and only tended to convince us that nothing flatters vanity or confirms obstinacy in kings more than repeated petitioning—and nothing has contributed more than that very measure to make the kings of Europe absolute. Witness Denmark and Sweden. Wherefore, since nothing but blows will do, for God's sake let us come to a final separation, and not leave the next generation to be cutting throats under the violated unmeaning names of parent and child.

To say they will never attempt it again is idle and visionary; we thought so at the repeal of the Stamp Act, yet a year or two undeceived us; as well may we suppose that nations which have been once defeated will never renew the quarrel.

As to government matters, it is not in the power of Britain to do this continent justice. The business of it will soon be too weighty and intricate to be managed with any tolerable degree of convenience by a power so distant from us and so very ignorant of us; for if they cannot conquer us, they cannot govern us. To be always running three or four thousand miles with a tale or a petition, waiting four or five months for an answer, which, when obtained, requires five or six more to explain it in, will in a few years be looked upon as folly and childishness. There was a time when it was proper, and there is a proper time for it to cease.

Small islands not capable of protecting themselves are the proper objects for kingdoms to take under their care, but there is something very absurd in supposing a continent to be perpetually governed by an island. In no instance has nature made the satellite larger than its primary planet; and as England and America, with respect to each other, reverse the common order of nature, it is evident they belong to different systems—England to Europe, America to itself.

I am not induced by motives of pride, party, or resentment to espouse the doctrine of separation and independence; I am clearly, positively, and conscientiously persuaded that it is the true interest of this continent to be so; that everything short of *that* is mere patchwork, that it can afford no lasting felicity—that it is leaving the sword to our children, and shrinking back at a time when a little more, a little further, would have rendered this continent the glory of the earth.

As Britain has not manifested the least inclination toward a compromise, we may be assured that no terms can be obtained worthy the acceptance of the continent, or any ways equal to the expense of blood and treasure we have been already put to.

The object contended for ought always to bear some just proportion to the expense. The removal of [Lord] North, or the whole detestable junto, is a matter unworthy the millions we have expended. A temporary stoppage of trade was an inconvenience which would have sufficiently balanced the repeal of all the acts complained of, had such repeals been obtained; but if the whole continent must take up arms, if every man must be a soldier, it is scarcely worth our while to fight against a contemptible ministry only. Dearly, dearly do we pay for the repeal of the acts, if that is all we fight for; in a just estimation it is as great a folly to pay a Bunker Hill price for law as for land. As I have always considered the independence of this continent as an event which sooner or later must arrive, so from the late rapid progress of the continent to maturity, the event cannot be far off. Wherefore, on the breaking out of hostilities, it was not worth the while to have disputed a matter which time would have finally redressed, unless we meant to be in earnest; otherwise it is like wasting an estate on a suit at law to regulate the trespasses of a tenant whose lease is just expiring. No man was a warmer wisher for a reconciliation than myself before the fatal nineteenth of April 1775, but the moment the event of that day was made known I rejected the hardened, sullen-tempered Pharaoh of England forever and disdain the wretch that, with the pretended title of father of his people, can unfeelingly hear of their slaughter and composedly sleep with their blood upon his soul.

But admitting that matters were now made up, what would be the event? I answer, the ruin of the continent. And that for several reasons:

First. The powers of governing still remaining in the hands of the king, he will have a negative over the whole legislation of this continent. And as he has shown himself such an inveterate enemy to liberty and discovered such a thirst for arbitrary power, is he or is he not a proper man to say to these colonies, "You shall make no laws but what I please!"? And is there any inhabitant of America so ignorant as not to know that, according to what is called the "present Constitution," that this continent can make no laws but what the king gives leave to; and is there any man so unwise as not to see that (considering what has happened) he will suffer no law to be made here but such as suits *his* purpose? We may be as effectually enslaved by the want of laws in America as by submitting to laws made for us in England. After matters are made up (as it is called), can there be any doubt but the whole power of the crown will be exerted to keep this continent as low and humble as possible? Instead of going forward we shall go backward, or be perpetually quarrelling, or ridiculously petitioning. We are already greater than the king wishes us to be, and will he not hereafter endeavor to make us less? To bring the matter to one point, is the power who is jealous of our prosperity a proper power to govern us? Whoever says "No" to this question is an independent, for independence means no more than whether we shall make our own laws or whether the king, the greatest enemy this continent has or can have, shall tell us "there shall be no laws but such as I like."

But the king, you will say, has a negative in England; the people there can make no laws without his consent. In point of right and good order, there is something very ridiculous that a youth of twenty-one (which has often happened) shall say to several millions of people older and wiser than himself, "I forbid this or that act of yours to be law." But in this place I decline this sort of reply, though I will never cease to expose the absurdity of it, and only answer that England being the king's residence, and America not so, makes quite another case. The king's negative *here* is ten times more dangerous and fatal than it can be in England; for *there* he will scarcely refuse his consent to a bill for putting England into as strong a state of defense as possible, and in America he would never suffer such a bill to be passed.

America is only a secondary object in the system of British politics. England consults the good of *this* country no farther than it answers her *own* purpose. Wherefore her own interest leads her to suppress the growth of *ours* in every case which does not promote her advantage or in the least interferes with it. A pretty state we should soon be in under such a secondhand government, considering what has happened! Men do not change from enemies to friends by the alteration of a name. And in order to show that reconciliation now is a dangerous doctrine, I affirm *that it would be policy in the king at this time to repeal the acts, for the sake of reinstating himself in the government of the provinces,* in order that *he may accomplish by craft and subtlety in the long run what he cannot do by force and violence in the short one.* Reconciliation and ruin are nearly related.

Secondly. That as even the best terms which we can expect to obtain can amount to no more than a temporary expedient, or a kind of government by guardianship, which can last no longer than till the colonies come of age, so the general face and state of things in the interim will be unsettled and unpromising. Emigrants of property will not choose to come to a country whose form of government hangs but by a thread, and who is every day tottering on the brink of commotion and disturbance; and numbers of the present inhabitants would lay hold of the interval to dispose of their effects and quit the continent.

But the most powerful of all arguments is that nothing but independence, i.e., a continental form of government, can keep the peace of the continent and preserve it inviolate from civil wars. I dread the event of a reconciliation with Britain now, as it is more than probable that it will be followed by a revolt somewhere or other, the consequences of which may be far more fatal than all the malice of Britain.

Thousands are already ruined by British barbarity (thousands more will probably suffer the same fate). Those men have other feelings than us who have nothing suffered. All they now possess is liberty; what they before enjoyed is sacrificed to its service, and having nothing more to lose they disdain submission. Besides, the general temper of the colonies toward a British government will be like that of a youth who is nearly out of his time; they will care very little about her. And a government which cannot preserve the peace is no government at all, and in that case we pay our money for nothing; and pray what is it that Britain can do, whose power will be wholly on paper, should a civil tumult break out the very day after reconciliation? I have heard some men say, many of whom I believe spoke without thinking, that they dreaded an independence, fearing that it would produce civil war. It is but seldom that our first thoughts are truly correct, and that is the case here; for there are ten times more to dread from a patched-up connection than from independence. I make the sufferer's case my own, and I protest that, were I driven from house and home, my property destroyed, and my circumstances ruined, that as a man, sensible of injuries, I could never relish the doctrine of reconciliation or consider myself bound thereby.

The colonies have manifested such a spirit of good order and obedience to continental government as is sufficient to make every reasonable person easy and happy on that head. No man can assign the least pretense for his fears on any other grounds than such as are truly childish and ridiculous, viz., that one colony will be striving for superiority over another.

Where there are no distinctions, there can be no superiority; perfect equality affords no temptation. The republics of Europe are all (and we may say always) in peace. Holland and Switzerland are without wars, foreign or domestic. Monarchical governments, it is true, are never long at rest; the crown itself is a temptation to enterprising ruffians at home; and that degree of pride and insolence ever attendant on regal authority swells into a rupture with foreign powers in instances where a republican government, by being formed on more natural principles, would negotiate the mistake.

If there is any true cause of fear respecting independence, it is because no plan is yet laid down. Men do not see their way out. Wherefore, as an opening into that business, I offer the following hints, at the same time modestly affirming that I have no other opinion of them myself than that they may be the means of giving rise to something better. Could the straggling thoughts of individuals be collected, they would frequently form materials for wise and able men to improve into useful matter.

Let the assemblies be annual, with a president only. The representation more equal, their business wholly domestic, and subject to the authority of a Continental Congress.

Let each colony be divided into six, eight, or ten convenient districts, each district to send a proper number of delegates to Congress, so that each colony send at least thirty. The whole number in Congress will be at least 390. Each Congress to sit and to choose a president by the following method: When the delegates are met, let a colony be taken from the whole thirteen colonies by lot, after which let the whole Congress choose (by ballot) a president from out of the delegates of *that* province. In the next Congress, let a colony be taken by lot from twelve only, omitting that colony from which the president was taken in the former Congress, and so proceeding on till the whole thirteen shall have had their proper rotation. And in order that nothing may pass into a law but what is satisfactorily just, not less than three fifths of the Congress to be called a majority. He that will promote discord under a government so equally formed as this would have joined Lucifer in his revolt.

But where, says some, is the king of America? I'll tell you, friend, he reigns above, and does not make havoc of mankind like the royal brute of Britain. Yet that we may not appear to be defective even in earthly honors, let a day be solemnly set apart for proclaiming the charter; let it be brought forth placed on the divine law, the word of God; let a crown be placed thereon, by which the world may know that, so far as we approve of monarchy, that in America *the law is king.* For as in absolute governments the king is law, so in free countries the law *ought* to be king; and there ought to be no other. But lest any ill use should afterward arise, let the crown at the conclusion of the ceremony be demolished and scattered among the people, whose right it is.

A government of our own is our natural right; and when a man seriously reflects on the precariousness of human affairs, he will become convinced that it is infinitely wiser and safer to form a Constitution of our own in a cool, deliberate manner while we have it in our power than to trust such an interesting event to time and chance. If we omit it now, some Massanello [an adventurer] may hereafter arise who, laying hold of popular disquietudes, may collect together the desperate and the discontented, and by assuming to themselves the powers of government may sweep away the liberties of the continent like a deluge. Should the government of America return again into the hands of Britain, the tottering situation of things will be a temptation for some desperate adventurer to try his fortune, and in such a case what relief can Britain give? Ere she could hear the news, the fatal business might be done, and ourselves suffering like the wretched Britons under the oppression of the conqueror. Ye that oppose independence now, ye know not what ye do; ye are opening a door to eternal tyranny by keeping vacant the seat of government. There are thousands and tens of thousands who would think it glorious to expel from the continent that barbarous and hellish power which has stirred up the Indians and the Negroes to destroy us; the cruelty has a double guilt: it is dealing brutally by us and treacherously by them.

To talk of friendship with those in whom our reason forbids us to have faith and our affections, wounded through a thousand pores, instruct us to detest is madness and folly. Every day wears out the little remains of kindred between us and them; and can there be any reason to hope that, as the relationship expires, the affection will increase, or that we shall agree better when we have ten times more and greater concerns to quarrel over than ever?

Ye that tell us of harmony and reconciliation, can ye restore to us the time that is past? Can ye give to prostitution its former innocence? Neither can ye reconcile Britain and America. The last cord now is broken, the people of England are presenting addresses against us. There are injuries which nature cannot forgive; she would cease to be nature if she did. As well can the lover forgive the ravisher of his mistress as the continent forgive the murders of Britain. The Almighty has implanted in us these unextinguishable feelings for good and wise purposes. They are the guardians of his image in our hearts. They distinguish us from the herd of common animals. The social compact would dissolve and justice be extirpated [from] the earth, or have only a casual existence, were we callous to the touches of affection. The robber and the murderer would often escape unpunished did not the injuries which our tempers sustain provoke us into justice.

O ye that love mankind! Ye that dare oppose not only the tyranny but the tyrant, stand forth! Every spot of the Old World is overrun with oppression. Freedom has been hunted round the globe. Asia and Africa have long expelled her. Europe regards her like a stranger, and England has given her warning to depart. O! receive the fugitive, and prepare in time an asylum for mankind.

12

The States at War

The legend of George Washington is such a commonplace to students of American history that there is a real danger in his grandeur overcoming his very significant contributions to the new nation. Washington's first major public role was Commander-in-Chief of the Continental Army, but his service in the French and Indian War as General Braddock's aide, his efforts in 1755 at the age of twenty-three to organize Virginia's defenses, and his fifteen years of service in the House of Burgesses, all prepared him well for this position.

His letters, which were written during the War, reveal time and again that it was no easy matter to forge an army out of the raw American farmer. Moreover, even during this great crisis, there was a surprising amount of debate and discussion over the place of the military in a republican government: Should the army be professional? What ought to be the position of the political arm of the government (here the Continental Congress) toward the military? Could an army be clothed and equipped without far greater coercion than the several states seemed prepared to accept? Would an army once victorious accept dissolution, or might it vie for control of the government? If ultimately, the new republic and its army reached a *modus vivendi* and managed to conduct a successful war against the British, much of the credit belongs to Washington.

THE WRITINGS
OF GEORGE WASHINGTON

1   To the President of Congress

Camp at Cambridge July 10, 1775

Sir,

I arrived safe at this Place on the 3d inst., after a Journey attended with a good deal of Fatigue, and retarded by necessary Attentions to the successive Civilities which accompanied me in my whole Rout. Upon my arrival, I immediately visited the several Posts occupied by our Troops, and as soon as the Weather permitted,

From *The Writings of George Washington*, Worthington C. Ford, ed. (New York, 1891), III: 8–18; IV: 438–451; VI: 257–265; IX: 102–109; XI: 330–334.

reconnoitred those of the Enemy. I found the latter strongly entrench'd on Bunker's Hill about a Mile from Charlestown, and advanced about half a Mile from the Place of the last Action. The Bulk of their Army commanded by Genl. Howe, lays on Bunker's Hill, and the Remainder on Roxbury Neck, except the Light Horse, and a few Men in the Town of Boston. On our side we have thrown up Intrenchments on Winter and Prospect Hills, the Enemies camp in full View at the Distance of little more than a Mile. The Troops in this Town are intirely of the Massachusetts: The Remainder of the Rhode Island Men, are at Sewall's Farm: Two Regiments of Connecticut and 9 of the Massachusetts are at Roxbury. The Residue of the Army, to the Number of about 700, are posted in several small Towns along the Coast, to prevent the Depredations of the Enemy: Upon the whole, I think myself authorized to say, that considering the great Extent of Line, and the nature of the Ground we are as well secured as could be expected in so short a Time and under the Disadvantages we labour. These consist in a Want of Engineers to construct proper Works and direct the men, a Want of Tools, and a sufficient Number of Men to man the Works in Case of an attack.

It is our unanimous Opinion to hold and defend these Works as long as possible. The Discouragement it would give the Men and its contrary Effects on the ministerial Troops, thus to abandon our Incampment in their Face, form'd with so much Labor, added to the certain Destruction of a considerable and valuable Extent of Country, and our Uncertainty of finding a Place in all Respects so capable of making a stand, are leading Reasons for this Determination: at the same Time we are very sensible of the Difficulties which attend the Defence of Lines of so great extent, and the Dangers which may ensue from such a Division of the Army.

My earnest Wishes to comply with the Instructions of the Congress in making an early and complete Return of the State of the Army, has led into an involuntary Delay in addressing you, which has given me much Concern. Having given orders for this Purpose immediately on my Arrival, I was led from Day to Day to expect they would come in, and therefore detained the Messenger. They are not now so complete as I could wish, but much Allowance is to be made for Inexperience in Forms, and a Liberty which has been taken (not given) on this subject. These Reasons I flatter myself will no longer exist, and of Consequence more Regularity and exactness in future prevail.

We labor under great Disadvantages for Want of Tents, for tho' they have been help'd out by a Collection of now useless sails from the Sea Port Towns, the Number is yet far short of our Necessities. The Colleges and Houses of this Town are necessarily occupied by the Troops which affords another Reason for keeping our present Situation: But I most sincerely wish the whole Army was properly provided to take the Field, as I am well assured, that besides greater Expedition and Activity in case of Alarm, it would highly conduce to Health and discipline. As Materials are not to be had here, I would beg leave to recommend the procuring a farther supply from Philadelphia as soon as possible.

I should be extremely deficient in Gratitude, as well as Justice, if I did not take the first opportuny to acknowledge the Readiness and Attention which the provincial Congress and different Committees have shewn to make every Thing as convenient and agreeable as possible: but there is a vital and inherent Principle of Delay incompatible with military service in transacting Business thro' such numerous and different Channels. I esteem it therefore my Duty to represent the Inconvenience that must unavoidably ensue from a dependence on a Number of Persons for supplies, and submit it to the Consideration of the Congress whether the publick Service will not be best promoted by appointing a Commissary General for these purposes.

I find myself already much embarrassed for Want of a Military Chest; these embarrassments will increase every day: I must therefore request that Money may be forwarded as soon as Possible. The want of this most necessary Article, will I fear produce great Inconveniences if not prevented by an early Attention. I find the Army in general, and the Troops raised in Massachusetts in particular, very deficient in necessary Cloathing. Upon Inquiry there appears no Probability of obtaining any supplies in this Quarter. And the best Consideration of this Matter I am able to form, I am of Opinion that a Number of hunting Shirts not less than 10,000, would in a great Degree remove this Difficulty in the cheapest and quickest manner. I know nothing in a speculative View more trivial, yet if put in Practice would have a happier Tendency to unite the Men, and abolish those Provincial Distinctions which lead to Jealousy and Dissatisfaction. In a former part of this Letter I mentioned the want of Engineers; I can hardly express the Disappointment I have experienced on this Subject. The Skill of those we have, being very imperfect and confined to the mere manual Exercise of Cannon: Whereas—the War in which we are engaged requires a Knowledge comprehending the Duties of the Field and Fortifications. If any Persons thus qualified are to be found in the Southern Colonies, it would be of great publick Service to forward them with all expedition. Upon the Article of Ammunition I must re-echo the former Complaints on this Subject: We are so exceedingly destitute, that our Artillery will be of little Use without a supply both large and seasonable: What we have must be reserved for the small Arms, and that managed with the utmost Frugality.

2   To the President of Congress

On the Heights of Haerlem, 24 September, 1776

Sir,

From the hours allotted to sleep, I will borrow a few moments to convey my thoughts on sundry important matters to Congress. I shall offer them with the sincerity, which ought to characterize a man of candor, and with the freedom, which may be used in giving useful information without incurring the imputation of presumption.

We are now, as it were, upon the eve of another dissolution of our army. The remembrance of the difficulties, which happened upon that occasion last year, and the consequences, which might have followed the change if proper advantages had been taken by the enemy, added to a knowledge of the present temper and situation of the troops, reflect but a very gloomy prospect in the appearances of things now, and satisfy me beyond the possibility of doubt, that, unless some speedy and effectual measures are adopted by Congress, our cause will be lost. It is in vain to expect, that any more than a trifling part of this army will again engage in the service on the encourgement offered by Congress. When men find that their townsmen and companions are receiving twenty, thirty, and more dollars for a few months' service, which is truly the case, it cannot be expected, without using compulsion; and to force them into the service would answer no valuable purpose. When men are irritated, and their passions inflamed, they fly hastily and cheerfully to arms; but, after the first emotions are over, to expect among such people as compose the bulk of an army, that they are influenced by any other principles than those of interest, is to look for what never did, and I fear never will happen; the Congress will deceive themselves, therefore, if they expect it. A soldier, reasoned with upon the goodness of the cause he is engaged in, and the inestimable rights he is contending for, hears you with patience, and acknowledges the truth of your observations, but adds that it is of no more importance to him than to others. The officer makes you the same reply, with this further remark, that his pay will not support him, and he cannot ruin himself and family to serve his country, when every member of the community is equally interested, and benefitted by his labors. The few, therefore, who act upon principles of disinterestedness, comparatively speaking, are no more than a drop in the ocean.

It becomes evident to me than, that, as this contest is not likely to be the work of a day, as the war must be carried on systematically, and to do it you must have good officers, there are in my judgment no other possible means to obtain them but by establishing your army upon a permanent footing, and giving your officers good pay. This will induce gentlemen and men of character to engage; and, till the bulk of your officers is composed of such persons as are actuated by principles of honor and a spirit of enterprise, you have little to expect from them. They ought to have such allowances, as will enable them to live like and support the character of gentlemen, and not be driven by a scanty pittance to the low and dirty arts, which many of them practise, to filch from the public more than the difference of pay would amount to, upon an ample allowance. Besides, something is due to the man, who puts his life in your hands, hazards his health, and forsakes the sweets of domestic enjoyment. Why a captain in the Continental service should receive no more than five shillings currency per day for performing the same duties, that an officer of the same rank in the British service receives ten shillings for, I never could conceive; especially when the latter is provided with every necessary he requires upon the best terms, and the former can scarce procure them at any rate. There is nothing that gives a man consequence and renders him fit for command, like a support that renders him independent of every body but the state he serves.

With respect to the men, nothing but a good bounty can obtain them upon a permanent establishment; and for no shorter time, than the continuance of the war, ought they to be engaged; as facts incontestably prove, that the difficuly and cost of enlistments increase with time. When the army was first raised at Cambridge, I am persuaded the men might have been got, without a bounty, for the war. After this, they began to see that the contest was not likely to end so speedily as was imagined, and to feel their consequence by remarking, that, to get in their militia in the course of the last year, many towns were induced to give them a bounty.

If the present opportunity is slipped, I am persuaded that twelve months more will increase our difficulties fourfold. I shall therefore take the freedom of giving it as my opinion, that a good bounty should be immediately offered, aided by the proffer of at least a hundred or a hundred and fifty acres of land, and a suit of clothes and blanket to each non-comissioned officer and soldier; as I have good authority for saying, that, however high the men's pay may appear, it is barely sufficient, in the present scarcity and dearness of all kinds of goods, to keep them in clothes, much less afford support to their families.

If this encouragement then is given to the men, and such pay allowed the officers as will induce gentlemen of character and liberal sentiments to engage, and proper care and precaution are used in the nomination, (having more regard to the characters of persons, than to the number of men they can enlist,) we should in a little time have an army able to cope with any that can be opposed to it, as there are excellent materials to form one out of. But while the only merit an officer possesses is his ability to raise men, while those men consider and treat him as an equal, and, in the character of an officer, regard him no more than a broomstick, being mixed together as one common herd, no order nor discipline can prevail; nor will the officer ever meet with that respect, which is essentially necessaary to due subordination.

To place any dependence upon militia is assuredly resting upon a broken staff. Men just dragged from the tender scenes of domestic life, unaccustomed to the din of arms, totally unacquainted with every kind of military skill, (which being followed by want of confidence in themselves, when opposed to troops regularly trained, disciplined, and appointed, superior in knowledge and superior in arms,) makes them timid and ready to fly from their own shadows. Besides the sudden change in their manner of living, (particularly in the lodging,) brings on sickness in many, impatience in all, and such an unconquerable desire of returing to their respective homes, that it not only produces shameful and scandalous desertions among themselves, but infuses the like spirit in others. Again, men accustomed to unbounded freedom and no control cannot brooke the restraint, which is indispensably necessary to the good order and government of an army; without which, licentiousness and every kind of disorder triumphantly reign. To bring men to a proper degree of subordination is not the work of a day, a month, or even a year; and, unhappily for us and the cause we are engaged in, the little discipline I have been laboring to establish in the army under my immediate command is in a manner done away, by having such a mixture of troops, as have been called together within these few months.

The jealousy of a standing army, and the evils to be apprehended from one, are remote, and, in my judgment, situated and circumstanced as we are, not at all to be dreaded; but the consequence of wanting one, according to my ideas formed from the present view of things, is certain and inevitable ruin. Another matter highly worthy of attention is, that other rules and regulations may be adopted for the government of the army, than those now in existence; otherwise the army, but for the name, might as well be disbanded. For the most atrocious offences, one or two instances only excepted, a man receives no more than thirty-nine lashes; and these, perhaps, through the collusion of the officer, who is to see it inflicted, are given in such a manner as to become rather a matter of sport than punishment.

It is evident that this punishment is inadequate to many crimes it is assigned to. As a proof of it, thirty or forty soldiers will desert at a time, and of late a practice prevails (as you will see by my letter of the 22d) of the most alarming nature and which will, if it cannot be checked, prove fatal both to the country and army; I mean the infamous practice of plundering. For, under the idea of Tory property, or property that may fall into the hands of the enemy, no man is secure in his effects, and scarcely in his person. In order to get at them, we have several instances of people being frightened out of their houses, under pretence of those houses being ordered to be burnt, and this is done with a view of seizing the goods; nay, in order that the villany may be more effectually concealed, some houses have actually been burnt, to cover the theft. I have, with some others, used my utmost endeavors to stop this horrid practice; but under the present lust after plunder, and want of laws to punish offenders, I might almost as well attempt to remove Mount Atlas.

An army formed of good officers moves like clockwork; but there is no situation upon earth less enviable, nor more distressing, than that person's, who is at the head of troops which are regardless of order and discipline, and who are unprovided with almost every necessary. In a word, the difficulties, which have for ever surrounded me since I have been in the service, and kept my mind constantly upon the stretch, the wounds, which my feelings as an officer have received by a thousand things, which have happened contrary to my expectation and wishes; the effect of my own conduct, and present appearance of things, so little pleasing to myself, as to render it a matter of no surprise to me if I should stand capitally censured by Congress; added to a consciousness of my inability to govern an army composed of such discordant parts, and under such a variety of intricate and perplexing circumstances;—induces not only a belief, but a thorough conviction in my mind, that it will be impossible, unless there is a thorough change in our military system, for me to conduct matters in such a manner as to give satisfaction to the public, which is all the recompense I aim at, or ever wished for.

3 To the President of Congress

Valley Forge, 23 December, 1777
Sir,

Full as I was in my representation of the matters in the commissary's department yesterday, fresh and more powerful reasons oblige me to add, that I am now convinced beyond a doubt, that, unless some great and capital change suddenly takes in that line, this army must inevitably be reduced to one or other of these three things; starve, dissolve, or disperse in order to obtain subsistence in the best manner they can. Rest assured, Sir, this is not an exaggerated picture, and that I have abundant reason to suppose what I say.

Yesterday afternoon, receiving information that the enemy in force had left the city, and were advancing towards Derby with the apparent design to forage, and draw subsistence from that part of the country, I ordered the troops to be in readiness, that I might give every opposition in my power; when behold, to my great mortification, I was not only informed, but convinced, that the men were unable to stir on account of provision, and that a dangerous mutiny, begun the night before, and which with difficulty was suppressed by the spirited exertions of some officers, was still much to be apprehended for want of this article. This brought forth the only commissary in the purchasing line in this camp; and, with him, this melancholy and alarming truth, that he had not a single hoof of any kind to slaughter, and not more than twenty-five barrels of flour! From hence form an opinion of our situation when I add, that he could not tell when to expect any.

All I could do under these circumstances, was to send out a few light parties to watch and harass the enemy, whilst other parties were instantly detached different ways to collect, if possible, as much provision as would satisfy the present pressing wants of the soldiery. But will this answer? No, Sir; three or four days of bad weather would prove our destruction. What then is to become of the army this winter? And if we are so often without provisions now, what is to become of us in the spring, when our force will be collected, with the aid perhaps of militia to take advantage of an early campaign, before the enemy can be reinforced? These are considerations of great magnitude, meriting the closest attention; finding that the inactivity of the army, whether for want of provisions, clothes, or other essentials, is charged to my account, not only by the common vulgar but by those in power, it is time to speak plain in exculpation of myself. With truth, then, I can declare, that no man in my opinion ever had his measures more impeded than I have, by every department of the army.

Since the month of July we have had no assistance from the quartermaster-general, and to want of assistance from this department the commissary-general charges great part of his deficiency.

The soap vinegar, and other articles allowed by Congress, we see none of, nor have we seen them, I believe, since the battle of Brandywine. The first, indeed, we have now little occasion for; few men having more than one shirt, many only the moiety of one, and some none at all. In addition as a further proof of the inability of an army, under the circumstances of this, to perform the common duties of soldiers, (besides a number of men confined to hospitals for want of shoes, and others in farmers' houses on the same account,) we have, by a field-return this day made, no less than two thousand eight hundred and ninety-eight men now in camp unfit for duty, because they are barefoot and otherwise naked. By the same return it appears, that our whole strength in Continental troops, including the eastern brigades, which have joined us since the surrender of General Burgoyne, exclusive of the Maryland troops sent to Wilmington, amounts to no more than eight thousand two hundred in camp fit for duty; notwithstanding which, and that since the 4th instant, our numbers fit for duty, from the hardships and exposures they have undergone, particularly on account of blankets (numbers having been obliged, and still are, to sit up all night by fires, instead of taking comfortable rest in a natural and common way), have decreased near two thousand men.

We find gentlemen, without knowing whether the army was really going into winter-quarters or not I can assure those gentlemen, that it is a much easier and less distressing thing to draw remonstrances in a comfortable room by a good fireside, than to occupy a cold, bleak hill, and sleep under frost and snow, without clothes or blankets. However, although they seem to have little feeling for the naked and distressed soldiers, I feel superabundantly for them, and, from my soul, I pity those miseries, which it is neither in my power to relieve or prevent.

It is for these reasons, therefore, that I have dwelt upon the subject; and it adds not a little to my other difficulties and distress to find, that much more is expected of me than is possible to be performed, and that upon the ground of safety and policy I am obliged to conceal the true state of the army from public view, and thereby expose myself to detraction and calumny. The honorable committee of Congress went from camp fully possessed of my sentiments respecting the establishment of this army, the necessity of auditors of accounts, the appointment of officers, and new arrangements. I have no need, therefore, to be prolix upon these subjects, but I refer to the committee. I shall add a word or two to show, first, the necessity of some better provision for binding the officers by the tie of interest to the service, as no day nor scarce an hour passes without the offer of a resigned commission (otherwise I much doubt the practicability of holding the army together much longer, and in this I shall probably be thought the more sincere, when I freely declare, that I do not myself expect to derive the smallest benefit from any establishment that Congress may adopt, otherwise than as a member of the community at large in the good, which I am persuaded will result from the measure, by making better officers and better troops); and, secondly, to point out the necessity of making the appointments and arrangements without loss of time. We have not more than three months, in which to prepare a great deal of business. If we let these slip or waste, we shall be laboring under the same difficulties all next campaign, as we have been this, to rectify mistakes and bring things to order.

In short, there is as much to be done in preparing for a campaign, as in the active part of it. Every thing depends upon the preparation that is made in the several departments, and the success or misfortunes of the next campaign will more than probably originate with our activity or supineness during this winter.

4 To Lieutenant-Colonel John Laurens
About to Sail for France to Confer with This Ally

New Windsor, 15 January, 1781

Dear Sir,

In compliance with your request I shall commit to writing the result of our conferences on the present state of American affairs, in which I have given you my ideas with that freedom and explicitness, which the objects of your commission, my entire confidence in you, and the exigency demand. To me it appears evident:

That, considering the diffused population of these States, the consequent difficulty of drawing together its resources, the composition and temper of *a part* of the inhabitants, the want of a sufficient stock of national wealth as a foundation for revenue, and the almost total extinction of commerce, the efforts we have been compelled to make for carrying on the war have exceeded the natural abilities of this country, and by degrees brought it to a crisis, which renders immediate and efficacious succors from abroad indispensable to its safety.

That the patience of the army, from an almost uninterrupted series of complicated distress, is now nearly exhausted, and their discontents matured to an extremity, which has recently had very disagreeable consequences, and which demonstrates the absolute necessity of speedy relief, a relief not within the compass of our means. You are too well acquainted with all their sufferings for want of clothing, for want of provisions, for want of pay.

That, the people being dissatisfied with the mode of supporting the war, there is cause to apprehend, that evils actually felt in the prosecution may weaken those sentiments which began it, founded, not on immediate sufferings, but on a speculative apprehension of future sufferings from the loss of their liberties. There is danger, that a commercial and free people, little accustomed to heavy burthens, pressed by impositions of a new and odious kind, may not make a proper allowance for the necessity of the conjuncture, and may imagine they have only exchanged one tyranny for another.

That, from all the foregoing considerations result, 1st, absolute necessity of an immediate, ample, and efficacious succor in money, large enough to be a foundation for substantial arrangements of finance, to revive public credit, and give vigor to future operations; 2dly, the vast importance of a decided effort of the allied arms on this continent, the ensuing campaign, to effectuate once for all the great objects of the alliance, the liberty and independence of these States. Without the first we may make a feeble and expiring effort the next campaign, in all probability the period to our opposition. With it, we should be in a condition to continue the war, as long as the obstinacy of the enemy might require. The first is essential to the latter; both combined would bring the contest to a glorious issue, crown the obligations, which America already feels to the magnanimity and generosity of her ally, and perpetuate the union by all the ties of gratitude and affection, as well as mutual advantage, which alone can render it solid and indissoluble.

That, next to a loan of money, a constant naval superiority on these coasts is the object most interesting. This would instantly reduce the enemy to a difficult defensive, and, by removing all prospect of extending their acquisitions, would take away the motives for prosecuting the war. Indeed, it is not to be conceived how they could subsist a large force in this country, if we had the command of the seas, to interrupt the regular transmission of supplies from Europe. This superiority, (with an aid in money,) would enable us to convert the war into a vigorous offensive. I say nothing of the advantages to the trade of both nations, nor how infinitely it would facilitate our supplies. With respect to us, it seems to be one of *two* deciding points; and it appears, too, to be the interest of our allies, abstracted from the immediate benefits to this country, to transfer the naval war to America. The number of ports friendly to them, hostile to the British, the materials for repairing their disabled ships, the extensive supplies towards the subsistence of their fleet, are circumstances which would give them a palpable advantage in the contest of these seas.

123

That no nation will have it more in its power to repay what it borrows than this. Our debts are hitherto small. The vast and valuable tracts of unlocated lands, the variety and fertility of climates and soils, the advantages of every kind which we possess for commerce, insure to this country a rapid advancement in population and prosperity, and a certainty, its independence being established, of redeeming in a short term of years the comparatively inconsiderable debts it may have occasion to contract.

That, notwithstanding the difficulties under which we labor, and the inquietudes prevailing among the people, there is still a fund of inclination and resource in the country, equal to great and continued exertions, provided we have it in our power to stop the progess of disgust, by changing the present system, and adopting another more consonant with the spirit of the nation, and more capable of activity and energy in public measures; of which a powerful succor of money must be the basis. The people are discontented; but it is, with the feeble and oppressive mode of conducting the war, not with the war itself. They are not unwilling to contribute to its support, but they are unwilling to do it in a way that renders private property precarious; a necessary consequence of the fluctuation of the national currency, and of the inability of government to perform its engagements oftentimes coercively made. A large majority are still firmly attached to the independence of these States, abhor a reunion with Great Britain, and are affectionate to the alliance with France; but this disposition cannot supply the place of means customary and essential in war, nor can we rely on its duration amidst the perplexities, oppressions, and misfortunes, that attend the want of them.

If the foregoing observations are of any use to you, I shall be happy. I wish you a safe and pleasant voyage, the full accomplishment of your mission, and a speedy return; being, with sentiments of perfect friendship, regard, and affection, dear Sir, &c.

5   Farewell Orders to the Armies of the United States

Rocky Hill, near Princeton, [Sunday] 2 November 1783

The United States in Congress assembled, after giving the most honorable testimony to the merits of the federal armies, and presenting them with the thanks of their country for their long, eminent and faithful services, having thought proper, by their proclamation bearing date the 18th day of October last, to discharge such part of the troops as were engaged for the war, and to permit the officers on furlough to retire from service from and after to-morrow; which proclamation having been communicated in the public papers for the information and government of all concerned, it only remains for the Commander-in-chief to address himself once more, and that for the last time, to the armies of the United States (however widely dispersed the individuals who compose them may be), and to bid them an affectionate, a long farewell.

But before the Commander-in-chief takes his final leave of those he holds most dear, he wishes to indulge himself a few moments in calling to mind a slight review of the past. He will then take the liberty of exploring with his military friends their future prospects, of advising the general line of conduct, which, in his opinion, ought to be pursued; and he will conclude the address by expressing the obligations he feels himself under for the spirited and able assistance he has experienced from them, in the performance of an arduous office.

A contemplation of the complete attainment (at a period earlier than could have been expected) of the object, for which we contended against so formidable a power, cannot but inspire us with astonishment and gratitude. The disadvantageous circumstances on our part, under which the war was undertaken, can never be forgotten. The singular interpositions of Providence in our feeble condition were such, as could scarcely escape the attention of the most unobserving; while the unparalleled perseverance of the armies of the United States, through almost every possible suffering and discouragement for the space of eight long years, was little short of a standing miracle.

It is not the meaning nor within the compass of this address, to detail the hardships peculiarly incident to our service, or to describe the distresses, which in several instances have resulted from the extremes of hunger and nakedness, combined with the rigors of an inclement season; nor is it necessary to dwell on the dark side of our past affairs. Every American officer and soldier must now console himself for any unpleasant circumstances, which may have occurred, by a recollection of the uncommon scenes in which he has been called to act no inglorious part, and the astonishing events of which he has been a witness; events which have seldom, if ever before, taken place on the stage of human action; nor can they probably ever happen again. For who has before seen a disciplined army formed at once from such raw materials? Who, that was not a witness, could imagine, that the most violent local prejudices would cease so soon; and that men, who came from the different parts of the continent, strongly disposed by the habits of education to despise and quarrel with each other, would instantly become but one patriotic band of brothers? Or who, that was not on the spot, can trace the steps by which such a wonderful revolution has been effected, and such a glorious period put to all our warlike toils?

It is universally acknowledged, that the enlarged prospects of happiness, opened by the confirmation of our independence and sovereignty, almost exceeds the power of description. And shall not the brave men, who have contributed so essentially to these inestimable acquisitions, retiring victorious from the field of war to the field of agriculture, participate in all the blessings, which have been obtained? In such a republic, who will exclude them from the rights of citizens, and the fruits of their labors? In such a country, so happily circumstanced, the pursuits of commerce and the cultivation of the soil will unfold to industry the certain road to competence. To those hardy soldiers, who are actuated by the spirit of adventure, the fisheries will afford ample and profitable employment; and the extensive and fertile regions of the West will yield a most happy asylum to those, who, fond of domestic enjoyment, are seeking for personal independence. Nor is it possible to conceive, that any one of the United States will prefer a national bankruptcy, and a dissolution of the Union, to a compliance with the requisitions of Congress, and the

125

payment of its just debts; so that the officers and soldiers may expect considerable assistance, in recommencing their civil occupations, from the sums due to them from the public, which must and will most inevitably be paid.

In order to effect this desirable purpose, and to remove the prejudices, which may have taken posession of the minds of any of the good people of the States, it is earnestly recommended to all the troops, that, with strong attachments to the Union, they should carry with them into civil society the most conciliating dispositions, and that they should prove themselves not less virtuous and useful as citizens, than they have been persevering and victorious as soldiers. What though there should be some envious individuals, who are unwilling to pay the debt the public has contracted, or to yield the tribute due to merit; yet let such unworthy treatment produce no invective, or any instance of intemperate conduct. Let it be remembered, that the unbiassed voice of the free citizens of the United States has promised the just reward and given the merited applause. Let it be known and remembered, that the reputation of the federal armies is established beyond the reach of malevolence; and let a consciousness of their achievements and fame still incite the men, who composed them, to honorable actions; under the persuasion that the private virtues of economy, prudence, and industry, will not be less amiable in civil life, than the more splendid qualities of valor, perseverance, and enterprise were in the field. Every one may rest assured, that much, very much, of the future happiness of the officers and men, will depend upon the wise and manly conduct, which shall be adopted by them when they are mingled with the great body of the community. And, although the General has so frequently given it as his opinion in the most public and explicit manner, that, unless the principles of the Federal Government were properly supported, and the powers of the Union increased, the honor, dignity, and justice of the nation would be lost forever; yet he cannot help repeating, on this occasion, so interesting a sentiment, and leaving it as his last injunction to every officer and every soldier, who may view the subject in the same serious point of light, to add his best endeavors to those of his worthy fellow citizens towards effecting these great and valuable purposes, on which our very existence as a nation so materially depends.

The Commander-in-chief conceives little is now wanting, to enable the soldier, to change the military character into that of the citizen, but that steady and decent tenor of behavior, which has generally distinguished, not only the army under his immediate command, but the different detachments and separate armies, through the course of the war. From their good sense and prudence he anticipates the happiest consequences; and, while he congratulates them on the glorious occasion, which renders their services in the field no longer necessary, he wishes to express the strong obligations he feels himself under for the assistance he has received from every class and in every instance. He presents his thanks in the most serious and affectionate manner to the general officers, as well for their counsel on many interesting occasions, as for their ardor in promoting the success of the plans he had adopted; to the commandants of regiments and corps, and to the other officers, for their great zeal and attention in carrying his orders promptly into execution; to the staff, for their alacrity and exactness in performing the duties of their several departments; and to the non-commissioned officers and private soldiers, for their extraordinary patience and suffering, as well as their invincible fortitude in action. To the various branches of the army, the General takes this last and solemn opportunity of professing his inviolable attachment and friendship. He wishes more than bare professions were in his power; that he were really able to be useful to them all in future life. He flatters himself, however, they will do him the justice to believe, that whatever could with propriety be attempted by him has been done.

And being now to conclude these his last public orders, to take his ultimate leave in a short time of the military character, and to bid a final adieu to the armies he has so long had the honor to command, he can only again offer in their behalf his recommendations to their grateful country, and his prayers to the God of armies. May ample justice be done them here, and may the choicest of Heaven's favors, both here and hereafter, attend those, who, under the Divine auspices, have secured innumerable blessings for others. With these wishes and this benediction, the Commander-in-chief is about to retire from service. The curtain of separation will soon be drawn, and the military scene to him will be closed for ever.

Ratifying the Constitution

Although the men who gathered in Philadelphia during the summer of 1787 were united on the need for a stronger government to replace the Confederation of the States, many of their countrymen vehemently disagreed. When the work of the Convention went before the states for ratification—at least nine would have to approve it for the new government to go into effect—its basic goals were often hotly debated. Some states, particularly weak ones like Georgia or Delaware, immediately ratified the document. But in others, New York and Virginia, for example, there were closely fought contests over the fate of the new government.

It is no easy matter to know what divided the Federalists—those who favored the new Constitution—from the Anti-Federalists. The following selections from the debate in the Virginia State Ratifying Convention offer some interesting clues. Was one camp more democratic than the other? Read the arguments of Anti-Federalist, George Mason. Was the other camp more interested in paying the war debt in full value for personal as well as public reasons? Look at the arguments of Federalists like Edmund Randolph and James Madison. But one must also be attentive to other issues: Were some participants more certain than others that the new government would not trample the liberties of the people? If so, what gave one group but not the other this confidence? These questions are a starting point for understanding why some men became Federalists, and others, Anti-Federalists.

THE VIRGINIA DEBATES

Mr. George Mason. Mr. Chairman, whether the Constitution be good or bad, the present clause clearly discovers that it is a national government, and no longer a Confederation. I mean that clause which gives the first hint of the general government laying direct taxes. The assumption of this power of laying direct taxes does, of itself, entirely change the confederation of the states into one consolidated government. This power, being at discretion, unconfined, and without any kind of control, must carry every thing before it. The very idea of converting what was

From *The Debates in the Several Conventions on the Adoption of the Federal Constitution*, Jonathan Elliot, ed. (Washington, D.C., 1836), III: 30–38, 80–84.

formerly a confederation to a consolidated government, is totally subversive of every principle which has hitherto governed us. This power is calculated to annihilate totally the state governments. Will the people of this great community submit to be individually taxed by two different and distinct powers? Will they suffer themselves to be doubly harassed? These two concurrent powers cannot exist long together; the one will destroy the other: the general government being paramount to, and in every respect more powerful than the state governments, the latter must give way to the former. Is it to be supposed that one national government will suit so extensive a country, embracing so many climates, and containing inhabitants so very different in manners, habits, and customs? It is ascertained, by history, that there never was a government over a very extensive country without destroying the liberties of the people: history also, supported by the opinions of the best writers, shows us that monarchy may suit a large territory, and despotic governments ever so extensive a country, but that popular governments can only exist in small territories. Is there a single example, on the face of the earth, to support a contrary opinion? Where is there one exception to this general rule? Was there ever an instance of a general national government extending over so extensive a country, abounding in such a variety of climates, &c., where the people retained their liberty? I solemnly declare that no man is a greater friend to a firm union of the American states than I am; but, sir, if this great end can be obtained without hazarding the rights of the people, why should we recur to such dangerous principles? Requisitions have been often refused, sometimes from an impossibility of complying with them; often from that great variety of circumstances which retards the collection of moneys; and perhaps sometimes from a wilful design of procrastinating. But why shall we give up to the national government this power, so dangerous in its nature, and for which its members will not have sufficient information? Is it not well known that what would be a proper tax in one state would be grievous in another? The gentleman who hath favored us with a eulogium in favor of this system, must, after all the encomiums he has been pleased to bestow upon it, acknowledge that our federal representatives must be unacquainted with the situation of their constituents. Sixty-five members cannot possibly know the situation and circumstances of all the inhabitants of this immense continent. When a certain sum comes to be taxed, and the mode of levying to be fixed, they will lay the tax on that article which will be most productive and easiest in the collection, without consulting the real circumstances or convenience of a country, with which, in fact, they cannot be sufficiently acquainted.

The mode of levying taxes is of the utmost consequence; and yet here it is to be determined by those who have neither knowledge of our situation, nor a common interest with us, nor a fellow-feeling for us.

Why should we give up this dangerous power of individual taxation? Why leave the manner of laying taxes to those who, in the nature of things, cannot be acquainted with the situation of those on whom they are to impose them, when it can be done by those who are well acquainted with it?

I candidly acknowledge the inefficacy of the Confederation; but requisitions have been made which were impossible to be complied with—requisitions for more gold and silver than were in the United States. If we give the general government the power of demanding their quotas of the states, with an alternative of laying direct taxes in case of non-compliance, then the mischief would be avoided; and the certainty of this conditional power would, in all human probability, prevent the application, and the sums necessary for the Union would be then laid by the states, by those who know how it can best be raised, by those who have a fellow-feeling for us. Give me leave to say, that the sum raised one way with convenience and ease, would be very oppressive another way. Why, then, not leave this power to be exercised by those who know the mode most convenient for the inhabitants, and not by those who must necessarily apportion it in such manner as shall be oppressive?

With respect to the representation so much applauded, I cannot think it such a full and free one as it is represented; but I must candidly acknowledge that this defect results from the very nature of the government. It would be impossible to have a full and adequate representation in the general government; it would be too expensive and too unwieldy. We are, then, under the necessity of having this a very inadequate representation. Is this general representation to be compared with the real, actual, substantial representation of the state legislatures? It cannot bear a comparison. To make representation real and actual, the number of representatives ought to be adequate; they ought to mix with the people, think as they think, feel as they feel,—ought to be perfectly amenable to them, and thoroughly acquainted with their interest and condition. Now, these great ingredients are either not at all, or in a small degree, to be found in our federal representatives; so that we have no real, actual, substantial representation: but I acknowledge it results from the nature of the government. The necessity of this inconvenience may appear a sufficient reason not to argue against it; but, sir, it clearly shows that we ought to give power with a sparing hand to a government thus imperfectly constructed. To a government which, in the nature of things, cannot but be defective, no powers ought to be given but such as are absolutely necessary. There is one thing in it which I conceive to be extremely dangerous. Gentlemen may talk of public virtue and confidence; we shall be told that the House of Representatives will consist of the most virtuous men on the continent, and that in their hands we may trust our dearest rights. This, like all other assemblies, will be composed of some bad and some good men; and, considering the natural lust of power so inherent in man, I fear the thirst of power will prevail to oppress the people.

But my principal objection is, that the Confederation is converted to one general consolidated government, which, from my best judgment of it, (and which perhaps will be shown, in the course of this discussion, to be really well founded,) is one of the worst curses that can possibly befall a nation. Does any man suppose that one general national government can exist in so extensive a country as this? I hope that a government may be framed which may suit us, by drawing a line between the general and state governments, and prevent that dangerous clashing of interest and power, which must, as it now stands, terminate in the destruction of one or the other. When we come to the judiciary, we shall be more convinced that this government will terminate in the annihilation of the state governments: the question then will be, whether a consolidated government can preserve the freedom and secure the rights of the people.

If such amendments be introduced as shall exclude danger, I shall most gladly put my hand to it. When such amendments as shall, from the best information, secure the great essential rights of the people, shall be agreed to by gentlemen, I shall most heartily make the greatest concessions, and concur in any reasonable measure to obtain the desirable end of conciliation and unanimity. An indispensable amendment in this case is, that Congress shall not exercise the power of raising direct taxes till the states shall have refused to comply with the requisitions of Congress. On this condition it may be granted; but I see no reason to grant it unconditionally, as the states can raise the taxes with more ease, and lay them on the inhabitants with more propriety, than it is possible for the general government to do. If Congress hath this power without control, the taxes will be laid by those who have no fellow-feeling or acquaintance with the people. This is my objection to the article now under consideration. It is a very great and important one. I therefore beg gentlemen to consider it. Should this power be restrained, I shall withdraw my objections to this part of the Constitution; but as it stands, it is an objection so strong in my mind, that its amendment is with me a *sine qua non* of its adoption. I wish for such amendments, and such only, as are necessary to secure the dearest rights of the people.

Mr. Pendleton. Mr. Chairman, my worthy friend has expressed great uneasiness in his mind, and informed us that a great many of our citizens are also extremely uneasy, at the proposal of changing our government; but that, a year ago, before this fatal system was thought of, the public mind was at perfect repose. It is necessary to inquire whether the public mind was at ease on the subject, and if it be since disturbed, what was the cause. What was the situation of this country before the meeting of the federal Convention? Our general government was totally inadequate to the purpose of its institution; our commerce decayed; our finances deranged; public and private credit destroyed: these and many other national evils rendered necessary the meeting of that Convention. If the public mind was then at ease, it did not result from a conviction of being in a happy and easy situation: it must have been an inactive, unaccountable stupor. The federal Convention devised the paper on your table as a remedy to remove our political diseases. What has created the public uneasiness since? Not public reports, which are not to be depended upon; but mistaken apprehensions of danger, drawn from observations on government which do not apply to us. When we come to inquire into the origin of most governments of the world, we shall find that they are generally dictated by a conqueror, at the point of the sword, or are the offspring of confusion, when a great popular leader, taking advantage of circumstances, if not producing them, restores order at the expense of liberty, and becomes the tyrant over the people. It may well be supposed that, in forming a government of this sort, it will not be favorable to liberty: the conqueror will take care of his own emoluments, and have little concern for the interest of the people. In either case, the interest and ambition of a despot, and not the good of the people, have given the tone to the government. A government thus formed must necessarily create a continual war between the governors and governed.

Writers consider the two parties (the people and tyrants) as in a state of perpetual warfare, and sound the alarm to the people. But what is our case? We are perfectly free from sedition and war: we are not yet in confusion: we are left to consider our real happiness and security: we want to secure these objects: we know they cannot be attained without government. Is there a single man, in this committee, of a contrary opinion? What was it that brought us from a state of nature to society, but to secure happiness? And can society be formed without government? Personify government: apply to it as a friend to assist you, and it will grant your request. This is the only government founded in real compact. There is no quarrel between government and liberty; the former is the shield and protector of the latter. The war is between government and licentiousness, faction, turbulence, and other violations of the rules of society, to preserve liberty. Where is the cause of alarm? We, the people, possessing all power, form a government, such as we think will secure happiness: and suppose, in adopting this plan, we should be mistaken in the end; where is the cause of alarm on that quarter? In the same plan we point out an easy and quiet method of reforming what may be found amiss. No, but, say gentlemen, we have put the introduction of that method in the hands of our servants, who will interrupt it from motives of self-interest. What then? We will resist, did my friend say? conveying an idea of force. Who shall dare to resist the people? No, we will assemble in Convention; wholly recall our delegated powers, or reform them so as to prevent such abuse; and punish those servants who have perverted powers, designed for our happiness, to their own emolument. Here, then, sir, there is no cause of alarm on this side; but on the other side, rejecting of government, and dissolving of the Union, produce confusion and despotism.

But an objection is made to the form: the expression, We, the people, is thought improper. Permit me to ask the gentlemen who made this objection, who but the people can delegate powers? Who but the people have a right to form government? The expression is a common one, and a favorite one with me. The representatives of the people, by their authority, is a mode wholly inessential. If the objection be, that the Union ought to be not of the people, but of the state governments, then I think the choice of the former very happy and proper. What have the state governments to do with it? Were they to determine, the people would not, in that case, be the judges upon what terms it was adopted.

But the power of the Convention is doubted. What is the power? To propose, not to determine. This power of proposing was very broad; it extended to remove all defects in government: the members of that Convention, who were to consider all the defects in our general government, were not confined to any particular plan. Were they deceived? This is the proper question here. Then the question must be between this government and the Confederation. The latter is no government at all. It has been said that it has carried us, through a dangerous war, to a happy issue. Not that Confederation, but common danger, and the spirit of America, were bonds of our union: union and unanimity, and not that insignificant paper, carried us through that dangerous war. "United, we stand; divided, we fall!" echoed and reëchoed through America—from Congress to the drunken carpenter—was effectual, and procured the end of our wishes, though now forgotten by gentlemen, if such there be, who incline to let go this stronghold, to catch at feathers; for such all substituted projects may prove.

This spirit had nearly reached the end of its power when relieved by peace. It was the spirit of America, and not the Confederation, that carried us through the war: thus I prove it. The moment of peace showed the imbecility of the federal government: Congress was empowered to make war and peace; a peace they made, giving us the great object, independence, and yielding us a territory that exceeded my most sanguine expectations. Unfortunately, a single disagreeable clause, not the object of the war, has retarded the performance of the treaty on our part. Congress could only recommend its performance, not enforce it; our last Assembly (to their honor be it said) put this on its proper grounds—on honorable grounds; it was as much as they ought to have done. This single instance shows the imbecility of the Confederation; the debts contracted by the war were unpaid; demands were made on Congress; all that Congress was able to do was to make an estimate of the debt, and proportion it among the several states; they sent on the requisitions, from time to time, to the states, for their respective quotas. These were either complied with partially, or not at all. Repeated demands on Congress distressed that honorable body; but they were unable to fulfill those engagements, as they so earnestly wished. What was the idea of other nations respecting America? What was the idea entertained of us by those nations to whom we were so much indebted? The inefficacy of the general government warranted an idea that we had no government at all. Improvements were proposed, and agreed to by twelve states; but were interrupted, because the little state of Rhode Island refused to accede to them. This was a further proof of the imbecility of that government. Need I multiply instances to show that it is wholly ineffectual for the purposes of its institution? Its whole progress since the peace proves it.

Shall we then, sir, continue under such a government, or shall we introduce that kind of government which shall produce the real happiness and security of the people? When gentlemen say that we ought not to introduce this new government, but strengthen the hands of Congress, they ought to be explicit. In what manner shall this be done? If the union of the states be necessary, government must be equally so; for without the latter, the former cannot be effected. Government must then have its complete powers, or be ineffectual; a legislature to fix rules, impose sanctions, and point out the punishment of the transgressors of these rules; an executive to watch over officers, and bring them to punishment; a judiciary, to guard the innocent, and fix the guilty, by a fair trial. Without an executive, offenders would not be brought to punishment; without a judiciary, any man might be taken up, convicted, and punished without a trial. Hence the necessity of having these three branches. Would any gentleman in this committee agree to vest these three powers in one body—Congress? No. Hence the necessity of a new organization and distribution of those powers. If there be any feature in this government which is not republican, it would be exceptionable. From all the public servants responsibility is secured, by their being representatives, mediate or immediate, for short terms, and their powers defined. It is, on the whole complexion of it, a government of laws, not of men.

But it is represented to be a consolidated government, annihilating that of the states—a consolidated government, which so extensive a territory as the United

States cannot admit of, without terminating in despotism. If this be such a government, I will confess, with my worthy friend, that it is inadmissible over such a territory as this country. Let us consider whether it be such a government or not. I should understand a consolidated government to be that which should have the sole and exclusive power, legislative, executive, and judicial, without any limitation. Is this such a government? Or can it be changed to such a one? It only extends to the general purposes of the Union. It does not intermeddle with the local, particular affairs of the states. Can Congress legislate for the state of Virginia? Can they make a law altering the form of transferring property, or the rule of descents, in Virginia? In one word, can they make a single law for the individual, exclusive purpose of any one state? It is the interest of the federal to preserve the state governments; upon the latter the existence of the former depends: the Senate derives its existence immediately from the state legislatures; and the representatives and President are elected under their direction and control; they also preserve order among the citizens of their respective states, and without order and peace no society can possibly exist. Unless, therefore, there be state legislatures to continue the existence of Congress, and preserve order and peace among the inhabitants, this general government, which gentlemen suppose will annihilate the state governments, must itself be destroyed. When, therefore, the federal government is, in so many respects, so absolutely dependent on the state governments, I wonder how any gentleman, reflecting on the subject, could have conceived an idea of a possibility of the former destroying the latter.

Mr. Madison then arose.— I shall not attempt to make impressions by any ardent professions of zeal for the public welfare. We know the principles of every man will, and ought to be, judged, not by his professions and declarations, but by his conduct; by that criterion, I mean, in common with every other member, to be judged; and, should it prove unfavorable to my reputation, yet it is a criterion from which I will by no means depart. Comparisons have been made between the friends of this Constitution and those who oppose it: although I disapprove of such comparisons, I trust that, in point of truth, honor, candor, and rectitude of motives, the friends of this system, here and in other states, are not inferior to its opponents. But professions of attachment to the public good, and comparisons of parties, ought not to govern or influence us now. We ought, sir, to examine the Constitution on its own merits solely: we are to inquire whether it will promote the public happiness: its aptitude to produce this desirable object ought to be the exclusive subject of our present researches. In this pursuit, we ought not to address our arguments to the feelings and passions, but to those understandings and judgments which were selected by the people of this country, to decide this great question by a calm and rational investigation.

Before I proceed to make some additions to the reasons which have been adduced by my honorable friend over the way, I must take the liberty to make some observations on what was said by another gentleman, (Mr. Patrick Henry.) He told us that this Constitution ought to be rejected because it endangered the public liberty, in his opinion, in many instances. Give me leave to make one answer to that observation: Let the dangers which this system is supposed to be replete with be clearly pointed out: if any dangerous and unnecessary powers be given to the general legislature, let them be plainly demonstrated; and let us not rest satisfied with general assertions of danger, without examination. If powers be necessary, apparent danger is not a sufficient reason against conceding them. He has suggested that licentiousness has seldom produced the loss of liberty; but that the tyranny of rulers has almost always effected it. Since the general civilization of mankind, I believe there are more instances of the abridgment of the freedom of the people by gradual and silent encroachments of those in power, than by violent and sudden usurpations; but, on a candid examination of history, we shall find that turbulence, violence, and abuse of power, by the majority trampling on the rights of the minority, have produced factions and commotions, which, in republics, have, more frequently than any other cause, produced despotism. If we go over the whole history of ancient and modern republics, we shall find their destruction to have generally resulted from those causes. If we consider the peculiar situation of the United States, and what are the sources of that diversity of sentiment which pervades its inhabitants, we shall find great danger to fear that the same causes may terminate here in the same fatal effects which they produced in those republics. This danger ought to be wisely guarded against. Perhaps, in the progress of this discussion, it will appear that the only possible remedy for those evils, and means of preserving and protecting the principles of republicanism, will be found in that very system which is now exclaimed against as the parent of oppression.

I must confess I have not been able to find his usual consistency in the gentleman's argument on this occasion. He informs us that the people of the country are at perfect repose—that is, every man enjoys the fruits of his labor peaceably and securely, and that every thing is in perfect tranquillity and safety. I wish sincerely, sir, this were true. If this be their happy situation, why has every state acknowledged the contrary? Why were deputies from all the states sent to the general Convention? Why have complaints of national and individual distresses been echoed and reechoed throughout the continent? Why has our general government been so shamefully disgraced, and our Constitution violated? Wherefore have laws been made to authorize a change, and wherefore are we now assembled here? A federal government is formed for the protection of its individual members. Ours has attacked itself with impunity. Its authority has been disobeyed and despised. I think I perceive a glaring inconsistency in another of his arguments. He complains of this Constitution, because it requires the consent of at least three fourths of the states to introduce amendments which shall be necessary for the happiness of the people. The assent of so many he urges as too great an obstacle to the admission of salutary amendments, which, he strongly insists, ought to be at the will of a bare majority. We hear this argument, at the very moment we are called upon to assign reasons for proposing a constitution which puts it in the power of nine states to abolish the present inadequate, unsafe, and pernicious Confederation! In the first case, he asserts that a majority ought to have the power of altering the government, when found to be inadequate to the security of public happiness. In the last case, he affirms that even three fourths of the community have not a right to alter a government which experience has proved to be subversive of national felicity! nay, that the most necessary and urgent alterations cannot be made without the absolute unanimity of all the states! Does not the thirteenth article of the Confederation expressly require that no alteration shall be made without the unanimous consent of all the states? Could any thing in theory be more perniciously improvident and injudicious than this submission of the will of the majority to the most trifling minority? Have not experience and practice actually manifested this theoretical inconvenience to be extremely impolitic? Let me mention one fact, which I conceive must carry conviction to the mind of any one: the smallest state in the Union has obstructed every attempt to reform the government; that little member has repeatedly disobeyed and counteracted the general authority; nay, has even supplied the enemies of its country with provisions. Twelve states had agreed to certain improvements which were proposed, being thought absolutely necessary to preserve the existence of the general government; but as these improvements, though really indispensable, could not, by the Confederation, be introduced into it without the consent of every state, the refractory dissent of that little state prevented their adoption. The inconveniences resulting from this requisition, of unanimous concurrence in alterations in the Confederation, must be known to every member in this Convention; it is therefore needless to remind them of them. Is it not self-evident that a trifling minority ought not to bind the majority? Would not foreign influence be exerted with facility over a small minority? Would the honorable gentleman agree to continue the most radical defects in the old system, because the petty state of Rhode Island would not agree to remove them?

The honorable member then told us that there was no instance of power once transferred being voluntarily renounced. Not to produce European examples, which may probably be done before the rising of this Convention, have we not seen already, in seven states, (and probably in an eighth state,) legislatures surrendering some of the most important powers they possessed? But, sir, by this government, powers are not given to any particular set of men; they are in the hands of the people; delegated to their representatives chosen for short terms; to representatives responsible to the people, and whose situation is perfectly similar to their own. As long as this is the case we have no danger to apprehend. When the gentleman called our recollection to the usual effects of the concession of powers, and imputed the loss of liberty generally to open tyranny, I wish he had gone on farther. Upon his review of history, he would have found that the loss of liberty very often resulted from factions and divisions; from local considerations, which eternally lead to quarrels; he would have found internal dissensions to have more frequently demolished civil liberty, than a tenacious disposition in rulers to retain any stipulated powers.

14

The New American

One of the most perceptive accounts of the reality and promise of American life after the Revolution was written not by a native, but by a newcomer, St. John de Crevecoeur. Born in Normandy, France, Crevecoeur received his formal education in England and then migrated to French Canada in 1754. He served with General Montcalm in the French and Indian War, and after the French defeat he moved to the British colonies. He lived in New York between 1769 and 1780, working as a farmer.

As Crevecoeur thought about his adopted land, he wondered what held this heterogeneous people together. As an immigrant, he was properly sensitive to the incredible diversity of the inhabitants—they seemed to come from every European nation. And yet, Crevecoeur also recognized that life in the New World transformed the European. The dynamics of this process of change and its implications for the United States were the basic questions that Crevecoeur set out to answer when he made his famous inquiry: What is an American?

LETTERS FROM
AN AMERICAN FARMER
St. John de Crevecoeur

WHAT IS AN AMERICAN

I wish I could be acquainted with the feelings and thoughts which must agitate the heart and present themselves to the mind of an enlightened Englishman, when he first lands on this continent. He must greatly rejoice that he lived at a time to see this fair country discovered and settled; he must necessarily feel a share of national pride, when he views the chain of settlements which embellishes these extended shores. When he says to himself, this is the work of my countrymen, who, when convulsed by factions, afflicted by a variety of miseries and wants, restless and impatient, took refuge here. They brought along with them their national genius, to which they principally owe what liberty they enjoy, and what substance they possess. Here he sees the industry of his native country displayed in a new manner, and traces in their works the embryos of all the arts, sciences, and ingenuity which

From *Letters from an American Farmer* (first published 1782; reprinted, New York, 1912), Chapter III.

flourish in Europe. Here he beholds fair cities, substantial villages, extensive fields, an immense country filled with decent houses, good roads, orchards, meadows, and bridges, where a hundred years ago all was wild, woody, and uncultivated! What a train of pleasing ideas this fair spectacle must suggest; it is a prospect which must inspire a good citizen with the most heartfelt pleasure. The difficulty consists in the manner of viewing so extensive a scene. He is arrived on a new continent; a modern society offers itself to his contemplation, different from what he had hitherto seen. It is not composed, as in Europe, of great lords who possess everything, and of a herd of people who have nothing. Here are no aristocratical families, no courts, no kings, no bishops, no ecclesiastical dominion, no invisible power giving to a few a very visible one; no great manufacturers employing thousands, no great refinements of luxury. The rich and the poor are not so far removed from each other as they are in Europe. Some few towns excepted, we are all tillers of the earth, from Nova Scotia to West Florida. We are a people of cultivators, scattered over an immense territory, communicating with each other by means of good roads and navigable rivers, united by the silken bands of mild government, all respecting the laws, without dreading their power, because they are equitable. We are all animated with the spirit of an industry which is unfettered and unrestrained, because each person works for himself. If he travels through our rural districts he views not the hostile castle, and the haughty mansion, contrasted with the clay-built hut and miserable cabin, where cattle and men help to keep each other warm, and dwell in meanness, smoke, and indigence. A pleasing uniformity of decent competence appears throughout our habitations. The meanest of our log-houses is a dry and comfortable habitation. Lawyer or merchant are the fairest titles our towns afford; that of a farmer is the only appellation of the rural inhabitants of our country. It must take some time ere he can reconcile himself to our dictionary, which is but short in words of dignity, and names of honour. There, on a Sunday, he sees a congregation of respectable farmers and their wives, all clad in neat homespun, well mounted, or riding in their own humble waggons. There is not among them an esquire, saving the unlettered magistrate. There he sees a parson as simple as his flock, a farmer who does not riot on the labour of others. We have no princes, for whom we toil, starve, and bleed: we are the most perfect society now existing in the world. Here man is free as he ought to be; nor is this pleasing equality so transitory as many others are. Many ages will not see the shores of our great lakes replenished with inland nations, nor the unknown bounds of North America entirely peopled. Who can tell how far it extends? Who can tell the millions of men whom it will feed and contain? for no European foot has as yet travelled half the extent of this mighty continent!

The next wish of this traveller will be to know whence came all these people? they are a mixture of English, Scotch, Irish, French, Dutch, Germans, and Swedes. From this promiscuous breed, that race now called Americans have arisen. The eastern provinces must indeed be excepted, as being the unmixed descendants of Englishmen. I have heard many wish that they had been more intermixed also: for my part, I am no wisher, and think it much better as it has happened. They exhibit a most conspicuous figure in this great and variegated picture; they too enter for a great share in the pleasing perspective displayed in these thirteen provinces. I know it is fashionable to reflect on them, but I respect them for what they have done; for the accuracy and wisdom with which they have settled their territory; for the decency of their manners; for their early love of letters; their ancient college, the first in this hemisphere; for their industry; which to me who am but a farmer, is the criterion of everything. There never was a people, situated as they are, who with so ungrateful a soil have done more in so short a time. Do you think that the monarchical ingredients which are more prevalent in other governments, have purged them from all foul stains? Their histories assert the contrary.

In this great American asylum, the poor of Europe have by some means met together, and in consequence of various causes; to what purpose should they ask one another what countrymen they are? Alas, two thirds of them had no country. Can a wretch who wanders about, who works and starves, whose life is a continual scene of sore affliction or pinching penury; can that man call England or any other kingdom his country? A country that had no bread for him, whose fields procured him no harvest, who met with nothing but the frowns of the rich, the severity of the laws, with jails and punishments; who owned not a single foot of the extensive surface of this planet? No! urged by a variety of motives, here they came. Every thing has tended to regenerate them; new laws, a new mode of living, a new social system; here they are become men: in Europe they were as so many useless plants, wanting vegetative mould, and refreshing showers; they withered, and were mowed down by want, hunger, and war; but now by the power of transplantation, like all other plants they have taken root and flourished! Formerly they were not numbered in any civil lists of their country, except in those of the poor; here they rank as citizens. By what invisible power has this surprising metamorphosis been performed? By that of the laws and that of their industry. The laws, the indulgent laws, protect them as they arrive, stamping on them the symbol of adoption; they receive ample rewards for their labours; these accumulated rewards procure them lands; those lands confer on them the title of freemen, and to that title every benefit is affixed which men can possibly require. This is the great operation daily performed by our laws. From whence proceed these laws? From our government. Whence the government? It is derived from the original genius and strong desire of the people ratified and confirmed by the crown. This is the great chain which links us all, this is the picture which every province exhibits, Nova Scotia excepted. There the crown has done all; either there were no people who had genius, or it was not much attended to: the consequence is, that the province is very thinly inhabited indeed; the power of the crown in conjunction with the musketos has prevented men from settling there. Yet some parts of it flourished once, and it contained a mild harmless set of people. But for the fault of a few leaders, the whole were banished. The greatest political error the crown ever committed in America, was to cut off men from a country which wanted nothing but men!

What attachment can a poor European emigrant have for a country where he had nothing? The knowledge of the language, the love of a few kindred as poor as himself, were the only cords that tied him: his country is now that which gives him land, bread, protection, and consequence: *Ubi panis ibi patria,* is the motto of all emigrants. What then is the American, this new man? He is either an European, or the descendant of an European, hence that strange mixture of blood, which you will find in no other country. I could point out to you a family whose grandfather was an Englishman, whose wife was Dutch, whose son married a French woman, and whose present four sons have now four wives of different nations. *He* is an American, who, leaving behind him all his ancient prejudices and manners, receives new ones from the new mode of life he has embraced, the new government he obeys, and the new rank he holds. He becomes an American by being received in the broad lap of our great *Alma Mater*. Here individuals of all nations are melted into a new race of men, whose labours and posterity will one day cause great changes in the world. Americans are the western pilgrims, who are carrying along with them that great mass of arts, sciences, vigour, and industry which began long since in the east; they will finish the great circle. The Americans were once scattered all over Europe; here they are incorporated into one of the finest systems of population which has ever appeared, and which will hereafter become distinct by the power of the different climates they inhabit. The American ought therefore to love this country much better than that wherein either he or his forefathers were born. Here the rewards of his industry follow with equal steps the progress of his labour; his labour is founded on the basis of nature, *self-interest;* can it want a stronger allurement? Wives and children, who before in vain demanded of him a morsel of bread, now, fat and frolicsome, gladly help their father to clear those fields whence exuberant crops are to arise to feed and to clothe them all; without any part being claimed, either by a despotic prince, a rich abbot, or a mighty lord. Here religion demands but little of him; a small voluntary salary to the minister, and gratitude to God; can he refuse these? The American is a new man, who acts upon new principles; he must therefore entertain new ideas, and form new opinions. From involuntary idleness, servile dependence, penury, and useless labour, he has passed to toils of a very different nature, rewarded by ample subsistence.—This is an American.

British America is divided into many provinces, forming a large association, scattered along a coast 1500 miles extent and about 200 wide. This society I would fain examine, at least such as it appears in the middle provinces; if it does not afford that variety of tinges and gradations which may be observed in Europe, we have colours peculiar to ourselves. For instance, it is natural to conceive that those who live near the sea, must be very different from those who live in the woods; the intermediate space will afford a separate and distinct class.

Men are like plants; the goodness and flavour of the fruit proceeds from the peculiar soil and exposition in which they grow. We are nothing but what we derive from the air we breathe, the climate we inhabit, the government we obey, the system of religion we profess, and the nature of our employment. Here you will find but few crimes; these have acquired as yet no root among us. I wish I was able to trace all my ideas; if my ignorance prevents me from describing them properly, I hope I shall be able to delineate a few of the outlines, which are all I propose.

Those who live near the sea, feed more on fish than on flesh, and often encounter that boisterous element. This renders them more bold and enterprising;

this leads them to neglect the confined occupations of the land. They see and converse with a variety of people; their intercourse with mankind becomes extensive. The sea inspires them with a love of traffic, a desire of transporting produce from one place to another; and leads them to a variety of resources which supply the place of labour. Those who inhabit the middle settlements, by far the most numerous, must be very different; the simple cultivation of the earth purifies them, but the indulgences of the government, the soft remonstrances of religion, the rank of independent freeholders, must necessarily inspire them with sentiments, very little known in Europe among people of the same class. What do I say? Europe has no such class of men; the early knowledge they acquire, the early bargains they make, give them a great degree of sagacity. As freemen they will be litigious; pride and obstinacy are often the cause of law suits; the nature of our laws and governments may be another. As citizens it is easy to imagine, that they will carefully read the newspapers, enter into every political disquisition, freely blame or censure governors and others. As farmers they will be careful and anxious to get as much as they can, because what they get is their own. As northern men they will love the cheerful cup. As Christians, religion curbs them not in their opinions; the general indulgence leaves every one to think for themselves in spiritual matters; the laws inspect our actions, our thoughts are left to God. Industry, good living, selfishness, litigiousness, country politics, the pride of freemen, religious indifference, are their characteristics. If you recede still farther from the sea, you will come into more modern settlements; they exhibit the same strong lineaments, in a ruder appearance. Religion seems to have still less influence, and their manners are less improved.

Now we arrive near the great woods, near the last inhabited districts; there men seem to be placed still farther beyond the reach of government, which in some measure leaves them to themselves. How can it pervade every corner; as they were driven there by misfortunes, necessity of beginnings, desire of acquiring large tracts of land, idleness, frequent want of economy, ancient debts; the re-union of such people does not afford a very pleasing spectacle. When discord, want of unity and friendship; when either drunkenness or idleness prevail in such remote districts; contention, inactivity, and wretchedness must ensue. There are not the same remedies to these evils as in a long established community. The few magistrates they have, are in general little better than the rest; they are often in a perfect state of war; that of man against man, somtimes decided by blows, sometimes by means of the law; that of man against every wild inhabitant of these venerable woods, of which they are come to dispossess them. There men appear to be no better than carnivorous animals of a superior rank, living on the flesh of wild animals when they can catch them, and when they are not able, they subsist on grain. He who would wish to see America in its proper light, and have a true idea of its feeble beginnings and barbarous rudiments, must visit our extended line of frontiers where the last settlers dwell, and where he may see the first labours of settlement, the mode of clearing the earth, in all their different appearances; where men are wholly left dependent on their native tempers, and on the spur of uncertain industry, which often fails when not sanctified by the efficacy of a few moral rules. There, remote from the power of example and check of shame, many families exhibit the most hideous parts of our society. They are a kind of forlorn hope, preceding by ten or twelve years the most respectable army of veterans which come after them. In that space, prosperity will polish some, vice and the law will drive off the rest, who uniting again with others like themselves will recede still farther; making room for more industrious people, who will finish their improvements, convert the loghouse into a convenient habitation, and rejoicing that the first heavy labours are finished, will change in a few years that hitherto barbarous country into a fine fertile, well regulated district. Such is our progress, such is the march of the Europeans toward the interior parts of this continent. In all societies there are off-casts; this impure part serves as our precursors or pioneers; my father himself was one of that class, but he came upon honest principles, and was therefore one of the few who held fast; by good conduct and temperance, he transmitted to me his fair inheritance, when not above one in fourteen of his contemporaries had the same good fortune.

Forty years ago this smiling country was thus inhabited; it is now purged, a general decency of manners prevails throughout, and such has been the fate of our best countries.

Exclusive of those general characteristics, each province has its own, founded on the government, climate, mode of husbandry, customs, and peculiarity of circumstances. Europeans submit insensibly to these great powers, and become, in the course of a few generations, not only Americans in general, but either Pennsylvanians, Virginians, or provincials under some other name. Whoever traverses the continent must easily observe those strong differences, which will grow more evident in time. The inhabitants of Canada, Massachusetts, the middle provinces, the southern ones will be as different as their climates; their only points of unity will be those of religion and language.

Europe contains hardly any other distinctions but lords and tenants; this fair country alone is settled by freeholders, the possessors of the soil they cultivate, members of the government they obey, and the framers of their own laws, by means of their representatives. This is a thought which you have taught me to cherish; our difference from Europe, far from diminishing, rather adds to our usefulness and consequences as men and subjects. Had our forefathers remained there, they would only have crowded it, and perhaps prolonged those convulsions which had shook it so long. Every industrious European who transports himself here, may be compared to a sprout growing at the foot of a great tree; it enjoys and draws but a little portion of sap; wrench it from the parent roots, transplant it, and it will become a tree bearing fruit also. Colonists are therefore entitled to the consideration due to the most useful subjects; a hundred families barely existing in some parts of Scotland, will here in six years, cause an annual exportation of 10,000 bushels of wheat: 100 bushels being but a common quantity for an industrious family to sell, if they cultivate good land. It is here then that the idle may be employed, the useless become useful, and the poor become rich; but by riches I do not mean gold and silver, we have but little of those metals; I mean a better sort of wealth, cleared lands, cattle, good houses, good clothes, and an increase of people to enjoy them.

There is no wonder that this country has so many charms, and presents to

Europeans so many temptations to remain in it. A traveller in Europe becomes a stranger as soon as he quits his own kingdom; but it is otherwise here. We know, properly speaking, no strangers; this is every person's country; the variety of our soils, situations, climates, governments, and produce, hath something which must please everybody. No sooner does an European arrive, no matter of what condition, than his eyes are opened upon the fair prospect; he hears his language spoke, he retraces many of his own country manners, he perpetually hears the names of families and towns with which he is acquainted; he sees happiness and prosperity in all places disseminated; he meets with hospitality, kindness, and plenty everywhere; he beholds hardly any poor, he seldom hears of punishments and executions; and he wonders at the elegance of our towns, those miracles of industry and freedom. He cannot admire enough our rural districts, our convenient roads, good taverns, and our many accommodations; he involuntarily loves a country where everything is so lovely. When in England, he was a mere Englishman; here he stands on a larger portion of the globe, not less than its fourth part, and may see the productions of the north, in iron and naval stores; the provisions of Ireland, the grain of Egypt, the indigo, the rice of China. He does not find, as in Europe, a crowded society, where every place is over-stocked; he does not feel that perpetual collision of parties, that difficulty of beginning, that contention which oversets so many. There is room for everybody in America; has he any particular talent, or industry? he exerts it in order to procure a livelihood, and it succeeds. Is he a merchant? the avenues of trade are infinite; is he eminent in any respect? he will be employed and respected. Does he love a country life? pleasant farms present themselves; he may purchase what he wants, and thereby become an American farmer. Is he a labourer, sober and industrious? he need not go many miles, nor receive many informations before he will be hired, well fed at the table of his employer, and paid four or five times more than he can get in Europe. Does he want uncultivated lands? thousands of acres present themselves, which he may purchase cheap. Whatever be his talents or inclinations, if they are moderate, he may satisfy them. I do not mean that every one who comes will grow rich in little time; no, but he may procure an easy, decent maintenance, by his industry. Instead of starving he will be fed, instead of being idle he will have employment; and these are riches enough for such men as come over here. The rich stay in Europe, it is only the middling and the poor that emigrate. Would you wish to travel in independent idleness, from north to south, you will find easy access, and the most cheerful reception at every house; society without ostentation, good cheer without pride, and every decent diversion which the country affords, with little expense. It is no wonder that the European who has lived here a few years, is desirous to remain; Europe with all its pomp, is not to be compared to this continent, for men of middle stations, or labourers.

An European, when he first arrives, seems limited in his intentions, as well as in his views; but he very suddenly alters his scale; two hundred miles formerly appeared a very great distance, it is now but a trifle; he no sooner breathes our air than he forms schemes, and embarks in designs he never would have thought of in his own country. There the plenitude of society confines many useful ideas, and often extinguishes the most laudable schemes which here ripen into maturity. Thus Europeans become Americans. This great metamorphosis has a double effect, it extinguishes all his European prejudices, he forgets that mechanism of subordination, that servility of disposition which poverty had taught him; and sometimes he is apt to forget too much, often passing from one extreme to the other. If he is a good man, he forms schemes of future prosperity, he proposes to educate his children better than he has been educated himself; he thinks of future modes of conduct, feels an ardour to labour he never felt before. Pride steps in and leads him to everything that the laws do not forbid: he respects them; with a heart-felt gratitude he looks toward the east, toward that insular government from whose wisdom all his new felicity is derived, and under whose wings and protection he now lives. These reflections constitute him the good man and the good subject. Ye poor Europeans, ye, who sweat, and work for the great—ye, who are obliged to give so many sheaves to the church, so many to your lords, so many to your government, and have hardly any left for yourselves—ye, who are held in less estimation than favourite hunters or useless lap-dogs—ye, who only breathe the air of nature, because it cannot be withheld from you; it is here that ye can conceive the possibility of those feelings I have been describing; it is here the laws of naturalisation invite every one to partake of our great labours and felicity, to till unrented, untaxed lands!

After a foreigner from any part of Europe is arrived, and become a citizen; let him devoutly listen to the voice of our great parent, which says to him, "Welcome to my shores, distressed European; bless the hour in which thou didst see my verdant fields, my fair navigable rivers, and my green mountains!—If thou wilt work, I have bread for thee; if thou wilt be honest, sober, and industrious, I have greater rewards to confer on thee—ease and independence. I will give thee fields to feed and clothe thee; a comfortable fireside to sit by, and tell thy children by what means thou hast prospered; and a decent bed to repose on. I shall endow thee beside with the immunities of a freeman. If thou wilt carefully educate thy children, teach them gratitude to God, and reverence to that government, that philanthropic government, which has collected here so many men and made them happy. I will also provide for thy progeny; and to every good man this ought to be the most holy, the most powerful, the most earnest wish he can possibly form, as well as the most consolatory prospect when he dies. Go thou and work and till; thou shalt prosper, provided thou be just, grateful, and industrious."

15

The Congress Begins

William Maclay (1743–1804) was a Pennsylvania attorney and landowner who served for some years in the state legislature. In 1789 he was elected a United States Senator for Pennsylvania, but was defeated for re-election in 1791 by a Federalist. Maclay's journal is one of our few sources for the early congressional debates for at this time no official record was being prepared for the public.

As an opponent of Hamilton's financial program, Maclay fought the chartering of the United States Bank and defended the interests of small farmers. Since Jefferson did not arrive in New York until the spring of 1790, almost a year after the new government began operations, Maclay was a leader of the group fearing a revival of monarchical oppression. The depth of his suspicions is a reminder of the experimental and innovative character of republican government in the late eighteenth century and the anxiety of many Americans concerning the future of the Constitution.

THE JOURNAL
OF WILLIAM MACLAY

28th April, 1789

This day I ought to note with some extraordinary mark. I had dressed and was about to set out, when General Washington, the greatest man in the world, paid me a visit. I met him at the foot of the stairs. Mr. Wynkoop just came in. We asked him to take a seat. He excused himself on account of the number of his visits. We accompanied him to the door. He made us complaisant bows—one before he mounted and the other as he went away on horseback.

I may as well minute a remark here as anywhere else, and, indeed, I wish it were otherwise, not for what we have, but for what others want; but we have really more republican plainness and sincere openness of behavior in Pennsylvania than in any other place I have ever been. I was impressed with a different opinion until I have had full opportunity of observing the gentlemen of New England, and sorry indeed am I to say it, but no people in the Union dwell more on trivial distinctions and matters of mere form. They really seem to show a readiness to stand on punctilio and ceremony. A little learning is a dangerous thing ('tis said). May not the same be said of breeding? It is certainly true that people little used with

From *The Journal of William Maclay* (New York, 1890, 1927), 4–12, 22–25, 27–28, 49, 106–114.

company are more apt to take offense, and are less easy, than men much versant in public life. They are an unmixed people in New England, and used only to see neighbors like themselves; and when once an error of behavior has crept in among them, there is small chance of its being cured; for, should they go abroad, being early used to a ceremonious and reserved behavior, and believing that good manners consists entirely in punctilios, they only add a few more stiffened airs to their deportment, excluding good humor, affability of conversation, and accommodation of temper and sentiment as qualities too vulgar for a gentleman.

30 April, Thursday

This is a great, important day. Goddess of etiquette, assist me while I describe it. The Senate met. The Vice-President rose in the most solemn manner. This son of *Adam* seemed impressed with deeper gravity, yet what shall I think of him? He often, in the midst of his most important airs—I believe when he is at loss for expressions (and this he often is, wrapped up, I suppose, in the contemplation of his own importance)—suffers an unmeaning kind of vacant laugh to escape him. This was the case to-day, and really to me bore the air of ridiculing the farce he was acting. "Gentlemen, I wish for the direction of the Senate. The President will, I suppose, address the Congress. How shall I behave? How shall we receive it? Shall it be standing or sitting?"

Here followed a considerable deal of talk from him which I could make nothing of. Mr. Lee began with the House of Commons (as is usual with him), then the House of Lords, then the King, and then back again. The result of his information was, that the Lords sat and the Commons stood on the delivery of the King's speech. Mr. Izard got up and told how often he had been in the Houses of Parliament. He said a great deal of what he had seen there. [He] made, however, this sagacious discovery, that the Commons stood because they had no seats to sit on, being arrived at the bar of the House of Lords. It was discovered after some time that the King sat, too, and had his robes and crown on.

Mr. Adams got up again and said he had been very often indeed at the Parliament on those occasions, but there always was such a crowd, and *ladies along*, that for his part he could not say how it was. Mr. Carrol got up to declare that he thought it of no consequence how it was in Great Britain; they were no rule to us, etc. But all at once the Secretary, who had been out, whispered to the Chair that the Clerk from the Representatives was at the door with a communication. Gentlemen of the Senate, how shall he be received? A silly kind of resolution of the committee on that business had been laid on the table some days ago. The amount of it was that each House should communicate to the other what and how they chose; it concluded, however, something in this way: That everything should be done with all the *propriety* that was *proper*. The question was, Shall this be adopted, that we may know how to receive the Clerk? It was objected [that] this will throw no light on the subject; it will leave you where you are. Mr. Lee brought the House of Commons before us again. He reprobated the rule; declared that the Clerk should not come within the bar of the House; that the proper mode was for the Sergeant-at-Arms, with the mace of his shoulder, to meet the Clerk at the door and receive his communication; we are not, however, provided for this ceremonious way of doing business, having neither mace nor sergeant nor Masters in Chancery, who carry down bills from the English Lords.

Here we sat an hour and ten minutes before the President arrived—this delay was owing to Lee, Izard, and Dalton, who had stayed with us while the Speaker came in, instead of going to attend the President. The President advanced between the Senate and Representatives, bowing to each. He was placed in the chair by the Vice-President; the Senate with their president on the right, the Speaker and the Representatives on his left. The Vice-President rose and addressed a short sentence to him. The import of it was that he should now take the oath of office as President. He seemed to have forgot half what he was to say, for he made a dead pause and stood for some time, to appearance, in a vacant mood. He finished with a formal bow, and the President was conducted out of the middle window into the gallery, and the oath was administered by the Chancellor. Notice that the business done was communicated to the crowd by proclamation, etc., who gave three cheers, and repeated it on the President's bowing to them.

As the company returned into the Senate chamber, the President took the chair and the Senators and Representatives their seats. He rose, and all arose also, and addressed them (see the address). This great man was agitated and embarrassed more than ever he was by the leveled cannon or pointed musket. He trembled, and several times could scarce make out to read, though it must be supposed he had often read it before. He put part of the fingers of his left hand into the side of what I think the tailors call the fall of the breeches changing the paper into his left hand. After some time he then did the same with some of the fingers of his right hand. When he came to the words *all the world,* he made a flourish with his right hand, which left rather an ungainly impression. I sincerely, for my part, wished all set ceremony in the hands of the dancing-masters, and that this first of men had read off his address in the plainest manner, without ever taking his eyes from the paper, for I felt hurt that he was not first in everything. He was dressed in deep brown, with metal buttons, with an eagle on them, white stockings, a bag, and sword.

From the hall there was a grand procession to Saint Paul's Church, where prayers were said by the Bishop. The procession was well conducted and without accident, as far as I have heard. The militia were all under arms, lined the street near the church, made a good figure, and behaved well.

The Senate returned to their chamber after service, formed, and took up the address. Our Vice-President called it *his most gracious speech.* I can not approve of this. A committee was appointed on it—Johnson, Carrol, Patterson. Adjourned. In the evening there were grand fireworks.

May 1st

Attended at the Hall at eleven. The prayers were over and the minutes reading. When we came to the minute of the speech it stood, *His most gracious speech.* I looked all around the Senate. Every countenance seemed to wear a blank. The Secretary was going on: I must speak or nobody would. "Mr. President, we have lately had a hard struggle for our liberty against kingly authority. The minds of men are still heated: everything related to that species of government is odious to the people. The words prefixed to the President's speech are the same that are

147

usually placed before the speech of his Britannic Majesty. I know they will give offense. I consider them as improper. I therefore move that they be struck out, and that it stand simply address or speech, as may be judged most suitable."

Mr. Adams rose in his chair and expressed the greatest surprise that anything should be objected to on account of its being taken from the practice of that Government under which we had lived so long and happily formerly; that he was for a dignified and respectable government, and as far as he knew the sentiments of people they thought as he did; that for his part he was one of the first in the late contest [the Revolution], and, if *he could have thought of this, he never would have drawn his sword.*

Painful as it was, I had to contend with the Chair. I admitted that the people of the colonies (now States) had enjoyed formerly great happiness under that species of government, but the abuses of that Government under which they had smarted had taught them what they had to fear from that kind of government; that there had been a revolution in the sentiments of people respecting government equally great as that which had happened in the Government itself; that even the modes of it were now abhorred; that the enemies of the Constitution had objected to it the facility there would be of transition from it to kingly government and all the trappings and splendor of royalty; that if such a thing as this appeared on our minutes, they would not fail to represent it as the first step of the ladder in the ascent to royalty. The Vice-President rose a second time, and declared that he could not possibly conceive that any person could take offense at it.

Up now rose Mr. Read, and declared for the paragraph. He saw no reason to object to it because the British speeches were styled *most gracious.* If we chose to object to words because they had been used in the same sense in Britain, we should soon be at a loss to do business. I had to reply. "It is time enough to submit to necessity when it exists. At present we are at no loss for words. The words speech or address without any addition will suit us well enough."

The unequivocal declaration that he would never have drawn his sword, etc., has drawn my mind to the following remarks: that the motives of the actors in the late Revolution were various can not be doubted. The abolishing of royalty, the extinguishment of patronage and dependencies attached to that form of government, were the exalted motives of many revolutionists, and these were the improvements meant by them to be made of the war which was forced on us by Britisth aggression—in fine, the amelioration of government and bettering the condition of mankind. These ends and none other were publicly avowed, and all our constitutions and public acts were formed in this spirit. Yet there were not wanting a party whose motives were different. They wished for the loaves and fishes of government, and cared for nothing else but a translation of the diadem and scepter from London to Boston, New York, or Philadelphia; or, in other words, the creation of a new monarchy in America, and to form niches for themselves in the temple of royalty.

This spirit manifested itself strongly among the officers at the close of the war, and I have been afraid the army would not have been disbanded if the common soldiers could have been kept together. This spirit they developed in the Order of Cincinnati, where I trust it will spend itself in a harmless flame and soon become extinguished. That Mr. Adams should, however, so unequivocally avow this motive, at a time when a republican form of government is secure to every State in the Union, appears to me a mark of extreme folly.

Mem., 1790

It is worthy of remark that about this time a spirit of reformation broke out in France which finally abolished all titles and every trace of the feudal system. Strange, indeed, that in that very country [America], where the flame of freedom had been kindled, an attempt should be made to introduce these absurdities and humiliating distinctions which the hand of reason, aided by our example, was prostrating in the heart of Europe. I, however, will endeavor (as I have hitherto done) to use the resentment of the Representatives to defeat Mr. Adams and others on the subject of titles. The pompous and lordly distinctions which the Senate have manifested a disposition to establish between the two Houses have nettled the Representatives, and this business of titles may be considered as part of the same tune. While we are debating on titles I will, through the Speaker, Mr. Muhlenberg, and other friends, get the idea suggested of answering the President's address without any title, in contempt of our deliberations, which still continue on that subject. This once effected, will confound them [the Senators] completely, and establish a precedent they will not dare to violate.

May 8th

Attended a joint committee on the papers of the old Congress. Made progress in the business. Agreed to meet at half-past ten on Monday and report. Senate formed. The Secretary, as usual, had made some mistakes, which were rectified, and now Mr. Elsworth moved for the report of the Joint Committee to be taken up on the subject of titles. It was accordingly done. Mr. Lee led the business. He took his old ground—all the world, civilized and savage, called for titles; that there must be something in human nature that occasioned this general consent; that, therefore, he conceived it was right. Here he began to enumerate many nations who gave titles—such as Venice, Genoa, and others. The Greeks and Romans, it was said, had no titles, "but" (making a profound bow to the Chair) "you were pleased to set us right in this with respect to the Conscript Fathers the other day." Here he repeated the Vice-President's speech of the 23d ultimo [April], almost verbatim all over.

Mr. Elsworth rose. He had a paper in his hat, which he looked constantly at. He repeated almost all that Mr. Lee had said, but got on the subject of kings—declared that the sentence in the primer of *fear God and honor the king* was of great importance; that kings were of divine appointment; that Saul, the head and shoulders taller than the rest of the people, was elected by God and anointed by his appointment.

I sat, after he had done, for a considerable time, to see if anybody would rise. At last I got up and first answered Lee as well as I could with nearly the same arguments, drawn from the Constitution, as I had used on the 23d ult. I mentioned that within the space of twenty years back more light had been thrown on the subject of governments and on human affairs in general than for several generations before; that this light of knowledge had diminished the veneration for titles, and that mankind now considered themselves as little bound to imitate the follies of civilized nations as the brutalities of savages; that the abuse of power and the fear of bloody masters had extorted titles as well as adoration, in some instances from the trembling crowd; that the impression now on the minds of the citizens of these States was that of horror for kingly authority.

Izard got up. He dwelt almost entirely on the antiquity of kingly government. He could not, however, well get further back than Philip of Macedon. He seemed to have forgot both Homer and the Bible. He urged for something equivalent to nobility having been common among the Romans, for they had three names that seemed to answer to honorable, or something like it, before and something behind. He did not say Esquire. Mr. Carrol rose and took my side of the question. He followed nearly the track I had been in, and dwelt much on the information that was now abroad in the world. He spoke against kings. Mr. Lee and Mr. Izard were both up again. Elsworth was up again. Langdon was up several times, but spoke short each time. Patterson was up, but there was no knowing which side he was of. Mr. Lee considered him as against him and answered him, but Patterson finally voted with Lee. The Vice-President repeatedly helped the speakers for titles. Esworth was enumerating how common the appellation of President was. The Vice-President put him in mind that there were presidents of fire companies and of a cricket club. Mr. Lee at another time was saying he believed some of the States authorized title by their Constitutions. The Vice-President, from the chair, told him that Connecticut did it. At sundry other times he interfered in a like manner. I had been frequently up to answer new points during the debate.

I collected myself for a last effort. I read the clause in the Constitution against titles of nobility; showed that the spirit of it was against not only granting titles by Congress, but against the permission of foreign potentates granting *any titles whatever;* that as to kingly government, it was equally out of the question, as a republican government was guaranteed to every State in the Union; that they were both equally forbidden fruit of the Constitution. I called the attention of the House to the consequences that were like to follow; that gentlemen seemed to court a rupture with the other House. The Representatives had adopted the report, and were this day acting on it, or according to the spirit of the report. We were proposing a title. Our conduct would mark us to the world as actuated by the spirit of dissension, and the characters of the Houses would be as aristocratic and democratical.

The report [of the Committee on Titles] was, however, rejected. "Excellency" was moved for as a title by Mr. Izard. It was withdrawn by Mr. Izard, and "highness" with some prefatory word, proposed by Mr. Lee. Now long harangues were made in favor of this title. "Elective" was placed before. It was insisted that such a dignified title would add greatly to the weight and authority of the Government both at home and abroad. I declared myself totally of a different opinion; that at present it was impossible to add to the respect entertained for General Washington; that if you gave him the title of any foreign prince or potentate, a belief would follow that the manners of that prince and his modes of government would be adopted by the President. (Mr. Lee had, just before I got up, read over a list of the titles of all the princes and potentates of the earth, marking where the word "highness" occurred. The Grand Turk had it, all the princes of Germany had [it], sons and daughters of crown heads, etc.) That particularly "elective highness," which sounded nearly like "electoral highness," would have a most ungrateful sound to many thousands of industrious citizens who had fled from German oppression; that "highness" was part of the title of a prince or princes of the blood, and was often given to dukes; that it was degrading our President to place him on a par with any prince of any blood in Europe, nor was there one of them that could enter the list of true glory with him.

But I will minute no more. The debate lasted till half after three o'clock, and it ended in appointing a committee to consider of a title to be given to the President. This whole silly business is the work of Mr. Adams and Mr. Lee; Izard follows Lee, and the New England men, who always herd together, follow Mr. Adams. Mr. Thompson says this used to be the case in the old Congress. I had, to be sure, the greatest share in this debate, and must now have completely sold (no, sold is a bad word, for I have got nothing for it) every particle of court favor, for a court our House seems determined on, and to run into all the fooleries, fopperies, fineries, and pomp of royal etiquette; and all this for Mr. Adams.

May 9th

Attended the Hall at ten o'clock to go on the Judicial Committee. Met many of the members. I know not the motive, but I never was received with more familiarity, nor quite so much, before by the members. Elsworth in particular seemed to show a kind of fondness. The Judicial Committee did no business. Senate formed. It took a long time to correct the minutes. Otis keeps them miserably. At length the committee came in and reported a title—*His Highness the President of the United States of America and Protector of the Rights of the Same.*

I rose. Mr. President, the Constitution of the United States has designated our Chief Magistrate by the appellation of the *President of the United States of America.* This is his title of office, nor can we alter, add to, or diminish it without infringing the Constitution. In like manner persons authorized to transact business with foreign powers are styled *Ambassadors, Public Ministers,* etc. To give them any other appellation would be an equal infringement. As to grades or orders or titles of nobility, nothing of the kind can be established by Congress.

Can, then, the President and Senate do that which is prohibited to the United States at large? Certainly not. Let us read the Constitution: *No title of nobility shall be granted by the United States.* The Constitution goes further. The servants of the public are prohibited from accepting them from any foreign state, king, or prince. So that the appellations and terms given to nobility in the Old World are contraband language in the United States, nor can we apply them to our citizens consistent with the Constitution. As to what the common people, soldiers, and sailors of foreign countries may think of us, I do not think it imports us much. Perhaps the less they think, or have occasion to think of us, the better.

But suppose this a desirable point, how is it to be gained? The English excepted, foreigners do not understand our language. We must use Hohen Mogende to a Dutchman. Beylerbey to a Turk or Algerine, and so of the rest. From the English indeed we may borrow terms that would not be wholly unintelligible to our own

151

citizens. But will they thank us for the compliment? Would not the plagiarism be more likely to be attended with contempt than respect among all of them? It has been admitted that all this is nonsense to the philosopher. I am ready to admit that every high-sounding, pompous appellation, descriptive of qualities which the object does not possess, must appear bombastic nonsense in the eye of every wise man. But I can not admit such an idea with respect to government itself. Philosophers have admitted not the utility but the necessity of it [government], and their labors have been directed to correct the vices and expose the follies which have been ingrafted upon it, and to reduce the practice of it to the principles of common sense, such as we see exemplified by the merchant, the mechanic, and the farmer, whose every act or operation tends to a productive or beneficial effect, and, above all, to illustrate this fact, that government was instituted for the benefit of the people, and that no act of government is justifiable that has not this for its object. Such has been the labor of philosophers with respect to government, and sorry indeed would I be if their labors should be in vain.

May 26th

Attended the Hall early. Was the first. Mr. Morris came next, the Vice-President next. I made an apology to the Vice-President for the absence of our chaplain, Mr. Linn. There had been some conversation yesterday in the Senate about the style of the Bishop. It had been entered on the minutes *right reverend*. The Vice-President revived the discourse; got at me about titles. I really never had opened my mouth on the affair of yesterday. He, however, addressed to me all he said, concluding: "You are against titles. But there are no people in the world so much in favor of titles as the people of America; and the Government never will be properly administered until they are adopted in the fullest manner." "We think differently, indeed, on the same subject. I am convinced that were we to adopt them in the fashion of Europe, we would ruin all. You have told us, sir, that they are idle in a philosophic point of view. Governments have been long at odds with common sense. I hope the conduct of America will reconcile them. Instead of adding respect to government, I consider that they would bring the personages who assume them into contempt and ridicule."

July 14th

The Senate met, and one of the bills for organizing one of the public departments—that of Foreign Affairs—was taken up. After being read, I begged leave of the Chair to submit some general observations, which, though apparently diffuse, I considered as pertinent to the bill before us, the first clause of which was, "There shall be an Executive Department," etc. There are a number of such bills, and may be many more, tending to direct the most minute particle of the President's conduct. If he is to be directed, how he shall do everything, it follows he must do nothing without direction. To what purpose, then, is the executive power lodged with the President, if he can do nothing without a law directing the mode, manner, and, of course, the thing to be done?" May not the two Houses of Congress, on this principle, pass a law depriving him of all powers? You may say it will not get his approbation. But two thirds of both Houses will make it a law without him, and the Constitution is undone at once.

Gentlemen may say, How is the Government then to proceed on these points? The simplest in the world. The President communicates to the Senate that he finds such and such officers necessary in the execution of the Government, and nominates the man. If the Senate approve, they will concur in the measure; if not, refuse their consent, etc., when the appointments are made. The President, in like manner, communicates to the House of Representatives that such appointments have taken place, and require adequate salaries. Then the House of Representatives might show their concurrence or disapprobation, by providing for the officer or not. I thought it my duty to mention these things, though I had not the vanity to think that I would make any proselytes in this stage of the business; and, perhaps, the best apology I could make was not to detain them long. I likewise said that, if the Senate were generally of my mind, a conference between the Houses should take place. But the sense of the House would appear on taking the question upon the first clause. The first clause was carried.

Now came the second clause. It was for the appointment of a chief clerk by the Secretary, who, in fact, was to be the principal, *"whenever the said principal officer shall be removed from office by the President of the United States."* There was a blank pause at the end of it. I was not in haste, but rose first: Mr. President, whoever attends strictly to the Constitution of the United States, will readily observe that the part assigned to the Senate was an important one—no less than that of being the great check, the regulator and corrector, or, if I may so speak, the balance of this Government. In their legislative capacity they not only have the concoction of all bills, orders, votes, or resolutions, but may originate any of them, save money bills. In the executive branch they have likewise power to check and regulate the proceedings of the President. Thus treaties, the highest and most important part of the Executive Department, must have a concurrence of two thirds of them. All appointments under the President and Vice-President, must be by their advice and consent, unless they concur in passing a law divesting themselves of this power. By the checks which are intrusted with them upon both the Executive and the other branch of the Legislature, the stability of the Government is evidently placed in their hands.

The approbation of the Senate was certainly meant to guard against the mistakes of the President in his appointments to office. I do not admit the doctrine of holding commissions 'during pleasure' as constitutional, and shall speak to that point presently. But, supposing for a moment, that to be the case, is not the same guard equally necessary to prevent improper steps in removals as in appointments? Certainly, common inference or induction can mean nothing short of this. It is a maxim in legislation as well as reason, and applies well in the present case, that it requires the same power to repeal as to enact. The depriving power should be the same as the appointing power.

But was this a point left at large by the Constitution? Certainly otherwise. Five or six times in our short Constitution is the trial by impeachment mentioned. In one place, the House of Representatives shall have the sole power of impeachment. In another, the Senate shall have the sole power to try impeachments. In a third, judgment shall not extend further than to removal from office, and disqualification to hold or enjoy offices, etc. The President shall not pardon in cases of impeachment. The President, Vice-President, and *all civil officers* of the United States, shall be removed from office on impeachment, etc. No part of the Constitution is so fully guarded as or more clearly expressed than this part of it. And most justly, too, for every good Government guards the reputation of her citizens as well as their life and property. Every turning out of office is attended with reproach, and the person so turned out is stigmatized with infamy. By means of impeachment a fair hearing and trial are secured to the party. Wthout this, what man of independent spirit would accept of such an office? Of what service can his abilities be to the community if afraid of the nod or beck of a superior? He must consult his will in every matter. Abject servility is most apt to mark the line of his conduct, and this on the one hand will not fail to be productive of despotism and tyranny on the other; for I consider mankind composed nearly of the same materials in America as in Asia, in the United States as in the East Indies. The Constitution certainly never contemplated any other mode of removing from office. The case is not omitted here; the most ample provision is made. If gentlemen do not like it, let them obtain an alteration of the Constitution; but this can not be done by law.

If the virtues of the present Chief Magistrate are brought forward as a reason for vesting him with extraordinary powers, no nation ever trod more dangerous ground. His virtues will depart with him, but the powers which you give him will remain, and if not properly guarded will be abused by future Presidents if they are men. This, however, is not the whole of the objection I have to the clause. A chief clerk is to be appointed, and this without any advice or consent of the Senate. This chief clerk, on the removal of the Secretary, will become the principal in the office, and so may remain during the presidency, for the Senate can not force the President into a nomination for a new officer. This is a direct stroke at the power of the Senate. Sir, I consider the clause as exceptional every way, and therefore move you to strike it out.

Langdon jumped up in haste; hoped the whole would not be struck out, but moved that the clause only of the President's removing should be struck out. Up rose Elsworth, and a most elaborate speech indeed did he make, but it was all drawn from writers on the distribution of government. The President was the executive officer. He was interfered with in the appointment, it is true, but not in the removal. The Constitution had taken one, but not the other, from him. Therefore, removal remained to him entire. He carefully avoided the subject of impeachment. He absolutely used the following expressions with regard to the President: *"It is sacrilege to touch a hair of his head, and we may as well lay the President's head on the block and strike it off with one blow."* The way he came to use these words was after having asserted that removing from office was his (the President's) privilege, we might as well do this as to deprive him of it. He [Elsworth] had sore eyes, and had a green silk over them. On pronouncing the last of the two sentences, he paused, put his handkerchief to his face, and either shed tears or affected to do so.

When he sat down both Butler and Izard sprang up. Butler, however, continued up. He began with a declaration that he came into the House in the most perfect state of indifference, and rather disposed to give the power in question to the President. But the arguments of the honorable gentleman from Connecticut [Elsworth], in endeavoring to support the clause, had convinced him, in the clearest manner, that the clause was highly improper, and he would vote against it. Izard now got at it, and spoke very long against the clause. Strong got up for the clause, and a most confused speech he made, indeed. I have notes of it, but think it really not worth answering, unless to show the folly of some things that he said. Dr. Johnson rose and told us twice before he proceeded far that he would not give an opinion on the power of the President. This man's conscience would not let him; he is a thorough-paced courtier, yet he wishes not to lose his interest with the President. However, his whole argument went against the clause, and at last he declared he was against the whole of it. Mr. Lee rose. He spoke long and pointedly against the clause. He repeated many of my arguments, but always was polite enough to acknowledge the mention I had made of them. He spoke from a paper which he held in his hand. He continued until it was past three o'clock, and an adjournment was called for and took place.

In looking over my notes I find I omitted to set down sundry arguments which I used. But no matter; I will not do it now.

July 15th

Senate met. Mr. Carrol showed impatience to be up first. He got up and spoke a considerable length of time. The burden of his discourse seemed to be the want of power in the President, and a desire of increasing it. Great complaints of what is called the *atrocious assumption of power in the States*. Many allusions to the power of the British kings. *The king can do no wrong.* If anything improper is done, it should be the Ministers that should answer. How strangely this man has changed!

The Collection bill was called for and read for the first time. Now Elsworth rose with a most lengthy debate. The first words he said were, "In this case the Constitution is our only rule, for we are sworn to support it." But [he] neither quoted it nor ever named it afterward except as follows. He said by allusion, "I buy a square acre of land. I buy the trees, water, and everything belonging to it. The executive power belongs to the President. The removing of officers is a tree on this acre. The power of removing is, therefore, his. It is in him. It is nowhere else. Thus we are under the necessity of ascertaining by implication where the power is." He called Dr. Johnson Thomas Aquinas by implication, too, and said things rather uncivil to some other of his opponents. Most carefully did he avoid entering on the subject of impeachment. After some time, however, he got fairly on new ground. Lamented the want of power in the President. Asked, Did we *ever quarrel* with the power of the Crown of Great Britain? No, we contended with the power of the Parliament. No one ever thought the power of the Crown too great. [He] said he was growing infirm, should die, and should not see it, but the Government would fail for want of power in the President. He would have power as far as he would be seen in his coach-and-six. "We must extend the executive arm." (Mr. Lee yesterday had said something about the Dutch.) "If we must have examples," said he, "let us draw them from the people whom we used always to imitate; from the nation who

155

have made all others bow before them, and not from the Dutch, who are divided and factious." He said a great deal more, but the above is all I minuted down at the time. Mr. Izard rose and answered. Mr. Butler rose and spoke. It was after three. Mr. Lee rose; said he had much to say, but would now only move an adjournment. As it was late, the House accordingly adjourned.

July 16th

Attended pretty early this morning. Many were, however, there before me. It was all huddling away in small parties. Our Vice-President was very busy indeed; running to every one. He openly attacked Mr. Lee before me on the subject in debate, and they were very loud on the business. I began to suspect that the court party had prevailed. Senate, however, met, and at it they went. Mr. Lee began, but I really believe the altercation, though not a violent one, which he had with the Vice-President had hurt him, for he was languid and much shorter than ever I had heard him on almost any subject. Mr. Patterson got up. For a long time you could not know what he would be at. After, however, he had warmed himself with his own discourse, as the Indians do with their war-songs, he said he was for the clause continuing. He had no sooner said so than he assumed a bolder tone of voice; flew over to England; extolled its Government; wished, in the most unequivocal language, that our President had the same powers; said, let us take a second view of England; repeating nearly the same thing. Let us take a third view of it, said he. And then he abused Parliament for having made themselves first triennial and lastly septennial. Speaking of the Constitution, he said expressly these words, speaking of the removing of officers: "There is not a word of removability in it." His argument was that the Executive held this as a matter of course.

Mr. Wyngate got up and said something for striking out. Mr. Read rose, and was swinging on his legs for an hour. He had to talk a great deal before he could bring himself to declare against the motion. But now a most curious scene opened. Dalton rose and said a number of things in the most hesitating and embarrassed manner. It was his recantation; [he] had just now altered his mind. From what had been said by the honorable gentleman from Jersey, he was now for the clause. Mr. Izard was so provoked that he jumped up; declared nothing had fallen from that gentleman that could possibly convince any man; that men might pretend so, but the thing was impossible.

Mr. Morris' face had reddened for some time. He rose hastily, threw censure on Mr. Izard; declared that the canting man behaved like a man of honor; that Patterson's arguments were good and sufficient to convince any man. The truth, however, was that everybody believed that John Adams was the great converter.

But now recantation was in fashion. Mr. Bassett recanted, too, though he said he had prepared himself on the other side. We now saw how it would go, and I could not help admiring the frugality of the court party in procuring recantations, or votes, which you please. After all the arguments were ended and the question taken the Senate was ten to ten, and the Vice-President with joy cried out, "It is not a vote!" without giving himself time to declare the division of the House and give his vote in order. Every man of our side, in giving his sentiments, spoke with great freedom, and seemed willing to avow his opinion in the openest manner. Not a man of the others who had made any speech to the merits of the matter, but went about it and about it. I called this singing the war-song, and I told Mr. Morris I would give him every one whom I heard sing the war-song; or, in other words, those who could not avow the vote they were fully minded to give until they had raised spirits enough by their own talk to enable them to do it. Grayson made a speech. It was not long, but he had in it this remarkable sentence: "The matter predicted by Mr. Henry is now coming to pass: consolidation is the object of the new Government, and the first attempt will be to destroy the Senate, as they are the representatives of the State Legislatures."

It has long been a maxim with me that no frame of government whatever would secure liberty or equal administration of justice to a people unless virtuous citizens were the legislators and Governors. I live not a day without finding new reason to subscribe to this doctrine. What avowed and repeated attempts have I seen to place the President above the powers stipulated for him by the Constitution!

The vote stood: For striking out—Butler, Izard, Langdon, Johnson, Wyngate, Few, Gunn, Grayson, Lee, Maclay—ten. Against striking out: Read, Bassett, Elsworth, Strong, Dalton, Patterson, Elmer, Morris, Henry, Carrol—ten; and John Adams.

16

The American Hero

Mason L. Weems (1759–1825), born in Maryland, was an Episcopal clergyman and book agent. After his ordination in England, he returned to America to spend most of his life wandering through the country selling books, some of which he wrote himself. Weems's emphasis on good works and religious piety was expressed in a series of biographies and moralizing tracts. Besides Washington, his subjects included Benjamin Franklin, William Penn, and the Revolutionary hero, General Francis Marion.

Of all his works, the most memorable was the study of Washington, which appeared for the first time in 1800, only months after the great man's death. Deliberately seeking to produce a best seller, Weems was remarkably successful; in the next one hundred years more than eighty printings were made, some of his episodes becoming staples of children's literature. Although Weems's inventiveness and imagination far outweighed his commitment to historical accuracy, this semifictional account profoundly influenced all subsequent biographers, positively or negatively. The popularity of his fables shows some of the qualities Americans demanded from their heroes, even though such standards were rarely attainable.

THE LIFE OF WASHINGTON
Mason L. Weems

CHAPTER II

BIRTH AND EDUCATION

To this day numbers of good Christians can hardly find faith to believe that Washington was, bona fide, *a Virginian! What! a buckskin!"* say they with a smile, *"George Washington a buckskin! pshaw! impossible! he was certainly an European: So great a man could never have been born in America."*

So *great a man could never have been born in America!* Why that's the very *prince of reasons* why he should have been born here! Nature, we know, is fond of

Reprinted by permission of the publishers from Marcus Cunliffe, editor, Mason L. Weems, *The Life of Washington*. Cambridge, Mass.: The Belknap Press of Harvard University Press, Copyright, 1962, by the President and Fellows of Harvard College. Pp. 6–12, 162–177, 181–182, 185–186.

harmonies; and *paria paribus,* that is, *great things to great,* is the rule she delights to work by. Where, for example, do we look for the *whale* "the biggest born of nature?" not, I trow, in a *millpond,* but in the main ocean; *"there go the great ships,"* and there are the spoutings of whales amidst their boiling foam.

By the same rule, where shall we look for Washington, the greatest among men, but in *America?* That greatest Continent, which, rising from beneath the frozen pole, stretches far and wide to the south, running almost *"whole the length of this vast terrene,"* and sustaining on her ample sides the roaring shock of half the watery globe. And equal to its size, is the furniture of this vast continent, where the Almighty has reared his cloud-capt mountains, and spread his sea-like lakes, and poured his mighty rivers, and hurled down his thundering cataracts in a style of the *sublime,* so far superior to any thing of the kind in the other continents, that we may fairly conclude that great men and great deeds are designed for America.

This seems to be the verdict of honest analogy; and accordingly we find America the honoured cradle of Washington, who was born on Pope's creek, in Westmoreland county, Virginia, the 22nd of February, 1732. His father, whose name was Augustin Washington, was also a Virginian, but his grandfather (John) was an Englishman, who came over and settled in Virginia in 1657.

His father fully persuaded that a marriage of virtuous love comes nearest to angelic life, early stepped up to the *altar* with glowing cheeks and joy sparkling eyes, while by his side, with soft warm hand, sweetly trembling in his, stood the angel form of the lovely Miss Dandridge.

After several years of great domestic happiness, Mr. Washington was separated by death, from this excellent woman, who left him and two children to lament her early fate.

Fully persuaded still, that *"it is not good for man to be alone,"* he renewed, for the second time, the chaste delights of matrimonial love. His consort was Miss Mary Ball, a young lady of fortune, and descended from one of the best families in Virginia.

. . . . By his first wife, Mr. Washington had two children, both sons—Lawrence and Augustin. By his second wife, he had five children, four sons and a daughter—George, Samuel, John, Charles, and Elizabeth. Those *over delicate* ones, who are ready to faint at thought of a second marriage, might do well to remember, that the greatest man that ever lived was the son of this second marriage! . . .

To assist his son to overcome that selfish spirit which too often leads children to fret and fight about trifles, was a notable care of Mr. Washington. For this purpose, of all the presents, such as cakes, fruit, &c. he received, he was always desired to give a liberal part to his play-mates. To enable him to do this with more alacrity, his father would remind him of the love which he would hereby gain, and the frequent presents which would in return be made *to him;* and also would tell of that great and good God, who delights above all things to see children love one another, and will assuredly reward them for acting so amiable a part. . . .

Never did the wise Ulysses take more pains with his beloved Telemachus, than did Mr. Washington with George, to inspire him with an *early love of truth.* "Truth, George," (said he) "is the loveliest quality of youth. I would ride fifty

159

miles, my son, to see the little boy whose heart is so *honest,* and his lips so *pure,* that we may depend on every word he says. O how lovely does such a child appear in the eyes of every body! His parents doat on him; his relations glory in him; they are constantly praising him to their children, whom they beg to imitate him. They are often sending for him, to visit them; and receive him, when he comes, with as much joy as if he were a little angel, come to set pretty examples to their children.

"But, Oh! how different, George, is the case with the boy who is so given to lying, that nobody can believe a word he says! He is looked at with aversion wherever he goes, and parents dread to see him come among their children. Oh, George! my son! rather than see you come to this pass, dear as you are to my heart, gladly would I assist to nail you up in your little coffin, and follow you to your grave. Hard, indeed, would it be to me to give up my son, whose little feet are always so ready to run about with me, and whose fondly looking eyes and sweet prattle make so large a part of my happiness: but still I would give him up, rather than see him a common liar.

"Pa, (said George very seriously) do I ever tell lies?"

"No, George, I *thank God* you do not, my son; and I rejoice in the hope you never will. At least, you shall never, from me, have cause to be guilty of so shameful a thing. Many parents, indeed, even compel their children to this vile practice, by barbarously beating them for every little fault; hence, on the next offence, the little terrified creature slips out a *lie!* just to escape the rod. But as to yourself, George, you know I have *always* told you, and now tell you again, that, whenever by accident you do any thing wrong, which must often be the case, as you are but a poor little boy yet, without *experience* or *knowledge,* never tell a falsehood to conceal it; but come *bravely* up, my son, like a *little man,* and tell me of it: and instead of beating you, George, I will but the more honour and love you for it, my dear."

This, you'll say, was sowing good seed!—Yes, it was: and the crop, thank God, was, as I believe it ever will be, where a man acts the true parent, that is, the *Guardian Angel,* by his child.

The following anecdote is a *case in point.* It is too valuable to be lost, and too true to be doubted; for it was communicated to me by the same excellent lady to whom I am indebted for the last.

"When George," said she, "was about six years old, he was made the wealthy master of a *hatchet!* of which, like most little boys, he was immoderately fond, and was constantly going about chopping every thing that came in his way. One day, in the garden, where he often amused himself hacking his mother's pea-sticks, he unluckily tried the edge of his hatchet on the body of a beautiful young English cherry-tree, which he barked so terribly, that I don't believe the tree ever got the better of it. The next morning the old gentleman finding out what had befallen his tree, which, by the by, was a great favourite, came into the house, and with much warmth asked for the mischievous author, declaring at the same time, that he would not have taken five guineas for his tree. Nobody could tell him any thing about it. Presently George and his hatchet made their appearance. *George,* said his father, *do you know who killed that beautiful little cherry-tree yonder in the garden?* This was a *tough question;* and George staggered under it for a moment; but quickly recovered himself: and looking at his father, with the sweet face of youth brightened with the inexpressible charm of all-conquering truth, he bravely cried out, *"I can't tell a lie, Pa; you know I can't tell a lie. I did cut it with my hatchet."*— *Run to my arms, you dearest boy,* cried his father in transports, *run to my arms; glad am I, George, that you killed my tree; for you have paid me for it a thousand fold. Such an act of heroism in my son, is more worth than a thousand trees, though blossomed with silver, and their fruits of purest gold.* . . .

CHAPTER XII

THE DEATH OF WASHINGTON

If the prayers of millions could have prevailed, Washington would have been immortal on earth. And if fulness of peace, riches, and honours could have rendered that immortality happy, Washington had been blessed indeed. But this world is not the place of true happiness. Though numberless are the satisfactions, which a prudence and virtue like Washington's may enjoy in this world, yet they fall short, infinite degrees, of that pure, unembittered felicity, which the Almighty parent has prepared in heaven for the spirits of the just.

To prepare for this immensity of bliss, is the real errand on which God sent us into the world. Our preparation consists in acquiring those great virtues, purity and love, which alone can make us *worthy* companions of angels, and fit partakers of their exalted delights. Washington had wisely spent life in acquiring the IMMORTAL VIRTUES. *"He had fought the good fight"* against his own unreasonable affections; *he had glorified God,* by exemplifying the charms of virtue to men; *he had borne the heat and burden of the day*—his *great* day of duty; and the evening (of old age) being come, the servant of God must now go to receive his wages. Happy Washington! If crowns and kingdoms could have purchased such peace as thine, such hopes big with immortality, with what begging earnestness would crowns and kingdoms have been offered by the mighty conquerors of the earth, in their dying moments of *terror* and *despair!*

On the 14th of December, 1799 (when he wanted but 9 weeks and 2 days of being 68 years old), he rode out to his mill, 3 miles distant. The day was raw and rainy. The following night he was attacked with a violent pain and inflammation of the throat. The lancet of one of his domestics was employed, but with no advantage. Early in the morning, Dr. Craik, the friend and physician of his youth and age, was sent for. Alarmed at the least appearance of danger threatening a life so dear to him, Dr. Craik advised to call in, immediately, the consulting assistance of his friends, the ingenious and learned Drs. Dick, of Alexandria, and Brown, of Port Tobacco. They came on the wings of speed. They felt the awfulness of their situation. The greatest of human beings was lying low: a life, of all others the most *revered,* the most *beloved,* was at stake. And if human skill could have saved—if the sword of genius, and the buckler of experience could have turned the stroke of death, Washington had still lived. But his *hour was come.*

It appears, that, from the commencement of the attack, he was favoured with a presentiment, that he was now laid down to rise no more. He took, however, the medicines that were offered him, but it was principally from a sense of *duty*.

It has been said that a man's death, is generally a copy of his life. It was Washington's case exactly. In his last illness he behaved with the firmness of a soldier, and the resignation of a christian.

The inflammation in his throat was attended with great pain, which he bore with the fortitude that became him. He was, once or twice, heard to say that, *had it pleased God, he should have been glad to die a little easier; but that he doubted not that it was for his good.*

Every hour now spread a sadder gloom over the scene. Despair sat on the faces of the physicians; for they saw that their art had failed! The strength of the mighty was departing from him; and death, with his sad harbingers, chills and paleness, was coming on apace.

Mount Vernon, which had long shone the queen of elegant joys, was now about to suffer a sad eclipse! an eclipse, which would soon be mournfully visible, not only through the United States, but throughout the whole world.

Sons and daughters of Columbia, gather yourselves together around the bed of your expiring father—around the last bed of him to whom under God you and your children owe many of the best blessings of this life. When Joseph the prime minister of Egypt heard his *shepherd father* was sick, he hastened up, to see him; and fell on his face and kissed him, and wept a long while. But Joseph had never received such services from Jacob as you have received from Washington. But we call you not to weep for Washington. We ask you not to view those eyes, now sunk and hollow, which formerly darted their lightning flashes against your enemies—nor to feel that heart, now faintly labouring, which so often throbbed with more than mortal joys when he saw his young countrymen charging like lions, upon the foes of liberty. No! we call you not to weep, but to rejoice. Washington, who so often conquered himself, is now about to conquer the last enemy.

Silent and sad, his physicians sat by his bedside, looking on him as he lay panting for breath. They thought on the past, and the tear swelled in their eyes. He marked it, and, stretching out his hand to them, and shaking his head, said, *"O no!—don't! don't!"* then with a delightful smile added, "I am dying, gentlemen: but, thank God, I am not afraid to die."

Feeling that the hour of his departure out of this world was at hand, he desired that every body would quit the room. They all went out, and according to his wish, left him—with his God.

There, by himself, like Moses alone on the top of Pisgah, he seeks the face of God. There, *by himself,* standing as on the awful boundary that divides time from eternity, that separates this world from the next, he cannot quit the long-frequented haunts of the one, nor launch away into the untried regions of the other, until (in humble imitation of the world's great Redeemer) he has poured forth into the bosom of his God those strong sensations which the solemnity of the situation naturally suggested.

With what angel fervour did he adore that *Almighty Love*, which, though inhabiting the heaven of heavens, deigned to wake his sleeping dust—framed him so fearfully in the womb—nursed him on a tender mother's *breast*—watched his helpless infancy—guarded his heedless youth—preserved him from the dominion of his passions—inspired him with the love of virtue—led him safely up to man—and, from such low beginnings, advanced him to such unparalleled usefulness and glory among men! These, and ten thousand other precious gifts heaped on him, unasked, many of them long before he had the knowledge to ask, overwhelmed his soul with gratitude unutterable, exalted to infinite heights his ideas of eternal love, and bade him without fear resign his departing spirit into the arms of his Redeemer God, whose mercies are over all his works.

He is now about to leave the great family of man, in which he has so long sojourned! The yearnings of his soul are over his brethren! How fervently does he adore that *goodness,* which enabled him to be so serviceable to them! That *grace,* which preserved him from injuring them by violence or fraud! How fervently does he pray that the *unsuffering kingdom of God may come,* and that the earth may be filled with the richest fruits of righteousness and peace!

He is now about to leave his *country!* that dear spot which gave him birth!—that dear spot for which he has so long watched and prayed, so long toiled and fought; and whose beloved children he has so often sought to gather, even as a hen gathereth her chickens under her wings. He sees them now spread abroad like flocks in goodly pastures; like favoured Israel in the land of promise. He remembers how God, by a mighty hand, and by an out-stretched arm, brought their fathers into this good land, a land flowing with milk and honey: and blessed them with the blessings of heaven above, and the earth beneath; with the blessings of LIBERTY and of PEACE, of RELIGION and of LAWS, above all other people. He sees that, through the rich mercies of God, they have now the precious opportunity to continue their country the GLORY of the earth, and a refuge for the poor and for the persecuted of all lands! The transporting sight of such a cloud of blessings, trembling close over the heads of his countrymen, together with the distressing uncertainty whether they will put forth their hands and enjoy them, shakes the *parent soul* of Washington with feelings *too strong* for his *dying frame!* The last tear that he is ever to shed now steals into his eye—the last groan that he is ever to heave is about to issue from his faintly labouring heart.

Feeling that the silver chord of life is loosing, and that his spirit is ready to quit her old companion the body, he extends himself on his bed—closes his eyes for the *last* time, with his own hands—folds his arms decently on his breast, then breathing out *"Father of mercies! take me to thyself,"*—he fell asleep.

Swift on angels' wings the brightening saint ascended; while voices more than human were heard (*in Fancy's ear*) warbling through the happy regions, and hymning the great procession towards the gates of heaven. His glorious coming was seen far off, and myriads of mighty angels hastened forth, with golden harps, to welcome the honoured stranger. High in front of the shouting hosts, were seen the beauteous forms of FRANKLIN, WARREN, MERCER, SCAMMEL, and of him who fell at Quebec, with all the virtuous patriots, who, on the side of Columbia, toiled or bled for *liberty* and *truth.* But oh! how changed from what they were, when, in

163

their days of flesh, bathed in sweat and blood, they fell at the parent feet of their weeping country! Not the homeliest infant suddenly springing into a soul-enchanting Hebe—not dreary winter, suddenly brightening into spring, with all her bloom and fragrance, ravishing the senses, could equal such glorious change. Oh! where are now their wrinkles and grey hairs? Where their ghastly wounds and clotted blood? Their forms are of the stature of angels—their robes like morning clouds streaked with gold—the stars of heaven, like crowns glitter on their heads—immortal youth, *celestial rosy red,* sits blooming on their cheeks; while infinite benignity and love beam from their eyes. Such were the forms of thy sons, O Columbia! such the brother band of thy martyred saints, that now poured forth from heaven's wide-opening gates, to meet thy Washington; to meet their beloved chief, who in the days of his mortality, had led their embattled squadrons to the war. At sight of him, even these *blessed spirits* seem to feel new raptures, and to look more dazzling bright. In joyous throngs they pour around him—they devour him with their eyes of love—they embrace him in transports of tenderness unutterable; while from their roseate cheeks, tears of joy, such as angels weep, roll down.

All that followed was too much for the over-dazzled eye of *Imagination.* She was seen to return, with the quick panting bosom and looks entranced of a fond mother, near swooning at sudden sight of a dear loved son, deemed *lost,* but now *found,* and raised to *kingly honours!* She was heard passionately to exclaim, with palms and eyes lifted to heaven, *"O, who can count the stars of Jacob, or number the fourth part of the blessings of Israel!—Let me die the death of Washington, and may my latter end be like his!"*

Let us now return to all that remained of Washington on the earth. He had expressly ordered in his will that he should be buried in a private *manner, and without any parade.* But this was impossible; for who could stay at home when it was said, *"to-day general Washington is to be buried!"* On the morning of the 18th, which was fixed on for his funeral, the people poured in by thousands to pay him the *last respect, and,* as they said, *to take their last look.* And, while they looked on him, nature stirred that at their hearts, which quickly brought the best blood into their cheeks, and rolled down the tears from their eyes. About two o'clock, they bore him to his long home, and buried him in his own family vault, near the banks of the great Potomac. And to this day, often as the ships of war pass that way, they waken up the thunder of their loudest guns, pointed to the spot, as if to tell the sleeping hero that he is not forgotten in his narrow dwelling.

The news of his death soon reached Philadelphia, where congress was then in session. A question of importance being on the carpet that day, the house, as usual, was much interested. But, soon as it was announced—"GENERAL WASHINGTON IS DEAD"—an instant stop was put to all business—the tongue of the orator was struck dumb—and a midnight silence ensued, save when it was interrupted by deepest sighs of the members, as, with drooping foreheads rested on their palms, they sat, each absorbed in mournful cogitation. Presently, as utterly unfit for business, both houses adjourned; and the members retired slow and sad to their lodgings, like men who had suddenly heard of the death of a father.

For several days hardly any thing was done in congress; hardly any thing thought of but to talk of and to praise the departed Washington. In this patriotic work all parties joined with equal alacrity and earnestness. In this all were *federalists,* all were *republicans.* Elegant addresses were exchanged between the two houses of congress and the president, and all of them replete with genius and gratitude.

Then, by unanimous consent, congress came to the following resolutions:

1st. That a grand marble monument should be erected at the city of Washington, under which, with permission of his lady, the body of the general should be deposited.

2d. That there should be a funeral procession from congress hall to the German Lutheran church to hear an oration delivered by one of the members of congress.

3d. That the members of congress should wear full mourning during the session.

4th. That it should be recommended to the people of the United States, to wear crape on the left arm, as mourning, for 30 days.

But, thank God, the people of the United States needed not the hint contained in the last resolution. Though they could not all very elegantly speak, yet their actions showed that they all very deeply *felt* what they owed to Washington. For in every city, village, and hamlet, the people were so struck on hearing of his death, that long before they heard of the resolution of congress, they ran together to ease their troubled minds in talking and hearing talk of Washington, and to devise some public mode of testifying their sorrow for his death. Every where throughout the continent, churches and court houses were hung in black, mourning was put on, processions were made, and sermons preached, while the crowded houses listened with pleasure to the praises of Washington, or sighed and wept when they heard of his toils and battles for his country.

CHAPTER XIII

CHARACTER OF WASHINGTON

When the children of the years to come, hearing his great name re-echoed from every lip, shall say to their fathers, *"what was it that raised Washington to such height of glory?"* let them be told that it was HIS GREAT TALENTS, CONSTANTLY GUIDED AND GUARDED BY RELIGION. For how shall man, *frail man,* prone to inglorious ease and pleasure, ever ascend the arduous steps of virtue, unless animated by the *mighty hopes* of religion? Or what shall stop him in his swift descent to infamy and vice, if unawed by that dread power which proclaims to the guilty that their secret crimes are seen, and shall not go unpunished? Hence the wise, in all ages, have pronounced, that *"there never was a truly great man without religion."*

There have, indeed, been *courageous generals,* and *cunning statesmen,* without religion, but mere courage or cunning, however paramount, never yet made a man great.

No! to be truly great, a man must have not only great talents, but those talents must be constantly exerted on great, i. e. good actions—*and perseveringly* too—for if he should turn aside to vice—farewel to his heroism. . . . But, sensual and grovelling as man is, what can incline and elevate him to those things like religion, that divine power, to whom alone it belongs to present those vast and eternal *goods* and *ills* which best alarm our fears, enrapture our hopes, inflame the worthiest loves, rouse the truest avarice, and in short touch every spring and passion of our souls in favour of virtue and noble actions. . . .

"There exists," says Washington, *"in the economy of nature, an inseparable connexion between duty and advantage."*—The whole life of this great man bears glorious witness to the truth of this his favourite aphorism. At the giddy age of fourteen, when the spirits of youth are all on tiptoe for freedom and adventures, he felt a strong desire to go to sea; but, very opposite to his wishes, his mother declared that she could not bear to part with him. His trial must have been very severe; for I have been told that a midshipman's commission was actually in his pocket—his trunk of clothes on board the ship—his honour in some sort pledged—his young companions importunate with him to go—and his whole soul panting for the promised pleasures of the voyage; but religion whispered *"honour thy mother, and grieve not the spirit of her who bore thee."*

Instantly the glorious boy sacrificed inclination to duty—dropt all thoughts of the voyage, and gave tears of joy to his widowed mother, in clasping to her bosom a dear child who could deny himself to make her happy. . . .

"Well," replied she embracing him tenderly, *"God, I hope, will reward my dear boy for this, some day or other."* Now see here, young reader, and learn that HE who prescribes our duty, is able to reward it. Had George left his fond mother to a broken heart, and gone off to sea, 'tis next to certain that he would never have taken that active part in the French and Indian war, which, by securing to him the hearts of his countrymen, paved the way for all his future greatness.

Now for another instance of the wonderful effect of religion on Washington's fortune. Shortly after returning from the war of Cuba, Lawrence (his *half* brother) was taken with the consumption, which made him so excessively fretful, that his *own* brother, Augustin, would seldom come near him. But George, whose heart was early under the softening and sweetening influences of religion, felt such a tenderness for his poor sick brother, that he not only put up with his peevishness, but seemed, from what I have been told, never so happy as when he was with him. He accompanied him to the island of Bermuda, in quest of health—and, after their return to Mount Vernon, often as his duty to lord Fairfax permitted, he would come down from the back woods to see him. And while with him he was always contriving or doing something to cheer and comfort his brother. Sometimes with his gun he would go out in quest of partridges and snipes, and other fine flavoured game, to tempt his brother's sickly appetite, and gain him strength. At other times he would sit for hours and read to him some entertaining book—and, when his cough came on, he would support his drooping head, and wipe the cold dew from his forehead, or the phlegm from his lips, and give him his medicine, or smooth his pillow; and all with such alacrity and artless tenderness as proved the sweetest cordial to his brother's spirits. For he was often heard to say to the Fairfax family, into which he married, that *"he should think nothing of his sickness, if he could but always have his brother George with him."* Well, what was the consequence? Why, when Lawrence came to die, he left almost the whole of his large estate to George, which served as another noble step to his future greatness. . . .

In the winter of '77, while Washington, with the American army lay encamped at Valley Forge, a certain good old FRIEND, of the respectable family and name of Potts, if I mistake not, had occasion to pass through the woods near head-quarters. Treading his way along the venerable grove, suddenly he heard the sound of a human voice, which as he advanced increased on his ear, and at length became like the voice of one speaking much in earnest. As he approached the spot with a cautious step, whom should he behold, in a dark natural bower of ancient oaks, but the commander in chief of the American armies on his knees at prayer! Motionless with surprise, friend Potts continued on the place till the general, having ended his devotions, arose, and, with a countenance of angel serenity, retired to headquarters: friend Potts then went home, and on entering his parlour called out to his wife, "Sarah, my dear! Sarah! All's well! all's well! George Washington will yet prevail!"

"What's the matter, Isaac?" replied she; "thee seems moved."

"Well, if I seem moved, 'tis no more than what I am. I have this day seen what I never expected. Thee knows that I always thought the sword and the gospel utterly inconsistent; and that no man could be a soldier and a christian at the same time. But George Washington has this day convinced me of my mistake."

He then related what he had seen, and concluded with this prophetical remark—"If George Washington be not a man of God, I am greatly deceived—and still more shall I be deceived if God do not, through him, work out a great salvation for America." . . .

"Of all the dispositions and habits which lead to the prosperity of a nation," says Washington, "religion is the indispensable support. Volumes could not trace all its connexions with private and public happiness. Let it simply be asked, where is the security for property, for reputation, for life itself, if there be no fear of God on the minds of those who give their oaths in courts of justice!"

But some will tell us, that *human laws* are sufficient for the purpose!

Human laws!—Human nonsense! For how often, even where the cries and screams of the wretched called aloud for lightning-speeded vengeance, have we not seen the sword of human law loiter in its coward scabbard, afraid of angry royalty? Did not that vile queen Jezebel, having a mind to compliment her husband with a vineyard belonging to poor Naboth, suborn a couple of villains to take a false oath against him, and then cause him to be dragged out with his little motherless, crying babes, and barbarously stoned to death?

Great God! what bloody tragedies have been acted on the poor ones of the earth, by kings and great men, who were *above* the laws, and had no sense of religion to keep them in awe!—And if men be not above the laws, yet what horrid crimes! what ruinous robberies! what wide-wasting flames! what cruel murders may they not commit in *secret,* if they be not withheld by the sacred arm of religion! "In vain, therefore," says WASHINGTON, "would that man claim the tribute of patriotism, who should do any thing to discountenance religion and morality, those great pillars of human happiness, those firmest props of the duties of men and citizens. The mere politician, equally with the pious man, ought to respect and cherish them."

But others have said, and with a serious face too, that a *sense of honour,* is sufficient to preserve men from base actions! O blasphemy to sense! Do we not daily hear of *men of honour,* by dice and cards, draining their fellow-citizens of the last cent, reducing them to a dung-hill, or driving them to a pistol? Do we not daily hear of *men of honour* corrupting their neighbours' wives and daughters, and then murdering their husbands and brothers in duels? Bind such selfish, such inhuman beings, by a sense of honour!! Why not bind roaring lions with cobwebs? "No," exclaims Washington, "whatever a sense of honour may do on men of refined education, and on minds of a peculiar structure, reason and experience both forbid us to expect that national morality can prevail, in exclusion of religious principles."

And truly Washington had abundant reason, from his own *happy experience*, to recommend religion so heartily to others.

For besides all those inestimable favours which he received from her at the hands of her celestial daughters, the *Virtues;* she threw over him her own magic mantle of *Character.* And it was this that immortalized Washington. By inspiring his countrymen with the profoundest veneration for him as the *best of men,* it naturally smoothed his way to supreme command; so that when War, that monster of hell, came on roaring against America, with all his death's heads and garments rolled in blood, the nation unanimously placed Washington at the head of their armies, from a natural persuasion that so good a man must be the peculiar favourite of Heaven, and the fastest friend of his country. How far this precious instinct in favour of goodness was corrected, or how far Washington's conduct was honourable to religion and glorious to himself and country, bright ages to come, and happy millions yet unborn, will, we hope, declare.

17

Spreading the Gospel

Lorenzo Dow (1777–1834) was one of the most famous, if eccentric, evangelists of his era. Born in Connecticut, he began his Methodist preaching while in his teens, traveling immense distances on horseback to carry the gospel into isolated rural areas of New England. After a trip to Europe he returned to spend some time preaching in the South, where he witnessed and helped inspire some of the violent ecstasies of camp meetings. His later years were spent preparing revised editions of his journals and issuing a series of pamphlets on various subjects. His preachings and writings were characteristically vivid and militant, suggesting the temperament of a man who willingly bore the hardships of itineracy and the hostility of the unconverted to carry his version of religious truth to frontier America.

THE JOURNAL
OF LORENZO DOW

I was born, October 16, 1777, in Coventry, Tolland County, State of Connecticut. My parents were born in the same town and descended from English ancestors. They had a son, and then three daughters, older than myself, and one daughter younger. They were very tender towards their children, and endeavored to educate them well, both in religion and common learning.

When I was two years old, I was taken sick; and my parents having been a long journey and returning homeward, heard of my dangerous illness, and that I was dead, and they expected to meet the people returning from my funeral. But to their joy, I was living; and beyond the expectation of all, I recovered.

When I was between three and four years old, one day, while I was at play with my companion, I suddenly fell into a muse about God and those places called heaven and hell, which I heard people converse about, so that I forgot my play, which my companion observing, desired to know the cause. I asked him if ever he said his prayers, morning or night; to which he replied, "No." Then said I, "You are wicked, and I will not play with you." So I quit his company and went into the house.

My mind, frequently on observing the works of creation, desired to know the cause of things; and I asked my parents many questions which they scarcely knew how to answer.

From *The Life, Travels, Labors, and Writings of Lorenzo Dow* (New York, 1859), 13–18, 20–22, 24, 27, 30–31, 126–127, 132–135, 155–157.

One day I was the means of killing a bird, and upon seeing it gasp, I was struck with horror. And upon seeing any beast struggle in death it made my heart beat hard, as it would cause the thoughts of my death to come into my mind. Death appeared such a terror to me, I sometimes wished that I might be translated as Enoch and Elijah were; and at other times I wished I had never been born.

When past the age of thirteen years, and about the time that JOHN WESLEY died, (1791), it pleased God to awaken my mind by a dream of the night, which was, that an old man came to me at mid-day, having a staff in his hand, and said to me, "Do you ever pray?" I told him, "No." Said he, "You must;" and then went away. He had not been long gone before he returned; and said again, "Do you pray?" I again said, "No." And after his departure I went out of doors, and was taken up by a whirlwind and carried above the skies. At length I discovered, across a gulf, as it were through a mist of darkness, a glorious place, in which was a throne of ivory overlaid with gold, and God sitting upon it, and Jesus Christ at his right hand, and angels and glorified spirits celebrating praise.—Oh! the joyful music! I thought the angel Gabriel came to the edge of heaven, holding a golden trumpet in his right hand, and cried to me with a mighty voice to know if I desired to come there. I told him I did. Said he, "You must go back to yonder world, and if you will be faithful to God, you shall come here in the end."

With reluctance I left the beautiful sight and came back to the earth again. And then I thought the old man came to me the third time and asked me if I had prayed. I told him I had. "Then," said he, "BE FAITHFUL, AND I WILL COME AND LET YOU KNOW AGAIN." I thought that was to be when I should be blest. And when I awakened, behold it was a dream. But it was strongly impressed on my mind, that this singular dream must be from God; and the way that I should know it, I should let my father know of it at such a time and in such a place, viz. as he would be feeding the cattle in the morning, which I accordingly did. No sooner had I done it than keen conviction seized my heart. I knew I was unprepared to die. Tears begun to run down plentifully, and I again resolved to seek the salvation of my soul. I began that day to pray in secret; but how to pray or what to pray for, I scarcely knew.

If now I had had any one to instruct me in the way and plan of salvation, I doubt not but I should have found salvation. But, alas, I felt like one wandering and benighted in an unknown wilderness, who wants both light and a guide. The Bible was like a sealed book; so mysterious I could not understand it. And in order to hear it explained, I applied to this person and that book; but got no satisfactory instruction. I frequently wished I had lived in the days of the prophets or apostles, that I could have had sure guides; for by the misconduct of professors, I thought there were no Bible saints in the land. Thus with sorrow many months heavily rolled away.

But at length, not finding what my soul desired, I began to examine the cause more closely, if possible to find it out: and immediately the doctrine of unconditional *reprobation* and particular *election* was exhibited to my view—that the state of all was unalterably fixed by God's *"eternal decrees."* Here discouragements arose, and I began to slacken my hand by degrees, until I entirely left off secret prayer, and could not bear to read or hear the scriptures, saying, "If God has foreordained whatever comes to pass, then all our labors are vain."

Feeling still condemnation in my breast, I concluded myself reprobated. Despair of mercy arose, hope was fled, and I was resolved to end my wretched life; concluding the longer I live, the more sin I shall commit, and the greater my punishment will be; but the shorter my life, the less sin, and of course the less punishment, and the sooner I shall know that the worst of my case. Accordingly I loaded a gun, and withdrew to a wilderness.

As I was about to put my intention into execution, a sudden solemn thought darted into my mind, "Stop and consider what you are about: if you end your life, you are undone for ever; but if you omit it a few days longer, it may be that something will turn up in your favor." This was attended with a small degree of hope, that if I waited a little while, it should not be altogether in vain. And I thought I felt thankful that God prevented me from sending my soul to everlasting misery.

About this time there was much talk about the people called Methodists, who were lately come into the western part of New England. There were various reports and opinions concerning them. Some said they were the deceivers that were to come in the last times; that such a delusive spirit attended them, that it was dangerous to hear them preach, lest they should lead people out of the good old way which they had been brought up in; and that they would deceive if possible the very elect. Some, on the other hand, said they were a good sort of people.

A certain man invited Hope Hull to come to his own town, who appointed a time when he would endeavor, if possible, to comply with his request. The day arrived, and the people flocked out from every quarter to hear, as they supposed, a new gospel. I went to the door and looked in to see a Methodist; but to my surprise he appeared like other men. I heard him preach from—"This is a faithful saying and worthy of all acception, that Christ Jesus came into the world to save sinners." And I thought he told me all that ever I did.

The next day he preached from these words: "Is there no balm in Gilead? Is there no Physician there? Why then is not the health of the daughter of my people recovered?" Jer. viii. 22.

As he drew the analogy between a person sick of a consumption and a sin-sick soul, he endeavored also to show how the real balm of Gilead would heal the consumption; and to spiritualize it, in the blood of Christ healing the soul; in which he described the way to heaven, and pointed out the way-marks, which I had never heard described so clearly before. I was convinced that this man enjoyed something that I was destitute of, and consequently that he was a servant of God.

He then got upon the application, and pointing his finger towards me, made this expression: "Sinner, there is a frowning Providence above your head, and a burning hell beneath your feet; and nothing but the brittle thread of life prevents your soul from falling into endless perdition. But, says the sinner, What must I do? You must pray. But I can't pray. If you don't pray, then you'll be damned." And as he brought out the last expression he either stamped with his foot on the box on which he stood, or smote with his hand upon the Bible, which both together came

171

home like a dagger to my heart. I had like to have fallen backwards from my seat, but saved myself by catching hold of my cousin who sat by my side, and I durst not stir for some time for fear lest I should tumble into hell. My sins, and the damnable nature of them, were in a moment exhibited to my view; and I was convinced that I was unprepared to die.

After the assembly was dismissed, I went out of doors. All nature seemed to wear a gloomy aspect; and every thing I cast my eyes upon seemed to bend itself against me, and wish me off the face of the earth.

I went to a funeral of one of my acquaintance the same day, but durst not look upon the corpse, for fear of becoming one myself. I durst not go near the grave, fearing lest I should fall in, and the earth come in upon me; for if I then died, I knew I must be undone. So I went home with a heavy heart.

I durst not close my eyes in sleep, until I first attempted to supplicate the throne of grace for preservation through the night. The next morning, as I went out of doors, a woman passing by told me that my cousin the evening before had found the pardoning love of God. This surprised me, that one of my companions was taken and I was left. I instantly came to a resolution to forsake my sins and seek the salvation of my soul. I made it my practice to pray thrice in a day for about the space of a week; when another of my cousins, brother to the former, was brought to cry for mercy in secret retirement in a garden, and his cries were so loud that he was heard upwards of a mile. The same evening he found comfort.

One evening there being, by my desire, a prayer-meeting appointed by the young converts, I set out to go; and on my way, by the side of a wood, I kneeled down and made a solemn promise to God, if he would pardon my sins and give me an evidence of my acceptance, that I would forsake all those things wherein I had formerly thought to have taken my happiness, and lead a religious life devoted to him; and with this promise I went to meeting.

I believe that many present felt the power of God. Saints were happy and sinners were weeping on every side: but I could not shed a tear. Then I thought within myself, if I could weep I would begin to take hope; but, oh! how hard is my heart! I went from one to another to know if there was any mercy for me. The young converts answered, "God is all love; he is all mercy." I replied, "God is just too, and justice will cut me down." I saw no way how God could be *just* and yet show me mercy.

When I got home, I went into my bedroom; and, kneeling down, I strove to look to God for mercy again; but found no comfort. I then lay down to rest, but durst not close my eyes in sleep, for fear I should never awake, until I awaked in endless misery.

I strove to plead with God for mercy, for several hours, as a man would plead for his life; until at length being weary in body, as the night was far spent, I fell into a slumber.

I thought I heard the voice of God's justice saying, "Take the unprofitable servant, and cast him into utter darkness." I put my hands together, and cried in my heart, "The time has been, that I might have had religion, but now it is too late; mercy's gate is shut against me, and my condemnation for ever sealed:—Lord, I give up; I submit; I yield; if there be mercy in heaven for me, let me know it; and if not, let me go down to hell and know the worst of my case." As these words flowed from my heart, I saw the Mediator step in, as it were, between the Father's justice and my soul, and these words were applied to my mind with great power; "Son! thy sins which are many are forgiven thee; thy faith hath saved thee; go in peace."

The burden of sin and guilt and the fear of hell vanished from my mind, as perceptibly as a hundred pounds weight falling from a man's shoulder; my soul flowed out in love to God, to his ways and to his people; yea, and to *all* mankind.

As soon as I obtained deliverance, I said in my heart, I have now found Jesus and his religion, but I will keep it to myself. But instantly my soul was so filled with peace, and love, and joy, that I could no more keep it to myself, seemingly, than a city set on a hill could be hid. At this time daylight dawned into the window. I arose, and went out of doors; and, behold, every thing I cast my eye upon, seemed to be speaking forth the praise and wonders of the Almighty. It appeared more like a new world than any thing else I can compare it to. This happiness is easier felt than described.

CHAPTER II

CALL TO PREACH, ETC.

One day being alone in a solitary place, whilst kneeling before God, these words were suddenly impressed on my mind: "Go ye into all the world, and preach the gospel to every creature." I instantly spoke out, "Lord, I am a child, I cannot go; I cannot preach." These words followed in my mind: "Arise, and go, for I have sent you." I said, "Send by whom thou wilt send, only not by me, for I am an ignorant, illiterate youth, not qualified for the important task." The reply was, "What God hath cleansed, call not thou common." I resisted the impression as a temptation of the devil; and then my Saviour withdrew from me the light of his countenance. I dared not believe that God had called me to preach, for fear of being deceived; and durst not disbelieve it, for fear of grieving the Spirit of God: thus I halted between two opinions.

1794

One day a prayer meeting being appointed in the town, and I feeling it my indispensable duty to go, I sought for my parents' consent in vain. Still, something was crying in my ears, "Go, go;" but fearing that my parents would call me a disobedient child, I resisted what I believe was required of me, and felt conscience to accuse me, and darkness to cover my mind. But at length, finding a spirit of prayer, I had faith to believe that God would bless me, though from the fourteenth of May to the ninth of June, I felt the sharp, keen, fiery darts of the enemy.

Sunday, October fifth, was the first time that I (with a trembling mind) attempted to open my mouth in public vocal prayer in the society.

A little previous to this time, upon considering what I must undergo if I entered upon the public ministry, I began to feel discouraged, and had thoughts of altering the situation of my life to excuse me from the work; but I could get no peace of

173

mind until I gave them entirely up, though my trials in this respect were exceedingly great.

Nov. 19th

My mind has been buffeted and greatly agitated, not tempted in the common sense of the word, so that my sleep departed from me, and caused me to walk and wring my hands for sorrow. Oh, *the corruption of wicked* nature! I feel the plague of a hard heart, and a mind prone to wander from God; something within which has need to be done away, and causes a burden, but no guilt, and from which discouragements frequently arise tending to slacken my hands.

I dreamed that I saw a man in a convulsion fit, and his countenance was expressive of hell. I asked a bystander what made his countenance look so horrible. Said he, "The man was sick and relating his past experience, his calls from time to time, and his promises to serve God; and how he had broke them; and now, said he, I am sealed over to eternal damnation, and instantly the convulsion seized him." This shocked me so much that I instantly awaked, and seemingly the man was before my eyes.

I dropped asleep again, and thought I saw all mankind in the air suspended by a brittle thread over hell, yet in a state of carnal security. I thought it to be my duty to tell them of it, and again awaked; and these words were applied to my mind with power: "There is a dispensation of the gospel committed unto you, and wo unto you if you preach not the gospel." I strove to turn my mind on something else; but it so strongly followed me, that I took it as a warning from God. And in the morning, to behold the beautiful sun to arise and shine into the window, whilst these words followed—"Unto you that fear my name, shall the Sun of Righteousness arise, with healing in his wings"—Oh! how happy I felt! The help of kings and priests is vain without the help of God.

December 31st

The year is now at a close. I see what I have passed through. What is to come the ensuing year, God only knows. But may the God of peace be with me, and grant me strength in proportion to my day, that I may endure to the end, and receive the crown of life. I felt my heart drawn to travel the world at large; but to trust God by faith, like the birds, for my daily bread was difficult, as my strength was small; and I shrunk from it.

CHAPTER III

MY BEGINNING TO TRAVEL

1796

March 30th. This morning early I set out for Rhode Island in quest of J. Lee, who was to attend a quarterly meeting there. As I was coming away, we joined in prayer, taking leave of each other; and as I got on my road, I looked about, and espied my mother looking after me until I got out of sight; this caused me some tender feelings afterwards.

Until this time I have enjoyed the comforts of a kind father's house; and oh! must I now become a wanderer and stranger upon earth until I get to my long-home!

Monday, October 10th

I rode twenty miles to Adams, and thence to Stanford: at these places we had refreshing seasons.

Wednesday, 12th

I rode thirty miles across the Green Mountain, in fifteen of which there was not a sign of a house; and the road being new, it frequently was almost impassable. However, I reached my appointment, and though weary in body, my soul was happy in God.

Leaving the state of Vermont, I crossed Connecticut river, through Northfield to Warwick, Massachusetts, where we had a refreshing season.

Thence I went to Orange, and preached in the Presbyterian meeting house, the clergyman having left the town. Being this day nineteen years old, I addressed myself to the youth. I spent a few days here; and, though meeting with some opposition, we had refreshing seasons.

October 20th

Satan pursues me from place to place. Oh! how can people dispute there being a devil! If they underwent as much as I do with his buffetings, they would dispute it no more. He throwing in his fiery darts, my mind is harassed like punching the body with forks and clubs. Oh that my Saviour would appear and sanctify my soul, and deliver me from all within that is contrary to purity!

23rd

I spoke in Hardwick to about four hundred people, thence went to Petersham and Wenchendon, to Fitchburgh, and likewise to Notown, where God gave me one spiritual child. Thence to Ashburnham, where we had some powerful times.

November 1st

I preached in Ringe, and a powerful work of God broke out shortly after, though some opposition attended it; but it was very solemn.

Some here, I trust, will bless God in the day of eternity that ever they saw my face in this vale of tears.

In my happiest moments I feel something that wants to be done away. Oh! the buffeting of Satan! if I never had any other hell, it would be enough.

Thence proceeded to Marlborough, where our meetings were not in vain.

Whilst I am preaching I feel happy. But as soon as I have done, I feel such horror, without guilt, by the buffetings of Satan, that I am ready to sink like a drowning man, sometimes to that degree that I have to hold my tongue between my teeth to keep from uttering blasphemous expressions; and I can get rid of these horrible feelings only by retirement in earnest prayer and exertion of faith in God.

Part Second

CHAPTER I

CAROLINAS AND TENNESSEE TOUR

October 28th, 1803

After an absence of about seven months, I arrived back in Georgia, having travelled upwards of four thousand miles. When I left this state, I was handsomely

175

equipped for travelling, by some friends whom God had raised me up in time of need, after my trials on my journey from New England. My equipment was as follows: My horse cost forty-five pounds, a decent saddle and cloth, portmanteau and bag, umbrella and lady's shove whip, a double suit of clothes, a blue broadcloth cloak (given me by a gentleman), shoes, stockings, cased hat, a valuable watch, with fifty-three dollars in my pocket for spending-money, &c., &c. But now on my return I had not the same valuable horse, and my watch I parted with for pecuniary aid to bear my expenses. My pantaloons were worn out, and my riding chevals were worn through in several places.

I had no stockings, shoes, nor moccasins, for the last several hundred miles, nor outer garment, having sold my cloak in West Florida. My coat and vest were worn through to my shirt; my hat-case and umbrella were spoiled by prongs of trees, whilst riding in the woods. Thus with decency I was scarcely able to get back to my friends as I would. It is true, I had many pounds and handsome presents offered me in my journey, but I could not feel freedom to receive them, only just what would serve my present necessity, to get along to my appointments, as I was such a stranger in the country, and so many to watch me (as an impostor) for evil, and but few to lift up my hands for good.

As I considered that the success and opening of many years depended on these days, I was not willing to give any occasion for the gospel to be blamed, or any occasion to hedge up my way. For it was with seriousness and consideration that I undertook these journeys, from conviction of duty, that God required it at my hands. And, knowing that impostors are fond of money, I was convinced that Satan would not be found wanting to whisper in the minds of the people, that my motives were sinister or impure.

Major John Oliver came and took me by the hand, calling me father, saying, "When you preached in Petersburgh last, your text was constantly ringing in my ears, for days together, whether I would deal kindly and truly with the Master, &c.; so I had no peace until I set out to seek the Lord: and since, my wife and I have been brought to rejoice in the Almighty."

He gave me a vest, pantaloons, umbrella, stockings, handkerchief, and a watch, &c. Another gave me a pair of shoes and a coat, a third, a cloak, and a few shillings for spending-money from some others. Thus I find that Providence, whose tender care is over all his works, by his kind hand is still preserving me. Oh, may I never betray his great cause committed to my charge!

February 14th

I had heard about a singularity called the *jerks or jerking exercise,* which appeared first near Knoxville in August last, to the great alarm of the people, which reports at first I considered as vague and false. But at length, like the Queen of Sheba, I set out to go and see for myself, and sent over these appointments into this country accordingly.

When I arrived in sight of this town, I saw hundreds of people collected in little bodies, and observing no place appointed for meeting, before I spoke to any, I got on a log and gave out a hymn; which caused them to assemble around, in solemn attentive silence. I observed several involuntary motions in the course of the meeting, which I considered as a specimen of the jerks. I rode seven miles behind a man across streams of water, and held meeting in the evening, being ten miles on my way.

In the night I grew uneasy, being twenty-five miles from my appointment for next morning at eleven o'clock. I prevailed on a young man to attempt carrying me with horses until day, which he thought was impracticable, considering the darkness of the night, and the thickness of the trees. Solitary shrieks were heard in these woods, which he told me were said to be the cries of murdered persons. At day we parted, being still seventeen miles from the spot, and the ground covered with a white frost. I had not proceeded far, before I came to a stream of water, from the springs of the mountain, which made it dreadful cold. In my heated state I had to wade this stream five times in the course of an hour, which I perceived so affected my body, that my strength began to fail. Fears began to arise that I must disappoint the people, till I observed some fresh tracks of horses, which casued me to exert every nerve to overtake them, in hopes of aid or assistance on my journey, and soon I saw them on an eminence. I shouted for them to stop till I came up. They inquired what I wanted? I replied, I had heard there was a meeting at Seversville by a stranger, and was going to it. They replied, that they had heard that a crazy man was to hold forth there, and were going also; and perceiving that I was weary, they invited me to ride: and soon our company was increased to forty or fifty, who fell in with us on the road from different plantations. At length I was interrogated whether I knew any thing about the preacher. I replied, "I have heard a good deal about him, and have heard him preach, but I have no great opinion of him." And thus the conversation continued for some miles before they found me out, which caused some color and smiles in the company. Thus, I got on to meeting; and after taking a cup of tea gratis, I began to speak to a vast audience, and I observed about thirty to have the jerks. Though they strove to keep still as they could, these emotions were involuntary and irresistible, as any unprejudiced eye might discern. Lawyer Porter, who had come a considerable distance, got his heart touched under the word, and being informed how I came to meeting, voluntarily lent me a horse to ride near one hundred miles, and gave me a dollar, though he had never seen me before.

Hence to Marysville, where I spoke to about one thousand five hundred; and many appeared to feel the word, but about fifty felt the jerks. At night I lodged with one of the Nicholites, a kind of Quakers who do not feel free to wear colored clothes. I spoke to a number of people at his house that night. Whilst at tea, I observed his daughter (who sat opposite to me at table) to have the jerks, and dropped the tea-cup from her hand in the violent agitation. I said to her, "Young woman, what is the matter?" She replied, "I have got the jerks." I asked her how long she had it? She observed, "A few days," and that it had been the means of the awakening and conversion of her soul, by stirring her up to serious consideration about her careless state, &c.

Sunday, February 19th, I spoke in Knoxville to hundreds more than could get into the courthouse, the governor being present. About one hundred and fifty appeared to have the jerking exercise, among whom was a circuit preacher

177

(Johnson) who had opposed them a little before, but he now had them powerfully; and I believe he would have fallen over three times had not the auditory been so crowded that he could not unless he fell perpendicularly.

After meeting, I rode eighteen miles to hold a meeting at night. The people of this settlement were mostly Quakers, and they had said (as I was informed) the Methodists and Presbyterians have the *jerks* because they *sing* and *pray* so much; but we are a still, peaceable people, wherefore we do not have them. However, about twenty of them came to the meeting, to hear one, as they said, somewhat in a Quaker line. But their usual stillness and silence was interrupted, for about a dozen of them had the jerks as keen and as powerful as any I had seen, so as to have occasioned a kind of grunt or groan when they would jerk. It appears that many have undervalued the great revival, and attempted to account for it altogether on natural principles; therefore it seems to me (from the best judgment I can form) that God hath seen proper to take this method to convince people, that he will work in a way to show his power, and sent the *jerks* as a sign of the times, partly in judgment for the people's unbelief, and yet as a mercy to convict people of divine realities.

I have seen Presbyterians, Methodists, Quakers, Baptists, Episcopalians, and Independents, exercised with the *jerks*—gentleman and lady, black and white, the aged and the youth, rich and poor, without exception; from which I infer, as it cannot be accounted for on natural principles, and carries such marks of involuntary motion, that it is no trifling matter. I believe that those who are most pious and given up to God, are rarely touched with it, and also those naturalists who wish and try to get it to philosophize upon it, are excepted. But the lukewarm, lazy, half-hearted, indolent professor is subject to it; and many of them I have seen, who, when it came upon them, would be alarmed and stirred up to redouble their diligence with God; and after they would get happy, were thankful it ever came upon them. Again, the wicked are frequently more afraid of it than the small-pox or yellow fever; these are subject to it. But the persecutors are more subject to it than any; and they sometimes have cursed, and swore, and damned it whilst jerking. There is no pain attending the jerks except they resist it, which if they do, it will weary them more in an hour than a day's labor, which shows that it requires the *consent* of the *will* to avoid suffering.

20th

I passed by a meeting-house, where I observed the undergrowth had been cut up for a camp-meeting, and from 50 to 100 saplings left breast-high, which to me appeared so slovenish that I could not but ask my guide the cause, who observed they were topped so high and left for the people to jerk by. This so excited my attention that I went over the ground to view it, and found where the people had laid hold of them and jerked so powerfully that they had kicked up the earth as a horse stamping flies. I observed some emotion both this day and night among the people. A Presbyterian minister (with whom I stayed) observed, "Yesterday whilst I was preaching some had the jerks, and a young man from North Carolina mimicked them out of derision, and was seized with them himself (which was the case with many others). He grew ashamed, and on attempting to mount his horse to go off, his foot jerked about so that he could not put it into the stirrup; some youngsters seeing this assisted him on, but he jerked so that he could not sit alone, and one got up to hold him on, which was done with difficulty. I observing this, went to him and asked him what he thought of it?" Said he, "I believe God sent it on me for my wickedness, and making so light of it in others;" and he requested me to pray for him.

I observed his wife had it; she said she was first attacked with it in bed. Dr. Nelson said he had frequently strove to get it in order to philosophize upon it, but could not, and observed they could not account for it on natural principles.

Friday, 19th

Camp-meeting commenced at Liberty. Here I saw the *jerks;* and some danced: a strange exercise indeed. However, it is involuntary, yet requires the consent of the will: i. e. the people are taken jerking irresistibly; and if they strive to resist it, it worries them much: yet is attended by no bodily pain, and those who are exercised to dance, (which in the pious seems an antidote to the jerks,), if they resist, it brings deadness and barrenness over the mind; but when they yield to it they feel happy, although it is a great cross. There is a heavenly smile and solemnity on the countenance, which carries a great conviction to the minds of beholders. Their eyes when dancing seem to be fixed upwards, as if upon an invisible object, and they lost to all below.

Sunday, 21st

I heard Doctor Tooley, a man of liberal education, who had been a noted deist, preach on the subject of the jerks and the dancing exercise. He brought ten passages of scripture to prove that dancing was once a religious exercise, but corrupted at Aaron's calf, and from thence young people got it for amusement. I believe the congregation and preachers were generally satisfied with his remarks.

Sunday, 25th

I spoke for the last time at Natchez. I visited Seltzertown, Greenville, and Gibson Port. This last place was a wilderness not two years ago, but now contains near thirty houses, with a courthouse and jail. We held a quarterly meeting on Clarke's creek. Some supposed I would get no campers, but at this quarterly meeting I wanted to know if there were any backsliders in the auditory, and if there were and they would come forward, I would pray with them. An old backslider, who had been happy in the old settlement, with tears came forward and fell upon his knees, and several followed his example. A panic seized the congregation, and a solemn awe ensued. We had a cry and shout, and it was a weeping, tender time. The devil was angry, and some without persecuted, saying, "Is God deaf, that they cannot worship him without such a noise?" though they perhaps would make a greater noise when drinking a toast. This prepared the way for the camp-meeting, and about thirty from this neighborhood went thirty miles or upwards, and encamped on the ground. The camp-meeting continued four days. The devil was angry at this also, and though his emissaries contrived various projects to raise a dust, their efforts proved ineffectual. In general there was good decorum, and about fifty were awakened, and five professed justifying faith; so that it may now be said that the country which was a refuge for scape-gallowses a few years since, in

Spanish times, is in a hopeful way, and the wilderness begins to bud and blossom as the rose, and the barren land becomes a fruitful field. I crossed the Mississippi into Louisiana, and visited several settlements, holding religious meetings. I believe there is a peculiar providence in such a vast territory falling to the United States, as liberty of conscience may now prevail as the country populates, which before was prohibited by the inquisition.

18

The Cost of Embargo

Henry Adams (1838–1918) was a great-grandson of one President and grandson of another. Although he failed to gain political power or prominence himself, he turned from his anger with the incivilities of the late nineteenth century to immerse himself in the chronicles of earlier, more inspiring eras. He became an accomplished historian, teaching for a number of years at Harvard before moving to Washington. There, he turned to the early national period, producing biographies of Albert Gallatin and John Randolph. In 1889 he published the first two volumes of his *History of the United States*, which covered the first administration of Jefferson. In the next two years he published seven more volumes, which went through 1816 and the last years of James Madison's Presidency.

Adams' portrait of Thomas Jefferson, his great-grandfather's friend and antagonist, was a masterful and ironic glimpse of unsuccessful statesmanship. The image of the great Republican leader, unintentionally destroying the sources of his political power in his desperate search to avoid war, was one of the great aesthetic accomplishments of the *History*. It was also, of course, a vindication and defense of Adams' own distinguished ancestor.

THE SECOND ADMINISTRATION OF THOMAS JEFFERSON
Henry Adams

CHAPTER XII

The embargo was an experiment in politics well worth making. In the scheme of President Jefferson's statesmanship, non-intercourse was the substitute for war,—the weapon of defence and coercion which saved the cost and danger of supporting army or navy, and spared America the brutalities of the Old World. Failure of the embargo meant in his mind not only a recurrence to the practice of war, but to every political and social evil that war had always brought in its train. In such a case the crimes and corruptions of Europe, which had been the object of his

From *History of the United States of America during the Second Administration of Thomas Jefferson* (New York, 1890), II: 272–289.

political fears, must, as he believed, sooner or later teem in the fat soil of America. To avert a disaster so vast, was a proper motive for statesmanship, and justified disregard for smaller interests. Jefferson understood better than his friends the importance of his experiment; and when in pursuing his object he trampled upon personal rights and public principles, he did so, as he avowed in the Louisiana purchase, because he believed that a higher public interest required the sacrifice:—

"My principle is, that the conveniences of our citizens shall yield reasonably, and their taste greatly, to the importance of giving the present experiment so fair a trial that on future occasions our legislators may know with certainty how far they may count on it as an engine for national purposes."

Hence came his repeated entreaties for severity, even to the point of violence and bloodshed:—

"I do consider the severe enforcement of the embargo to be of an importance not to be measured by money, for our future government as well as present objects."

Everywhere, on all occasions, he proclaimed that embargo was the alternative to war. The question next to be decided was brought by this means into the prominence it deserved. Of the two systems of statesmanship, which was the most costly,—which the most efficient?

The dread of war, radical in the Republican theory, sprang not so much from the supposed waste of life or resources as from the retroactive effects which war must exert upon the form of government; but the experience of a few months showed that the embargo as a system was rapidly leading to the same effects. Indeed, the embargo and the Louisiana purchase taken together were more destructive to the theory and practice of a Virginia republic than any foreign war was likely to be. Personal liberties and rights of property were more directly curtailed in the United States by embargo than in Great Britain by centuries of almost continuous foreign war. No one denied that a permanent embargo strained the Constitution to the uttermost tension; and even the Secretary of the Treasury and the President admitted that it required the exercise of the most arbitrary, odious, and dangerous powers. From this point of view the system was quickly seen to have few advantages. If American liberties must perish, they might as well be destroyed by war as be stifled by non-intercourse.

While the constitutional cost of the two systems was not altogether unlike, the economical cost was a point not easily settled. No one could say what might be the financial expense of embargo as compared with war. Yet Jefferson himself in the end admitted that the embargo had no claim to respect as an economical measure. The Boston Federalists estimated that the net American loss of income, exclusive of that on freights, could not be less than ten per cent for interest and profit on the whole export of the country,—or ten million eight hundred thousand dollars on a total export value of one hundred and eight millions. This estimate was extravagant, even if the embargo had been wholly responsible for cutting off American trade; it represented in fact the loss resulting to America from Napoleon's decrees, the British orders, and the embargo taken together. Yet at least the embargo was more destructive than war would have been to the interests of foreign commerce.

Even in the worst of foreign wars American commerce could not be wholly stopped,—some outlet for American produce must always remain open, some inward bound ships would always escape the watch of a blockading squadron. Even in 1814, after two years of war, and when the coast was stringently blockaded, the American Treasury collected six million dollars from imports; but in 1808, after the embargo was in full effect, the customs yielded only a few thousand dollars on cargoes that happened to be imported for some special purpose. The difference was loss, to the disadvantage of embargo. To this must be added loss of freight, decay of ships and produce, besides enforced idleness to a corresponding extent; and finally the cost of a war if the embargo system should fail.

In other respects the system was still costly. The citizen was not killed, but he was partially paralyzed. Government did not waste money or life, but prevented both money and labor from having their former value. If long continued, embargo must bankrupt the government almost as certainly as war; if not long continued, the immediate shock to industry was more destructive than war would have been. The expense of war proved, five years afterward, to be about thirty million dollars a year, and of this sum much the larger portion was pure loss; but in 1808, owing to the condition of Europe, the expense need not have exceeded twenty millions, and the means at hand were greater. The effect of the embargo was certainly no greater than the effect of war in stimulating domestic industry. In either case the stimulus was temporary and ineffective; but the embargo cut off the resources of credit and capital, while war gave both an artificial expansion. The result was that while embargo saved perhaps twenty millions of dollars a year and some thousands of lives which war would have consumed, it was still an expensive system, and in some respects more destructive than war itself to national wealth.

The economical was less serious than the moral problem. The strongest objection to war was not its waste of money or even of life; for money and life in political economy were worth no more than they could be made to produce. A worse evil was the lasting harm caused by war to the morals of mankind, which no system of economy could calculate. The reign of brute force and brutal methods corrupted and debauched society, making it blind to its own vices and ambitious only for mischief. Yet even on that ground the embargo had few advantages. The peaceable coercion which Jefferson tried to substitute for war was less brutal, but hardly less mischievous, than the evil it displaced. The embargo opened the sluice-gates of social corruption. Every citizen was tempted to evade or defy the laws. At every point along the coast and frontier the civil, military, and naval services were brought in contact with corruption; while every man in private life was placed under strong motives to corrupt. Every article produced or consumed in the country became an object of speculation; every form of industry became a form of gambling. The rich could alone profit in the end; while the poor must sacrifice at any loss the little they could produce.

If war made men brutal, at least it made them strong; it called out the qualities best fitted to survive in the struggle for existence. To risk life for one's country was no mean act even when done for selfish motives; and to die that others might more happily live was the highest act of self-sacrifice to be reached by man. War, with all

183

its horrors, could purify as well as debase; it dealt with high motives and vast interests; taught courage, discipline, and stern sense of duty. Jefferson must have asked himself in vain what lessons of heroism or duty were taught by his system of peaceable coercion, which turned every citizen into an enemy of the laws,—preaching the fear of war and of self-sacrifice, making many smugglers and traitors, but not a single hero.

If the cost of the embargo was extravagant in it effects on the Constitution, the economy, and the morals of the nation, its political cost to the party in power was ruinous. War could have worked no more violent revolution. The trial was too severe for human nature to endure. At a moment's notice, without avowing his true reasons, President Jefferson bade foreign commerce to cease. As the order was carried along the seacoast, every artisan dropped his tools, every merchant closed his doors, every ship was dismantled. American produce—wheat, timber, cotton, tobacco, rice—dropped in value or became unsalable; every imported article rose in price; wages stopped; swarms of debtors became bankrupt; thousands of sailors hung idle round the wharves trying to find employment on coasters, and escape to the West Indies or Nova Scotia. A reign of idleness began; and the men who were not already ruined felt that their ruin was only a matter of time.

The British traveller, Lambert, who visited New York in 1808, described it as resembling a place ravaged by pestilence:

"The port indeed was full of shipping, but they were dismantled and laid up; their decks were cleared, their hatches fastened down, and scarcely a sailor was to be found on board. Not a box, bale, cask, barrel, or package was to be seen upon the wharves. Many of the counting-houses were shut up, or advertised to be let; and the few solitary merchants, clerks, porters, and laborers that were to be seen were walking about with their hands in their pockets. The coffee-houses were almost empty; the streets, near the water-side, were almost deserted; the grass had begun to grow upon the wharves."

In New England, where the struggle of existence was keenest, the embargo struck like a thunderbolt, and society for a moment thought itself at an end. Foreign commerce and shipping were the life of the people,—the ocean, as Pickering said, was their farm. The outcry of suffering interests became every day more violent, as the public learned that this paralysis was not a matter of weeks, but of months or years. New Englanders as a class were a law-abiding people; but from the earliest moments of their history they had largely qualified their obedience to the law by the violence with which they abused and the ingenuity with which they evaded it. Against the embargo and Jefferson they concentrated the clamor and passion of their keen and earnest nature. Rich and poor, young and old, joined in the chorus; and one lad, barely in his teens, published what he called "The Embargo: a Satire,"—a boyish libel on Jefferson, which the famous poet and Democrat would afterward have given much to recall:—

"And thou, the scorn of every patriot name,
Thy country's ruin, and her councils' shame.

.   .   .   .

Go, wretch! Resign the Presidential chair,
Disclose thy secret measures, foul or fair;
Go search with curious eye for hornèd frogs
'Mid the wild waste of Louisiana bogs;
Or where Ohio rolls his turbid stream
Dig for huge bones, thy glory and thy theme."

The belief that Jefferson, sold to France, wished to destroy American commerce and to strike a deadly blow at New and Old England at once, maddened the sensitive temper of the people. Immense losses, sweeping away their savings and spreading bankruptcy through every village, gave ample cause for their complaints. Yet in truth, New England was better able to defy the embargo than she was willing to suppose. She lost nothing except profits which the belligerents had in any case confiscated; her timber would not harm for keeping, and her fish were safe in the ocean. The embargo gave her almost a monopoly of the American market for domestic manufactures; no part of the country was so well situated or so well equipped for smuggling. Above all, she could easily economize. The New Englander knew better than any other American how to cut down his expenses to the uttermost point of parsimony; and even when he became bankrupt he had but to begin anew. His energy, shrewdness, and education were a capital which the embargo could not destroy, but rather helped to improve.

The growers of wheat and live stock in the Middle States were more hardly treated. Their wheat, reduced in value from two dollars to seventy-five cents a bushel, became practically unsalable. Debarred a market for their produce at a moment when every article of common use tended to rise in cost, they were reduced to the necessity of living on the produce of their farms; but the task was not then so difficult as in later times, and the cities still furnished local markets not to be despised. The manufacturers of Pennsylvania could not but feel the stimulus of the new demand; so violent a system of protection was never applied to them before or since. Probably for that reason the embargo was not so unpopular in Pennsylvania as elsewhere, and Jefferson had nothing to fear from political revolution in this calm and plodding community.

The true burden of the embargo fell on the Southern States, but most severely upon the great State of Virginia. Slowly decaying, but still half patriarchal, Virginia society could neither economize nor liquidate. Tobacco was worthless; but four hundred thousand negro slaves must be clothed and fed, great establishments must be kept up, the social scale of living could not be reduced, and even bankruptcy could not clear a large landed estate without creating new encumbrances in a country where land and negroes were the only forms of property on which money could be raised. Stay-laws were tried, but served only to prolong the agony. With astonishing rapidity Virginia succumbed to ruin, while continuing to support the system that was draining her strength. No episode in American history was more touching than the generous devotion with which Virginia clung to the embargo, and drained the poison which her own President held obstinately to her lips. The cotton and rice States had less to lose, and could more easily bear brankruptcy; ruin was to them—except in Charleston—a word of little meaning; but the old society of

185

Virginia could never be restored. Amid the harsh warnings of John Randolph it saw its agonies approach; and its last representative, heir to all its honors and dignities, President Jefferson himself woke from his long dream of power only to find his own fortunes buried in the ruin he had made.

Except in a state of society verging on primitive civilization, the stoppage of all foreign intercourse could not have been attempted by peaceable means. The attempt to deprive the laborer of sugar, salt, tea, coffee, molasses, and rum; to treble the price of every yard of coarse cottons and woollens; to reduce by one half the wages of labor, and to double its burdens,—this was a trial more severe than war; and even when attempted by the whole continent of Europe, with all the resources of manufactures and wealth which the civilization of a thousand years had supplied, the experiment required the despotic power of Napoleon and the united armies of France, Austria, and Russia to carry it into effect. Even then it failed. Jefferson, Madison, and the Southern Republicans had no idea of the economical difficulties their system created, and were surprised to find American society so complex even in their own Southern States that the failure of two successive crops to find a sale threatened beggary to every rich planter from the Delaware to the Sabine. During the first few months, while ships continued to arrive from abroad and old stores were consumed at home, the full pressure of the embargo was not felt; but as the summer of 1808 passed, the outcry became violent. In the Southern States, almost by common consent debts remained unpaid and few men ventured to oppose a political system which was peculiarly a Southern invention; but in the Northern States, where the bankrupt laws were enforced and the habits of business were comparatively strict, the cost of the embargo was soon shown in the form of political revolution.

The relapse of Massachusetts to Federalism and the overthrow of Senator Adams in the spring of 1808 were the first signs of the political price which President Jefferson must pay for his passion of peace. In New York the prospect was little better. Governor Morgan Lewis, elected in 1804 over Aaron Burr by a combination of Clintons and Livingstons, was turned out of office in 1807 by the Clintons. Governor Daniel D. Tompkins, his successor, was supposed to be a representative of De Witt Clinton and Ambrose Spencer. To De Witt Clinton the State of New York seemed in 1807 a mere appendage,—a political property which he could control at will; and of all American politicians next to Aaron Burr none had shown such indifference to party as he. No one could predict his course, except that it would be shaped according to what seemed to be the interests of his ambition. He began by declaring himself against the embargo, and soon afterward declared himself for it. In truth, he was for or against it as the majority might decide; and in New York a majority could hardly fail to decide against the embargo. At the spring election of 1808, which took place about May 1, the Federalists made large gains in the legislature. The summer greatly increased their strength, until Madison's friends trembled for the result, and their language became despondent beyond reason. Gallatin, who knew best the difficulties created by the embargo, began to despair. June 29 he wrote: "From present appearances the Federalists will turn us out by 4th of March next." Ten days afterward he explained the reason of his fears: "I think that Vermont is lost; New Hampshire is in a bad neighborhood; and Pennsylvania is extremely doubtful." In August he thought the situation so serious that he warned the President:—

"There is almost an equal chance that if propositions from Great Britain, or other events, do not put it in our power to raise the embargo before the 1st of October, we will lose the Presidential election. I think that at this moment the Western States, Virginia, South Carolina, and perhaps Georgia are the only sound States, and that we will have a doubtful contest in every other."

Two causes saved Madison. In the first place, the opposition failed to concentrate its strength. Neither George Clinton nor James Monroe could control the whole body of opponents to the embargo. After waiting till the middle of August for some arrangement to be made, leading Federalists held a conference at New York, where they found themselves obliged, by the conduct of De Witt Clinton, to give up the hope of a coalition. Clinton decided not to risk his fortunes for the sake of his uncle the Vice-President; and this decision obliged the Federalists to put a candidate of their own in the field. They named C. C. Pinckney of South Carolina for President, and Rufus King of New York for Vice-President, as in 1804.

From the moment his opponents divided themselves among three candidates, Madison had nothing to fear; but even without this good fortune he possessed an advantage that weighed decisively in his favor. The State legislatures had been chosen chiefly in the spring or summer, when the embargo was still comparatively popular; and in most cases, but particularly in New York, the legislature still chose Presidential electors. The people expressed no direct opinion on national politics, except in regard to Congressmen. State after State deserted to the Federalists without affecting the general election. Early in September Vermont elected a Federalist governor, but the swarm of rotten boroughs in the State secured a Republican legislature, which immediately chose electors for Madison. The revolution in Vermont surrendered all New England to the Federalists. New Hampshire chose Presidential electors by popular vote; Rhode Island did the same,—and both States, by fair majorities, rejected Madison and voted for Pinckney. In Massachusetts and Connecticut the legislatures chose Federalist electors. Thus all New England declared against the Administration; and had Vermont been counted as she voted in September, the opposition would have received forty-five electoral votes from New England, where in 1804 it had received only nine. In New York the opponents of the embargo were very strong, and the nineteen electoral votes of that State might in a popular election have been taken from Madison. In this case Pennsylvania would have decided the result. Eighty-eight electoral votes were needed for a choice. New England, New York, and Delaware represented sixty-seven. Maryland and North Carolina were so doubtful that if Pennsylvania had deserted Madison, they would probably have followed her, and would have left the Republican party a wreck.

The choice of electors by the legislatures of Vermont and New York defeated all chance of overthrowing Madison; but apart from these accidents of management the result was already decided by the people of Pennsylvania. The wave of

Federalist success and political revolution stopped short in New York, and once more the Democracy of Pennsylvania steadied and saved the Administration. At the October election of 1808,—old Governor McKean having at last retired,—Simon Snyder was chosen governor by a majority of more than twenty thousand votes. The new governor was the candidate of Duane and the extreme Democrats; his triumph stopped the current of Federalist success, and enabled Madison's friends to drive hesitating Republicans back to their party. In Virginia, Monroe was obliged to retire from the contest, and his supporters dwindled in numbers until only two or three thousand went to the polls. In New York, De Witt Clinton contented himself with taking from Madison six of the nineteen electoral votes and giving them to Vice-President Clinton. Thus the result showed comparatively little sign of the true Republican loss; yet in the electoral college where in 1804 Jefferson had received the voices of one hundred and sixty-two electors, Madison in 1808 received only one hundred and twenty-two votes. The Federalist minority rose from fourteen to forty-seven.

In the elections to Congress the same effects were shown. The Federalists doubled their number of Congressmen, but the huge Republican majority could well bear reduction. The true character of the Eleventh Congress could not be foretold by the party vote. Many Nothern Republicans chosen to Congress were as hostile to the embargo as though they had been Federalists. Elected on the issue of embargo or anti-embargo, the Congress which was to last till March 5, 1811, was sure to be factious; but whether factious or united, it could have neither policy nor leader. The election decided its own issue. The true issue thenceforward was that of war; but on this point the people had not been asked to speak, and their representatives would not dare without their encouragement to act.

The Republican party by a supreme effort kept itself in office; but no one could fail to see that if nine months of embargo had so shattered Jefferson's power, another such year would shake the Union itself. The cost of this "engine for national purposes" exceeded all calculation. Financially, it emptied the Treasury, bankrupted the mercantile and agricultural class, and ground the poor beyond endurance. Constitutionally, it overrode every specified limit on arbitrary power and made Congress despotic, while it left no bounds to the authority which might be vested by Congress in the President. Morally, it sapped the nation's vital force, lowering its courage, paralyzing its energy, corrupting its principles, and arraying all the active elements of society in factious opposition to government or in secret paths of treason. Politically, it cost Jefferson the fruits of eight years painful labor for popularity, and brought the Union to the edge of a precipice.

Finally, frightful as the cost of this engine was, as a means of coercion the embargo evidently failed. The President complained of evasion, and declared that if the measure were faithfully executed it would produce the desired effect; but the people knew better. In truth, the law was faithfully executed. The price-lists of Liverpool and London, the published returns from Jamaica and Havana, proved that American produce was no longer to be bought abroad. On the continent of Europe commerce had ceased before the embargo was laid, and its coercive effects were far exceeded by Napoleon's own restrictions; yet not a sign came from Europe to show that Napoleon meant to give way. From England came an answer to the embargo, but not such as promised its success. On all sides evidence accumulated that the embargo, as an engine of coercion, needed a long period of time to produce a decided effect. The law of physics could easily be applied to politics; force could be converted only into its equivalent force. If the embargo—an exertion of force less violent than war—was to do the work of war, it must extend over a longer time the development of an equivalent energy. Wars lasted for many years, and the embargo must be calculated to last much longer than any war; but meanwhile the morals, courage, and political liberties of the American people must be perverted or destroyed; agriculture and shipping must perish; the Union itself could not be preserved.

Under the shock of these discoveries Jefferson's vast popularity vanished, and the labored fabric of his reputation fell in sudden and general ruin. America began slowly to struggle, under the consciousness of pain, toward a conviction that she must bear the common burdens of humanity, and fight with the weapons of other races in the same bloody arena; that she could not much longer delude herself with hopes of evading laws of Nature and instincts of life; and that her new statesmanship which made peace a passion could lead to no better result than had been reached by the barbarous system which made war a duty.

19

Two Presidents Reminisce

Relations between America's second and third Presidents were not always good. Friends in their youth, both struggling in the cause of national independence, their subsequent political careers revealed deep differences in their philosophies of government as they fought each other for office and influence. After Jefferson left the White House in 1809, however, it was possible to effect a reconcilation with Adams. Their ambitions dormant, their greatness achieved, they could reflect on the nature of the society they had formed. Between 1813 and 1826 Adams and Jefferson exchanged a remarkable series of letters, discussing not only the issues of the day but speculating on the future, reminiscing about the past, and trading anecdotes and erudition on an enormous variety of subjects.

The following two letters, written shortly after their reconciliation took place, reveal something of the philosophical differences that had divided them. Opposed in temperament, taste, and theory, the two men shared a vibrant curiosity about the world and a consuming interest in the fate of the Republic. Their deaths, occurring within hours of each other on the fiftieth anniversary of Independence, July 4, 1826, formed one of the most moving coincidences in American history.

THE ADAMS-JEFFERSON LETTERS

Jefferson to Adams

Monticello Oct. 28.13
Dear Sir

According to the reservation between us, of taking up one of the subjects of our correspondence at a time, I turn to your letters of Aug. 16. and Sep. 2.

I agree with you that there is a natural aristocracy among men. The grounds of this are virtue and talents. Formerly bodily powers gave place among the aristoi. But since the invention of gunpowder has armed the weak as well as the strong with

Reprinted with permission of The University of North Carolina Press from *The Adams-Jefferson Letters*, Lester J. Cappon, ed. (Chapel Hill, N.C., 1959), II: 387–392, 397–402. This book was published for the Institute of Early American History and Culture.

missile death, bodily strength, like beauty, good humor, politeness and other accomplishments, has become but an auxiliary ground of distinction. There is also an artificial aristocracy founded on wealth and birth, without either virtue or talents; for with these it would belong to the first class. The natural aristocracy I consider as the most precious gift of nature for the instruction, the trusts, and government of society. And indeed it would have been inconsistent in creation to have formed man for the social state, and not to have provided virtue and wisdom enough to manage the concerns of the society. May we not even say that that form of government is the best which provides the most effectually for a pure selection of these natural aristoi into the offices of government? The artificial aristocracy is a mischievous ingredient in government, and provision should be made to prevent it's ascendancy. On the question, What is the best provision, you and I differ; but we differ as rational friends using the free exercise of our own reason, and mutually indulging it's errors. *You* think it best to put the Pseudo-aristoi into a separate chamber of legislation where they may be hindered from doing mischief by their coordinate branches, and where also they may be a protection to wealth against the Agrarian and plundering enterprises of the Majority of the people. I think that to give them power in order to prevent them from doing mischief, is arming them for it, and increasing instead of remedying the evil. For if the coordinate branches can arrest their action, so may they that of the coordinates. Mischief may be done negatively as well as positively. Of this a cabal in the Senate of the U.S. has furnished many proofs. Nor do I believe them necessary to protect the wealthy; because enough of these will find their way into every branch of the legislation to protect themselves. From 15. to 20. legislatures of our own, in action for 30. years past, have proved that no fears of an equalisation of property are to be apprehended from them.

I think the best remedy is exactly that provided by all our constitutions, to leave to the citizens the free election and separation of the aristoi from the pseudo-aristoi, of the wheat from the chaff. In general they will elect the real good and wise. In some instances, wealth may corrupt, and birth blind them; but not in sufficient degree to endanger the society.

It is probable that our difference of opinion may in some measure be produced by a difference of character in those among whom we live. From what I have seen of Massachusets and Connecticut myself, and more from what I have heard, and the character given of the former by yourself, who know them so much better, there seems to be in those two states a traditionary reverence for certain families, which has rendered the offices of the government nearly hereditary in those families. I presume that from an early period of your history, members of these families happening to possess virtue and talents, have honestly exercised them for the good of the people, and by their services have endeared their names to them.

But altho' this hereditary succession to office with you may in some degree be founded in real family merit, yet in a much higher degree it has proceeded from your strict alliance of church and state. These families are canonised in the eyes of the people on the common principle 'you tickle me, and I will tickle you.' In Virginia we have nothing of this. Our clergy, before the revolution, having been secured against rivalship by fixed salaries, did not give themselves the trouble of acquiring influence over the people. Of wealth, there were great accumulations in particular families, handed down from generation to generation under the English law of entails. But the only object of ambition for the wealthy was a seat in the king's council. All their court then was paid to the crown and it's creatures; and they Philipised in all collisions between the king and people. Hence they were unpopular; and that unpopularity continues attached to their names. A Randolph, a Carter, or a Burwell must have great personal superiority over a common competitor to be elected by the people, even at this day.

At the first session of our legislature after the Declaration of Independence, we passed a law abolishing entails. And this was followed by one abolishing the privilege of Primogeniture, and dividing the lands of intestates equally among all their children, or other representatives. These laws, drawn by myself, laid the axe to the root of Pseudo-aristocracy. And had another which I prepared been adopted by the legislature, our work would have been compleat. It was a Bill for the more general diffusion of learning. This proposed to divide every county into wards of 5. or 6. miles square, like your townships; to establish in each ward a free school for reading, writing and common arithmetic; to provide for the annual selection of the best subjects from these schools who might receive at the public expence a higher degree of education at a district school; and from these district schools to select a certain number of the most promising subjects to be compleated at an University, where all the useful sciences should be taught. Worth and genius would thus have been sought out from every condition of life, and compleatly prepared by education for defeating the competition of wealth and birth for public trusts.

My proposition had for a further object to impart to these wards those portions of self-government for which they are best qualified, by confiding to them the care of their poor, their roads, police, elections, the nomination of jurors, administration of justice in small cases, elementary exercises of militia, in short, to have made them little republics, with a Warden at the head of each, for all those concerns which, being under their eye, they would better manage than the larger republics of the county or state. A general call of ward-meetings by their Wardens on the same day thro' the state would at any time produce the genuine sense of the people on any required point, and would enable the state to act in mass, as your people have so often done, and with so much effect, by their town meetings. The law for religious freedom, which made a part of this system, having put down the aristocracy of the clergy, and restored to the citizen the freedom of the mind, and those of entails and descents nurturing an equality of condition among them, this on Education would have raised the mass of the people to the high ground of moral respectability necessary to their own safety, and to orderly government; and would have compleated the great object of qualifying them to select the veritable aristoi, for the trusts of government. Altho' this law has not yet been acted on but in a small and inefficient degree, it is still considered as before the legislature, with other bills of the revised code, not yet taken up, and I have great hope that some patriotic spirit will, at a favorable moment, call it up, and make it the key-stone of the arch of our government.

With respect to Aristocracy, we should further consider that, before the establishment of the American states, nothing was known to History but the Man of the old world, crouded within limits either small or overcharged, and steeped in the vices which that situation generates. A government adapted to such men would be one thing; but a very different one that for the Man of these states. Here every one may have land to labor for himself if he chuses; or, preferring the exercise of any other industry, may exact for it such compensation as not only to afford a comfortable subsistence, but wherewith to provide for a cessation from labor in old age. Every one, by his property, or by his satisfactory situation, is interested in the support of law and order. And such men may safely and advantageously reserve to themselves a wholsome controul over their public affairs, and a degree of freedom, which in the hands of the Canaille of the cities of Europe, would be instantly perverted to the demolition and destruction of every thing public and private. The history of the last 25. years of France, and of the last 40. years in America, nay of it's last 200. years, proves the truth of both parts of this observation.

But even in Europe a change has sensibly taken place in the mind of Man. Science had liberated the ideas of those who read and reflect, and the American example had kindled feelings of right in the people. An insurrection has consequently begun, of science, talents and courage against rank and birth, which have fallen into contempt. It has failed in it's first effort, because the mobs of the cities, the instrument used for it's accomplishment, debased by ignorance, poverty and vice, could not be restrained to rational action. But the world will recover from the panic of this first catastrophe. Science is progressive, and talents and enterprize on the alert. Resort may be had to the people of the country, a more governable power from their principles and subordination; and rank, and birth, and tinsel-aristocracy will finally shrink into insignificance, even there. This however we have no right to meddle with. It suffices for us, if the moral and physical condition of our own citizens qualifies them to select the able and good for the direction of their government, with a recurrence of elections at such short periods as will enable them to displace an unfaithful servant before the mischief he meditates may be irremediable.

I have thus stated my opinion on a point on which we differ, not with a view to controversy, for we are both too old to change opinions which are the result of a long life of inquiry and reflection; but on the suggestion of a former letter of yours, that we ought not to die before we have explained ourselves to each other. We acted in perfect harmony thro' a long and perilous contest for our liberty and independance. A constitution has been acquired which, tho neither of us think perfect, yet both consider as competent to render our fellow-citizens the happiest and the securest on whom the sun has ever shone. If we do not think exactly alike as to it's imperfections, it matters little to our counry which, after devoting to it long lives of disinterested labor, we have delivered over to our successors in life, who will be able to take care of it, and of themselves. Ever and affectionately yours,

Th: Jefferson

Adams to Jefferson

Quincy November 15.13
Dear Sir

I cannot appease my melancholly commiseration for our Armies in this furious snow storm in any way so well as by studying your Letter of Oct. 28.

We are now explicitly agreed, in one important point, vizt. That "there is a natural Aristocracy among men; the grounds of which are Virtue and Talents."

You very justly indulge a little merriment upon this solemn subject of Aristocracy. I often laugh at it too, for there is nothing in this laughable world more ridiculous than the management of it by almost all the nations of the Earth. But while We smile, Mankind have reason to say to Us, as the froggs said to the Boys, What is Sport to you is Wounds and death to Us. When I consider the weakness, the folly, the Pride, the Vanity, the Selfishness, the Artifice, the low craft and meaning cunning, the want of Principle, the Avarice the unbounded Ambition, the unfeeling Cruelty of a majority of those (in all Nations) who are allowed an aristocratical influence; and on the other hand, the Stupidity with which the more numerous multitude, not only become their Dupes, but even love to be Taken in by their Tricks: I feel a stronger disposition to weep at their destiny, than to laugh at their Folly.

But tho' We have agreed in one point, in Words, it is not yet certain that We are perfectly agreed in Sense. Fashion has introduced an indeterminate Use of the Word "Talents." Education, Wealth, Strength, Beauty, Stature, Birth, Marriage, graceful Attitudes and Motions, Gait, Air, Complexion, Physiognomy, are Talents, as well as Genius and Science and learning. Any one of these Talents, that in fact commands or influences true Votes in Society, gives to the Man who possesses it, the Character of an Aristocrat, in my Sense of the Word.

Pick up, the first 100 men you meet, and make a Republick. Every Man will have an equal Vote. But when deliberations and discussions are opened it will be found that 25, by their Talents, Virtues being equal, will be able to carry 50 Votes. Every one of these 25, is an Aristocrat, in my Sense of the Word; whether he obtains his one Vote in Addition to his own, by his Birth Fortune, Figure, Eloquence, Science, learning, Craft Cunning, or even his Character for good fellowship and a bon vivant.

What gave Sir William Wallace his amazing Aristocratical Superiority? His Strength. What gave Mrs. Clark, her Aristocratical Influence to create Generals Admirals and Bishops? her Beauty. What gave Pompadour and Du Barry the Power of making Cardinals and Popes? their Beauty. You have seen the Palaces of Pompadour and Du Barry: and I have lived for years in the Hotel de Velentinois, with Franklin who had as many Virtues as any of them. In the investigation of the meaning of the Word "Talents" I could write 630 Pages, as pertinent as John Taylors of Hazelwood. But I will select a single Example: for female Aristocrats are nearly as formidable in Society as male.

A daughter of a green Grocer, walks the Streets in London dayly with a baskett of Cabbage, Sprouts, Dandlions and Spinage on her head. She is observed by the Painters to have a beautiful Face, an elegant figure, a graceful Step and a debonair. They hire her to Sitt. She complies, and is painted by forty Artists in a Circle around her. The scientific Sir William Hamilton outbids the Painters, sends her to Schools for a genteel Education and Marries her. This Lady not only causes the Tryumphs of the Nile of Copinhagen and Trafalgar, but seperates Naples from France and finally banishes the King and Queen from Sicilly. Such is the Aristocracy of the natural Talent of Beauty. Millions of Examples might be quoted from History sacred and profane, from Eve, Hannah, Deborah Susanna Abigail, Judith, Ruth, down to Hellen Madame de Maintenon and Mrs. Fitcherbert. For mercy's sake do not compell me to look to our chaste States and Territories, to find Women, one of whom lett go, would, in the Words of Holopherne's Guards "deceive the whole Earth."

The Proverbs of Theognis, like those of Solomon, are Observations on human nature, ordinary life, and civil Society, with moral reflections on the facts. I quoted him as a Witness of the Fact, that there was as much difference in the races of Men as in the breeds of Sheep; and as a sharp reprover and censurer of the sordid mercenary practice of disgracing Birth by preferring gold to it. Surely no authority can be more expressly in point to prove the existence of Inequalities, not of rights, but of moral intellectual and physical inqualities in Families, descents and Generations. If a descent from, pious, virtuous, wealthy litterary or scientific Ancestors is a letter of recommendation, or introduction in a Mans his favour, and enables him to influence only one vote in Addition to his own, he is an Aristocrat, for a democrat can have but one Vote. Aaron Burr had 100,000 Votes from the single Circumstance of his descent from President Burr and President Edwards.

Your commentary on the Proverbs of Theognis reminded me of two solemn Charactors, the one resembling John Bunyan, the other Scarron. The one John Torrey: the other Ben. Franklin. Torrey a Poet, an Enthusiast, a superstitious Bigot, once very gravely asked my Brother Cranch, "whether it would not be better for Mankind, if Children were always begotten from religious motives only"? Would not religion, in this sad case, have as little efficacy in encouraging procreation, as it has now in discouraging it? I should apprehend a decrease of population even in our Country where it increases so rapidly. In 1775 Franklin made a morning Visit, at Mrs. Yards to Sam. Adams and John. He was unusually loquacious. "Man, a rational Creature"! said Franklin. "Come, Let Us suppose a rational Man. Strip him of all his Appetites, especially of his hunger and thirst. He is in his Chamber, engaged in making Experiments, or in pursuing some Problem. He is highly entertained. At this moment a Servant Knocks, "Sir dinner is on Table." "Dinner! Pox! Pough! But what have you for dinner?" Ham and Chickens. "Ham"! "And must I break the chain of my thoughts, to go down and knaw a morsel of a damn'd Hogs Arse"? "Put aside your Ham." "I will dine tomorrow."

Take away Appetite and the present generation would not live a month and no future generation would ever exist. Thus the exalted dignity of human Nature would be annihilated and lost. And in my opinion, the whole loss would be of no more importance, than putting out a Candle, quenching a Torch, or crushing a Firefly, *if in this world only We have hope.*

Your distinction between natural and artificial Aristocracy does not appear to me well founded. Birth and Wealth are conferred on some Men, as imperiously by Nature, as Genius, Strength or Beauty. The Heir is honours and Riches, and power has often no more merit in procuring these Advantages, than he has in obtaining an handsome face or an elegant figure. When Aristocracies, are established by human Laws and honour Wealth and Power are made hereditary by municipal Laws and political Institutions, then I acknowledge artificial Aristocracy to commence: but this never commences, till Corruption in Elections becomes dominant and uncontroulable. But this artificial Aristocracy can never last. The everlasting Envys, Jealousies, Rivalries and quarrells among them, their cruel rapacities upon the poor ignorant People their followers, compell these to sett up Caesar, a Demagogue to be a Monarch and Master, pour mettre chacun a sa place ["to put each one in his place"]. Here you have the origin of all artificial Aristocracy, which is the origin of all Monarchy. And both artificial Aristocracy, and Monarchy, and civil, military, political and hierarchical Despotism, have all grown out of the natural Aristocracy of "Virtues and Talents." We, to be sure, are far remote from this. Many hundred years must roll away before We shall be corrupted. Our pure, virtuous, public spirited federative Republick will last for ever, govern the Globe and introduce the perfection of Man, his perfectability being already proved by Price Priestly, Condorcet Rousseau Diderot and Godwin.

"Mischief has been done by the Senate of U.S." I have known and felt more of this mischief, than Washington, Jefferson and Madison altoge [the]r. But this has been all caused by the constitutional Power of the Senate in Executive Business, which ought to be immediately, totally and eternally abolished.

Your distinction between the aristoi and pseudo aristoi, will not help the matter. I would trust one as soon as the other with unlimited Power. The Law wisely refuses an Oath as a witness in his own cause to the Saint as well as to the Sinner.

No Romance would be more amusing, than the History of your Virginian and our new England Aristocratical Families. Yet even in Rhode Island, where there has been no Clergy, no Church, and I had almost said, no State, and some People say no religion, there has been a constant respect for certain old Families. 57 or 58 years ago, in company with Col. Counsellor, Judge, John Chandler, whom I have quoted before, a Newspaper was brought in. The old Sage asked me to look for the News from Rhode Island and see how the Elections had gone there. I read the List of Wantons, Watsons, Greens, Whipples, Malbones etc. "I expected as much" said the aged Gentleman, "for I have always been of Opinion, that in the most popular Governments, the Elections will generally go in favour of the most ancient families." To this day when any of these Tribes and We may Add Ellerys, Channings Champlins etc are pleased to fall in with the popular current, they are sure to carry all before them.

You suppose a difference of Opinion between You and me, on the Subject of Aristocracy. I can find none. I dislike and detest hereditary honours, Offices

Emoluments established by Law. So do you. I am for ex[c]luding legal hereditary distinctions from the U.S. as long as possible. So are you. I only say that Mankind have not yet discovered any remedy against irresistable Corruption in Elections to Offices of great Power and Profit, but making them hereditary.

But will you say our Elections are pure? Be it so; upon the whole. But do you recollect in history, a more Corrupt Election than that of Aaron Burr to be President, or that of De Witt Clinton last year. By corruption, here I mean a sacrifice of every national Interest and honour, to private and party Objects.

I see the same Spirit in Virginia, that you and I see in Rhode Island and the rest of New England. In New York it is a struggle of Family Feuds. A fewdal Aristocracy. Pensylvania is a contest between German, Irish and old English Families. When Germans and Irish Unite, they give 30,000 majorities. There is virtually a White Rose and a Red Rose a Caesar and a Pompey in every State in this Union and Contests and dissentions will be as lasting. The Rivalry of Bourbons and Noailleses produced the French Revolution, and a similar Competition for Consideration and Influence, exists and prevails in every Village in the World.

Where will terminate the Rabies Agri ["madness for land"]? The Continent will be scattered over with Manors, much larger than Livingstons, Van Ranselaers or Phillips's. Even our Deacon Strong will have a Principality among you Southern Folk. What Inequality of Talents will be produced by these Land Jobbers?

Where tends the Mania for Banks? At my Table in Philadelphia, I once proposed to you to unite in endeavours to obtain an Amendment of the Constitution, prohibiting to the separate States the Power of creating Banks; but giving Congress Authority to establish one Bank, with a branch in each State; the whole limited to Ten Millions of dollars. Whether this Project was wise or unwise, I know not, for I had deliberated little on it then and have never thought it worth thinking much of since. But you spurned the Proposition from you with disdain.

This System of Banks begotten, hatched and brooded by Duer, Robert and Governeur Morris, Hamilton and Washington, I have always considered as a System of national Injustice. A Sacrifice of public and private Interest to a few Aristocratical Friends and Favourites. My scheme could have had no such Effect.

Verres plundered Temples and robbed a few rich Men; but he never made such ravages among private property in general, nor swindled so much out of the pocketts of the poor and the middle Class of People as these Banks have done. No people but this would have borne the Imposition so long. The People of Ireland would not bear Woods half pence. What Inequalities of Talent, have been introduced into this Country by these Aristocratical Banks!

Our Winthrops, Winslows, Bradfords, Saltonstalls, Quincys, Chandlers, Leonards Hutchinsons Olivers, Sewalls etc are precisely in the Situation of your Randolphs, Carters and Burwells, and Harrisons. Some of them unpopular for the part they took in the late revolution, but all respected for their names and connections and whenever they fall in with the popular Sentiments, are preferred, cetoris paribus to all others. When I was young, the Summum Bonum in Massachusetts, was to be worth ten thousand pounds Sterling, ride in a Chariot, be

Colonel of a Regiment of Militia and hold a seat in his Majesty's Council. No Mans Imagination aspired to any thing higher beneath the Skies. But these Plumbs, Chariots, Colonelships and counsellorships are recorded and will never be forgotten. No great Accumulations of Land were made by our early Settlers. Mr. Bausoin a French Refugee, made the first great Purchases and your General Dearborne, born under a fortunate Starr is now enjoying a large Portion of the Aristocratical sweets of them.

As I have no Amanuenses but females, and there is so much about generations in this letter that I dare not ask any one of them to copy it, and I cannot copy it myself I must beg of you to return it to me, your old Friend
    John Adams

20

The Appeal
of the New World

Frances Wright (1795–1852) was born in Scotland
and grew up a precocious and insatiable reader of
history and philosophy. Fascinated by the political and
social novelties of America, Fanny Wright sailed for
the New World in 1818, and spent more than two years
in the United States. Her letters of description back
home were numerous and detailed and, after returning
to England in 1821, she decided to publish some of
them as *Views of Society and Manners in America*. She
returned to the United States with Lafayette in 1824
and founded the experimental community of Nashoba
in Tennessee, where she tried to train and educate
Negro slaves as a means of integrating them into free
society. After many trips to Europe, an increasing involvement with utopian communities, and a career of
lecturing on education, social reform, free thought, and
women's rights, Fanny Wright died in 1852.

    Views of Society formed one of the most favorable
pictures of the new republic that a European had drawn
up to that time. Fanny Wright's enthusiasm for American institutions, with the crucial exception of slavery,
led often to distortions and misjudgments but reveal
something of the tremendous inspiration that the American experiment held for European reformers.

VIEWS OF SOCIETY AND MANNERS
IN AMERICA
Frances Wright

Agriculture

It were difficult, perhaps, to conceive man placed in a more enviable position than
he is as a cultivator of the soil in these states. Agriculture here assumes her most
cheerful aspect, and (some Europeans might smile doubtingly, but it is true) all
her ancient classic dignity, as when Rome summoned her consuls from the plough.
I have seen those who have raised their voice in the senate of their country, and

Reprinted by permission of the publishers from Paul R. Baker, editor, Frances Wright, *Views of
Society and Manners in America*. Cambridge, Mass.: The Belknap Press of Harvard University
Press, Copyright, 1963, by the President and Fellows of Harvard College. Pp. 99–101, 118–119,
194–202, 205–206, 208, 215–218, 267–270.

whose hands have fought her battles, walking beside the team and minutely directing every operation of husbandry, with the soil upon their garments and their countenances bronzed by the meridian sun. And how proudly does such a man tread his paternal fields! his ample domains improving under his hand, his garners full to overflowing, his table replenished with guests, and with a numerous offspring, whose nerves are braced by exercise and their minds invigorated by liberty. It was finely answered by an American citizen to a European who, looking around him, exclaimed, "Yes; this is all well. You have all the vulgar and the substantial, but I look in vain for the *ornamental*. Where are your ruins and your poetry?" "There are our ruins," replied the republican, pointing to a Revolutionary soldier who was turning up the glebe; and then, extending his hand over the plain that stretched before them, smiling with luxuriant farms and little villas, peeping out from beds of trees, "There is our poetry." . . .

The position of this country, its boundless territory, its varied soils and climates, its free institutions, and, favoured by these circumstances, the rapid increase of its population—all combine to generate in this people a spirit of daring enterprise as well as of proud independence. They spurn at little hindrances in narrow room, and prefer great difficulties in a wide horizon. In flying to the wilderness, they fly a thousand constraints which society must always impose, even under the fairest laws. They have here no longer to jostle with the crowd; their war is only with nature; their evils, therefore, are chiefly physical, and the comforts they may forego are amply compensated by the frets and cares from which they may be released. It is curious to consider the effect which this release from moral ills seems to have upon the constitution. Those who safely weather out the first hard seasoning, or who, from choosing their ground more judiciously, escape with but very little, are often found to live to an unusual age. It is a singular fact that the citizens of the new states are often remarkable for uncommon longevity and universally for uncommon stature. This cannot be accounted for by supposing that they are more exposed to air and exercise—the American farmer is this universally —and though universally the average of his stature is above that of Europeans, it were, perhaps, more just to ascribe this varying standard of bodily vigor to the less or greater pressure of mental solicitude. . . .

In the country, especially, service, however, well paid for, is a favour received. Every man is a farmer and a proprietor; few therefore can be procured to work for hire, and these must generally be brought from a distance. Country gentlemen complain much of this difficulty. Most things, however, have their good and their evil. I have remarked that the American gentry are possessed of much more personal activity than is common on other countries. They acquire, as children, the habit of doing for themselves what others require to be done for them, and are, besides, saved from the sin of insolence, which is often so early fixed in the young mind. Some foreigners will tell you that insolence here is with the poor. Each must speak from his own experience. I have never met with any, though I will confess that if I did it would offend me less than the insolence offered by the rich to the poor has done elsewhere. But insolence forms no characteristic of the American, whatever be his condition in life. I verily believe that you might travel from the

Canada frontier to the Gulf of Mexico, or from the Atlantic to the Missouri and never receive from a *native-born citizen* a rude word, it being understood always that you never *give one*.

On arriving at a tavern in this country, you excite no kind of *sensation*, come how you will. The master of the house bids you good day, and you walk in. Breakfast, dinner, and supper are prepared at stated times, to which you must generally contrive to accommodate. There are seldom more hands than enough to dispatch the necessary work. You are not therefore beset by half-a-dozen menials, imagining your wants before you know them yourself; make them known, however, and, if they be rational, they are generally answered with tolerable readiness, and I have invariably found with perfect civility. One thing I must notice, that you are never anywhere charged for attendance. The servant is not yours but the innkeeper's; no demands are made upon you except by the latter. This saves much trouble, and indeed is absolutely necessary in a house where the servant's labour is commonly too valuable to be laid at the mercy of every whimsical traveller. But this arrangement originates in another cause—the republican habits and feelings of the community. I honor the pride which makes a man unwilling to sell his personal service to a fellow creature; to come and go at the beck of another—is it not natural that there should be some unwillingness to do this? It is the last trade to which an American, man or woman, has recourse; still some must be driven to it, particularly of the latter sex, but she always assumes with you the manner of an equal. I have never in this country hired the attendance of any but native Americans, and never have met with an uncivil word, but I could perceive that neither would one have been taken. Honest, trusty, and proud, such is the American in service; there is a character here which all who can appreciate it will respect. . . .

Sectional Interests

Looking to the general plan of the central government, it will be seen with what extreme nicety the different interests of the multitudinous parts of this great confederacy are balanced, or employed as checks one upon the other. In the course of years these interests may be somewhat more distinctly marked than they are at present; some have even thought that they may be more strongly opposed. This appears more than doubtful. But even admitting the supposition, we cannot calculate the probable effects of this without counting for something the gradual strengthening of the national Union by the mixture of the people, the marriages and friendships conracted between the inhabitants of the different states, the tide of emigration, which shifts the population of one to the other, the course of prosperity enjoyed under a government more and more endeared as time more and more tries its widsom and imparts sanctity to its name. The time was when none or but a few of these sacred bonds existed, and still a friendly sympathy was not wanting among the different and uncemented communities scattered along the shores of the Atlantic.

During their colonial existence, the inhabitants of these states had but little intercourse with each other. Vast forests separated often the scanty population of the infant provinces. Varying climate and religion influenced also their customs and character; but still, however parted by trackless wastes, how little connected soever by the ties of private friendship, they had always two things in common—language and a fierce spirit of liberty, which sufficed to bind with a sure though invisible chain all the members of the scattered American family. The strength of this chain has seldom been fully appreciated by the enemies of America. They expected to break it even during the War of the Revolution, and were certain that it would of itself give way when the high-toned sentiment kept alive by a struggle for independence should subside, or when the pressure of common danger being removed, the necessity of cordial co-operation should not be equally apparent. Experience has hitherto happily disproved these calculations. The advantages of a vigorous and the blessings of a beneficent government, directing the energies and presiding over the welfare of the great whole, have been more and more felt and understood, while the influence of just laws, and still more the improved intercourse of the states one with another, have broken down prejudices and, in a great measure, obliterated distinctions of character among the different quarters of the republic.

The portion of the Union that has most generally preserved her ancient moral distinction is New England. The reason may be found in the rigidity of her early religious creed and in the greater separation of her people from the rest of the nation. Strictly moral, well-educated, industrious, and intelligent, but shrewd, cautious, and, as their neighbours say, at least, peculiarly long-sighted to their interests, the citizens of New England are the Scotch of America. Like them, they are inhabitants of a comparatively poor country and send forth legions of hardy adventurers to push their fortunes in richer climes. There is this difference, however, that the Scotchman traverses the world and gathers stores to spend them afterwards in his own barren hills, while the New Englander carries his penates with him and plants a colony on the shores of the Ohio, with no less satisfaction than he would have done on those of the Connecticut.

The nursery of backwoodsmen, New England, sends forth thousands and of course takes in few, so that her citizens are less exposed to the visitation of foreigners, and even to mixture with the people of other states, than is usual with their more southern neighbours. This has, perhaps, its advantages and disadvantages: it preserves to them all the virtues of a simple state of society, but with these also some of its prejudices; it serves to entrench them against luxury, but imparts to them something of a provincial character. Zealously attached to their own institutions, they have sometimes coldly espoused those of the nation. The Federal opposition chiefly proceeded from this quarter of the Union.

The political conduct of New England subsequent to the establishment of the federal government sunk her a little for some years in the esteem of the nation. The narrowness of her policy was charged to some peculiar selfishness of character in her people, but their conduct during the Revolutionary struggle redeems them from this charge and leads us to ascribe their errors to defect of judgment rather than to obliquity of principle. Since the war the liberal party, ever numerous, has gained the ascendant, and consequently the eastern states are resuming that place in the national councils which they originally held. . . . New York and Pennsylvania may perhaps be considered as the most *influential* states of the Union. . . . They are "the key-stones of the federal arch." Their rich and extensive territories seem to comprise all the interests into which the Union is divided. Commerce, agriculture, and manufactures are all powerfully represented by them on the floor of Congress. Their western division has much in common with the Mississippi states, and their eastern with those of the Atlantic. Their population stands conspicuous for national enterprise and enlightened policy, whether as regards the internal arrangement of their own republics or their share in the federal councils. These powerful states return no less than fifty members to Congress, being more than a fourth of the whole body. In proportion as the western states increase, this preponderance will be taken from them; in the meantime, however, it is in no case exerted to the prejudice of the general interests of the Union.

Whether it be from their wealth, or their more central position affording them the advantage of a free intercourse with the citizens of all the states of the Union, as well as foreigners from all parts of the world, the people of Pennsylvania and New York, but more particularly of the latter, have acquired a liberality of sentiment which imparts dignity to their public measures. They raise extensive funds, not only for the general education of their citizens (which is equally the case elsewhere), the founding of libraries, and seminaries of learning, but in the clearing of rivers, making roads and canals, and promoting other works of extensive utility, which might do honor to the richest empires of Europe. The progress of the New York state during the last thirty years is truly astonishing. Within this period, her population has more than quadrupled, and the value of property more than doubled. She has subdued the forest from Hudson to Erie and the Canadian frontier, and is now perfecting the navigation of all her great waters and connecting them with each other. . . .

No state in the Union can point to a longer line of public services than Virginia: she rung the first alarm of the Revolution by the mouth of her Patrick Henry; she led the army of patriots in the person of her Washington; she issued the Declaration of Independence from the pen of her Jefferson; she bound the first link of the federal Union by the hand of her Madison—she has given to the republic four of the purest patriots and wisest statesmen that ever steered the vessel of a state. . . .

The dignified position taken by Virginia in the national councils has placed her at the head of the republics of the South, whose policy, it may be remarked, has uniformly been liberal and patriotic and, on all essential points, in accordance with that of the central and western states. Whatever be the effect of black slavery upon the moral character of the southern population—and that upon *the mass* it must be deadly mischievous there can be no question—it has never been felt in the national Senate. Perhaps the arrangement has been prudent, or at least fortunate, which has somewhat tempered the democracy of American government in the south Atlantic states. By the existing constitution of Virginia and the states south of her, the qualifications required of a representative throw the legislative power into the hands of the more wealthy planters, a race of men no less distinguished for the polish of their manners and education than for liberal sentiments and general philanthropy. They are usually well-travelled in their own country and in Europe, possess enough wealth to be hospitable and seldom sufficient to be luxurious, and are thus, by education and condition, raised above the degrading influence which the possession of arbitrary power has on the human mind and the human heart. To the slight leaven of aristocracy, therefore, thrown into the institutions of Virginia and the Carolinas, we may, perhaps, attribute, in part, their generous and amiable bearing in the national councils. We must not omit, however, the ameliorating effect produced by the spread of education and the effect of liberal institutions on the white population generally. Even before the close of the Revolutionary War, Mr. Jefferson thought "a change already perceptible"; and we have a substantial proof that the change traced by that philosopher in the character of his fellow citizens was not imaginary, the first act of the Virginia legislature being the abolition of the slave trade. May she now set an example to her neighbouring states, as she then did to the world, by combating steadfastly the difficulties which her own fears or selfish interests may throw in the way of emancipation!

But the quarter of the republic to which the eye of a stranger turns with most curiosity is the vast region to the west of the Alleghenies. The character of these republics is necessarily as unique as their position, and their influence is already powerful upon the floor of Congress.

In glancing at their geographical position, the foreigner might hastily be led to consider them as growing rivals rather than friendly supporters of the Atlantic states. It will be found, however, that they are at present powerful cementers of the Union, and that the feelings and interests are such as to draw together the north and south divisions of the confederacy.

The new canals will probably draw off the produce of the western counties of New York to the Atlantic; still, however, a portion will find its way down the western waters, as their navigation shall be perfected from Erie to New Orleans. At all events, this route will continue to be preferred by the western counties of Pennsylvania, shortly destined to be the seat, if they are not so already, of flourishing manufactures. The advance made in this branch of industry during the last war and for some years previously has received some checks since the peace, but appears likely soon to proceed with redoubled energy.

It may be worth observing that there is something in the character of the American population, as well as in the diverse products of the soil, which seems favourable to the growth of manufactures. I do not allude merely to their mechanical ingenuity, which has shown itself in so many important inventions and improvements in shipbuilding, bridges, steamboat-navigation, implements of husbandry and machinery of all kinds, but to that proud feeling of independence, which disinclines them from many species of labour resorted to by Europeans. There are some farther peculiarities in the condition and character of the scattered population of the West, which rendered the birth of manufactures simultaneous with that of agriculture. In planting himself in the bosom of the wilderness, the settler is often entirely dependent upon his own industry for every article of food and raiment. While he wields the axe and turns up the soil, his wife plies the needle and the spinning wheel, and his children draw sugar from the maple and work at the loom. The finely watered state of Ohio affords so easy an egress for its internal produce that could a sure market have been found, it seems little likely that it would have attempted for many years any great establishments of domestic manufactures. But the policy of foreign countries threw so many checks in the way of the agriculturist and so completely suspended commerce that the new stimulus given to human industry was felt in the most remote corners of the Union.

The instantaneous effect produced by the commercial regulations of Europe, it seems almost impossible to credit; cotton mills and fulling mills, distilleries, and manufactories of every description, sprung, as it were, out of the earth, in city, town, village, and even on the forested shores of the western waters. The young Ohio, for instance, which had existed but eight years, in 1811 poured down the western waters woollen, flaxen, and cotton goods, of admirable but coarse texture, spirituous liquors, sugars, &c., to the value of two millions of dollars. . . .

The reviving ascendancy of the manufacturing over the commercial interest creates a strong community of feeling between the northern and western sections of the Union. Pittsburgh, the young Manchester of the United States, must always have the character of a western city, and its maritime port be New Orleans. Corinth was not more truly the eye of Greece than is Pittsburgh of America. Pennsylvania, in which it stands, uniting perfectly the characters of an Atlantic and a western state, is truly the keystone of the federal arch.

But if the new states are thus linked with the North, they have also some feelings in common with the South, and thus, drawing two ways, seem to consolidate that confederacy which Europeans have sometimes prophesied they would break. In the first place, Kentucky and Tennessee, the oldest members of this young family, have not only been peopled from Virginia and the Carolinas, but originally made part of those states. Generously released from their jurisdiction, they still retain a marked affection for their parents, and have, too, a community of evil with them, as well as of origin, in the form of black slavery. It is not unlikely that the mixture of slaveholding and nonslaveholding states to the west of the Alleghenies helps to balance the interests between the northern and southern sections of the Union on the floor of Congress. . . .

It is plain that in the course of a few generations the most populous and powerful division of the American family will be watered by the Mississippi, not the Atlantic. From the character of their infancy we may prophesy that the growing preponderance of the western republics will redound to the national honor and will draw more closely the social league, which binds together the great American family.

Bred up under the eye and fostered by the care of the federal government, they have attached themselves to the national institutions with a devotion of feeling unknown in the older parts of the republic. Their patriotism has all the ardor and their policy all the ingenuousness of youth. I have already had occasion to observe upon the enthusiasm with which they asserted the liberties and honor of their country during the last war. Their spirit throughout that contest was truly chivalrous. The anecdotes recorded not only of the valour, but of the romantic generosity of the western army of volunteers, might grace the noblest page of the

205

Revolutionary history. Nor have the people of the West shown themselves less generous in the Senate than the field. In the hall of the Representatives, they are invariably on the side of what is most honorable and high-minded. Even should they err, you feel that you would rather err with them than be wise with more long-headed or more cold-hearted politicians.

In considering America generally, one finds a character in her foreign to Europe —something which there would be accounted accounted visionary: a liberality of sentiment and a nationality of feeling, not founded upon the mere accident of birth, but upon the appreciation of that civil liberty to which she owes all her greatness and happiness. It is to be expected, however, that in the democracies of the West, these distinctions will be yet more peculiarly marked.

It seems to be a vulgar belief in Europe that the American wilderness is usually settled by the worst members of the community. The friend I write to is well aware that it is generally by the best. The love of liberty, which the emigrant bears with him from the shores of the Connecticut, the Hudson, or Potomac, is exalted and refined in the calm and seclusion of nature's primeval woods and boundless prairies. Some reckless spirits, spurning all law and social order, must doubtless mingle with the more virtuous crowd, but these rarely settle down as farmers. They start ahead of the advanced guard of civilization, and form a wandering troop of hunters, approximating in life and, sometimes, in character to the Indians, their associates. At other times they assume the occupation of shepherds, driving on their cattle from pasture to pasture, according as fancy leads them on from one fair prairie to another still fairer, or according as the approaching tide of population threatens to encroach upon their solitude and their wild dominion. . . .

I have given but a rude sketch of the great divisions of this republic; a subject of this kind admits not of much precision, or, at any rate, my pencil is not skilled enough to handle it ably. I wish you to observe, however, that the birth of the new states has tended to consolidate the Union, and that their growing importance is likely to be felt in the same manner, contrary to the calculations of long-sighted politicians, who foretold that as the integral parts of this great political structure should strengthen and multiply, the cement which held them together would crumble away, and that as the interests of the extended community should become more various, it would be distracted with more party animosities.

The fact is that every sapient prophecy with regard to America has been disproved. We were forewarned that she was too free, and her liberty has proved her security; too peaceable, and she has been found sufficient for her defence; too large, and her size has ensured her union. These numerous republics, scattered through so wide a range of territory, embracing all the climates and containing all the various products of the earth, seem destined, in the course of years, to form a world within themselves, independent alike of the treasures and the industry of all the other sections of the globe. . . . A people who have bled together for liberty, who equally appreciate and equally enjoy that liberty which their own blood or that of their fathers has purchased, who feel, too, that the liberty which they love has found her last asylum on their shores—such a people are bound together by ties of amity and citizenship far beyond what is usual in national communities. . . .

Education

The education of youth, which may be said to form the basis of American government, is in every state of the Union made a national concern. Upon this subject, therefore, the observations that apply to one may be considered as, more or less, applying to all. The portion of this widespread community that paid the earliest and most anxious attention to the instruction of its citizens was New England. This probably originated in the great democracy of her colonial institutions. Liberty and knowledge ever go hand in hand.

If the national policy of some of the New England states has been occasionally censurable, the internal arrangement of all amply redeems her character. There is not a more truly virtuous community in the world than that found in the democracies of the East. The beauty of their villages, the neatness and cleanliness of their houses, the simplicity of their manners, the sincerity of their religion, despoiled in a great measure of its former Calvinistic austerity, their domestic habits, pure morals, and well-administered laws must command the admiration and respect of every stranger. I was forcibly struck in Connecticut with the appearance of the children, neatly dressed, with their satchels on their arms and their faces blooming with health and cheerfulness, dropping their courtesy to the passenger as they trooped to school. The obeisance thus made is not rendered to station but to age. Like the young Spartans, the youth are taught to salute respectfully their superiors in years, and the artlessness and modesty with which the intelligent young creatures reply to the stranger's queries might give pleasure to Lycurgus himself.

The state of Connecticut has appropriated a fund of a million and a half of dollars to the suport of public schools. In Vermont, a certain portion of land has been laid off in every township, whose proceeds are devoted to the same purpose. In the other states, every township taxes itself to such amount as is necessary to defray the expense of schools, which teach reading, writing, and arithmetic to the whole population. In larger towns these schools teach geography and the rudiments of Latin. These establishments, supported at the common expense, are open to the whole youth, male and female, of the country. Other seminaries of a higher order are also maintained in the more populous districts, half the expense being discharged by appropriated funds and the remainder by a small charge laid on the scholar. The instruction here given fits the youth for the state colleges, of which there is one or more in every state. The university of Cambridge, in Massachusetts, is the oldest and, I believe, the most distinguished establishment of the kind existing in the Union.

Perhaps the number of colleges founded in this widespread family of republics may not, in general, be favourable to the growth of distinguished universities. It best answers, however, the object intended, which is not to raise a few very learned citizens but a well-informed and liberal-minded community. . . .

If we must seek the explanation of national manners in national institutions and early education, all the characteristics of the American admit of an easy explanation. The foreigner is at first surprised to find in the ordinary citizen that intelligence and those sentiments which he had been accustomed to seek in the writings of philosophers and the conversation of the most enlightened. The better half of our education in the Old World consists of unlearning: we have to unlearn when we come from the nursery, to unlearn again when we come from the school, and often to continue unlearning through life, and to quit the scene at last without having rid ourselves of half the false notions which had been implanted in our young minds. All this trouble is saved here. The impressions received in childhood are few and simple, as are all the elements of just knowledge. Whatever ideas may be acquired are learned from the page of truth and embrace principles often unknown to the most finished scholar of Europe. Nor is the *manner* in which education is here conducted without its influence in forming the character. I feel disposed at least to ascribe to it that mild friendliness of demeanor which distinguishes the American. It is violence that begets violence, and gentleness, gentleness. I have frequently heard it stated by West Indians that a slave invariably makes the hardest slave driver. In English schools it is well known that the worst-used *fag* becomes, in his turn, the most cruel tyrant, and in a British ship of war it will often be found that the merciless disciplinarian has learned his harshness in the school of suffering. The American, in his infancy, manhood, or age, never feels the hand of oppression. Violence is positively forbidden in the school, in the prisons, on shipboard, in the army; everywhere, in short, where authority is exercised, it must be exercised without appeal to the argument of a blow.

Not long since a master was dismissed from a public school, in a neighbouring state, for having struck a boy. The little fellow was transformed in a moment from a culprit to an accuser. "Do you dare to strike me? You are my teacher, but not my tyrant." The schoolroom made common cause in a moment, the fact was enquired into, and the master dismissed. No apology for the punishment was sought in the nature of the offence which might have provoked it. As my informer observed, "It was thought that the man who could not master his own passions was unfit to control the passions of others; besides, that he had infringed the rules of the school and forfeited the respect of his scholars." By this early exemption from arbitrary power, the boy acquires feelings and habits which abide with him through life. He feels his own importance as a human and a thinking being, and learns to regard violence as equally degrading to him who exercises it and to him who submits to it. You will perceive how the seeds of pride and gentleness are thus likely to spring up together in the same mind. In the proper union and tempering of these two qualities were, perhaps, found the perfection of national as well as of individual character.

In the education of women, New England seems hitherto to have been peculiarly liberal. The ladies of the eastern states are frequently possessed of the most solid acquirements, the modern and even the dead languages, and a wide scope of reading; the consequence is that their manners have the character of being more composed than those of my gay young friends in this quarter. I have already stated, in one of my earlier letters, that the public attention is now everywhere turned to the improvement of female education. In some states, colleges for girls are established under the eye of the legislature, in which are taught all those important branches of knowledge that your friend Dr. Rush conceived to be so requisite.

In other countries it may seem of little consequence to inculcate upon the female mind "the principles of government, and the obligations of patriotism," but it was wisely forseen by that venerable apostle of liberty that in a country where a mother is charged with the formation of an infant mind that is to be called in future to judge of the laws and support the liberties of a republic, the mother herself should well understand those laws and estimate those liberties. Personal accomplishments and the more ornamental branches of knowledge should certainly in America be made subordinate to solid information. This is perfectly the case with respect to the men; as yet the women have been educated too much after the European manner. French, Italian, dancing, drawing engage the hours of the one sex (and this but too commonly in a lax and careless way), while the more appropriate studies of the other are philosophy, history, political economy, and the exact sciences. It follows, consequently, that after the spirits of youth have somewhat subsided, the two sexes have less in common in their pursuits and turn of thinking than is desirable. A woman of a powerful intellect will of course seize upon the new topics presented to her by the conversation of her husband. The less vigorous or the more thoughtless mind is not easily brought to forego trifling pursuits for those which occupy the stronger reason of its companion.

I must remark that in no particular is the liberal philosophy of the Americans more honorably evinced than in the place which is awarded to women. The prejudices still to be found in Europe, though now indeed somewhat antiquated, which would confine the female library to romances, poetry, and belleslettres, and female conversation to the last new publication, new bonnet, and *pas seul,* are entirely unknown here. The women are assuming their place as thinking beings, not in despite of the men, but chiefly in consequence of their enlarged views and exertions as fathers and legislators. . . .

Slavery

And now, my dear friend, I approach the conclusion of the voluminous correspondence which I have addressed to you from this country. You contrive to persuade me that the information I have collected has often possessed for you the merit of novelty. I have, however, to regret that my personal observation has been confined to a portion of this vast country, the whole of whose surface merits the study of a more discerning traveller than myself. I own that as regards the southern states I have ever felt a secret reluctance to visit their territory. The sight of slavery is revolting everywhere, but to inhale the impure breath of its pestilence in the free winds of America is odious beyond all that the imagination can conceive. I do not mean to indulge in idle declamation either against the injustice of the masters or upon the degradation of the slave. This is a subject upon which it is difficult to reason, because it is so easy to feel. The difficulties that stand in the way of emancipation, I can perceive to be numerous; but should the masters content themselves with idly deploring the evil, instead of "setting their shoulder to the wheel" and actively working out its remedy, neither their courtesy in the drawing room, their virtues in domestic life, nor even their public services in the senate and the field will preserve the southern planters from the reprobation of their northern brethren, and the scorn of mankind. The Virginians are said to pride themselves upon the peculiar tenderness with which they visit the sceptre of authority upon their African vassals. As all those acquainted with the character of the Virginia planters, whether Americans or foreigners, appear to concur in bearing testimony to their humanity, it is probable that they are entitled to the praise which they claim. But in their position, justice should be held superior to humanity; to break the chains would be more generous than to gild them, and, whether we consider the interests of the master or the slave, decidedly more useful. It is true that this neither can nor ought to be done too hastily. To give liberty to a slave before he understands its value is, perhaps, rather to impose a penalty than to bestow a blessing; but it is not clear to me that the southern planters are duly exerting themselves to prepare the way for that change in the condition of their black population which they profess to think not only desirable but inevitable. From the conversation of some distinguished Virginians, I cannot but apprehend that they suffer themselves to be disheartened by the slender success which has hitherto attended the exertions of those philanthropists who have made the character and condition of the negro their study and care. "Look into the cabins of our free negroes," said an eminent individual, a native of Virginia, in conversing with me lately upon this subject; "you will find there little to encourage the idea that to impart the rights of freemen to our black population is to ameliorate their condition, or to elevate their character." It is undoubtedly true that the free negroes of Maryland and Virginia form the most wretched and consequently the most vicious portion of the black population. The most casual observation is sufficient to satisfy a stranger of the truth of this statement. I have not seen a miserable half-clad negro in either state whom I have not found, upon enquiry, to be in possession of liberty. But what argument is to be adduced from this? That to emancipate the African race would be to smite the land with a worse plague than that which defaces it already? The history of the negro in the northern states will save us from so revolting a conclusion. To argue that he constitutes, even there, the least valuable portion of the population, will not affect the question. If his character be there *improving,* a fact which none will deny, we have sufficient data upon which to ground the belief that he may, in time, be rendered a useful member of society, and that the vice and wretchedness which here dwell in the cabins of the emancipated negroes may be traced, in part, to the mixture of freedmen and slaves now observed in the black population. Were the whole race emancipated, their education would necessarily become a national object, the white population would be constrained to hire their service, and they themselves be under the necessity of selling it. At present, when restored by some generous planter to their birthright of liberty, the sons of Africa forfeit the protection of a master without securing the guardianship of the law. To their untutored minds, the gift of freedom is only a release from labour. Poor, ignorant, and lazy, it is impossible that they should not soon be vicious. To exonerate herself from the increasing weight of black pauperism, Virginia has imposed a restriction upon the benevolence of her citizens by a law which exacts of the citizen who emancipates his vassals that he shall remove them without the precincts of the state. . . . Why does not Virginia recur to the plan marked out by herself in the first year of her independence? Has she not virtue to execute what she had wisdom to conceive? She has made so many noble sacrifices to humanity and patriotism, her history records so many acts of heroism and disinterested generosity, that I am willing to persuade myself she is equal to this also. Nor can she be so blind to the future as not to perceive the consequences with which she is threatened, should she not take some active measures to eradicate the Egyptian plague which covers her soil. A servile war is the least of the evils which could befall her; the ruin of her moral character, the decay of her strength, the loss of her political importance, vice, indolence, degradation—these are the evils that will overtake her.

But I shall weary you with my commentaries upon an evil that is so far removed from your sight. Had you studied with me the history and character of the American republic, did you see in her so many seeds of excellence, so bright a dawning of national glory, so fair a promise of a brilliant meridian day, as your friend imagines that she can discern, you would share all that regret, impatience, and anxiety, with which she regards every stain that rests upon her morals, every danger that threatens her peace. An awful responsibility has devolved on the American nation; the liberties of mankind are entrusted to their guardianship; the honor of freedom is identified with the honor of their republic; the agents of tyranny are active in one hemisphere; may the children of liberty be equally active in the other! May they return with fresh ardor to the glorious work which they formerly encountered with so much success—in one word, may they realize the conviction lately expressed to me by their venerable President that "the day is not very far distant when a slave will not be found in America!"

PART THREE

The Problems
of Expansion, 1820–1876

In the 1820s a new generation matured and came to power in the United States. It had not participated in forging the nation, nor could it remember the debate on the Constitution or the events of 1776. This was, therefore, a time of acute testing for the republic. Were the values and goals of the Founding Fathers relevant or appropriate to their children and grandchildren? When Washington, Jefferson, Adams, and Madison were Presidents, hardly anyone doubted that the spirit of the Revolution was still alive. Citizens shared keen memories of fighting the Redcoats and few feared for the unity of the states; but now without these ties or experiences, a second and third generation might find their inherited traditions inapplicable as they confronted new problems and opportunities.

Moreover, the nation could not simply rely on old formulas or pat applications of tested principles. Pressing issues after 1820 demanded innovative and imaginative solutions. The Founding Fathers had imagined a country of sturdy freemen, tilling their own soil; but what was one to do with the growing number of textile factories in New England towns? They had believed that slavery would gradually disappear; but what was one to do when cotton fastened the institution firmly onto the South? They had imagined a nation of settled farmers; but what was one to do when countrymen refused to sit still and the lines of wagons moving westward swelled daily? They had invoked the general welfare and decried factionalism in politics; but what was one to say of burgeoning political parties and bitterly fought partisan election campaigns? The past was not a specific enough guide to the present problems.

After 1820, the United States began its growth as a major industrial nation, laying the foundation for the tremendous economic development that occurred after the Civil War. In 1830 the production of bituminous coal was barely over 100,000 tons; by 1860 it had climbed to 6,000,000 tons. In 1820 the manufacture of pig iron was only 54,000 tons; by 1860 it stood at 821,000 tons. By the turn of the next century these figures also would be dwarfed, but the first encounter with industrialism, the initial confrontation of the republic and the machine, occurred between 1820 and 1860.

The confrontation was frightening. Americans, surveying the English experience, feared that the factory might bring slums and violent strikes, and divide the nation as it degraded its laborers. Wealth and power might not be worth this cost; but, in fact, the United States avoided these dire results. Entrepreneurs, conscious of the dangers, prudently and paternally supervised the life of their workers. In Lowell, Massachusetts, for example, the textile-mill owners kept close watch over the young girls who tended the machines in company-sponsored boarding houses, and European travelers as well as local officials often testified to the moral integrity of the factory hands. Furthermore, there was long an acute shortage of labor in the first decades of the nineteenth century so that entrepreneurs not only invested in the newest labor-saving machinery but also tried to make working conditions as attractive as possible in order to recruit laborers to the factory. The founders of Lowell, hoping to draw New England farm girls to the mills, assured their families that the experience would be neither demeaning nor humiliating. Private profit and the workers' welfare often fitted together neatly. Finally, after 1840, an influx of immigrants supplied the factory owners' need for labor. The Europeans were docile. Coming from the country where they had faced starvation, the Irish, for instance, found the work hard but not intolerable. Owners became less paternal as immigrants increasingly made up the labor force. But many Americans had already concluded that industrialism would probably not corrupt the country.

The expanding plantation system transformed the South as extensively as the machine affected the North. The declining profits of tobacco cultivation at the end of the eighteenth century had persuaded many observers that slavery would not long survive. But the rise of textile manufacturing in England and New England created a large market for cotton. Factories called for more and more raw materials and the plantation turned to filling the demand.

For some Southerners the plantation style of life held an attraction. They treated their slaves favorably, delighted in social visits with neighbors, in holding local and state political office, and in living leisurely as gentlemen; but the more typical planter ran his establishment like a business, a cotton-growing factory requiring all the oversight and diligence of a capitalistic enterprise. He managed his work force rigorously to obtain the greatest return; he valued slaves for their market price, buying or selling accordingly. To maintain order and control he had recourse to coercion. But planters also bought obedience by keeping the perspectives of the slaves as limited as possible, to prevent them from imagining a life apart from slavery. Bennet Barrow, a wealthy Louisiana planter, advised his colleagues not to educate a slave or to allow him to visit with any frequency on other plantations or in towns. "You must," he also added, "make him as comfortable as possible at home . . . and by that means create in him a habit of perfect dependence on you." By varying combinations of these strategies, masters kept their slaves obediently at work. After 1830, few doubted the viability of the plantation system.

During these years Americans migrated westward in mounting numbers so that by 1860 almost as many people lived in the new states as in the original thirteen colonies. In the decades after 1820 Americans rapidly settled Ohio, Illinois, Indiana, Wisconsin, Michigan, and Missouri. By 1860, the North Central states held almost eight million people, and more than half of them had not been born in the region.

These circumstances might have fragmented the community and even the nation. It was one thing if masters did not know their slaves or owners their workers; but what would become of a community where neighbors did not know each other? Actually, however, migration encouraged rather than weakened community ties. The trip west and the first years of settlement forced men to rely upon each other for basic assistance. Neighbors banded together not only to construct houses but as vigilantes, to keep law and order. Moreover, without very many resources of their own, Western settlers turned frequently to the national government to build roads and supply troops, and generally to promote their welfare. They felt a national allegiance even more keenly than Easterners and Southerners.

The claims of the sections clashed in Washington, and the result was not always generous accommodation. Earlier, the focus of political attention usually had been on the state capitals. But even by the close of Washington's administration, national politics played an important part in the development of the country, and, whether for reasons of personality or ideology, the political scene was frequently stormy. At first, the strength of political organization fluctuated. At times there were bitter battles, at others good feeling prevailed. The accession of Andrew Jackson to the Presidency, however, sparked several lasting changes. First, elections became increasingly party-centered as Whigs and Democrats competed for support. Second, political organizations bcame more permanent and elaborate, feeding on the spoils of victory. Moreover, the two parties competed for power by attempting to capture wide public backing; the Whigs, abandoning all elitist notions in 1840, pursued mass support as keenly as the Jacksonians. As a result, voter participation reached unprecedented levels in Presidential elections. At the same time, national politics began to rival state politics in importance; more and more often, Washington became the appropriate place to seek assistance, to assert interests and ideas.

The outstanding quality of national politics after 1820, however, was sectionalism. Party organization was too new and weak to give members a national outlook. Men voted in Congress by states rather than by parties. They campaigned on election day under a party banner, but when it came time to make up their minds on an issue, they paid most attention to the interests of their state. Southerners tended to live together in Washington, and vote together in Congress; Western and Northern representatives were only slightly less clannish. Party loyalties were not strong enough to weaken sectional allegiance. Membership in a national organization like the Whigs or the Democrats was not vital enough to encourage a national perspective.

If no pressing questions had confronted the nation, sectionalism might have made little difference. But the country urgently needed guidance in settling the slavery problem, and national political institutions did not provide it. They were, of course, not alone in their failure; Protestant churches, for example, split over the issue; but when political parties also divided, civil war followed.

The first abolitional agitation coincided with the growing awareness that the peculiar institution would not die out of its own accord. To the abolitionists, slavery controverted the fundamental precepts of Christian morality as well as the basic ideals of the republic. Reformers convinced of the innate perfectibility of man were eagerly attempting to cure the insane, rehabilitate the criminal, and teach the deaf and dumb. They found it intolerable to accept the perpetuation of slavery in the United States. At first, audiences greeted their messages with little enthusiasm, but when slavery threatened to expand into the Western territories, more and more citizens thought it best to limit the institution. Southerners, for their part, reacted to all criticisms defensively and rigidly, preferring to block out the messages rather than try to reach a solution within a national framework. Convinced that their style of life, economic well-being, and physical safety depended on slavery, they saw themselves as a persecuted and misunderstood minority and retreated intellectually, socially, and politically inward.

The parties were unable to bridge these divisions. As other institutions splintered over the issue of slavery, the political arena became one of the last meeting places for all sections, offering a forum for discussion and a mechanism for effecting adjustments; but as Southerner separated from Northerner, the Democratic party became the party of the South, and the Republicans, successors to the Whigs, became the party of the North. This political reaction was all the more tragic for there was certainly in the North and West and in some parts of the South a vague but genuine sentiment for the union—a feeling that put the perpetuation of the United States above all other considerations. But the parties could not translate this emotion into workable political programs. Each side reiterated its demands; and when, in 1860, the South believed that Lincoln's election as President tipped the balance of power to the North, it took the final step of separation. The Union, rather than let its sisters depart in peace, resorted to arms. Even at the cost of civil war, it would not allow the nation to disintegrate.

Neither North nor South could marshall men and equipment speedily and efficiently, and quick success eluded both sides. Slowly over four years, the greater resources of the Union became increasingly important, and when General Ulysses S. Grant made full use of them, the North finally earned a hard-fought victory. The problems posed by peace were hardly less simple, and the Union did not reveal special skill or sensitivity in confronting them. The Republicans lacked any consistent or carefully considered program. They moved unsteadily from one measure to another, rarely considering the wider significance and implications of their actions. By the time military occupation was over in 1876, there were deep wounds that would take decades or longer to heal. The Union was preserved and the Negro free; but the North liberated the slaves without sustained attention to their welfare. It secured their political rights in law, but paid little attention to realities—political, social, or economic. The South, crushed and bitter, resented the harshness of military reconstruction, and when finally left to its own devices it all too often remained isolated in spirit and temperament. The nation in 1876 was still far from at peace with itself.

21

Morals and the Machine

The introduction of the machine and the factory in America was not without its difficulty, for, judging by the English experience, many observers feared for the moral welfare of the nation. In England they saw harsh working conditions and increasing friction between classes in strikes and labor organizations. Would the factory bring these evils to the new republic?

The founding of Lowell, Massachusetts, in the 1820s by a group of Boston entrepreneurs was a venture in profitmaking through the manufacture of textiles. But it was also an attempt to order industrial organization so as to prevent the noxious effects so prevalent in England. The two goals were not contradictory. The sponsors had to attract a large and reliable labor force, and in a country where small farmers predominated, this was no simple task. They decided to employ the young ladies of New England agricultural families. New England farming was not in so profitable a state that the families would not welcome some extra money. Still, fathers would have to be assured of their daughters' physical and moral welfare—the way the nation would have to be assured of the wholesome effects of industry. By design and good fortune, the Lowell entrepreneurs attracted a labor supply and helped convince the nation that industry could be controlled. The following selection by a Lowell minister, Henry A. Miles, was what the nation in general and fathers in particular wanted to hear.

LOWELL, AS IT WAS
AND AS IT IS
Henry A. Miles

Lowell has been highly commended by some, as a model community, for its good order, industry, spirit of intelligence, and general freedom from vice. It has been strongly condemned, by others, as a hotbed of corruption, tainting and polluting the whole land. We all, in New England, have an interest in knowing what are the exact facts of the case. We are destined to be a great manufacturing people. The

From *Lowell, As It Was and As It Is* (Lowell, 1845), 62–63, 67–76, 101–105, 129–135, 140–153, 160–161, 174–179, 214–215.

influences that go forth from Lowell, will go forth from many other manufacturing villages and cities. If these influences are pernicious, we have a great calamity impending over us. Rather than endure it, we should prefer to have every factory destroyed; the character of our sons and daughters being of infinitely more importance than any considerations "wherewithal they shall be clothed." If, on the other hand, a system has been introduced, carefully provided with checks and safeguards, and strong moral and conservative influences, it is our duty to see that this system be faithfully carried out, so as to prevent the disastrous results which have developed themselves in the manufacturing towns of other countries. Hence the topics above named assume the importance of the highest moral questions. They will justify and demand the most careful consideration. The author writes after a nine years' residence in this city, during which he has closely observed the working of the factory system, and has gathered a great amount of statistical facts which have a bearing upon this subject. He believes himself to be unaffected by any partisan views, as he stands wholly aside from the sphere of any interested motives. He enters upon this part of his work, feeling, in the outset, that he has no case, one way or the other, to make out.

A Lowell Boarding-House

Each of the long blocks of boarding-houses is divided into six or eight tenements, and are generally three stories high. These tenements are finished off in a style much above the common farm-houses of the country, and more nearly resemble the abodes of respectable mechanics in rural villages. They are all furnished with an abundant supply of water, and with suitable yards and out-buildings. These are constantly kept clean, the buildings well painted, and the premises thoroughly whitewashed every spring, at the Corporation's expense. The front room is usually the common eating-room of the house, and the kitchen is in the rear. The keeper of the house, (commonly a widow, with her family of children,) has her parlor in some part of the establishment; and in some houses there is a sitting-room for the use of the boarders. The remainder of the apartments are sleeping-rooms. In each of these are lodged two, four, and in some cases six boarders; and the room has an air of neatness and comfort, exceeding what most of the occupants have been accustomed to in their paternal homes. In many cases, these rooms are not sufficiently large for the number who occupy them; and oftentimes that attention is not paid to their ventilation which a due regard to health demands. These are points upon which a reform is called for; and, in the construction of new boarding-houses, this reform should be attempted. At the same time, it should in justice be added, that the evil alluded to is not peculiar to Lowell, and will not probably appear to be a crying one, if the case should be brought into comparison with many of the apartments of milliners and sempstresses in the boarding-houses of our cities.

As one important feature in the management of these houses, it deserves to be named that male operatives and female operatives do not board in the same tenement; and the following Regulations, printed by one of the companies, and given to each keeper of their houses, are here subjoined, as a simple statement of the rules generally observed by all the Corporations.

Regulations to be observed by persons occupying the Boarding-houses belonging to the Merrimack Manufacturing Company.

They must not board any persons not employed by the company, unless by special permission.

No disorderly or improper conduct must be allowed in the houses.

The doors must be closed at 10 o'clock in the evening; and no person admitted after that time, unless a sufficient excuse can be given.

Those who keep the houses, when required, must give an account of the number, names, and employment of their boarders; also with regard to their general conduct, and whether they are in the habit of attending public worship.

The buildings, both inside and out, and the yards about them, must be kept clean, and in good order. If the buildings or fences are injured, they will be repaired and charged to the occupant.

No one will be allowed to keep swine.

The hours of taking meals in these houses are uniform throughout all the Corporations in the city, and are as follows: Dinner—always at half past twelve o'clock. Breakfast—from November 1 to February 28, before going to work, and so early as to begin work as soon as it is light; through March at half past seven o'clock; from April 1 to September 19, at seven o'clock; and from September 20 to October 31, at half past seven o'clock. Supper—always after work at night, that is, after seven o'clock, from March 20 to September 19; after half-past seven o'clock, from September 20 to March 19. The time allowed for each meal is thirty minutes for breakfast, when that meal is taken after beginning work; for dinner, thirty minutes, from September 1 to April 30; and forty-five minutes from May 1 to August 31.

That this time is too short for a due regard to health, must be obvious to all. And yet it is probably as long as most business men allow to themselves; it is probably as long as is spent at the tables of more than half of our public hotels. For the sake of the operatives we wish that the time for meals was lengthened; but we do not see the propriety of calling in this quarter for a reform in those habits of hasty eating which pervade the whole country, and characterize our nation. The food that is furnished in these houses is of a substantial and wholesome kind, is neatly served, and in sufficient abundance. Operatives are under no compulsion to board in one tenement rather than another; it is for the interest of the boarding-house keeper, therefore, to have her bill of fare attractive.

The rents of the company's houses are purposely low, averaging only from one third to one half of what similar houses rent for in the city. There is no intention on the part of the Corporation to make any revenue from these houses. They are a great source of annual expense. But the advantages of supervision are more than an equivalent for this. No tenant is admitted who has not hitherto borne a good character, and who does not continue to sustain it. In many cases the tenant has long been keeper of the house, for six, eight, or twelve years, and is well known to hundreds of her girls as their adviser and friend and second mother.

The influence which this system of boarding-houses has exerted upon the good order and good morals of the place, has been vast and beneficent. By it the care and influence of the superintendent are extended over his operatives, while they are out of the mill, as well as while they are in it. Employing chiefly those who have no permanent residence in Lowell, but are only temporary boarders, upon any embarrassment of affairs they return to their country homes, and do not sink down here a helpless caste, clamouring for work, starving unless employed, and hence ready for a riot, for the destruction of property, and repeating here the scenes enacted in the manufacturing villages of England. To a very great degree the future condition of Lowell is dependent upon a faithful adhesion to this system; and it will deserve the serious consideration of those old towns which are now introducing steam mills, whether, if they do not provide boarding-houses, and employ chiefly other operatives than resident ones, they be not bringing in the seeds of future and alarming evil.

Hours of Labor

The following table shows the average hours per day of running the mills, throughout the year, on all the Corporations in Lowell:

	h.	m.		h.	m.
January	11	24	July	12	45
February	12	00	August	12	45
March	11	52	September	12	23
April	13	31	October	12	10
May	12	45	November	11	56
June	12	45	December	11	24

In addition to the above, it should be stated, that lamps are never lighted on Saturday evening, and that four holidays are allowed in the year, viz. Fast Day, Fourth of July, Thanksgiving Day, and Christmas Day.

No fact connected with the manufacturing business, has been so often, or so strongly objected to as this, which appears from the above table, that the average daily time of running the mills is twelve hours and ten minutes. It is no part of the object of this book to defend any thing which may be shown to be wrong, its sole purpose being a careful presentation of facts. Arguments are not needed to prove that toil, if it be continued for this length of time, each day, month after month, and year after year, is excessive, and too much for the tender frames of young women to bear. No one can more sincerely desire, than the writer of this book, that they had more leisure time for mental improvement and social enjoyment. It must be remembered, however, that their work is comparatively light. All the hard processes, not conducted by men, are performed by machines, the movements of which female operatives are required merely to oversee and adjust. And then as to their long confinement and care, there is a mitigation which, in discussions on this subject, has been almost altogether overlooked, but which is of such vital importance that it merits the most careful attention.

We have given above the hours per day of operating the mills. It must be well understood what this means. These are the hours for running the wheels. It does not follow that all operatives work this number of hours, or are in attendance this number of hours. This is not the case. By a system adjusted to secure this end, by keeping engaged a number of spare hands, by occasional permissions of absence, and by an allowed exchange of work among the girls, the average number of hours in which they are actually employed is not more than ten and a half. They are out to go shopping, to repair their clothes, to take care of themselves in any occasional illness, to see friends visiting the city, to call on sick friends here; nor are reasonable requests of this kind refused. Many of these girls, moreover, in the course of each year, take a vacation of a few weeks, to return to their homes. In these absences the work of the mill is not suspended. The wheels continue their revolutions for the prescribed number of hours. The processes are temporarily superintended by other hands. To suppose that every operative is on duty just as long as the machinery is in motion, is an error of the most deceptive kind. Yet this fallacy has been assumed in almost all the discussions on this subject. The fact has been overlooked of the great number of absences from the mills. These absences reduce the average of work-hours for the girls to the number just stated—ten and a half. This is not a mere assertion. It is a carefully ascertained, and well established fact, in verification of which proof will now be submitted.

Each overseer keeps a record of all the time his hands are employed, in days and quarter of days. These records, in one mill in the city, have been subjected to a thorough analysis. The space of time over which this analysis has been carried is one year. In Boott Mill, No. 1, there are one hundred and six girls who have been employed one year, working by the job. This is the whole number in that mill who are thus employed and have worked that time; and their time record gives the following results: Average number of days per year to each girl, two hundred and sixty and eighty-six one hundredths. Average number of hours per day, to each girl, ten hours and eight minutes.

Moral Police of the Corporations

It has been seen what a large amount of capital is here invested, and what manifold and extensive operations this capital sets in motion. The productiveness of these works depends upon one primary and indispensable condition—the existence of an industrious, sober, orderly, and moral class of operatives. Without this, the mills in Lowell would be worthless. Profits would be absorbed by cases of irregularity, carelessness, and neglect; while the existence of any great moral exposure in Lowell would cut off the supply of help from the virtuous homesteads of the country. Public morals and private interests, identical in all places, are here seen to be linked together in an indissoluble connection. Accordingly, the sagacity of self-interest, as well as more disinterested considerations, has led to the adoption of a strict system of moral police.

Before we proceed to notice the details of this system, there is one consideration bearing upon the character of our operatives, which must all the while be borne in mind. *We have no permanent factory population.* This is the wide gulf which separates the English manufacturing towns from Lowell. Only a very few of our operatives have their homes in this city. The most of them come from the distant interior of the country, as will be proved by statistical facts which will be presented in a subsequent chapter.

To the general fact, here noticed, should be added another, of scarcely less importance to a just comprehension of this subject,—*the female operatives Lowell do not work, on an average, more than four and a half years in the factories.* They then return to their homes, and their places are taken by their sisters, or by other female friends from their neighborhood.

Here, then, we have two important elements of difference between English and American operatives. The former are resident operatives, and are operatives for life, and constitute a permanent, dependent factory caste. The latter come from distant homes, to which in a few years they return, to be the wives of the farmers and mechanics of the country towns and villages. The English visitor to Lowell, when he finds it so hard to understand why American operatives are so superior to those of Leeds and Manchester, will do well to remember what a different class of females we have here to *begin* with—girls well educated in virtuous rural homes; nor must the Lowell manufacturer forget, that we forfeit the distinction, from that moment, when we cease to obtain such girls as the operatives of the city.

To obtain this constant importation of female hands from the country, it is necessary to secure *the moral protection of their characters while they are resident in Lowell.* This, therefore, is the chief object of that moral police referred to, some details of which will now be given.

It should be stated, in the outset, that no persons are employed on the Corporations who are addicted to intemperance, or who are known to be guilty of any immoralities of conduct. As the parent of all other vices, intemperance is most carefully excluded. Absolute freedom from intoxicating liquors is understood, throughout the city, to be a prerequisite to obtaining employment in the mills, and any person known to be addicted to their use is at once dismissed.

A more strictly and universally temperate class of persons cannot be found, than the nine thousand operatives of this city; and the fact is as well known to all others living here, as it is of some honest pride among themselves. In relation to other immoralities, it may be stated, that the suspicion of criminal conduct, association with suspected persons, and general and habitual light behavior and conversation, are regarded as sufficient reasons for dismissions, and for which delinquent operatives are discharged.

In respect to discharged operatives, there is a system observed, of such an effectual and salutary operation, that it deserves to be minutely described.

Any person wishing to leave a mill, is at liberty to do so, at any time, after giving a fortnight's notice. The operative so leaving, if of good character, and having worked a year, is entitled, as a matter of right, to an honorable discharge, made out after a printed form, with which every counting-room is supplied. That form is as follows:

Mr. or Miss —— ——, has been employed by the —— Manufacturing Company, in a —— Room, — years — months, and is honorably discharged.
—— ——, *Superintendent.*

LOWELL, —— ——

This discharge is a letter of recommendation to any other mill in the city, and not without its influence in procuring employment in any other mill in New England. A record of all such discharges is made in each counting-room, in a book kept for that purpose.

So much for honorable discharges. Those dishonorable have another treatment. The names of all persons dismissed for bad conduct, or who leave the mill irregularly, are also entered in a book kept for that purpose, and these names are sent to all the counting-rooms of the city, and are there entered on *their* books. *Such persons obtain no more employment throughout the city.* The question is put to each applicant, "Have you worked before in the city, and if so, where is your discharge?" If no discharge be presented, an inquiry of the applicant's name will enable the superintendent to know whether that name stands on his book of dishonorable discharges, and he is thus saved from taking in a corrupt or unworthy hand. This system, which has been in operation in Lowell from the beginning, is of great and important effect in driving unworthy persons from our city, and in preserving the high character of our operatives.

Any description of the moral care, studied by the Corporations, would be defective if it omitted a reference to the overseers. Every room in every mill has its first and second overseer. The former, or, in his absence, the latter, has the entire care of the room, taking in such operatives as he wants for the work of the room, assigning to them their employment, superintending each process, directing the repairs of disordered machinery, giving answers to questions of advice, and granting permissions of absence. At his small desk, near the door, where he can see all who go out or come in, the overseer may generally be found; and he is held responsible for the good order, propriety of conduct, and attention to business, of the operatives of that room. Hence, this is a post of much importance, and the good management of the mill is almost wholly dependent upon the character of its overseers. It is for this reason that peculiar care is exercised in their appointment. Raw hands, and of unknown characters, are never placed in this office. It is attained only by those who have either served a regular apprenticeship as machinists in the Repair Shop, or have become well known and well tried, as third hands, and assistant overseers. It is a post for which there are always many applicants, the pay being two dollars a day, with a good house, owned by the company, and rented at the reduced charge before notice. The overseers are almost universally married men, with families; and as a body, numbering about one hundred and eighty, in all, are among the most permanent residents, and most trustworthy and valuable citizens of the place. A large number of them are members of our churches, and are often chosen as council men in the city government, and representatives in the State legislature. The guiding and salutary influence which they exert over the operatives, is one of the most essential parts of the moral machinery of the mills.

As closely connected with the foregoing statements, the following note from a superintendent may be here republished, which was sent in reply to questions proposed to him in the Spring of 1841:—

Dear Sir:—

I employ in our mills, and in the various departments connected with them, thirty overseers, and as many second overseers. My overseers are married men, with families, with a single exception, and even he has engaged a tenement, and is to be married soon. Our second overseers are younger men, but upwards of twenty of them are married, and several others are soon to be married. Sixteen of our overseers are members of some regular church, and four of them are deacons. Ten of our second overseers are also members of the church, and one of them is the superintendent of a Sunday School. I have no hesitation in saying that in all the sterling requisites of character, in native intelligence, and practical good sense, in sound morality, and as active, useful, and exemplary citizens, they may, as a class, safely challenge comparison with any class in our community. I know not, among them all, an intemperate man, nor, at this time, even what is called a moderate drinker.

Yours truly,

Lowell, May 10, 1841

Still another source of trust which a Corporation has, for the good character of its operatives, is the moral control which they have over one another. Of course this control would be nothing among a generally corrupt and degraded class. But among virtuous and high-minded young women, who feel that they have the keeping of their characters, and that any stain upon their associates brings reproach upon themselves, the power of opinion becomes an ever-present, and ever-active restraint. A girl, *suspected* of immoralities, or serious improprieties of conduct, at once loses caste. Her fellow-boarders will at once leave the house, if the keeper does not dismiss the offender. In self-protection, therefore, the matron is obliged to put the offender away. Nor will her former companions walk with, or work with her; till at length, finding herself everywhere talked about, and pointed at, and shunned, she is obliged to relieve her fellow-operatives of a presence which they feel brings disgrace. From this power of opinion, there is no appeal; and as long as it is exerted in favor of propriety of behavior and purity of life, it is one of the most active and effectual safeguards of character.

It may not be out of place to present here the regulations, which are observed alike on all the Corporations, which are given to the operatives when they are first employed, and are posted up conspicuously in all the mills. They are as follows:—

Regulations to be Observed by All Persons Employed by the

——Manufacturing Company, in the Factories.

Every overseer is required to be punctual himself, and to see that those employed under him are so.

The overseers may, at their discretion, grant leave of absence to those employed under them, when there are sufficient spare hands in the room to supply their place; but when there are not sufficient spare hands, they are not allowed to grant leave of absence unless in cases of absolute necessity.

All persons are required to observe the regulations of the room in which they are employed. They are not allowed to be absent from their work without the consent of their overseer, except in case of sickness, and then they are required to send him word of the cause of their absence.

All persons are required to board in one of the boarding houses belonging to the company, and conform to the regulations of the house in which they board.

All persons are required to be constant in attendance on public worship, at one of the regular places of worship in this place.

Persons who do not comply with the above regulations will not be employed by the company.

Persons entering the employment of the company, are considered as engaging to work one year.

All persons intending to leave the employment of the company, are required to give notice of the same to their overseer, at least two weeks previous to the time of leaving.

Any one who shall take from the mills, or the yard, any yarn, cloth, or other article belonging to the company, will be considered guilty of STEALING—and prosecuted accordingly.

The above regulations are considered part of the contract with all persons entering the employment of the——Manufacturing Company. All persons who shall have complied with them, on leaving the employment of the company, shall be entitled to an honorable discharge, which will serve as a recommendation to any of the factories in Lowell. No one who shall not have complied with them will be entitled to such a discharge.

—— ——, Agent

Boarding-House Statistics

It has been before stated that in many cases the keepers of the boarding-houses retain their places for eight, ten, or twelve years. Standing in the place of parents to their girls, their future welfare is a matter of deep interest to these matrons, and frequently they have some knowledge of the after fortunes of their boarders, through sisters and neighbors, who have succeeded them in the mills. It, hence, appeared probable, that by extensive and careful inquiries of the matrons, important facts might be collected in respect to the health and character of their girls, while boarders, and of their honorable standing in life, after they had retired from Lowell. For this purpose a series of questions was prepared, copies of which were handed to three or four matrons on each Corporation, and their written replies have been returned to the author, and will here be subjoined. There was no selection of houses from which to seek returns, and there is no selection of returns so as to present only favorable cases.

The questions were as follows:—

1. How long have you kept a boarding-house on this Corporation?
2. How many boarders have you now?
3. How many boarders have you had in all since you kept the house?
4. How many of your girls have, to your knowledge, been married?
5. How many have died?
6. How many have gone home sick?
7. How many of your boarders have been dismissed from the Corporation for bad conduct?
8. Have you ever had much sickness in your house?

9. How many cases do you think, which have lasted a week, and have had the care of a physician?

The replies will be copied exactly as they were returned.

Case 1. Have kept a boarding-house on the Appleton four and a half years; have now nineteen boarders; have had probably, in all, a hundred and fifty; knows of ten of these that have been married; not one of her girls, while a boarder, has died; three have gone home sick; none of her boarders have been dismissed for bad conduct; have had but little sickness; perhaps eight cases that have lasted a week, and had the care of a physician.

Case 2. Have kept a boarding-house on the Hamilton nineteen years; have now sixteen boarders; have had twenty-five, upon an average, all the time; know of over two hundred of my girls that have been married, having kept an account of them till within two years past; only one of my boarders has died in my house; fifteen have gone home sick; one of my boarders has been dismissed from the Corporation for bad conduct; never have had much sickness; perhaps ten cases corresponding to the description in Question 9.

Case 3. Have kept a boarding-house on the Lowell Corporation eleven years; have now twenty-five boarders; have had, perhaps, two hundred in all; know of as many as fifty of them that have been married; not one has died in my house; none have ever been sent home sick; one of my boarders was turned off from the Corporation for bad conduct; have had very little sickness in my house; can remember but eleven cases that have lasted a week and been attended by a physician.

Case 4. Have kept a boarding-house on the Merrimack for twelve years; have now sixteen boarders; presume I have had four hundred in all; can remember eighty of these that have been married; none have died at my house; have heard of the death of eleven; three have gone home sick; none dismissed from my house for bad conduct; have had but little sickness in my house, perhaps ten or twelve cases that have lasted a week.

Case 5. Have kept a boarding-house on the Appleton, eight years and seven months; have now sixteen boarders; cannot tell how many I have had in all, perhaps two hundred and seventy-five; know of forty-five of my girls that have been married; eight have died; twelve have gone home sick; none have been dismissed from my house for bad conduct; have had much sickness in my house, should think as many as twenty cases lasting a week.

Case 6. Have kept a boarding-house on the Hamilton for nineteen years; have now nineteen boarders; probably have had three hundred in all; can recollect only nineteen of my girls that have been married; two have died from my house; twelve have gone home sick; three have been dismissed for bad conduct; never have had much sickness; can remember fourteen cases lasting a week.

Case 7. Have been matron on the Merrimack nine years; have now sixteen boarders; have had two hundred and fifteen since I kept the house; know of sixty of my girls who have been married; three have died in my house, and have heard of the death of six others; seven have gone home sick; none have been dismissed from my house for bad conduct; never have had much sickness, not more than seven or eight cases lasting a week.

22

Life on a Southern Plantation

No easy generalizations can describe slave life on antebellum American plantations. There were important differences between being a slave in the Upper South and the Lower South, between working on a large plantation and a small one, between serving a kind resident planter and a narrow-minded overseer. Yet, the institution of slavery shared more common characteristics than differences. A black on one plantation may have had a few more amenities than his counterpart on another—but both served in bondage and labored for the economic welfare of their masters.

It is difficult to re-create the style of slave life; for obvious reasons slaves left almost no written legacy of servitude. Yet a good many records do survive of plantation life, set down, to be sure, by the owners. This selection is excerpted from the records of Bennet H. Barrow (1811–1854), a cotton planter in Louisiana. Barrow inherited his lands from his father and ran a lucrative plantation. He lived well, indulged in the proper sports, and had some interest in politics but never held an office above the parish level. He seems to have been very much a man of his day, sharing the virtues and vices of his peers. He kept his records well, and, from them, one can piece together some notion of what it was like to be a slave in the pre-Civil War South.

THE DIARY OF BENNET H. BARROW

1 Rules of Highland Plantation (May 1838)

No negro shall leave the place at any time without my permission, or in my absence that of the Driver the driver in that case being responsible, for the cause of such absence. which ought never to be omitted to be enquired into—

The Driver should never leave the plantation, unless on business of the plantation—

From Edwin Adams Davis, *Plantation Life in the Florida Parishes of Louisiana, 1836–1846, as Reflected in the Diary of Bennet H. Barrow* (New York: Columbia University Press, 1943), 126–136, 392–399, 406–410, 427–437. Copyright 1943 Columbia University Press.

No negro shall be allowed to marry out of the plantation

No negro shall be allowed to sell anything without my express permission   I have ever maintained the doctrine that my negroes have no time Whatever, that they are always liable to my call without questioning for a moment the propriety, of it, I adhere to this on the grounds of expediency and right. The verry security of the plantation requires that a general and uniform control over the people of it should be exercised. Who are to protect the plantation from the intrusions of ill designed persons When evry body is a broad? Who can tell the moment When a plantation might be threatened with destruction from Fire—could the flames be arrested if the negroes are scattered throughout the neighborhood, seeking their amusement. Are these not duties of great importance, and in which evry negro himself is deeply interested   to render this part of the rule justly applicable, however, it would be necessary that such a settled arrangement should exist on the plantation as to make it unnecessary for a negro to leave it—or to have a good plea for doing so—You must, therefore make him as comfortable at Home as possible, affording him What is essentially necessary for his happiness—you must provide for him Your self and by that means creat in him a habit of perfect dependence on you—Allow it ounce to be understood by a negro that he is to provide for himself, and you that moment give him an undeniable claim on you for a portion of his time to make this provision, and should you from necessity, or any other cause, encroach upon his time—disappointment and discontent are seriously felt—if I employ a labourer to perform a certain quantum of work per day and I agree to pay him a certain amount for the performance of said work When he has accomplished it I of course have no further claim on him for his time or services—but how different is it with a slave—Who can calculate the exact profit or expence of a slave one year with another,   if I furnish my negro with evry necessary of life, without the least care on his part—if I support him in sickness, however long it may be, and pay all his expenses, though he does nothing—if I maintain him in his old age, when he is incapable of rendering either himself or myself any service, am I not entitled to an exclusive right to his time   good feelings, and a sense of propriety would all ways prevent unnecessary employment on the Sabbath, and policy would check any exaction of excessive labor in common—Whatever other privileges I allow the Driver, he is not suffered to send any negro off the plantation, unless he sends him to me or some extraordinary circumstances arises that could make it proper that a message should be sent to a neighbour for as his transactions are confined solely to the plantation there rarely could exist a necessity to communicate with me,   if he sends him for his own purpose, he is answerable for his absence as the negro would be, did he go away without any permission at all—I never give a negro a Pass to go from home without he first states particularly where he wishes to go, and assigns a cause for his desiring to be absent. if he offers a good reason, I never refuse, but otherwise, I never grant him a Pass, and feel satisfied that no practice is more prejudicial to the community, and to the negros themselves, and that of giving them general Pass'es—to go Where they please   I am so opposed to this plan that I never permit any negro to remain on my plantation, whose Pass does not authorize him expressly to come to it—Some think that after a negro has done his work it is an act of oppression to confine him to the plantation, when he might be strolling about the neighborhood for his amusement and recreation—this is certainly a mistaken humanity. Habit is evry thing—The negro who is accustomed to remain constantly at Home, is just as satisfied with the society on the plantation as that which he would find elsewhere, and the verry restrictions laid upon him being equally imposed on others, he does not feel them, for society is kept at Home for them—As the Driver is answerable for the good conduct of the negroes, and the proper application of their time he ought always to be present to attend, otherwise he could never with propriety be charged with neglect, in which case all responsibility would be at an End—No rule that I have stated is of more importance than that relating to negroes marrying out of the plantation   it seems to me, from What observations I have made it is utterly impossible to have any method, or regularity When the men and women are permitted to take wives and husbands indiscriminately off the plantation,   negroes are verry much desposed to pursue a course of this kind, and without being able to assign any good reason, though the motive can be readily perceived, and is a strong one with them, but one that tends not in the Least to the benefit of the Master, or their ultimate good. the inconveniences that at once strikes one as arising out of such a practice are these—

First—in allowing the men to marry out of the plantation, you give them an uncontrolable right to be frequently absent

2d Wherever their wives live, there they consider their homes, consequently they are indifferent to the interest of the plantation to which they actually belong—

3d—it creates a feeling of independance, from being, of right, out of the control of the masters for a time—

4th—They are repeatedly exposed to temptation from meeting and asociating with negroes from different directions, and with various habits & vices—

5th—Where there are several women on a plantation, they may have husbands from different plantations belonging to different persons. These men posess different habits are acustomed to different treatment, and have different privileges, so your plantation every day becomes a rendeezvous of a medly of characters. Negroes who have the privilege of a monthly Passes to go where they please, and at any hour that they say they have finished their work, to leave their Master's plan'tn come into yours about midday, When your negroes are at work, and the Driver engaged, they either take possession of houses their wives live—and go to sleep or stroll about in perfect idleness—feeling themselves accessible to every thing. What an example to those at work at the time—can any circumstance be more Intrusive of good order and contentment

Sixthly—When a man and his wife belong to different persons, they are liable to be separated from each other, as well as their children, either by caprice of either of the parties, or When there is a sale of property—this keeps up an unsettled state of things, and gives rise to repeated now connections—it might be asked how does this rule answer when there are several men on a plantation and few women—or vice versa, When there several women, & few men—For to adopt rules merely because they are good in themselves and not to pursue a plan Which would make them applicable, would be Fallacious—I prefer giving them money of Christmas to their making any thing, thereby creating an interest with you and yours. &c. I furnish my negroes regularly with their full share of allowance weakly. 4 pound & 5 pound of meat to evry thing that goes in the field—2 pound over 4 years   1½ between 15 months and 4 years old—Clear good meat—I give them cloths twice a year, two suits—one pair shoues for winter   evry third year a blanket—"single negro—two." I supply them with tobacco   if a negro is suffered to sell any thing he chooses without any inquiry being made, a spirit of trafficing at once is created. to carry this on, both means and time are necessary, neither of which is he of right possessed. A negro would not be content to sell only What he raises or makes or either corn (should he be permitted) or poultry, or the like, but he would sell a part of his allowance allso, and would be tempted to commit robberies to obtain things to sell. Besides, he would never go through his work carefully, particularly When other engagements more interesting and pleasing are constantly passing through his mind, but would be apt to slight his work   That the general conduct of master has a verry considerable influence on the character and habits of his slave, will be readily admitted. When a master is uniform in his own habits & conduct, his slaves know his wishes, and What they are to expect if they act in opposition to, or conformity with them, therefore, the more order and contentment Exist.

A plantation might be considered as a piece of machinery, to operate successfully, all of its parts should be uniform and exact, and the impelling force regular and steady; and the master, if he pretended at all to attend to his business, should be their impelling force.

If a master exhibits no extraordinary interest in the proceedings on his plantation, it is hardly to be expected that any other feelings but apathy, and perfect indifference could exist with his negroes, and it would be unreasonable for him, Who as the princaple incitements, And is careless, to expect attention and exaction from those, Who have no other interest than to avoid the displeasure of their master. in the different departments on the plantation as much destinction and separation are kept up as possible with a view to create responsibility—The Driver has a directed charge of every thing, but there are subordinate persons, who take the more immediate care of the different departments. For instance, I make one persons answerable for my stock. Horses cattle hogs &c.   another the plantation utensials &c.   one the sick—one the poultry. another providing for and taking care of the children whose parents are in the field &c. As good a plan as could be adopted, to establish security and good order on the plantation is that of constituting a watch at night, consisting of two or more men. they are answerable of all trespasses commited during their watch, unless they produce the offender. or give immediate alarm. When the protection of a plantation is left to the negroes generally, you at once perceive the truth of the maxim that what is evry one's business, is no one's business. but when a regular watch is Established, Each in turn performs his tour of duty, so that the most careless is at times, made to be observant and watchful—the verry act of organizing a watch bespeaks a care and attention on the part of a master, Which, has the due influence on the negro—

Most of the above rules "in fact with the exception of the last" I have adopted since 1833. And with success—get your negroes ounce disciplined and planting is a

231

pleasure—A H[ell] without it never have an Overseer—Every negro to come up Sunday after their allowance Clean & head well combed—it gives pride to every one, the fact of master feeling proud of them, When clean &c.

Never allow any man to talk to your negros, nothing more injurious.

2   The Diary (September) 1838

September 1

Clear   warm—picking above   best picking this year—3 sick   gave evry cotton picker a light Whipping for picking trashy cotten

    2   Clear   wind North—and quit cool—sudden change—hands averged higher yesterday than they have this year—163—upwards of 20 Bales out—Ten Bales behind last year & 30 Bales behind 1836—difference in the season

    3   Clear. quite cold. picking cotten Gns place—good picking—started all my Gins—don't like the appearance of my crop. most ragged looking crop I ever had. bent & broke down—2 sick—3 lame &c.

    4   Clear   wind East—cool. picking home (above) since dinner

    5   Cloudy   wind East—best picking today I've had this year—went to Ruffins with Family—and went in the swamp Killing Aligators—after dinner went driving   started two large Bucks in Wades field—stood on the roade between Roberts and Ruffins—one came through—Sidney Flower took first Shot standing—neither of his *shots* were fatal—ran to me   missed first fire   second wounded him verry badly—ran short distance & stoped. nearly falling—Ruffin shot at him behind —ran short distance & fell—Hounds still after the other Deer—our shooting turned it Back—went in pursuit of the *1st one* he jumped up some few steps from us—and ran a mile—by this time it was dark   4 dogs came to us and we followed it—jumped it between my field and the lower part Lane place—Came running directly to us—and had Ruffins Horse of stood would have touched him   fired as it passed (missed) ran few steps dogs bayed it—found him standing. erect head & tail up ready for battle—gave him another loade. ran short distance   dogs caught him—hour after night—verry Large and fat   4 prongs

    6 Few clouds. cool mornings—Took jos Bell—Fanny Bell & Grey Luzbourough colts of Lucillas up to train—also Pressure & Dick Haile—a strong string —O. jacob cut the end of his right Fore finger nearly off—two others slightly cut—with Broad ax—avreage 170 pound Cotten yesterday—appearance of rain to night sprinkle

    7   Few clouds—wind East—fine picking. averaged 183 yesterday—cotten 40 Bales out last night—30 Bales behind last year at this time. went down to see john Joor   his cotten has suffered verry much for want of rain

    8   Cloudy   warm—hand generally did not pick as well yesterday as day before—fine picking—highest yesterday & this year 260. Atean small boy Owens the best boy I ever saw

    9   Clear   pleasant   hands picked Finely yesterday   aveaged 209

    10   Clear   verry cool morning—upwards of 50 Bales out 30 odd Gined   fine picking

11   Clear cool morning. Four first rate cotten pickers sick hands picked well yesterday   Atean 300. Dave L. 310.   highest this year—sent to Town after my Bagging & rope. waiting for it 3 weaks past—Knocked the blind Teeth out of my Grey Luzbourough Colt. Little Independence.

12   Clear cool mornings—5 sick   picking above—20 Bales out at Gns pressing Home—the best cotten and best picking in upper new corn land cotten I ever saw

13   Clear cool morning—weighd cotten in the field—5 sick   Augue & Fever

14   Cloudy   warm—most of the hands picked well yesterday highest 325 Atean—will have picked off of the new corn land above (50 acres) 25 Bales   at least 50 Bales to pick—averaged yesterday 209—25 Bales pressed last night

15   Cloudy. *sprinkling* of rain—Hands picked higher yesterday than they have done this year—Avreaged 226—Owens boy 13 years old picked 200—best boy I ever saw. verry light sprinkle rain this evening.

16   Stormy looking day. great deal of rain last night and still raining—wind from the East. hands picked well yesterday   highest average this year 234½

17   dark & Cloudy—wind South—women spinning   men & trash gang trashing cotten and raising House—Between 90 & 100 Bales out. 49 Pressed   70 Gind in No

18   Cloudy damp morning—some rain at noon. picking cotten since Breakfast—went driving with james Leak   Dr Desmont and Sidney Flower. started two Fawns in my field, ran some time. dogs quit them.

19   Clear pleasant morning—62 Bales pressed last night—Cotten bend down verry much from wind on Sunday—between 90 & 100 Bales out in No—Went hunting in my field   started 3 Deer. Killed a fine young Buck—Several joined me afterwards—went driving on the swamp—started a Deer   dogs ran off—in coming out of the drive started a Bear. only one dog—he became too much frightened to do any thing

20   Clear   pleasant   picking P. Rice bottom—hands pick well considering the storm—several sick

21   Verry Foggy morning—Com'enced hauling Cotten this morning—1st shipment—Bales will avreage 470 lbs   upwards of 100 out in No   100 & 15 of 400. this time last year had out 125—25 behind last year. owing to the season—cotten more backward in opening—at first picking—never had Cotten picked more trashy than yesterday. And to day by dinner—some few picked badly—5 sick & 2 children

22   Considerable rain before Breakfast, Appearance of a bad day—pressing—4 sick—Caught Darcas with dirt in cotton bag last night. weighed 15 pounds—Tom Beauf picked badly yesterday morning   Whiped him. few Cuts—left the field some time in the evening without his Cotton and have not seen him since—He is in the habit of doing so yearly. except last year   Heavy rains during the day   women spinning—trashing Cotten   men & children—Tom B. showed himself—"sick"—Cotten picked since the storm looks verry badly—Cotten market opened this year at 13 & 13¾ cts—Bagging & *cordage* 20 & 24 and 8½ & 9 cts—Porke from $16 to $24 a Barrel—Never com'ence hauling Cotten that it did'ent

233

rain—worked the ford at Little Creek in the Gns field—Wind blowing cool from the North since 2 oclock—Here I am sitting with the Baby in my lap "Bennet B." Emily criticising the History of Georgia—Caroline and John at all Kinds of mischief

23 Clear verry cool wind from the North—nine degrees colder than yesterday morning—intend most of the hands to dry and trash Cotten to day. Frank Kish Henry & Isreal pressed Bales to day. $1 each—Killed Wild Cow this morning. as Fat as could well be

24 Clear quit cold—P. Dhoertys Gin House *Burnt* down on Friday night Last. light enoughf at my scaffold yard to read names & figures on the sleight —& at least 5 miles—Mr. Tisdale our Trainer came down from K.y yesterday— had my cart Wheels tired yesterday at Ruffins

25 Clear cool—went to Town—hauled 49 Bales to Ratliffs Landing yesterday—12 to Town to day 61 in all—went driving yesterday Killed two Fawns—and one young Buck in my Gns field with the most singular Horns I ever heard of or Saw—verry fat—several sick. most this year

26 Clear pleasant weather. Shiped to day Eighty Bales Cotten. verry fine —6 or 7 Lying up—picked badly for two days past—Cotten Selling 14 cts

27 Clear pleasant—went hunting in the swamp in company of Dr Desmont J. Leake, & Mr Pain from Isle of Madeaira—a large wine importer—verry Large— Killed 3 Deer. lost Mr Pain, stayed untill after dark firing Guns &c. the old gentleman found the brier and Came up to Ruffins well scratched & bloody— he refused to call Leake by his name—having lost a cargo of Wine. Vessel springing a *Leak*

28 Cloudy cool wind from the North—jno Joor sent a hand up to ex-change with me, yesterday, his hands pick verry badly—Dennis and Tom "*Beauf*" ran off on Wednesday—Dennis came in yesterday morning after I went hunting. "Sick"—left the Sick House this morning—if I can see either of them and have a gun at the time will let them have the contents of it—Dennis returned to the Sick House at dinner

29 Foggy morning—warm day A G. Barrow—Dr Walker & Wm Munson stayed with me last night went Hunting to day Munson missed—Emily went to Woodville yesterday—Hands picked better yesterday than they have done. since the storm—avreged 200. Tom B. went to picking Cotten this morning—did'ent bring his Cotten to be weighed—came to me after I went to Bed

3   Slave Births: 1835–1839

Mother	Child	Date of Birth	Comments
L. Lucy	Louisa	October 5, 1835	
Mary		September 15, 1835	
Margaret	Orange	February 1, 1836	
Cealy	Jane Bello	April 22, 1836	
Candis	Issac	August 1, 1836	

Sidney		July 10, 1836	Born dead
Maria	Kitty	July 10, 1836	
Harriet	Ned	November 20, 1836	
Patty		December 19, 1836	Died
Leah	Adeline	March 6, 1837	
Margaret	Edmond	September 21, 1837	Died
Mary	Rose	January 9, 1838	
Sidney	Robert	February 21, 1838	
Edny		June 7, 1838	
Fanny		July 4, 1838	Died
Jane		September 29, 1838	Died
Candis		October 12, 1838	Died
Maria	Horrace	November 30, 1838	
Harriet	Sally	December 2, 1838	
Leah		December 10, 1838	Died
L. Lucey	Anzy	March , 1839	
Luce	Jobe	June 10, 1839	
Patty	Vina	July 20, 1839	
L. Hannah	Mathilda	July 20, 1839	
Mary	Elsa	July 23, 1839	
Luckey		July 26, 1839	Dwindled away

4   Slave Deaths: 1836–1839

Old Rheuben	1836	60 years	
Old Betty	1836	65 years	Found dead. Cripple 5 years.
Billy	1836		Died of worms 6 hours after taken
Nelly	1837	26 years	Died 24 hours after I saw her. Received some injury. In the family way.
Easter	1837	50 years	Died of Pleurisy, drinking, &c. Relapse, died very suddenly. Great loss.
William	1837	3 years	Died suddenly. Worms.
Hanover	1837	6 years	Died of worms, suddenly.
George	1837	30 years	Drowned in attempting to cross L. Creek in Gns field at dark, and in a verry heavy storm, on a mule. Irreparable loss in every respect. September 6.
Edny's child	1838	one week old	Died of Lock jaw, June 13.
Candis' child	1838	one week old	Died of Lock jaw, October 19.
Harriet's Ned	1838		Died suddenly, December 1.
Fanny's child		4 months old	Died from carelessness.
Jane's child			Died from disease of mother.
Leah's child	1838	one week old	December 17.
Sidney's child	1839	2 years old	Sick for 10 or 12 days. Recovering. Caught violent cold and sore throat. Strangled, died in 24 hours after relapse. September 19.

5   Misconduct and Punishments: 1840–1841

Darcas		Left the field without the consent of the Driver. Pretending to be sick.
Anica		Filthiness, in the milk and butter. Her and Darcas alike. December 10, 1840 improved very much.
Peter		Told me several lies Christmas, Drunkard, etc.
Candis		Saw Dennis while runaway.
Jenney		Saw Dennis while runaway.
Patience		Not trashing cotten well. Leaving yellow locks in it etc.
Julia		Not trashing cotten well.
Bet	X*	Not trashing cotten well.
Creasy		Not trashing cotten well.
F. Jerry		For going to town with very dirty clothes and keeping himself so, "generally."
Patty		Inattention to work and herself.
Lavenia		Inattention to work and herself.
L. Hannah		For taking rails and breaking good ones.
O. Hannah	X	Not trashing cotton enough. Found the gin stopped every time I've been down at the Gns. place.
Bet	X	Not trashing cotton enough.
Harriet		Not trashing cotton enough, and dirty clothes.
F. Jerry	X	Up too late and out of his house.
D. Bartley	X	Up after 10 o'clock.
Wade	X	Up after 10 o'clock.
Wash		Carelessness with his plough, horses, gear, etc.
Ralph	X	Neglect of his horses.
Randall		Up too late, sleeping in chair, etc.
Dave L.		Neglect in hauling cotton repeatedly.
D. Bartley	X	For not picking as well as he can, etc.
F. Jerry	X	For not picking as well as he can, etc.
Wash	X	Behaving very badly this season, so far.
T. Jim	X	Not picking well.
Fanny	X	Not picking well.
Creasy		Bad conduct, impudence to Driver and neglected work.
G. Jerry	X	Neglect in planting peas, and slow.
Jenny	X	Neglect in planting peas, and slow.
Patience	X	Did not go in the field till breakfast "late" and told the Driver "Alfred" she was sick and had been to the house for a dose of oil, and told me the same, found she had not been and she acknowledged the lie, but told Margaret she would give her some cloth if she would get the earache and tell Patty she had been here after oil, etc. And told me a dozen lies while questioning her. Gave her a very severe whipping.
Levi	X	Carelessness with his oxen and talking to the workman. Neglect of business.
Maria		For not reporting herself when sick. Remained in the Quarter 3 days without my knowledge.

Patty		And all the house ones for general bad conduct. Can't let a peach get ripe, etc.
Jane		The meanest negro living. Filth in cooking. Saw me coming to the house at 120. left the kitchen, etc. Of[f] near two days, foiled her having anything to do with anyone, and chained at nights.
O. Fill	X	Not reporting the plough hands for injuring the cotton covering up bottom limbs, etc.
Demps		Sound beating with my stick. Impudence of manner.
Atean	X	Covering up cotton limbs with ploughs.
Luce		Neglect of child. Its foot burnt.
Jim		Inattention to work, moving seed and impudence to Driver.
G. Jerry		Inattention to work.
Lize	X	Inattention to work.
Bet	XX	Careless in dropping seed, disowning it, etc.
Anica		Meaness to the sick, and hiding from me, etc.
Dennis		Severity to his mules.
Patty		For going over to Dr. Walker's during my absence, etc.
Milley	X	For going over to Dr. Walker's during my absence, etc.
Israel	X	Hiding from work. Moving cotton, etc. and not picking.

* X signifies whipping.
** XX signifies unusually severe whipping.

6   Inventory of the Estate of Bennet H. Barrow

Succession of Bennett H. Barrow, deceased

State of Louisiana, Parish of West Feliciana

Be it Remembered, that on this the fourteenth day of June in the year of our Lord One thousand eight hundred and fifty-four, I, Bertrand Haralson, Recorder in and for said Parish. Have attended this day, at the late residence of Bennett H. Barrow, deceased, for making an Inventory and appraisement of all the property, real and personal, belonging to Bennett H. Barrow, deceased.

The following is a true Proces Verbal of the Separate Estate of the deceased;

SLAVES	
Stephen, aged 6 years, valued at two hundred 50 dollars	250.00
Roden, aged 5 years, valued at two hundred dollars	200.00
Jack, aged 51 years, valued at eight hundred dollars	800.00
Eliza, aged 44 years, valued at five hundred dollars	500.00
Bazil, aged 20 years, valued at six hundred dollars	600.00
Little Cato, aged 37 years, valued at six hundred dollars	600.00
Hetty, aged 36 years, valued at five hundred dollars	500.00
Amos, an infant, valued at fifty dollars	50.00
Temps, aged 43 years, valued at fifty dollars	50.00
Lindy, aged 23 years, valued at seven hundred dollars	700.00
Virginia, aged 2 years, valued at One hundred & fifty dollars	150.00
Sidney, aged 39 years, valued at six hundred & fifty dollars	650.00
Aggy, aged 20 years, valued at seven hundred & fifty dollars	750.00

Angelle, an infant, valued at fifty dollars	50.00
Cynthis, aged 13 years, valued at four hundred dollars	400.00
Suckey, aged 9 years, valued at three hundred dollars	300.00
Spencer, aged 7 years, valued at three hundred dollars	300.00
Nelly, aged 5 years, valued at two hundred dollars	200.00
Litty, an infant, valued at fifty dollars	50.00
Rosiese, aged 4 years, valued at two hundred dollars	200.00
Fanny, aged 33 years, valued at Seven hundred dollars	700.00
Little Judy, aged 13 years, valued at five hundred dollars	500.00
Ralph, aged 34 years, valued at four hundred dollars	400.00
Ester Jim, aged 34 years, valued at nine hundred & fifty dollars	950.00
Little Nancy, aged 18 years, valued at seven hundred dollars	700.00
Old Suckey, aged 56 years, valued at One hundred dollars	100.00
Rachael, aged 25 years, valued at Six hundred dollars	600.00
Emeline, aged 4 years, valued at one hundred & fifty dollars	150.00
Essex, an infant, valued at One Hundred dollars	100.00
Mathew, aged 20 years, valued at eight hundred & fifty dollars	850.00
Israel, aged 37 years, valued at eight hundred dollars	800.00
Lucy, aged 71 years, valued at ten dollars	10.00
Lavinia, aged 31 years, valued at Seven hundred & fifty dollars	750.00
Annis, aged 13 years, valued at five hundred dollars	500.00
Polly, aged 8 years, valued at three hundred & fifty dollars	350.00
Caroline, aged 6 years, valued at Two hundred & fifty dollars	250.00
Josephine, aged 4 years, valued at One hundred & fifty dollars	150.00
Angeline, aged 2 years, valued at One hundred dollars	100.00
Dave, aged 46 years, valued at Seven hundred dollars	700.00
Little Jim, aged 24 years, valued at nine hundred dollars	900.00
Maria, aged 19 years, valued at six hundred dollars	600.00
Old Jimmy, aged 59 years, valued at five dollars sic [sick]	005.00
Nat, aged 28 years, valued at Eight hundred & fifty dollars	850.00
Levy, aged 39 years, valued at four hundred & fifty dollars	450.00
Grace, aged 29 years, valued at six hundred dollars	600.00
Little Jack, aged 9 years, valued at three hundred dollars	300.00
Gilson, aged 7 years, valued at two hundred dollars	200.00
Edward, aged 2 years, valued at One Hundred & fifty dollars	150.00
Dennis, aged 44 years, valued at nine hundred & fifty dollars	950.00
Ettienne, aged 37 years, valued at One thousand dollars	1,000.00
Dicy, aged 4 years, valued at two hundred dollars	200.00
Randel, aged 1 years, valued at one hundred dollars	100.00
Jeny, aged 39 years, valued at nine hundred dollars	900.00
Milly, aged 29 years, valued at six hundred dollars	600.00
Kesiah, aged 10 years, valued at three hundred dollars	300.00
Lotty, aged 7 years, valued at two hundred dollars	200.00
Minerva, aged 3 years, valued at one hundred & fifty	150.00
Patience, aged 43 years, valued at five hundred dollars	500.00
Ester Nat, aged 29 years, valued at Seven hundred dollars	700.00
Josh, aged 69 years, valued at One hundred dollars	100.00
Leah, aged 33 years, valued at Seven hundred & fifty dollars	750.00
Littleton, aged 21 years, valued at nine hundred dollars	900.00

23

The Appeal of Jackson

The political supporters of Andrew Jackson were an odd mixture—frontiersmen, small bankers, commercial farmers, businessmen starting out on their careers. Jackson's style may be part of the explanation for this coalition. A military hero, he appeared very much a leader and a man of the people. But there was another important ingredient in Jackson's appeal and that was his conception that the proper government was limited government. He was a strict constructionist of the Constitution. Jackson's nationalism was beyond question but he did not seek to extend the powers of the federal government at the expense of the state. In fact, quite the reverse was true, and in the 1830s this stance had wide support, albeit for very different reasons. Under this principle, for example, the government would stay out of central banking, leaving it to state institutions—a move that would free more funds for circulation and please eager businessmen looking for capital and ambitious farmers wanting to purchase more lands.

The strict constructionist side of Jacksonian politics was especially evident in the President's veto of the Maysville Internal Improvements Act. How was it that the hero of the Westerner denied him federal support for a road? The event is described in full detail by one of Jackson's most important advisers and his successor in the Presidency, Martin Van Buren. The account is obviously by a loyal friend—but a critical reading will illuminate a very important facet of Jacksonian democracy.

THE AUTOBIOGRAPHY OF MARTIN VAN BUREN

Having for several years made the subject of Internal Improvements by the Federal Government my study, apprehensions of the evils their prosecution, as the Constitution stood, might entail upon the Country had become grave, and sincerely believing that the adverse current which had set in that direction might and could only be arrested thro' the General's extraordinary popularity I early and assidu-

Reprinted with permission from *The Autobiography of Martin Van Buren*, John C. Fitzpatrick, ed., Fourteenth Report of the Historical Manuscripts Commission, American Historical Association, June 14, 1919, 312–328, 337–338.

ously pressed the matter upon his consideration. He embraced my suggestions not only with alacrity but with that lively zeal with which he received every proposition which he thought could be made conducive to the public good. I propose to give a succinct account of the steps that proceeded from our conversations; and I will first briefly notice some of the General's characteristic qualities by which their advancement was essentially promoted. It is however far from my intention to attempt a complete portraiture of individual character. I am conscious that such attempts often, not to say generally, manifest the ambition of the author to shew his skill in depicting a perfectly good or an absolutely bad character instead of a desire to portray his subject as he really was, and that the picture, when finished is thus a reflection of his imagination rather than a reliable representation of real life. I hope to make the world better acquainted with the true character of Andrew Jackson than it was before, but I design to do this chiefly by correct reports of what he said and did on great occasions.

Although firm to the last degree in the execution of his resolution when once formed, I never knew a man more free from conceit, or one to whom it was to a greater extent a pleasure, as well as a recognized duty, to listen patiently to what might be said to him upon any subject under consideration until the time for action had arrived. Akin to his disposition in this regard was his readiness to acknowledge error whenever an occasion to do so was presented and a willingness to give full credit to his co-actors on important occasions without ever pausing to consider how much of the merit he awarded was at the expense of that due to himself. In this spirit he received the aid of those associated with him in the public service in the preparation of the public documents that were issued under his name, wholly indifferent in regard to the extent to which their participation was known, solicitous only that they should be understood by those to whom they were addressed as a true record of his opinions, his resolutions and his acts. That point secured he cared little either as to the form of words in which they were expressed, or as to the agency through which the particular exposition was concocted.

Neither, I need scarcely say, was he in the habit of talking, much less of boasting of his own achievements. Content with the part he had actually taken in the conduct and solution of any important public question and never having reason to complain of the opinions formed and expressed of his acts by a large majority of his Countrymen he had neither a desire nor a motive to parade his own or to shine in borrowed plumes.

I have already spoken of Gen. Jackson's early preference for the self-denying theory and strict-construction doctrines of the old republican school. But the principle of internal improvements by the Federal Government, so far from being acted upon when he was first in Congress, was, disavowed by the great leader of the administration, and a large share of Gen. Jackson's time was spent in the camp whilst the subject was debated by the rising men of the day from 1816 to 1823, when he re-appeared on the floor of Congress. There was besides a peculiarity in his position at the latter period which, tho' it could not—as nothing could—lead him, to do wrong when it became necessary to act, was nevertheless well calculated to lessen somewhat, for the moment at least, his active participation in this particular branch of legislation. To give to that peculiarity the weight to which it was entitled the reader must bear in mind the influence exerted by Pennsylvania in bringing Gen. Jackson forward for the Presidency, an influence which will not I think be over-estimated when it is regarded as having controlled the result; and this consideration deserves to be constantly remembered whilst canvassing the merits of his subsequent course upon several very important points.

Pennsylvania is in every sense of the word a great state and worthy of high respect—great in her material resources and great in the constant industry, the morality and general intelligence of her People. When to the credit she derives from these sources is added that which has naturally accrued from the moderate and sound character of her general course it will be seen how well she has deserved the honor shewn her by her sister States in the title with which they have distinguished her of "the key stone of the arch of the Union."

It is nevertheless true that she has for a long time presented a favorable field for the agitation of political questions which address themselves to special interests in the communities upon which they are pressed. Internal Improvements by the Federal Government, a high protective tariff and a Bank of the United States had, for many years before Gen. Jackson's accession to the Presidency, been regarded as favorite measures with the good people of Pennsylvania. In respect to the first, which is now the subject of our consideration, both of the great Reports of the Committees on Roads and Canals, at the period when it embraced a large share of the attention of Congress, were from Pennsylvanians,—Mr. Wilson and Mr. Hemphill. Yet these measures and the question of the removal of the Indians, which had so strongly excited their misdirected sympathies, were destined to be the principal domestic subjects on which Gen. Jackson's Administration, if he succeeded in the election, was to be employed. With the two last, (the Bank and the Tariff) he had made himself familiar and as to them his course was fixed; and, foreseeing the necessity he would be under upon those points to run counter to the wishes of his Pennsylvania friends at the very threshold of his administration, it was natural that a man of his generous temper, and of whose character fidelity to friendship was the crowning grace, should have been desirous to avoid any addition to the issues between himself and his no less generous supporters, as far as that could be avoided without dereliction of duty.

It was under such circumstances, and never having made the constitutional question in relation to the power of Congress over the matter a subject of critical examination, that he voted in 1823–4 and 5, in favor of the acts "to provide for the necessary surveys for roads and canals", and "authorizing a subscription to the stock of the Chesapeake and Delaware Canal Company" and a few other propositions of similar import, which votes were vehemently urged, by his opponents, against his subsequent course.

None but the men who were active and conspicuous in the service of the Federal Government at that day, and of these now few remain amongst us, can form any adequate opinion of the power and influence which those who had embarked their political fortunes in attempts to commit the General Government irretrievably to the promotion and construction of Internal Improvements, had acquired both in Congress and among the most alert and enterprising portions of the People. The wild spirit of speculation, to whose career our ever growing and ever moving population and our expanded and expanding territory offered the fairest field, became wilder over the prospect before it and the wits of Congressmen were severely tasked in devising and causing to be surveyed and brought forward under captivating disguises the thousand local improvements with which they designed to dazzle and seduce their constituents. It required an extraordinary degree of resolution in a public man to attempt to resist a passion that had become so rampant, but this consideration might stimulate but could not discourage Gen. Jackson so long as he was convinced that the course presented for his consideration was the path of duty. He was unfeignedly grateful to Pennsylvania for what she had done for him, he knew well that upon this question as upon those of the removal of the Indians and of the Bank she had taken a lead in the wrong direction, he was extremely loth to add another to the great points upon which his duty would compel him to throw himself in the way of her gratification, but for all and against all such appeals and motives he promptly opposed the suggestions of right, and the ever present and ever operative sense of an official obligation superior to personal feeling.

He appreciated to their full extent the arguments in support of the inexpediency of the legislation which he was asked to arrest, whilst the Constitution remained unaltered, but preferred to meet the question on constitutional grounds. No Cabinet councils were called: not another member of the Cabinet was consulted before his decision had become irrevocable. It was understood between us that I should keep an eye upon the movements of Congress and bring to his notice the first Bill upon which I might think his interference would be preferable, and that when such a case was presented, we would take up the question of Constitutional power and examine it deliberately and fully.

The Bill authorizing a subscription to the stock of the Maysville, Washington, Paris and Lexington Turnpike-road Company appeared to me to present the looked for occasion. Its local character was incontestably established by the fact that the road commenced and ended in the same State. It had passed the House and could undoubtedly pass the Senate. The road was in Mr. Clay's own State and Mr. Clay was, the General thought—whether rightfully or not is now immaterial,—pressing the measure and the question it involved upon him rather for political effect than for public ends, and it was his preference, in accordance with a sound military axiom to make his enemy's territory the theatre of the war whenever that was practicable.

I brought the subject to the President's notice during one of our daily rides, immediately after the passage of the Bill by the House and proposed to send him on our return the brief of which I have spoken and of which I had before promised him a perusal. I had myself no hesitation in respect to the course that ought to be pursued and spoke of it accordingly. He received my suggestions favorably, appeared sensible of the importance of the proposed step and at parting begged me not to delay sending him the brief—which was done as soon as I got to my house.

Within five days after the passage of the Bill by the House of Representatives I received from him the following note.

(PRIVATE)

May 4th, 1830

My Dear Sir,

I have been engaged to day as long as my head and eyes would permit, poring over the manuscript you handed me; as far as I have been able to decipher it I think it one of the most lucid expositions of the Constitution and historical accounts of the departure by Congress from its true principles that I have ever met with.

It furnishes clear views upon the constitutional powers of Congress. The inability of Congress under the Constitution to apply the funds of the Government to private, not national purposes I never had a doubt of. The Kentucky road bill involves this very power and I think it right boldly to meet it at the threshold. With this object in view I wish to have an interview with you and consult upon this subject that the constitutional points may be arranged to bear upon it with clearness so that the people may fully understand it.

Can I see you this evening or Thursday morning?

Your friend

Andrew Jackson

MR. VAN BUREN

TO THE PRESIDENT

My Dear Sir,

I thank you for your favorable opinion of the notes. This matter has for a few days past borne heavily on my mind, and brought it to the precise conclusion stated in your note. Under this impression I had actually commenced throwing my ideas on paper to be submitted to you when I should get through, to see whether it is not possible to defeat the aim of our adversaries in either respect, viz; whether it be to draw you into the approval of a Bill most emphatically *local*, and thus endeavor to saddle you with the latitudinarian notions upon which the late administration acted, or to compel you to take a stand against internal improvements generally, and thus draw to their aid all those who are interested in the ten thousand schemes which events and the course of the Government for a few past years have engendered. I think I see land, and that it will be in our power to serve the Country and at the same time counteract the machinations of those who mingle their selfish and ambitious views in the matter. We shall have time enough; the Bill has not yet passed the Senate and you have, you know, ten days after that.

Yours truly

M. Van Buren

W. May 4th 1830

I requested him some days after to obtain from the Secretary of the Treasury the financial statement which [later] accompanied the *veto*-Message, and received in reply the following spirited note.

(PRIVATE)

May 15th, 1830

Dear Sir,

Your note is received. I am happy that you have been looking at the proceedings of Congress. The appropriations now exceed the available funds in the Treasury, and the estimates always exceed the real amount available. I have just called upon the

Secretary of the Treasury for the amount of the estimated available balance on the 1st January 1831.

The people expected reform retrenchment and economy in the administration of this Government. This was the cry from Maine to Louisiana, and instead of these the great object of Congress, *it would seem*, is to make mine one of the most extravagant administrations since the commencement of the Government. This must not be; The Federal Constitution must be obeyed, State-rights preserved, our national debt *must be paid, direct taxes and loans avoided* and the Federal union preserved. These are the objects I have in view, and regardless of all consequences, will carry into effect.

Yr. friend

A. J.

Mr. V. B. Sec. of State

Let me see you this evening or in the morning.

Not one out of twenty of the opposition members believed that President Jackson, notwithstanding his proverbial indifference to the assumption of responsibility, in respect to measures he believed to be right, would venture to veto an act for the internal improvement of the Country in the then state of public opinion upon the subject and after the votes he had so recently given in favor of such acts. If they had thought otherwise they would not have presented him a Bill so purely local in its character. Apprehensive that they would, when his designs became known to them, change their course in that respect, and avail themselves of the selfish views and unsettled opinions of a sufficient number of those who had been elected as Jackson men to substitute a Bill for a work more national in its pretensions, I was extremely solicitous that nothing should be said upon the subject until it should be too late for such a step, and pressed that point upon the General. It was the only one, I knew, that required to be pressed and it was, moreover, that which I was persuaded would be the most difficult for him. He was entirely unreserved in his public dealings—the People, he thought, should know every thing and "give it to Blair" (or *Blar* as he pronounced it)—was almost always his prompt direction when ever any information was brought to him which affected or might affect the public interest.

Col. Johnson, of Kentucky, was induced by Western members, who had been alarmed by floating rumors, to sound the President and if he found that there existed danger of such a result to remonstrate with him, in their names and his own, against a *veto*. At the moment of his appearance the President and myself were engaged in an examination of the exposé of the state of the Treasury to which I have referred, and alone. After a delay natural to a man possessed as the Colonel was of much real delicacy of feeling and having an awkward commission in hand, he said that he had called at the instance of many friends to have some conversation with the General upon a very delicate subject and was deterred from entering upon it by an apprehension that he might give offense. He was kindly told to dismiss such fears, and assured that as the President reposed unqualified confidence in his friendship he could say nothing on any public matter that would give offense. He then spoke of the rumors in circulation, of the feelings of the General's Western friends in regard to the subject of them, of his apprehensions of the uses that Mr. Clay would make of a veto, and encouraged by the General's apparent interest, and warmed by his own, he extended his open hand and exclaimed "General! If this hand were an anvil on which the sledge hammer of the smith was descending and a fly were to light upon it in time to receive the blow he would not crush it more effectually than you will crush your friends in Kentucky if you veto that Bill!" Gen. Jackson evidently excited by the bold figure and energetic manner of Col. Johnson, rose from his seat and advanced towards the latter, who also quitted his chair, and the following questions and answers succeeded very rapidly: "Sir, have you looked at the condition of the Treasury—at the amount of money that it contains—at the appropriations already made by Congress—at the amount of other unavoidable claims upon it?"—"No! General, I have not! But there has always been money enough to satisfy appropriations and I do not doubt there will be now!"—"Well, I have, and this is the result," (repeating the substance of the Treasury exhibit,) "and you see there is no money to be expended as my friends desire. Now, I stand committed before the Country to pay off the National Debt, at the earliest practicable moment; this pledge I am determined to redeem, and I cannot do this if I consent to encrease it without necessity. Are you willing—are my friends willing to lay taxes to pay for internal improvements?—for be assured I will not borrow a cent except in cases of absolute necessity!"—"No!" replied the Colonel, "that would be worse than a *veto!*"

These emphatic declarations delivered with unusual earnestness and in that peculiarly impressive manner for which he was remarkable when excited quite overcrowed the Colonel who picked up the green bag which he usually carried during the session and manifested a disposition to retreat. As he was about to leave I remarked to him that he had evidently made up his mind that the General had determined to veto the Bill at all events, but that when he reflected how much of the President's earnestness was occasioned by his own strong speech and how natural it was for a man to become excited when he has two sets of friends, in whom he has equal confidence, urging him in different directions, he would be less confident in his conclusion. Reminded by this observation that he had suffered the guard which he had imposed on himself to be broken down by the Colonel's *sledge-hammer,* the General told him that he was giving the matter a thorough investigation and that their friends might be assured that he would not make up his mind without looking at every side of it,—that he was obliged to him for what he had said and wished all his friends to speak to him as plainly.

The Colonel with his accustomed urbanity deported himself as if reassured and appeared to consider the case not so desperate as he had at first imagined, but his manner was assumed for the purpose of quieting my apprehensions which he perceived and understood. When he returned to the House he replied to the eager enquiries of his Western friends that the General had thanked him and assured him that he would thoroughly examine the subject, but his private opinion decidedly was that nothing less than a voice from Heaven would prevent the old man from vetoing the Bill, and he doubted whether that would!

Still so strong was the impression derived from Gen. Jackson's habit of never concealing his views upon a subject on which his mind was made up, that the

245

incredulity of the members was but slightly removed by the Colonel's report: what he would do in the matter remained an open question to the last. The consequence was that the importunities of his friends were increased, but as the detailed account of Col. Johnson's embassy discouraged direct remonstrances with the President they were addressed to me, and in my efforts to keep both sides quiet by statements of the difficulties with which the subject was environed by reason of the conflicting struggles of the friends of the Administration, I exposed my own course to some suspicion or affected suspicion in the end. The General told me, on my return from England, that one of the charges brought against me by Mr. Calhoun's friends, to justify the rejection of my nomination as Minister, was that I had been opposed to the *veto* and had tried to prevent him from interposing it.

The impression among the General's Western friends, that he would destroy his popularity by a *veto*, was universal and prevailed also extensively among those from the North. The Pennsylvania members generally were rampant in their opposition and most of them voted for the Bill after the *veto* was interposed. Being with him to a very late hour the night before the Message was sent up, he asked me to take an early breakfast with him, as Congress was on the point of breaking up, and would therefore meet at an early hour. On going up stairs to his office, he leaning on my arm on account of his extreme physical weakness, I observed that our friends were frightened. "Yes," he replied,—"but don't mind that! The thing is here" (placing his hand on the breast-pocket of his coat) "and shall be sent up as soon as Congress convenes."

It was sent up that morning and a scene ensued that baffled all our calculations. If there was any sentiment among our opponents which we knew to be universal, before the reading of the *veto*-Message, it was that it would prove the political death warrant of the Administration and we were prepared to hear denunciations against the violence and destructive effects of the measure and the reckless insult offered to the House by the President in sending it. But no such clamor arose, and the first and principal objection that was made against the Message, when the reading was finished, and which was persevered in to the end, was that it was "an *electioneering document*" sent to Congress for political effect!—and that the "*hand of the magician*" was visible in every line of it!

It was indeed received with unbounded satisfaction by the great body of the disinterested and genuine friends of the Administration throughout the Country. Col. Hayne, of South Carolina, at the great Charleston dinner given to inaugurate nullification, and thro' its means to put that Administration to the severest trial that any had ever been exposed to in our Country spoke of the *veto as* "the most auspicious event which had taken place in the history of the Country for years past." I refer but to one other of those acceptable exhibitions of public feeling which pervaded the Union, tho' less imposing in form not less gratifying. Col. [Robert] Ramsay, one of the Representatives from Pennsylvania, an excitable but honest man and true patriot, irritated almost beyond endurance by the *veto*, followed us from the Capitol to the White House, after the close of the session, and, presuming on the strength of his friendship for the General, fairly upbraided him for his course. The latter bore his reproaches, for such they really were altho' intended only as a remonstrance which he thought allowable in a devoted friend, with a degree of mildness that excited my admiration, begging the dissatisfied representative to say no more upon the subject until he had seen his constituents and venturing to prophesy that he would find them pleased with the veto. The worthy Pennsylvanian received the intimation as an additional injury and parted from us in an exceedingly bad humor. A short time afterwards, as I was one day approaching the President he held up to me in an exultant manner, a paper which proved to be a letter from our good friend Ramsay in which he announced the confirmation of the General's prediction and acknowledged that, in that case at least, the latter had known his constituents better than he himself had known them.

And yet this measure was but the entering wedge to the course of action by which that powerful combination known as the Internal Improvement party was broken asunder and finally annihilated. The power which a combined influence of that description, addressing itself to the strongest passion of man's nature and wielded by a triumvirate of active and able young statesmen as a means through which to achieve for themselves the glittering prize of the Presidency, operating in conjunction with minor classes of politicians, looking in the same general direction and backed by a little army of cunning contractors, is capable of exerting in communities so excitable as our own, can easily be imagined. The danger in offending and the difficulty of resisting such an influence were equally apparent. The utmost prudence was required in respect to the ground that should be occupied by the President in the first step that he was to take in the prosecution of the great reform that he had in view. His own past course increased the necessity of great circumspection at the start. His name was, in very deed, a tower of strength, but prudence as well as sound principle dictated that their partiality should not be put to an unreasonable test by the ground he now took, on an occasion of intense interest, in a document which, as we all well knew, would have to pass through the severest scrutiny.

In view of this state of things the *veto*-Message assumed the following positions:—

1st. The construction of Internal Improvements under the authority of the Federal Government was not authorized by the Constitution.

2nd. Altho' the true view of the Constitution in regard to the power of appropriation was probably that taken in Madison's Report concerning the alien and sedition laws, by which it was confined to cases where the particular measure which the appropriation was designed to promote was within the enumerated authorities vested in Congress, yet every Administration of the Government had, in respect to appropriations of money only adopted in practice (several cases of which were mentioned) a more enlarged construction of the power. This course, it was supposed, had been so long and so extensively persisted in as to render it difficult, if not impracticable, to bring the operations of the Government back to the construction first referred to. The Message nowhere admitted that the more enlarged construction which had obtained so strong a foothold, was a true exposition of the Constitution, and it conceded that its restriction against abuse, viz., that the works which might be thus aided should be "of a general, not

247

local—National, not State" character, a disregard of which distinction would of necessity lead to the subversion of the Federal System, was unsafe, arbitrary in its nature and inefficient.

3d. Although he might not feel it to be his duty to interpose the Executive veto against the passage of Bills appropriating money for the construction of such works as were authorized by the States, and were National in their character the President did not wish to be understood as assenting to the expediency of embarking the General Government in a system of that kind at this time; but he could never give his approval to a measure having the character of that under consideration, not being able to regard it in any other light than as a measure of a purely local character; or if it could be considered National no further distinction between the appropriate duties of the General and State Governments need be attempted, for there could be no local interest that might not, under such a construction, be denominated, with equal propriety, National.

His *veto* was placed on that specific ground, and the rest of the Message was principally taken up in discussing the propriety and expediency of deferring all other action upon the subject, even of appropriations for National works until the Public Debt should be paid and amendments of the Constitution adopted by which such appropriation could be protected against the abuses to which they were exposed.

For seven years of General Jackson's administration was the general subject thus banished from the halls of Congress and by my election as his successor that virtual interdict (if it may be so termed) was extended to eleven years. It was in consequence of the steps of which I have spoken that the project of a system of Internal Improvements by the Federal Government was—there is every reason to believe—forever withdrawn from the action of that Government. Not that any such consequence can be attributed to the opinion or action of any man who may for a season be placed at its head, for no one conversant with human nature or with the course of political events will ever expect with confidence such a result from such causes. The opinion I have expressed is founded on more potent considerations. Every effort in the direction referred to was certainly suspended for eleven years and other fields of exertion in behalf of such works were soon found and occupied. To a people as impulsive as ours eleven years of denial and delay are almost equivalent to an eternal veto, and those who maintained that the passion for Internal Improvements, so rampant at the seat of the Federal Government at the commencement of the Jackson administration, would seek other and constitutional directions for its gratification, if that could be perseveringly denied to it there for even a shorter period, stand justified by the event. All of the works of that character which it was ever hoped might prove safe and useful to the Country, have been made by or under the authority of the State Governments. All motive for enlisting the interference of the National Government for generations to come, has thus been superseded. In the cases of wild and unprofitable or speculative projects, losses, to the extent of many millions, which the Treasury would have sustained if these works had been constructed under Federal authority, have fallen with a weight diminished by the vigilance inspired by private interest and by State supervision, upon the shoulders of those who expected to make money by them, instead of emptying the national coffers, to be recruited by taxes collected from the mass of the people who would have derived no exclusive advantages from their success.

We have had two administrations of the Federal Government whose politics were of the Governmental-improvement stamp, but none of the old projects have been brought forward—resolutions in favour of Internal Improvements have been dropped from the partisan platforms of the party that suported those administrations. The theory and the practice—except as to cases not involved in the general question—are both exploded as regards the action of the Federal Government and the signal advantages which the Country has reaped from this result will be elsewhere noticed.

24

The Log Cabin Campaign

The election of 1840 has often been described as the first modern American political campaign. Both the Whigs and the Democrats turned their best efforts to appealing to the public to support their party in the November election. There was nothing unusual in this for the Jacksonians; they had prided themselves since 1828 on their rapport with all the voters. For the Whigs, however, this was unprecedented strategy, marking their abandonment of any notion that a political organization could win power in the United States by looking exclusively for the support of the prosperous. As a result of the two-party competition in 1840, a greater percentage of eligible voters participated in the election than in any previous national contest.

The tactic may have been new to the Whigs, but they practiced it like old hands. From their selection of a candidate, William Henry Harrison, to their organization of parades and rallies, they showed themselves quick learners. These selections—a newspaper account of a Harrison parade, a Harrison stump speech, and a Harrison song—testify to their skills. There is also a good look at the content and style of American politics in 1840.

THE ELECTION OF 1840

1 Rally for William Henry Harrison in St. Louis, Missouri, as Reported by the St. Louis *New Era*

We cannot believe that any friend of Harrison could, in his most sanguine moments, have anticipated so glorious a day, such a turn-out of the people, as was witnessed on Tuesday last in this city. Everything was auspicious. The heavens, the air, the earth, all seemed to have combined to assist in doing honor to the services, the patriotism and the virtues of William Henry Harrison. Never have we seen so much enthusiasm, so much honest, impassioned and eloquent feeling displayed in the countenances and bursting from the lips of freemen. It was a day of jubilee. The people felt that the time had come when they could breathe freely—when they were about to cast from them the incubus of a polluted and abandoned party, and when they could look forward to better and happier days in store for them and for

From *The Election of 1840*, A. B. Norton, ed. (1888), I: 141–146, 150–151, 245–253, II: 21–22.

the country. The city itself bore, in some respects, the remarkable character of a Sabbath day. By the Whigs, and even among the Democrats, there was little work done. The doors of all places of business were closed, and nothing was thought of on this carnival day but joy and gratitude. We shall, ourselves, give such an account of the proceedings as our time and opportunities permitted us to gather, leaving it to the imagination to fill up the *tout ensemble* of the picture.

Preparations had been made for the reception and entertainment of the company, by the proper committees, at Mrs. Ashley's residence. The extensive park was so arranged as to accommodate the throng of persons who were expected. Seats were erected for the officers of the day, for the speakers and for the ladies. At the hour appointed by the marshal of the day, the people commenced to assemble at the court house, and several associations and crafts were formed in the procession as they advanced on the ground. While this was going on, the steamboats bringing delegations from St. Charles, Hannibal, Adams county, Ill., and Alton, arrived at the wharf, with banners unfurled to the breeze, and presenting a most cheering sight. The order of procession, so far as we have been able to obtain it, was as follows:

Music: Brass band.

1. Banner, borne by farmers from the northern part of St. Louis township. This banner represented the "Raising of the Siege of Fort Meigs" and bore as its motto, "It Has Pleased Providence, We Are Victorious." (Harrison's dispatch.)

2. Officers and members of the Tippecanoe club, preceded by the president, Col. John O'Fallon, with a splendid banner, representing a hemisphere surmounted by an American eagle, strangling with his beak a serpent, its folds grasped within its talons, and its head having the face of a fox in the throes of death. Above was a rainbow, emblematic of hope, in which was the name of the club. Below the hemisphere was the motto, "The Victor in '11, Will be the Victor in '40." On the reverse side, the letters "T. C." The members six abreast.

3. Log cabin committee, six abreast.

4. The president and vice-presidents of the day.

5. Soldiers who served under Harrison in the late war—in a car, adorned with banners on each side—one, a view of a steamboat named Tippecanoe, with a sign board, "For Washington City." On the other, a view of the cabin at North Bend, the farmer at his plow, with the inscription, "Harrison, the Old Soldier, Honest Man, and Pure Patriot."

6. Invited guests in carriages.

7. Citizens on foot, six abreast, bearing banners inscribed, "Harrison, the Friend of Pre-emption Rights," "One Term for the Presidency;" "Harrison, the People's Candidate;" "Harrison, the People's Sober Second Thought;" "Harrison, He Never Lost a Battle;" "Harrison, the Protector of the Pioneers of the West;" "Harrison, Tyler and Reform;" "Harrison, the Poor Man's Friend;" "Harrison, the Friend of Equal Laws and Equal Rights."

8. Citizens on horseback, six abreast.

9. Delegation from Columbia Bottom.

10. Canoe, "North Bend."

251

11. Boys with banners, upon one of which was inscribed, "Our Country's Hope," and on another, "Just as the Twig is Bent, the Tree's Inclined."

These boys belonged to the several schools of the city; were regularly marshaled, and presented, by the regularity of their conduct, a most interesting spectacle.

12. Laborers, with their horses and carts, shovels, picks, etc., with a banner bearing the inscription, "Harrison, the Poor Man's Friend—We Want Work."

13. A printing press on a platform with banners, and the pressman striking off Tippecanoe songs, and distributing them to the throng of people as they passed along, followed in order by the members of the craft.

14. Drays, with barrels of hard cider.

15. A log cabin mounted on wheels, and drawn by six beautiful horses, followed by the craft of carpenters in great numbers. Over the door of the cabin, the words, "The String of the Latch Never Pulled In."

16. The blacksmiths, with forge, bellows, etc., mounted on cars, the men at work. Banner, "We Strike for Our Country's Good."

17. The joiners and cabinet-makers; a miniature shop mounted on wheels; men at work; the craft following it.

18. A large canoe, drawn by six horses, and filled with men.

19. Two canoes, mounted, and filled by sailors.

20. Fort Meigs, in miniature, 40 by 15 feet, drawn by nine yoke of oxen. The interior filled with soldiers, in the usual dress of that day, hunting shirts, leggins, leather breeches, etc.; and one of the men a participant in the defense of Fort Meigs. At every bastion of the fort the muzzle of a piece of ordnance protruded itself, and from another point a piece of artillery was fired, at short intervals, during the day. The whole was most admirably got up, and reflects much credit upon the friends of "Old Tip," to be found at the "Floating Dock."

21. Delegation of brickmakers, with apparatus, clay, etc., and men at work.

22. Delegation of bricklayers, with a beautiful banner, representing a log cabin, brick house going up, etc., and followed by the craft, six abreast.

Band of music.

23. Delegation from Carondelet.

24. Delegation from Belleville, Ill., with banners.

25. Delegation from Alton, with canoe, drawn by four horses, and banners representing the state of the country, the peculiar notions of the Loco Foco party about the reduction of the prices of labor to the standard of the hard-money countries of Europe and of Cuba; a sub-treasury box, with illustrations, etc. One of the banners bore the inscription, "Connecticut Election, 4,600 Majority; Rhode Island, 1,500 Majority;" and a cunning looking fellow, with his thumb on his nose, and twisting his fingers in regular Samuel Weller style, saying, "You Can't Come It, Matty." This delegation numbered about two hundred men.

26. Delegations from Hannibal and Pike counties with banners, etc.

27. Delegation from Rockport with a log cabin, canoe, banners, etc.

28. Delegation from St. Charles, with banners bearing the names of the

twenty-six States, borne by as many individuals, and having with them a handsome canoe drawn by four horses.

Arrived at the southern extremity of the park, the procession halted and formed in open order, the rear passing to the front.

The people were then successively addressed by Mr. John Hogan, of Illinois.

Colonel John O'Fallon was then called for, and mounted on Fort Meigs, he thus addressed the people:

My Fellow Citizens:

I feel deeply sensible of the honor you confer upon me by calling me to address this vast concourse of intelligent freemen. My pursuits in life have led me into retirement; I am wholly unused to speaking in public.

Aware that my known acquaintance with the eventful scenes which we have this day assembled to commemorate, is the only reason for this call, I shall, consequently, in responding to it, state something of what I know in relation to them.

I had the honor of serving under General Harrison at the battle of Tippecanoe, during the seige of Fort Meigs, and at the battle of the Thames. I can say that, from the commencement to the termination of his military services in the last war, I was almost constantly by his side. I was familiar with his conduct as governor and superintendent of Indian affairs of the Territory of Indiana, and after the return of peace, as commissioner to treat with all the hostile Indians of the last war in the Northwest, for the establishment of a permanent reconciliation and peace. I saw also much of General Harrison whilst he was in the Congress of the United States.

Opportunities have thus been afforded me of knowing him in all the relations of life, as an officer and as a man, and of being enabled to form a pretty correct estimate of his military and civil services, as well as his qualifications and fitness for office. I know him to be open and brave in his disposition, of active and industrious habits, uncompromising in his principles, above all guile and intrigue, and a pure, honest, noble-minded man, with a heart ever overflowing with warm and generous sympathies for his fellow-man. As a military man, his daring, chivalrous courage inspired his men with confidence and spread dismay and terror to his enemies. In all his plans he was successful. In all his engagements he was victorious. He has filled all the various civil and military offices committed to him by his country, with sound judgment and spotless fidelity. In every situation he was cautious and prudent, firm and energetic, and his decisions always judicious. His acquirements as a scholar are varied and extensive, his principles as a statesman sound, pure and republican.

If chosen President he will be the President of the people rather than of a party. The Government will then be administered for the general good and welfare.

His election will be the dawn of a new era! The reform of the abuses of a most corrupt, profligate and oppressive Government. Then will end the ten years' war upon the currency and institutions of the country. The hard-money cry and hard times will disappear together. Then will cease further attempts to increase the wages of the office-holders and reduce the wages of the people to the standard of European labor.

Then shall we see restored the general prosperity of the people, by giving them a sound local currency, mixed with a currency of a uniform value throughout the land. The revival of commerce, of trade, enterprise and general confidence. Then the return of happier, more peaceful and more prosperous days, when cheerfulness and plenty will, once more, smile around the poor man's table.

About the close of the meeting the following resolutions were adopted with three cheers:

Resolved, That the Whig young men of St. Louis county will respond to the call for a young men's convention at Rocheport on the 20th of June, and that the cause of old Tippecanoe shall not suffer because they are not on the ground.

Resolved, That five hundred of the real "log cabin and hard cider boys" of St. Louis county will stand at a corner of the Rocheport cabin on the 18th, and join in the convention of the 20th, when they hope to meet ten thousand of their brethren and join with them in doing honor to the farmer-statesmen of the West.

Resolved, That a committee of twenty be appointed to select the five hundred who shall go.

After the adoption of these resolutions, a song was sung, and the company dispersed.

2   A Stump Speech of William Henry Harrison, at Fort Greenville, to the Citizens of Ohio and Indiana

Friends and Fellow-citizens:

It is with no slight emotion that I undertake to address you on this occasion. Nor am I a little embarrassed for words wherein to express my deep sense of your kindness towards me, manifested by the friendliness and magnanimity of your greeting. My heart yields up to you the homage of its deepest gratitude, though my tongue expresses it not.

Fellow-citizens, you are all aware of the position that I occupy before the American people—being a candidate of a portion of them for the Presidency of the United States. It will doubtless be said by some that I am here for the purpose of electioneering for myself; that I have come to solicit your votes; but believe me gentlemen, this is not the case. I am present on this occasion but as an invited guest of citizens of Darke. It is my deliberate opinion and sincere desire that the bestowment of office should be the free act of the people, and I have no wish to bias their judgment unjustly in my favor. But, notwithstanding my wish and determination not to engage as a politician in the pending canvass for officers to administer the General Government, although I would have preferred to remain with my family in *the peace and quiet of our log cabin at the Bend,* rather than become engaged in political or other disputes as the advocate of my own rectitude of conduct, yet, from the continued torrent of calumny that has been poured upon me, from the slanders, abuses, and obloquy which have been promulgated and circulated to my discredit, designed to asperse and blacken my character, and from the villainous and false charges urged against me by the pensioned presses of this administration, my attendance at this celebration appeared to have been made an act of necessity, a step which I was compelled to take for self-defense. Chiefly for this purpose have I come among you, and trusting you will all perceive the propriety of its course, it seems superfluous to add any further reasons for its adoption.

Years ago, fellow-citizens, when I left this spot—for aught I knew, for the last time—I had little idea of the surprising change which would be wrought in its appearance during the time which has supervened. Never did I expect to stand here and behold such a scene as this. It resembles somewhat the recent *siege* of "Old Fort Meigs." I am now sixty-seven years of age. I have therefore lived to behold much of the glory of my country; I have seen the palmy days of this Republic; and especially have I witnessed many of the brilliant events which have characterized the growing greatness of the lovely West; but this very day and its incidents mark an epoch in my own history the like of which I have seldom experienced. It is now twenty-five years since I was at Fort Greenville—then surrounded by a dense forest dark and dreary. At that period there was scarce a log cabin between Greenville and Cincinnati—all between was one entire, unbroken wilderness. How wonderfully and how speedily have the giant woods bowed their stately tops to the industry and enterprise of Western pioneers, as if some magic power had cleaved them from the earth! And now in their stead what do we behold? Broad, cultivated fields, flowery gardens, and happy homes. Delightful picture—gratifying change! Proud reflection! that this transition of things is the result of the handiwork of Western people—of American freemen.

Fellow-citizens, you have undoubtedly seen it oftentimes stated in a certain class of newspapers that I am a very decrepit old man, obliged to hobble about on crutches; that I was caged up, and that I could not speak loud enough to be heard more than four or five feet distant, in consequence of which last misfortune I am stigmatized with the cognomen of "General Mum." You now perceive, however, that these stories are false. But there are some more serious matters charged against me, which I shall take the liberty to prove untrue. You know it has been said by some that I have no principles; that I dare not avow any principles and that I am kept under the surveillance of a "committee." All this is false—unconditionally false.

Now, with regard to the political condition of our common country, I trust there is no impropriety in my addressing you upon subjects concerning the public weal. What means this "great commotion" among the people of this great nation? What are the insufferable grievances which have driven so many thousands, nay, millions, of the American people into the council for the purpose of devising measures for their mutual relief? Wherefore do they cry aloud as with one voice, Reform! Our country is in peril! The public morals are corrupted. How has it been done? "To the victors belong the spoils," say our rulers. What are the consequences? Ask the hundred public defaulters throughout the land! Ask the hirelings of corruption who are proffering "power and place" as bribes to secure votes! Ask the subsidized press what governs its operations, and it will open its iron jaws and answer you in a voice loud enough to shake the Pyramids—Money! Money! I speak not at random—facts bear me testimony. The principle is boldly avowed, as well as put in practice by men in high places, that falsehood is justifiable in order to accomplish their purposes. Why this laxity in the morals of our rulers and their followers? Did they inherit depravity from their ancestors? How does it come that such recklessness of truth and justice is manifested of late by some individuals among us? Why some of the causes produce these evils I have already intimated. There are others. Intense party spirit destroys patriotism.

A celebrated Grecian commander once said, and said truly: "Where virtue is best rewarded, there will virtue most prevail." It is even so, a wise and true saying. But how has the practice of your Government of late accorded with this maxim? It is proverbial with the advocates of monarchy in the Old World that republics are ungrateful. How does your experience for the last few years give the lie to this proposition? Nay, fellow-citizens, I fear that this Government affords many examples which tend but too strongly to verify the proverb. Among other instances of manifest ingratitude, to only one will I here recur. I mean the removal from office, without cause or provocation, save a difference of opinion with the President, of Gen. Solomon Van Rensselaer, of New York. He was a noble friend of ours in the "winter of our discontent." I became acquainted with him when, like myself, he was a young officer in General Wayne's army. I found him an agreeable, social companion, as well as a brave and magnanimous soldier. He assisted in fighting the battles of his country; aye, for your behoof, my countrymen, his blood has been poured out upon the soil of Ohio. The bullets of your enemies have pierced his body while fighting in defense of your interests. And not only on the plains of Ohio has he stood between danger and his country, but in other places likewise. In the sanguinary battle of Queenstown he received six wounds from his country's foes. Well, what is his reward? After having spent the flower of his youth and the vigor of his manly prime in the service of his country as a soldier, he was called by the American people to serve them in a civil capacity. He obeyed the call with thankfulness of heart. But he has been cruelly driven out of the service by the administration, and why? Because, fellow-citizens, he was the friend of the companion of his youth; because he would not forsake a fellow-soldier; because he was my incorruptible friend; and because the emoluments of his office were wanted to reward the partisan services of a supporter of my political competitor. "Ah, there's the rub!" But you, my friends, I am confident, will not long permit such wrong to the men who "righted your wrongs" in olden times.

Fellow-citizens, you know that my opponents call me a Federalist. But I deny the charge: I am not—I never was a Federalist. Federalists are in favor of concentrating power in the hands of the executive; Democrats are in favor of the retention of power by the people. I am, and ever have been, a Democratic Republican. My former practices will bear me out in what I say. When I was governor of Indiana Territory, I was vested with despotic power, and had I chosen to exercise it, I might have governed that people with a rod of iron. But being a child of the Revolution, and bred to its principles, I believed in the right and the ability of the people to govern themselves; and they were always permitted to enjoy that high privilege. I had the power to prorogue, adjourn and dissolve the legislature, to lay off the new counties and establish seats of justice; to appoint sheriffs and other officers. But never did I interpose my prerogative to defeat the wishes of a majority of the people. The people chose their own officers, and I invariably confirmed their choice; where they preferred to have their county seats, there I located them; they made their own laws and I ratified them. *I never vetoed a bill in my life.*

But I have been denounced as a bank man. Well, let it go. I am so far a bank man as I believe every rational Republican ought to be, and no further. The Constitution of the United States makes it the duty of the Government to provide ways and means for the collection and disbursement of the public revenue. If the people deem it necessary to the proper discharge of the functions of their Government to create a national bank, properly guarded and regulated, I shall be the last man, if elected President, to set up my authority against that of the millions of American freemen. It is needful to have a larger money circulation in a land of liberty than in an empire of despotism. Destroy the poor man's credit and you destroy his capital. The peasant who toils incessantly to maintain his famishing household, in the hard money countries of Europe, rarely if ever becomes the noble lord who pastures his "flocks upon a thousand hills." There are necessarily difficulties connected with every form and system of the Government, but it should be the aim and object of the statesman to form the best institutions within this power to make for the good of his country.

Fellow-citizens, I cannot forbear inviting your attention to the concerns of your Government, in the welfare of which all good citizens feel a deep interest. I warn you to watch your rulers. Remember, "Eternal vigilance is the price of liberty." When I looked around upon the dangers which seem to be suspended as by a hair over this people, I tremble for the safety of this Republic. In an evil hour has the Chief Magistrate of this nation been transformed into a monarch and despot at pleasure! To show that this is the case I need but refer you to the profound and philosophical historian, Gibbon, who says, "The obvious definition of monarchy seems to be that of a State in which a *single person,* by whatsoever name he may be distinguished, *is intrusted with the execution of the law, the management of the revenue, and the command of the army.*" Is not Martin Van Buren intrusted with these functions? Most assuredly he is. Call him by whatsoever title you choose, President, executive, chief magistrate, consul, king, stadtholder, it does not alter the nature of his power; that remains the same, unchanged, and the President, therefore, possesses all the functions necessary to constitute a monarch. You have often heard of the "moneyed influence of the country" denounced while it yet remained in the hands of the people, as dangerous to public liberty.

Have you, then, no apprehension, no fear of a moneyed influence, equal to that of half the nation, concentrated in the hands of a single individual, at the same time possessing two other of the most potent powers that belong to our Government? The great Julius Caesar—the conquering Julius has said, "Give me soldiers and I will get money; give me money and I will get soldiers." The public purse is already confided to the hands of the President; a respectable army is also under his control, and it is in contemplation by the administration to add to the present military force of the United States an army of 200,000 men. American freemen, pause and reflect. Meditate before you act. Matters of the highest moment depend upon your action and await your decision. There may be no ambitious Caesar among us who will dare to use the ample means now combined in the hands of the President for the subversion of our liberties, but the exceptions to ambitious men so inclined are so few that they but fortify the rule. Look around you, fellow-citizens. Are you girt with your armor or have you surrendered it to another? The "sentinels upon the watch tower of freedom"—have they been true to their trusts, or have they slept? I warn you, my countrymen, against the danger of neglecting your duty. Power is always stealing from the many to the few. Beware how you intrust our rights to the keeping of any man. They are never so secure as when protected by your own shield and defended by yourselves with your own weapons.

In conclusion fellow-citizens, indulge me in a few remarks in regard to my old fellow-soldiers. A small number of them are here by my side. They stood by me in battle, firm and invincible, in by-gone days. Some of them are remnants of the Revolution—soldiers with whom I served under the gallant Wayne. Where, my brethren, are our companions in danger on the field of strife? Alas! many of them are taking their final repose in the calm and peace of death!

The old soldiers, one by one, are dwindling away—gliding as it were down the river of time into the haven of long-sought rest. But a few of them even now are remaining to sorrow in gladness for the ingratitude of their country. When this country was a dismal howling wilderness those warriors were exposing themselves to danger and disease in the unwholesome swamps and morasses of the West, by guarding and defending our frontiers. Many of them became present victims to the malaria of the marshes and the insalubrity of the climate, others returned to their houses with disease engendered in their systems, but to linger for a time, and perhaps waste away with consumption; while yet smaller portions still remain among us, though generally shattered in constitution and feeble in health. Why is it, fellow-citizens, that these old soldiers of General Wayne's army have never been repaid for their services, or been allowed pensions by our Government? The nation is much indebted to them, and justice requires that the debt should be paid, and I could never die in peace, and feel no sting of remorse, if I were to permit their claims to pass unnoticed, and without making an effort, when opportunity offered, to have them satisfied.

Fellow-citizens, my character has been most grossly and wantonly assailed by the dangerous demagogues of the administration party. They have falsely charged me with the commission of almost every crime which is denominated such that man can be guilty of. My character, which I had fondly hoped to preserve unsullied as a boon and an example for my family, has been much more traduced and belied within the few months past, and, for this reason I have sometimes regretted that your predilection had made me a candidate for office; but, nevertheless, I claim no sympathy of the public on that score. I only desire you to examine my past conduct, to read the history of your country and ascertain my political course heretofore, and the principles on which I have ever acted, and if you find that my doctrines are unsound and unworthy of your support, it is your sacred duty to reject them. I ask not your sympathy or favor. I want but common justice. Let me have a fair trial, and, whatever may be your verdict, I shall be satisfied. Investigate matters fairly and honestly; compare the doctrines and practices of my adversaries with mine, and then decide as you shall think right and proper. Cast aside your prejudices and predilections, and vote only from principle. It is your duty to do so. Heed not the censure of knavish politicians who reproach you with the name of "turn coat," etc. *It is not approbrious to turn from a party to your country.* We should despise the odium sought to be heaped upon us by designing men, from their selfish motives, as they despise truth and honesty.

Hoping that the right may prevail and make our country prosperous, I will only add the wish that you may long enjoy its blessings, maintain its free institutions, and rejoice in the independence of happy freemen.

3   **Tippecanoe Songs of 1840**

THE LOG CABIN AND HARD CIDER CANDIDATE

TUNE, "AULD LANG SYNE"
Should good old cider be despised,
       And ne'er regarded more?
Should plain log cabins be despised,
       Our fathers built of yore?
For the true old style, my boys!
       For the true old style?
Let's take a mug of cider, now,
       For the true old style.

We've tried experiments enough
       Of fashions new and vain,
And now we long to settle down
       To good old times again.
For the good old ways, my boys!
       For the good old ways,
Let's take a mug of cider, now,
       For the good old ways.

We've tried your purse-proud lords, who love
       In palaces to shine;
But we'll have a plowman President
       Of the Cincinnatus line.
For old North Bend, my boys!
       For old North Bend,
We'll take a mug of cider, yet,
       For old North Bend.

We've tried the "greatest and the best,"
       And found him bad enough;
And he who "in the footsteps treads"

Is yet more sorry stuff.
For the brave old Thames, my boys!
        For the brave old Thames,
We'll take a mug of cider, yet,
        For the brave old Thames.

Then give 's a hand, my boys!
        And here's a hand for you,
And we'll quaff the good old cider yet
        For Old Tippecanoe.
For Old Tippecanoe, my boys!
        For Old Tippecanoe,
We'll take a mug of cider, yet,
        For Old Tippecanoe.

And surely you'll give your good vote,
        And surely I will, too;
And we'll clear the way to the White House, yet,
        For Old Tippecanoe.
For Tip-pe-canoe, my boys,
        For Tip-pe-canoe,
We'll take a mug of cider, yet,
        For Tippecanoe.

25

Violence in Politics

The violence that marked other aspects of American life finally came to affect its politics also. Mob action against abolition agitators, and the great Southern fear and occasional reality of slave revolts, had their counterpart, at least symbolically, on the floor of the United States Senate on May 22, 1856. Having recently concluded a long and bitter denunciation of the affairs in Kansas, including personal attacks on Senators Butler and Douglas, Massachusetts Senator Charles Sumner was writing letters at his chamber desk when suddenly he was brutally clubbed by South Carolina Congressman Preston Brooks, a relative of Senator Butler. This outburst of violence on the Senate floor became the occasion for further sectional recriminations. The Southern press applauded Brooks while many Northerners made Sumner a martyr to his cause.

In the course of these events, one more national institution had proved itself incapable of withstanding the tensions of the day. The issue of slavery tore organization after organization apart. It prompted Northern men to attack their neighbors for voicing unpopular opinions; it led Southerners into frantic efforts to minimize the possibility of slave revolts. When violence and bitterness overtook the political leaders of the nation, time was running out. Failures to come to grips with the issue threatened the worst consequences. The nation soon experienced them all in the form of the Civil War.

THE WORKS OF CHARLES SUMNER

1   Charles Sumner Addresses the Senate on the Issue of Kansas, May 19-20, 1856

You are now called to redress a great wrong. Seldom in the history of nations is such a question presented. Tariffs, army bills, navy bills, land bills, are important, and justly occupy your care; but these all belong to the course of ordinary legislation. As means and instruments only, they are necessarily subordinate to the

From *The Works of Charles Sumner* (Boston, 1871), IV: 137–151, 260–264; 278–279, 312–313.

conservation of Government itself. Grant them or deny them, in greater or less degree, and you inflict no shock. The machinery of Government continues to move. The State does not cease to exist. Far otherwise is it with the eminent question now before you, involving, as it does, Liberty in a broad Territory, and also involving the peace of the whole country, with our good name in history forevermore.

Take down your map, Sir, and you will find that the Territory of Kansas, more than any other region, occupies the middle spot of North America, equally distant from the Atlantic on the east and the Pacific on the west, from the frozen waters of Hudson's Bay on the north and the tepid Gulf Stream on the south,—constituting the precise geographical centre of the whole vast Continent. To such advantages of situation, on the very highway between two oceans, are added a soil of unsurpassed richness, and a fascinating, undulating beauty of surface, with a health-giving climate, calculated to nurture a powerful and generous people, worthy to be a central pivot of American institutions. Against this Territory, thus fortunate in position and population, a Crime has been committed which is without example in the records of the Past. Not in plundered provinces or in the cruelties of selfish governors will you find its parallel.

The wickedness which I now begin to expose is immeasurably aggravated by the motive which prompted it. Not in any common lust for power did this uncommon tragedy have its origin. It is the rape of a virgin Territory, compelling it to the hateful embrace of Slavery; and it may be clearly traced to a depraved desire for a new Slave State, hideous offspring of such a crime, in the hope of adding to the power of Slavery in the National Government. Yes, Sir, when the whole world, alike Christian and Turk, is rising up to condemn this wrong, making it a hissing to the nations, here in our Republic, *force*—ay, Sir, FORCE—is openly employed in compelling Kansas to this pollution, and all for the sake of political power. There is the simple fact, which you will vainly attempt to deny, but which in itself presents an essential wickedness that makes other public crimes seem like public virtues.

This enormity, vast beyond comparison, swells to dimension of crime which the imagination toils in vain to grasp, when it is understood that for this purpose are hazarded the horrors of intestine feud, not only in this distant Territory, but everywhere throughout the country. The muster has begun. The strife is no longer local, but national. Even now, while I speak, portents lower in the horizon, threatening to darken the land, which already palpitates with the mutterings of civil war. The fury of the propagandists, and the calm determination of their opponents, are diffused from the distant Territory over wide-spread communities, and the whole country, in all its extent, marshalling hostile divisions, and foreshadowing a conflict which, unless happily averted by the triumph of Freedom, will become war,—fratricidal, parricidal war,—with an accumulated wickedness beyond that of any war in human annals, justly provoking the avenging judgment of Providence and the avenging pen of History. Such is the Crime which you are to judge. The criminal also must be dragged into day, that you may see and measure the power by which all this wrong is sustained. From no common source could it proceed. In its perpetration was needed a spirit of vaulting ambition which would hesitate at nothing; a hardihood of purpose insensible to the judgment of mankind; a madness for Slavery, in spite of Constitution, laws, and all the great examples of our history; also a consciousness of power such as comes from the habit of power; a combination of energies found only in a hundred arms directed by a hundred eyes; a control of Public Opinion through venal pens and a prostituted press; an ability to subsidize crowds in every vocation of life,—the politician with his local importance, the lawyer with his subtle tongue, and even the authority of the judge on the bench,—with a familiar use of men in places high and low, so that none, from the President to the lowest border postmaster, should decline to be its tool: all these things, and more, were needed, and they were found in the Slave Power of our Republic. There, Sir, stands the criminal, all unmasked before you, heartless, grasping, and tyrannical: for this is the Power behind—greater than any President—which succors and sustains the Crime. Nay, the proceedings I now arraign derive their fearful consequence only from this connection.

Such is the Crime and such the criminal which it is my duty to expose; and, by the blessing of God, this duty shall be done completely to the end. But this will not be enough. The Apologies which, with strange hardihood, are offered for the Crime must be torn away, so that it shall stand forth without a single rag or fig-leaf to cover its vileness. And, finally, the True Remedy must be shown. The subject is complex in relations, as it is transcendent in importance; and yet, if I am honored by your attention, I hope to present it clearly in all its parts, while I conduct you to the inevitable conclusion that Kansas must be admitted at once, with her present Constitution, as a State of this Union, and give a new star to the blue field of our National Flag. And here I derive satisfaction from the thought, that the cause is so strong in itself as to bear even the infirmities of its advocates; nor can it require anything beyond that simplicity of treatment and moderation of manner which I desire to cultivate. Its true character is such, that, like Hercules, it will conquer just so soon as it is recognized.

I must say something of a general character, particularly in response to what has fallen from Senators who have raised themselves to eminence on this floor in championship of human wrong: I mean the Senator from South Carolina [Mr. BUTLER] and the Senator from Illinois [Mr. DOUGLAS], who, though unlike as Don Quixote and Sancho Panza, yet, like this couple, sally forth together in the same adventure. I regret much to miss the elder Senator from his seat; but the cause against which he has run a tilt, with such ebullition of animosity, demands that the opportunity of exposing him should not be lost; and it is for the cause that I speak. The Senator from South Carolina has read many books of chivalry, and believes himself a chivalrous knight, with sentiments of honor and courage. Of course he has chosen a mistress to whom he has made his vows, and who, though ugly to others, is always lovely to him,—though polluted in the sight of the world, is chaste in his sight: I mean the harlot Slavery. For her his tongue is always profuse in words. Let her be impeached in character, or any proposition he made to shut her out from the extension of her wantonness, and no extravagance of manner or hardihood of assertion is then too great for this Senator. The frenzy of Don

263

Quixote in behalf of his wench Dulcinea del Toboso is all surpassed. The asserted rights of Slavery, which shock equality of all kinds, are cloaked by a fantastic claim of equality. If the Slave States cannot enjoy what, in mockery of the great fathers of the Republic, he misnames Equality under the Constitution,—in other words, the full power in the National Territories to compel fellow-men to unpaid toil, to separate husband and wife, and to sell little children at the auction-block,—then, Sir, the chivalric Senator will conduct the State of South Carolina out of the Union! Heroic knight! Exalted Senator! A second Moses come for a second exodus!

Not content with this poor menace, which we have been twice told was "measured," the Senator, in the unrestrained chivalry of his nature, has undertaken to apply opprobrious words to those who differ from him on this floor. He calls them "sectional and fanatical"; and resistance to the Usurpation of Kansas he denounces as "an uncalculating fanaticism." To be sure, these charges lack all grace of originality and all sentiment of truth; but the adventurous Senator does not hesitate. He is the uncompromising, unblushing representative on this floor of a flagrant *sectionalism,* now domineering over the Republic,—and yet, with a ludicrous ignorance of his own position, unable to see himself as others see him, or with an effrontery which even his white head ought not to protect from rebuke, he applies to those here who resist his *sectionalism* the very epithet which designates himself. The men who strive to bring back the Government to its original policy, when Freedom and not Slavery was national, while Slavery and not Freedom was sectional, he arraigns as *sectional.* This will not do. It involves too great a perversion of terms. I tell that Senator that it is to himself, and to the "organization" of which he is the "committed advocate," that this epithet belongs. I now fasten it upon them. For myself, I care little for names; but, since the question is raised here, I affirm that the Republican party of the Union is in no just sense *sectional,* but, more than any other party, *national,*—and that it now goes forth to dislodge from the high places that tyrannical sectionalism of which the Senator from South Carolina is one of the maddest zealots.

To the charge of fanaticism I also reply. Sir, fanaticism is found in an enthusiasm or exaggeration of opinion, particularly on religious subjects; but there may be fanaticism for evil as well as for good. Now I will not deny that there are persons among us loving Liberty too well for personal good in a selfish generation. Such there may be; and, for the sake of their example, would that there were more! In calling them "fanatics," you cast contumely upon the noble army of martyrs, from the earliest day down to this hour,—upon the great tribunes of human rights, by whom life, liberty, and happiness on earth have been secured,—upon the long line of devoted patriots, who, throughout history, have truly loved their country,—and upon all who, in noble aspiration for the general good, and in forgetfulness of self, have stood out before their age, and gathered into their generous bosoms the shafts of tyranny and wrong, in order to make a pathway for Truth.

As the Senator from South Carolina is the Don Quixote, so the Senator from Illinois [Mr. DOUGLAS] is the squire of Slavery, its very Sancho Panza, ready to do its humiliating offices. This Senator, in his labored address vindicating his labored report,—piling one mass of elaborate error upon another mass,—constrained himself, as you will remember, to unfamiliar decencies of speech. But I go back now to an earlier occasion, when, true to native impulses, he threw into this discussion, "for a charm of powerful trouble," personalities most discreditable to this body. I will not stop to repel imputations which he cast upon myself; but I mention them to remind you of the "sweltered venom sleeping got," which, with other poisoned ingredients, he cast into the caldron of this debate. Of other things I speak. Standing on this floor, the Senator issued his rescript requiring submission to the Usurped Power of Kansas; and this was accompanied by a manner—all his own—befitting the tyrannical threat. Very well. Let the Senator try. I tell him now that he cannot enforce any such submission. The Senator, with the Slave Power at his back, is strong; but he is not strong enough for this purpose. He is bold. He shrinks from nothing. Like Danton, he may cry, *"De l'audace! encore de l'audace! et toujours de l'audace!"* but even his audacity cannot compass this work. The Senator copies the British officer who with boastful swagger said that with the end of his sword he would cram the "stamps" down the throats of the American people; and he will meet a similar failure. He may convulse this country with civil feud. Like the ancient madman, he may set fire to this Temple of Constitutional Liberty, grander than Ephesian dome; but he cannot enforce obedience to that tyrannical Usurpation.

The Senator dreams that he can subdue the North. He disclaims the open threat but his conduct implies it. How little that Senator knows himself, or the strength of the cause which he persecutes! He is but mortal man; against him is immortal principle. With finite power he wrestles with the infinite, and he must fall. Against him are stronger battalions than any marshalled by mortal arm,—the inborn, ineradicable, invincible sentiments of the human heart; against him is Nature with all her subtile forces; against him is God. Let him try to subdue these.

2   Congressman Preston Brooks
Describes His Actions

In the Senate of the United States on the 19th and 20th May Mr. Sumner of Mass delivered a speech in which he reflected injuriously upon the State of South Carolina and was particularly offensive to Senator Butler who is my relative. I preferred to see the published 'Speech and saw it for the first time on wednesday morning.

The objectionable passages are to be found on the 5th 29th and 30th pages of Mr. Sumners Speech.

As soon as I had read the speech I felt it to be my duty to inflict some return for the insult to my State and my relative. On wednesday I took a seat in the Capitol grounds, expecting Mr. Sumner to pass. While going down the lower steps of the Capitol I met Mr. Edmundson of Va., who is my personal friend, and asked him to walk with me to the seat. I then informed him that it was my purpose to see Mr. Sumner and that as he might be accompanied by several of his friends I desired him to remain with me as a witness and for nothing else. I also enjoined upon him on no account to interfere. Mr. Sumner did not pass by while we were so seated though we remained until ½ past 12 o'clock. My colleague Mr. Keitt joined us a few moments before we returned to the House and so did Senator Johnson of Arkansas. Neither of them was informed of my purpose during that day. During night of Wednesday and about 10 o'clock I informed my colleagues Mr. Keitt and Mr. Orr. of my purpose. The next morning at eleven o'clock I took my position in the Porter's lodge to intercept Mr. Sumner. I again waited until half past 12 o'clock—the hour at which both Houses of Congress meet. While in the Porter's lodge Mr. Edmundson on his way to the Capitol saw me and came in of his own accord. He and I went to the House together. Mr. Keitt went that morning to baltimore.

Being twice disappointed I determined to keep my eye on Mr. Sumner and knowing that the Senate would adjourn at an early hour, I went to the senate and stood without the bar until it did adjourn. Mr. Sumner continued within the Hall, though he did not all the time retain his Seat. He had upon his desk a large number of his speeches and was, when not interupted, employed in franking them. Several ladies continued in the Hall some on the floor and some in the gallery.

I waited until the last lady left and then approached Mr. Sumner in front and said—Mr Sumner I have read your last speech with care and as much impartiality as is possible under the circumstances, and I feel it my duty to say that you have libeled my State and slandered my kinsman who is aged and absent and I have come to punish you for it. As I uttered the word punish Mr. Sumner offered to rise and when about half erect I struck him a slight blow with the smaller end of my cane. He then rose fully erect and endeavoured to make a battle. I was then compelled to strike him harder than I had intended. About the fifth blow he ceased to resist and I moderated my blows. I continued to strike Mr. S. until he fell when I ceased. I did not strike Mr. Sumner after he had fallen. The Cane used by me was an ordinary walking stick made of gutta percha and hollow. I used it because it was light and elastic and because I fancied it would not break. The Cane had been presented to me by a friend full three months past. It had a thin gold head and was not loaded or even heavy. Mr. Sumner was never struck with the larger end of the Cane. When Mr. Crittenden took hold of me and said something like "don't kill him," I replied that I had no wish to injure him seriously, but only to flogg him.

I went to the Senate alone, asked no one to go or to be with me. Indeed no one knew of my purpose to assail Mr. Sumner in the Senate. It was not my purpose or desire to assault him in the Senate, nor would I have done so, had it not become manifest that he would remain in his seat to a very late hour. The three gentlemen who alone knew of my purpose were neither present when the attack was made. Neither Mr. Orr or Mr. Edmundson were present at any time of the affray to my knowledge. Mr. Keitt came up when it was about half over.

I deem it proper to add that the assault upon Mr. Sumner was not because of his political principles, but because of the insulting language used in reference to my State and absent relative.

28 May 1856

P. S. Brooks

3   Charles Sumner Testifies on the Event

In the House of Representatives, on the day after the assault, Hon. Lewis D. Campbell, of Ohio, moved a Select Committee of five "to investigate the subject, and to report the facts, with such resolutions in reference thereto as in their judgments may be proper and necessary for the vindication of the character of the House." The resolution was adopted.

The Committee visited Mr. Sumner at his house.

"Hon. Charles Sumner, being sworn, testified.

"*Question* (by Mr. Campbell).   What do you know of the facts connected with the assault alleged to have been made upon you in the Senate Chamber by Hon. Mr. Brooks, of South Carolina, on Thursday, May 22, 1856?

"*Answer.*   I attended the Senate as usual on Thursday, the 22d of May. After some formal business, a message was received from the House of Representatives, announcing the death of a member of that body from Missouri. This was followed by a brief tribute to the deceased from Mr. Geyer, of Missouri, when, according to usage, and out of respect to the deceased, the Senate adjourned.

"Instead of leaving the Chamber with the rest on the adjournment, I continued in my seat, occupied with my pen. While thus intent, in order to be in season for the mail, which was soon to close, I was approached by several persons who desired to speak with me; but I answered them promptly and briefly, excusing myself, for the reason that I was much engaged. When the last of these left me, I drew my armchair close to my desk, and, with my legs under the desk, continued writing. My attention at this time was so entirely withdrawn from all other objects, that, though there must have been many persons on the floor of the Senate, I saw nobody.

"While thus intent, with my head bent over my writing, I was addressed by a person who had approached the front of my desk so entirely unobserved that I was not aware of his presence until I heard my name pronounced. As I looked up, with pen in hand, I saw a tall man, whose countenance was not familiar, standing directly over me, and at the same moment caught these words: 'I have read your speech twice over carefully. It is a libel on South Carolina, and Mr. Butler, who is a relative of mine——' While these words were still passing from his lips, he commenced a succession of blows with a heavy cane on my bare head, by the first of which I was stunned so as to lose sight. I no longer saw my assailant, nor any person or object in the room. What I did afterwards was done almost unconsciously, acting under the instinct of self-defence. With head already bent down, I rose from my seat, wrenching up my desk, which was screwed to the floor, and then pressed forward, while my assailant continued his blows. I have no other consciousness until I found myself ten feet forward, in front of my desk, lying on the floor of the Senate, with my bleeding head supported on the knee of a gentleman, whom I soon recognized, by voice and countenance, as Mr. Morgan, of New York. Other persons there were about me offering me friendly assistance; but I did not recognize any of them. Others there were at a distance, looking on and offering no assistance, of whom I recognized only Mr. Douglas, of Illinois, Mr. Toombs, of Georgia, and I thought also my assailant, standing between them.

"I was helped from the floor and conducted into the lobby of the Senate, where I was placed upon a sofa. Of those who helped me to this place I have no recollection. As I entered the lobby, I recognized Mr. Slidell, of Louisiana, who retreated; but I recognized no one else until some time later, as I supposed, when I felt a friendly grasp of the hand, which seemed to come from Mr. Campbell, of Ohio. I have a vague impression that Mr. Bright, President of the Senate, spoke to me while I was lying on the floor of the Senate or in the lobby.

"I make this statement in answer to the interrogatory of the Committee, and offer it as presenting completely all my recollections of the assault and of the attending circumstances, whether immediately before or immediately after. I desire to add, that, besides the words which I have given as uttered by my assailant, I have an indistinct recollection of the words, 'old man'; but these are so enveloped in the mist which ensued from the first blow, that I am not sure whether they were uttered or not.

"*Ques.* (by Mr. Greenwood). How long do you suppose it was after the adjournment of the Senate before this occurrence took place?

"*Ans.* I am very much at a loss to say whether it was half an hour or fifteen minutes: I should say ranging from fifteen minutes to half an hour, more or less; perhaps not more than fifteen minutes. I have already testified that I was so much absorbed with what I was doing at my desk, that I took very little note of anything, not even of time.

"*Ques.* (by Mr. Cobb). Was the first blow you received from Mr. Brooks before he had finished the sentence?

"*Ans.* I have no recollection beyond what I have stated.

"*Ques.* My question was, whether a blow was struck before Mr. Brooks finished the remark to you which you have just quoted?

"*Ans.* The blow came down with the close of the sentence.

"*Ques.* Then the sentence was closed before the blow was struck?

"*Ans.* It seemed to me that the blow came in the middle of an unfinished sentence. In the statement I have made I used the language, 'While these words were still passing from his lips, he commenced a succession of blows.' I heard distinctly the words I have given; I heard the words 'a relative of mine,' and then it seemed to me there was a break, and I have left it as an unfinished sentence, the sequel of which I did not hear on account of the blows.

"*Ques.* (by Mr. Campbell). Did you, at any time between the delivery of your speech referred to and the time when you were attacked, receive any intimation, in writing or otherwise, that Mr. Brooks intended to attack you?

"*Ans.* Never, directly or indirectly; nor had I the most remote suspicion of any attack, nor was I in any way prepared for an attack. I had no arms or means of defence of any kind. I was, in fact, entirely defenceless at the time, except so far as my natural strength went. In other words, I had no arms either about my person or in my desk. Nor did I ever wear arms in my life. I have always lived in a civilized community, where wearing arms has not been considered necessary. When I had finished my speech my colleague came to me and said, 'I am going home with you to-day; several of us are going home with you.' Said I, 'None of that, Wilson.' And instead of waiting for him, or allowing him to accompany me home, I shot off just as I should any other day. While on my way from the Capitol, I overtook Mr. Seward, with whom I had engaged to dine. We walked together as far as the omnibuses. He then proposed that we should take an omnibus, which I declined, stating that I must go to the printing-office to look over proofs. I therefore walked alone, overtaking one or two persons on the way. I have referred to this remark of my colleague in answer to your question, whether I had in any way been put on my guard?

"*Ques.* (by Mr. Cobb).   What do you attribute the remark of your colleague to? In other words, was it founded upon an apprehension growing out of what you had said in your speech?

"*Ans.*   I understand that it was. He has told me since that a member of the House had put him on his guard, but he did not mention it to me at the time. I suspected no danger, and therefore I treated what he said to me as trifling.

"*Ques.* (by Mr. Pennington).   Have you ever defied or invited violence?

"*Ans.*   Never, at any time.

"*Ques.*   State what was the condition of your clothing after this violence, when you were taken from the Chamber.

"*Ans.*   I was in such a condition at the time that I was unaware of the blood on my clothes. I know little about it until after I reached my room, when I took my clothes off. The shirt, around the neck and collar, was soaked with blood. The waistcoat had many marks of blood upon it; also the trousers. The broadcloth coat was covered with blood on the shoulders so thickly that the blood had soaked through the cloth, even through the padding, and appeared on the inside; there was also a great deal of blood on the back of the coat and its sides.

"*Ques.*   Were you aware of the intention of Mr. Brooks to strike or inflict a blow before the blow was felt?

"*Ans.*   I had not the remotest suspicion of it until I felt the blow on my head.

"*Ques.* (by Mr. Campbell).   Do you know how often you were struck?

"*Ans.*   I have not the most remote idea.

"*Ques.*   How many wounds have you upon your head?

"*Ans.*   I have two principal wounds upon my head, and several bruises on my hands and arms. The doctor will describe them more particularly than I am able to.

"*Ques.* (by Mr. Cobb).   You stated, that, when Mr. Brooks approached you, he remarked that he had read your speech, and it was a libel upon his State and upon his relative. I will ask you, if you had, prior to that assault, in any speech, made any personal allusions to Mr. Brooks's relative, Mr. Butler, or to the State of South Carolina, to which Mr. Brooks applied this remark?

"*Ans.*   At the time my assailant addressed me I did not know who he was, least of all did I suppose him to be a relative of Mr. Butler. In a speech recently made in the Senate I have alluded to the State of South Carolina, and to Mr. Butler; but I

269

have never said anything which was not in just response to his speeches, according to parliamentary usage, nor anything which can be called a libel upon South Carolina or Mr. Butler."

4   The Response of the Southern Press: The Richmond Enquirer, June 9, 1856

It is idle to think of union or peace or truce with Sumner or Sumner's friends. Catiline was purity itself, compared to the Massachusetts Senator, and his friends are no better than he. They are all (we mean the leading and conspicuous ones) avowed and active traitors. . . . Sumner and Sumner's friends must be punished and silenced. Government which cannot suppress such crimes as theirs has failed of its purpose. Either such wretches must be hung or put in the penitentiary, or the South should prepare at once to quit the Union. We would not jeopard the religion and morality of the South to save a Union that had failed for every useful purpose. Let us tell the North at once, If you cannot suppress the treasonable action, and silence the foul, licentious, and infidel propagandism of such men as Stephen Pearl Andrews, Wendell Phillips, Beecher, Garrison, Sumner, and their negro and female associates, let us part in peace.

Your sympathy for Sumner has shaken our confidence in your capacity for self-government more than all your past history, full of evil portents as that has been. He had just avowed his complicity in designs far more diabolical than those of Catiline or Cethegus,—nay, transcending in iniquity all that the genius of a Milton has attributed to his fallen angels. We are not surprised that he should be hailed as hero and saint, for his proposed war on everything sacred and divine, by that Pandemonium where the blasphemous Garrison, and Parker, and Andrews, with their runaway negroes and masculine women, congregate.

In the main, the press of the South applaud the conduct of Mr. Brooks, without condition or limitation. Our approbation, at least, is entire and unreserved. We consider the act good in conception, better in execution, and best of all in consequence. The vulgar Abolitionists in the Senate are getting above themselves. They have been humored until they forget their position. They have grown saucy, and dare to be impudent to gentlemen! Now, they are a low, mean, scurvy set, with some little book-learning, but as utterly devoid of spirit or honor as a pack of curs. Intrenched behind 'privilege,' they fancy they can slander the South and insult its representatives with impunity. The truth is, they have been suffered to run too long without collars. They must be lashed into submission. Sumner, in particular, ought to have nine-and-thirty early every morning. He is a great strapping fellow, and could stand the cowhide beautifully. Brooks frightened him, and at the first blow of the cane he bellowed like a bull-calf. There is the blackguard Wilson, an ignorant Natick cobbler, swaggering in excess of muscle, and absolutely dying for a beating. Will not somebody take him in hand? Hale is another huge, red-faced, sweating scoundrel, whom some gentleman should kick and cuff until he abates something of his impudent talk. These men are perpetually abusing the people and representatives of the South, for tyrants, robbers, ruffians, adulterers, and what not. Shall we stand it?

Mr. Brooks has initiated this salutary discipline, and he deserves applause for the bold, judicious manner in which he chastised the scamp Sumner. It was a proper act, done at the proper time, and in the proper place.

5 Abolitionist Wendell Phillips Addresses a Boston Audience Immediately after the Clubbing

Nobody needs now to read this speech of Charles Sumner to know whether it is good. We measure the amount of the charge by the length of the rebound. [*Cheers.*] When the spear, driven to the quick, makes the Devil start up in his own likeness, we may be sure it is the spear of Ithuriel. [*Great applause.*] That is my way of measuring the speech which has produced this glorious result. Oh, yes, glorious! for the world will yet cover every one of those scars with laurels. [*Enthusiastic cheering.*] Sir, he *must* not die! We need him yet, as the vanguard leader of the hosts of Liberty. No, he shall yet come forth from that sick-chamber, and every gallant heart in the Commonwealth be ready to kiss his very footsteps. [*Loud cheers.*]

Perhaps, Mr. Chairman and fellow-citizens, I am wrong; but I accept that speech of my loved and honored friend, and with an unmixed approbation,—read it with envious admiration,—take it all. [*Cheers.*] Yes, what word is there in it that any one of us would not have been proud to utter? Not one! [*Great applause.*] In utter scorn of the sickly taste, of the effeminate scholarship, that starts back, in delicate horror, at a bold illustration, I dare to say there is no animal God has condescended to make that man may not venture to name. [*Applause.*] And if any ground of complaint is supposable in regard to this comparison, which shocks the delicacy of some men and some presses, it is the animal, not Mr. Douglas, that has reason to complain. [*Thunders of applause, renewed again and again.*]

Mr. Chairman, there are some characters whose worth is so clear and self-evident, so tried and approved, so much without flaw, that we lay them on the shelf,—and when we hear of any act attributed to them, no matter in what doubtful terms it be related, we judge the single act by the totality of the character, by our knowledge of the whole man, letting a lifetime of uprightness explain a doubtful hour. Now, with regard to our honored Senator, we know that his taste, intellect, and heart are all of this quality,—a total, unflawed gem; and I know, when we get the full and complete report of what he said, the *ipsissima verba* in which it was spoken, that the most fastidious taste of the most delicate scholar will not be able to place finger on a word of Charles Sumner which the truest gentleman would not gladly indorse. [*Loud cheers.*] I place the foot of my uttermost contempt on those members of the press of Boston that have anything to say in criticism of his language, while he lies thus prostrate and speechless,—our champion beaten to the ground for the noblest word Massachusetts ever spoke in the Senate. [*Prolonged applause.*]

271

26

The Bloodbath of War

The Civil War set section against section in one of the bloodiest conflicts ever fought. The day of the mercenary was over; weapons had improved while medical skills had not, and the result in losses of lives could reach tragic proportions.

The first Union generals used their armies cautiously, hesitating to enter battle unless confident of the outcome. Typically, troops were inactive and generals gained the reputation of being slow. Casualties were low, but the Union was not faring well. The appointment of Grant to head the army changed everything. He was prepared to fight and take the costs. Perhaps no other campaign so vividly demonstrates Grant's tactics as the battles fought in May 1864 between his forces and those of General Robert E. Lee at the Wilderness and the Spotsylvania Courthouse.

Colonel Charles Wainwright, a Union artillery commander, kept a detailed diary of these events. He did not play a major role in them, but he had access to accurate information; he observed well, and recorded what he learned. His account follows the action at the Wilderness beginning May 5 and at Spotsylvania beginning May 10. Wainwright understood that in terms of territory won the battles were stalemates, or, indeed, Lee's victories. But his record made clear that with Grant willing to fight a war of attrition, the Union resources would eventually bring victory.

THE PERSONAL JOURNALS OF COLONEL CHARLES S. WAINWRIGHT

May 3, [1864], Tuesday

Everything is packed, and we only wait the hour of midnight in order to start. Orders have been coming in thick and fast all day; an army is as bad as a woman starting on a journey, so much to be done at the last moment.

It seems that notwithstanding General Meade's appeal to their honour, there are a number of men inclined to be fractious under the idea that their term of service is

Reprinted with permission of Allan Nevins from *A Diary of Battle: The Personal Journals of Colonel Charles S. Wainwright, 1861–1865*, Allan Nevins, ed. (New York, 1962), pp. 347–349, 352–357, 359–360, 362–365, 367–381.

already out; he now sends notice that all such be shot without trial if they do not step out to the music.

This afternoon General Warren had his division commanders and myself at his quarters, shewed us his orders, and explained tomorrow's move. We are to try to get around Lee, between him and Richmond, and so force him to fight on our own ground. My batteries, with two forage waggons each, start at midnight, pass through Stevensburg, and then follow in rear of the First and Third Divisions. The ammunition and all the rest of the waggons, together with half of the ambulances, move off to Chancellorsville and we are warned that we shall not see them again for five days. The night is soft but cloudy, with some signs of rain; now the roads are capital. Our general officers, that I have talked with, are very sanguine; Grant is said to be perfectly confident. God grant that their expectations be more realized.

When I reached Warren's quarters Wadsworth only was there. He insisted on having my opinion as to which way we were to move, whether around Lee's right or left; and when I told him I had no opinion, having nothing to found one on, declared I must be a regular, I was so non-committal. Would that it were characteristic of all regulars never to give an opinion on subjects they knew nothing about; and if the people at home, newspaper editors and correspondents, and also the politicians at Washington, would take a leaf out of the same book, it would save the country millions of money, and many a poor fellow in our army his life.

Old Wilderness Tavern, May 4, Wednesday

It was nearly two o'clock this morning when we got our orders to haul out. I had managed a few short snatches of sleep before that time, but do not improve in my ability to go off at any moment and in any place. There is a kind of weird excitement in this starting at midnight. The senses seemed doubly awake to every impression—the batteries gathering around my quarters in the darkness; the moving of lanterns, and the hailing of the men; then the distant sound of the hoofs of the aide's horse who brings the final order to start. Sleepy as I always am at such times, I have a certain amount of enjoyment in it all. We got off without much trouble.

Great care was taken not to make any more fires than usual, so as not to attract the attention of the enemy; otherwise the darkness and distance were a quite sufficient cover to our movement. Through Stevensburg, on towards Shepherd's Grove for another mile or so, and then across country through a byroad, we had it all to ourselves. When we arrived at the head of the Germanna Plank Road we had to wait an hour for the two divisions which were to precede us to file by. It was nine o'clock by the time I reached the ford. After crossing, General Warren directed me to divide the batteries among the infantry divisions for the march through the Wilderness. I hated to break them up so on the first day's march, before I had time to look after them all, but an unbroken string of artillery over a mile long was certainly somewhat risky through these dense woods.

Lacy House, May 5, Thursday

This is the second anniversary of my first battle and has been celebrated in due form. Two years ago, I went into the battle of Williamsburg on the 5th of May; one year after I was in the battle of Chancellorsville; today we have been at it for the

273

third time, and though I have not been under very much fire myself, I have had quite a smell of gunpowder, and am two guns short tonight. We have made no progress today, and virtually hold the same position we did yesterday.

May 6, Friday

Grant ordered us to attack along our whole front this morning at five o'clock, but Lee got ahead of us, and pitched into Sedgwick's right. The fight there, all musketry, was hot but not very long: report said that we had the advantage.

Soon after sunrise the head of Burnside's column arrived. They went into the wood by a road from the south corner of the opening here, and pushed on I don't know how far. Burnside himself remained at the very opening of the road, where he fixed his headquarters. The number of staff officers who kept continually riding back to him was something wonderful; nor did his division commanders seem satisfied with sending, but came themselves a number of times: so that I got a very poor impression of the corps.

About noon Hancock was attacked in his advanced position and driven back. This was another very hard fight, and we all waited most impatiently to hear Burnside's men begin, but not a shot was fired by them; at least none to speak of until it was quiet again in front of the Second Corps; then there was an hour or two of musketry but amounting to nothing. There is a great deal of feeling here about this, and I could see that Warren and Meade were very sore about it too, though the latter said nothing. Burnside somehow is never up to the mark when the tug comes. In the evening, about their usual time, Lee pitched into Hancock again, and they had a third heavy fight, but without any gain on either side I hear.

This day's fight has been a terrible one. Our losses are variously estimated at from 10,000 to 15,000 at headquarters, and we hold no more ground than we did last night. Among our lost is General Wadsworth reported killed within the rebel lines; Getty, Webb, and Baxter are said to be wounded; and a General Hays in the Second Corps killed. I know nothing of the plan of battle, if indeed there was any, or could be in such a dense wilderness; but I cannot help thinking that had Burnside pushed in as he was expected to, things might have been very different. Lee's loses, too, must have been very heavy, as he was the attacking party quite as much as we were. Patrick tells me he has received about 1,700 prisoners: these report that General Longstreet was wounded on Hancock's front today. My own command has not fired a shot. Burnside and his staff occupy the Lacy house. We have our tents pitched in the courtyard at night and taken down in the morning.

May 7, Saturday

Things have been quiet all today: no movement of importance has been made on either side so far as I can learn. Our skirmish line was pushed forward in the morning, but Lee was everywhere found strongly entrenched and consequently no attack was made. The losses in this corps have been very heavy; some 6,000 or 7,000 as near as I can ascertain. My batteries remain as they were and have entrenched themselves.

As we came to this point, the rebel sharpshooters opened a very ugly fire on us from the other side of the valley, say four hundred yards off, especially from the wood to the left of the road where they lay thick behind large fallen trees. A couple of batteries of twelve-pounders also opened, from over the open part of the opposite knoll to our right of the road, a very ugly fire of shrapnel, their guns being entirely hid by the knoll.

The rebel guns, just equal in number and description to my own, were, quite hid by the knoll behind which they stood; we could only see the puffs of smoke from their explosions. It followed as a matter of course that they fired too high. My own gunners did the same, and it was with great difficulty that I got them down. At last, however, I did so as to make almost every shot strike the top of the knoll just on what was to us the skyline. When I had also got them to burst their shot as they struck, we shut the rebs up in five minutes; probably their guns were withdrawn.

The whole affair lasted half an hour, and was one of the prettiest little duels I have seen. The enemy had decidedly the advantage in ground, but they lost it by keeping too much under cover; otherwise it was a very even match, both sides firing shrapnel entirely. Had they run their guns up to the top of the knoll so as to get a good sight of us, the chances are that we should have got the worst of it, for their skirmishers hurt us badly. From behind the logs where they lay, a dozen or twenty would fire by command at the same object. They let fly at us when I first arrived with most of my staff and orderlies; being all on horseback in the open ground, it is a great wonder that none of us were hit. Supposing that the fire was drawn by the evidence of a general officer, I sent all off into the wood.

Our men and the batteries, meanwhile, as well as the enemy, entrenched themselves. The day's fight has been anything but encouraging. Lee by this time has all his force in our front, and tonight will doubtless make his position secure. Grant will not be able to force his way through by this route without a hard fight if he succeeds then. Our men did not go in today with any spirit; indeed, it is hard work to get any up after marching all night.

I feel awfully tired tonight, now the excitement is over, having had not a wink of sleep for forty hours; and pretty miserable, too, for my waggon has broken down again, and we are consequently minus everything, forcing me to sponge upon corps headquarters for my supper and night's lodging. They received me very kindly, and served a very good meal considering: their purveyor goes along himself and furnishes the whole concern.

Grant evidently means to fight all his troops. The Heavies who must number over 3,000 strong formed a brigade under Colonel Kitching, Sixth New York Artillery, and were placed on the left of the Third Division, across the valley road to Parker's Store.

About dark, General Warren informed me that the whole army was to move during the night for Lee's right, and shewed me Meade's order. I wish that I could have got a copy of it. So near as I can remember all trains were ordered to Chancellorsville; we were to lead off the troops so soon as it was quite dark.

May 8, Sunday

The night was cloudy, and exceeding dark: The road, which was not wide and made a thorough cut all along here, was literally jammed with troops moving one step at a time. Never before did I see such slow progress made: certainly not over half a mile an hour, if that. Nor could I get around them, for it was so dark that you could not see at all where your horse was stepping.

As we pushed along in this way, every lighted pipe being distinctly seen in the darkness, a lot of pack mules from one of Griffin's head brigades, who had got frightened at something, came down the line on a run. Their great wide packs cleared a broad road through the middle of the line, and their numbers were constantly increased by other mules and horses which they frightened in their passage as much as themselves. Beyond this I rode nearly two miles without coming across anything that could be called a column. At Meade's headquarters I found them all asleep, but thought this straggling of the column of sufficient importance to wake Williams up and tell him of it, as I did not know what might be depending on time. Every officer and man was doubtless very tired and the night was very dark, but it is to me impossible to understand the perfect indifference with which officers allow their men to lag and break ranks for such little things. The fact of our march at night was enough to tell every man that we wanted to reach some place without Lee's knowing it.

When I reached General Warren, I found them all quietly eating their breakfast. Perhaps it was on account of my having made such a fuss along the road about the time lost by our corps, so that I felt chagrined; but I certainly thought then that both Warren and Meade were not pushing matters as much as they ought, considering how important it was to reach Spotsylvania Court House before Lee; and now that we have not got there at all today, I am quite sure of it. Warren had no control, I presume, over the division of cavalry under Merritt which was ahead of us; but he should have, as ranking officer at the head of the column, been charged with the securing of a good position at the Court House and have had control of all troops engaged in doing this, or else Meade should have been on the ground himself, I feel sure that had our column been properly pushed we might have got up to Merritt at least an hour before daylight; which would have given the men that much time for rest and breakfast. If then Merritt had pushed ahead at five o'clock, with Warren's corps close behind him, there is no doubt we should have been ahead of Lee, and got hold of the Court House.

About six-thirty o'clock Merritt reported that the enemy were too strong for him, and Warren was ordered to clear the way for himself.

There are also two other civilians at corps headquarters: Hendricks, a reporter for the *Herald,* and Reverend Doctor Winslow, Sanitary Commission Agent. The former seems a nice sort of a man and as he sends off a messenger every evening with his report, I may be able to get letters through. At any rate, I shall be able to give him an exact account of any officers who fall, and they will know at home that I am safe if I do not figure in the *Herald*'s list. Dr. Winslow is a famous old trump. I met him first on the field of Chancellorsville and introduced myself, he being an own cousin of father's; I was astonished tonight to see how well he bore all the fatigues and inconveniences of this hard life; he was as jolly as anyone and made himself agreeable to all. Warren was colonel of Duryea's Zouaves, with which the doctor and his family first entered the service, and is very much attached to him. I say the "doctor and his family first entered the service," for they all came, he as chaplain, his wife as nurse, and three boys in the line.

Alsop Farm, May 9, Monday

About midnight we were awakened with orders that no move would be made today; we were to rest, fill up supplies of all sorts; make returns so far as possible, and straighten out generally. Quite strong works had been thrown up during the night, but the rebel sharpshooters still made it hot there. Quite early in the day these skirmishers inflicted a terrible loss on us by killing General Sedgwick. He was shot dead a few feet from Mink's left piece, near the rejunction of the roads. No greater loss could have befallen us; certainly none which would have been so much mourned. "Uncle John" was loved by his men as no other corps commander ever was in this army.

Alsop Farm, May 10, Tuesday

This has been a day of hard fighting and heavy loss, without a commensurate gain, if indeed we have gained any thing. A number of attacks have been made all along the line by portions of the Second, Fifth, and Sixth Corps. So far as I can find out they seem to have been weak affairs in almost every case, and unsupported; and mere shoving forward of a brigade or two now here now there, like a chess-player shoving out his pieces and then drawing them right back. There may have been some plan in it, but in my ignorance I cannot help thinking that one big, well-sustained attack at one point would have been much more likely to succeed. None of those made accomplished anything except Upton's, which was very brilliant, as he carried the works at the point of the bayonet without firing a shot, and brought out nine hundred prisoners. But he was not supported at all, and had to fall back at once. Probably his loss was smaller than that of any of the unsuccessful brigades: men will never learn that the greatest safety is in pushing ahead. Upton will certainly get his star now.

May 11, Wednesday

One day fighting and then a day of rest seems to be the new order. Yesterday was fighting day; this has been a day of rest, so called. That is, we have not made any attacks nor been attacked; but all hands have been on the alert, not knowing what might turn up. To officers of sufficient rank to have any responsibility such a day is almost as tiring as one of actual fighting, for they are kept on strain the whole time by reports of the enemy moving here and gathering there.

It is now eight days since we left Culpeper, during seven of which there has been more or less fighting. It is said now that the men stood up to their work much better yesterday than they did in the Wilderness, and that the losses on both sides are very heavy. Our total loss up to this time is variously estimated at from 20,000 to 30,000; including four generals killed.

An unusually large proportion of the wounds are slight, owing to the fighting being mostly in the wood. The weather has been very hot and dusty, so that the men have suffered much, while the wounded must have undergone intolerable agonies during the long ride from here to Belle Plaine, where our base now is. This afternoon we had a nice refreshing thunder shower, which will help us much. Water is good in this district, and ice is found in sufficient quantities for all hospital uses.

Laurel Hill, May 12, Thursday

This has been a day of fighting fully equal to any that we have had as to severity and loss, but for once with the advantage decidedly on our side. The Second Corps had all moved around to the left of the Sixth during the night, and at daylight made an attack in force, the whole corps being thrown in at once. I do not know any of the particulars of it, and saw nothing but the long line of prisoners as they came to the rear. General Meade in his congratulatory order says Hancock captured forty guns and seven thousand prisoners, "driving the enemy entirely from his works." The number of guns and prisoners is very likely overestimated; nor has Lee yet entirely left his works. Still, we have made a big haul of prisoners, and certainly got more guns than have ever before been taken or lost at once by this army; Lee has spent the whole day in efforts to recapture it, making such fierce attacks that although our men were now behind works, it has been all they could do to hold their own. Our loss during the day is estimated from 5,000 all the way up to 10,000.

Of course nothing has been talked of all day save this morning's success; every incident reported, whether true or not, is rapidly passed from mouth to mouth through the whole army. The following is fact. When the two rebel generals were brought to Hancock, he, having known them both before the war, offered his hand. Johnson took it and behaved like a man, but Steuart, who is from Baltimore, drew himself up and said that "under present circumstances he could not take General Hancock's hand." Hancock at once replied "under no other circumstances would it be offered to a rebel." It was very good.

Officers just in from the captured salient, where the fighting is still going on, say that there has been no one spot like it in the whole war. A perfect rampart of dead lie on either side of the captured works. A number of the guns have not been got over the works yet, and neither side is willing to let the other take them off. I hear that 20,000 reinforcements are expected up tonight.

May 13, Friday

It commenced raining last night and has kept at it pretty steadily all today. The day has been a veritable day of rest to the men and all, for both sides were too much exhausted to do anything, even if the weather had been more propitious. Lee has given up all hopes of recovering the ground lost to Hancock, and has fallen back about a mile at this point to his second line.

Our reinforcements have not yet made their appearance. We need them, for this army is very rapidly dwindling. General Grant, I hear, says that he never knew what fighting was before. A new move is to be tried tonight, the order for which has just come. This corps is to move around to the left of Burnside and attack at daylight tomorrow. It is a terrible night for a march, though it be but seven miles.

Today I received the first letters from home since leaving Culpeper. Though only ten days, it seems months since I last heard, making the answers to questions written before that read very queer; the subjects having been entirely forgotten. The latest was dated on the 6th. They had just heard of our starting, not of the commencement of fighting. I have got a line off almost every day, Mr. Hendricks, the *Herald* reporter, kindly sending them with his dispatches.

In our domestic affairs we manage to rub along, not expecting much luxury in eating or comfort in sleeping such times as these. I wonder how I manage to get on with only four or six hours' sleep, who need eight or nine ordinarily; but excitement does wonders. Dr. Thompson's boy acts as cook. He does quite tolerably, considering; better a good deal than Ben. Fried potatoes in his "pièce de résistance."

Beverly House, May 14, Saturday

My march last night was a hard one and a most extraordinary. I started at ten o'clock with all the batteries, making, together with their waggons, some one hundred and twenty carriages. The night was dark as Erebus to begin with, but a dense fog and drizzling rain increased the darkness soon after midnight. Our road at first lay directly to the rear, and was encumbered with endless trains on their way to Belle Plaine. I had to exert the full force of my authority and constantly appeal to the spread eagle on my shoulders in order to get past these endless trains. Sometimes even these did not avail, when main force had to be resorted to, and their waggons forcibly turned out of the road.

There has been more or less skirmishing during the day, and my batteries have done some firing, but we have had no heavy fighting.

It has rained pretty much all day. The whole country is a sea of mud, especially around the house here, where the ground has been trod up by men and horses. Indoors the floor is covered with an inch of mud; but notwithstanding that, Warren, his staff, myself, and my staff are spreading our blankets on the muddy floor for our night's lodging. The roof leaks, too, so that small streams of water drop through onto us; while a few signs of blood around show that the house was used as a hospital early in the day. Such a pig sty one would hesitate to enter at home—certainly without thick-soled boots and turning up one's pants. But here it seems a blessing, and I expect to sleep soundly, for it is near forty-eight hours since I closed my eyes. We lay tonight in our spurs, fearing the enemy may try us, as our men have been too tired today to do much in the way of entrenching themselves. All my batteries have been moved to the north side of the bridge for the night.

May 15, Sunday

A quiet day, although it is Sunday, which is somewhat extraordinary for, without its being intended, Sunday has seemed to be heretofore the day of hardest work. Perhaps it is only because the day being properly a day of rest, we notice it all the more when it ceases to be so. By "a quiet day" I only mean comparatively so, for skirmishing is going on incessantly, and more or less wounded constantly coming in from the front, but there has been no attack on either side, nor any artillery firing on our side.

May 16, Monday

Another day of quiet: Grant seems to be nonplused and to have got to the end of his tether. Things remain just as they were yesterday. We got a little feed for our horses last night, but we have orders not to feed more than four pounds a day, barely enough to keep life in a horse provided he had nothing to do.

279

It has cleared off at last, and the ground is drying up rapidly. I managed to get a bath and clean clothes in my tent, which was a luxury no one can imagine who has not been living as we have since we left Culpeper. I cannot imagine how the line officers of infantry manage, for they have no means of carrying aught with them beyond what they have on their backs. They must simply go dirty: a fortnight without a change is something awful to contemplate.

I got a couple of hours to run up to Army Headquarters this afternoon. They being only some three-quarters of a mile back I could hear any alarm on our front and return in five minutes. I learned there that by the last returns our losses are over 35,000 up to last night; which is more than I supposed More than 20,000 fell in the Wilderness, beside some 6,000 reported prisoners. These are about all the prisoners we have lost, while we have nearly double that number of the enemy. Their loss in killed and wounded must be near two-thirds as great as ours, which with the 10,000 captured will make a hole in their strength.

May 17, Tuesday

Have been busy all day reorganizing my command, for it almost amounts to that. Late last night the order came to reduce all batteries to six guns, shipping off the surplus guns and ordnance stores at Belle Plaine.

A number of stragglers, runaways from the battlefield, have been brought back to the army; who are ordered to be tried at once, and executed where found guilty. The reinforcements are said to be fairly on their way up at last. A big move is on foot for the night. The Second and Sixth Corps to return to the old ground on the right and pitch in there; great things are hoped from it by Grant. I fear he will not find Lee asleep.

May 18, Wednesday

The movement last night was carried out on time, so that two divisions of the Second Corps attacked at daylight. But they found that Lee had covered his front here with acres of slashing, which was almost impenetrable of itself; rebel batteries too swept the whole front, and infantry enough were there to make success impossible. Our men, especially the Irish Brigade, are said to have behaved admirably. They made a number of attempts to get through the fallen timber, but were unable to reach the rebel works. Our losses are said to have been considerable; that for the enemy could hardly have been anything. All attempt on that flank is given up, and now the whole army, including the Ninth Corps, is to be swung around again on to our left.

May 19, Thursday

Everything remained quiet during the morning.

This evening I got a batch of letters from home down to the 13th. They had not then received any of my pencil notes, which I have sent off nearly every day; but the papers had given full accounts, and they were congratulating themselves on my name not being in the long lists of killed and wounded, which certainly look fearful in print. Of course, the whole city was in a state of terrible anxiety, while they appear to have received a better idea of our success than we have here. I also got a letter from Major Reynolds. He gives the following as the idea prevalent through the Western army: "We expect Lieutenant-General Grant will march right into

Richmond: if he fails it will be because he has not his old troops with him. The Army of the Potomac never did anything." Reynolds and the Twentieth Corps of course know better than this, but their easy victories at the West have given them this notion. Had they been here the last fortnight, they might have been induced to say with Grant: "I never knew what fighting was before."

The trial of deserters has been pushed forward rapidly. Several are to be shot tomorrow morning. Now is the time to do it; the punishment should be so sure and speedy that cowards will be more afraid of running away than of standing.

May 20, Friday

The days have been clear of late, not very warm; but there is a heavy fog every night, which keeps things in a state of chronic dampness and nastiness; bad and uncomfortable enough for us who lodge under a roof, and must be much worse for *outsiders*.

Things have been very quiet today; no attempt on either side. Indeed Lee seems to have determined to act altogether on the defensive of late; and Grant to be quite nonplused as to what to do: he evidently has not found any weak spot opposite our left, or there would have been fighting today. Now he has concluded to give Spotsylvania up altogether as a bad job, and we have orders this evening to march in the morning. I am to withdraw all my batteries before daylight, and previous to that to erect brush screens in front of them on the works so that the enemy will not know that they are withdrawn. I suspect that they will make a shrewd guess at it, however. The wounded are all to be sent to Fredericksburg, and everything indicates a longer detour this time than heretofore.

May 21, Bivouac, Saturday

Our corps started at ten A.M. this morning, getting off without any serious trouble, though the enemy did open from some of their batteries and knock over a few men.

Our march today has not been a severe one, the roads being good and unobstructed. We are bound for Hanover Junction: at least that is the point Grant hopes to get possession of before Lee.

So has ended the battle of Spotsylvania Court House, for I suppose that properly speaking all our fighting around that point was one battle. Yet it bore more of the likeness of an irregular siege than of a pitched battle, for all the engagements were actual assaults on works. Grant was foiled there as he was in the Wilderness, so that the victory, so far as there was any, rests again with Lee. Yet we did somewhat better than in the Wilderness; for, as near as I can learn, our losses have not been nearly so great, while the enemy's have been heavier. I may be mistaken in this, but believe I am correct.

27

Reconstruction in the South

The question of Reconstruction—by what procedures were Southern states to be readmitted to the Union—raised exceptionally difficult and complex issues. The South was not a foreign territory to be occupied and governed without a grave concern for the consequences. These were states, and a war had been fought to keep them within the Union; now with victory, an enemy of four years had to be brought back into the nation. There was also the thorny problem of the freed slave—what part was he to play in the social, economic, and political life of the states? Did he need federal protection from former slaveowners? How quickly should he be given full citizenship? Congress would have had a difficult enough time with these issues had all its members shared the best of will. But distrust, whether of Andrew Johnson or the South, and bitter invective, whether from honest indignation or political strategy, all too often colored debates and decisions.

It was from this atmosphere that reporter Charles Nordhoff went in 1875 to investigate the condition of the South for the *New York Herald*. Nordhoff came to the United States as a child, grew up in Cincinnati, and after a few years as a merchant seaman became a journalist and editor. A staunch Union supporter during the war, he published several pamphlets and tracts on its behalf. He spent five months on his Southern assignment and his findings, even his own prejudices, make clear just how complex Americans found the problems of Reconstruction.

THE COTTON STATES
IN 1875
Charles Nordhoff

It was my fortune to spend the winter of 1874–'75 in Washington, in almost daily attendance upon the debates of Congress, and in more or less intimate friendly relations with many of its leading members, of both parties. The Southern question was, during the whole of the three months' session, that which attracted most attention, and was in public and private most earnestly discussed. The Louisiana

From *The Cotton States in the Spring and Summer of 1875* (New York, 1876), 9–25.

affair, the Vicksburg riot, the Alabama question, the Arkansas muddle, were all the topics of continual excited conversation in and out of Congress. I was extremely desirous to find a basis of fact on which to found a trustworthy opinion of the condition of the South; but was constantly confused by statements apparently partisan, and, at any rate, unsatisfactory.

Under these circumstances I accepted gladly an offer from Mr. Bennett to make for him an exploration of the principal Southern States, and see for myself what I had vainly tried to discover by questioning others. My journey began early in March, and ended in July. I visited successively Arkansas, Louisiana, Mississippi, Alabama, North Carolina, and Georgia; and the results of my observations were printed in letters to the *New York Herald*. These letters, with some additions and corrections, form the larger part of the present volume.

Though my letters consisted almost entirely of statements of fact, I found, from first to last, opinions and conclusions imputed to me, by partisan writers, which I did not and do not entertain. It was but natural, perhaps, that each side should accept such facts as served its purposes, and draw inferences from them which were not my own. But I do not wish to be misunderstood, and propose, therefore, to prefix to the record of my observations my own deductions. And to make clear my point of view, it is proper to say that I am a Republican, and have never voted any other Federal ticket than the Republican; I have been opposed to slavery as long as I have had an opinion on any subject except sugar-candy and tops; and I am a thorough believer in the capacity of the people to rule themselves, even if they are very ignorant, better than any body else can rule them.

The following, then, are the conclusions I draw from my observations in the Cotton States:

There is not, in any of the States of which I speak, any desire for a new war; any hostility to the Union; any even remote wish to re-enslave the blacks; any hope or expectation of repealing any constitutional amendment, or in any way curtailing the rights of the blacks as citizens. The former slave-holders understand perfectly that the blacks can not be re-enslaved. "They have been free, and they would drive us out of the country if they thought we were about to re-enslave them. They are a quiet and peaceable people, except when they are exasperated; but then they are terrible. A black mob is a ruthless and savage thing," said a Southern man to me; and another remarked, "If ever you, in the North, want to re-enslave the negroes, you must give us three months' notice, so that we may all move out, with our wives and children. They were a source of constant anxiety to us when we held them in slavery. To attempt to re-enslave them would be only to invite them to murder us, and lay the country waste."

In Mississippi alone did I find politicians silly enough to talk about the Caucasian race, and the natural incapacity of the negro for self-government; and even there the best Republicans told me that these noisy Democratic demagogues were but a small, though aggressive and not unpowerful, minority; and even in Mississippi, a strong Republican, a Federal law officer, an honest and faithful man, assured me that the northern half of the State, which, with the exception of the region lying about Vicksburg, is the most prone to occasional violence and disorder, was, when I was there, to his personal knowledge, as peaceful and orderly as any part of New York or Ohio.

That the Southern whites should rejoice over their defeat, now, is impossible. That their grandchildren will, I hope and believe. What we have a right to require is, that they shall accept the situation; and that they do. What they have a right to ask of us is, that we shall give them a fair chance under the new order of things; and that we have so far too greatly failed to do. What the Southern Republican too often requires is that the Southern Democrat should humiliate himself, and make penitent confession that slavery was a sin, that secession was wrong, and that the war was an inexcusable crime. Is it fair or just to demand this?

The Southern Republicans seem to me unfair and unreasonable in another way. They complain constantly that the Southern whites still admire and are faithful to their own leaders; and that they like to talk about the bravery of the South during the war, and about the great qualities of their leading men. There seems to me something childish, and even cowardly, in this complaint. The Southern man who fought and believed in it, would be a despicable being if he should now turn around and blacken the characters of his generals and political leaders, or if he should not think with pride of the feats of arms and of endurance of his side.

Moreover, it is a fact that the men of brains, of influence, of intelligence, in the South, did, almost to a man, consent to secession, and take an active part in the war against the Union. It was, I believe, and most of them now believe, a great blunder on their part; but they have paid a heavy penalty for their mistake, for most of them were wealthy, and are now poor.

As to ostracism of Northern men, it stands thus: In all the States I have seen, the Republican reconstructors did shamefully rob the people. In several of them they continue to do so. Now, all the Republicans in the South are not dishonest; but whoever, in a State like Louisiana or Mississippi now, and Arkansas, Alabama, and others formerly, acts with the Republicans, actually lends his support and countenance to corrupt men. Is it strange that, if he is ever so honest himself, he is disliked for his political course?

As to "intimidation," it is a serious mistake to imagine this exclusively a Democratic proceeding in the South. It has been practiced in the last three years quite as much, and even more rigorously, by the Republicans. The negroes are the most savage intimidators of all. In many localities which I visited, it was as much as a negro's life was worth to vote the Democratic ticket; and even to refuse to obey the caucus of his party caused him to be denounced as "BOLTER," and to be forsaken by his friends, and even by his wife or sweetheart. That there has also been Democratic intimidation is undeniable; but it does not belong to the Southern Republicans to complain of it.

Wherever one of these States has fallen under the control of Democrats, this has been followed by important financial reforms; economy of administration; and, as in Arkansas and Alabama, by the restoration of peace and good-will.

In Louisiana and Mississippi, which remain under Republican control, there is a continuance of barefaced corruption, and of efforts, made by a class of unscrupulous demagogues, to set the races in hostility against each other.

The misconduct of the Republican rulers in all these States has driven out of their party the great mass of the white people, the property-owners, tax-payers, and persons of intelligence and honesty. At first a considerable proportion of these were ranged on the Republican side. Now, in all the States I have mentioned, except in North Carolina, the Republican party consists almost exclusively of the negroes and the Federal office-holders, with, in Louisiana and Mississippi, the Republican State and county officers also.

Thus has been perpetuated what is called the "color-line" in politics, the Democratic party being composed of the great mass of the whites, including almost the entire body of those who own property, pay taxes, or have intelligence; while the Republican party is composed almost altogether of the negroes, who are, as a body, illiterate, without property, and easily misled by appeals to their fears, and to their gratitude to "General Grant," who is to them the embodiment of the Federal power.

This division of political parties on the race or color-line has been a great calamity to the Southern States.

It had its origin in the refusal of the Southern whites, after the war, to recognize the equal political rights of the blacks; and their attempts, in State legislatures, to pass laws hostile to them. This folly has been bitterly regretted by the wiser men in the South. A Mississippian said to me, "It was a great blunder. We could have better afforded to educate and train the colored people, and fit them for the duties of citizenship, than to have had them alienated from us." He was right; it was a great, though probably an inevitable, blunder. It flung the negro into the hands of the so-called Republicans in the Southern States, and these, by adroitly appealing to his fears and to his gratitude to the Federal Government, and by encouraging his desire for official power and spoils, have maintained the color-line in politics, and by its means kept themselves in power.

One of the most intelligent and excellent men I met in Louisiana told me that in 1872 he had made a thorough canvass of the part of the State in which he lives, addressing himself entirely to the colored people, by whom he is liked and trusted, and trying to explain to them the necessity for honest local government, and their interest in the matter. "But," said he, "I presently became aware that I was followed by a Republican, an illiterate and low-lived man, whom no colored man would have trusted with five dollars, but who overturned all my arguments by whispering, 'Don't believe what he tells you; they only want to put you back into slavery.' "

The Federal office-holders are largely to blame for the continuance of this evil. They are a very numerous class in every Southern State; and have far greater influence than their fellows in Northern States, especially over the blacks, who have been taught to regard them as their guardians, and political guides and leaders. They are too often, and in the majority of cases indeed, *but by no means in all,* men of low character, Republicans by trade, and of no influence except among the negroes, to whom the lowest Federal officer, even a deputy-marshal's deputy, is a very powerful being, armed with the whole strength of the Federal Government.

The color-line is maintained mostly by Republican politicians, but they are helped by a part of the Democratic politicians, who see their advantage in having the white vote massed upon their side.

Human nature being what it is, no one can be surprised that the Republican leaders who found it easy to mass the colored vote, who found also the Federal power flung into their hands, and themselves its ministers, who by these means alone have been able to maintain themselves in power, regardless entirely of the use they made of this power—that under these conditions they should become and remain both weak and corrupt.

Inevitably in such cases there must be a feeling of hostility by the whites toward the blacks, and it is an evidence of the good nature of the mass of whites that, in the main, they conduct themselves toward the blacks kindly and justly. They concentrate their dislike upon the men who have misled and now misuse the black vote, and this I can not call unjust. It is commonly said, "The negroes are not to blame; they do not know any better."

On the other hand, as the feeling is intense, it is often undiscriminating, and includes the just with the unjust among the Republicans. Hence what is called "ostracism" will last just as long as the color-line is maintained, and as long as Republicans maintain themselves in power by the help of the black vote, and by Federal influence. That this feeling of dislike and suspicion toward Northern men often goes to an unjust and unreasonable extent is very true, and it is not easy for a Northern man to hear with patience stories showing its manifestations.

The evil influence of the mass of Federal office-holders in most of these States is an important, but with us in the North unsuspected, element in protracting ill-feeling and preventing a political settlement. They have very great influence; they are the party leaders; if they do not show themselves zealous Republicans, they are removed; and they are interested in keeping men of brains and influence out of their party. Unfortunately, they have been allowed to control; and the Federal Administration has rejected the assistance in the management of these States of the only men whose help would have been important and effective; namely, the natural leaders of the Southern people.

There was, in those Southern States which I have visited, for some years after the war and up to the year 1868, or in some cases 1870, much disorder, and a condition of lawlessness toward the blacks—a disposition, greatest in the more distant and obscure regions—to trample them underfoot, to deny their equal rights, and to injure or kill them on slight or no provocations. The tremendous change in the social arrangements of the Southern States required time as well as laws and force to be accepted. The Southern whites had suffered a defeat which was sore to bear, and on top of this they saw their slaves—their most valuable and cherished property—taken away and made free, and not only free, but their political equals. One needs to go into the far South to know what this really meant, and what deep resentment and irritation it inevitably bred.

At the same time came the attempt of President Johnson to re-arrange the

286

Southern States in a manner which the wisest and best Democrats I have met in the South have declared to me was unwise and productive of disorder.

I believe that there was, during some years, a necessity for the interference of the Federal power to repress disorders and crimes which would otherwise have spread, and inflicted, perhaps, irretrievable blows on society itself. But, after all, I am persuaded time was the great and real healer of disorders, as well as differences. We of the North do not always remember that even in the farthest South there were large property interests, important industries, many elements of civilization which can not bear long-continued disorders; and, moreover, that the men of the South are Americans, like ourselves, having, by nature or long training a love of order and permanence, and certain, therefore, to reconstitute society upon the new basis prescribed to them, and to do it by their own efforts, so soon as they were made to feel that the new order of things was inevitable.

That there were, during some years after the war, shocking crimes in the States I have visited, no man can deny; but a grave wrong is done when those days are now brought up and those deeds recited to describe the South of to-day.

There was, after 1868, in all the States I have seen, great misgovernment, as I have said, mostly by men who called themselves Republicans, but who were for the greater part adventurers, camp-followers, soldiers of fortune, not a few who had been Democrats and "Copperheads" during the war, or Secessionists, and engaged in the rebellion—some Northern men, but also many native Southerners.

This misgovernment has been various. Its most marked or prominent features were the unscrupulous greed and pecuniary corruption of the rulers and their subordinates, who, in a multitude of cases, notably in Arkansas and Louisiana, were not better than common robbers.

But public robbery was, after all, not the worst crime of the men who arose in the name of the Republican party to govern these Southern States. The gravest offense of these "Republican" State governments was their total neglect of the first duty of rulers, to maintain the peace and execute justice. They did not enforce the laws; they corrupted the judiciary; they played unscrupulously upon the ignorant fears of the blacks and upon their new-born cupidity; they used remorselessly the vilest tools for the vilest purposes; they encouraged disorder, so that they might the more effectually appeal to the Federal power and to the Northern people for help to maintain them in the places they so grossly and shamelessly abused.

The injury done to a community by the total failure of its rulers to maintain order, repress crime, and execute justice, is more seriously felt in Louisiana than in any other of the States of which I am speaking. It is a wonder to me that society has not entirely gone to pieces in that State; and I became persuaded that its white population possesses uncommonly high qualities when I saw that, in spite of an incredible misgovernment, which encouraged every vice and crime, which shame-lessly corrupted the very fountains and sources of justice, and made the rulers a terror to the peaceably inclined—in spite of this, order and peace have been gradually restored and are now maintained, and this by the efforts of the people chiefly.

No thoughtful man can see Louisiana as I saw it last spring without gaining a

287

high respect for its white people. The State is to-day as fit for self-government as Ohio or New York. The attitude of the races there toward each other is essentially kindly, and only the continuous efforts of black and white demagogues of the basest kind keep them apart politically. The majority of the white people of the State are well disposed, anxious for an upright government, ready to help honest and wise rulers, if they could only get them, to maintain peace and order. I sincerely believe that whenever they are relieved from Federal oppression—and in their case it is the worst kind of oppression—they will set up a government essentially honest and just, and will deal fairly and justly with the colored citizens.

No thoughtful man can examine the history of the last ten years in the South, as he may hear it on the spot and from both parties, without being convinced that it was absolutely necessary to the security of the blacks, and the permanent peace of the Southern communities, to give the negro, ignorant, poor, and helpless as he was, every political right and privilege which any other citizen enjoys. That he should vote and that he should be capable of holding office was necessary, I am persuaded, to make him personally secure, and, what is of more importance, to convert him from a *freedman* into a *free man*.

That he has not always conducted himself well in the exercise of his political rights is perfectly and lamentably true; but this is less his fault than that of the bad white men who introduced him to political life. But, on the other hand, the vote has given him what nothing else could give—a substantive existence; it has made him a part of the State. Wherever, as in Arkansas, the political settlement nears completion, and the color-line is broken, his political equality will help—slowly, but certainly—to make him a respectable person. I will add that in this view many Southern Democrats concur. "If the North had not given the negroes suffrage, it would have had to hold our States under an exclusively military government for ten years," said such a man to me.

General manhood suffrage is undoubtedly a danger to a community where, as in these States, the entire body of ignorance and poverty has been massed by adroit politicians upon one side. The attempt to continue for even four years longer such a state of things as has been by Federal force maintained in Louisiana would either cause a necessary and entirely justifiable revolt there, or totally destroy society.

There are scores of parishes and counties where the colored voters are to the white as four, six, eight, and even ten to one; where, therefore, ignorant men, without property, and with no self-restraint or sense of honor in pecuniary trusts, would continue to rule absolutely; to levy taxes which others must pay; to elect judges and fiduciary officers out of their own number; to be the tools of the least scrupulous and the most greedy wretches in the community. There are scores of parishes and counties in Louisiana, Alabama, and Mississippi, where the voice of the people is not the voice of God, but the voice of the worst thief in the community.

But the moment the color-line is broken, the conditions of the problem are essentially changed. Brains and honesty have once more a chance to come to the top. The negro, whose vote will be important to both parties, will find security in that fact. No politician will be so silly as to encroach upon his rights, or allow his opponents to do so; and the black man appears to me to have a sense of respectability which will prevent him, unencouraged by demagogues, from trying to force himself into positions for which he is unfit. He will have his fair chance, and he has no right to more.

Whenever the Federal interference in all its shapes ceases, it will be found, I believe, that the negroes will not at first cast a full vote; take away petty Federal "organizers," and the negro, left face to face with the white man, hearing both sides for the first time; knowing by experience, as he will presently, that the Democrat is not a monster, and that a Democratic victory does not mean his reenslavement, will lose much of his interest in elections. "They won't vote unless they have white organizers," is the universal testimony of the Republican leaders wherever I have been.

Of course, as soon as parties are re-arranged on a sound and natural basis, the negro vote will re-appear; for the leaders of each party, the Whig or Republican and the Democrat, will do their utmost to get his vote, and therein will be the absolute security of the black man. I believe, however, that for many years to come, until a new generation arrives at manhood perhaps, and, at any rate, until the black man becomes generally an independent farmer, he will be largely influenced in his political affiliations by the white. He will vote as his employer, or the planter from whom he rents land, or the white man whom he most trusts, and with whom, perhaps, he deposits his savings, tells him is best for his own interest. He will, perhaps, in the cities, sell his registration certificate, as in Montgomery in May last. But, at any rate, he will vote or not, as he pleases. And it is far better for him that he should act under such influences than that his vote should be massed against the property and intelligence of the white people to achieve the purposes of unscrupulous demagogues.

It struck me as probable and natural that some constitutional modification of the suffrage should come about in such States as Louisiana and Mississippi. An education qualification, applied equally to white and black, seemed to me evident. But the reply was, that it is impossible. These States have a considerable population of poor and illiterate whites, who would resist to the uttermost—now, at least any limitation which would affect them. "It is more probable that we shall make the State Senate represent property, leaving the House open to every body," said a Louisiana Republican to me; but even that would only make a dead-lock, and is a poor expedient to evade a difficulty. The real cure, I imagine, lies—after the breaking of the color-line—in general and even compulsory education. But there is room for wide statesmanship in many of the Southern States.

The negro, in the main, is industrious. Free labor is an undoubted success in the South. The negro works; he raises cotton and corn, sugar and rice, and it is infinitely to his credit that he continues to do so, and, according to the universal testimony, works more steadfastly and effectively this year than ever before since 1865, in spite of the political hurly-burly in which he has lived for the last ten years.

Nor ought we of the North to forget that a part of the credit of the negroes' industry to-day is due to the Southern planters, who have been wise enough to adapt themselves to the tremendous change in their labor system, and honest enough not to discourage the ignorant free laborer by wronging him of his earnings or by driving unjust bargains with him.

The system of planting on shares, which prevails in most of the cotton region I have seen, appears to me admirable in every respect. It tends to make the laborer independent and self-helpful, by throwing him on his own resources. He gets the reward of his own skill and industry, and has the greatest motive to impel him to steadfast labor and to self-denial.

I have satisfied myself, too, that the black man gets, wherever I have been, a fair share of the crop he makes. If anywhere he suffers wrong, it is at the hands of poor farmers, who cultivate a thin soil, and are themselves poor and generally ignorant.

The black laborer earns enough, but he does not save his money. In the heart of the cotton country, a negro depending on his own labor alone, with the help of his wife in the picking season, may live and have from seventy-five to one hundred and twenty-five dollars clear money in hand at the close of the season. If he has several half-grown boys able to help him in the field, he may support his family during the year, and have from one hundred and seventy-five to two hundred dollars clear money at the year's end. Few laborers as ignorant as the average plantation negro can do as well anywhere in the world.

Of course he lives poorly; but he thrives on corn-meal and bacon, and has few doctor's bills to pay. Unfortunately, as yet, he commonly spends his money like a sailor or a miner, or any other improvident white man. Very few lay by their earnings; yet the deposits in the Freedmen's Bank showed how very considerable were the savings of the few; and I am sorry to say that the criminal mismanagement of this trust has struck a serious blow in the South, for it has given a fresh impetus to the spendthrift habits of the blacks.

They have as yet far less desire to own farms than I hoped to find. They are, like almost all rude people, fond of owning an acre or a house lot; and in Southern towns and cities it is common to find them such owners. But, except in Georgia, a comparatively small number, as yet, are freeholders in the best sense of the word. This, however, will come with time. They have been free but ten years, and in that time have been unsettled by the stress of politics, and have scarcely known, until within the last two years, whether their freedom was a substantial fact, or only a pleasant dream. Moreover, they have, very naturally, enjoyed the spending of their own money, and have had to acquire mules, farm implements, household goods, not to speak of very ancient and shabby buggies, sham jewelry, and gewgaws of all kinds.

The character of the Southern negro is essentially kindly and good. He is not naturally quarrelsome, and his vices are mostly those which he retains from slavery. For instance, it is the almost universal complaint of the planters that they can not keep stock, either cattle or hogs. It is the bad custom in the South to turn such animals into the woods to shift more or less for themselves, and here they fall a prey to the colored men, who kill and eat them. They have not yet learned to respect property rights so loosely asserted. But this will come with time. Nor are the planters' chickens safe. In fact, petty theft is a common vice of the plantation negro. He learned it as a slave, and has yet unlearned it.

They are anxious to send their children to school, and the colored schools are more abundant in those States which I have seen than I expected to find them. I think it may be said that the colored people, so far, have got their fair share of schools and school money. In such places as New Orleans, Mobile, Selma, and Montgomery, the colored schools are excellently managed and liberally provided for. By general consent of both colors, there are no mixed schools; nor would it be wise to force this anywhere.

It must be remembered that few of the Southern States had public schools before the war. The whites are unaccustomed to them; and enlightened and influential Democrats, as in Georgia, have difficulty in obtaining appropriations for schools sufficient to place these on a sound basis. The poorer whites are still in doubt about the usefulness of a thorough public-school system. But wherever I have been the blacks have a fair share of school privileges.

I come last to speak of the future of the Southern States: I was deeply impressed with the natural wealth, mostly undeveloped, of the States I saw. The South contains the greatest body of rich but unreclaimed soil on this continent. Louisiana seems to me to have elements of wealth as great as California. Georgia has a great future as a manufacturing State, and will, I believe, within a few years tempt millions of Northern and European capital into her borders to engage in manufactures.

Almost everywhere, except in Louisiana, Mississippi, and perhaps Arkansas, I noticed an increase of the towns. I saw many new buildings, and others going up; and observant Southern men remarked upon this to me also. Wherever the people have been even moderately prosperous, these improvements begin to make a show.

As wealth once more begins to accumulate, some other and sound forms of investment are, and will be, sought for it. It will be turned into houses, town improvements, and, above all, I believe, into factories of various kinds. Of course, the accumulations of the community will no longer be in so few hands as before; but this also is already found to be a great advantage in the South, where employments are becoming more varied, and there is more work for mechanics of different kinds.

I noticed, also, at many points a tendency to a more varied agriculture; to smaller farms; to the cultivation of fruits and vegetables for distant markets; and in these ways much remains to be done, which, when done, will very greatly increase the wealth of the Southern States.

No one who has seen the States of which I speak can doubt that they have before them a remarkable future. Nothing but long-continued political disturbances can prevent them from making very rapid strides in wealth. Their climate fits them for a greater variety of products than any of our Northern States.

Meantime it is a fact that, if the planters are poor, they owe but little money. There is no doubt that there has been much suffering in the South since the war among a class of people who formerly scarcely knew what even prudent economy meant. The emancipation of the slaves destroyed at a blow, for the slave-owners, the greater part of the accumulated capital of these States. The labor is still there. The community will presently be wealthier than ever. But in the redistribution of this wealth the former wealthy class is reduced to moderate means. It is by no means a public calamity; but it makes many individuals gloomy and hopeless, and is one cause of the general depression.

These are my conclusions concerning those Southern States which I have seen. If they are unfavorable to the Republican rule there, I am sorry for it. No men ever had a greater opportunity to serve their fellow-men and their nation than the Republicans who undertook the work of reconstruction in the South; and they could not have desired greater power than was given them. Had they used their power as statesmen, or even only as honest and unselfish citizens, not only would the States I speak of to-day have been prosperous, and their people of both races contented and happy, but there would now have been, in every one of them, a substantial and powerful Republican party. Nor are the Northern Republican leaders without blame in this matter. They chose for their allies in the South men like Spencer in Alabama, Ames in Mississippi, Kellogg and Packard in Louisiana, Dorsey and Brooks in Arkansas, not to speak of hundreds of subordinate instruments, corrupt, weak, or self-seeking. They suffered the most shameless public plundering to go on in those States without inquiry. They confided the Federal power and patronage to men, many of whom would to-day be in State-prisons if they had their dues. And they have, as the result of their carelessness, seen State after State fall into the hands of the Democrats, and, in a large part of the Union, the name of Republican made odious to all honest and intelligent men; while they have crushed to the earth a considerable number of honest Republicans in the South, who, naturally, found no favor in the eyes of such men as Spencer and Ames.

PART FOUR

Industrialization, 1850–1890

In the four decades between 1850 and 1890 the United States underwent a stunning economic and social transformation. Midcentury America was an agricultural and rural society. It had more slaves than factory workers and still more independent farmers. Only one-eighth of its population lived in cities of more than eight thousand. The United States ranked well behind England, France, and Germany in the value of its manufactured goods.

By 1890 nearly one-third of the American population lived in cities, and the remaining two-thirds were tied to the swelling urban industrial centers in a variety of ways. The United States was the leading industrial power of the world; its manufactures almost equalled those of England, France, and Germany combined! As late as 1880, American rural and urban real estate were of approximately equal value, $10 billion. Ten years later, farm property had risen to $13 billion, urban property to $26 billion! The gross national product more than doubled between the end of the Civil War and 1890.

An efficient national transportation and communications network was laid down in these years. Railroad mileage increased eighteen-fold, shipping costs fell dramatically. The telegraph, and later the telephone, allowed instant contact between cities on opposite sides of the continent. These and other developments called into being a national distribution system for goods and services. Woolworth's five-and-ten-cent stores, the A & P grocery chain, Montgomery Ward's mail-order catalog, Macy's, and nationally advertised brand names like Baker's chocolate, Singer sewing machines, Swift meats, and Kellogg's cornflakes all appeared during this era.

The availability of a national market spurred specialization, increased production, and created costly new labor-saving machines. The giant textile factories built in Lowell, Massachusetts, in the 1820s were rare exceptions to the general pattern. By 1890 firms employing several thousand operatives were commonplace. The prospect of sales to millions of customers across the country made it profitable to invest in elaborate machines and processes that could make a product more cheaply than the individual craftsman, utilizing relatively unskilled working men and women.

The new technology, however, required investment on a scale few individual entrepreneurs could provide. The dominant form of business organization quickly became the limited liability corporation, not the family firm, generating its capital by selling its stock to the public through investment bankers like J. P. Morgan. There were a variety of attempts by major corporations to obtain primacy and protection from competition by purchase of rivals, pools, mergers, and trust agreements.

The rising city was the point of concentration for much of the explosive economic energy unleashed during this period, and the spectacular growth of the cities was a dramatic symbol of the emergence of a new America. No less than one hundred and one American cities doubled their population in the 1880s. The new factories were in many cases outside the major urban centers—Homestead, Pennsylvania; Pullman, Illinois; and Winston, North Carolina; for instance—but the control of manufacturing gravitated toward the metropolis, for there the financing, distribution, and sales were accomplished. The growth of the cities and the consequent need to build housing, roads, warehouses, bridges, water and sewage systems was itself an increasingly important source of economic dynamism as the nineteenth century drew to a close.

Even the prairie farmer, hundreds of miles from a factory or large city, found his way of life transformed. The American farmer had never been a true peasant, securely rooted in a plot of land that had been his family's for generations. He had always been a restless soul, quick to scent new opportunity and to move on in search of it, and he was likely to concentrate his efforts on the production of a cash crop—cotton, tobacco, and rice in the South, corn, wheat, meat, and dairy products elsewhere—for sale at a market. Farming was usually a business for him, and speculative. Gains from selling his farm for more than he paid for it were often on his mind. But in this period, farming became more of a business, and a more dangerous business than ever before. Improved transportation and communications opened up vast new areas that had never been available for cultivation before, and drew farm products from these areas into a world-wide market. There were tempting new opportunities for profit, but a number of new risks as well. The market fluctuated more wildly than ever before, responding now to events far across the seas. The farmer was more likely to be living on borrowed money, due to both the competitive pressure to invest in new farm equipment and improvements and to the temptation to accumulate large land-holdings on the assumption that prosperity would continue forever. The city, and city institutions—the bank, the railroad, the grain exchange—seemed increasingly to control his life, and it was the city to which his children drifted when they came of age.

Most Americans in this era were becoming richer in material terms. Real wages in manufacturing edged slowly upward, though interrupted by depressions in the late 1850s and the 1870s. The owners and managers of the growing corporations as well as their lesser white collar employees received some fraction of the new wealth generated by improved productivity. Even the farmers, despite their bitter protests in the 1880s and 1890s, shared to some degree in these gains. There were large groups of desperately poor people in the new America—the tenement dwellers Jacob Riis describes in *How the Other Half Lives*, for instance; but few were deprived of all opportunities for increased economic security and social mobility. The poorest tended to be those most recently arrived in the urban, industrial world, from the farms of Europe or of rural America. In time they found their way out of the slums, for the most part, and into the American mainstream.

A booming economy and a fluid social order lent credence to the optimism of Horatio Alger, Russell Conwell, and other preachers of the gospel of success. Belief in the sacredness of hard work had deep roots in the American past; the values Lucy Larcom learned in early childhood could be traced back to Benjamin Franklin and even to Puritan divines of the seventeenth century. But in the latter half of the nineteenth century these ideas became a national obsession, and in the process were vulgarized to the point where many believed that worldly wealth was the ultimate measure of human worth. The gospel of wealth, fortified by Darwinian ideals about the survival of the fittest, was used to excuse ruthless business practices and cold disregard of the sufferings of the unfortunate. The social philosophy of Conwell met with criticism, especially toward the end of the period, but a sufficient number of Americans were surviving and prospering in the new order to give Social Darwinism and laissez-faire political economy considerable plausibility for a time.

Despite the optimism fostered by an expansive social and economic setting, many Americans felt significant reservations about the new order. There was some nostalgia for the old ways, and revulsion from the machine and the dollar. For all of his commitment to progress, Mark Twain preferred the steamboat to the screeching locomotive, and he looked wistfully backward to Tom Sawyer and Huck Finn's life in sleepy Hannibal, Missouri. There was popular suspicion of the new class of fabulously wealthy "robber barons" who accumulated unprecedented fortunes in the Gilded Age, often by methods that seemed incomprehensible if not positively immoral. If the poor were not getting poorer, the rich were getting very much richer, and the contrast between the two became increasingly sharp. The cities were bursting at the seams with newcomers, many of them packed like sardines into dark, dirty tenements. The newcomers were often immigrants, speaking strange tongues, practicing alien ways. Every year more Americans were exposed to the harsh discipline of the factory, and to the disintegrating pressures of life in the urban jungle. Although industrial America produced more wealth, the national market was more sensitive to fluctuations; undreamed of prosperity in boom times was followed by devastating setbacks at other times. The social order had changed more radically and more rapidly than the typical American's conception of it, and it is probable that the ordinary citizen felt more helpless, more driven, more at the mercy of implacable external forces at the end of the period than at the beginning.

The national political system in this era did not prove very responsive to these new difficulties and concerns. The major efforts of the national government to deal with the problems generated by rapid urbanization and industrialization came after 1890, though some states made significant attempts in this period. Discontented groups sought to influence public policy in accord with their preferences—the farmers, through the Granger movement, the Greenback party, and the Farmer's Alliances, workingmen through the Knights of Labor. But there was truth in the harsh insistence of the hard-headed founder of the American Federation of Labor, Samuel Gompers, that the accumulation and disciplined exercise of economic power would produce greater benefits than moralistic appeals for humanitarian legislation. Groups capable of improving their market position through concerted action—skilled artisans, corporate leaders in many industries, certain professionals, and others—flourished. Less readily organized groups—unskilled workers, small shop-keepers, Negroes, small farmers—fared less well.

In the years between 1850 and 1890 modern America was born. The material achievements of the new society were impressive. Whether the uneasiness, the discontent, the bewildering complexity, and the group conflict it had generated could be satisfactorily dealt with, however, it was left to the future to determine.

28

A Boom Town and the Making of a Millionaire

William Dean Howells, one of the finest novelists of late-nineteenth century America, provides here a vivid sketch of how the discovery of a natural gas field transformed a Midwestern community and one of its residents. Born in a small town in Ohio in 1837, Howells came to Boston shortly after the close of the Civil War and quickly won national eminence as editor of the *Atlantic Monthly* and as a prolific and popular novelist and literary critic. His rise to fame coincided with the birth of modern America. The rise of the city and the factory, the nationalization of American business, and the moral and political challenges these developments posed to older American values were the dominant themes of this era; it was Howells more than any other single figure who saw to it that American writers explored these issues. His philosophy of "literary realism" rejected the romantic, sentimental, and melodramatic and urged that the writer's first task was careful social observation and the realistic portrayal of everyday life. In his most famous work, *The Rise of Silas Lapham* (1885), Howells grappled with the ethical dilemmas confronted by an old-fashioned businessman in an increasingly impersonal and amoral economy. The following scene is drawn from perhaps his finest book, *A Hazard of New Fortunes* (1890), a brilliant critique of the oil tycoon Dryfoos and the class he represented.

A HAZARD OF NEW FORTUNES
William Dean Howells

"Yes, yes," said Fulkerson. "Well, the natural-gas country is worth seeing. I don't mean the Pittsburgh gas-fields, but out in Northern Ohio and Indiana around Moffitt—that's the place in the heart of the gas region that they've been booming so. Yes, you ought to see that country. If you haven't got any idea how old the country looks. You remember how the fields used to be all full of stumps?"

From *A Hazard of New Fortunes* (New York, 1911), 92–101.

"I should think so."

"Well, you won't see any stumps now. All that country out around Moffitt is just as smooth as a checker-board, and looks as old as England. You know how we used to burn the stumps out; and then somebody invented a stump-extractor, and we pulled them out with a yoke of oxen. Now they just touch 'em off with a little dynamite, and they've got a cellar dug and filled up with kindling ready for housekeeping whenever you want it. Only they haven't got any use for kindling in that country—all gas. I rode along on the cars through those level black fields at corn-planting time, and every once in a while I'd come to a place with a piece of ragged old stove-pipe stickin' up out of the ground, and blazing away like forty, and a fellow ploughing all round it and not minding it any more than if it was spring violets. Horses didn't notice it, either. Well, they've always known about the gas out there; they say there are places in the woods where it's been burning ever since the country was settled.

"But when you come in sight of Moffitt—my, oh, my! Well, you come in smell of it about as soon. That gas out there ain't odorless, like the Pittsburgh gas, and so it's perfectly safe; but the smell isn't bad—about as bad as the finest kind of benzine. Well, the first thing that strikes you when you come to Moffitt is the notion that there has been a good warm, growing rain, and the town's come up overnight. That's in the suburbs, the annexes, and additions. But it ain't shabby—no shanty-town business; nice brick and frame houses, some of 'em Queen Anne style, and all of 'em looking as if they had come to stay. And when you drive up from the depot you think everybody's moving. Everything seems to be piled into the street; old houses made over, and new ones going up everywhere. You know the kind of street Main Street always used to be in our section—half plank-road and turnpike, and the rest mud-hole, and a lot of stores and doggeries strung along with false fronts a story higher than the back, and here and there a decent building with the gable end to the public; and a court-house and jail and two taverns and three or four churches. Well, they're all there in Moffitt yet, but architecture has struck it hard, and they've got a lot of new buildings that needn't be ashamed of themselves anywhere; the new court-house is as big as St. Peter's, and the Grand Opera-House is in the highest style of the art. You can't buy a lot on that street for much less than you can buy a lot in New York—or you couldn't when the boom was on; I saw the place just when the boom was in its prime. I went out there to work the newspapers in the syndicate business, and I got one of their men to write me a real bright, snappy account of the gas; and they just took me in their arms and showed me everything. Well, it *was* wonderful, and it was beautiful, too! To see a whole community stirred up like that was—just like a big boy, all hope and high spirits, and no discount on the remotest future; nothing but perpetual boom to the end of time—I tell you it warmed your blood. Why, there were some things about it that made you think what a nice kind of world this would be if people ever took hold together, instead of each fellow fighting it out on his own hook, and devil take the hindmost. They made up their minds at Moffitt that if they wanted their town to grow they'd got to keep their gas public property. So they extended their corporation line so as to take in pretty much the whole gas region round there; and then the city took possession of every well that was put down, and held it for the common good. Anybody that's a mind to come to Moffitt and start any kind of manufacture can have all the gas he wants *free*; and for fifteen dollars a year you can have all the gas you want to heat and light your private house. The people hold on to it for themselves, and, as I say, it's a grand sight to see a whole community hanging together and working for the good of all, instead of splitting up into as many different cut-throats as there are able-bodied citizens. See that fellow?" Fulkerson broke off, and indicated with a twirl of his head a short, dark, foreign-looking man going out of the door. "They say that fellow's a Socialist. I think it's a shame they're allowed to come here. If they don't like the way we manage our affairs let 'em stay at home," Fulkerson continued. "They do a lot of mischief, shooting off their mouths round here. I believe in free speech and all that; but I'd like to see these fellows shut up in jail and left to jaw one another to death. *We* don't want any of their poison."

"Well," Fulkerson resumed, "they took me round everywhere in Moffitt, and showed me their big wells—lit 'em up for a private view, and let me hear them purr with the soft accents of a mass-meeting of locomotives. Why, when they let one of these wells loose in a meadow that they'd piped it into temporarily, it drove the flame away forty feet from the mouth of the pipe and blew it over half an acre of ground. They say when they let one of their big wells burn away all winter before they had learned how to control it, that well kept up a little summer all around it; the grass stayed green, and the flowers bloomed all through the winter. *I* don't know whether it's so or not. But I can believe anything of natural gas. My! but it was beautiful when they turned on the full force of that well and shot a roman candle into the gas—that's the way they light it—and a plume of fire about twenty feet wide and seventy-five feet high, all red and yellow and violet, jumped into the sky, and that big roar shook the ground under your feet! You felt like saying: 'Don't trouble yourself; I'm perfectly convinced. I believe in Moffitt.' We-e-e-ll!" drawled Fulkerson, with a long breath, "that's where I met old Dryfoos."

"Oh yes!—Dryfoos," said March.

"Yes," Fulkerson laughed. "We've got round to Dryfoos again. I thought I could cut a long story short, but I seem to be cutting a short story long. If you're not in a hurry, though—"

"Not in the least. Go on as long as you like."

"I met him there in the office of a real-estate man—speculator, of course; everybody was, in Moffitt; but a first-rate fellow, and public-spirited as all get-out; and when Dryfoos left he told me about him. Dryfoos was an old Pennsylvania Dutch farmer, about three or four miles out of Moffitt, and he'd lived there pretty much all his life; father was one of the first settlers. Everybody knew he had the right stuff in him, but he was slower than molasses in January, like those Pennsylvania Dutch. He'd got together the largest and handsomest farm anywhere around there; and he was making money on it, just like he was in some business somewhere; he was a very intelligent man; he took the papers and kept himself posted; but he was awfully old-fashioned in his ideas. He hung on to the doctrines as well as the dollars of the dads; it was a real thing with him. Well, when the boom began to come he hated it awfully, and he fought it. He used to write communications to the weekly newspaper in Moffitt—they've got three dailies there now—and throw cold water on the boom. He couldn't catch on no way. It made him sick to hear the clack that went on about the gas the whole while, and that stirred up the neighborhood and got into his family. Whenever he'd hear of a man that had been offered a big price for his land and was going to sell out and move into town, he'd go and labor with him and try to talk him out of it, and tell him how long his fifteen or twenty thousand would last him to live on, and shake the Standard Oil Company before him, and try to make him believe it wouldn't be five years before the Standard owned the whole region.

"Of course, he couldn't do anything with them. When a man's offered a big price for his farm, he don't care whether it's by a secret emissary from the Standard Oil or not; he's going to sell and get the better of the other fellow if he can. Dryfoos couldn't keep the boom out of his own family even. His wife was with him. She thought whatever he said and did was just as right as if it had been thundered down from Sinai. But the young folks were sceptical, especially the girls that had been away to school. The boy that had been kept at home because he couldn't be spared from helping his father manage the farm was more like him, but they contrived to stir the boy up with the hot end of the boom, too. So when a fellow came along one day and offered old Dryfoos a cool hundred thousand for his farm, it was all up with Dryfoos. He'd 'a' liked to 'a' kept the offer to himself and not done anything about it, but his vanity wouldn't let him do that; and when he let it out in his family the girls outvoted him. They just *made* him sell.

"He wouldn't sell all. He kept about eighty acres that was off in one piece by itself, but the three hundred that had the old brick house on it, and the big barn—that went, and Dryfoos bought him a place in Moffitt and moved into town to live on the interest of his money. Just what he had scolded and ridiculed everybody else for doing. Well, they say that at first he seemed like he would go crazy. He hadn't anything to do. He took a fancy to that land-agent, and he used to go and set in his office and ask him what he should do. 'I hain't got any horses, I hain't got any cows, I hain't got any pigs, I hain't got any chickens. I hain't got anything to do from sun-up to sun-down.' The fellow said the tears used to run down the old fellow's cheeks, and if he hadn't been so busy himself he believed he should 'a' cried, too. But most o' people thought old Dryfoos was down in the mouth because he hadn't asked more for his farm, when he wanted to buy it back and found they held it at a hundred and fifty thousand. People couldn't believe he was just homesick and heartsick for the old place. Well, perhaps he *was* sorry he hadn't asked more; that's human nature, *too*.

"After a while something happened. That land-agent used to tell Dryfoos to get out to Europe with his money and see life a little, or go and live in Washington, where he could *be* somebody; but Dryfoos wouldn't, and he kept listening to the talk there, and all of a sudden he caught on. He came into that fellow's one day with a plan for cutting up the eighty acres he'd kept into town lots; and he'd got it all plotted out so well, and had so many practical ideas about it, that the fellow was astonished. He went right in with him, as far as Dryfoos would let him, and glad of the chance; and they were working the thing for all it was worth when I struck Moffitt. Old Dryfoos wanted me to go out and see the Dryfoos & Hendry Addition—guess he thought maybe I'd write it up; and he drove me out there himself. Well, it was funny to see a town made: streets driven through; two rows of shade-trees, hard and soft, planted; cellars dug and houses put up—regular Queen Anne style, too, with stained glass—all at once. Dryfoos apologized for the streets because they were hand-made; said they expected their street-making machine Tuesday, and then they intended to *push* things."

Fulkerson enjoyed the effect of his picture on March for a moment, and then went on: "He was mighty intelligent, too, and he questioned me up about my business as sharp as *I* ever was questioned; seemed to kind of strike his fancy; I guess he wanted to find out if there was any money in it. He was making money, hand over hand, then; and he never stopped speculating and improving till he'd scraped together three or four hundred thousand dollars; they said a million, but they like round numbers at Moffitt, and I guess half a million would lay over it comfortably and leave a few thousands to spare, probably. Then he came on to New York."

Fulkerson struck a match against the ribbed side of the porcelain cup that held the matches in the centre of the table, and lit a cigarette, which he began to smoke, throwing his head back with a leisurely effect, as if he had got to the end of at least as much of his story as he meant to tell without prompting.

March asked him the desired question. "What in the world for?"

Fulkerson took out his cigarette and said, with a smile: "To spend his money, and get his daughters into the old Knickerbocker society. Maybe he thought they were all the same kind of Dutch."

"And has he succeeded?"

"Well, they're not social leaders yet. But it's only a question of time—generation or two—especially if time's money, and if *Every Other Week* is the success it's bound to be."

"You don't mean to say, Fulkerson," said March, with a half-doubting, half-daunted laugh, "that *he's* your Angel?"

"That's what I mean to say," returned Fulkerson. "I ran onto him in Broadway one day last summer. If you ever saw anybody in your life, you're sure to meet him in Broadway again, sooner or later. That's the philosophy of the bunco business; country people from the same neighborhood are sure to run up against each other the first time they come to New York. I put out my hand, and I said, 'Isn't this Mr. Dryfoos from Moffitt?' He didn't seem to have any use for my hand; he let me keep it, and he squared those old lips of his till his imperial stuck straight out. Ever see Bernhardt in 'L'Etrangère'? Well, the American husband is old Dryfoos all over; no mustache, and hay-colored chin-whiskers cut slanting from the corners of his mouth. He cocked his little gray eyes at me, and says he: "Yes, young man; my name *is* Dryfoos, and I'm from Moffitt. But I don't want no present of Longfellow's Works, illustrated; and I don't want to taste no fine teas; but I know a policeman that does; and if you're the son of my old friend Squire Strohfeldt, you'd better get out.' 'Well, then,' said I, 'how would you like to go into the newspaper syndicate business?' He gave another look at me, and then he burst out laughing, and he grabbed my hand, and he just froze to it. I never saw anybody so glad.

"Well, the long and the short of it was that I asked him round here to Maroni's to dinner; and before we broke up for the night we had settled the financial side of the plan that's brought you to New York. I can see," said Fulkerson, who had kept his eyes fast on March's face, "that you don't more than half like the idea of Dryfoos. It ought to give you more confidence in the thing than you ever had. You needn't be afraid," he added, with some feeling, "that I talked Dryfoos into the thing for my own advantage."

"Oh, my dear Fulkerson!" March protested, all the more fervently because he was really a little guilty.

"Well, of course not! I didn't mean you were. But I just happened to tell him what I wanted to go into when I could see my way to it, and he caught on of his own accord. The fact is," said Fulkerson, "I guess I'd better make a clean breast of it, now I'm at it. Dryfoos wanted to get something for that boy of his to do. He's in railroads himself, and he's in mines and other things, and he keeps busy, and he can't bear to have his boy hanging round the house doing nothing, like as if he was a girl. I told him that the great object of a rich man was to get his son into just that fix, but he couldn't seem to see it, and the boy hated it himself. He's got a good head, and he wanted to study for the ministry when they were all living together out on the farm; but his father had the old-fashioned ideas about that. You know they used to think that any sort of stuff was good enough to make a preacher out of; but they wanted the good timber for business; and so the old man wouldn't let him. You'll see the fellow; you'll like him; he's no fool, I can tell you; and he's going to be our publisher, nominally at first and actually when I've taught him the ropes a little."

29

The Gospel of Success

Baptist minister Russell Conwell was among the most popular lecturers of his day and one of the leading prophets of the gospel of success. The industrial transformation of America in the latter half of the nineteenth century produced an enormous body of popular literature and speech emphasizing the virtues of aggressive individualism and earnest pursuit of the main chance. Americans had always been committed to self-help, always interested in success, but never before had there been so stark and crude an identification between virtue and money-making. An advertisement for a patent medicine in a newspaper of this period could state quite innocently, "The first object in life with the American people is to get rich; the second how to retain their health. The first can be obtained by energy, honesty, and saving; the second, by using Green's August Flower." The main elements of success creed were summed up well in Conwell's famous "Acres of Diamonds" speech. It was delivered an estimated six thousand times, and netted Conwell a small fortune in lecture fees, part of which he employed to found the Baptist institution, Temple University, in Philadelphia. The version printed here was given in Philadelphia, as several of its remarks indicate. When on the lecture circuit Conwell made a habit of arriving early enough in a new community to obtain local anecdotes consistent with his general theme, which he then inserted where appropriate.

ACRES OF DIAMONDS
Russell Conwell

When going down the Tigris and Euphrates rivers many years ago with a party of English travelers I found myself under the direction of an old Arab guide whom we hired up at Bagdad, and I have often thought how that guide resembled our barbers in certain mental characteristics. He thought that it was not only his duty to guide us down those rivers, and do what he was paid for doing, but also to entertain us with stories curious and weird, ancient and modern, strange and familiar. Many of them I have forgotten, and I am glad I have, but there is one I shall never forget.

From pp. 3–9, 15–24 of *Acres of Diamonds* by Russell H. Conwell. Copyright 1905 by Harper & Brothers. Reprinted by permission of Harper & Row, Publishers.

Said he, "I will tell you a story now which I reserve for my particular friends." When he emphasized the words "particular friends," I listened, and I have ever been glad I did. I really feel devoutly thankful, that there are 1,674 young men who have been carried through college by this lecture who are also glad that I did listen. The old guide told me that there once lived not far from the River Indus an ancient Persian by the name of Ali Hafed. He said that Ali Hafed owned a very large farm, that he had orchards, grain-fields, and gardens; that he had money at interest, and was a wealthy and contented man. He was contented because he was wealthy, and wealthy because he was contented. One day there visited that old Persian farmer one of those ancient Buddhist priests, one of the wise men of the East. He sat down by the fire and told the old farmer how this world of ours was made. He said that this world was once a mere bank of fog, and that the Almighty thrust His finger into this bank of fog, and began slowly to move His finger around, increasing the speed until at last He whirled this bank of fog into a solid ball of fire. Then it went rolling through the universe, burning its way through other banks of fog, and condensed the moisture without, until it fell in floods of rain upon its hot surface, and cooled the outward crust. Then the internal fires bursting outward through the crust threw up the mountains and hills, the valleys, the plains and prairies of this wonderful world of ours. If this internal molten mass came bursting out and cooled very quickly it became granite; less quickly copper, less quickly silver, less quickly gold, and, after gold, diamonds were made.

Said the old priest, "A diamond is a congealed drop of sunlight." Now that is literally scientifically true, that a diamond is an actual deposit of carbon from the sun. The old priest told Ali Hafed that if he had one diamond the size of his thumb he could purchase the county, and if he had a mine of diamonds he could place his children upon thrones through the influence of their great wealth.

Ali Hafed heard all about diamonds, how much they were worth, and went to his bed that night a poor man. He had not lost anything, but he was poor because he was discontented, and discontented because he feared he was poor. He said, "I want a mine of diamonds," and he lay awake all night.

Early in the morning he sought out the priest. I know by experience that a priest is very cross when awakened early in the morning, and when he shook that old priest out of his dreams, Ali Hafed said to him:

"Will you tell me where I can find diamonds?"

"Diamonds! What do you want with diamonds?" "Why, I wish to be immensely rich." "Well, then, go along and find them. That is all you have to do; go and find them, and then you have them." "But I don't know where to go." "Well, if you will find a river that runs through white sands, between high mountains, in those white sands you will always find diamonds." "I don't believe there is any such river." "Oh yes, there are plenty of them. All you have to do is to go and find them, and then you have them." Said Ali Hafed, "I will go."

So he sold his farm, collected his money, left his family in charge of a neighbor, and away he went in search of diamonds. He began his search, very properly to my mind, at the Mountains of the Moon. Afterward he came around into Palestine, then wandered on into Europe, and at last when his money was all spent and he was in rags, wretchedness, and poverty, he stood on the shore of that bay at Barcelona, in Spain, when a great tidal wave came rolling in between the pillars of Hercules, and the poor, afflicted, suffering, dying man could not resist the awful temptation to cast himself into that incoming tide, and he sank beneath its foaming crest, never to rise in this life again.

When that old guide had told me that awfully sad story he stopped the camel I was riding on and went back to fix the baggage that was coming off another camel, and I had an opportunity to muse over his story while he was gone. I remember saying to myself, "Why did he reserve that story for his 'particular friends'?" There seemed to be no beginning, no middle, no end, nothing to it. That was the first story I had ever heard told in my life, and would be the first one I ever read, in which the hero was killed in the first chapter. I had but one chapter of that story, and the hero was dead.

When the guide came back and took up the halter of my camel, he went right ahead with the story, into the second chapter, just as though there had been no break. The man who purchased Ali Hafed's farm one day led his camel into the garden to drink, and as that camel put its nose into the shallow water of that garden brook, Ali Hafed's successor noticed a curious flash of light from the white sands of the stream. He pulled out a black stone having an eye of light reflecting all the hues of the rainbow. He took the pebble into the house and put it on the mantel which covers the central fires, and forgot all about it.

A few days later this same old priest came in to visit Ali Hafed's successor, and the moment he opened that drawing-room door he saw that flash of light on the mantel, and he rushed up to it, and shouted: "Here is a diamond! Has Ali Hafed returned?" "Oh no, Ali Hafed has not returned, and that is not a diamond. That is nothing but a stone we found right out here in our own garden." "But," said the priest, "I tell you I know a diamond when I see it. I know positively that is a diamond."

Then together they rushed out into that old garden and stirred up the white sands with their fingers, and lo! there came up other more beautiful and valuable gems than the first. "Thus," said the guide to me, and, friends, it is historically true, "was discovered the diamond-mine of Golconda, the most magnificent diamond-mine in all the history of mankind, excelling the Kimberly itself. The Kohinoor, and the Orloff of the crown jewels of England and Russia, the largest on earth, came from that mine."

When that old Arab guide told me the second chapter of his story, he then took off his Turkish cap and swung it around in the air again to get my attention to the moral. Those Arab guides have morals to their stories, although they are not always moral. As he swung his hat, he said to me, "Had Ali Hafed remained at home and dug in his own cellar, or underneath his own wheat-fields, or in his own garden, instead of wretchedness, starvation, and death by suicide in a strange land, he would have had 'acres of diamonds.' For every acre of that old farm, yes, every shovelful, afterward revealed gems which since have decorated the crowns of monarchs."

As I come here to-night and look around this audience I am seeing again what through these fifty years I have continually seen—men that are making precisely that same mistake. I often wish I could see the younger people, and would that the Academy had been filled to-night with our high-school scholars and our grammar-school scholars, that I could have them to talk to. While I would have preferred such an audience as that, because they are most susceptible, as they have not grown up into their prejudices as we have, they have not gotten into any custom that they cannot break, they have not met with any failures as we have; and while I could perhaps do such an audience as that more good than I can do grown-up people, yet I will do the best I can with the material I have. I say to you that you have "acres of diamonds" in Philadelphia right where you now live. "Oh," but you will say, "you cannot know much about your city if you think there are any 'acres of diamonds' here."

But it serves simply to illustrate my thought, which I emphasize by saying if you do not have the actual diamond-mines literally you have all that they would be good for to you. Because now that the Queen of England has given the greatest compliment ever conferred upon American woman for her attire because she did not appear with any jewels at all at the late reception in England, it has almost done away with the use of diamonds anyhow. All you would care for would be the few you would wear if you wish to be modest, and the rest you would sell for money.

Now then, I say again that the opportunity to get rich, to attain unto great wealth, is here in Philadelphia now, within the reach of almost every man and woman who hears me speak to-night, and I mean just what I say. I have not come to this platform even under these circumstances to recite something to you. I have come to tell you what in God's sight I believe to be the truth, and if the years of life have been of any value to me in the attainment of common sense, I know I am right; that the men and women sitting here, who found it difficult perhaps to buy a ticket to this lecture or gathering to-night, have within their reach "acres of diamonds," opportunities to get largely wealthy. There never was a place on earth more adapted than the city of Philadelphia to-day, and never in the history of the world did a poor man without capital have such an opportunity to get rich quickly and honestly as he has now in our city. I say it is the truth, and I want you to accept it as such; for if you think I have come to simply recite something, then I would better not be here. I have no time to waste in any such talk, but to say the things I believe, and unless some of you get richer for what I am saying to-night my time is wasted.

I say that you ought to get rich, and it is your duty to get rich. How many of my pious brethren say to me, "Do you, a Christian minister, spend your time going up and down the country advising young people to get rich, to get money?" "Yes, of course I do." They say, "Isn't that awful! Why don't you preach the gospel instead of preaching about man's making money?" "Because to make money honestly is to preach the gospel." That is the reason. The men who get rich may be the most honest men you find in the community.

"Oh," but says some young man here to-night, "I have been told all my life that if a person has money he is very dishonest and dishonorable and mean and contemptible." My friend, that is the reason why you have none, because you have that idea of people. The foundation of your faith is altogether false. Let me say here clearly, and say it briefly, though subject to discussion which I have not time for here, ninety-eight out of one hundred of the rich men of America are honest. That is why they are rich. That is why they are trusted with money. That is why they carry on great enterprises and find plenty of people to work with them. It is because they are honest men.

Says another young man, "I hear sometimes of men thet get millions of dollars dishonestly." Yes, of course you do, and so do I. But they are so rare a thing in fact that the newspapers talk about them all the time as a matter of news until you get the idea that all the other rich men got rich dishonestly.

My friend, you take and drive me—if you furnish the auto—out into the suburbs of Philadelphia, and introduce me to the people who own their homes around this great city, those beautiful homes with gardens and flowers, those magnificent homes so lovely in their art, and I will introduce you to the very best people in character as well as in enterprise in our city, and you know I will. A man is not really a true man until he owns his own home, and they that own their homes are made more honorable and honest and pure, and true and economical and careful, by owning the home.

For a man to have money, even in large sums, is not an inconsistent thing. We preach against covetousness, and you know we do, in the pulpit, and oftentimes preach against it so long and use the terms about "filthy lucre" so extremely that Christians get the idea that when we stand in the pulpit we believe it is wicked for any man to have money—until the collection-basket goes around, and then we almost swear at the people because they don't give more money. Oh, the inconsistency of such doctrines as that!

Money is power, and you ought to be reasonably ambitious to have it. You ought because you can do more good with it than you could without it. Money printed your Bible, money builds your churches, money sends your missionaries, and money pays your preachers, and you would not have many of them, either, if you did not pay them. I am always willing that my church should raise my salary, because the church that pays the largest salary always raises it the easiest. You never knew an exception to it in your life. The man who gets the largest salary can do the most good with the power that is furnished to him. Of course he can if his spirit be right to use it for what it is given to him.

I say, then, you ought to have money. If you can honestly attain unto riches in Philadelphia, it is your Christian and godly duty to do so. It is an awful mistake of these pious people to think you must be awfully poor in order to be pious.

Some men say, "Don't you sympathize with the poor people?" Of course I do, or else I would not have been lecturing these years. I won't give in but what I sympathize with the poor, but the number of poor who are to be sympathized with is very small. To sympathize with a man whom God has punished for his sins, thus to help him when God would still continue a just punishment, is to do wrong, no doubt about it, and we do that more than we help those who are deserving. While we should sympathize with God's poor—that is, those who cannot help themselves—let us remember there is not a poor person in the United States who was not made poor by his own shortcomings, or by the shortcomings of some one else. It is all wrong to be poor, anyhow. Let us give in to that argument and pass that to one side.

A gentleman gets up back there, and says, "Don't you think there are some things in this world that are better than money?" Of course I do, but I am talking about money now. Of course there are some things higher than money. Oh yes, I know by the grave that has left me standing alone that there are some things in this world that are higher and sweeter and purer than money. Well do I know there are some things higher and grander than gold. Love is the grandest thing on God's earth, but fortunate the lover who has plenty of money. Money is power, money is force, money will do good as well as harm. In the hands of good men and women it could accomplish, and it has accomplished, good.

I hate to leave that behind me. I heard a man get up in a prayer-meeting in our city and thank the Lord he was "one of God's poor." Well, I wonder what his wife thinks about that? She earns all the money that comes into that house, and he smokes a part of that on the veranda. I don't want to see any more of the Lord's poor of that kind, and I don't believe the Lord does. And yet there are some people who think in order to be pious you must be awfully poor and awfully dirty. That does not follow at all. While we sympathize with the poor, let us not teach a doctrine like that.

Yet the age is prejudiced against advising a Christian man (or, as a Jew would say, a godly man) from attaining unto wealth. The prejudice is so universal and the years are far enough back, I think, for me to safely mention that years ago up at Temple University there was a young man in our theological school who thought he was the only pious student in that department. He came into my office one evening and sat down by my desk, and said to me: "Mr. President, I think it is my duty sir, to come in and labor with you." "What has happened now?" Said he, "I heard you say at the Academy, at the Peirce School commencement, that you thought it was an honorable ambition for a young man to desire to have wealth, and that you thought it made him temperate, made him anxious to have a good name, and made him industrious. You spoke about man's ambition to have money helping to make him a good man. Sir, I have come to tell you the Holy Bible says that 'money is the root of all evil.'"

I told him I had never seen it in the Bible, and advised him to go out into the chapel and get the Bible, and show me the place. So out he went for the Bible, and soon he stalked into my office with the Bible open, with all the bigoted pride of the narrow sectarian, or of one who founds his Christianity on some misinterpretation of Scripture. He flung the Bible down on my desk, and fairly squealed into my ear: "There it is, Mr. President; you can read it for yourself." I said to him: "Well, young man, you will learn when you get a little older that you cannot trust another denomination to read the Bible for you. You belong to another denomination. You are taught in the theological school, however, that emphasis is exegesis. Now, will you take that Bible and read it yourself, and give the proper emphasis to it?"

He took the Bible, and proudly read, " 'The love of money is the root of all evil.' "

Then he had it right, and when one does quote aright from that same old Book he quotes the absolute truth. I have lived through fifty years of the mightiest battle that old Book has ever fought, and I have lived to see its banners flying free; for never in the history of this world did the great minds of earth so universally agree that the Bible is true—all true—as they do at this very hour.

So I say that when he quoted right, of course he quoted the absolute truth. "The love of money is the root of all evil." He who tries to attain unto it too quickly, or dishonestly, will fall into many snares, no doubt about that. The love of money. What is that? It is making an idol of money, and idolatry pure and simple everywhere is condemned by the Holy Scriptures and by man's common sense. The man that worships the dollar instead of thinking of the purposes for which it ought to be used, the man who idolizes simply money, the miser that hordes his money in the cellar, or hides it in his stocking, or refuses to invest it where it will do the world good, that man who hugs the dollar until the eagle squeals has in him the root of all evil.

30

A New England Girl
Confronts the Factory

Lucy Larcom, later a schoolteacher and a highly successful writer for the juvenile market, was forced to work for several years in the gigantic cotton mills of Lowell, Massachusetts, starting at the tender age of eleven. She was a somewhat unusual girl, as this selection from her autobiography makes clear; and it should be noted that she describes a pre-1850 phase of industrial history; late nineteenth-century factory life was more difficult to describe in such rosy terms. The peculiar system of labor recruitment sketched here—the reliance upon farm girls who lived in the strictly controlled company boarding houses and worked for a brief period before departing for marriage—proved difficult to transplant to other cities. By the 1840s, even in Lowell itself, the labor force was becoming more permanent, more heavily immigrant in origin, and less contented; but the values and personal resources upon which Lucy Larcom drew in adjusting to the factory environment were not the exclusive property of New England girls of the Age of Jackson, but a heritage to which many other Americans and Americanized immigrants were exposed.

A NEW ENGLAND
GIRLHOOD
Lucy Larcom

During my father's life, a few years before my birth, his thoughts had been turned towards the new manufacturing town growing up on the banks of the Merrimack. He had once taken a journey there, with the possibility in his mind of making the place his home, his limited income furnishing no adequate promise of a maintenance for his large family of daughters. From the beginning, Lowell had a high reputation for good order, morality, piety, and all that was dear to the old-fashioned New Englander's heart.

After his death, my mother's thoughts naturally followed the direction his had taken; and seeing no other opening for herself, she sold her small estate, and moved

From *A New England Girlhood, Outlined from Memory* (Boston, 1889), 145–146, 153–157, 164–165, 167–169, 175–176, 199–201.

to Lowell, with the intention of taking a corporation-house for mill-girl boarders. Some of the family objected, for the Old World traditions about factory life were anything but attractive; and they were current in New England until the experiment at Lowell had shown that independent and intelligent workers invariably give their own character to their occupation. My mother had visited Lowell, and she was willing and glad, knowing all about the place, to make it our home.

Most of my mother's boarders were from New Hampshire and Vermont, and there was a fresh, breezy sociability about them which made them seem almost like a different race of beings from any we children had hitherto known.

We helped a little about the housework, before and after school, making beds, trimming lamps, and washing dishes. The heaviest work was done by a strong Irish girl, my mother always attending to the cooking herself. She was, however, a better caterer than the circumstances required or permitted. She liked to make nice things for the table, and, having been accustomed to an abundant supply, could never learn to economize. At a dollar and a quarter a week for board, (the price allowed for mill-girls by the corporations) great care in expenditure was necessary. It was not in my mother's nature closely to calculate costs, and in this way there came to be a continually increasing leak in the family purse. The older members of the family did everything they could, but it was not enough. I heard it said one day, in a distressed tone, "The children will have to leave school and go into the mill."

There were many pros and cons between my mother and sisters before this was positively decided. The mill-agent did not want to take us two little girls, but consented on condition we should be sure to attend school the full number of months prescribed each year. I, the younger one, was then between eleven and twelve years old.

I listened to all that was said about it, very much fearing that I should not be permitted to do the coveted work. For the feeling had already frequently come to me, that I was the one too many in the overcrowded family nest. Once, before we left our old home, I had heard a neighbor condoling with my mother because there were so many of us, and her emphatic reply had been a great relief to my mind:—

"There isn't one more than I want. I could not spare a single one of my children."

But her difficulties were increasing, and I thought it would be a pleasure to feel that I was not a trouble or burden or expense to anybody. So I went to my first day's work in the mill with a light heart. The novelty of it made it seem easy, and it really was not hard, just to change the bobbins on the spinning-frames every three quarters of an hour or so, with half a dozen other little girls who were doing the same thing. When I came back at night, the family began to pity me for my long, tiresome day's work, but I laughed and said,—

"Why, it is nothing but fun. It is just like play."

And for a little while it was only a new amusement; I liked it better than going to school and "making believe" I was learning when I was not. And there was a great deal of play mixed with it. We were not occupied more than half the time. The intervals were spent frolicking around among the spinning-frames, teasing and talking to the older girls, or entertaining ourselves with games and stories in a

311

corner, or exploring, with the overseer's permission, the mysteries of the carding-room, the dressing-room, and the weaving-room.

I never cared much for machinery. The buzzing and hissing and whizzing of pulleys and rollers and spindles and flyers around me often grew tiresome. I could not see into their complications, or feel interested in them. But in a room below us we were sometimes allowed to peer in through a sort of blind door at the great water-wheel that carried the works of the whole mill. It was so huge that we could only watch a few of its spokes at a time, and part of its dripping rim, moving with a slow, measured strength through the darkness that shut it in. It impressed me with something of the awe which comes to us in thinking of the great Power which keeps the mechanism of the universe in motion. Even now, the remembrance of its large, mysterious movement, in which every little motion of every noisy little wheel was involved, brings back to me a verse from one of my favorite hymns:—

Our lives through various scenes are drawn,
    And vexed by traffic cares,
While Thine eternal thought moves on
    Thy undisturbed affairs.

There were compensations for being shut in to daily toil so early. The mill itself had its lessons for us. But it was not, and could not be, the right sort of life for a child, and we were happy in the knowledge that, at the longest, our employment was only to be temporary.

When I took my next three months at the grammar school, everything there was changed, and I too was changed. The teachers were kind, and thorough in their instruction; and my mind seemed to have been ploughed up during that year of work, so that knowledge took root in it easily. It was a great delight to me to study, and at the end of the three months the master told me that I was prepared for the high school.

But alas! I could not go. The little money I could earn—one dollar a week, besides the price of my board—was needed in the family, and I must return to the mill. It was a severe disappointment to me, though I did not say so at home. I did not at all accept the conclusion of a neighbor whom I heard talking about it with my mother. His daughter was going to the high school, and my mother was telling him how sorry she was that I could not.

"Oh," he said, in a soothing tone, "my girl hasn't got any such head-piece as yours has. Your girl doesn't need to go."

Of course I knew that whatever sort of a "head-piece" I had, I did need and want just that very opportunity to study. I think the resolution was then formed, inwardly, that I *would* go to school again, some time, whatever happened. I went back to my work, but now without enthusiasm. I had looked through an open door that I was not willing to see shut upon me.

I began to reflect upon life rather seriously for a girl of twelve or thirteen. What was I here for? What could I make of myself? Must I submit to be carried along with the current, and do just what everybody else did? No: I knew I should not do that, for there was a certain Myself who was always starting up with her own original plan or aspiration before me, and who was quite indifferent as to what people generally thought.

Well, I would find out what this Myself was good for, and that she should be!

It was but the presumption of extreme youth. How gladly would I know now, after these long years, just why I was sent into the world, and whether I have in any degree fulfilled the purpose of my being!

In the older times it was seldom said to little girls, as it always has been said to boys, that they ought to have some definite plan, while they were children, what to be and do when they were grown up. There was usually but one path open before them, to become good wives and housekeepers. And the ambition of most girls was to follow their mother's footsteps in this direction; a natural and laudable ambition. But girls, as well as boys, must often have been conscious of their own peculiar capabilities,—must have desired to cultivate and make use of their individual powers. When I was growing up, they had already begun to be encouraged to do so. We were often told that it was our duty to develop any talent we might possess, or at least to learn to do some one thing which the world needed, or which would make it a pleasanter world.

The gray stone walls of St. Anne's church and rectory made a picturesque spot in the middle of the town, remaining still as a lasting monument to the religious purpose which animated the first manufacturers. The church arose close to the oldest corporation (the "Merrimack"), and seemed a part of it, and a part, also, of the original idea of the place itself which was always a city of worshipers, although it came to be filled with a population which preferred meeting-houses to churches. I admired the church greatly. I had never before seen a real one; never anything but a plain frame meeting-house; and it and its benign, apostolic-looking rector were like a leaf out of an English story-book.

And so, also, was the tiny white cottage nearly opposite, set in the middle of a pretty flower-garden that sloped down to the canal. In the garden there was almost always a sweet little girl in a pink gown and white sunbonnet gathering flowers when I passed that way, and I often went out of my path to do so. These relieved the monotony of the shanty-like shops which bordered the main street. The town had sprung up with a mushroom-rapidity, and there was no attempt at veiling the newness of its bricks and mortar, its boards and paint.

But there were buildings that had their own individuality, and asserted it. One of these was a mud-cabin with a thatched roof, that looked as if it had emigrated bodily from the bogs of Ireland. It had settled itself down into a green hollow by the roadside, and it looked as much at home with the lilac-tinted crane's-bill and yellow buttercups as if it had never lost sight of the shamrocks of Erin.

Now, too, my childish desire to see a real beggar was gratified. Straggling petitioners for "cold victuals" hung around our back yard, always of Hibernian extraction; and a slice of bread was rewarded with a shower of benedictions that lost itself upon us in the flood of its own incomprehensible brogue.

At home I was among children of my own age, for some cousins and other acquaintances had come to live and work with us. We had our evening frolics and entertainments together, and we always made the most of our brief holiday hours. We had also with us now the sister Emilie of my fairy-tale memories, who had grown into a strong, earnest-hearted woman. We all looked up to her as our model, and the ideal of our heroine-worship; for our deference to her in every way did amount to that.

She watched over us, gave us needed reproof and commendation, rarely cosseted us, but rather made us laugh at what many would have considered the hardships of our lot. She taught us not only to accept the circumstances in which we found ourselves, but to win from them courage and strength. When we came in shivering from our work, through a snow-storm, complaining of numb hands and feet, she would say cheerily, "But it doesn't make you any warmer to *say* you are cold"; and this was typical of the way she took life generally, and tried to have us take it. She was constantly denying herself for our sakes, without making us feel that he was doing so. But she did not let us get into the bad habit of pitying ourselves because we were not as "well off" as many other children. And indeed we considered ourselves pleasantly situated; but the best of it all was that we had *her*.

Her theories for herself, and her practice, too, were rather severe; but we tried to follow them, according to our weaker abilities. Her custom was, for instance, to take a full cold bath every morning before she went to her work, even though the water was chiefly broken ice; and we did the same whenever we could be resolute enough. It required both nerve and will to do this at five o'clock on a zero morning, in a room without a fire; but it helped us to harden ourselves, while we formed a good habit. The working-day in winter began at the very earliest daylight, and ended at half-past seven in the evening.

Another habit of hers was to keep always beside her at her daily work something to study or to think about. At first it was "Watts on the Improvement of the Mind," arranged as a textbook, with questions and answers, by the minister of Beverly who had made the thought of the millennium such a reality to his people. She quite wore this book out, carrying it about with her in her working-dress pocket. After that, "Locke on the Understanding" was used in the same way. She must have known both books through and through by heart. Then she read Combe and Abercrombie, and discussed their physics and metaphysics with our girl boarders, some of whom had remarkably acute and well-balanced minds. Her own seemed to have turned from its early bent toward the romantic, her taste being now for serious and practical, though sometimes abstruse, themes.

At this time I had learned to do a spinner's work, and I obtained permission to tend some frames that sood directly in front of the river-windows, with only them and the wall behind me, extending half the length of the mill,—and one young woman beside me, at the farther end of the row. She was a sober, mature person, who scarcely thought it worth her while to speak often to a child like me; and I was, when with strangers, rather a reserved girl; so I kept myself occupied with the river, my work, and my thoughts. And the river and my thoughts flowed on together, the happiest of companions. Like a loitering pilgrim, it sparkled up to me in recognition as it glided along, and bore away my little frets and fatigues on its bosom. When the work "went well," I sat in the window-seat, and let my fancies fly whither they would,—downward to the sea, or upward to the hills that hid the mountain-cradle of the Merrimack.

The printed regulations forbade us to bring books into the mill, so I made my window-seat into a small library of poetry, pasting its side all over with newspaper clippings. In those days we had only weekly papers, and they had always a "poet's corner," where standard writers were well represented, with anonymous ones, also. I was not, of course, much of a critic. I chose my verses for their sentiment, and because I wanted to commit them to memory; sometimes it was a long poem, sometimes a hymn, sometimes only a stray verse. Mrs. Hemans sang with me,—

Far away, o'er the blue hills far away;
and I learned and loved her "Better Land," and

If thou hast crushed a flower,
and "Kindred Hearts."

We used sometimes to see it claimed, in public prints, that it would be better for all of us mill-girls to be working in families, at domestic service, than to be where we were.

Perhaps the difficulties of modern housekeepers did begin with the opening of the Lowell factories. Country girls were naturally independent, and the feeling that at this new work the few hours they had of every-day leisure were entirely their own was a satisfaction to them. They preferred it to going out as "hired help." It was like a young man's pleasure in entering upon business for himself. Girls had never tried that experiment before, and they liked it. It brought out in them a dormant strength of character which the world did not previously see, but now fully acknowledges. Of course they had a right to continue at that freer kind of work as long as they chose, although their doing so increased the perplexities of the housekeeping problem for themselves even, since many of them were to become, and did become, American house-mistresses.

It would be a step towards the settlement of this vexed and vexing question if girls would decline to classify each other by their occupations, which among us are usually only temporary, and are continually shifting from one pair of hands to another. Changes of fortune come so abruptly that the millionaire's daughter of to-day may be glad to earn her living by sewing or sweeping tomorrow.

It is the first duty of every woman to recognize the mutual bond of universal womanhood. Let her ask herself whether she would like to hear herself or her sister spoken of as a shop-girl, or a factory-girl, or a servant-girl, if necessity had compelled her for a time to be employed in either of the ways indicated. If she would shrink from it a little, then she is a little inhuman when she puts her unknown human sisters who are so occupied into a class by themselves, feeling herself to be somewhat their superior. She is really the superior person who has accepted her work and is doing it faithfully, whatever it is. This designating others by their casual employments prevents one from making real distinctions, from knowing persons as persons. A false standard is set up in the minds of those who classify and of those who are classified.

Perhaps it is chiefly the fault of ladies themselves that the word "lady" has nearly lost its original meaning (a noble one) indicating sympathy and service;—

315

bread-giver to those who are in need. The idea that it means something external in dress or circumstances has been too generally adopted by rich and poor; and this, coupled with the sweeping notion that in our country one person is just as good as another, has led to ridiculous results, like that of saleswomen calling themselves "salesladies." I have even heard a chambermaid at a hotel introduce herself to guests as "the chamberlady."

I do not believe that any Lowell mill-girl was even absurd enough to wish to be known as a "factory-lady," although most of them knew that "factory-girl" did not represent a high type of womanhood in the Old World. But they themselves belonged to the New World, not to the Old; and they were making their own traditions, to hand down to their Republican descendants,—one of which was and is that honest work has no need to assert itself or to humble itself in a nation like ours, but simply to take its place as one of the foundation-stones of the Republic.

31

How the Other Half Lived

Newspaper reporter Jacob Riis, a Danish-born immigrant who had been trapped in destitution in the slums of New York city in the 1870s, won national prominence in 1890 with his biting exposé of New York tenement-house life, *How the Other Half Lives*. Riis was simplistic in his assumption that bad housing conditions were the principal source of social pathology, and that improving the dwellings of poor people without changing other features of their social environment—for example, their low and irregular wages—would transform their lives; nor did he even devise an effective program for upgrading slum housing. He exaggerated what might be accomplished through charitable housing experiments, "philanthropy plus five percent," and he was a victim of the urban renewal fallacy still alive in contemporary America, assuming that tearing down delapidated buildings is itself progress, never asking what would happen to the poor people displaced by demolition. But Riis performed a valuable service in bringing the seamy side of American urban life to public attention, and he made an interesting beginning toward a sociology of immigrant adjustment and assimilation to the urban environment.

HOW THE OTHER HALF LIVES
Jacob Riis

To-day, what is a tenement? The law defines it as a house "occupied by three or more families, living independently and doing their cooking on the premises; or by more than two families on a floor, so living and cooking and having a common right in the halls, stairways, yards, etc." That is the legal meaning, and includes flats and apartment-houses, with which we have nothing to do. In its narrower sense the typical tenement was thus described when last arraigned before the bar of public justice: "It generally a brick building from four to six stories high on the street, frequently with a store on the first floor which, when used for the sale of liquor, has a side opening for the benefit of the inmates and to evade the Sunday law; four families occupy each floor, and a set of rooms consists of one or two dark

From *How the Other Half Lives: Studies among the Tenements of New York* (New York, 1890), 17–20, 24–27, 43–46, 104–119, 136–141.

closets, used as bedrooms, with a living room twelve feet by ten. The staircase is too often a dark well in the center of the house, and no direct through ventilation is possible, each family being separated from the other by partitions. Frequently the rear of the lot is occupied by another building of three stories high with two families on a floor." The picture is nearly as true to-day as ten years ago, and will be for a long time to come. The dim light admitted by the air-shaft shines upon greater crowds than ever. Tenements are still "good property," and the poverty of the poor man his destruction. A barrack down town where he *has to live* because he is poor brings in a third more rent than a decent flat house in Harlem. The statement once made a sensation that between seventy and eighty children has been found in one tenement. It no longer excites even passing attention, when the sanitary police report counting 101 adults and 91 children in a Crosby Street house, one of twins, built together. The children in the other, if I am not mistaken, numbered 89, a total of 180 for two tenements! Or when a midnight inspection in Mulberry Street unearths a hundred and fifty "lodgers" sleeping on filthy floors in two buildings. Spite of brown-stone trimmings, plate-glass and mosaic vestibule floors, the water does not rise in summer to the second story, while the beer flows unchecked to the all-night picnics on the roof. The saloon with the side-door and the landlord divide the prosperity of the place between them, and the tenant, in sullen submission, foots the bills.

Where are the tenements of to-day? Say rather: where are they not? In fifty years they have crept up from the Fourth Ward slums and the Five Points the whole length of the island, and have polluted the Annexed District to the Westchester line. Crowding all the lower wards, wherever business leaves a foot of ground unclaimed; strung along both rivers, like ball and chain tied to the foot of every street, and filling up Harlem with their restless, pent-up multitudes, they hold within their clutch the wealth and business of New York, hold them at their mercy in the day of mob-rule and wrath. The bullet-proof shutters, the stacks of hand-grenades, and the Gatling guns of the Sub-Treasury are tacit admissions of the fact and of the quality of the mercy expected. The tenements to-day are New York, harboring three-fourths of its population. When another generation shall have doubled the census of our city, and to that vast army of workers, held captive by poverty, the very name of home shall be as a bitter mockery, what will the harvest be?

Cherry Street. Be a little careful, please! The hall is dark and you might stumble over the children pitching pennies back there. Not that it would hurt them: kicks and cuffs are their daily diet. They have little else. Here where the hall turns and dives into utter darkness is a step, and another, another. A flight of stairs. You can feel your way, if you cannot see it. Close? Yes! What would you have? All the fresh air that ever enters these stairs comes from the hall-door that is forever slamming, and from the windows of dark bedrooms that in turn receive from the stairs their sole supply of the elements God meant to be free, but man deals out with such niggardly hand. That was a woman filling her pail by the hydrant you just bumped against. The sinks are in the hallway, that all the tenants may have access—and all be poisoned alike by their summer stenches. Hear the pump squeak! It is the lullaby of tenement-house babes. In summer, when a thousand thirsty throats pant for a cooling drink in this block, it is worked in vain. But the saloon, whose open door you passed in the hall, is always there. The smell of it has followed you up. Here is a door. Listen! That short hacking cough, that tiny, helpless wail—what do they mean? They mean that the soiled bow of white you saw on the door downstairs will have another story to tell—Oh! a sadly familiar story—before the day is at an end. The child is dying with measles. With half a chance it might have lived; but it had none. That dark bedroom killed it.

"It was took all of a suddint," says the mother, smoothing the throbbing little body with trembling hands. There is no unkindness in the rough voice of the man in the jumper, who sits by the window grimly smoking a clay pipe, with the little life ebbing out in his sight, bitter as his words sound: "Hush, Mary! If we cannot keep the baby, need we complain—such as we?"

Such as we! What if the words ring in your ears as we grope our way up the stairs and down from floor to floor, listening to the sounds behind the closed doors—some of quarrelling, some of coarse songs, more of profanity. They are true. When the summer heats come with their suffering they have meaning more terrible than words can tell. Come over here. Step carefully over this baby—it is a baby, spite of its rags and dirt—under these iron bridges called fire-escapes, but loaded down, despite the incessant watchfulness of the firemen, with broken household goods, with wash-tubs and barrels, over which no man could climb from a fire. This gap between dingy brick-walls is the yard. That strip of smoke-colored sky up there is the heaven of these people. Do you wonder the name does not attract them to the churches? That baby's parents live in the rear tenement here. She is at last as clean as the steps we are now climbing. There are plenty of houses with half a hundred such in. The tenement is much like the one in front we just left, only fouler, closer, darker—we will not say more cheerless. The word is a mockery. A hundred thousand people lived in rear tenements in New York last year. Here is a room neater than the rest. The woman, a stout matron with hard lines of care in her face, is at the wash-tub. "I try to keep the childer clean," she says, apologetically, but with a hopeless glance around. The spice of hot soapsuds is added to the air already tainted with the smell of boiling cabbage, of rags and uncleanliness all about. It makes an overpowering compound. It is Thursday, but patched linen is hung upon the pulley-line from the window. There is no Monday cleaning in the tenements. It is wash-day all the week round, for a change of clothing is scarce among the poor. They are poverty's honest badge, these perennial lines of rags hung out to dry, those that are not the washerwoman's professional shingle. The true line to be drawn between pauperism and honest poverty is the clothes-line. With it begins the effort to be clean that is the first and the best evidence of a desire to be honest.

The poorest immigrant comes here with the purpose and ambition to better himself and, given half a chance, might be reasonably expected to make the most of it. To the false plea that he prefers the squalid homes in which his kind are housed there could be no better answer. The truth is, his half chance has too long been wanting, and for the bad result he has been unjustly blamed.

As emigration from east to west follows the latitude, so does the foreign influx in New York distribute itself along certain well-defined lines that waver and break only under the stronger pressure of a more gregarious race or the encroachments of inexorable business. A feeling of dependence upon mutual effort, natural to strangers in a strange land, unacquainted with its language and customs, sufficiently accounts for this.

The Irishman is the true cosmopolitan immigrant. All-pervading, he shares his lodging with perfect impartiality with the Italian, the Greek, and the "Dutchman," yielding only to sheer force of numbers, and objects equally to them all. A map of the city, colored to designate nationalities, would show more stripes than on the skin of a zebra, and more colors than any rainbow. The city on such a map would fall into two great halves, green for the Irish prevailing in the West Side tenement districts, and blue for the Germans on the East Side. But intermingled with these ground colors would be an odd variety of tints that would give the whole the appearance of an extraordinary crazy-quilt. From down in the Sixth Ward, upon the site of the old Collect Pond that in the days of the fathers drained the hills which are no more, the red of the Italian would be seen forcing its way northward along the line of Mulberry Street to the quarter of the French purple on Bleecker Street and South Fifth Avenue, to lose itself and reappear, after a lapse of miles, in the "Little Italy" of Harlem, east of Second Avenue. Dashes of red, sharply defined, would be seen strung through the Annexed District, northward to the city line. On the West Side the red would be seen overrunning the old Africa of Thompson Street, pushing the black of the negro rapidly uptown, against querulous but unavailing protests, occupying his home, his church, his trade and all, with merciless impartiality. There is a church in Mulberry Street that has stood for two generations as a sort of milestone of these migrations. Built originally for the worship of staid New Yorkers of the "old stock," it was engulfed by the colored tide, when the draft-riots drove the negroes out of reach of Cherry Street and the Five Points. Within the past decade the advance wave of the Italian onset reached it, and to-day the arms of United Italy adorn its front. The negroes have made a stand at several points along Seventh and Eighth Avenues; but their main body, still pursued by the Italian foe, is on the march yet, and the black mark will be found overshadowing to-day many blocks on the East Side, with One Hundredth Street as the centre, where colonies of them have settled recently.

Hardly less aggressive than the Italian, the Russian and Polish Jew, having overrun the district between Rivington and Division Streets, east of the Bowery, to the point of suffocation, is filling the tenements of the old Seventh Ward to the river front, and disputing with the Italian every foot of available space in the back alleys of Mulberry Street. The two races, differing hopelessly in much, have this in common: they carry their slums with them wherever they go, if allowed to do it. Little Italy already rivals its parent, the "Bend," in foulness. Other nationalities that begin at the bottom make a fresh start when crowded up the ladder. Happily both are manageable, the one by rabbinical, the other by the civil law. Between the dull gray of the Jew, his favorite color, and the Italian red, would be seen squeezed in on the map a sharp streak of yellow, marking the narrow boundaries of Chinatown. Dovetailed in with the German population, the poor but thrifty Bohemian might be picked out by the sombre hue of his life as of his philosophy, struggling against heavy odds in the big human bee-hives of the East Side. Colonies of his people extend northward, with long lapses of space, from below the Cooper Institute more than three miles. The Bohemian is the only foreigner with any considerable representation in the city who counts no wealthy man of his race, none who has not to work hard for a living, or has got beyond the reach of the tenement.

Down near the Battery the West Side emerald would be soiled by a dirty stain, spreading rapidly like a splash of ink on a sheet of blotting paper, headquarters of the Arab tribe, that in a single year has swelled from the original dozen to twelve hundred, intent, every mother's son, on trade and barter. Dots and dashes of color here and there would show where the Finnish sailors worship their djumala (God), the Greek pedlars the ancient name of their race, and the Swiss the goddess of thrift. And so on to the end of the long register, all toiling together in the galling fetters of the tenement. Were the question raised who makes the most of life thus mortgaged, who resists most stubbornly its levelling tendency—knows how to drag even the barracks upward a part of the way at least toward the ideal plane of the home—the palm must be unhesitatingly awarded the Teuton. The Italian and the poor Jew rise only by compulsion. The Chinaman does not rise at all; here, as at home, he simply remains stationary. The Irishman's genius runs to public affairs rather than domestic life; wherever he is mustered in force the saloon is the gorgeous centre of political activity. The German struggles vainly to learn his trick; his Teutonic wit is too heavy, and the political ladder he raises from his saloon usually too short or too clumsy to reach the desired goal. The best part of his life is lived at home, and he makes himself a home independent of the surroundings, giving the lie to the saying, unhappily become a maxim of social truth, that pauperism and drunkenness naturally grow in the tenements. He makes the most of his tenement, and it should be added that whenever and as soon as he can save up money enough, he gets out and never crosses the threshold of one again.

The tenements grow taller, and the gaps in their ranks close up rapidly as we cross the Bowery and, leaving Chinatown and the Italians behind, invade the Hebrew quarter. Baxter Street, with its interminable rows of old clothes shops and its brigades of pullers-in—nicknamed "the Bay" in honor, perhaps, of the tars who lay to there after a cruise to stock up their togs, or maybe after the "schooners" of beer plentifully bespoke in that latitude—Bayard Street, with its synagogues and its crowds, gave us a foretaste of it. No need of asking here where we are. The jargon of the street, the signs of the sidewalk, the manner and dress of the people, their unmistakable physiognomy, betray their race at every step. Men with queer skull-caps, venerable beard, and the outlandish long-skirted kaftan of the Russian Jew, elbow the ugliest and the handsomest women in the land. The contrast is startling. The old women are hags; the young, houris. Wives and mothers at sixteen, at thirty they are old. So thoroughly has the chosen people crowded out the Gentiles in the Tenth Ward that, when the great Jewish holidays come around every year, the public schools in the district have practically to close up. Of their thousands of pupils scarce a handful come to school. Nor is there any suspicion that the rest are playing hookey. They stay honestly home to celebrate. There is no mistaking it: we are in Jewtown.

It is said that nowhere in the world are so many people crowded together on a square mile as here. The average five-story tenement adds a story or two to its stature in Ludlow Street and an extra building on the rear lot, and yet the sign "To Let" is the rarest of all there. Here is one seven stories high. The sanitary policeman whose beat this is will tell you that it contains thirty-six families, but the term has a widely different meaning here and on the avenues. In this house, where a case of small-pox was reported, there were fifty-eight babies and thirty-eight children that were over five years of age. In Essex Street two small rooms in a six-story tenement were made to hold a "family" of father and mother, twelve children, and six boarders. The boarder plays as important a part in the domestic economy of Jewtown as the lodger in the Mulberry Street Bend. These are samples of the packing of the population that has run up the record here to the rate of three hundred and thirty thousand per square mile. The densest crowding of Old London, I pointed out before, never got beyond a hundred and seventy-five thousand. Even the alley is crowded out. Through dark hallways and filthy cellars, crowded, as is every foot of the street, with dirty children, the settlements in the rear are reached. Thieves know how to find them when pursued by the police, and the tramps that sneak in on chilly nights to fight for the warm spot in the yard over some baker's oven. They are out of place in this hive of busy industry, and they know it. It has nothing in common with them or with their philosophy of life, that the world owes the idler a living. Life here means the hardest kind of work almost from the cradle. The world as a debtor has no credit in Jewtown. Its promise to pay wouldn't buy one of the old hats that are hawked about Hester Street, unless backed by security representing labor done at lowest market rates. But this army of workers must have bread. It is cheap and filling, and bakeries abound. Wherever they are in the tenements the tramp will skulk in, if he can. There is such a tramps' roost in the rear of a tenement near the lower end of Ludlow Street, that is never without its tenants in winter. By a judicious practice of flopping over on the stone pavement at intervals, and thus warming one side at a time, and with an empty box to put the feet in, it is possible to keep reasonably comfortable there even on a rainy night. In summer the yard is the only one in the neighborhood that does not do duty as a public dormitory.

Thrift is the watchword of Jewtown, as of its people the world over. It is at once its strength and its fatal weakness, its cardinal virtue and its foul disgrace. Become an over-mastering passion with these people who come here in droves from Eastern Europe to escape persecution, from which freedom could be bought only with gold, it has enslaved them in bondage worse than that from which they fled. Money is their God. Life itself is of little value compared with even the leanest bank account. In no other spot does life wear so intensely bald and materialistic an aspect as in Ludlow Street. Over and over again I have met with instances of these Polish or Russian Jews deliberately starving themselves to the point of physical exhaustion, while working night and day at a tremendous pressure to save a little money. An avenging Nemesis pursues this headlong hunt for wealth; there is no worse paid class anywhere. I once put the question to one of their own people, who, being a pawnbroker, and an unusually intelligent and charitable one, certainly enjoyed the advantage of a practical view of the situation: "Whence the many wretchedly poor people in such a colony of workers, where poverty, from a misfortune, has become a reproach, dreaded as the plague?"

"Immigration," he said, "brings us a lot. In five years it has averaged twenty-five thousand a year, of which more than seventy per cent, have stayed in New York. Half of them require and receive aid from the Hebrew Charities from the very start, lest they starve. That is one explanation. There is another class than the one that cannot get work: those who have had too much of it; who have worked and hoarded and lived, crowded together like pigs, on the scantiest fare and the worst to be got, bound to save whatever their earnings, until, worn out, they could work no longer. Then their hoards were soon exhausted. That is their story." And I knew that what he said was true.

Penury and poverty are wedded everywhere to dirt and disease, and Jewtown is no exception. It could not well be otherwise in such crowds, considering especially their low intellectual status. The managers of the Eastern Dispensary, which is in the very heart of their district, told the whole story when they said: "The diseases these people suffer from are not due to intemperance or immorality, but to ignorance, want of suitable food, and the foul air in which they live and work." The homes of the Hebrew quarter are its workshops also. Reference will be made to the economic conditions under which they work in a succeeding chapter. Here we are concerned simply with the fact. You are made fully aware of it before you have travelled the length of a single block in any of these East Side streets, by the whir of a thousand sewing-machines, worked at high pressure from earliest dawn till mind and muscle give out together. Every member of the family, from the youngest to the oldest, bears a hand, shut in the qualmy rooms, where meals are cooked and clothing washed and dried besides, the live-long day. It is not unusual to find a dozen persons—men, women, and children—at work in a single small room. The fact accounts for the contrast that strikes with wonder the observer who comes across from the Bend. Over there the entire population seems possessed of an uncontrollable impulse to get out into the street; here all its energies appear to be bent upon keeping in and away from it. Not that the streets are deserted. The overflow from these tenements is enough to make a crowd anywhere. The children alone would do it. Not old enough to work and no room for play, that is their story. In the home the child's place is usurped by the lodger, who performs the service of the Irishman's pig—pays the rent. In the street the army of hucksters crowd him out. Typhus fever and small-pox are bred here, and help solve the question what to do with him. Filth diseases both, they sprout naturally among the hordes that bring the germs with them from across the sea, and whose first instinct is to hide their sick lest the authorities carry them off to the hospital to be slaughtered, as they firmly believe. The health officers are on constant and sharp lookout for hidden fever-nests. Considering that half of the ready-made clothes that are sold in the big stores, if not a good deal more than half, are made in these tenement rooms, this is not excessive caution. It has happened more than once that a child recovering from small-pox, and in the most contagious stage of the disease, has been found crawling among heaps of half-finished clothing that the next day would be offered for sale on the counter of a Broadway store; or that a typhus fever patient has been discovered in a room whence perhaps a hundred coats had been sent home that week, each one with the wearer's death-warrant, unseen and unsuspected, basted in the lining.

Attached to many of the synagogues, which among the poorest Jews frequently consist of a scantily furnished room in a rear tenement, with a few wooden stools or benches for the congregation, are Talmudic schools that absorb a share of the growing youth. The school-master is not rarely a man of some attainments who has been stranded there, his native instinct for money-making having been smothered in the process that has made of him a learned man. It was of such a school in Eldridge Street that the wicked Isaac Iacob, who killed his enemy, his wife, and himself in one day, was janitor. But the majority of the children seek the public schools, where they are received sometimes with some misgivings on the part of the teachers, who find it necessary to inculcate lessons of cleanliness in the worst cases by practical demonstration with wash-bowl and soap. "He took hold of the soap as if it were some animal," said one of these teachers to me after such an experiment upon a new pupil, "and wiped three fingers across his face. He called that washing." In the Allen Street public school the experienced principal has embodied among the elementary lessons, to keep constantly before the children the duty that clearly lies next to their hands, a characteristic exercise. The question is asked daily from the teacher's desk: "What must I do to be healthy?" and the whole school responds:

I must keep my skin clean,
Wear clean clothes,
Breathe pure air,
And live in the sunlight.

It seems little less than biting sarcasm to hear them say it, for to not a few of them all these things are known only by name. In their everyday life there is nothing even to suggest any of them. Only the demand of religious custom has power to make their parents clean up at stated intervals, and the young naturally are no better. As scholars, the children of the most ignorant Polish Jew keep fairly abreast of their more favored playmates, until it comes to mental arithmetic, when they leave them behind with a bound. It is surprising to see how strong the instinct of dollars and cents is in them. They can count, and correctly, almost before they can talk.

Thursday night and Friday morning are bargain days in the "Pig-market." Then is the time to study the ways of this peculiar people to the best advantage. A common pulse beats in the quarters of the Polish Jews and in the Mulberry Bend, though they have little else in common. Life over yonder in fine weather is a perpetual holiday, here a veritable tread-mill of industry. Friday brings out all the latent color and picturesqueness of the Italians, as of these Semites. The crowds and the common poverty are the bonds of sympathy between them. The Pig-market is in Hester Street, extending either way from Ludlow Street, and up and down the side streets two or three blocks, as the state of trade demands. The name was given to it probably in derision, for pork is the one ware that is not on sale in the Pig-market. There is scarcely anything else that can be hawked from a wagon that is not to be found, and at ridiculously low prices. Bandannas and tin cups at two cents, peaches at a cent a quart, "damaged" eggs for a song, hats for a quarter, and spectacles, warranted to suit the eye, at the optician's who has opened shop on a Hester Street door-step, for thirty-five cents; frowsy-looking chickens and half-plucked geese, hung by the neck and protesting with wildly strutting feet even in death against the outrage, are the great staple of the market. Half or a quarter of a chicken can be bought here by those who cannot afford a whole. It took more than ten years of persistent effort on the part of the sanitary authorities to drive the trade in live fowl from the streets to the fowl-market on Gouverneur Slip, where the killing is now done according to Jewish rite by priests detailed for the purpose by the chief rabbi. Since then they have had a characteristic rumpus, that involved the entire Jewish community, over the fees for killing and the mode of collecting them. Here is a woman churning horse-radish on a machine she has chained and padlocked to a tree on the sidewalk, lest someone steal it. Beside her a butcher's stand with cuts at prices the avenues never dreamed of. Old coats are hawked for fifty cents, "as good as new," and "pants"—there are no trousers in Jewtown, only pants—at anything that can be got. There is a knot of half a dozen "pants" pedlars in the middle of the street, twice as many men of their own race fingering their wares and plucking at the seams with the anxious scrutiny of would-be buyers, though none of them has the least idea of investing in a pair. Yes, stop! This baker, fresh from his trough, bare-headed and with bare arms, has made an offer: for this pair thirty cents; a dollar and forty was the price asked. The pedlar shrugs his shoulders, and turns up his hands with a half pitying, wholly indignant air. What does the baker take him for? Such pants—. The baker has turned to go. With a jump like a panther's, the man with the pants has him by the sleeve. Will he give eighty cents? Sixty? Fifty? So help him, they are dirt cheap at that. Lose, will he, on the trade, lose all the profit of his day's peddling. The baker goes on unmoved. Forty then? What, not forty? Take them then for thirty, and wreck the life of a poor man. And the baker takes them and goes, well knowing that at least twenty cents of the thirty, two hundred per cent., were clear profit, if indeed the "pants" cost the pedlar anything.

The suspender pedlar is the mystery of the Pig-market, omnipresent and unfathomable. He is met at every step with his wares dangling over his shoulder, down his back, and in front. Millions of suspenders thus perambulate Jewtown all day on a sort of dress parade. Why suspenders, is the puzzle, and where do they all go to? The "pants" of Jewtown hang down with a common accord, as if they had never known the support of suspenders. It appears to be as characteristic a trait of the race as the long beard and the Sabbath silk hat of ancient pedigree. I have asked again and again. No one has ever been able to tell me what becomes of the suspenders of Jewtown. Perhaps they are hung up as bric-à-brac in its homes, or laid away and saved up as the equivalent of cash. I cannot tell. I only know that more suspenders are hawked about the Pig-market every day than would supply the whole of New York for a year, were they all bought and turned to use.

The crowds that jostle each other at the wagons and about the sidewalk shops, where a gutter plank on two ash-barrels does duty for a counter! Pushing, struggling, babbling, and shouting in foreign tongues, a veritable Babel of confusion. An English word falls upon the ear almost with a sense of shock, as something unexpected and strange. In the midst of it all there is a sudden wild scattering, a hustling of things from the street into dark cellars, into back-yards and by-ways, a slamming and locking of doors hidden under the improvised shelves and counters. The health officers' cart is coming down the street, preceded and followed by stalwart policemen, who shovel up with scant ceremony the eatables—musty bread, decayed fish and stale vegetables—indifferent to the curses that are showered on them from stoops and windows, and carry them off to the dump. In the wake of the wagon, as it maks its way to th East River after the raid, follow a line of despoiled hucksters shouting defiance from a safe distance. Their clamor dies away with the noise of the market. The endless panorama of the tenements, rows upon rows, between stony streets, stretches to the north, to the south, and to the west as far as the eye reaches.

Evil as the part is which the tenement plays in Jewtown as the pretext for circumventing the law that was made to benefit and relieve the tenant, we have not far to go to find it in even a worse role. If the tenement is here continually dragged into the eye of public condemnation and scorn, it is because in one way or another it is found directly responsible for, or intimately associated with, three-fourths of the miseries of the poor. In the Bohemian quarter it is made the vehicle for enforcing upon a proud race a slavery as real as any that ever disgraced the South. Not content with simply robbing the tenant, the owner, in the dual capacity of landlord and employer, reduces him to virtual serfdom by making his becoming *his* tenant, on such terms as he sees fit to make, the condition of employment at wages likewise of his own making. It does not help the case that this landlord employer, almost always a Jew, is frequently of the thrifty Polish race just described.

Probably more than half of all the Bohemians in this city are cigarmakers, and it is the herding of these in great numbers in the so-called tenement factories, where the cheapest grade of work is done at the lowest wages, that constitutes at once their greatest hardship and the chief grudge of other workmen against them. The manufacturer who owns, say, from three or four, to a dozen or more tenements contiguous to his shop, fills them up with these people, charging them outrageous rents, and demanding often even a preliminary deposit of five dollars "key money;" deals them out tobacco by the week, and devotes the rest of his energies to the paring down of wages to within a peg or two of the point where the tenant rebels in desperation. When he does rebel, he is given the alternative of submission, or eviction with entire loss of employment. His needs determine the issue. Usually he is not in a position to hesitate long. Unlike the Polish Jew, whose example of untiring industry he emulates, he has seldom much laid up against a rainy day. He is fond of a glass of beer, and likes to live as well as his means will permit. The shop triumphs, and fetters more galling than ever are forged for the tenant. In the opposite case, the newspapers have to record the throwing upon the street of a small army of people, with pitiful cases of destitution and family misery.

Men, women and children work together seven days in the week in these cheerless tenements to make a living for the family, from the break of day till far into the night. Often the wife is the original cigarmaker from the old home, the husband having adopted her trade here as a matter of necessity, because, knowing no word of English, he could get no other work. As they state the cause of the bitter hostility of the trades unions, she was the primary bone of contention in the day of the early Bohemian immigration. The unions refused to admit the women, and, as the support of the family depended upon her to a large extent, such terms as were offered had to be accepted. The manufacturer has ever since industriously fanned the antagonism between the unions and his hands, for his own advantage. The victory rests with him, since the Court of Appeals decided that the law, passed a few years ago, to prohibit cigarmaking in tenements was unconstitutional, and thus put an end to the struggle.

The sore grievances I found were the miserable wages and the enormous rents exacted for the minimum of accommodation. And surely these stand for enough of suffering. Take a row of houses in East Tenth Street as an instance. They contained thirty-five families of cigarmakers, with probably not half a dozen persons in the whole lot of them, outside of the children, who could speak a word of English, though many had been in the country half a lifetime. This room with two windows giving on the street, and a rear attachment without windows, called a bedroom by courtesy, is rented at $12.25 a month. In the front room man and wife work at the bench from six in the morning till nine at night. They make a team, stripping the tobacco leaves together; then he makes the filler, and she rolls the wrapper on and finishes the cigar. For a thousand they receive $3.75, and can turn out together three thousand cigars a week. The point has been reached where the rebellion comes in, and the workers in these tenements are just now on a strike, demanding $5.00 and $5.50 for their work. The manufacturer having refused, they are expecting hourly to be served with notice to quit their homes, and the going of a stranger among them excites their resentment, until his errand is explained. While we are in the house, the ultimatum of the "boss" is received. He will give $3.75 a thousand, not another cent. Our host is a man of seeming intelligence, yet he has been nine years in New York and knows neither English nor German. Three bright little children play about the floor.

His neighbor on the same floor has been here fifteen years, but shakes his head when asked if he can speak English. He answers in a few broken syllables when addressed in German. With $11.75 rent to pay for like accommodation, he has the advantage of his oldest boy's work besides his wife's at the bench. Three properly make a team, and these three can turn out four thousand cigars a week, at $3.75. This Bohemian has a large family; there are four children, too small to work, to be cared for. A comparison of the domestic bill of fare between Tenth and Ludlow Streets results in the discovery that this Bohemian's butcher's bill for the week, with meat at twelve cents a pound as in Ludlow Street, is from two dollars and a half to three dollars. The Polish Jew fed as big a family on one pound of meat a day. The difference proves to be typical.

32

The Making of a Monopoly

In this early essay published in the *Atlantic Monthly* in 1881, Henry Demerast Lloyd, later to win fame for his fiery denunciation of big business, *Wealth Against Commonwealth* (1894), provides a bitter description of some of the methods by which John D. Rockefeller's Standard Oil Company achieved for a time a monopoly over oil refining. Lloyd was insufficiently appreciative of the increased efficiency Rockefeller brought to the chaotic oil industry, but his sense of moral outrage at the devious techniques pictured here and his fear of the concentration of so much power in one organization were widely shared by Americans of his day. By the 1890s Lloyd was less inclined to look back in nostalgia toward an economy of intensely competitive small producers, and had come to favor public ownership of the great corporations; but most of his countrymen were slow to abandon their faith in free competition and their distrust of government.

STORY
OF A GREAT MONOPOLY
Henry Demarest Lloyd

When Commodore Vanderbilt began the world he had nothing, and there were no steamboats or railroads. He was thirty-five years old when the first locomotive was put into use in America. When he died, railroads had become the greatest force in modern industry, and Vanderbilt was the richest man of Europe or America, and the largest owner of railroads in the world. He used the finest business brains of his day and the franchise of the state to build up a kingdom within the republic, and like a king he bequeathed his wealth and power to his eldest son. Bancroft's History of the United States and our railroad system were begun at the same time. The history is not yet finished, but the railroads owe on stocks and bonds $4,600,000,000, more than twice our national debt of $2,220,000,000, and tax the people annually $490,000,000, one and a half times more than the government's revenue last year of $274,000,000. More than any other class, our railroad men have developed the country, and tried its institutions. The evasion of almost all taxes by the New York Central Railroad has thrown upon the people of New York State more than a fair share of the cost of government, and illustrates some of the methods by which the rich are making the poor poorer. Violations of trust by Credit Mobiliers, Jay Gould's wealth and the poverty of Erie stockholders, such

From "Story of a Great Monopoly," *Atlantic Monthly*, March, 1881.

corruption of legislatures as gave the Pacific Mail its subsidies, and nicknamed New Jersey "The State of Camden and Amboy," are sins against public and private faith on a scale impossible in the early days of republics and corporations. A lawsuit still pending, though begun ten years ago by a citizen of Chicago, to recover the value of baggage destroyed by the Pennsylvania Railroad; Judge Barnard's midnight orders for the Erie ring; the surrender of its judicial integrity by the supreme court of Pennsylvania at the bidding of the Pennsylvania Railroad, as charged before Congress by President Gowen, of the Reading Railroad; the veto by the Standard Oil Company of the enactment of a law by the Pennsylvania legislature to carry out the provision of the constitution of the State that every one should have equal rights on the railroads,—these are a few of the many things that have happened to kill the confidence of our citizens in the laws and the administration of justice. No other system of taxation has borne as heavily on the people as those extortions and inequalities of railroad charges which caused the granger outburst in the West, and the recent uprising in New York. In the actual physical violence with which railroads have taken their rights of way through more than one American city, and in the railroad strikes of 1876 and 1877 with the anarchy that came with them, there are social disorders we hoped never to see in America. These incidents in railroad history show most of the points where we fail, as between man and man, employer and employed, the public and the corporation, the state and the citizen, to maintain the equities of "government"—and employment—"of the people, by the people, for the people."

Our treatment of "the railroad problem" will show the quality and calibre of our political sense. It will go far in foreshadowing the future lines of our social and political growth. It may indicate whether the American democracy, like all the democratic experiments which have preceded it, is to become extinct because the people had not wit enough or virtue enough to make the common good supreme.

The remarkable series of eight railroad strikes, which began during the Centennial Exposition of the prosperity of our first century and the perfection of our institutions, culminated on July 16, 1877, in the strike on the Baltimore and Ohio Railroad at Martinsburg, West Virginia. This spread into the greatest labor disturbance on record. For a fortnight there was an American Reign of Terror. We have forgotten it,—that is, it has taught us nothing; but if Freeman outlives us to finish his History of Federal Government from the Achaian League to the Disruption of the United States, he will give more than one chapter to the labor rising of 1877. The strike at Martinsburg was instantly felt at Chicago and Baltimore in the stoppage of shipments. In a few hours the Baltimore and Ohio, one of the chief commercial arteries of Maryland, Virginia, West Virginia, Ohio, Indiana, and Illinois, was shut up. The strike spread to the Pennsylvania, the Erie and the New York Central railroads, and to the Great Western lines, with their countless branches, as far west as Omaha and Topeka, and as far south as the Ohio River and the Texas Pacific. The feeling of the railroad employés all over the country was expressed by the address of those of the Pennsylvania Railroad to its stockholders. The stockholders were reminded that "many of the railroad's men did not average wages of more than seventy-five cents a day;" that "the influence of the road had been used to destroy the business of its best customers, the oil producers, for the purpose of building up individual interests." "What is the result? The traffic has almost disappeared from the Pennsylvania Railroad, and in place of $7,-000,000 revenue this year, although shipments are in excess of last year, your road will receive scarcely half the amount. This alone would have enabled your company to pay us enough for a living." The address also refers pointedly to the abuses of fast freight lines, rolling-stock companies, and other railroad inventions for switching business into private pockets. Other workingmen followed the example of the railroad employés. At Zanesville, Ohio, fifty manufactories stopped work. Baltimore ceased to export petroleum. The rolling mills, foundries, and refineries of Cleveland were closed. Chicago, St. Louis, Cincinnati, all the cities large and small, had the same experience. At Indianapolis, next to Chicago the largest point for the eastward shipment of produce, all traffic was stopped except on the two roads that were in the hands of the national government. At Erie, Pa., the railroad struck, and notwithstanding the remonstrance of the employés refused to forward passengers or the United States mails. The grain and cattle of the farmer ceased to move to market, and the large centres of population began to calculate the chances of famine. New York's supply of Western cattle and grain was cut off. Meat rose three cents a pound in one day, while Cleveland telegraphed that hogs, sheep, beeves, and poultry billed for New York were dying on the side-tracks there. Merchants could not sell, manufacturers could not work, banks could not lend. The country went to the verge of panic, for the banks, in the absence of remittances, had resolved to close if the blockade lasted a few days longer. President Garrett, of the Baltimore and Ohio Railroad, wrote that his "great national highway could be restored to public use only by the interposition of the United States army." President Scott, of the Pennsylvania Railroad, telegraphed the authorities at Washington, "I fear that unless the general government will assume the responsibility of order throughout the land, the anarchy which is now present will become more terrible than has ever been known in the history of the world." The governors of ten States—West Virginia, Maryland, New Jersey, New York, Pennsylvania, Ohio, Illinois, Wisconsin, Missouri, and Kentucky—issued dispersing proclamations which did not disperse. The governors of four of them—West Virginia, Maryland, Pennsylvania, and Illinois—appealed to the national government for help against domestic insurrection, which the State could not suppress. The president of the United States issued two national proclamations to the insurgents. The state troops were almost useless, as in nearly all cases they fraternized with the strikers. All the national troops that could be spared from the Indian frontier and the South were ordered back to the centres of civilization. The regulars were welcomed by the frightened people of Chicago with cheers which those who heard will never forget. Armed guards were placed at all the public buildings of Washington, and ironclads were ordered up for the protection of the national capital. Cabinet meetings were continuous. General Winfield S. Hancock was sent to Baltimore to take command, General Sherman was called back from the West, and General Schofield was ordered from West Point into active service. Barricades, in the French style, were thrown up by the voters of Baltimore. New York and Philadelphia were heavily garrisoned. In Philadelphia every avenue of approach to the Pennsylvania Railroad was patrolled, and the city was under a guard of six thousand armed men, with eight batteries of artillery. There were encounters between troops and voters, with loss of life, at Martinsburg, Baltimore, Pittsburg, Chicago, Reading, Buffalo, Scranton, and San Francisco. In the scene at Pittsburg, there was every horror of revolution. Citizens and soldiers were killed, the soldiers were put to flight, and the town left at the mercy of the mob. Railroad cars, depots, hotels, stores, elevators, private houses, were gutted and burned. The city has just compromised for $1,810,000 claims for damages to the amount of $2,938,460, and has still heavy claims to settle. The situation was described at this point by a leading newspaper as one of "civil war with the accompanying horrors of murder, conflagration, rapine, and pillage." These were days of greater bloodshed, more actual suffering, and wider alarm in the North than that part of the country experienced at any time during the civil war, except when Lee invaded Pennsylvania. As late as August 3d, the beautiful valley of the Wyoming, in Pennsylvania, was a military camp, traversed by trains loaded with Gatling guns and bayonets, and was guarded by Governor Hartranft in person with five thousand soldiers. These strikes, penetrating twelve States and causing insurrections in ten of them, paralyzed the operation of twenty thousand miles of railroad, and directly and indirectly threw one million men temporarily out of employment. While they lasted they caused greater losses than any blockade which has been made by sea or land in the history of war. Non-sensational observers, like the Massachusetts Board of Railroad Commissioners, look to see the outburst repeated, possibly to secure a rise of wages. The movement of the railroad trains of this country is literally the circulation of its blood. Evidently, from the facts we have recited, the States cannot prevent its arrest by the struggle between these giant forces within society, outside the law.

Kerosene has become, by its cheapness, the people's light the world over. In the United States we used 220,000,000 gallons of petroleum last year. It has come into such demand abroad that our exports of it increased from 79,458,888 gallons in 1868, to 417,648,544 in 1879. It goes all over Europe, and to the far East. The Oriental demand for it is increasing faster than any other. We are assured by the eloquent petroleum editor of the New York Shipping List that "it blazes across the ruins of Babylon and waste Persepolis," and that "all over Polynesia, and Far Cathay, in Burmah, in Siam, in Java, the bronzed denizens toil and dream, smoke opium and swallow hasheesh, woo and win, love and hate, and sicken and die under the rays of this wonderful product of our fruitful caverns." However that may be, it is statistically true that China and the East Indies took over 10,000,000 gallons in 1877, and nearly 25,000,000 gallons in 1878. After articles of food, this country has but one export, cotton, more valuable than petroleum. It was worth $61,789,438 in our foreign trade in 1877; $46,574,974 in 1878; and $18,546,642 in the five months ending November 30, 1879. In the United States, in the cities as well as the country, petroleum is the general illuminator. We use more kerosene lamps than Bibles. The raw material of this world's light is produced in a territory beginning with Cattaraugus County in New York, and extending southwesterly through eight or nine counties of Pennsylvania, making a belt about one hundred

331

and fifty miles long, and twelve or fifteen miles wide, and then, with an interval, running into West Virginia, Kentucky, and Tennessee, where the yield is unimportant. The bulk of the oil comes from two counties, Cattaraugus in New York, and McKean in Pennsylvania. There are a few places elsewhere that produce rock oil, such as the shales of England, Wales, and Scotland, but the oil is so poor that American kerosene, after being carried thousands of miles, can undersell it. Very few of the forty millions of people in the United States who burn kerosene know that its production, manufacture, and export, its price at home and abroad, have been controlled for years by a single corporation,—the Standard Oil Company. This company began in a partnership, in the early years of the civil war, between Samuel Andrews and John Rockefeller in Cleveland. Rockefeller had been a bookkeeper in some interior town in Ohio, and had afterwards made a few thousand dollars by keeping a flour store in Cleveland. Andrews had been a day laborer in refineries, and so poor that his wife took in sewing. He found a way of refining by which more kerosene could be got out of a barrel of petroleum than by any other method, and set up for himself a ten-barrel still in Cleveland, by which he cleared $500 in six months. Andrews' still and Rockefeller's savings have grown into the Standard Oil Company. It has a capital, nominally $3,500,000, but really much more, on which it divides among its stockholders every year millions of dollars of profits. It has refineries at Cleveland, Baltimore, and New York. Its own acid works, glue factories, hardware stores, and barrel shops supply it with all the accessories it needs in its business. It has bought land at Indianapolis on which to erect the largest barrel factory in the country. It has drawn its check for $1,000,000 to suppress a rival. It buys 30,000 to 40,000 barrels of crude oil a day, at a price fixed by itself, and makes special contracts with the railroads for the transportation of 13,000,000 to 14,000,000 barrels of oil a year. The four quarters of the globe are partitioned among the members of the Standard combinations. One has the control of the China trade; another that of some country of Europe; another that of the United States. In New York, you cannot buy oil for East Indian export from the house that has been given the European trade; reciprocally, the East Indian house is not allowed to sell for export to Europe. The Standard produces only one fiftieth or sixtieth of our petroleum, but dictates the price of all, and refines nine tenths. Circulars are issued at intervals by which the price of oil is fixed for all the cities of the country, except New York, where a little competition survives. Such is the indifference of the Standard Oil Company to railroad charges that the price is made the same for points so far apart as Terre Haute, Chicago, and Keokuk. There is not to-day a merchant in Chicago, or in any other city in the New England, Western, or Southern States, dealing in kerosene, whose prices are not fixed for him by the Standard. In all cases these prices are graded so that a merchant in one city cannot export to another. Chicago, Cincinnati, or Cleveland is not allowed to supply the tributary towns. That is done by the Standard itself, which runs oil in its own tank cars to all the principal points of distribution. This corporation has driven into bankruptcy, or out of business, or into union with itself, all the petroleum refineries of the country except five in New York, and a few of little consequence in Western Pennsylvania. Nobody knows how many millions Rockefeller is worth. Current gossip among his business acquaintance in Cleveland puts his income last year at a figure second only, if second at all, to that of Vanderbilt. His partner, Samuel Andrews, the poor English day laborer, retired years ago with millions. Just who the Standard Oil Company are, exactly what their capital is, and what are their relations to the railroads, nobody knows except in part. Their officers refused to testify before the supreme court of Pennsylvania, the last New York Railroad Investigating Committee, and a committee of Congress. The New York committee found there was nothing to be learned from them, and was compelled to confess its inability to ascertain as much as it desired to know "of this mysterious organization, whose business and transactions are of such a character that its members declined giving a history or description, lest their testimony be used to convict them of crime."

Their great business capacity would have insured the managers of the Standard success, but the means by which they achieved monopoly was by conspiracy with the railroads. Mr. Simon Sterne, counsel for the merchants of New York in the New York investigation, declared that the relations of the railroads to the Standard exhibited "the most shameless perversion of the duties of a common carrier to private ends that has taken place in the history of the world." The Standard killed its rivals, in brief, by getting the great trunk lines to refuse to give them transportation. Commodore Vanderbilt is reported to have said that there was but one man—Rockefeller—who could dictate to him. Whether or not Vanderbilt said it, Rockefeller did it. The Standard has done everything with the Pennsylvania legislature, except refine it. In 1876 its organization was brought before Congress, and referred to a committee. A prominent member of the Standard, not a member of Congress, conducted the farce of inquiry from behind the seat of the chairman. Another member of the company, who was a member of Congress, came with the financial officer of the company before the committee, and sustained him in his refusal to testify about the organization, its members, or its relations with the railroads. The committee never reported. The facts they suppressed must be hunted out through newspaper articles, memorials from the oil producers and refiners, records of lawsuits, reports of chambers of commerce and of legislative investigating committees, and other miscellaneous sources of information.

The contract is in print by which the Pennsylvania Railroad agreed with the Standard, under the name of the South Improvement Company, to double the freights on oil to everybody, but to repay the Standard one dollar for every barrel of oil it shipped, and one dollar for every barrel any of its competitors shipped. This contract was produced in Congress, and was stigmatized by Representative Conger as "the most damnable and startling evidence yet produced of the possibility of railroad monopoly." Ostensibly this contract was given up, in deference to the whirlwind of indignation it excited. But Rockefeller, the manager of the Standard, was a man who could learn from defeat. He made no more tell-tale contracts that could be printed. He effected secret arrangements with the Pennsylvania, the New York Central, the Erie, and the Atlantic and Great Western. What influences he used to make the railroad managers pliable may probably be guessed from the fact that one quarter of the stock of the Acme Oil Company, a partner in the Standard combination, on which heavy monthly dividends are paid, is owned by persons whose names Rockefeller would never reveal, which Mr. Archbold, the president of the company, said under oath he had not been told, and which the supreme court of Pennsylvania has not yet been able to find out. The Standard succeeded in getting from Mr. Vanderbilt free transportation for its crude oil from the wells in Pennsylvania, one hundred and fifty miles, to the refineries at Cleveland, and back. This stamped out competing refineries at Pittsburgh, and created much of the raw material of the riots of July, 1877. Vanderbilt signed an agreement, March 25, 1872, that "all agreements for the transportation of oil after this date shall be upon a basis of perfect equality," and ever since has given the Standard special rates and privileges. He has paid it back in rebates millions of dollars, which have enabled it to crush out all competitors, although many of them, like the Octave Oil Company and the Titusville refiners, had done all their business over his road till they went into bankruptcy, broken by his contracts with the Standard. He united with the Erie in a war on the Pennsylvania Railroad, to force it to sell to the Standard all its refineries, and the great pipe lines by which the oil, like Croton water in the mains, was carried from the wells to the railroads. He then joined with the Erie and the Pennsylvania in a similar attack on the Baltimore and Ohio, which had to sell out to the Standard. So the Standard obtained the control of all the pipe lines and of the transportation, of everything, in fact, as a witness said before the New York Railroad Investigating Committee, except the bodies of the producers. Mr. Vanderbilt began, as did the Erie and Pennsylvania railroad kings, with paying back to the Standard, but to no other shipper, ten per cent. of its freight bills. He continued making one concession after another, till when he was doing the business for other shippers at $1.40 and $1.25 a barrel, he charged the Standard only eighty and eighty-one cents, and this was afterwards reduced to sixty cents a barrel. During the war against the Pennsylvania road to make it sell out to the Standard, the New York Central carried oil for less than nothing. Besides the other allowances, Mr. Vanderbilt paid the Standard through its alias, the American Transfer Company, a rebate of thirty-five cents a barrel on all the crude oil shipped by it or its competitors. When the oil producers, whom the Standard had cut off from all access to the world except through it, sought an exit through an out-of-the-way railroad and the Erie Canal, or down the Ohio River hundreds of miles to Huntingdon, thence by the Chesapeake and Ohio Railroad to Richmond, and so to the sea, Mr. Vanderbilt lowered his rates to the Standard so that it could undersell any one who used these devious routes. When the producers, June, 1879, completed their own tidewater pipe line, 104 miles long, to a junction with the Reading Railroad, obtaining in this way a direct connection with the seaboard, Mr. Vanderbilt reduced his rate to the public from $1.40 to $1.25 a barrel to thirty-five and twenty-five cents, and charged the Standard twenty, fifteen, finally but ten cents. For ten cents Mr. Vanderbilt hauled for the Standard a barrel weighing 390 pounds over 400 miles, and hauled back the empty cars, at the same time that he charged forty-five cents for hauling a can of milk weighing ninety pounds for sixty miles. So closely had the Standard octopus gripped itself about Mr. Vanderbilt that even at the outside rates its competitors could not get transportation from him. He

334

allowed the Standard to become the owner of all the oil cars run over his road, and of all his terminal facilities for oil. As the Standard owned all but 200 of the oil cars run on the Erie, and leased all that road's terminal facilities, it could charge its rivals anything it pleased for the privileges of New York harbor. When Mr. Vanderbilt was questioned by Mr. Simon Sterne, of the New York committee, about these and other things, his answers were, "I don't know," "I forget," "I don't remember," to 116 questions out of 249 by actual count. At a time when the Standard Oil Company through its other self, the American Transfer Company, was receiving from the New York Central thirty-five cents a barrel on all oil shipped by itself or its competitors, and was getting other rebates which cost the New York Central over $2,000,000 from October 17, 1877, to March 31, 1879, Mr. Vanderbilt testified positively before the New York Investigating Committee that he knew nothing whatever about the American Transfer Company, its officers, or the payments to it.

33

The Impulse
toward Labor Organization

In his testimony before the United States Industrial Commission investigating "the relations between labor and capital" in 1900, Samuel Gompers expounds the philosophy of disciplined struggle that allowed his American Federation of Labor to triumph over its rival the Knights of Labor in the 1880s. Unlike the Knights of Labor, the American Federation of Labor was the organ of the skilled elite of American labor, and the great mass of unskilled, semiskilled, and service workers remained outside its ranks. But Gompers was probably correct in his belief that at a time when the presuppositions of employers, and indeed of most middle-class Americans, were hostile to union organization, it was necessary to concentrate on the task of building strength among workers who had special skills and hence market power.

TESTIMONY BEFORE THE U.S. INDUSTRIAL COMMISSION
Samuel Gompers

Gompers.   It is the purpose of organized labor to bring the number of strikes down to a minimum, and in order to accomplish that we try to be better prepared for them.

Q.   What is the result in the last 10 years? Have strikes decreased or increased—that is, compared with the increase of organized labor?—A.   During the first year of organizations, as a rule, there are strikes. When workmen remain organized for any considerable length of time, strikes are reduced in number. It is a peculiar fact that when workmen are unorganized they imagine their employers are almighty and themselves absolutely impotent. When workmen organize for the first time, this transformation takes place: they imagine their employers absolutely impotent and themselves almighty, and the result of it is there is conflict. The employer, so far as strikes begun in his establishment are concerned, resents immediately the assumption of the workmen to appear by committee. He has been accustomed to look upon himself, as to his factory or his establishment, as "monarch of all he surveys" with undisputed sway, and the fact that his employees have an entity as an organization, to be represented by a committee, is something

From *Report of the U.S. Industrial Commission on the Relations and Conditions of Capital and Labor* (Washington, D.C., 1901), VII: 606–608, 617–618, 642–646, 655.

unheard of by him and absolutely intolerable. He imagines immediately that it is a question as to his right to his property: imagines immediately that his property is threatened, and surrounds himself with such safeguards—as the lamented Gladstone once said, "The entire resources of civilization had not yet been exhausted"—arms everybody who swears loyalty to the company, and often surrounds himself with a mercenary armed force, and all the wiles and devices that the acumen of our legal friends can suggest are always employed to overcome, overawe these "mutineers" against his authority.

Q.   To what extent, if any, is the employer, in your judgment, responsible for that condition of affairs?—A.   To the same extent that the bourgeois of France, the royalists of France, were responsible in cowing the people of France, which resulted in the revolution and the brutality manifested by the people when they got power. The employers have simply cut wages whenever they thought it convenient. They looked upon their employees as part of the machinery; to exhibit, perhaps, some little sympathy when one was very critically injured or suffering, and then expected the worship of them all; the cutting of wages time and again, in season and out of season; the discharge of a man who proposed to exercise his right as a man, whether it was as a workman or as a citizen; and so on, driving practically the courage and heart out of the man; and when, through some incident, of which there are thousands, the men are organized of their own volition, quite frequently they touch shoulders for the first time outside of the shop—they touch shoulders, and the thrill simply enthuses them and intoxicates them with new-found power. It is only after the organization has administered a very costly lesson to the employer, and it is only after the workmen themselves have felt the pangs of hunger, perhaps, or other sacrifices resultant from strikes they suffer when unprepared, unorganized, that they are more careful of each other—both sides. They organize and try to meet each other and discuss with each other, and the better the workmen are organized the more able are they to convince the employer that there is an ethical side to the demands of labor. It required 40,000 people in the city of New York in my own trade in 1877 to demonstrate to the employers that we had a right to be heard in our own defense of our trade, and an opportunity to be heard in our own interests. It cost the miners of the country, in 1897, 16 weeks of suffering to secure a national conference and a national agreement. It cost the railroad brotherhoods long months of suffering, many of them sacrificing their positions, in the railroad strike of 1877, and in the Chicago, Burlington and Quincy strike, of the same year, to secure from the employers the right to be heard through committees, their representatives—that is, their committees of the organization to secure these rights. Workmen have had to stand the brunt of the suffering. The American Republic was not established without some suffering, without some sacrifice, and no tangible right has yet been achieved in the interest of the people unless it has been secured by sacrifices and persistency. After a while we become a little more tolerant to each other and recognize all have rights; get around the table and chaff each other; all recognize that they were not so reasonable in the beginning. Now we propose to meet and discuss our interests, and if we can not agree we propose in a more reasonable way to conduct our contests, each to decide how to hold out and bring

337

the other one to terms. A strike, too, is to industry as the right that the British people contended for in placing in the House of Commons the power to close the purse strings to the Government. The rights of the British people were secured in two centuries—between 1500 and 1600—more than ever before, by the securing of that power to withhold the supplies; tied up the purse strings and compelled the Crown to yield. A strike on the part of workmen is to close production and compel better terms and more rights to be acceded to the producers. The economic results of strikes to workers have been advantageous. Without strikes their rights would not have been considered. It is not that workmen or organized labor desires the strike, but it will tenaciously hold to the right to strike. We recognize that peaceful industry is necessary to successful civilized life, but the right to strike and the preparation to strike is the greatest preventive to strikes. If the workmen were to make up their minds to-morrow that they would under no circumstances strike, the employers would do all the striking for them in the way of lesser wages and longer hours of labor.

Q.   The whole philosophy is contest and conquest?—A.   Except when there be like power on both sides; then it becomes reason, by the power on both sides; it then comes to reason rather than contest and conquest. It becomes a matter then of reason; and, as I tried to say in the earlier part of my testimony, no matter how just a cause is, unless that cause is backed up with power to enforce it, it is going to be crushed and annihilated. I tried to illustrate some time ago this proposition by the fact that when England has a dispute with the Afghanistans she immediately proceeds to bombard them unless they acquiesce in her demands; and she would have done the same thing in Venezuela; but when England has a dispute with the United States, she says, "Let us arbitrate" this question; and I think the United States in this regard, or any other nation, is not any different in that regard at all; and the employers are practically in the same position. When the strike occurred at Pullman, Mr. Pullman said he had nothing to arbitrate. His people were unorganized, but he met the committees; not now; he don't meet anyone now; but he used to meet the committees of his unorganized workmen; and the railroad managers—they simply throw their unorganized workmen into the streets if they have any grievances or supposed grievances, but when it comes to organized engineers, firemen, or conductors, or trainmen, who have fairly well organized unions, why, they meet them in conference, pat them on the back sometimes, and say they are jolly good fellows. The economic results to the workers have been invariably beneficial. Even strikes which have been lost have had their good, beneficial results upon the workers. For after all the question must be looked upon in a comprehensive, in a broad way. If the workers, say, have struck for an increase in wages, and the employers refuse to concede them, and finally defeat the workmen, yet as a matter of fact it is almost invariably the case that those who have taken the places of the men who went on strike were themselves receiving less wages before doing so. It is seldom, if ever, that a workman will go from a position where he receives higher wages to take the place of a striker at lower wages. It therefore shows that those who take the places of the strikers improve their material position in the matter of wages. It is asserted that those who strike are compelled to look out for other positions, which is naturally true; but in only isolated cases do they accept positions which pay them less than those they struck against; so that in the sum total of it there is an economic and social advantage. Strikes have convinced the employers of the economic advantage of reduced hours of labor; strikes have rid many a trade of the "jerry builder;" of the fraudulent employer who won't pay wages; strikes have enforced lien laws for wages, where laws have been previously unable to secure the payment; strikes have organized employers as well as employees; strikes have made strong and independent men who were for a long period of years cowards; strikes have made a more independent citizenship of men who often voted simply because it pleased the boss; strikes have given men greater lease of life; strikes have resulted in higher wages, better homes, and demand for better things; strikes have organized wage-earners, too. The strike has taken the place of the barbarous weapons of the dirk and bludgeon. Strikes in the modern sense can occur only in civilized countries.

Q. Does the community at large suffer from strikes?—A. Seldom, if any, except temporarily. It is alleged by some that strikes diminish the wealth of a community and do irreparable injury. If a strike takes place and is not adjusted, it is the very best evidence, of itself, that the community is not suffering for the want of that article. If the community would begin to suffer for that article, employers would immediately concede the demand of the strikers, and the time which is lost in the strike is always made up in a greater continuity of industry after the strike is closed. It is seldom, if ever, workmen are continually employed throughout the entire year. A strike is simply a transferring of the time when idleness shall occur from the advantage of the employer to the advantage of the employees.

Q. So that you would say that the introduction of new machinery does not make a permanent displacement of labor?—A. It would, were it not for the extent of the movement of the wage earners to reduce the hours of labor. When the wage earners do not reduce their hours of labor in proportion to the progress made in the introduction of machinery, new tools, and the division and subdivision of labor, then there is a greater number who are unemployed.

Q. When you say that new machinery, bringing in more rapid processes of production, has lightened the toil of the operatives?—A. No. The organizations of labor have lightened the toil of the workingman, if the toil has been lightened. As a matter of fact, the velocity with which machinery is now run calls forth the expenditure of nearly all the physical and mental force which the wage-earner can give to industry. In substantiation of my negative answer to your question, I would call attention to the fact that after the introduction of machinery, machinery propelled by the motive power of steam, the hours of labor of the working people were from sunup to sundown, and the machinery, which was costly, was not of advantage to the possessor unless it could be operated for a longer period than from sunup to sundown, and it was in that case as perhaps in all, that necessity, being the mother of invention, that which was absent was forthcoming; that was, artificial light to take the place of the rays of the sun after it had set for the day, and with the introduction of artificial light, gas, came the lengthening of the hours of labor of the working people both of the United States and continental Europe. Wherever machinery was at all introduced the object was to have the machinery operated as long as possible, and with the aid of gas the opportunity came. The organizations of

339

the working people were very fragmentary, and few and weak. The hours of labor were lengthened until lives were destroyed by the thousands; and then came the introduction of woman and child labor. There was no restrictive legislation for them; and then came the efforts of the organizations of labor that called forth a yearning and cry of the whole human family against the slaughter of the innocents in the factories of Great Britain particularly, and subsequently in the United States. And it was the power of organized labor—first in feeling that its cause was right, that men and women were being cut down in their manhood and womanhood and childhood, dwarfed or killed, that in a few generations the working people were bound to deteriorate physically, mentally, and morally; that they were deteriorating physically, mentally, and morally; and their ability as producers of wealth would have been destroyed in a few generations had the possessors of machines at that time continued in full sway—it was the efforts of the trade unions of Great Britain, first in their protests, second, in their strikes, and third in their appeals to the public conscience which called forth the factory legislation which limited the hours of labor of women and children in certain industries. Only a few years ago the counsel for the Arkwright Club of Massachusetts said, in a hearing before the labor committee of the Massachusetts legislature in opposition to a bill to limit hours of labor: "If you take the women and children out of the industry, why you take the very heart out of it." And regardless of the brutality of the remark, it was held that if the law limited the hours of labor of the women and children the mill owners would close down the mill and thus close it for men, too. It is for that reason I call attention to the attorney's remark—that with the factory legislation of Great Britain limiting the hours of labor of women and children in several of the industries, it practically secured a reduction in the hours of labor of the male adults also.

Q. In this year of combinations and consolidations and so-called trusts, part of the press and some public men have classified labor associations as connected with and a part of this trust body. What do you say to that classification of labor organizations with capitalistic trusts?—A. I think it is unjustifiable to make that charge against organized labor. Organized labor's efforts are directed to bring within the fold of the organization everyone who works at the trade, everyone who works for wages. The effort is to extend the organization to everyone. You can not break into a trust, and it is our effort to try to make it unprofitable for the workers to break out or longer remain out of the union. One is a close corporation, and the other is an organization world-wide in its effect and influence for good, and the effort is to have the entire body of workers members of the organization.

Q. Is it general that these unions invite the cooperation and the membership of good workmen who have not been associated in labor before?—A. The testimony I gave last April before your commission covers that question partly, but I would say that while we then had 475 general organizers, we now have 550. Where we then had 3 special paid organizers for the American Federation of Labor, we now have 15. There is not a national union in the entire country that has not from 3 to 10 special traveling organizers, whose sole duty it is to try and bring the unorganized workmen within the fold of the union, and to share the benefits of organized effort.

Q. So you would say that the trades union itself is not particularly a selfish organization, for the benefit of those who are first incorporated into it, and to the immediate membership that is attached to it locally: that its influence is wider?—A. Decidedly wider. There is a difference between the contracted selfishness and the broad selfishness that finds one's good served by serving others; by benefiting others. We know that our movement is largely hampered, our progress is hindered, by the large number of unorganized men, and to bring the unorganized within the pale of the organization would make our effort all the more successful and the struggle less intense.

Q. What effect do you think these combinations of capital, or so-called trusts, will have, so far as the interests of organized labor are concerned, for good or for evil?—A. I should prefer that the future shall determine that. Our attitude toward the trusts, I should say, would be largely determined by the attitude of the trusts toward organized labor. It can't be taken as a general proposition. There have been some trusts where, in absorbing, say, some nonunion establishment, and the organization of labor of that trade has had contracts with the different union establishments before the trust was formed, the result of the trust in that particular case has been that the nonunion establishment, paying way below the scale, became part of the trust, became unionized, and an agreement reached increasing wages, reducing hours, and recognizing union conditions. On the other hand, again, there have been trusts where union establishments have been absorbed, and they have become nonunion, so there is no real hard and fast rule by which this question can be determined from our standpoint. We view the trust from the standpoint that they are our employers, and the employer who is fair to us, whether an individual, or a collection of individuals, an aggregation of individuals in the form of a corporation or a trust, matters little to us so long as we obtain the fair conditions—that condition that we regard as fair compensation or reward for our labor.

Q. So far as the whole body of workmen of the United States are concerned, organized or unorganized, do you think that those consolidated bodies where they reach a capitalization of say one hundred, one hundred and fifty, or two hundred millions are really abnormal in the conduct of our business, and are they not. through the great control they have of capital and influence, through legislation and otherwise, rather a menace to the welfare of the country at large?—A. Yes; from some of the causes I have tried to indicate; not necessarily the possession of the wealth, but it is the abuse of the possession.

Q. In other words, you are not particularly afraid, as the head of a great organization, of the large accumulations of wealth, provided that, either through legislation or public opinion, the abuses of that wealth can be regulated?—A. I believe that as time goes on the wage-earners will continue to become larger sharers per dollar of the wealth produced. I have no fear as to the future of organized labor. I have no fear as to the future of labor. This morning I indicated the fact that there is a constant struggle which has been going on from time immemorial between the wealth possessors and those who produce wealth, and that struggle has manifested itself in different forms, at different times, in different countries. That struggle has continued up to date, and will continue so long as there are divers interests between the two. Now, if the wealth possessors, now in form of trusts,

341

make their attitude more unbearable to labor, become more oppressive than ever to labor, it may make the struggle more intense and more bitter; but the struggle is to be met, and will be met; it is only a question whether it shall manifest itself in the power of organization of labor on the one hand and the power of organized wealth on the other, within the bounds of reason, making material concessions, and realizing the development that is continually going on, and the natural desire and the natural right of labor to be continually sharing larger in the product of labor, the social evolution taking place, or whether the trusts, through the intense antagonism that they may manifest toward labor, make that fight all the more bitter, all the more intense. I have not any fear as to the future. My only fear is—and there is something I want to obviate, that I am trying to give my life's work to obviate, that the struggle shall not be so bitter and costly.

Q. Suppose it is thought best on the part of capital to call in as a cooperative factor the forces of labor organized, especially in the profit sharing, or cooperative, or other form of just division of profits in the wealth producers, and wealth itself, would you say that organized labor would accept conditions of that kind in preference to the wage system that they have now?—A. I would say that judging from the history of such efforts in the past, I would look upon such propositions with a very great deal of suspicion. There have been few, if any, of these concerns that have been even comparatively fair to their employees. The average employer who has indulged in this single-handed scheme to solve the social problem has gotten out of the workers all that there was in them and all their vitality, and made the mold prematurely, to the tune of 5 or 10 years of their lives. They made the worker work harder, longer hours, and when the employees of other concerns in the same line of trade were enjoying increased wages, shorter hours of labor, and other improvements, tending to the material progress of the worker, the employees of the concern where so-called profit sharing was the system at the end of the year found themselves receiving lower wages for harder work than were those who were not under that beneficent system.

Q. Then you would say that practically attempts made in this country in the line of profit sharing, and mutuality between the employer and employee in the sharing of profits of the production, have been failures?—A. There are few exceptions. So long as our present social system shall last, it is positively ludicrous for any concern or few concerns to attempt to solve the social problem for themselves. It is just as ludicrous and ridiculous as it is for a number of well-meaning people, well-meaning workmen, to make up their minds to enter upon a colonization scheme of cooperation. They isolate themselves from the world— even if their purpose is a success, if their scheme is a success, they have simply emancipated themselves from the world, and are contributing nothing toward the solution of the struggle; yes, they have hindered the struggle, for, as a rule, these people are discontented with the wrongs that exist, but, though manifesting some little thought and ability, deprive the people who are struggling from the benefits of that knowledge and discontent; so in the sum total, it is depriving the movement for social improvement, economic advancement, of the intelligence, and independence, and manhood, and character of these people who isolate themselves from the rest of the world. And so it is with those profit-sharing concerns, perhaps prompted by no other cause than that of philanthropy or desire to solve the problem. That is not the way it must be solved; you can not solve the social problem without taking into consideration the human family. There is no such thing as solving the social problem without incorporating the whole human family.

Q. Would the general proposition be that the worker should be a sharer in the profits of production? Then ought he to be a sharer in the losses of production?—A. We have so little that we can afford to do with nothing less than what we have.

Q. In other words you think the wage-scale system is on a minimum?—A. The wage scale, sliding often—but there is a minimum or a life line, below which we object it shall go. If an employer of labor can not conduct business by paying a minimum and living wage let him get out of business and make room for someone else who can pay it. We contend that it is a libel upon the human family to say that any industry, to be successfully conducted, can not afford to pay a living wage to the producers of the article in that industry.

Q. You believe in the wage system then, rather than in partnership?—A. I can not assent to that. I know that we are operating under the wage system. As to what system will ever come to take its place I am not prepared to say. I have given this subject much thought; I have read the works of the most advanced economists, competent economists in all schools of thought—the trade unionist, the socialist, the anarchist, the single taxer, the cooperationist, etc. I am not prepared to say, after having read, and with an honest endeavor to arrive at a conclusion—I am not prepared to say that either of their propositions are logical, scientific, or natural. I know that we are living under the wage system, and so long as that lasts, it is our purpose to secure a continually larger share for labor, for the wealth producers. Whether the time shall come, as this constantly increasing share to labor goes on, when profits shall be entirely eliminated, and the full product of labor, the net result of production, go to the laborer, thus abolishing the wage system; or whether, on the other hand, through the theory of the anarchist, there should be an abolition of all title in land other than its occupation and use, the abolition of the monopoly of the private issuance of money, the abolition of the patent system—whether we will return to the first principles; or whether, under the single tax, taxing the land to the full value of it—I am perfectly willing that the future shall determine and work out. I know that as the workers more thoroughly organize, and continually become larger sharers in the product of their toil, they will have the better opportunities for their physical and mental cultivation instilled into them, higher hopes and aspirations, and they will be the better prepared to meet the problems that will then confront them. For the present it is our purpose to secure better conditions and instill a larger amount of manhood and independence into the hearts and minds of the workers, and to broaden their mental sphere and the sphere of their affections.

Q. Is it not true that for many years, the tendency to improved condition of the working people of this country has been very marked, and that to-day they are larger sharers in their product than ever before?—A. That is true; yes, and it is wholly due to the efforts of their own organization.

Q. You would not agree to the statement sometimes made that the conditions

343

of the working man are growing worse and worse?—A.   Oh, that is perfectly absurd.

Q.   Of course you lay the improved conditions to the organization of labor?—A.   Yes. That can be easily proven, for, as a matter of fact, where the workers remain unorganized, as a rule they have not shared in the great improvements that the working people have who have been organized, and, judging from cause and effect, one can easily determine that that for which I contend is a fact. During the entire industrial revival of industry of 1884 to 1886 and 1887, the textile workers in Cohoes, N.Y., I think, were the only body of working people in the country who suffered a reduction of wages, despite the revival of industry. They were unorganized. But, of course, I want to say this in connection with this matter: In our present economic condition of society we have with a very great degree of regularity a period of these industrial panics that the student can determine almost with the exactness that an astronomer does of the comets, the coming of these periods of industrial crises. Quite a number do not observe this economic phenomena. The worker knows that during these industrial panics he is out of a job; and you might have all the philosophy in the world, all the facts in the world to demonstrate the truthfulness of your position, but he is out of a job, and he can not understand that there has been any social improvement, not even that he has improved beyond the condition of his forefathers 10 centuries ago; he knows he is out of a job, and he is hungry, and the prospects of something in the future are very remote, and to him the world has been growing worse all the time; the world is in an awful condition, and it is in an awful condition truly, and we must remember this, when we consider the social progress; we must not compare this year with the last, or last year with the year before, but compare it for a century by decades, then the marvelous progress can be easily observed. One, of course, can not—unless he is as old as my friend, Major Farquhar—go back a century, but most of us young men can go back 20 or 30 years; we can mark the condition, and that which we do not know of our own knowledge we can ascertain of truthful recorders.

Q.   To what do you attribute the vastly superior condition of the American workingmen over the European; the social condition; the advanced, you might say, scale of wages paid in America over the European condition?—A.   First, the working people of Europe have emerged from a condition of slavery and serfdom to that of wage laborers. The workingmen of America have not had this hereditary condition of slavery and serfdom. There has been no special status for them as slaves or serfs, and in theory, at least, they were supposed to be equals to all others.

Another reason is the climatic conditions that obtain in our country. The changes from extreme heat to extreme cold make the people more active, more nervous; accelerates their motion, accelerates their thought; again, the vast domain of land, rich soil, that even to-day is beyond speculation, much less the knowledge of our own people—all these things have contributed to a better material condition for the working people of our country. I should add, I think, that the climate conditions, requiring better food, more nutritious food, better clothing, more comfortable clothing, better houses, better homes, have all been contributing factors for the workers to insist upon receiving—to secure these things in the shape of higher wages.

Q.   He demands higher wages and gets them?—A.   Yes.

Q. Comparatively higher wages?—A. He gets higher wages; comparatively higher wages.

Then again I will say that the productivity of the American laborer is far greater than that of his brother workman in any part of the world.

Q. How do you rate that?—A. I can not begin to tell you. I can say, however, that in every mechanical trade, when European workmen come over to this country and stand beside their American fellow workingmen it simply dazes them—the velocity of motion, the deftness, the quickness, the constant strain. The European bricklayer, the European carpenter, the European compositor-printer, the European tailor comes over here and works in the shop, or factory, or office, and he is simply intoxicated by the rapidity of the movements of the American workingman, and it is some months, with the greatest endeavor, before he can at all come near the production of the American workingman. He must do it in time or he will go without a job.

Q. The capital that is employed in productive industry sustains very close relation with labor, so there ought to be a very great harmony of interests between the owners of that capital and the owners of labor?—A. There has never yet existed identity of interests between buyer and seller of an article. If you have anything to sell and I want to buy it your interest and mine are not identical

Q. Is there not a possibility that the day will come when they will be substantially identical, when they recognize each other's rights?—A. I should regard that upon the same plan as I would the panaceas that are offered by our populists, socialists, anarchists, and single-tax friends, as very remote and very far removed, if that time should ever come. I am perfectly satisfied to fight the battles of to-day, of those here, and those that come to-morrow, so their conditions may be improved, and they may be better prepared to fight in the contests or solve the problems that may be presented to them. The hope for a perfect millennium—well, it don't come every night; it don't come with the twinkling of the eye; it is a matter which we have got to work out, and every step that the workers make or take, every vantage point gained, is a solution in itself. I have often inquired of men who have ready-made patent solutions of this social problem, and I want to say to you, sir, that I have them offered to me on an average of two or three a week, and they are all equally unsatisfactory. I maintain that we are solving the problem every day; we are solving the problems as they confront us. One would imagine by what is often considered as the solution of the problem that it is going to fall among us, that a world cataclysm is going to take place; that there is going to be a social revolution; that we will go to bed one night under the present system and the morrow morning wake up with a revolution in full blast, and the next day organize a Heaven on earth. That is not the way that progress is made; that is not the way the social evolution is brought about; that is not the way the human family are going to have interests advanced. We are solving the problem day after day. As we get an hour's more leisure every day it means millions of golden hours, of opportunities, to the human family. As we get 25 cents a day wages increase it means another solution, another problem solved, and brings us nearer the time when a greater degree of justice and fair dealing will obtain among men.

345

34

In Defense
of the Status Quo

In the last third of the nineteenth century Yale professor William Graham Sumner skillfully turned Charles Darwin's conception of "the survival of the fittest" to the defense of rugged individualism and laissez-faire political economy. While his essay "The Absurd Effort to Make the World Over" was published a few years after 1890, the terminal date of the present section, it summed up arguments he had widely disseminated in the 1870s and 1880s. Popular discontent with the workings of the economy was growing steadily, and a diverse band of critics and reformers—Henry George, Edmund Bellamy, Howells, Riis, Lloyd, and others—was finding a wider audience. In response Sumner offered a thoughtful defense of the status quo and a sharp critique of the assumptions of reformers. His emphasis upon the inexorable evolution of modern society toward greater organization, however, could have been used to justify the program of a Samuel Gompers as well as a John D. Rockefeller, and soon "Reform Darwinist" thinkers like sociologist Lester Frank Ward were to do just that.

THE ABSURD EFFORT
TO MAKE THE WORLD OVER
William Graham Sumner

It will not probably be denied that the burden of proof is on those who affirm that our social condition is utterly diseased and in need of radical regeneration. My task at present, therefore, is entirely negative and critical: to examine the allegations of fact and the doctrines which are put forward to prove the correctness of the diagnosis and to warrant the use of the remedies proposed

The propositions put forward by social reformers nowadays are chiefly of two kinds. There are assertions in historical form, chiefly in regard to the comparison of existing with earlier social states, which are plainly based on defective historical knowledge, or at most on current stock historical dicta which are uncritical and incorrect. Writers very often assert that something never existed before because they do not know that it ever existed before, or that something is worse than ever

From *War and Other Essays* (New Haven, Conn., 1911), 195–210.

before because they are not possessed of detailed information about what has existed before. The other class of propositions consists of dogmatic statements which, whether true or not, are unverifiable. This class of propositions is the pest and bane of current economic and social discussion. Upon a more or less superficial view of some phenomenon a suggestion arises which is embodied in a philosophical proposition and promulgated as a truth. From the form and nature of such propositions they can always be brought under the head of "ethics." This word at least gives them an air of elevated sentiment and purpose, which is the only warrant they possess. It is impossible to test or verify them by any investigation or logical process whatsoever. It is therefore very difficult for anyone who feels a high responsibility for historical statements, and who absolutely rejects any statement which is unverifiable, to find a common platform for discussion or to join issue satisfactorily in taking the negative.

When anyone asserts that the class of skilled and unskilled manual laborers of the United States is worse off now in respect to diet, clothing, lodgings, furniture, fuel, and lights; in respect to the age at which they can marry; the number of children they can provide for; the start in life which they can give to their children, and their chances of accumulating capital, than they ever have been at any former time, he makes a reckless assertion for which no facts have been offered in proof. Upon an appeal to facts, the contrary of this assertion would be clearly established. It suffices, therefore, to challenge those who are responsible for the assertion to make it good.

If it is said that the employed class are under much more stringent discipline than they were thirty years ago or earlier, it is true. It is not true that there has been any qualitative change in this respect within thirty years, but it is true that a movement which began at the first settlement of the country has been advancing with constant acceleration and has become a noticeable feature within our time. This movement is the advance in the industrial organization. The first settlement was made by agriculturists, and for a long time there was scarcely any organization. There were scattered farmers, each working for himself, and some small towns with only rudimentary commerce and handicrafts. As the country has filled up, the arts and professions have been differentiated and the industrial organization has been advancing. This fact and its significance has hardly been noticed at all; but the stage of the industrial organization existing at any time, and the rate of advance in its development, are the absolutely controlling social facts. Nine-tenths of the socialistic and semi-socialistic, and sentimental or ethical, suggestions by which we are overwhelmed come from failure to understand the phenomena of the industrial organization and its expansion. It controls us all because we are all in it. It creates the conditions of our existence, sets the limits of our social activity, regulates the bonds of our social relations, determines our conceptions of good and evil, suggests our life-philosophy, molds our inherited political institutions, and reforms the oldest and toughest customs, like marriage and property. I repeat that the turmoil of heterogeneous and antagonistic social whims and speculations in which we live is due to the failure to understand what the industrial organization is and its all-pervading control over human life, while the traditions of our school of

347

philosophy lead us always to approach the industrial organization, not from the side of objective study, but from that of philosophical doctrine. Hence it is that we find that the method of measuring what we see happening by what are called ethical standards, and of proposing to attack the phenomena by methods thence deduced, is so popular.

The advance of a new country from the very simplest social coordination up to the highest organization is a most interesting and instructive chance to study the development of the organization. It has of course been attended all the way along by stricter subordination and higher discipline. All organization implies restriction of liberty. The gain of power is won by narrowing individual range. The methods of business in colonial days were loose and slack to an inconceivable degree. The movement of industry has been all the time toward promptitude, punctuality, and reliability. It has been attended all the way by lamentations about the good old times; about the decline of small industries; about the lost spirit of comradeship between employer and employee; about the narrowing of the interests of the workman; about his conversion into a machine or into a "ware," and about industrial war. These lamentations have all had reference to unquestionable phenomena attendant on advancing organization. In all occupations the same movement is discernible—in the learned professions, in schools, in trade, commerce, and transportation. It is to go on faster than ever, now that the continent is filled up by the first superficial layer of population over its whole extent and the intensification of industry has begun. The great inventions both make the intension of the organization possible and make it inevitable, with all its consequences, whatever they may be. I must expect to be told here, according to the current fashions of thinking, that we ought to control the development of the organization. The first instinct of the modern man is to get a law passed to forbid or prevent what, in his wisdom, he disapproves. A thing which is inevitable, however, is one which we cannot control. We have to make up our minds to it, adjust ourselves to it, and sit down to live with it. Its inevitableness may be disputed, in which case we must re-examine it; but if our analysis is correct, when we reach what is inevitable we reach the end, and our regulations must apply to ourselves, not to the social facts.

Now the intensification of the social organization is what gives us greater social power. It is to it that we owe our increased comfort and abundance. We are none of us ready to sacrifice this. On the contrary, we want more of it. We would not return to the colonial simplicity and the colonial exiguity if we could. If not, then we must pay the price. Our life is bounded on every side by conditions. We can have this if we will agree to submit to that. In the case of industrial power and product the great condition is combination of force under discipline and strict coordination. Hence the wild language about wage-slavery and capitalistic tyranny.

In any state of society no great achievements can be produced without great force. Formerly great force was attainable only by slavery aggregating the power of great numbers of men. Roman civilization was built on this. Ours has been built on steam. It is to be built on electricity. Then we are all forced into an organization around these natural forces and adapted to the methods or their application; and although we indulge in rhetoric about political liberty, nevertheless we find ourselves bound tight in a new set of conditions, which control the modes of our existence and determine the directions in which alone economic and social liberty can go.

If it is said that there are some persons in our time who have become rapidly and in a great degree rich, it is true; if it is said that large aggregations of wealth in the control of individuals is a social danger, it is not true.

The movement of the industrial organization which has just been described has brought out a great demand for men capable of managing great enterprises. Such have been called "captains of industry." The analogy with military leaders suggested by this name is not misleading. The great leaders in the development of the industrial organization need those talents of executive and administrative skill, power to command, courage, and fortitude, which were formerly called for in military affairs and scarcely anywhere else. The industrial army is also as dependent on its captains as a military body is on its generals. One of the worst features of the existing system is that the employees have a constant risk in their employer. If he is not competent to manage the business with success, they suffer with him. Capital also is dependent on the skill of the captain of industry for the certainty and magnitude of its profits. Under these circumstances there has been a great demand for men having the requisite ability for this function. As the organization has advanced, with more impersonal bonds of coherence and wider scope of operations, the value of this functionary has rapidly increased. The possession of the requisite ability is a natural monopoly. Consequently, all the conditions have concurred to give to those who possessed this monopoly excessive and constantly advancing rates of remuneration.

Another social function of the first importance in an intense organization is the solution of those crises in the operation of it which are called the conjuncture of the market. It is through the market that the lines of relation run which preserve the system in harmonious and rhythmical operation. The conjuncture is the momentary sharper misadjudgment of supply and demand which indicates that a redistribution of productive effort is called for. The industrial organization needs to be insured against these conjunctures, which, if neglected, produce a crisis and catastrophe; and it needs that they shall be anticipated and guarded against as far as skill and foresight can do it. The rewards of this function for the bankers and capitalists who perform it are very great. The captains of industry and the capitalists who operate on the conjuncture, therefore, if they are successful, win, in these days, great fortunes in a short time. There are no earnings which are more legitimate or for which greater services are rendered to the whole industrial body. The popular notions about this matter really assume that all the wealth accumulated by these classes of persons would be here just the same if they had not existed. They are supposed to have appropriated it out of the common stock. This is so far from being true that, on the contrary, their own wealth would not be but for themselves; and besides that, millions more of wealth, many-fold greater than their own, scattered in the hands of thousands, would not exist but for them.

Within the last two years I have traveled from end to end of the German

349

Empire several times on all kinds of trains. I reached the conviction, looking at the matter from the passenger's standpoint, that, if the Germans could find a Vanderbilt and put their railroads in his hands for twenty-five years, letting him reorganize the system and make twenty-five million dollars out of it for himself in that period, they would make an excellent bargain.

But it is repeated until it has become a commonplace which people are afraid to question, that there is some social danger in the possession of large amounts of wealth by individuals. I ask, Why? I heard a lecture two years ago by a man who holds perhaps the first chair of political economy in the world. He said, among other things, that there was great danger in our day from great accumulations; that this danger ought to be met by taxation, and he referred to the fortune of the Rothschilds and to the great fortunes made in America to prove his point. He omitted, however, to state in what the danger consisted or to specify what harm has ever been done by the Rothschild fortunes or by the great fortunes accumulated in America. It seemed to me that the assertions he was making, and the measures he was recommending, ex-cathedra, were very serious to be thrown out so recklessly. It is hardly to be expected that novelists, popular magazinists, amateur economists, and politicians will be more responsible. It would be easy, however, to show what good is done by accumulations of capital in a few hands—that is, under close and direct management, permitting prompt and accurate application; also to tell what harm is done by loose and unfounded denunciations of any social component or any social group. In the recent debates on the income tax the assumption that great accumulations of wealth are socially harmful and ought to be broken down by taxation was treated as an axiom, and we had direct proof how dangerous it is to fit out the average politician with such unverified and unverifiable dogmas as his warrant for his modes of handling the direful tool of taxation.

Great figures are set out as to the magnitude of certain fortunes and the proportionate amount of the national wealth held by a fraction of the population, and eloquent exclamation-points are set against them. If the figures were beyond criticism, what would they prove? Where is the rich man who is oppressing anybody? If there was one, the newspapers would ring with it. The facts about the accumulation of wealth do not constitute a plutocracy, as I will show below. Wealth, in itself considered, is only power, like steam, or electricity, or knowledge. The question of its good or ill turns on the question how it will be used. To prove any harm in aggregations of wealth it must be shown that great wealth is, as a rule, in the ordinary course of social affairs, put to a mischievous use. This cannot be shown beyond the very slightest degree, if at all.

Therefore, all the allegations of general mischief, social corruption, wrong, and evil in our society must be referred back to those who make them for particulars and specifications. As they are offered to us we cannot allow them to stand, because we discern in them faulty observation of facts, or incorrect interpretation of facts, or a construction of facts according to some philosophy, or misunderstanding of phenomena and their relations, or incorrect inferences, or crooked deductions.

Assuming, however, that the charges against the existing "capitalistic"—that is, industrial—order of things are established, it is proposed to remedy the ill by reconstructing the industrial system on the principles of democracy. Once more we must untangle the snarl of half ideas and muddled facts.

Democracy is, of course, a word of conjure with. We have a democratic-republican political system, and we like it so well that we are prone to take any new step which can be recommended as "democratic" or which will round some "principle" of democracy to a fuller fulfillment. Everything connected with this domain of political thought is crusted over with false historical traditions, cheap philosophy, and undefined terms, but it is useless to try to criticize it. The whole drift of the world for five hundred years has been toward democracy. That drift, produced by great discoveries and inventions, and by the discovery of a new continent, has raised the middle class out of the servile class. In alliance with the crown they crushed the feudal classes. They made the crown absolute in order to do it. Then they turned against the crown and, with the aid of the handicraftsmen and peasants, conquered it. Now the next conflict which must inevitably come is that between the middle capitalist class and the proletariat, as the word has come to be used. If a certain construction is put on this conflict, it may be called that between democracy and plutocracy, for it seems that industrialism must be developed into plutocracy by the conflict itself. That is the conflict which stands before civilized society to-day. All the signs of the times indicate its commencement, and it is big with fate to mankind and to civilization.

Although we cannot criticize democracy profitably, it may be said of it, with reference to our present subject, that up to this time democracy never has done anything, either in politics, social affairs, or industry, to prove its power to bless mankind. If we confine our attention to the United States, there are three difficulties with regard to its alleged achievements, and they all have the most serious bearing on the proposed democratization of industry.

1. The time during which democracy has been tried in the United States is too short to warrant any inferences. A century or two is a very short time in the life of political institutions, and if the circumstances change rapidly during the period the experiment is vitiated.

2. The greatest question of all about American democracy is whether it is a cause or a consequence. It is popularly assumed to be a cause, and we ascribe to its beneficent action all the political vitality, all the easiness of social relations, all the industrial activity and enterprise which we experience and which we value and enjoy. I submit, however, that, on a more thorough examination of the matter, we shall find that democracy is a consequence. There are economic and sociological causes for our political vitality and vigor, for the ease and elasticity of our social relations, and for our industrial power and success. Those causes have also produced democracy, given it success, and have made its faults and errors innocuous. Indeed, in any true philosophy, it must be held that in the economic forces which control the material prosperity of a population lie the real causes of its political institutions, its social class-adjustments, its industrial prosperity, its moral code, and its world-philosophy. If democracy and the industrial system are both products of the economic conditions which exist, it is plainly absurd to set democracy to defeat those conditions in the control of industry. If, however, it is

351

not true that democracy is a consequence, and I am well aware that very few people believe it, then we must go back to the view that democracy is a cause. That being so, it is difficult to see how democracy, which has had a clear field here in America, is not responsible for the ills which Mr. Bellamy and his comrades in opinion see in our present social state, and it is difficult to see the grounds of asking us to intrust it also with industry. The first and chief proof of success of political measures and systems is that, under them, society advances in health and vigor and that industry develops without causing social disease. If this has not been the case in America, American democracy has not succeeded. Neither is it easy to see how the masses, if they have undertaken to rule, can escape the responsibilities of ruling, especially so far as the consequences affect themselves. If, then, they have brought all this distress upon themselves under the present system, what becomes of the argument for extending the system to a direct and complete control of industry?

3. It is by no means certain that democracy in the United States has not, up to this time, been living on a capital inherited from aristocracy and industrialism. We have no pure democracy. Our democracy is limited at every turn by institutions which were developed in England in connection with industrialism and aristocracy, and these institutions are of the essence of our system. While our people are passionately democratic in temper and will not tolerate a doctrine that one man is not as good as another, they have common sense enough to know that he is not; and it seems that they love and cling to the conservative institutions quite as strongly as they do to the democratic philosophy. They are, therefore, ruled by men who talk philosophy and govern by the institutions. Now it is open to Mr. Bellamy to say that the reason why democracy in America seems to be open to the charge made in the last paragraph, of responsibility for all the ill which he now finds in our society, is because it has been infected with industrialism (capitalism); but in that case he must widen the scope of his proposition and undertake to purify democracy before turning industry over to it. The socialists generally seem to think that they make their undertakings easier when they widen their scope, and make them easiest when they propose to remake everything; but in truth social tasks increase in difficulty in an enormous ratio as they are widened in scope.

The question, therefore, arises, if it is proposed to reorganize the social system on the principles of American democracy, whether the institutions of industrialism are to be retained. If so, all the virus of capitalism will be retained. It is forgotten, in many schemes of social reformation in which it is proposed to mix what we like with what we do not like, in order to extirpate the latter, that each must undergo a reaction from the other, and that what we like may be extirpated by what we do not like. We may find that instead of democratizing capitalism we have capitalized democracy—that is, have brought in plutocracy. Plutocracy is a political system in which the ruling force is wealth. The denunciation of capital which we hear from all the reformers is the most eloquent proof that the greatest power in the world to-day is capital. They know that it is, and confess it most when they deny it most strenuously. At present the power of capital is social and industrial, and only in a small degree political. So far as capital is political, it is on account of political abuses, such as tariffs and special legislation on the one hand and legislative strikes on the other. These conditions exist in the democracy to which it is proposed to transfer the industries. What does that mean except bringing all the power of capital once for all into the political arena and precipitating the conflict of democracy and plutocracy at once? Can anyone imagine that the masterfulness, the overbearing disposition, the greed of gain, and the ruthlessness in methods, which are the faults of the master of industry at his worst, would cease when he was a functionary of the State, which had relieved him of risk and endowed him with authority? Can anyone imagine that politicians would no longer be corruptly fond of money, intriguing, and crafty when they were charged, not only with patronage and government contracts, but also with factories, stores, ships, and railroads? Could we expect anything except that, when the politician and the master of industry were joined in one, we should have the vices of both unchecked by the restraints of either? In any socialistic state there will be one set of positions which will offer chances of wealth beyond the wildest dreams of avarice; *viz.*, on the governing committees. Then there will be rich men whose wealth will indeed be a menace to social interests, and instead of industrial peace there will be such war as no one has dreamed of yet: the war between the political ins and outs—that is, between those who are on the committee and those who want to get on it.

We must not drop the subject of democracy without one word more. The Greeks already had occasion to notice a most serious distinction between two principles of democracy which lie at its roots. Plutarch says that Solon got the archonship in part by promising equality, which some understood of esteem and dignity, others of measure and number. There is one democratic principle which means that each man should be esteemed for his merit and worth, for just what he is, without regard to birth, wealth, rank, or other adventitious circumstances. The other principle is that each one of us ought to be equal to all the others in what he gets and enjoys. The first principle is only partially realizable, but, so far as it goes, it is elevating and socially progressive and profitable. The second is not capable of an intelligible statement. The first is a principle of industrialism. It proceeds from and is intelligible only in a society built on the industrial virtues, free endeavor, security of property, and repression of the baser vices; that is, in a society whose industrial system is built on labor and exchange. The other is only a rule of division for robbers who have to divide plunder or monks who have to divide gifts. If, therefore, we want to democratize industry in the sense of the first principle, we need only perfect what we have now, especially on its political side. If we try to democratize it in the sense of the other principle, we corrupt politics at one stroke; we enter upon an industrial enterprise which will waste capital and bring us all to poverty, and we set loose greed and envy as ruling social passions.

If this poor old world is as bad as they say, one more reflection may check the zeal of the headlong reformer. It is at any rate a tough old world. It has taken its trend and curvature and all its twists and tangles from a long course of formation. All its wry and crooked gnarls and knobs are therefore stiff and stubborn. If we puny men by our arts can do anything at all to straighten them, it will only be by modifying the tendencies of some of the forces at work, so that, after a sufficient time, their action may be changed a little and slowly the lines of movement may be

353

modified. This effort, however, can at most be only slight, and it will take a long time. In the meantime spontaneous forces will be at work, compared with which our efforts are like those of a man trying to deflect a river, and these forces will have changed the whole problem before our interferences have time to make themselves felt. The great stream of time and earthly things will sweep on just the same in spite of us. It bears with it now all the errors and follies of the past, the wreckage of all the philosophies, the fragments of all the civilizations, the wisdom of all the abandoned ethical systems, the debris of all the institutions, and the penalties of all the mistakes. It is only in imagination that we stand by and look at and criticize it and plan to change it. Everyone of us is a child of his age and cannot get out of it. He is in the stream and is swept along with it. All his sciences and philosophy come to him out of it. Therefore the tide will not be changed by us. It will swallow up both us and our experiments. It will absorb the efforts at change and take them into itself as new but trivial components, and the great movement of tradition and work will go on unchanged by our fads and schemes. The things which will change it are the great discoveries and inventions, the new reactions inside the social organism, and the changes in the earth itself on account of changes in the cosmical forces. These causes will make of it just what, in fidelity to them, it ought to be. The men will be carried along with it and be made by it. The utmost they can do by their cleverness will be to note and record their course as they are carried along, which is what we do now, and is that which leads us to the vain fancy that we can make or guide the movement. That is why it is the greatest folly of which a man can be capable, to sit down with a slate and pencil to plan out a new social world.

PART FIVE

The Quest for Order, 1890–1929

Describing the ferment of reform in the first decade of the twentieth century, Theodore Roosevelt found "a condition of excitement and irritation in the public mind." In the twenty-two years between 1890 and 1912, many Americans began to question the political and social justice of their society. The sources for this era of reform were varied, and their origins were old; but in the scope and variety of evils attacked, the era was unprecedented, provoked by a restless urge to re-examine the nature of the American dream.

Economic distress caused some of the excitement. American farmers were learning that hard work and technical success were not enough. Despite their immense acreages of wheat, corn, and cotton, despite the growing market for their cattle and grain in the huge cities of the Eastern seaboard and across the ocean in Europe, farm prices had not kept pace with the wants and needs of American farmers. Angered by the rising costs of transportation, dismayed by the obvious contrasts between their own living styles and those of the rising businessmen and professionals, many farmers turned to political action. The targets of their denunciations varied, but in the early 1890s many farmers hoped that government manipulation of currency, principally increasing the monetization of silver, would solve their problems. The formation of the Populist Party represented the peak of agrarian political action, and even though it was unsuccessful, the bitterness and despair that its rhetoric recorded aroused other Americans to reconsider inequities in the nation's economic life.

Farmers were not alone in searching for radical methods to re-establish their position. Rapid industrialization had concentrated thousands of ill-paid and resentful workers in the great new factories and coal mines which were powering America's enormous growth. Industrialists were frequently ignorant of or unsympathetic toward their employees' problems. When strikers sought to gain reduced hours or higher wages through collective action, magnates turned to the police powers of the state to protect their private interests, or else relied on armies of mercenaries to force labor into a more compromising mood. The 1880s and 1890s witnessed a series of savage strikes in the United States, which destroyed unions without producing an alternative way of solving the basic conflicts dividing management and labor. Many Americans brooded about the consequences of a clash they saw as inevitable and bloody. Under the spur of larger profits, firms began to combine and multiply in size, until their working forces were enormous. The huge and increasingly impersonal corporations were an object of fear, not only to workers, but to consumers and small businessmen who worried that in the race toward bigness older freedoms and opportunities that had been regarded as distinctively American were being lost.

The perils of size were nowhere more apparent than in the enormous new cities created by migration from the farms and from Europe. In the city the contrasts of civilized life were shockingly exposed. Journalists, economists, social workers, and clergymen returned from voyages of exploration to the slums and sweatshops with a sense of horror and outrage. Technological inventions like the automobile and electric traction, bridge-building and subway construction, structural steel skyscrapers and high-speed elevators, were helping to meet the city's most elementary problems of communication and transport, but the social disasters of inadequate housing, delinquency, epidemic disease, prostitution, and family desertion seemed larger than ever before. Groups of clergymen sought to return their churches to a role in the life of the masses by becoming involved in causes for social justice, and expanding their religious activities to include entertainment, recreation, and socializing. Members of Protestant sects, uneasy and sometimes afraid of the alien religious heritage that urban immigrants carried with them from the Old World, launched aggressive revival campaigns to convert the new Americans to their faith and social values.

The city was also discovered by lay reformers, disturbed by the breakdown of community institutions and anxious to provide surrogates for them. The settlement-house movement was probably the most memorable of these efforts to restore some sense of order and belonging to the fragmented and fast-moving life of the great cities. Immigrant families, caught between nostalgia for older ways and a desire to adjust rapidly to new demands, coped painfully with the novel independence of their children. Settlements offered club life and music, art classes and dances, remedial instruction and sports to ease the entrance of these youngsters into an alien world, and to restore some unity and purpose to the disrupted living patterns of their parents. Older ethnic traditions, church life and village associations, native theater and foreign language newspapers added vitality to urban culture, while they also gave some structure to the daily lives of former peasants and village artisans.

The wealthy were also seeking structure for their lives, and ways of expressing their newly won fortunes and prestige. Private schools, country clubs, opera houses, and museums testified to their desire for isolation from the masses, on the one hand, and their interest in display, on the other. The high arts of music, drama, painting, and sculpture were patronized by rich Americans with industry and often with taste, but their pretensions and ignorance frequently called down the contempt and anger of working people, whose own culture and values they ignored. The resulting lack of communication would be bridged, to a slight extent, by the appearance of the infant motion-picture industry, but in these years social reformers worried about the melodrama and cheap violence of popular entertainments and sought ways of countering them in community-sponsored recreation programs.

Immigrants and aristocrats were not the only groups divided by cultural preferences. In these years the first massive migrations northward by Southern Negroes brought new groups to American cities. Increasingly severe segregation laws and practical disenfranchisement in the South posed a dilemma for Negro leadership. Followers of Booker T. Washington's gradualist program, which emphasized the acquisition of occupational skills, clashed with more determined radicals led by W. E. B. DuBois, who advocated more militancy and aggressiveness in demanding political equality. Despite its gravity, however, the problem of integrating American Negroes into the life of the country did not receive the sustained attention of many reformers, whose energy was focused instead on relieving the problems of the cities, and stating the objections of the middle classes to the curse of bigness.

Many of these reform leaders, coming out of educated, reasonably comfortable Protestant backgrounds, were aroused by the spectacle of corrupt municipal governments and underhanded business practices; both seemed to produce wasteful and constraining results, increasing the costs that taxpayers and consumers were forced to pay, without increasing the services and benefits they received. Urban journalists like Lincoln Steffens, magazine contributors like Ida Tarbell and David Graham Phillips, earned for themselves the sobriquet of "muckrakers" for their delight in exposing the grimy and suspect aspects of business and government; but the man who gave them that title, Theodore Roosevelt, became himself a hero to reformers of this generation, a gifted publicist who brought to the White House a sense of drama and excitement that had been missing for forty years. Roosevelt's friends and appointees helped bring a new sense of purpose to the activities of the federal government, so long dwarfed by the giant operations of big business. Under the prodding of progressives the first efforts were made to bring social security to millions of laborers, through experimental workmen's compensation programs, new minimum wage and maximum hour laws, and renewed attacks on the attempts of large corporations to fix prices and restrain trade for their own profit. Roosevelt's efforts in the field of conservation were particularly attractive to the middle-class

357

activists who supported him; humanitarianism combined with efficiency in stimulating them to political involvement, and programs that promised to conserve more effectively the nation's resources, even while they curbed the rapacious practices of private industry, were sure to win their applause.

Roosevelt's reform commitments were not total or radical. His nostalgia was for older value systems, not for the small-scale individualistic America of the midnineteenth century. He accepted the responsibility of size, in foreign as well as domestic relations, and was an active supporter of a more aggressive diplomacy, particularly since the Spanish-American War, in which he participated, had brought a sense of imperial destiny to millions of Americans. The issue of annexing territories was bitterly debated, with participants acting from a variety of motives. Anti-imperialists feared not only the regimenting effects of overseas expansion but they brooded also about the social dangers of amalgamating alien racial groups. Already the millions of immigrants from eastern and central Europe were deemed a menace to older values by conservative leaders, who argued that if the policy of unlimited immigration were continued, Americans would be committing race suicide. Though their efforts were still unsuccessful by 1912, they had scored impressive gains and had attracted wide support. Doctrines of eugenic improvement and racial inferiority illustrated the paradoxes that seemingly scientific research could bring along with it.

But the ugly side of foreign expansion and American self-confidence was counterbalanced by the undeniable energy and originality of the Progressive Idea. Lawyers, professors, journalists, and clergymen were joining together to find new ways of purging government of its political insensitivities and bringing to the dependent and the deprived at least a taste of the promise of American life. Political experiments like the primary, the initiative, and the referendum sought to restore a sense of contact and meaning to the individual's relationship with government. Governors, mayors, and Congressmen dramatized efforts to revise old municipal codes, to discover more equitable methods of taxation, to beautify an increasingly ugly physical environment, to use the resources of government to inspect and standardize foods and drugs, to improve the vitality of public-school systems and toy with expanding the curricula, to control the vast transportation and communications networks whose franchises were often bought with bribery and extortion, and to extend the protection of the state to women and children victimized by the demands of the industrial system. Many of these efforts left basic problems untouched and were far from solving the misery of millions of toiling farmers and workers; but they had indicated the possibilities of collective action and introduced a new generation to the excitement of political reform.

Above all, the urge for improvement that dominated the politics and social life of the first decade of the century led many Americans to reconsider the purposes of their national life, to examine the costs that growth carried with it. Old ideas of mission and special purpose, which had characterized the American experiment in previous centuries, were expressed now in a new language, suited to the complexities of the twentieth century. In rhetoric that was both flamboyant and inspiring, political leaders sought to reassure their troubled countrymen that the possibilities of power were good as well as dangerous and that the people could again become their own masters. Artists and writers, as well as politicians, were discovering new patterns of beauty and new possibilities of order in the vast commercial and technological monuments being erected across the nation. This sense of optimism and energy was no substitute for answers to the problems and frequently was marred by nostalgia and moral narrowness. Nonetheless the thrust of progress had finally brought with it a self-consciousness and insight that was indispensable for future national development. Material growth alone was no longer sufficient to guarantee the country's safety, and, by expressing their hopes as well as fears, Progressive leaders articulated modern versions of an older dream of dignity.

Then, in the summer of 1914, the murder of an Austrian prince at Sarajevo touched off the greatest armed conflict Europe had ever witnessed. By September, the great powers had begun to pour giant armies into a seemingly inexhaustible sink of death and destruction. Americans would enter this war, optimistically and confidently carrying the Progressive spirit of domestic reform into the world arena. But disillusionment grew quickly, first about ventures abroad, then about conditions at home. The 1920s, for all the popular notions of a roaring time, with flappers frenetically dancing the Charleston in gay speakeasies, was a decade marked by the most fundamental kinds of doubts and fears, an era when Americans were hard put to accept external responsibilities or to tolerate internal differences. Their responses ranged from private escapism to public repression. The 1920s, in other words, was an era not so much of song and dance as of isolationism, prohibition, immigration restriction, and the Ku Klux Klan.

Although Woodrow Wilson won re-election in 1916 on the slogan, "He kept us out of war," the President did not keep his promise very long. No doubt Wilson and his countrymen would have preferred to remain neutral in World War I; there were the many problems of industrialism, and no tradition was stronger than avoiding entanglement in European affairs. Yet they were drawn into the conflict, as Wilson, a proud and moralistic man, insisted on exercising and defending the right of neutral American ships to carry on trade. When the German command decided that all-out submarine warfare could bring victory and ignored the rights of neutrals to execute the strategy, American ships were sunk and Wilson had no choice except to ask Congress to declare war; but to compensate the nation, Wilson promised in the best Progressive tradition that this would be no ordinary war. It would accomplish nothing less than to end all wars, and to make the world safe for democracy. Rather than insist that our national self-interest was at stake or that an Allied victory was critical to America's immediate welfare, Wilson turned the war into a crusade, elevating participation to the highest possible plane. Indeed the rhetoric made it seem that the very millennium would accompany the peace.

However, peace brought conferences and further entanglements in the intricacies of European diplomacy, unavoidable compromises, and eventual disillusionments. Wilson went to meet the Allies at Paris and tried his best to keep the treaty negotiations as open and as democratic as possible; still, secret treaties often undermined his efforts. He argued vigorously and persuasively for self-determination for hitherto dependent nationalities, but all too often the ambitions of victorious powers determined the drawing of new boundary lines.

Yet Wilson achieved one critical victory: the creation of a League of Nations that would, he believed, be able to correct any errors or injustices. Linking it to the peace treaty as the best guarantee of future world security, Wilson returned home to defend his work.

Critics, especially in the Senate, immediately took him to task. They pointed to every instance in the peace treaty where the provisions had fallen short of Wilson's ideals, reiterating their distrust of European diplomatic maneuvers. They made the focus of their attacks the League, asserting that membership would imperil national sovereignty, that American troops would be at the beck and call of an international power. Wilson explained that the commitments would be moral, not legal, and that only Congress could declare war, but still the debate and stances hardened. A majority of the electorate would probably have preferred the country to join the League, but Wilson could not translate popular sentiments into a legislative victory. He suddenly fell ill in the midst of the battle, and his debility, his heavy-handed moralism, and his lack of political astuteness together with the determination of hard-core opponents combined to defeat the League. All the promises of war and peace evaporated.

These events cast a pall over the next decade, breeding a deep and widely shared cynicism. Wilson became the President who promised peace and delivered war; Americans were deceived by Allied propaganda or were the helpless victims of the munitions makers in search of greater profits. The promises of a war to end all wars rang hollow in the 1920s and robbed all ideological or high-sounding phrases of meaning. Having been taken in by one set of grandiose promises, Americans were not going to open themselves to similar disappointments again. Isolationism came to dominate public opinion. The country would have no part of the notion that power brought responsibility in world affairs. It turned its back on Europe—and as Franklin D. Roosevelt would discover in the 1930s, it would not easily be persuaded to change posture.

Americans also abandoned during this decade the Progressive faith that immigrants would easily and creditably integrate into the society. Progressives had confidently sponsored a variety of institutions to assimilate the newcomer: schools, settlement houses, and charitable organizations taught the immigrant to substitute American customs for eastern or southern European ones. These institutions, to be sure, showed little respect for Old World traditions and were impatient with non-American ways of doing things; but they operated on a voluntary basis, without threat or compulsion, hoping to set a persuasive example. In the 1920s, however, Americans grew far more distrustful of the immigrant and uneasy with the implications of a heterogeneous society. They were angry, on the one hand, that immigrants did not disappear or totally assimilate into the melting pot; they were jealous, on the other hand, when immigrants made advances in politics, business, or culture. Without the essential optimism of the Progressives, this generation turned from persuasion to coercion, from voluntary institutions to binding laws, moving at once to cut off the flow of newcomers and to harass those already here.

One of the first results of this shift was Prohibition as expressed in the Eighteenth Amendment, adopted in 1919, outlawing the sale of liquor. Convinced that it was no coincidence that bars and taverns flourished in lower-class immigrant neighborhoods, many Americans concluded that drinking made the immigrant poor, disorderly, and dangerous. Drunkedness was an unwelcome remnant of corrupt Old World customs, and by avoiding temptation, the immigrant could become a hard-working citizen and better American. No longer certain that persuasion would do, the country turned to compulsory legislation. Prohibition, still half-rooted in the Progressive era, was a mild step compared to later measures. Indeed one of the reasons that Prohibition was never vigorously enforced through the 1920s was because the groups that supported it most eagerly at first soon turned to still more coercive and compulsory measures: immigration restriction and Ku Klux Klan activities.

The movement for immigration restriction achieved its major goals in the 1920s. Congressional legislation not only limited the total number of immigrants but placed special restrictions on those from southern and eastern Europe. The law established yearly quotas for various national groups; and to insure that the newer immigrants—the Poles, the Slovaks, the Italians, the Jews—would no longer compose the bulk of entering foreigners, it based the quotas on the percentages of immigrants here in 1890. The date was carefully chosen, for very few of these groups were as yet present in any size. The popular rationale for this decision rested on the prevailing theories of race superiority and inferiority—arguments that enjoyed a great vogue during these years. The Anglo-Saxons stood at the highest end of the scale; Africans were at the bottom, and the Mediterranean types (Jews and Italians) near them. Popular prejudice armed with a specious but general theory combined effectively to cut off the flow of immigrants.

The Ku Klux Klan for its part tried to make life as terrifying as possible for immigrants already here, especially the Catholics. Although Southern in inspiration and origins, the bulk of the Klan's membership and activities in the 1920s centered in Midwestern and border states, often in cities with mixed populations like Chicago or Indianapolis. The Klan filled two critical functions for its members. First, through ceremonies, passwords, costumes, and marches, it gave the lower middle-class Americans a sense of comradeship and excitement, enlivening life in dull, drab, and isolated small towns, supplying a sense of identity and belonging in larger cities. Secondly, and most important, it permitted members to express frustrations and prejudices against anyone or anything that was different. Bewildered by change, threatened by the unfamiliar, frightened that others were making their mark in a changing America while they stood still, Klansmen donned masks, burned crosses, and somehow hoped to preserve their importance and their values.

They achieved some victories. They saw in Prohibition a national law that wrote their values into the Constitution; they saw in immigration restriction a confirmation of their mistrust of foreigners; but soon internal corruption and

361

scandal struck the Klan, and condemnations of the secret organization increased. By the end of the decade the Klan was practically dead. Still its power and influence in the 1920s were testimony to the extraordinary fears that gripped many Americans.

The more serious problems confronting the nation in this decade received far too little attention. Caught up in worrying about immigrants and intemperance, Americans did not look closely at their economy to see whether the surface prosperity went very deep. Well before the Depression, farmers had fallen on hard times; having expanded their production during World War I, they now faced glutted markets at home and abroad. Labor-union victories in the first decade of the twentieth century were not maintained into the 1920s, and the bulk of workers had no protection against wage reductions or unemployment. Moreover, no one looked with any care at business practices, content to abdicate the task of regulation; but business did not fulfill its responsibility adequately. The manipulation of the stock market was the outstanding example of the unchecked dominance of private over public welfare. These failings became only too apparent when Black Friday 1929, crash day at Wall Street, signaled the start of a decade-long depression.

The nation's political leaders sat undisturbed, content to utter truisms rather than educate the public to necessary reforms. The Presidents set the tone. Warren Harding was a jovial, warm-hearted, and incompetent President, who also had the misfortune of being betrayed by his friends. Corruption during his administration was even more widespread than during the worst days of the Gilded Age. His successor Calvin Coolidge had risen to national prominence as the Governor who broke a Boston police strike; in the White House he was known as a man of few words rather than for the quality of anything he said or did. Perhaps the most qualified was Herbert Hoover. His reputation as a brilliant administrator was well earned. In charge of distributing American war relief to Europe, he fulfilled the task efficiently and humanely; but as President he was a prisoner of his unwavering hostility to any interference by government in the economy. He too was content to let matters take their own course, even in the first years of the Depression. With these men in the White House, it was not surprising that a good part of the nation never understood the irrationality of its fears or the issues that needed its attention. One of Franklin D. Roosevelt's many accomplishments would be the skillful education in realities that he gave his countrymen.

35

The Omaha Convention
of 1892

The farmer's revolt against the inequities of American life reached a political climax in the summer of 1892 when the People's Party met in Omaha to nominate a Presidential candidate. For years farmers had been complaining about the low prices of their crops, and the high prices of railroads, telephones, storaging, and servicing, which had cut their profit margins almost to a vanishing point. With the two major political parties apparently impervious to their demands, the protestors decided to organize their own vehicle, and in Omaha they nominated an old Greenbacker and Civil War veteran, James B. Weaver, as their candidate on a platform aimed at monopolies and wealthy interests. The Convention was a picturesque assemblage of men and women who felt outside the mainstream of recent American events. They sought to purify American life with an almost evangelical fervor. Some of the flavor of their rhetoric, as well as the substance of their program, is contained in the following account, published by the Populist's that same year.

THE LIFE AND PUBLIC SERVICES
OF JAMES BAIRD WEAVER
E. A. Allen

The National Convention of the People's Party convened in Omaha at 10 o'clock, Saturday, July 2d, 1892. Long before the hour of gathering the vast hall was crowded with visitors. The scene presented characteristics of a great National Convention. There was one significant difference between the gathering and the national conclaves of the Democratic and Republican Parties held a few days ago.

In the Convention the politician was conspicuously absent. Tactics and subterfuge gave place to open declarations, and all there was of politics at this Convention was on the surface and was plainly manifested in every demonstration that occasion afforded. Indeed, there was little of that competition for factional advantage that is typical of all other National Conventions. Everybody seemed to be in a congratulatory mood over the large attendance to the Convention, and there was a general determination that harmony should be preserved on all questions, and

From *The Life and Public Services of James Baird Weaver* (n.p., 1892), 53–66, 75–77, 96–101.

that the most available man should be selected to lead the fight in the coming campaign.

Even in the Convention, the People's Party would seem anxious to preserve an individuality and to set at defiance an example of two great Parties whose National Conventions have been held.

By 11 o'clock the part of the hall allotted to delegates was fairly well filled, most of the delegates being present, but in much confusion.

The general remark was that it was a fine looking body of men. Strong and striking physiognomies were present. Cranks and odd creatures, however, were occasionally seen. Before the Convention was called to order straw hats predominated. Compared with the Minneapolis and Chicago Conventions the Omaha Convention was not so well dressed, though it appeared by no means poverty stricken.

The extensive preparations made by the Democrats at the Wigwam at Chicago, and by the Republicans at Minneapolis, are noted by their absence at the Coliseum at Omaha. Nevertheless, the building presented a gay and inviting appearance, as the delegates began to assemble, and as the hour for the meeting approached an exhibition of enthusiasm was added to this sprightliness, which could not be exceeded if the hall would contain 100,000 instead of one-tenth that number.

The circular building had been arranged in terraces, with a number of outlets, which prevented anything approaching confusion. Flags and banners floated from every pillar and arch, and the display of evergreens is something in the nature of triumphal arches, not the less inviting because of their scarcity, adding a degree of freshness to the scene. The delegates were slow in arriving. The press were first to enter, and delegation after delegation followed, and the hall became full of industrial leaders in straw hats and breezy attire, in keeping with the day.

There was a slight lull as Chairman Taubeneck, of the National Committee, announced that the first National Convention of the People's Party was now convened in regular session. Then followed a burst of applause. Prayer was offered by Rev. Diffenbacher, a well known Alliance man. Mayor Bemis, of Omaha, heartily welcomed the delegates, and then Ben Terrell, of Texas, was introduced as "the hero of the Alliance movement from its earliest day."

Prolonged cheers greeted Mr. Terrell's appearance. Mr. Terrell paid a graceful tribute to Omaha's Mayor and continued: "This Convention is indeed a protest against present conditions. It is utterly impossible to stay the movement. If every leader of this movement, I care not who he is, be he Powderly (cheers) or Weaver, that we trust above all men as a patriotic man, or whoever you may name—if they were to-day to put themselves in opposition the movement would sweep over them and their names be forgotten. (Applause.)

"Never before in this country has such a Convention been assembled. I believe there is no man here seeking position. I have never before attended a Convention where every man desired success to everything and was perfectly willing to lay down personal ambition to secure it.

"As to the South, I want to say it is imbued with the same spirit you are. (Cheers.) The South will vote for the man who stands on the St. Louis platform, be he who he may, and the man from the South who does not share this spirit had better leave the hall." (Cheers.) The speaker then declared that the People's Party had ended sectionalism, and for that alone was entitled to the gratitude of the people.

C. H. Ellington, of Georgia, was introduced as temporary Chairman, and in his speech of acceptance he said: "Ladies and gentlemen, fellow-countrymen and brethren—I salute you. From far-off Georgia, the great Empire State of the South, I come to greet you. Language fails me. It is impossible to tell my high appreciation of the honor this greatest of Conventions has conferred upon me by electing me to the Temporary Chairmanship. But when my mind turns to the great purpose for which we have met—its mighty depth, length, breadth, its wonderful conception, all that is wrapped up in what it means to us to be defeated and what it would mean should victory crown our efforts—all these things crowd upon me, and I long for the tongue of Gabriel, whose trumpet tones shall reach to the farthest end of the globe, rousing and convening the people wherever its sound shall fall upon them.

"In all the history of this country, the land of the free, the home of the brave, there has never been another such gathering of people. (Applause.) North, South, East or West are to-day mingling their hosts together in a sense and for a purpose never before realized in this country. (Applause.) When, in the early days of this new country, our forefathers fought for their liberty and won, it was with a different foe and by use of different means. The battlefield which settled the fight was a long, bloody one. Again, when we fought in the late rivalry, though between brother and brother, between those who were bone of the same bone and flesh of the same flesh, the fight was a bloody one, and now, for the first time, the classes in these United States are marching and marshaling their armies for the greatest struggle the world ever saw. (Cheers.) A mortal combat is on, and the ballot will be the weapon of war. (Cheers.)

"The eyes of the world are upon us. Some are looking at us with hate and fear in their hearts, while others are watching us prayerfully, anxiously and hopefully. Nothing would give more joy to our opponents than to see this vast assemblage disagree. They want us to bicker and wrangle. Hundreds of pens stand ready to note the first word of discord, and in every direction the wires are waiting to transmit the hoped-for news. Brethren, friends, let us disappoint them and from the very beginning shake hands upon this one point that harmony, unity and good will shall prevail. (Cheers.) Let us lay aside all selfish individual feeling, all personal ambition that may by any possibility tend to disharmonize, and coming together in the spirit of pure fractional feeling, determined that the dominant principle shall be patriotism, pure and simple, and the desire for the general and permanent prosperity of the people. (Cheers.) I believe it is possible for this representative body to meet, counsel, perform its work and adjourn without one single word of discord, one atom of hateful strife to mar and deface its glorious record. To this end I am absolutely, untiringly at your service. We have reached the crisis in our history, and this meeting will show, whether or not we measure up the responsibilities of the hour.

"The subscribers here desire to tender you our utmost thanks. Nothing would please us better than to meet with you, that we might clasp hands and exchange with you words of encouragement as the co-workers in the great struggle now going on between the people and those who live and fatten through class laws and the violation of the law. But, however pleasant it might be for us to meet and enjoy a general hand-shaking, yet in our opinion those of us who are not delegates should remain here to watch the work which the people have given us to do.

"The two Wall Street Parties have held their Conventions. They have nominated their canditates and are marshalling their hosts. One side is engaged in 'putting the rascals out,' the other in 'keeping them in.' They have no aims or objects but the spoils of office, while the people are sinking from affluence to penury, and laborers in the cities, factories, shops and mines are dying of starvation and by Pinkerton bullets. It is the mission of our new party, then, to restore to the people their God-given rights and the scepter of the Government; to restore the people their lands and their confiscated highways, and to wrest from corporations and money kings the control of the people's money and all the other appliances of commerce and of our Christian civilization. We have full faith in your united wisdom. We believe you will select for our great party of the people standard-bearers who are worthy of the times and the occasion, and you will arrange the necessary details for a vigorous and successful campaign. The times are auspicious. Men are everywhere surrendering their party predjudices and trampling under foot old party lines. They are crying out on all sides—North, South, East and West—'What must we do to be saved.' Let us on with the work so nobly begun by our patriotic fathers, that the Government of the people, by the people, and for the people shall not perish from the earth.

"Accept, gentlemen, our fraternal regards, and may the great Ruler of Nations guide your councils."

W. A. Peffer, U. S. Senate

Ignatius Donnelly, of Minnesota, was introduced, pending the Committee's report, and spoke at length on the issues of the People's party:

"I do not mean," said Mr. Donnelly, "to indulge in any words of idle compliments—for the dignity of the occasion forbids it—when I say that no greater body of men has ever assembled upon this continent than those who sit here to-day, since those men met who formulated the immortal Declaration of Independence.

"It is in many respects the most astonishing gathering this country has ever seen—a Convention without a single tool or instrument of monopoly in its midst; a Convention whose every man has paid the expenses of his journey thither and his return, or which have been paid by a man as poor as himself. (Cheers.)

"There is not in this gathering a single President of a railroad (cheers); there is not a single representative of an army or rings which are robbing and sucking the life blood out of the American people. (Cheers.)

"I can not help but think of the astounding contrast this body presents to the Conventions which have recently met in Minneapolis and Chicago. One little point emphasizes the difference, and should be sufficient in itself to show the American people who are its friends.

"There are in this Convention delegates from the distant State of California, and they could not obtain the same railroad concessions that are granted to the National Conventions. They are here at a cost, as I am informed, of $150 to each of them. I am told that there are delegates here from Wyoming who traveled 300 miles in farm-wagons to reach the nearest depot where they could take the train for Omaha. (Cries of "Hurrah for Wyoming.")

"One hundred and sixteen years of national life under the management of two great parties has given us, according to the different estimates, from 8,000 to 30,000 millionaires, and 1,500,000 tramps, while the whole land is blistered with mortgages and the whole people are steeped to the lips in poverty. My friends, every great fight that was ever made in the past for right and liberty culminates in this present gathering. Every battlefield of the past fought to make men more free, more happy and more prosperous, has shed the fruits of victory upon this great assemblage. (Cheers.) What a contrast to that Minneapolis Convention. The leading man of that body, the man most petted, and dined and wined, was Chauncey M. Depew, twenty times a millionaire, President of two railroad companies and representative of the Vanderbilt's $200,000,000. Why he could not sneeze but the Republican papers had pictures of him in every point of the process. (Laughter and cheers.) I had a debate the other day in Minnesota, with a representative speaker of the Republican party, and I challenged him to point to a man in the great Convention who could be mentioned in one breath with the great philanthropist and humanitarian who founded the Republican party. Where is your Horace Greeley, your Charles Sumner, your Wendell Phillips, your Abraham Lincoln? I asked him to point me out a single friend of labor in the Convention, a single friend of the farmer, a single friend of the mechanic; what was the answer? I was given as an example of the philanthropist, Fred Douglass. (Cheers.) 'Why,' I replied, 'you have to go out of your own color to find an example.' (Cheers.)

"And when I asked for another name, I was given the name of William McKinley, Jr., (laughter) a man who put up the tariff for the benefit of the protectionist manufacturers to increase burdens of the people. That is Republican philanthropy. It would be a miracle if the American people had not by this time appreciated Bill McKinley's philanthropy. I want it understood that I am not saying anything against the rank and fame of either of these parties. (Cries of "Good.") The whole American people have been in one or the other of these parties, and as the American people are, in my judgment, the best and noblest people on the face of the earth, it would not become me to accuse either of them, but the leaders, the politics and the Conventions of these parties, are legitimate subjects for comment. They point in the direction of this terrible power of pleutocracy that has got the whole country by the throat."

In conclusion Mr. Donnelly said: "I am willing that the Southern delegates to this Convention should meet and agree upon a candidate for President, and I will pledge for the man so nominated the unanimous support of Minnesota; I can promise you the solid Electoral vote of Minnesota for the People's Party. I believe that I can promise that Nebraska will go the same way, and North and South Carolina and Georgia. I know that we can count on Kansas. I tell you, there is no such word as fail, so far as this movement is concerned."

It was the desire of the People's Party delegates to set an example for sobriety and the observance of the Sabbath Day for the other political parties. The necessity for such a course may be better understood by reading the following, taken from a prominent Chicago paper:

"The Democrats do not mean to be outdone by the Republicans. The drunkenness and debauchery that characterized the Minneapolis Convention have been equaled, if not surpassed, by the Democrats in session in Chicago. With the first arrival of delegations and boomers the carnival of drink began. Saturday night squads of drunken men could be seen reeling from saloon to saloon. Sunday matters got worse. Sunday night a mob of yelling, half-drunken men crowded the lobby of the Palmer House, and in nearly every saloon within a mile of the center of the city crowds of men could be found drinking, fighting, cursing, and shouting for Cleveland, Hill, Boies, Gorman, or some other candidate. The dens of the 'levee' were crowded with men wearing badges indicating their choice for President. A little after midnight Sunday the Calumet Club, of Maryland, arrived, and, headed by a brass band, marched up to the Tremont House. Five minutes after breaking ranks they lined up four deep before the long bar of the Tremont House, waiting for drinks. The bar rooms and saloons had made great preparations. Chicago's capacity in a saloon line is very large under ordinary circumstances. There are hundreds of dens and gin shops within a radius of a mile of the court-house. On Sunday night they all did a tremendous business. Their capacity was taxed to its utmost. Monday night was even worse. More delegates and boomers had arrived. The crowds were large. Vice and drunkenness did not abate in the least, but grew visible. At midnight carriages were rolling down the streets, filled with drunken, shouting men. The yells of intoxicated men resounded through the streets and pandemonium broke loose. Down on the dark avenues, where vice reigns supreme, was a terrible scene. The streets were filled with carriages carrying enthusiastic delegates from place to place. Wine, beer, and whisky flowed like water, and the shouts of the revelers could be heard on every side. Crowds of men filed out of one gilded gin-shop and den only to enter another a few doors away. The scenes that were enacted were too disgraceful to print.

"Not until the gray light of morning appeared did the shouts of the revelers die away. One by one, overcome by liquor and tired out with the night's debauch, they fell into a drunken sleep. The saloon-keepers and den-owners counted over the harvest they had reaped, safely stowed away their ill-gotten gains, and congratulated themselves on the character of the representatives of the great political party that had gathered in this city.

"These men were to assemble a few hours later to help select the candidates of one of the large parties for the highest offices in our nation. They were to frame a platform of principles to guide the legislation of the United States. They were preparing for this task in a manner which should strike terror to the hearts of the patriotic, sober manhood of this country. And their preparation for this important service was a drunken debauch! Is it possible that Christian men can train and vote with a party which is represented by so many of this class of citizens?"

People's Party Platform

ADOPTED AT OMAHA, NEB., JULY 4, 1892

Preamble

Assembled upon the one hundred and sixteenth anniversary of the Declaration of Independence, the People's party of America, in their first National Convention, invoking upon their action the blessing of Almighty God, puts forth, in the name and on behalf of the people of this country, the following preamble and declaration of principles:

The conditions which surround us best justify our cooperation. We meet in the midst of a nation brought to the verge of political and material ruin; corruption dominates the ballot-box, the Legislature, the Congress, and touching even the ermine of the bench. The people are demoralized; most of the States have been compelled to isolate the voters at the polling places to prevent universal intimidation or bribery. The newspapers are subsidized or muzzled; public opinion silenced; business prostrated; our homes covered with mortgages, labor impoverished, and the land concentrating in the hands of the capitalists.

The urban workmen are denied the rights of organization for self protection; imported, pauperized labor beats down their wages; a hireling standing army, unrecognized by our laws, is established to shoot them down, and they are rapidly degenerating into European conditions. The fruits of the toil of millions are boldly stolen to build up colossal fortunes for a few, unprecedented in the history of mankind; and the possessors of these, in turn, despise the republic and endanger liberty. From the same prolific womb of governmental injustice we breed the two great classes—tramps and millionaires. The national power to create money is appropriated to enrich bond-holders; a vast public debt, payable in legal tender currency, has been funded into gold-bearing bonds, thereby adding millions to the burdens of the people.

Silver which has been used as coin since the dawn of history, has been demonetized to add to the purchasing power of gold by decreasing the value of all forms of property as well as human labor, and the supply of currency is purposely abridged to fatten usurers, bankrupt enterprise and enslave industry. A vast conspiracy against mankind has been organized on two continents, and is rapidly taken possession of the world. If not met and overthrown at once it forbodes terrible social convultions, the destruction of civilization or the establishment of an absolute despotism.

We have witnessed for more than a quarter of a century the struggles of the two great political parties for power and plunder, while grievous wrongs have been inflicted on the suffering people. We charge that the controlling influences dominating both these parties have permitted the existing dreadful conditions to develop without serious effort to prevent or restrain them. Neither do they promise any substantial reform. They have agreed together to ignore, in the coming campaign, every issue but one. They propose to drown the outcries of a plundered people with the uproar of a sham battle over the tariff, so that capitalists, corporations, national banks, trusts, watered stock, the demonetization of silver and

369

the oppression of the usurers may all be lost sight of. They propose to sacrifice our homes, lives and children on the altar of Mammon; to destroy the multitude in order to secure corruption funds from the millionaires.

Assembled on the anniversary of the birth of our nation, and filled with the spirit of the grand generation who established our independence, we seek to restore the government of the Republic to the hands of the "plain people," with whose class it originated. We assert our purpose to be identical with the purposes of the national constitution: To form a more perfect union, establish justice, insure domestic tranquility, provide for the common defense, promote the general welfare, and secure the blessing of liberty for ourselves and our posterity.

We declare that this republic can only endure as a free government while built upon the love of the whole people for each other and for the nation; that it cannot be pinned together by bayonets; that the civil war is over, and that every passion and resentment which grew out of it must die with it, and that we must be in fact, as we are in name, one united brotherhood of free men.

Our country finds itself confronted by conditions for which there is no precedent in the history of the world; our annual agricultural productions amount to billions of dollars in value, which must within a few weeks perhaps be exchanged for billions of dollars of commodities consumed in their production; the existing currency supply is wholly inadequate to make this exchange. The results are falling prices, the formation of combines and rings, the impoverishment of the producing class. We pledge ourselves that if given power we will labor to correct these evils by wise and reasonable legislation in accordance with the terms of our platform.

We believe that the powers of government should be expanded as in the case of the postal service, as rapidly and as far as the good sense of an intelligent people and the teachings of experience shall justify, to the end that oppression, injustice and poverty shall eventually cease in the land.

While our sympathies, as a party of reform, are naturally upon the side of every proposition that will tend to make men intelligent, virtuous and temperate, we nevertheless regard these questions, important as they are, subordinate to the great issues now pressing for solution, and upon which not only our individual prosperity, but the very existence of free institutions depends; and we ask all men to first help us determine whether we are to have a republic to administer before we differ as to the condition upon which it is to be administered, believing that the forces of reform this day organized will never cease to move forward until every wrong is remedied and the equal rights and equal privileges securely established for all the men and women of the country. We declare therefore,

1. That the union of the labor forces of the United States, this day consummated shall be permanent and perpetual. May its spirit come into all hearts for the salvation of the republic and the uplifting of mankind.

2. Wealth belongs to him who creates it, and every dollar taken from industry, without an equivalent, is robbery. "If any will not work, neither shall he eat." The interests of rural and civic labor are the same; their enemies are identical.

We believe that the time has come when the railroad corporations will either own the people or the people must own the railroads, and should the government enter upon the work of owning the managing any or all railroads, we should favor an amendment to the constitution by which all persons engaged in the government service shall be placed under civil service regulation of the most rigid character, so as to prevent the increase of the power of the national administration by the use of such additional government employes.

Finance. First

We demand a national currency, safe, sound and flexible, issued by the general government only, a full legal tender for all debts, public and private; and that without the use of banking corporations, a just, equitable and efficient means of distribution direct to the people at a tax not to exceed 2 per cent to be provided as set forth in the subtreasury plan of the Farmers' Alliance, or some better system; also by payment in discharge of its obligations for public improvements.

a. We demand the free and unlimited coinage of silver.

b. We demand that the amount of circulating medium be speedily increased to not less than $50 per capita.

c. We demand a graduated income tax.

d. We believe that the money of the country should be kept as much as possible in the hands of the people, and hence we demand all national and State revenue shall be limited to the necessary expenses of the government economically and honestly administered.

e. We demand that postal savings banks be established by the government for the safe deposit of the earnings of the people and to facilitate exchange.

Land. Second

The land, including all the natural resources of wealth, is the heritage of all the people and should not be monopolized for speculative purposes, and alien ownership of land should be prohibited. All land now held by railroads and other corporations in excess of their actual needs, and all lands now owned by aliens, should be reclaimed by the government, and held for actual settlers only.

Transportation. Third

Transportation being a means of exchange and a public necessity, the government should own and operate the railroads in the interest of the people.

a. The telegraph and telephone, like the post-office system, being a necessity for the transmission of news, should be owned and operated by the government in the interest of the people.

The reading of nearly every plank of the platform proper was received with some applause. The free silver plank was enthusiastically greeted with cheers, and the Government ownership of the railroads plank again got a tumultous greeting, in which it was noticeable that Nebraska, Georgia, Kansas and Texas led. Applause and cries of "Amen" from all parts of the house was the reception accorded the paragraph favoring Government control of the telephone and telegraph lines. A regular Baptist camp-meeting chorus greeted the land plank.

The conclusion of the reading of the platform was warmly greeted. Its adoption was instantly moved, and, though a Missouri delegate was striving for some

371

unknown purpose to get recognition, it was put through by unanimous consent, the whole Convention rising in advance of the Chair and adopting the platform almost before he could move its adoption.

At once on the adoption of the platform the Convention broke over all restraint and went wild in a demonstration that had a likeness to description of enthusiastic Bastile demonstrations in France. The whole Convention, delegates and audience, rose to their feet and the first platform of the People's party was ushered into the world with a scene of enthusiasm, though not in absolute length, almost equal to the cyclonic ovation which greeted the mention of the name of James G. Blaine, at Minneapolis. That scene lasted thirty-one minutes, and this scene between twenty and twenty-five minutes.

It began by the Convention rising in their chairs, cheering, swinging coats, which had been taken off on account of the heat, waving hats and fans, and throwing things in the air. All the delegates were on their feet and the stage was crowded with members of the Committee on Resolutions. Several delegates seized Branch, of Georgia, Chairman, and trotted him up and down the main aisle on their shoulders.

The uproar continued tremendously. As if by a flash a number of delegates seized the uprights used to hold the placards designating the place of State delegations in the hall, and rushed with them to the platform, forming a cordon about the whole platform. Banners were also borne there. The New Yorkers seized old man Lloyd, of New York, whose beaming, ruddy, face, long, white locks and beard gave him a Rip Van Winkle aspect, and, bearing him on their shoulders, placed him in the very front of the phalanx on the stage, where he was handed a baton, and enthusiastically beat time to the wild cheering of the crowd.

36

The Negro's Strategy

However bright the promise of the Progressive Era seemed to many reformers, the American Negro continued to experience degradation and repression, North and South. Lynchings, segregation, economic deprivation, and legal discrimination of all sorts made life bleak for millions of black Americans.

Solutions to the problem varied. One of the most influential programs was offered by Booker T. Washington (1856–1915), born a slave in Virginia. After emancipation, Washington managed to attend school, and in 1872 he entered Hampton Institute, where he worked his way through as a janitor. Some years later Washington was asked to take charge of a newly established Negro normal school (for training teachers) in Tuskegee, Alabama. Washington developed there a nationally famous educational center, and established a world-wide reputation as a spokesman for the American Negro. His program of industrial progress, self-help, personal discipline, and political moderation was epitomized in his famous 1893 address in Atlanta, the text of which follows.

Washington was willing to sacrifice immediate political equality for economic advances; others angrily refused to do so. W. E. B. DuBois (1868–1963), a Harvard-trained sociologist, expressed a more radical view. As the twentieth century proceeded, his objectives gained greater support, and DuBois went on to help found the NAACP, carrying forth an active career of political leadership and creative scholarship.

UP FROM SLAVERY
Booker T. Washington

In my early life I used to cherish a feeling of ill will toward any one who spoke in bitter terms against the Negro, or who advocated measures that tended to oppress the black man or take from him opportunities for growth in the most complete manner. Now, whenever I hear any one advocating measures that are meant to curtail the development of another, I pity the individual who would do this. I know that the one who makes this mistake does so because of his lack of opportunity for

From *Up from Slavery, An Autobiography* (New York, 1901), 203–204, 206, 208–213, 215–226, 229–230, 234–237.

the highest kind of growth. I pity him because I know that he is trying to stop the progress of the world, and because I know that in time the development and the ceaseless advance of humanity will make him ashamed of his weak and narrow position. One might as well try to stop the progress of a mighty railroad train by throwing his body across the track, as to try to stop the growth of the world in the direction of giving mankind more intelligence, more culture, more skill, more liberty, and in the direction of extending more sympathy and more brotherly kindness.

I now come to that one of the incidents in my life which seems to have excited the greatest amount of interest, and which perhaps went farther than anything else in giving me a reputation that in a sense might be called National. I refer to the address which I delivered at the opening of the Atlanta Cotton states and International Exposition, at Atlanta, Ga., September 18, 1895.

The directors of the Exposition decided that it would be a fitting recognition of the coloured race to erect a large and attractive building which should be devoted wholly to showing the progress of the Negro since freedom. It was further decided to have the building designed and erected wholly by Negro mechanics. This plan was carried out. In design, beauty, and general finish the Negro Building was equal to the others on the grounds.

As the day for the opening of the Exposition drew near, the Board of Directors began preparing the programme for the opening exercises. In the discussion from day to day of the various features of this programme, the question came up as to the advisability of putting a member of the Negro race on for one of the opening addresses, since the Negroes had been asked to take such a prominent part in the Exposition. It was argued, further, that such recognition would mark the good feeling prevailing between the two races. After the question had been canvassed for several days, the directors voted unanimously to ask me to deliver one of the opening-day addresses, and in a few days after that I received the official invitation.

The receiving of this invitation brought to me a sense of responsibility that it would be hard for any one not placed in my position to appreciate. What were my feelings when this invitation came to me? I remembered that I had been a slave; that my early years had been spent in the lowest depths of poverty and ignorance, and that I had had little opportunity to prepare me for such a responsibility as this. It was only a few years before that time that any white man in the audience might have claimed me as his slave; and it was easily possible that some of my former owners might be present to hear me speak.

I knew, too, that this was the first time in the entire history of the Negro that a member of my race had been asked to speak from the same platform with white Southern men and women on any important National occasion. I was asked now to speak to an audience composed of the wealth and culture of the white South, the representatives of my former masters. I knew, too, that while the greater part of my audience would be composed of Southern people, yet there would be present a large number of Northern whites, as well as a great many men and women of my own race.

I was determined to say nothing that I did not feel from the bottom of my heart to be true and right. When the invitation came to me, there was not one word of intimation as to what I should say or as to what I should omit. In this I felt that the Board of Directors had paid a tribute to me. They knew that by one sentence I could have blasted, in a large degree, the success of the Exposition. I was also painfully conscious of the fact that, while I must be true to my own race in my utterances, I had it in my power to make such an ill-timed address.

On the morning of September 17, together with Mrs. Washington and my three children, I started for Atlanta. I felt a good deal as I suppose a man feels when he is on his way to the gallows. In passing through the town of Tuskegee I met a white farmer who lived some distance out in the country. In a jesting manner this man said: "Washington, you have spoken before the Northern white people, the Negroes in the South, and to us country white people in the South; but in Atlanta, to-morrow, you will have before you the Northern whites, the Southern whites, and the Negroes all together. I am afraid that you have got yourself into a tight place." This farmer diagnosed the situation correctly, but his frank words did not add anything to my comfort.

Early in the morning a committee called to escort me to my place in the procession which was to march to the Exposition grounds. In this procession were prominent coloured citizens in carriages, as well as several Negro military organizations. I noted that the Exposition officials seemed to go out of their way to see that all of the coloured people in the procession were properly placed and properly treated.

The room was very large, and well suited to public speaking. When I entered the room, there were vigorous cheers from the coloured portion of the audience, and faint cheers from some of the white people. I had been told, while I had been in Atlanta, that while many white people were going to be present to hear me speak, simply out of curiosity, and that others who would be present would be in full sympathy with me, there was a still larger element of the audience which would consist of those who were going to be present for the purpose of hearing me make a fool of myself, or, at least, of hearing me say some foolish thing, so that they could say to the officials who had invited me to speak, "I told you so!"

When I arose to speak, there was considerable cheering, especially from the coloured people. As I remember it now, the thing that was uppermost in my mind was the desire to say something that would cement the friendship of the races and bring about hearty coöperation between them. So far as my outward surroundings were concerned, the only thing that I recall distinctly now is that when I got up, I saw thousands of eyes looking intently into my face. The following is the address which I delivered:—

**Mr. President and Gentlemen
of the Board of Directors and Citizens**

One-third of the population of the South is of the Negro race. No enterprise seeking the material, civil, or moral welfare of this section can disregard this element of our population and reach the highest success. I but convey to you, Mr.

President and Directors, the sentiment of the masses of my race when I say that in no way have the value and manhood of the American Negro been more fittingly and generously recognized than by the managers of this magnificant Exposition at every stage of its progress. It is a recognition that will do more to cement the friendship of the two races than any occurrence since the dawn of our freedom.

Not only this, but the opportunity here afforded will awaken among us a new era of industrial progress. Ignorant and inexperienced, it is not strange that in the first years of our new life we began at the top instead of at the bottom; that a seat in Congress or the state legislature was more sought than real estate or industrial skill; that the political convention of stump speaking had more attractions than starting a dairy farm or truck garden.

A ship lost at sea for many days suddenly sighted a friendly vessel. From the mast of the unfortunate vessel was seen a signal, "Water, water: we die of thirst!" The answer from the friendly vessel at once came back, "Cast down your bucket where you are." A second time the signal, "Water, water; send us water!" ran up from the distressed vessel, and was answered, "Cast down your bucket where you are." And a third and fourth signal for water was answered, "Cast down your bucket where you are." The captain of the distressed vessel, at last heeding the injunction, cast down his bucket, and it came up full of fresh, sparkling water from the mouth of the Amazon River. To those of my race who depend on bettering their condition in a foreign land or who underestimate the importance of cultivating friendly relations with the Southern white man, who is their next-door neighbour, I would say: "Cast down your bucket where you are"—cast it down in making friends in every manly way of the people of all races by whom we are surrounded.

Cast it down in agriculture, mechanics, in commerce, in domestic service, and in the professions. And in this connection it is well to bear in mind that whatever other sins the South may be called to bear, when it comes to business, pure and simple, it is in the South that the Negro is given a man's chance in the commercial world, and in nothing is this Exposition more eloquent than in emphasizing this chance. Our greatest danger is that in the great leap from slavery to freedom we may overlook the fact that the masses of us are to live by the productions of our hands, and fail to keep in mind that we shall prosper in proportion as we learn to dignify and glorify common labour and put brains and skill into the common occupations of life; shall prosper in proportion as we learn to draw the line between the superficial and the substantial, the ornamental gewgaws of life and the useful. No race can prosper till it learns that there is as much dignity in tilling a field as in writing a poem. It is at the bottom of life we must begin, and not at the top. Nor should we permit our grievances to overshadow our opportunities.

To those of the white race who look to the incoming of those of foreign birth and strange tongue and habits for the prosperity of the South, were I permitted I would repeat what I say to my own race, "Cast down your bucket where you are." Cast it down among the eight millions of Negroes whose habits you know, whose fidelity and love you have tested in days when to have proved treacherous meant the ruin of your firesides. Cast down your bucket among these people who have, without strikes and labour wars, tilled your fields, cleared your forests, builded your railroads and cities, and brought forth treasures from the bowels of the earth, and helped make possible this magnificent representation of the progress of the South. Casting down your bucket among my people, helping and encouraging them as you are doing on these grounds, and to education of head, hand, and heart, you will find that they will buy your surplus land, make blossom the waste places in your fields, and run your factories. While doing this, you can be sure in the future, as in the past, that you and your families will be surrounded by the most patient, faithful, law-abiding, and unresentful people that the world has seen. As we have proved our loyalty to you in the past, in nursing your children, watching by the sick-bed of your mothers and fathers, and often following them with tear-dimmed eyes to their graves, so in the future, in our humble way, we shall stand by you with a devotion that no foreigner can approach, ready to lay down our lives, if need be, in defence of yours, interlacing our industrial, commercial, civil, and religious life with yours in a way that shall make the interests of both races one. In all things that are purely social we can be as separate as the fingers, yet one as the hand in all things essential to mutual progress.

There is no defence or security for any of us except in the highest intelligence and development of all. If anywhere there are efforts tending to curtail the fullest growth of the Negro, let these efforts be turned into stimulating, encouraging, and making him the most useful and intelligent citizen. Effort or means so invested will pay a thousand per cent interest. These efforts will be twice blessed—"blessing him that gives and him that takes."

There is no escape through law of man or God from the inevitable:—

The laws of changeless justice bind
Oppressor with oppressed;
And close as sin and suffering joined
We march to fate abreast.

Nearly sixteen millions of hands will aid you in pulling the load upward, or they will pull against you the load downward. We shall constitute one-third and more of the ignorance and crime of the South, or one-third its intelligence and progress; we shall contribute one-third to the business and industrial prosperity of the South, or we shall prove a veritable body of death, stagnating, depressing, retarding every effort to advance the body politic.

Gentlemen of the Exposition, as we present to you our humble effort at an exhibition of our progress, you must not expect overmuch. Starting thirty years ago with ownership here and there in a few quilts and pumpkins and chickens (gathered from miscellaneous sources), remember the path that has led from these to the inventions and production of agricultural implements, buggies, steam-engines, newspapers, books, statuary, carving, paintings, the management of drug-stores and banks, has not been trodden without contact with thorns and thistles. While we take pride in what we exhibit as a result of our independent efforts, we do not for a moment forget that our part in this exhibition would fall far short of your expectations but for the constant help that has come to our educational life, not only from the Southern states, but especially from Northern philanthropists, who have made their gifts a constant stream of blessing and encouragement.

The wisest among my race understand that the agitation of questions of social equality is the extremest folly, and that progress in the enjoyment of all the privileges that will come to us must be the result of severe and constant struggle rather than of artificial forcing. No race that has anything to contribute to the markets of the world is long in any degree ostracized. It is important and right that all privileges of the law be ours, but it is vastly more important that we be prepared for the exercises of these privileges. The opportunity to earn a dollar in a factory just now is worth infinitely more than the opportunity to spend a dollar in an opera-house.

In conclusion, may I repeat that nothing in thirty years has given us more hope and encouragement, and drawn us so near to you of the white race, as this opportunity offered by the Exposition; and here bending, as it were, over the altar that represents the results of the struggles of your race and mine, both starting practically empty-handed three decades ago. I pledge that in your effort to work out the great and intricate problem which God has laid at the doors of the South, you shall have at all times the patient, sympathetic help of my race; only let this be constantly in mind, that, while from representations in these buildings of the product of field, of forest, of mine, of factory, letters, and art, much good will come, yet far above and beyond material benefits will be that higher good, that, let us pray God, will come, in a blotting out of sectional differences and racial animosities and suspicions, in a determination to administer absolute justice, in a willing obedience among all classes to the mandates of law. This, then, coupled with our material prosperity, will bring into our beloved South a new heaven and a new earth.

The first thing that I remember, after I had finished speaking, was that Governor Bullock rushed across the platform and took me by the hand, and that others did the same. I received so many and such hearty congratulations that I found it difficult to get out of the building. I did not appreciate to any degree, however, the impression which my address seemed to have made, until the next morning, when I went into the business part of the city. As soon as I was recognized, I was surprised to find myself pointed out and surrounded by a crowd of men who wished to shake hands with me. This was kept up on every street on to which I went, to an extent which embarrassed me so much that I went back to my boarding-place. The next morning I returned to Tuskegee. At the station in Atlanta, and at almost all of the stations at which the train stopped between that city and Tuskegee, I found a crowd of people anxious to shake hands with me.

The papers in all parts of the United States published the address in full, and for months afterward there were complimentary editorial references to it. Mr. Clark Howell, the editor of the Atlanta *Constitution,* telegraphed to a New York paper, among other words, the following, "I do not exaggerate when I say that Professor Booker T. Washington's address yesterday was one of the most notable speeches, both as to character and as to the warmth of its reception, ever delivered to a Southern audience. The address was a revelation. The whole speech is a platform upon which blacks and whites can stand with full justice to each other."

The coloured people and the coloured newspapers at first seemed to be greatly pleased with the character of my Atlanta address, as well as with its reception. But after the first burst of enthusiasm began to die away, and the coloured people began reading the speech in cold type, some of them seemed to feel that they had been hypnotized. They seemed to feel that I had been too liberal in my remarks toward the Southern whites, and that I had not spoken out strongly enough for what they termed the "rights" of the race. For a while there was a reaction, so far as a certain element of my own race was concerned, but later these reactionary ones seemed to have been won over to my way of believing and acting.

I am often asked to express myself more freely than I do upon the political condition and the political future of my race. These recollections of my experience in Atlanta give me the opportunity to do so briefly. My own belief is, although I have never before said so in so many words, that the time will come when the Negro in the South will be accorded all the political rights which his ability, character, and material possessions entitle him to. I think, though, that the opportunity to freely exercise such political rights will not come in any large degree through outside or artificial forcing, but will be accorded to the Negro by the Southern white people themselves, and that they will protect him in the exercise of those rights. Just as soon as the South gets over the old feeling that it is being forced by "foreigners," or "aliens," to do something which it does not want to do, I believe that the change in the direction that I have indicated is going to begin. In fact, there are indications that it is already beginning in a slight degree.

I believe it is the duty of the Negro—as the greater part of the race is already doing—to deport himself modestly in regard to political claims, depending upon the slow but sure influences that proceed from the possession of property, intelligence, and high character for the full recognition of his political rights. I think that the according of the full exercise of political rights is going to be a matter of natural, slow growth, not an over-night, gourd-vine affair. I do not believe that the Negro should cease voting, for a man cannot learn the exercise of self-government by ceasing to vote any more than a boy can learn to swim by keeping out of the water, but I do believe that in his voting he should more and more be influenced by those of intelligence and character who are his next-door neighbours.

I know coloured men who, through the encouragement, help, and advice of Southern white people, have accumulated thousands of dollars' worth of property, but who, at the same time, would never think of going to those same persons for advice concerning the casting of their ballots. This, it seems to me, is unwise and unreasonable, and should cease. In saying this I do not mean that the Negro should truckle, or not vote from principle, for the instant he ceases to vote from principle he loses the confidence and respect of the Southern white man even.

As a rule, I believe in universal, free suffrage, but I believe that in the South we are confronted with peculiar conditions that justify the protection of the ballot in many of the states, for a while at least, either by an educational test, a property test, or by both combined; but whatever tests are required, they should be made to apply with equal and exact justice to both races.

THE SOULS OF BLACK FOLK
W. E. B. DuBois

Mr. Washington represents in Negro thought the old attitude of adjustment and submission; but adjustment at such a peculiar time as to make his programme unique. This is an age of unusual economic development, and Mr. Washington's programme naturally takes an economic cast, becoming a gospel of Work and Money to such an extent as apparently almost completely to overshadow the higher aims of life. Moreover, this is an age when the more advanced races are coming in closer contact with the less developed races, and the race-feeling is therefore intensified; and Mr. Washington's programme practically accepts the alleged inferiority of the Negro races. Again, in our own land, the reaction from the sentiment of war time has given impetus to race-prejudice against Negroes, and Mr. Washington withdraws many of the high demands of Negroes as men and American citizens. In other periods of intensified prejudice all the Negro's tendency to self-assertion has been called forth; at this period a policy of submission is advocated. In the history of nearly all other races and peoples the doctrine preached at such crises has been that manly self-respect is worth more than lands and houses, and that a people who voluntarily surrender such respect, or cease striving for it, are not worth civilizing.

In answer to this, it has been claimed that the Negro can survive only through submission. Mr. Washington distinctly asks that black people give up, at least for the present, three things,—

First, political power,

Second, insistence on civil rights,

Third, higher education of Negro youth,—

and concentrate all their energies on industrial education, the accumulation of wealth, and the conciliation of the South. This policy has been courageously and insistently advocated for over fifteen years, and has been triumphant for perhaps ten years. As a result of this tender of the palm-branch, what has been the return? In these years there have occurred:

1. The disfranchisement of the Negro.

2. The legal creation of a distinct status of civil inferiority for the Negro.

3. The steady withdrawal of aid from institutions for the higher training of the Negro.

These movements are not, to be sure, direct results of Mr. Washington's teachings; but his propaganda has, without a shadow of doubt, helped their speedier accomplishment. The question then comes: Is it possible, and probable, that nine millions of men can make effective progress in economic lines if they are deprived of political rights, made a servile caste, and allowed only the most meagre

From *The Souls of Black Folk* (Chicago, 1904), 50–59.

chance for developing their exceptional men? If history and reason give any distinct answer to these questions, it is an emphatic *No*. And Mr. Washington thus faces the triple paradox of his career:

1. He is striving nobly to make Negro artisans business men and property-owners; but it is utterly impossible, under modern competitive methods, for workingmen and property-owners to defend their rights and exist without the right of suffrage.

2. He insists on thrift and self-respect, but at the same time counsels a silent submission to civic inferiority such as is bound to sap the manhood of any race in the long run.

3. He advocates common-school and industrial training, and depreciates institutions of higher learning; but neither the Negro common-schools, nor Tuskegee itself, could remain open a day were it not for teachers trained in Negro colleges, or trained by their graduates.

In failing thus to state plainly and unequivocally the legitimate demands of their people, even at the cost of opposing an honored leader, the thinking classes of American Negroes would shirk a heavy repsonsibility,—a responsibility to themselves, a responsibility to the struggling masses, a responsibility to the darker races of men whose future depends so largely on this American experiment, but especially a responsibility to this nation,—this common Fatherland. It is wrong to encourage a man or a people in evil-doing; it is wrong to aid and abet a national crime simply because it is unpopular not to do so. The growing spirit of kindliness and reconciliation between the North and South after the frightful difference of a generation ago ought to be a source of deep congratulation to all, and especially to those whose mistreatment caused the war; but if that reconciliation is to be marked by the industrial slavery and civic death of those same black men, with permanent legislation into a position of inferiority, then those black men, if they are really men, are called upon by every consideration of patriotism and loyalty to oppose such a course by all civilized methods, even though such opposition involves disagreement with Mr. Booker T. Washington. We have no right to sit silently by while the inevitable seeds are sown for a harvest of disaster to our children, black and white.

It would be unjust to Mr. Washington not to acknowledge that in several instances he has opposed movements in the South which were unjust to the Negro; he sent memorials to the Louisiana and Alabama constitutional conventions, he has spoken against lynching, and in other ways has openly or silently set his influence against sinister schemes and unfortunate happenings. Notwithstanding this, it is equally true to assert that on the whole the distinct impression left by Mr. Washington's propaganda is, first, that the South is justified in its present attitude toward the Negro because of the Negro's degradation; secondly, that the prime cause of the Negro's failure to rise more quickly is his wrong education in the past; and, thirdly, that his future rise depends primarily on his own efforts. Each of these propositions is a dangerous half-truth. The supplementary truths must never be lost sight of: first, slavery and race-prejudice are potent if not sufficient causes of the Negro's position; second, industrial and common-school training were necessarily slow in planting because they had to await the black teachers trained by higher institutions,—it being extremely doubtful if any essentially different development was possible, and certainly a Tuskegee was unthinkable before 1880; and, third, while it is a great faith to say that the Negro must strive and strive mightily to help himself, it is equally true that unless his striving be not simply seconded, but rather aroused and encouraged, by the initiative of the richer and wiser environing group, he cannot hope for great success.

In his failure to realize and impress this last point, Mr. Washington is especially to be criticised. His doctrine has tended to make the whites, North and South, shift the burden of the Negro problem to the Negro's shoulders and stand aside as critical and rather pessimistic spectators; when in fact the burden belongs to the nation, and the hands of none of us are clean if we bend not our energies to righting these great wrongs.

The South ought to be led, by candid and honest criticism, to assert her better self and do her full duty to the race she has cruelly wronged and is still wronging. The North—her co-partner in guilt—cannot salve her conscience by plastering it with gold. We cannot settle this problem by diplomacy and suaveness, by "policy" alone. If worse come to worst, can the moral fibre of this country survive the slow throttling and murder of nine millions of men?

The black men of America have a duty to perform, a duty stern and delicate,—a forward movement to oppose a part of the work of their greatest leader. So far as Mr. Washington preaches Thrift, Patience, and Industrial Training for the masses, we must hold up his hands and strive with him, rejoicing in his honors and glorying in the strength of this Joshua called of God and of man to lead the headless host. But so far as Mr. Washington apologizes for injustice, North or South, does not rightly value the privilege and duty of voting, belittles the emasculating effects of caste distinctions, and opposes the higher training and ambition of our brighter minds,—so far as he, the South, or the Nation, does this—we must unceasingly and firmly oppose them. By every civilized and peaceful method we must strive for the rights which the world accords to men, clinging unwaveringly to those great words which the sons of the Fathers would fain forget: "We hold these truths to be self-evident: That all men are created equal; that they are endowed by their Creator with certain unalienable rights; that among these are life, liberty, and the pursuit of happiness."

37

The House of Dreams

Jane Addams (1860–1935) was one of the great social reformers of her era. The daughter of an Illinois miller and state senator, she graduated from college intending to become a physician, but after her health failed she abandoned her plans and spent some years traveling in Europe. During a second trip there she was inspired by the work of Toynbee Hall, a settlement in London, and returned to America to begin the country's first great settlement house, Hull House, in Chicago. There she gathered artists, educators, and social workers to help repair the social damage caused by immigration, urbanization, and industrialization. Through nurseries, women's clubs, lectures, theater groups, gymnasiums, she sought to restore a sense of community participation and generational understanding to the people of her neighborhood.

The tact and energy of Miss Addams were matched by her writing skills; in a series of notable books she popularized the causes of social work, community reconstruction, women's rights, and peace. Her works were tied together by a desire to reassert older moral and ethical values in a vocabulary that made them meaningful to victims of rapid change. In 1931, several years before her death, she received the Nobel Peace Prize.

THE HOUSE
OF DREAMS
Jane Addams

To the preoccupied adult who is prone to use the city street as a mere passageway from one hurried duty to another, nothing is more touching than his encounter with a group of children and young people who are emerging from a theater with the magic of the play still thick upon them. They look up and down the familiar street scarcely recognizing it and quite unable to determine the direction of home. From a tangle of "make believe" they gravely scrutinize the real world which they are so reluctant to reënter, reminding one of the absorbed gaze of a child who is groping his way back from fairy-land whither the story has completely transported him.

"Going to the show" for thousands of young people in every industrial city is the only possible road to the realm of mystery and romance; the theater is the only

From *The Spirit of Youth and the City Streets* (New York, 1905), 75–103.

place where they can satisfy that craving for a conception of life higher than that which the actual world offers them. In a very real sense the drama and the drama alone performs for them the office of art as is clearly revealed in their blundering demand stated in many forms for "a play unlike life." The theater becomes to them a "veritable house of dreams" infinitely more real than the noisy streets and the crowded factories.

This first simple demand upon the theater for romance is closely allied to one more complex which might be described as a search for solace and distraction in those moments of first awakening from the glamour of a youth's interpretation of life to the sterner realities which are thrust upon his consciousness. These perceptions which inevitably "close around" and imprison the spirit of youth are perhaps never so grim as the case of the wage-earning child. We can all recall our own moments of revolt against life's actualities, our reluctance to admit that all life was to be as unheroic and uneventful as that which we saw about us, it was too unbearable that "this was all there was" and we tried every possible avenue of escape. As we made an effort to believe, in spite of what we saw, that life was noble and harmonious, as we stubbornly clung to poesy in contradiction to the testimony of our senses, so we see thousands of young people thronging the theaters bent in their turn upon the same quest. The drama provides a transition between the romantic conceptions which they vainly struggle to keep intact and life's cruelties and trivialities which they refuse to admit. A child whose imagination has been cultivated is able to do this for himself through reading and reverie, but for the overworked city youth of meager education, perhaps nothing but the theater is able to perform this important office.

The theater also has a strange power to forecast life for the youth. Each boy comes from our ancestral past not "in entire forgetfulness," and quite as he unconsciously uses ancient war-cries in his street play, so he longs to reproduce and to see set before him the valors and vengeances of a society embodying a much more primitive state of morality than that in which he finds himself. Mr. Patten has pointed out that the elemental action which the stage presents, the old emotions of love and jealousy, of revenge and daring take the thoughts of the spectator back into deep and well worn channels in which his mind runs with a sense of rest afforded by nothing else. The cheap drama brings cause and effect, will power and action, once more into relation and gives a man the thrilling conviction that he may yet be master of his fate. The youth of course, quite unconscious of this psychology, views the deeds of the hero simply as a forecast of his own future and it is this fascinating view of his own career which draws the boy to "shows" of all sorts. They can scarcely be too improbable for him, portraying, as they do, his belief in his own prowess. A series of slides which has lately been very popular in the five-cent theaters of Chicago, portrayed five masked men breaking into a humble dwelling, killing the father of the family and carrying away the family treasure. The golden-haired son of the house, aged seven, vows eternal vengeance on the spot, and follows one villain after another to his doom. The execution of each is shown in lurid detail, and the last slide of the series depicts the hero, aged ten, kneeling upon his father's grave counting on the fingers of one hand the number of men that he has killed, and thanking God that he has been permitted to be an instrument of vengeance.

In another series of slides, a poor woman is wearily bending over some sewing, a baby is crying in the cradle, and two little boys of nine and ten are asking for food. In despair the mother sends them out into the street to beg, but instead they steal a revolver from a pawn shop and with it kill a Chinese laundryman, robbing him of $200. They rush home with the treasure which is found by the mother in the baby's cradle, wereupon she and her sons fall upon their knees and send up a prayer of thankfulness for this timely and heaven-sent assistance.

Is it not astounding that a city allows thousands of its youth to fill their impressionable minds with these absurdities which certainly will become the foundation for their working moral codes and the data from which they will judge the proprieties of life!

It is as if a child, starved at home, should be forced to go out and search for food, selecting, quite naturally, not that which is nourishing but that which is exciting and appealing to his outward sense, often in his ignorance and foolishness blundering into substances which are filthy and poisonous.

Out of my twenty years' experience at Hull-House I can recall all sorts of pilfering, petty larcenies, and even burglaries, due to that never ceasing effort on the part of boys to procure theater tickets. I can also recall indirect efforts towards the same end which are most pitiful. I remember the remorse of a young girl of fifteen who was brought into the Juvenile Court after a night spent weeping in the cellar of her home because she had stolen a mass of artificial flowers with which to trim a hat. She stated that she had taken the flowers because she was afraid of losing the attention of a young man whom she had heard say that "a girl has to be dressy if she expects to be seen." This young man was the only one who had ever taken her to the theater and if he failed her, she was sure that she would never go again, and she sobbed out incoherently that she "couldn't live at all without it." Apparently the blankness and grayness of life itself had been broken for her only by the portrayal of a different world.

One boy whom I had known from babyhood began to take money from his mother from the time he was seven years old, and after he was ten she regularly gave him money for the play Saturday evening. However, the Saturday performance, "starting him off like," he always went twice again on Sunday, procuring the money in all sorts of illicit ways. Practically all of his earnings after he was fourteen were spent in this way to satisfy the insatiable desire to know of the great adventures of the wide world which the more fortunate boy takes out in reading Homer and Stevenson.

In talking with his mother, I was reminded of my experience one Sunday afternoon in Russia when the employees of a large factory were seated in an open-air theater, watching with breathless interest the presentation of folk stories. I was told that troupes of actors went from one manufacturing establishment to another presenting the simple elements of history and literature to the illiterate employees. This tendency to slake the thirst for adventure by viewing the drama is, of course, but a blind and primitive effort in the direction of culture; for "he who makes himself its vessel and bearer thereby acquires a freedom from the blindness and soul poverty of daily existence."

It is partly in response to this need that more sophisticated young people often go to the theater, hoping to find a clue to life's perplexities. Many times the bewildered hero reminds one of Emerson's description of Margaret Fuller, "I don't know where I am going, follow me"; nevertheless, the stage is dealing with the moral themes in which the public is most interested.

And while many young people go to the theater if only to see represented, and to hear discussed, the themes which seem to them so tragically important, there is no doubt that what they hear there, flimsy and poor as it often is, easily becomes their actual moral guide. In moments of moral crisis they turn to the sayings of the hero who found himself in a similar plight. The sayings may not be profound, but at least they are applicable to conduct. In the last few years scores of plays have been put upon the stage whose titles might be easily translated into proper headings for sociological lectures or sermons, without including the plays of Ibsen, Shaw and Hauptmann, which deal so directly with moral issues that the moralists themselves wince under their teachings and declare them brutal. But it is this very brutality which the over-refined and complicated city dwellers often crave. Moral teaching has become so intricate, creeds so metaphysical, that in a state of absolute reaction they demand definite instruction for daily living. Their whole-hearted acceptance of the teaching corroborates the statement recently made by an English playwright that "The theater is literally making the minds of our urban populations today. It is a huge factory of sentiment, of character, of points of honor, of conceptions of conduct, of everything that finally determines the destiny of a nation. The theater is not only a place of amusement, it is a place of culture, a place where people learn how to think, act, and feel." Seldom, however, do we associate the theater with our plans for civic righteousness, although it has become so important a factor in city life.

One Sunday evening last winter an investigation was made of four hundred and sixty six theaters in the city of Chicago, and it was discovered that in the majority of them the leading theme was revenge; the lover following his rival; the outraged husband seeking his wife's paramour; or the wiping out by death of a blot on a hitherto unstained honor. It was estimated that one sixth of the entire population of the city had attended the theaters on that day. At that same moment the churches throughout the city were preaching the gospel of good will. Is not this a striking commentary upon the contradictory influences to which the city youth is constantly subjected!

This discrepancy between the church and the stage is at times apparently recognized by the five-cent theater itself, and a blundering attempt is made to suffuse the songs and moving pictures with piety. Nothing could more absurdly demonstrate this attempt than a song, illustrated by pictures, describing the adventures of a young man who follows a pretty girl through street after street in the hope of "snatching a kiss from her ruby lips." The young man is overjoyed when a sudden wind storm drives the girl to shelter under an archway, and he is about to succeed in his attempt when the good Lord, "ever watchful over innocence," makes the same wind "blow a cloud of dust into the eyes of the rubberneck," and "his foul purpose is foiled." This attempt at piety is also shown in a series of films depicting Bible stories and the Passion Play at Oberammergau, forecasting the time when the moving film will be viewed as a mere mechanical device for the use of the church, the school and the library, as well as for the theater.

At present, however, most improbable tales hold the attention of the youth of the city night after night, and feed his starved imagination as nothing else succeeds in doing. In addition to these fascinations, the five-cent theater is also fast becoming the general social center and club house in many crowded neighborhoods. It is easy of access from the street, the entire family of parents and children can attend for a comparatively small sum of money, and the performance lasts for at least an hour; and, in some of the humbler theaters, the spectators are not disturbed for a second hour.

The room which contains the mimic stage is small and cozy, and less formal than the regular theater, and there is much more gossip and social life as if the foyer and pit were mingled. The very darkness of the room, necessary for an exhibition of the films, is an added attraction to many young people, for whom the space is filled with the glamour of love making.

Hundreds of young people attend these five-cent theaters every evening in the week, including Sunday, and what is seen and heard there becomes the sole topic of conversation, forming the ground pattern of their social life. That mutual understanding which in another social circle is provided by books, travel and all the arts, is here compressed into the topics suggested by the play.

The young people attend the five-cent theaters in groups, with something of the "gang" instinct, boasting of the films and stunts in "our theater." They find a certain advantage in attending one theater regularly, for the *habitués* are often invited to come upon the stage on "amateur nights," which occur at least once a week in all the theaters. This is, of course, a most exciting experience. If the "stunt" does not meet with the approval of the audience, the performer is greeted with jeers and a long hook pulls him off the stage; if, on the other hand, he succeeds in pleasing the audience, he may be paid for his performance and later register with a booking agency, the address of which is supplied by the obliging manager, and thus he fancies that a lucrative and exciting career is opening before him. Almost every night at six o'clock a long line of children may be seen waiting at the entrance of these booking agencies, of which there are fifteen that are well known in Chicago.

Thus, the only art which is constantly placed before the eyes of "the temperamental youth" is a debased form of dramatic art, and a vulgar type of music, for the success of a song in these theaters depends not so much upon its musical rendition as upon the vulgarity of its appeal. In a song which held the stage of a cheap theater in Chicago for weeks, the young singer was helped out by a bit of mirror from which she threw a flash of light into the faces of successive boys whom she selected from the audience as she sang the refrain, "You are my Affinity." Many popular songs relate the vulgar experiences of a city man

387

wandering from amusement park to bathing beach in search of flirtations. It may be that these "stunts" and recitals of city adventure contain the nucleus of coming poesy and romance, as the songs and recitals of the early minstrels sprang directly from the life of the people, but all the more does the effort need help and direction, both in the development of its technique and the material of its themes.

The few attempts which have been made in this direction are astonishingly rewarding to those who regard the power of self-expression as one of the most precious boons of education. The Children's Theater in New York is the most successful example, but every settlement in which dramatics have been systematically fostered can also testify to a surprisingly quick response to this form of art on the part of young people. The Hull-House Theater is constantly besieged by children clamoring to "take part" in the plays of Schiller, Shakespeare, and Molière, although they know it means weeks of rehearsal and the complete memorizing of "stiff" lines. The audiences sit enthralled by the final rendition and other children whose tastes have supposedly been debased by constant vaudeville, are pathetically eager to come again and again. Even when still more is required from the young actors, research into the special historic period, copying costumes from old plates, hours of labor that the "th" may be restored to its proper place in English speech, their enthusiasm is unquenched. But quite aside from its educational possibilities one never ceases to marvel at the power of even a mimic stage to afford to the young a magic space in which life may be lived in efflorescence, where manners may be courtly and elaborate without exciting ridicule, where the sequence of events is impressive and comprehensible. Order and beauty of life is what the adolescent youth craves above all else as the younger child indefatigably demands his story. "Is this where the most beautiful princess in the world lives?" asks a little girl peering into the door of the Hull-House Theater, or "Does Alice in Wonderland always stay here?" It is much easier for her to put her feeling into words than it is for the youth who has enchantingly rendered the gentle poetry of Ben Jonson's "Sad Shepherd," or for him who has walked the boards as Southey's Wat Tyler. His association, however, is quite as clinging and magical as in the child's although he can only say, "Gee, I wish I could always feel the way I did that night. Something would be doing then." Nothing of the artist's pleasure, nor of the revelation of that larger world which surrounds and completes our own, is lost to him because a careful technique has been exacted,—on the contrary this has only dignified and enhanced it. It would also be easy to illustrate youth's eagerness for artistic expression from the recitals given by the pupils of the New York Music School Settlement, or by those of the Hull-House Music School. These attempts also combine social life with the training of the artistic sense and in this approximate the fascinations of the five-cent theater.

This spring a group of young girls accustomed to the life of a five-cent theater, reluctantly refused an invitation to go to the country for a day's outing because the return on a late train would compel them to miss one evening's performance. They found it impossible to tear themselves away not only from the excitements of the theater itself but from the gaiety of the crowd of young men and girls invariably gathered outside discussing the sensational posters.

A steady English shopkeeper lately complained that unless he provided his four daughters with the money for the five-cent theaters every evening they would steal it from his till, and he feared that they might be driven to procure it in even more illicit ways. Because his entire family life had been thus disrupted he gloomily asserted that "this cheap show had ruined his home and was the curse of America." This father was able to formulate the anxiety of many immigrant parents who are absolutely bewildered by the keen absorption of their children in the cheap theater. This anxiety is not, indeed, without foundation. An eminent alienist of Chicago states that he has had a number of patients among neurotic children whose emotional natures have been so over-wrought by the crude appeal to which they had been so constantly subjected in the theaters, that they have become victims of hallucination and mental disorder. The statement of this physician may be the first note of alarm which will awaken the city to its duty in regard to the theater, so that it shall at least be made safe and sane for the city child whose senses are already so abnormally developed.

This testimony of a physician that the conditions are actually pathological, may at last induce us to bestir ourselves in regard to procuring a more wholesome form of public recreation. Many efforts in social amelioration have been undertaken only after such exposures; in the meantime, while the occasional child is driven distraught, a hundred children permanently injure their eyes watching the moving films, and hundreds more seriously model their conduct upon the standards set before them on this mimic stage.

Three boys, aged nine, eleven and thirteen years, who had recently seen depicted the adventures of frontier life including the holding up of a stage coach and the lassoing of the driver, spent weeks planning to lasso, murder, and rob a neighborhood milkman, who started on his route at four o'clock in the morning. They made their headquarters in a barn and saved enough money to buy a revolver, adopting as their watchword the phrase "Dead Men Tell no Tales." One spring morning the conspirators, with their faces covered with black cloth, lay "in ambush" for the milkman. Fortunately for him, as the lariat was thrown the horse shied, and, although the shot was appropriately fired, the milkman's life was saved. Such a direct influence of the theater is by no means rare, even among older boys. Thirteen young lads were brought into the Municipal Court in Chicago during the first week that "Raffles, the Amateur Cracksman" was upon the stage, each one with an outfit of burglar's tools in his possession, and each one shamefacedly admitting that the gentlemanly burglar in the play had suggested to him a career of similar adventure.

In so far as the illusions of the theater succeed in giving youth the rest and recreation which comes from following a more primitive code of morality, it has a close relation to the function performed by public games. It is, of course, less valuable because the sense of participation is largely confined to the emotions and the imagination, and does not involve the entire nature.

We might illustrate by the "Wild West Show" in which the onlooking boy imagines himself an active participant. The scouts, the Indians, the bucking ponies, are his real intimate companions and occupy his entire mind. In contrast with this

389

we have the omnipresent game of tag which is, doubtless, also founded upon the chase. It gives the boy exercise and momentary echoes of the old excitement, but it is barren of suggestion and quickly degenerates into horse-play.

Well considered public games easily carried out in a park or athletic field, might both fill the mind with the imaginative material constantly supplied by the theater, and also afford the activity which the cramped muscles of the town dweller so sorely need. Even the unquestioned ability which the theater possesses to bring men together into a common mood and to afford them a mutual topic of conversation, is better accomplished with the one national game which we already possess, and might be infinitely extended through the organization of other public games.

The theater even now by no means competes with the baseball league games which are attended by thousands of men and boys who, during the entire summer, discuss the respective standing of each nine and the relative merits of every player. During the noon hour all the employees of a city factory gather in the nearest vacant lot to cheer their own home team in its practice for the next game with the nine of a neighboring manufacturing establishment and on a Saturday afternoon the entire male population of the city betakes itself to the baseball field; the ordinary means of transportation are supplemented by gay stage-coaches and huge automobiles, noisy with blowing horns and decked with gay pennants. The enormous crowd of cheering men and boys are talkative, good-natured, full of the holiday spirit, and absolutely released from the grind of life. They are lifted out of their individual affairs and so fused together that a man cannot tell whether it is his own shout or another's that fills his ears; whether it is his own coat or another's that he is wildly waving to celebrate a victory. He does not call the stranger who sits next to him his "brother" but he unconsciously embraces him in an overwhelming outburst of kindly feeling when the favorite player makes a home run. Does not this contain a suggestion of the undoubted power of public recreation to bring together all classes of a community in the modern city unhappily so full of devices for keeping men apart?

Already some American cities are making a beginning toward more adequate public recreation. Boston has its municipal gymnasiums, cricket fields, and golf grounds. Chicago has seventeen parks with playing fields, gymnasiums and baths, which at present enroll thousands of young people. These same parks are provided with beautiful halls which are used for many purposes, rent free, and are given over to any group of young people who wish to conduct dancing parties subject to city supervision and chaperonage. Many social clubs have deserted neighboring saloon halls for these municipal drawing rooms beautifully decorated with growing plants supplied by the park greenhouses, and flooded with electric lights supplied by the park power house. In the saloon halls the young people were obliged to "pass money freely over the bar," and in order to make the most of the occasion they usually stayed until morning. At such times the economic necessity itself would override the counsels of the more temperate, and the thrifty door keeper would not insist upon invitations but would take in any one who had the "price of a ticket." The free rent in the park hall, the good food in the park restaurant, supplied at cost, have made three parties closing at eleven o'clock no more expensive than one party breaking up at daylight, too often in disorder.

Is not this an argument that the drinking, the late hours, the lack of decorum, are directly traceable to the commercial enterprise which ministers to pleasure in order to drag it into excess because excess is more profitable? To thus commercialize pleasure is as monstrous as it is to commercialize art. It is intolerable that the city does not take over this function of making provision for pleasure, as wise communities in Sweden and South Carolina have taken the sale of alcohol out of the hands of enterprising publicans.

We are only beginning to understand what might be done through the festival, the street procession, the band of marching musicians, orchestral music in public squares or parks, with the magic power they all possess to formulate the sense of companionship and solidarity. The experiments which are being made in public schools to celebrate the national holidays, the changing seasons, the birthdays of heroes, the planting of trees, are slowly developing little ceremonials which may in time work out into pageants of genuine beauty and significance. No other nation has so unparalleled an opportunity to do this through its schools as we have, for no other nation has so wide-spreading a school system, while the enthusiasm of children and their natural ability to express their emotions through symbols, gives the securest possible foundation to this growing effort.

The city schools of New York have effected the organization of high school girls into groups for folk dancing. These old forms of dancing which have been worked out in many lands and through long experiences, safeguard unwary and dangerous expression and yet afford a vehicle through which the gaiety of youth may flow. Their forms are indeed those which lie at the basis of all good breeding, forms which at once express and restrain, urge forward and set limits.

One may also see another center of growth for public recreation and the beginning of a pageantry for the people in the many small parks and athletic fields which almost every American city is hastening to provide for its young. These small parks have innumerable athletic teams, each with its distinctive uniform, with track meets and match games arranged with the teams from other parks and from the public schools; choruses of trade unionists or of patriotic societies fill the park halls with eager listeners. Labor Day processions are yearly becoming more carefully planned and more picturesque in character, as the desire to make an overwhelming impression with mere size gives way to a growing ambition to set forth the significance of the craft and the skill of the workman. At moments they almost rival the dignified showing of the processions of the German Turn Vereins which are also often seen in our city streets.

The many foreign colonies which are found in all American cities afford an enormous reserve of material for public recreation and street festival. They not only celebrate the feasts and holidays of the fatherland, but have each their own public expression for their mutual benefit societies and for the observance of American anniversaries. From the gay celebration of the Scandinavians when war was averted and two neighboring nations were united, to the equally gay celebration of the centenary of Garibaldi's birth; from the Chinese dragon cleverly trailing its way through the streets, to the Greek banners flung out in honor of immortal heroes, there is an infinite variety of suggestions and possibilities for public recreation and for the corporate expression of stirring emotions. After all, what is the function of art but to preserve in permanent and beautiful form those emotions and solaces which cheer life and make it kindlier, more heroic and easier to comprehend; which lift the mind of the worker from the harshness and loneliness of his task, and, by connecting him with what has gone before, free him from a sense of isolation and hardship?

Were American cities really eager for municipal art, they would cherish as genuine beginnings the tarentella danced so interminably at Italian weddings; the primitive Greek pipe played throughout the long summer nights; the Bohemian theaters crowded with eager Slavophiles; the Hungarian musicians strolling from street to street; the fervid oratory of the young Russian preaching social righteousness in the open square.

Many Chicago citizens who attended the first annual meeting of the National Playground Association of America, will never forget the long summer day in the large playing field filled during the morning with hundreds of little children romping through the kindergarten games, in the afternoon with the young men and girls contending in athletic sports; and the evening light made gay by the bright colored garments of Italians, Lithuanians, Norwegians, and a dozen other nationalities, reproducing their old dances and festivals for the pleasure of the more stolid Americans. Was this a forecast of what we may yet see accomplished through a dozen agencies promoting public recreation which are springing up in every city of America, as they already are found in the large towns of Scotland and England?

Let us cherish these experiments as the most precious beginnings of an attempt to supply the recreational needs of our industrial cities. To fail to provide for the recreation of youth, is not only to deprive all of them of their natural form of expression, but is certain to subject some of them to the overwhelming temptation of illicit and soul-destroying pleasures. To insist that young people shall forecast their rose-colored future only in a house of dreams, is to deprive the real world of that warmth and reassurance which it so sorely needs and to which it is justly entitled; furthermore, we are left outside with a sense of dreariness, in company with that shadow which already lurks only around the corner for most of us—a skepticism of life's value.

392

38

Mr. Dooley on Culture

Martin Dooley, the "Sage of Archer Avenue," was the creation of a Chicago journalist and humorist, Finley Peter Dunne (1867–1936). Dunne, who worked on a series of Chicago newspapers, introduced his alter ego, an Irish saloon-keeper, in 1893. For the next twenty-five years, in newspaper columns, magazines, and books, Mr. Dooley, in a rich native brogue, gave his comments on the great events and personages of the day. Generally on the side of the underdog, an enemy to pretense and pomposity of all sorts, Mr. Dooley punctured a whole series of sacred cows. Imperialism, immigration restrictionists, racial bigots, and trusts were among his targets, but his more general subject was the human condition itself.

"Oh, well," said Mr. Hennessy, "we are as th' Lord made us."

"No," said Mr. Dooley, "lave us be fair. Lave us take some iv th' blame oursilves."

ART PATRONAGE

"I see in this pa-aper," said Mr. Dooley, "they'se a fellow kickin' because an American painther ain't got anny chanst again' foreign compytition."

"Sure," said Mr. Hennessy; "he's aisy displaced. I niver knew th' business to be betther. Wages is high an' 'tis a comfortable thrade barrin' colic."

"I don't mane that kind iv painthers," said Mr. Dooley. "I don't mane th' wans that paint ye'er barn, but th' wans that paints a pitcher iv ye'er barn an' wants to sell it to ye f'r more thin th' barn is worth. This man says no matther how industhrees an American painther is, no matther if he puts on his overalls arly in th' mornin' an' goes out with a laddher an' whales away all day long, he can hardly arn a livin', while th' pauper artists iv Europe is fairly rowlin' in th' lap iv luxury. Manny a la-ad that started in life with th' intintion iv makin' th' wurruld f'rget that what's his name—Hogan's frind—ye know who I mane—Michael Angelo—ever lived, is now glad to get a job decoratin' mountain scenery with th' latest news about th' little liver pills.

"Ye see, Hinnissy, whin a man gets hold iv a large hatful iv money, wan iv th' first things he does is to buy some art. Up to th' time whin th' top blew off th' stock market, he bought his art out iv th' front window iv a news an' station'ry shop or

From [Finley Peter Dunne] "Art Patronage," *Observations by Mr. Dooley* (New York and London, 1906), 41–46.

had it put in be th' paperhanger. He took th' Sundah pa-apers that ar-re a gr-reat help if ye're collectin' art, an' he had some pitchers iv fruit that looks nachral enough to ate, d'ye mind, a paintin' iv a deer like th' wan he shot at in th' Manotowish counthry in Eighty-eight, an' a livin' likeness iv a Lake Supeeryor white fish on a silver plate. That was th' peeryod, mind ye, whin th' iron dogs howled on his lawn an' people come miles an' miles f'r to see a grotto made out iv relics iv th' Chicago fire.

"Manetime his daughter was illustratin' suspinders an' illuminatin' china plates an' becomin' artistic, an' afther awhile whin th' time come that he had to keep a man at th' dure to sweep out th' small bills, she give him a good push to'rd betther things. Besides, his pardner down th' sthreet had begun collectin' pitchers, an' ivry time he wint abroad th' mannyfacthrers iv pitcher frames bought new autymobills f'r th' Champs All Easy. So 'twas a soft matther f'r our frind Higbie to be persuaded that he ought to be a pathron iv art, an' he wint abroad detarmined to buy a bunch iv chromos that'd make people come out iv th' gallery iv his pardner down th' sthreet stiflin' their laughter in their hands.

"Now ye'd think seein' that he made his money in this counthry, he'd pathronize American art. Ye'd believe he'd sind wurrud down to his agent f'r to secure forty feet iv Evansville be moonlight an' be con-tint. But he don't.

"Ye don't catch Higbie changin' iv anny iv his dividends on domestic finished art. He jumps on a boat an' goes sthraight acrost to th' centhral deepo. The first thing he gets is a porthrait iv himsilf be wan iv th' gr-reat modhren masthers, Sargent be name. This here Sargent, Hogan tells me, used to live in this counthry, an' faith, if he'd stayed here ye might see him to-day on a stagin'. But he had a mind in his head an' he tore off f'r Europe th' way a duck hunter goes f'r a rice swamp. Afther awhile, Higbie shows up, an' says he: 'I'm Higbie iv th' Non-Adhesive Consolidated Glue Company,' he says. 'Can ye do me?' 'I can an' will,' says Sargent. 'I'll do ye good. How much have ye got?' he says. 'Get some more an' come around,' he says. An' Higbie puts on his Prince Albert coat an' laves it open so that ye can see his watch charm—th' crown iv Poland with th' Kohinoor in th' top iv it— an' me frind Sargent does him brown an' red. He don't give him th' pitcher iv coorse. If ye have ye'er porthrait painted be a gr-reat painther, it's ye'er porthrait but 'tis his pitcher, an' he keeps it till ye don't look that way anny more. So Higbie's porthrait is hung up in a gallery an' th' doctors brings people to see it that ar-re sufferin' fr'm narvous dyspepsia to cheer thim up. Th' pa-apers says 'tis fine. 'Number 108 shows Sargent at his best. There is the same marvellous ticknick that th' great master displayed in his cillybrated take-off on Mrs. Maenheimer in last year's gallery. Th' skill an' ease with which th' painther has made a monkey iv his victim are beyond praise. Sargent has torn th' sordid heart out iv th' wretched crather an' exposed it to th' wurruld. Th' wicked, ugly little eyes, th' crooked nose, th' huge graspin' hands, tell th' story iv this miscreant's character as completely as if they were written in so manny wurruds, while th' artist, with wondherful malice, has painted onto th' face a smile iv sickenin' silf-complacency that is positively disgustin'. No artist iv our day has succeeded so well in showin' up th' maneness iv th' people he has mugged. We ondershtand that th' atrocious Higbie paid wan hundherd thousan' dollars f'r this comic valentine. It is worth th' money to ivrybody but him.'

"But Higbie don't see th' pa-aper. He's over in Paris. Th' chimes are rung, bonefires are lighted in th' sthreets an' th' Pannyma Comp'ny declares a dividend whin he enters th' city. They'se such a demand f'r paint that th' supply runs out an' manny gr-reat imprishonist pitcher facthries is foorced to use bluein'. Higbie ordhers paintin's be th' ton, th' r-runnin' foot, th' foot pound, th' car load. He insthructs th' pitcher facthries to wurruk night an' day till his artistic sowl is satisfied. We follow his coorse in th' pa-apers. 'Th' cillybrated Gainsborough that niver wud be missed has been captured be Misther Higbie, th' American millyionaire. Th' price paid is said to be wan hundherd thousan' dollars. Th' pitcher riprisints a lady in a large hat fondlin' a cow. It is wan iv th' finest Gainsboroughs painted be th' Gainsborough Mannyfacthrin' comp'ny iv Manchester. At th' las' public sale, it was sold f'r thirty dollars. Misther Higbie has also purchased th' cillybrated Schmartzmeister Boogooroo, wan iv th' mos' horrible examples iv this delightful painther's style. He is now negotyatin' with th' well-known dealer Moosoo Mortheimer f'r th' intire output iv th' Barabazah School. Yisterdah in a call on th' janial dealer, th' name iv th' cillybrated painther Mooney was mintioned. "How manny pitchers has he painted?" "Four hundherd and forty-three thousan' at ilivin o'clock to-day," says th' dealer. "But four hundherd thousan' iv thim ar-re in America." "Get th' r-est iv thim f'r me," says th' connysoor. "What did ye say th' gintleman's name was?" We ondershtand that Misther Mooney has had to put in two new four-deck machines to meet th' ordhers, which include thirty green an' mauve haystacks, forty blue barns or childher at play, an' no less thin ninety riprisintations iv mornin' at sea, moonlight avenin', flock iv sheep, or whativer ye may call thim.'

"An whin he comes home, he hangs thim in his house, so that his friends can't turn around without takin' off a pasthral scene on their coats, an' he pastes th' price on th' frame, an' whin he dies, he laves his pitcher to some definceless art museem. An' there ye ar-re.

"So I tell ye, Hinnissy, if I was a young an' ambitious American painther, I'd go to Europe. Whin Hannigan was over there, he met a young man that painted that fine head iv Murphy that looks so much like Casey that hangs in Schwartzmeister's back room. 'Ar-re ye still at th' art?' says Hannigan. 'I am,' says th' young man. 'How does it go?' asks Hannigan. 'I've more thin I can do,' says th' young man. 'Since steel rails got so high, I've had to hire an assistant. Ye see, I didn't get on in Chicago. Me "Bridgepoort in a Fog" was th' on'y pitcher I sold, an' a sausage mannyfacthrer bought that because his facthry was in it. I come over here, an' so's me pitchers will have a fair show, I sign annywan's name ye want to thim. Ye've heerd iv Michael Angelo? That's me. Y've heerd iv Gainsborough? That's me. Ye've heerd iv Millet, th' boy that painted th' pitcher give away with th' colored supplimint iv th' Sundah Howl? That's me. Yis, sir, th' rale name iv near ivry distinguished painther iv modhren times is Remsen K. Smith. Whin ye go home, if ye see a good painther an' glazier that'd like a job as assistant Rimbrandt f'r th' American thrade, sind him to me. F'r,' he says, 'th' on'y place an American artist can make a livin' is here. Charity f'r artists,' he says, 'begins abroad,' he says."

"Well," said Mr. Hennessy, "perhaps a bum Europeen pitcher is betther thin a good American pitcher."

"Perhaps so," said Mr. Dooley. "I think it is so. Annyhow, no matther how bad a painther he is, annywan that can get money out iv an American millyionaire is an artist an' desarves it. There's th' rale art. I wish it was taught in th' schools. I'd like to see an exhibition at th' Museem with 'Check iv American Gintleman, dhrawn fr'm life,' hung on th' wall."

THE CARNEGIE LIBRARIES

"Has Andhrew Carnaygie given ye a libry yet?" asked Mr. Dooley.

"Not that I know iv," said Mr. Hennessy.

"He will," said Mr. Dooley. "Ye'll not escape him. Befure he dies he hopes to crowd a libry on ivry man, woman, an' child in th' counthry. He's given thim to cities, towns, villages, an' whistlin' stations. They're tearin' down gas-houses an' poor-houses to put up libries. Befure another year, ivry house in Pittsburg that ain't a blast-furnace will be a Carnaygie libry. In some places all th' buildin's is libries. If ye write him f'r an autygraft he sinds ye a libry. No beggar is iver turned impty-handed fr'm th' dure. Th' pan-handler knocks an' asts f'r a glass iv milk an' a roll. 'No, sir,' says Andhrew Carnaygie. 'I will not pauperize this onworthy man.' Nawthin is worst f'r a beggar-man thin to make a pauper iv him. Yet it shall not be said iv me that I give nawthin' to th' poor. Saunders, give him a libry, an' if he still insists on a roll tell him to roll th' libry. F'r I'm humorous as well as wise,' he says."

"Does he give th' books that go with it?" asked Mr. Hennessy.

"Books?" said Mr. Dooley. "What ar-re ye talkin' about? D'ye know what a libry is? I suppose ye think it's a place where a man can go, haul down wan iv his fav'rite authors fr'm th' shelf, an' take a nap in it. That's not a Carnaygie libry. A Carnaygie libry is a large, brown-stone, impenethrible buildin' with th' name iv th' maker blown on th' dure. Libry, fr'm th' Greek wurruds, libus, a book, an' ary, sildom,—sildom a book. A Carnaygie libry is archytechoor, not lithrachoor. Lithrachoor will be riprisinted. Th' most cillybrated dead authors will be honored be havin' their names painted on th' wall in distinguished comp'ny, as thus: Andhrew Carnaygie, Shakespeare; Andhrew Carnaygie, Byron; Andhrew Carnaygie, Bobby Burns; Andhrew Carnaygie, an' so on. Ivry author is guaranteed a place next to pure readin' matther like a bakin' powdher advertisemint, so that whin a man comes along that niver heerd iv Shakespeare he'll know he was somebody, because there he is on th' wall. That's th' dead authors. Th' live authors will stand outside an' wish they were dead."

From [Finley Peter Dunne] "The Carnegie Libraries," *Dissertations by Mr. Dooley* (New York and London, 1906), 177–182.

"He's havin' gr-reat spoort with it. I r-read his speech th' other day, whin he laid th' corner-stone iv th' libry at Pianola, Ioway. Th' entire popylation iv this lithry cinter gathered to see an' hear him. There was th' postmaster an' his wife, th' blacksmith an' his fam'ly, the station agent, mine host iv th' Farmers' Exchange, an' some sthray live stock. 'Ladies an' gintlemen,' says he. 'Modesty compels me to say nawthin' on this occasion, but I am not be be bulldozed,' he says. 'I can't tell ye how much pleasure I take in disthributin' monymints to th' humble name around which has gathered so manny hon'rable associations with mesilf. I have been a very busy little man all me life, but I like hard wurruk, an' givin' away me money is th' hardest wurruk I iver did. It fairly makes me teeth ache to part with it. But there's wan consolation. I cheer mesilf with th' thought that no matther how much money I give it don't do anny particular person anny good. Th' worst thing ye can do f'r anny man is to do him good. I pass by th' organ-grinder on th' corner with a savage glare. I bate th' monkey on th' head whin he comes up smilin' to me window, an' hurl him down on his impecyoonyous owner. None iv me money goes into th' little tin cup. I cud kick a hospital, an' I lave Wall Sthreet to look afther th' widow an' th' orphan. Th' submerged tenth, thim that can't get hold iv a good chunk iv th' goods, I wud cut off fr'm th' rest iv th' wurruld an' prevint fr'm bearin' th' haughty name iv papa or th' still lovelier name iv ma. So far I've got on'y half me wish in this matther.

" 'I don't want poverty an' crime to go on. I intind to stop it. But how? It's been holdin' its own f'r cinchries. Some iv th' gr-reatest iv former minds has undertook to prevint it an' has failed. They didn't know how. Modesty wud prevint me agin fr'm sayin' that I know how, but that's nayether here nor there. I do. Th' way to abolish poverty an' bust crime is to put up a brown-stone buildin' in ivry town in th' counthry with me name over it. That's th' way. I suppose th' raison it wasn't thried befure was that no man iver had such a name. 'Tis thrue me efforts is not appreciated ivrywhere. I offer a city a libry, an' oftentimes it replies an' asks me f'r something to pay off th' school debt. I rayceive degraded pettyshuns fr'm so-called proud methropolises f'r a gas-house in place iv a libry. I pass thim by with scorn. All I ask iv a city in rayturn f'r a fifty-thousan'-dollar libry is that it shall raise wan millyon dollars to maintain th' buildin' an' keep me name shiny, an' if it won't do that much f'r lithrachoor, th' divvle take it, it's onworthy iv th' name iv an American city. What ivry community needs is taxes an' lithrachoor. I give thim both. Three cheers f'r a libry an' a bonded debt! Lithrachoor, taxation, an' Andhrew Carnaygie, wan an' insiprable, now an' foriver! They'se nawthin' so good as a good book. It's betther thin food; it's betther thin money. I have made money an' books, an' I like me books betther thin me money. Others don't, but I do. With these few wurruds I will con-clude. Modesty wud prevint me fr'm sayin' more, but I have to catch a thrain, an' cannot go on. I stake ye to this libry, which ye will have as soon as ye raise th' money to keep it goin'. Stock it with useful readin', an' some day ye're otherwise pauper an' criminal childher will come to know me name whin I am gone an' there's no wan left to tell it thim.'

"Whin th' historyan comes to write th' histhry iv th' West he'll say: 'Pianola, Ioway, was a prosperous town till th' failure iv th' corn crop in nineteen hundherd an' wan, an' th' Carnaygie libry in nineteen hundherd an' two. Th' govermint ast f'r thirty dollars to pave Main Sthreet with wooden blocks, but th' gr-reat philanthropist was firm, an' the libry was sawed off on th' town. Th' public schools, th' wurruk-house, th' wather wurruks, an' th' other penal instichoochions was at wanst closed, an' th' people begun to wurruk to support th' libry. In five years th' popylation had deserted th' town to escape taxation, an' now, as Mr. Carnaygie promised, poverty an' crime has been abolished in th' place, th' janitor iv th' buildin' bein' honest an' well paid.'

"Isn't it good f'r lithrachoor, says ye? Sure, I think not, Hinnissy. Libries niver encouraged lithrachoor anny more thin tombstones encourage livin'. No wan iver wrote annythin' because he was tol' that a hundherd years fr'm now his books might be taken down fr'm a shelf in a granite sepulcher an' some wan wud write 'Good' or 'This man is crazy' in th' margin. What lithrachoor needs is fillin' food. If Andhrew wud put a kitchen in th' libries an' build some bunks or even swing a few hammocks where livin' authors cud crawl in at night an' sleep while waitin' f'r this enlightened nation to wake up an' discover th' Shakespeares now on th' turf, he wud be givin' a rale boost to lithrachoor. With th' smoke curlin' fr'm th' chimbley, an' hundherds iv potes settin' aroun' a table loaded down with pancakes an' talkin' pothry an' prize-fightin', with hundherds iv other potes stacked up nately in th' sleep-in'-rooms an' snorin' in wan gran' chorus, with their wives holdin' down good-payin' jobs as libraryans or cooks, an' their happy little childher playin' through th' marble corrydors, Andhrew Carnaygie wud not have lived in vain. Maybe that's th' on'y way he knows how to live. I don't believe in libries. They pauperize lithrachoor. I'm f'r helpin' th' boys that's now on th' job. I know a pote in Halsted Sthreet that wanst wrote a pome beginnin', 'All th' wealth iv Ind,' that he sold to a magazine f'r two dollars, payable on publycation. Lithrachoor don't need advancin'. What it needs is advances f'r th' lithrachoors. Ye can't shake down posterity f'r th' price.

"All th' same, I like Andhrew Carnaygie. Him an' me ar-re agreed on that point. I like him because he ain't shamed to give publicly. Ye don't find him puttin' on false whiskers an' turnin' up his coat-collar whin he goes out to be benivolent. No, sir. Ivry time he dhrops a dollar it makes a noise like a waither fallin' down-stairs with a tray iv dishes. He's givin' th' way we'd all like to give. I niver put annything in th' poor-box, but I wud if Father Kelly wud rig up like wan iv thim slot-machines, so that whin I stuck in a nickel me name wud appear over th' altar in red letters. But whin I put a dollar in th' plate I get back about two yards an' hurl it so hard that th' good man turns around to see who done it. Do good be stealth, says I, but see that th' burglar-alarm is set. Anny benivolent money I hand out I want to talk about me. Him that giveth to th' poor, they say, lindeth to th' Lord; but in these days we look f'r quick returns on our invistmints. I like Andhrew Carnaygie, an', as he says, he puts his whole soul into th' wurruk."

"What's he mane be that?" asked Mr. Hennessy.

"He manes," said Mr. Dooley, "that he's gin'rous. Ivry time he gives a libry he gives himsilf away in a speech."

39

The Melting Pot

Two hundred and fifty years after the first settlements, millions of immigrants were still making their way from Europe to the New World. Between 1890 and 1912 many of them came from southern and eastern Europe, escaping conditions of great poverty and oppression. Like the seventeenth-century colonists, these immigrants had to make great adjustments, but their difficulties were compounded by special religious and linguistic traditions, and the need to come to terms with a national history that was already more than a century old.

Mary Antin (1881–1949) was one who managed the adjustments and exploited her handicaps to brilliant advantage. Brought to Boston from Russian Poland in 1894, she showed great precocity as a child, writing poems printed in local newspapers. As a child she also wrote, in Yiddish, a moving account of her long journey, *From Polotzk to Boston*; but her mastery of English was equally impressive, as revealed in the pages of *The Promised Land*. This account of growing up in a new country, searching for the meaning of citizenship and liberty even while trying to retain some older memories and values, was unusual for its eloquence if not for its contents. In articulating her own passage to adulthood, Mary Antin was describing the experience of a generation.

THE PROMISED LAND
Mary Antin

Memory may take a rest while I copy from a contemporaneous document the story of the great voyage. In accordance with my promise to my uncle, I wrote, during my first months in America, a detailed account of our adventures between Polotzk and Boston. Ink was cheap, and the epistle, in Yiddish, occupied me for many hot summer hours.

On a gray wet morning in early April we set out for the frontier. This was the real beginning of our journey, and all my faculties of observation were alert. I took note of everything,—the weather, the trains, the bustle of railroad stations, our fellow passengers, and the family mood at every stage of our progress.

From *The Promised Land* (Boston and New York, 1912), 169–170, 172, 175–179, 222–228, 270–275.

The bags and bundles which composed our travelling outfit were much more bulky than valuable. A trifling sum of money, the steamer ticket, and the foreign passport were the magic agents by means of which we hoped to span the five thousand miles of earth and water between us and my father. The passport was supposed to pass us over the frontier without any trouble, but on account of the prevalence of cholera in some parts of the country, the poorer sort of travellers, such as emigrants, were subjected, at this time, to more than ordinary supervision and regulation.

The phrases "we were told to do this" and "told to do that" occur again and again in my narrative, and the most effective handling of the facts could give no more vivid picture of the proceedings. We emigrants were herded at the stations, packed in the cars, and driven from place to place like cattle.

We arrived in Hamburg early one morning, after a long night in the crowded cars. We were marched up to a strange vehicle, long and narrow and high, drawn by two horses and commanded by a mute driver. We were piled up on this wagon, our baggage was thrown after us, and we started on a sight-seeing tour across the city of Hamburg.

The smiles and shivers fairly crowded each other in some parts of our career.

Suddenly, when everything interesting seemed at an end, we all recollected how long it was since we had started on our funny ride. Hours, we thought, and still the horses ran. Now we rode through quieter streets where there were fewer shops and more wooden houses. Still the horses seemed to have just started. I looked over our perch again. Something made me think of a description I had read of criminals being carried on long journeys in uncomfortable things—like this? Well, it was strange—this long, long drive, the conveyance, no word of explanation; and all, though going different ways, being packed off together. We were strangers; the driver knew it. He might take us anywhere—how could we tell?

Yes, we are frightened. We are very still. Some Polish women over there have fallen asleep, and the rest of us look such a picture of woe, and yet so funny, it is a sight to see and remember.

Our mysterious ride came to an end on the outskirts of the city, where we were once more lined up, cross-questioned, disinfected, labelled, and pigeonholed.

This last place of detention turned out to be a prison. "Quarantine" they called it, and there was a great deal of it—two weeks of it. Two weeks within high brick walls, several hundred of us herded in half a dozen compartments,—numbered compartments,—sleeping in rows, like sick people in a hospital; with roll-call morning and night, and short rations three times a day; with never a sign of the free world beyond our barred windows; with anxiety and longing and homesickness in our hearts, and in our ears the unfamiliar voice of the invisible ocean, which drew and repelled us at the same time. The fortnight in quarantine was not an episode; it was an epoch, divisible into eras, periods, events.

Our turn came at last. We were conducted through the gate of departure, and after some hours of bewildering manœuvres, described in great detail in the report to my uncle, we found ourselves—we five frightened pilgrims from Polotzk—on the deck of a great big steamship afloat on the strange big waters of the ocean.

For sixteen days the ship was our world. My letter dwells solemnly on the details of the life at sea, as if afraid to cheat my uncle of the smallest circumstance. It does not shrink from describing the torments of seasickness; it notes every change in the weather. A rough night is described, when the ship pitched and rolled so that people were thrown from their berths; days and nights when we crawled through dense fogs, our foghorn drawing answering warnings from invisible ships. The perils of the sea were not minimized in the imagination of us inexperienced voyagers. The captain and his officers ate their dinners, smoked their pipes and slept soundly in their turns, while we frightened emigrants turned our faces to the wall and awaited our watery graves.

All this while the seasickness lasted. Then came happy hours on deck, with fugitive sunshine, birds atop the crested waves, band music and dancing and fun. I explored the ship, made friends with officers and crew, or pursued my thoughts in quiet nooks. It was my first experience of the ocean, and I was profoundly moved.

Oh, what solemn thoughts I had! How deeply I felt the greatness, the power of the scene! The immeasurable distance from horizon to horizon; the huge billows forever changing their shapes—now only a wavy and rolling plain, now a chain of great mountains, coming and going farther away; then a town in the distance, perhaps, with spires and towers and buildings of gigantic dimensions; and mostly a vast mass of uncertain shapes, knocking against each other in fury, and seething and foaming in their anger; the gray sky, with its mountains of gloomy clouds, flying, moving with the waves, as it seemed, very near them; the absence of any object besides the one ship; and the deep, solemn groans of the sea, sounding as if all the voices of the world had been turned into sighs and then gathered into that one mournful sound—so deeply did I feel the presence of these things, that the feeling became one of awe, both painful and sweet, and stirring and warming, and deep and calm and grand.

I would imagine myself all alone on the ocean, and Robinson Crusoe was very real to me. I was alone sometimes. I was aware of no human presence; I was conscious only of sea and sky and something I did not understand. And as I listened to its solemn voice, I felt as if I had found a friend, and knew that I loved the ocean. It seemed as if it were within as well as without, part of myself; and I wondered how I had lived without it, and if I could ever part with it.

And so suffering, fearing, brooding, rejoicing, we crept nearer and nearer to the coveted shore, until, on a glorious May morning, six weeks after our departure from Polotzk, our eyes beheld the Promised Land, and my father received us in his arms.

The public school has done its best for us foreigners, and for the country, when it has made us into good Americans. I am glad it is mine to tell how the miracle was wrought in one case. You should be glad to hear of it, you born Americans; for it is the story of the growth of your country; of the flocking of your brothers and sisters from the far ends of the earth to the flag you love; of the recruiting of your armies of workers, thinkers, and leaders. And you will be glad to hear of it, my comrades in adoption; for it is a rehearsal of your own experience, the thrill and wonder of which your own hearts have felt.

How long would you say, wise reader, it takes to make an American? By the middle of my second year in school I had reached the sixth grade. When, after the Christmas holidays, we began to study the life of Washington, running through a

401

summary of the Revolution, and the early days of the Republic, it seemed to me that all my reading and study had been idle until then. The reader, the arithmetic, the song book, that had so fascinated me until now, became suddenly sober exercise books, tools wherewith to hew a way to the source of inspiration. When the teacher read to us out of a big book with many bookmarks in it, I sat rigid with attention in my little chair, my hands tightly clasped on the edge of my desk; and I painfully held my breath, to prevent sighs of disappointment escaping, as I saw the teacher skip the parts between bookmarks. When the class read, and it came my turn, my voice shook and the book trembled in my hands. I could not pronounce the name of George Washington without a pause. Never had I prayed, never had I chanted the songs of David, never had I called upon the Most Holy, in such utter reverence and worship as I repeated the simple sentences of my child's story of the patriot. I gazed with adoration at the portraits of George and Martha Washington, till I could see them with my eyes shut. And whereas formerly my self-consciousness had bordered on conceit, and I thought myself an uncommon person, parading my schoolbooks through the streets, and swelling with pride when a teacher detained me in conversation, now I grew humble all at once, seeing how insignificant I was beside the Great.

As I read about the noble boy who would not tell a lie to save himself from punishment, I was for the first time truly repentant of my sins. Formerly I had fasted and prayed and made sacrifice on the Day of Atonement, but it was more than half play, in mimicry of my elders. I had no real horror of sin, and I knew so many ways of escaping punishment. I am sure my family, my neighbors, my teachers in Polotzk—all my world, in fact—strove together, by example and precept, to teach me goodness. Saintliness had a new incarnation in about every third person I knew. I did respect the saints, but I could not help seeing that most of them were a little bit stupid, and that mischief was much more fun than piety. Goodness, as I had known it, was respectable, but not necessarily admirable. The people I really admired, like my Uncle Solomon, and Cousin Rachel, were those who preached the least and laughed the most. My sister Frieda was perfectly good, but she did not think the less of me because I played tricks. What I loved in my friends was not inimitable. One could be downright good if one really wanted to. One could be learned if one had books and teachers. One could sing funny songs and tell anecdotes if one travelled about and picked up such things, like one's uncles and cousins. But a human being strictly good, perfectly wise, and unfailingly valiant, all at the same time, I had never heard or dreamed of. This wonderful George Washington was as inimitable as he was irreproachable. Even if I had never, never told a lie, I could not compare myself to George Washington; for I was not brave—I was afraid to go out when snowballs whizzed—and I could never be the First President of the United States.

So I was forced to revise my own estimate of myself. But the twin of my new-born humility, paradoxical as it may seem, was a sense of dignity I had never known before. For if I found that I was a person of small consequence, I discovered at the same time that I was more nobly related than I had ever supposed. I had relatives and friends who were notable people by the old standards,—I had never been ashamed of my family,—but this George Washington, who died long before I was born, was like a king in greatness, and he and I were Fellow Citizens. There was a great deal about Fellow Citizens in the patriotic literature we read at this time; and I knew from my father how he was a Citizen, through the process of naturalization, and how I also was a citizen, by virtue of my relation to him. Undoubtedly I was a Fellow Citizen, and George Washington was another. It thrilled me to realize what sudden greatness had fallen on me; and at the same time it sobered me, as with a sense of responsibility. I strove to conduct myself as befitted a Fellow Citizen.

Before books came into my life, I was given to star-gazing and daydreaming. When books were given me, I fell upon them as a glutton pounces on his meat after a period of enforced starvation. I lived with my nose in a book, and took no notice of the alternations of the sun and stars. But now, after the advent of George Washington and the American Revolution, I began to dream again. I strayed on the common after school instead of hurrying home to read. I hung on fence rails, my pet book forgotten under my arm, and gazed off to the yellow-streaked February sunset, and beyond, and beyond. I was no longer the central figure of my dreams; the dry weeds in the lane crackled beneath the tread of Heroes.

What more could America give a child? Ah, much more! As I read how the patriots planned the Revolution, and the women gave their sons to die in battle, and the heroes led to victory, and the rejoicing people set up the Republic, it dawned on me gradually what was meant by *my country*. The people all desiring noble things, and striving for them together, defying their oppressors, giving their lives for each other—all this it was that made *my country*. It was not a thing that I *understood*; I could not go home and tell Frieda about it, as I told her other things I learned at school. But I knew one could say "my country" and *feel* it, as one felt "God" or "myself." My teacher, my schoolmates, Miss Dillingham, George Washington himself could not mean more than I when they said "my country," after I had once felt it. For the Country was for all the Citizens, and *I was a Citizen*. And when we stood up to sing "America," I shouted the words with all my might. I was in very earnest proclaiming to the world my love for my new-found country.

I love thy rock and rills,
Thy woods and templed hills.

Boston Harbor, Crescent Beach, Chelsea Square—all was hallowed ground to me. As the day approached when the school was to hold exercises in honor of Washington's Birthday, the halls resounded at all hours with the strains of patriotic songs; and I, who was a model of the attentive pupil, more than once lost my place in the lesson as I strained to hear, through closed doors, some neighboring class rehearsing "The Star-Spangled Banner." If the doors happened to open, and the chorus broke out unveiled—

O! say, does that Star-Spangled Banner yet wave
O'er the land of the free, and the home of the brave?—

delicious tremors ran up and down my spine, and I was faint with suppressed enthusiasm.

Where had been my country until now? What flag had I loved? What heroes had

403

I worshipped? The very names of these things had been unknown to me. Well I knew that Polotzk was not my country. It was *goluth*—exile. On many occasions in the year we prayed to God to lead us out of exile. The beautiful Passover service closed with the words, "Next year, may we be in Jerusalem." On childish lips, indeed, those words were no conscious aspiration; we repeated the Hebrew syllables after our elders, but without their hope and longing. Still not a child among us was too young to feel in his own flesh the lash of the oppressor. We knew what it was to be Jews in exile, from the spiteful treatment we suffered at the hands of the smallest urchin who crossed himself; and thence we knew that Israel had good reason to pray for deliverance. But the story of the Exodus was not history to me in the sense that the story of the American Revolution was. It was more like a glorious myth, a belief in which had the effect of cutting me off from the actual world, by linking me with a world of phantoms. Those moments of exaltation which the contemplation of the Biblical past afforded us, allowing us to call ourselves the children of princes, served but to tinge with a more poignant sense of disinheritance the long humdrum stretches of our life. In very truth we were a people without a country. Surrounded by mocking foes and detractors, it was difficult for me to realize the persons of my people's heroes or the events in which they moved. Except in moments of abstraction from the world around me, I scarcely understood that Jerusalem was an actual spot on the earth, where once the Kings of the Bible, real people, like my neighbors in Polotzk, ruled in puissant majesty. For the conditions of our civil life did not permit us to cultivate a spirit of nationalism. The freedom of worship that was grudgingly granted within the narrow limits of the Pale by no means included the right to set up openly any ideal of a Hebrew State, any hero other than the Czar. What we children picked up of our ancient political history was confused with the miraculous story of the Creation, with the supernatural legends and hazy associations of Bible lore.

So it came to pass that we did not know what *my country* could mean to a man. And as we had no country, so we had no flag to love. It was by no far-fetched symbolism that the banner of the House of Romanoff became the emblem of our latter-day bondage in our eyes. Even a child would know how to hate the flag that we were forced, on pain of severe penalties, to hoist above our housetops, in celebration of the advent of one of our oppressers. And as it was with country and flag, so it was with heroes of war. We hated the uniform of the soldier, to the last brass button. On the person of a Gentile, it was the symbol of tyranny; on the person of a Jew, it was the emblem of shame.

So a little Jewish girl in Polotzk was apt to grow up hungry-minded and empty-hearted; and if, still in her outreaching youth, she was set down in a land of outspoken patriotism, she was likely to love her new country with a great love, and to embrace its heroes in a great worship. Naturalization, with us Russian Jews, may mean more than the adoption of the immigrant by America. It may mean the adoption of America by the immigrant.

It was characteristic of the looseness of our family discipline at this time that nobody was seriously interested in our visits to Morgan Chapel. Our time was our own, after school duties and household tasks were done. Joseph sold newspapers after school; I swept and washed dishes; Dora minded the baby. For the rest, we amused ourselves as best we could. Father and mother were preoccupied with the store day and night; and not so much with weighing and measuring and making change as with figuring out how long it would take the outstanding accounts to ruin the business entirely. If my mother had scruples against her children resorting to a building with a cross on it, she did not have time to formulate them. If my father heard us talking about Morgan Chapel, he dismissed the subject with a sarcastic characterization, and wanted to know if we were going to join the Salvation Army next; but he did not seriously care, and he was willing that the children should have a good time. And if my parents had objected to Morgan Chapel, was the sidewalk in front of the saloon a better place for us children to spend the evening? They could not have argued with us very long, so they hardly argued at all.

In Polotzk we had been trained and watched, our days had been regulated, our conduct prescribed. In America, suddenly, we were let loose on the street. Why? Because my father having renounced his faith, and my mother being uncertain of hers, they had no particular creed to hold us to. The conception of a system of ethics independent of religion could not at once enter as an active principle in their life; so that they could give a child no reason why to be truthful or kind. And as with religion, so it fared with other branches of our domestic education. Chaos took the place of system; uncertainty, inconsistency undermined discipline. My parents knew only that they desired us to be like American children; and seeing how their neighbors gave their children boundless liberty, they turned us also loose, never doubting but that the American way was the best way. In public deportment, in etiquette, in all matters of social intercourse, they had no standards to go by, seeing that America was not Polotzk. In their bewilderment and uncertainty they must trust us children to learn from such models as the tenements afforded. More than this, they must step down from their throne of parental authority, and take the law from their children's mouths; for they had no other means of finding out what was good American form. The result was that laxity of domestic organization, that inversion of normal relations which makes for friction, and which sometimes ends in breaking up a family that was formerly united and happy.

This sad process of disintegration of home life may be observed in almost any immigrant family of our class and with our traditions and aspirations. It is part of the process of Americanization; an upheaval preceding the state of repose. It is the cross that the first and second generations must bear, an involuntary sacrifice for the sake of the future generations. These are the pains of adjustment, as racking as the pains of birth. And as the mother forgets her agonies in the bliss of clasping her babe to her breast, so the bent and heart-sore immigrant forgets exile and homesickness and ridicule and loss and estrangement, when he beholds his sons and daughters moving as Americans among Americans.

On Wheeler Street there were no real homes. There were miserable flats of three or four rooms, or fewer, in which families that did not practise race suicide cooked, washed, and ate; slept from two to four in a bed, in windowless bedrooms;

quarrelled in the gray morning, and made up in the smoky evening; tormented each other, supported each other, saved each other, drove each other out of the house. But there was no common life in any form that means life. There was no room for it, for one thing. Beds and cribs took up most of the floor space, disorder packed the interspaces. The centre table in the "parlor" was not loaded with books. It held, invariably, a photograph album and an ornamental lamp with a paper shade; and the lamp was usually out of order. So there was as little motive for a common life as there was room. The yard was only big enough for the perennial rubbish heap. The narrow sidewalk was crowded. What were the people to do with themselves? There were the saloons, the missions, the libraries, the cheap amusement places, and the neighborhood houses. People selected their resorts according to their tastes. The children, let it be thankfully recorded, flocked mostly to the clubs; the little girls to sew, cook, dance, and play games; the little boys to hammer and paste, mend chairs, debate, and govern a toy republic. All these, of course, are forms of baptism by soap and water.

Our neighborhood went in search of salvation to Morgan Memorial Hall, Barnard Memorial, Morgan Chapel aforementioned, and some other clean places that lighted a candle in their window. My brother, my sister Dora, and I were introduced to some of the clubs by our young neighbors, and we were glad to go. For our home also gave us little besides meals in the kitchen and beds in the dark. What with the six of us, and the store, and the baby, and sometimes a "greener" or two from Polotzk, whom we lodged as a matter of course till they found a permanent home—what with such a company and the size of our tenement, we needed to get out almost as much as our neighbors' children. I say almost; for our parlor we managed to keep pretty clear, and the lamp on our centre table was always in order, and its light fell often on an open book. Still, it was part of the life of Wheeler Street to belong to clubs, so we belonged.

I didn't care for sewing or cooking, so I joined a dancing-club; and even here I was a failure. I had been a very good dancer in Russia, but here I found all the steps different, and I did not have the courage to go out in the middle of the slippery floor and mince it and toe it in front of the teacher. When I retired to a corner and tried to play dominoes, I became suddenly shy of my partner; and I never could win a game of checkers, although formerly I used to beat my father at it. I tried to be friends with a little girl I had known in Chelsea, but she met my advances coldly. She lived on Appleton Street, which was too aristocratic to mix with Wheeler Street. Geraldine was studying elocution, and she wore a scarlet cape and hood, and she was going on the stage by and by. I acknowledged that her sense of superiority was well-founded, and retired farther into my corner, for the first time conscious of my shabbiness and lowliness.

I looked on at the dancing until I could endure it no longer. Overcome by a sense of isolation and unfitness, I slipped out of the room, avoiding the teacher's eye, and went home to write melancholy poetry.

What had come over me? Why was I, the confident, the ambitious, suddenly grown so shy and meek? Why was the candidate for encyclopædic immortality overawed by a scarlet hood? Why did I, a very tomboy yesterday, suddenly find my playmates stupid, and hide-and-seek a bore? I did not know why. I only knew that I was lonely and troubled and sore; and I went home to write sad poetry.

I shall never forget the pattern of the red carpet in our parlor,—we had achieved a carpet since Chelsea days,—because I lay for hours face down on the floor, writing poetry on a screechy slate. When I had perfected my verses, and copied them fair on the famous blue-lined note paper, and saw that I had made a very pathetic poem indeed, I felt better. And this happened over and over again. I gave up the dancing-club, I ceased to know the rowdy little boys, and I wrote melancholy poetry oftener, and felt better. The centre table became my study. I read much, and mooned between chapters, and wrote long letters to Miss Dillingham.

For some time I wrote to her almost daily. That was when I found in my heart such depths of woe as I could not pack into rhyme. And finally there came a day when I could utter my trouble in neither verse nor prose, and I implored Miss Dillingham to come to me and hear my sorrowful revelations. But I did not want her to come to the house. In the house there was no privacy; I could not talk. Would she meet me on Boston Common at such and such a time?

Would she? She was a devoted friend, and a wise woman. She met me on Boston Common. It was a gray autumn day—was it not actually drizzling?—and I was cold sitting on the bench; but I was thrilled through and through with the sense of the magnitude of my troubles, and of the romantic nature of the rendezvous.

Who that was even half awake when he was growing up does not know what all these symptoms betokened? Miss Dillingham understood, and she wisely gave me no inkling of her diagnosis. She let me talk and kept a grave face. She did not belittle my troubles—I made specific charges against my home, members of my family, and life in general; she did not say that I would get over them, that every growing girl suffers from the blues; that I was, in brief, a little goose stretching my wings for flight. She told me rather that it would be noble to bear my sorrows bravely, to soothe those who irritated me, to live each day with all my might. She reminded me of great men and women who have suffered, and who overcame their troubles by living and working. And she sent me home amazingly comforted, my pettiness and self-consciousness routed by the quiet influence of her gray eyes searching mine. This, or something like this, had to be repeated many times, as anybody will know who was present at the slow birth of his manhood. From now on, for some years, of course, I must weep and laugh out of season, stand on tiptoe to pluck the stars in heaven, love and hate immoderately, propound theories of the destiny of man, and not know what is going on in my own heart.

40

A Visitor's America

Like many other foreigners, English men of letters took great interest in the development of American society. What distinguished their concern was the stream of books they issued to acquaint the world with their conclusions. Dickens, Thackeray, Anthony Trollope, Matthew Arnold, and Oscar Wilde all visited the United States and recorded their impressions. In 1912 the novelist Arnold Bennett (1867–1931) joined this list, spending several weeks in America before returning home to pen his observations. A versatile and accomplished writer who catered to many levels of taste, Bennett caught something of the energy and concentration of American life, in the days just preceding World War I. Present-day problems and prejudices, as well as distinctive features of the prewar era, are embedded in Bennett's picture of the new technology and the world of business.

YOUR UNITED STATES
Arnold Bennett

What strikes and frightens the backward European as much as anything in the United States is the efficiency and fearful universality of the telephone. Just as I think of the big cities as agglomerations pierced everywhere by elevator-shafts full of movement, so I think of them as being threaded, under pavements and over roofs and between floors and ceilings and between walls, by millions upon millions of live filaments that unite all the privacies of the organism—and destroy them in order to make one immense publicity! I do not mean that Europe has failed to adopt the telephone, nor that in Europe there are no hotels with the dreadful curse of an active telephone in every room. But I do mean that the European telephone is a toy, and a somewhat clumsy one, compared with the inexorable seriousness of the American telephone. Many otherwise highly civilized Europeans are as timid in addressing a telephone as they would be in addressing a royal sovereign. The average European middle-class householder still speaks of his telephone, if he has one, in the same falsely casual tone as the corresponding American is liable to speak of his motor-car. It is naught—a negligible trifle—but somehow it comes into the conversation!

"How odd!" you exclaim. And you are right. It is we Europeans who are wrong, through no particular fault of our own.

The American is ruthlessly logical about the telephone. The only occasion on

From *Your United States* (New York and London, 1912), 73–98.

which I was in really serious danger of being taken for a madman in the United States was when, in a Chicago hotel, I permanently removed the receiver from the telephone in a room designed (doubtless ironically) for slumber. The whole hotel was appalled. Half Chicago shuddered. In response to the prayer of a deputation from the management I restored the receiver. On the horrified face of the deputation I could read the unspoken query: "Is it conceivable that you have been in this country a month without understanding that the United States is primarily nothing but a vast congeries of telephone-cabins?" Yes, I yielded and admired! And I surmise that on my next visit I shall find a telephone on every table of every restaurant that respects itself.

It is the efficiency of the telephone that makes it irresistible to a great people whose passion is to "get results" —the instancey with which the communication is given, and the clear loudness of the telephone's voice in reply to yours: phenomena utterly unknown in Europe. Were I to inhabit the United States, I too should become a victim of the telephone habit, as it is practised in its most advanced form in those suburban communities to which I have already incidentally referred at the end of the previous chapter. There a woman takes to the telephone as women in more decadent lands take to morphia. You can see her at morn at her bedroom window, pouring confidences into her telephone, thus combining the joy of an innocent vice with the healthy freshness of breeze and sunshine. It has happened to me to sit in a drawing-room, where people gathered round the telephone as Europeans gather around a fire, and to hear immediately after the ejaculation of a number into the telephone a sharp ring from outside through the open window, and then to hear in answer to the question, "What are you going to wear to-night?" two absolutely simultaneous replies, one loudly from the telephone across the room, and the other faintlier from a charming human voice across the garden: "I don't know. What are you?" Such may be the pleasing secondary scientific effect of telephoning to the lady next door on a warm afternoon.

Now it was obvious that behind the apparently simple exterior aspects of any telephone system there must be an intricate and marvelous secret organization. In Europe my curiosity would probably never have been excited by the thought of that organization—at home one accepts everything as of course!—but, in the United States, partly because the telephone is so much more wonderful and terrible there, and partly because in a foreign land one is apt to have strange caprices, I allowed myself to become the prey of a desire to see the arcanum concealed at the other end of all the wires; and thus, one day, under the high protection of a demigod of the electrical world, I paid a visit to a telephone-exchange in New York, and saw therein what nine hundred and ninety-nine out of every thousand of the most ardent telephone-users seldom think about and will never see.

A murmuring sound, as of an infinity of scholars in a prim school conning their lessons, and a long row of young women seated in a dim radiance on a long row of precisely similar stools, before a long apparatus of holes and pegs and pieces of elastic cord, all extremely intent: that was the first broad impression. One saw at once that none of these young women had a single moment to spare; they were all involved in the tremendous machine, part of it, keeping pace with it and in it, and not daring to take their eyes off it for an instant, lest they should sin against it. What they were droning about it was impossible to guess; for if one stationed oneself close to any particular rapt young woman, she seemed to utter no sound, but simply and without ceasing to peg and unpeg holes at random among the thousands of holes before her, apparently in obedience to the signaling of faint, tiny lights that in thousands continually expired and were rekindled. (It was so that these tiny lights should be distinguishable that the illumination of the secret and finely appointed chamber was kept dim.) Throughout the whole length of the apparatus the colored elastic cords to which the pegs were attached kept crossing one another in fantastic patterns.

We who had entered were ignored. We might have been ghosts, invisible and inaudible. Even the supervisors, less-young women set in authority, did not turn to glance at us as they moved restlessly peering behind the stools. And yet somehow I could hear the delicate shoulders of all the young women saying, without speech: "Here come these tyrants and taskmasters again, who have invented this exercise which nearly but not quite cracks our little brains for us! They know exactly how much they can get out of us, and they get it. They are cleverer than us and more power than us; and we have to submit to their discipline. But—" And afar off I could hear: "What are you going to wear to-night?" "Will you dine with me to-night?" "I want two seats." "Very well, thanks, and how is Mrs. . . . ?" "When can I see you to-morrow?" "I'll take your offer for those bonds." . . . And I could see the interiors of innumerable offices and drawing-rooms. . . . But of course I could hear and see nothing really except the intent drone and quick gesturing of those completely absorbed young creatures in the dim radiance, on stools precisely similar.

I understood why the telephone service was so efficient. I understood not merely from the demeanor of the long row of young women, but from everything else I had seen in the exact and diabolically ingenious ordering of the whole establishment.

We were silent for a time, as though we had entered a church. We were, perhaps unconsciously, abashed by the intensity of the absorption of these neat young women. After a while one of the guides, one of the inscrutable beings who had helped to invent and construct the astounding organism, began in a low voice on the forlorn hope of making me comprehend the mechanism of a telephone-call and its response. And I began on the forlorn hope of persuading him by intelligent acting that I did comprehend. We each made a little progress. I could not tell him that, though I genuinely and humbly admired his particular variety of genius, what interested me in the affair was not the mechanics, but the human equation. As a professional reader of faces, I glanced as well as I could sideways at those bent girls' faces to see if they were happy. An absurd inquiry! Do *I* look happy when I'm at work, I wonder! Did they then look reasonably content? Well, I came to the conclusion that they looked like most other faces—neither one thing nor the other. Still, in a great establishment, I would sooner search for sociological information in the faces of the employed than in the managerial rules.

"What do they earn?" I asked, when we emerged from the ten-atmosphere pressure of that intense absorption. (Of course I knew that no young women could possibly for any length of time be as intensely absorbed as these appeared to be. But the illusion was there, and it was effective.)

I learned that even the lowest beginner earned five dollars a week. It was just the sum I was paying for a pair of clean sheets every night at a grand hotel. And that the salary rose to six, seven, eight, eleven, and even fourteen dollars for supervisors, who, however, had to stand on their feet seven and a half hours a day, as shopgirls do for ten hours a day; and that in general the girls had thirty minutes for lunch, and a day off every week, and that the Company supplied them gratuitously with tea, coffee, sugar, couches, newspapers, arm-chairs, and fresh air, of which last fifty fresh cubic feet were pumped in for every operator every minute.

Said the demigod of the electrical world, condescendingly: "All this telephone business is done on a mere few hundred horse-power. Come away, and I'll show you electricity in bulk."

And I went away with him, thoughtful. In spite of the inhuman perfection of its functioning, that exchange was a very human place indeed. It brilliantly solved some problems; it raised others. Excessively difficult to find any fault whatever in it! A marvelous service, achieved under strictly hygienic conditions—and young women must make their way through the world! And yet—Yes, a very human place indeed!

The demigods of the electric world do not condescend to move about in petrol motor-cars. In the exercise of a natural and charming coquetry they insist on electrical traction, and it was in the most modern and soundless electric brougham that we arrived at nightfall under the overhanging cornice-eaves of two gigantic Florentine palaces—just such looming palaces, they appeared in the dark, as may be seen in any central street of Florence, with a cinema-show blazing its signs on the ground floor, and Heaven knows what remnants of Italian aristocracy in the mysterious upper stories. Having entered one of the palaces, simultaneously with a tornado of wind, we passed through long, deserted, narrow galleries, lined with thousands of small, caged compartments containing "transformers," and on each compartment was a label bearing always the same words: "Danger, 6,600 volts." "Danger, 6,600 volts." "Danger, 6,600 volts." A wondrous relief when we had escaped with our lives from the menace of those innumerable volts! And then we stood on a high platform surrounded by handles, switches, signals—apparatus enough to put all New York into darkness, or to annihilate it in an instant by the unloosing of terrible cohorts of volts!—and faced an enormous white hall, sparsely peopled by a few colossal machines that seemed to be revolving and oscillating about their business with the fatalism of conquered and resigned leviathans. Immaculately clean, inconceivably tidy, shimmering with brilliant light under its lofty and beautiful ceiling, shaking and roaring with the terrific thunder of its own vitality, this hall in which no common voice could make itself heard produced nevertheless an effect of magical stillness, silence, and solitude. We were alone in it, save that now and then in the far-distant spaces a figure might flit and disappear between the huge glinting columns of metal. It was a hall enchanted and inexplicable. I understood nothing of it. But I understood that half the electricity of New York was being generated by its engines of a hundred and fifty thousand horse-power, and that if the spell were lifted the elevators of New York would be immediately paralyzed, and the twenty million lights expire beneath the eyes of a startled population. I could have gazed at it to this day, and brooded to this day upon the human imaginations that had perfected it; but I was led off, hypnotized, to see the furnaces and boilers under the earth. And even there we were almost alone, to such an extent had one sort of senseless matter been compelled to take charge of another sort of senseless matter. The odyssey of the coal that was lifted high out of ships on the tide beyond, to fall ultimately into the furnaces within, scarcely touched by the hand-wielded shovel, was by itself epical. Fresh air pouring in at the rate of twenty-four million cubic feet per hour cooled the entire palace, and gave to these stoke-holes the uncanny quality of refrigerators. The lowest horror of the steamship had been abolished here.

I was tempted to say: "This alone is fit to be called the heart of New York!"

But was it necessary to come to America in order to see and describe telephone-exchanges and electrical power-houses? Do not these wonders exist in all the cities of earth? They do, but not to quite the same degree of wondrousness. Hat-shops, and fine hat-shops, exist in New York, but not to quite the same degree of wondrousness as in Paris. People sing in New York, but not with quite the same natural lyricism as in Naples. The great civilizations all present the same features; but it is just the differences in degree between the same feature in this civilization and in that—it is just these differences which together constitute and illustrate the idiosyncrasy of each. It seems to me that the brains and the imagination of America shone superlatively in the conception and ordering of its vast organizations of human beings, and of machinery, and of the two combined. By them I was more profoundly attracted, impressed, and inspired than by any other non-spiritual phenomena whatever in the United States. For me they were the proudest material achievements, and essentially the most poetical achievements, of the United States. And that is why I am dwelling on them.

Further, there are business organizations in America of a species which do not flourish at all in Europe. For example, the "mail-order house," whose secrets were very generously displayed to me in Chicago—a peculiar establishment which sells merely everything (except patent-medicines)—on condition that you order it by post. Go into that house with money in your palm, and ask for a fan or a flail or a fur-coat or a fountain-pen or a fiddle, and you will be requested to return home and write a letter about the proposed purchase, and stamp the letter and drop it into a mail-box, and then to wait till the article arrives at your door. That house is one of the most spectacular and pleasing proofs that the inhabitants of the United States are thinly scattered over an enormous area, in tiny groups, often quite isolated from stores. On the day of my visit sixty thousand letters had been received, and every executable order contained in these was executed before closing time, by the co-ordinated efforts of over four thousand female employees and over three thousand males. The conception would make Europe dizzy. Imagine a merchant in Moscow trying to inaugurate such a scheme!

A little machine no bigger than a soup-plate will open hundreds of envelopes at once. They are all the same, those envelopes; they have even less individuality than sheep being sheared, but when the contents of one—any one at random—are put into your hand, something human and distinctive is put into your hand. I read the caligraphy on a blue sheet of paper, and it was written by a woman in Wyoming, a neat, earnest, harassed, and possibly rather harassing woman, and she wanted all sorts of things and wanted them intensely—I could see that with clearness. This complex purchase was an important event in her year. So far as her imagination went, only one mail-order would reach the Chicago house that morning, and the entire establishment would be strained to meet it.

Then the blue sheet was taken from me and thrust into the system, and therein lost to me. I was taken to a mysteriously rumbling shaft of broad diameter, that pierced all the floors of the house and had trap-doors on each floor. And when one of the trap-doors was opened I saw packages of all descriptions racing after one another down spiral planes within the shaft. There were several of these great shafts—with divisions for mail, express, and freight traffic—and packages were ceaselessly racing down all of them, laden with the objects desired by the woman of Wyoming and her fifty-nine-thousand-odd fellow-customers of the day. At first it seemed to me impossible that that earnest, impatient woman in Wyoming should get precisely what she wanted; it seemed to me impossible that some mistake should not occur in all that noisy fever of rushing activity. But after I had followed an order, and seen it filled and checked, my opinion was that a mistake would be the most miraculous phenomenon in that establishment. I felt quite reassured on behalf of Wyoming.

And then I was suddenly in a room where six hundred billing-machines were being clicked at once by six hundred young women, a fantastic aural nightmare, though none of the young women appeared to be conscious that anything bizarre was going on. . . . And then I was in a printing-shop, where several lightning machines spent their whole time every day in printing the most popular work of reference in the United States, a bulky book full of pictures, with an annual circulation of five and a half million copies—the general catalogue of the firm. For the first time I realized the true meaning of the word "popularity"—and sighed. . . .

And then it was lunch-time for about a couple of thousand employees, and in the boundless restaurant I witnessed the working of the devices which enabled these legions to choose their meals, and pay for them (cost price) in a few moments, and without advanced mathematical calculations. The young head of the restaurant showed me, with pride, a menu of over a hundred dishes—Austrian, German, Hungarian, Italian, Scotch, French, and American; at prices from one cent up as high as ten cents (prime roast-beef)—and at the foot of the menu was his personal appeal: "*I* desire to extend to you a cordial invitation to inspect," etc. "*My* constant aim will be," etc. Yet it was not *his* restaurant. It was the firm's restaurant. Here I had a curious illustration of an admirable characteristic of American business methods that was always striking me—namely, the real delegation of responsibility. An American board of direction will put a man in charge of a department, as a viceroy over a province, saying, as it were: "This is yours. Do as

413

you please with it. We will watch the results." A marked contrast this with the centralizing of authority which seems to be ever proceeding in Europe, and which breeds in all classes at all ages—especially in France—a morbid fear and horror of accepting responsibility.

Later, I was on the ground level, in the midst of an enormous apparent confusion—the target for all the packages and baskets, big and little, that shot every instant in a continuous stream from those spiral planes, and slid dangerously at me along the floors. Here were the packers. I saw a packer deal with a collected order, and in this order were a number of tiny cookery utensils, a four-cent curling-iron, a brush, and two incredibly ugly pink china mugs, inscribed in cheap gilt respectively with the words "Father" and "Mother." Throughout my stay in America no moment came to me more dramatically than this moment, and none has remained more vividly in my mind. All the daily domestic life of the small communities in the wilds of the West and the Middle West, and in the wilds of the back streets of the great towns, seemed to be revealed to me by the contents of that basket, as the packer wrapped up and protected one article after another. I had been compelled to abandon a visitation of the West and of the small communities everywhere, and I was sorry. But here in a microcosm I thought I saw the simple reality of the backbone of all America, a symbol of the millions of the little plain people, who ultimately make possible the glory of the world-renowned streets and institutions in dazzling cities.

There was something indescribably touching in that curling-iron and those two mugs. I could see the table on which the mugs would soon proudly stand, and "father" and "mother" and children there at, and I could see the hand heating the curling-iron and applying it. I could see the whole little home and the whole life of the little home. . . . And afterward, as I wandered through the warehouses— pyramids of the same chair, cupboards full of the same cheap violin, stacks of the same album of music, acres of the same carpet and wallpaper, tons of the same gramophone, hundreds of tons of the same sewing-machine and lawn-mower—I felt as if I had been made free of the secrets of every village in every State of the Union, and as if I had lived in every little house and cottage thereof all my life! Almost no sense of beauty in those tremendous supplies of merchandise, but a lot of honesty, self-respect, and ambition fulfilled. I tell you I could hear the engaged couples discussing ardently over the pages of the catalogue what manner of bedroom suite they would buy, and what design of sideboard. . . .

Finally, I arrived at the firm's private railway station, where a score or more trucks were being laden with the multifarious boxes, bales, and parcels, all to leave that evening for romantic destinations such as Oregon, Texas, and Wyoming. Yes, the package of the woman of Wyoming's desire would ultimately be placed somewhere in one of those trucks! It was going to start off toward her that very night!

Impressive as this establishment was, finely as it illustrated the national genius for organization, it yet lacked necessarily, on account of the nature of its activity, those outward phenomena of splendor which charm the stranger's eye in the great central houses of New York, and which seem designed to sum up all that is most characteristic and most dazzling in the business methods of the United States. These central houses are not soiled by the touch of actual merchandise. Nothing more squalid than ink ever enters their gates. They traffic with symbols only, and the symbols, no matter what they stand for, are never in themselves sordid. The men who have created these houses seem to have realized that, from their situation and their importance, a special effort toward representative magnificence was their pleasing duty, and to have made the effort with a superb prodigality and an astounding ingenuity.

Take, for a good, glorious example, the very large insurance company, conscious that the eyes of the world are upon it, and that the entire United States is expecting it to uphold the national pride. All the splendors of all the sky-scrapers are united in its building. Its foyer and grand staircase will sustain comparison with those of the Paris Opéra. You might think you were going into a place of entertainment! And, as a fact, you are! This affair, with nearly four thousand clerks, is the huge toy and pastime of a group of millionaires who have discovered a way of honestly amusing themselves while gaining applause and advertisement. Within the foyer and beyond the staircase, notice the outer rooms, partitioned off by bronze grilles, looming darkly gorgeous in an eternal windowless twilight studded with the beautiful glowing green disks of electric-lamp shades; and under each disk a human head bent over the black-and-red magic of ledgers! The desired effect is at once obtained, and it is wonderful. Then lose yourself in and out of the ascending and descending elevators, and among the unending multitudes of clerks, and along the corridors of marble (total length exactly measured and recorded). You will be struck dumb. And immediately you begin to recover your speech you will be struck dumb again. . . .

Other houses, as has been seen, provide good meals for their employees at cost price. This house, then, will provide excellent meals, free of charge! It will install the most expensive kitchens and richly spacious restaurants. It will serve the delicate repasts with dignity. "Does all this lessen the wages?" No, not in theory. But in practice, and whether the management wishes or not, it must come out of the wages. "Why do you do it?" you ask the department chief, who apparently gets far more fun out of the contemplation of these refectories than out of the contemplation of premiums received and claims paid. "It is better for the employees," he says. "But we do it because it is better for us. It pays us. Good food, physical comfort, agreeable environment, scientific ventilation—all these things pay us. We get results from them." He does not mention horses, but you feel that the comparison is with horses. A horse, or a clerk, or an artisan—it pays equally well to treat all of them well. This is one of the latest discoveries of economic science, a discovery not yet universally understood.

I say you do not mention horses, and you certainly must not hint that the men in authority may have been actuated by motives of humanity. You must believe what you are told—that the sole motive is to get results. The eagerness with which all heads of model establishments would disavow to me any thought of being humane was affecting in its *naiveté*; it had that touch of ingenuous wistfulness which I remarked everywhere in America—and nowhere more than in the demeanor of many mercantile highnesses. (I hardly expect Americans to understand just what I mean here.) It was as if they would blush at being caught in an act of humanity, like school-boys caught praying. Still, to my mind, the white purity of their desire to get financial results was often muddied by the dark stain of a humane motive. I may be wrong (as people say), but I know I am not (as people think).

The further you advance into the penetralia of this arch-exemplar of American organization and profusion, the more you are amazed by the imaginative perfection of its detail: as well in the system of filing for instant reference fifty million separate documents, as in the planning of a concert-hall for the diversion of the human machines.

As we went into the immense concert-hall a group of girls were giving an informal concert among themselves. When lunch is served on the premises with chronographic exactitude, the thirty-five minutes allowed for the meal give an appreciable margin for music and play. A young woman was just finishing a florid song. The concert was suspended, and the whole party began to move humbly away at this august incursion.

"Sing it again; do, please!" the departmental chief suggested. And the florid song. The concert was suspended, and the whole party began to move humbly away the group fled, the thirty-five minutes being doubtless up. The departmental chief looked at me in silence, content, as much as to say: "This is how we do business in America." And I thought, "Yet another way of getting results!"

But sometimes the creators of the organization, who had provided everything, had been obliged to confess that they had omitted from their designs certain factors of evolution. Hat-cupboards were a feature of the women's offices—delightful specimens of sound cabinetry. And still, millinery was lying about all over the place, giving it an air of feminine occupation that was extremely exciting to a student on his travels. The truth was that none of those hats would go into the cupboards. Fashion had worsted the organization completely. Departmental chiefs had nothing to do but acquiesce in this startling untidiness. Either they must wait till the circumference of hats lessened again, or they must tear down the whole structure and rebuild it with due regard to hats.

Finally, we approached the sacred lair and fastness of the president, whose massive portrait I had already seen on several walls. Spaciousness and magnificence increased. Ceilings rose in height, marble was softened by the thick pile of carpets. Mahogany and gold shone more luxuriously. I was introduced into the vast ante-chamber of the presidential secretaries, and by the chief of them inducted through polished and gleaming barriers into the presence-chamber itself: a noble apartment, an apartment surpassing dreams and expectations, conceived and executed in a spirit of majestic prodigality. The president had not been afraid. And his costly audacity was splendidly justified of itself. This man had a sense of the romantic, of the dramatic, of the fit. And the qualities in him and his *état major* which had commanded the success of the entire enterprise were well shown in the brilliant symbolism of that room's grandiosity. . . . And there was the president's portrait again, gorgeously framed.

He came in through another door, an old man of superb physique, and after a little while he was relating to me the early struggles of his company. "My wife used to say that for ten years she never saw me," he remarked.

I asked him what his distractions were, now that the strain was over and his ambitions so gloriously achieved. He replied that occasionally he went for a drive in his automobile.

"And what do you do with yourself in the evenings?" I inquired.

He seemed a little disconcerted by this perhaps unaccustomed bluntness.

"Oh," he said, casually, "I read insurance literature."

He had the conscious mien and manners of a reigning prince. His courtesy and affability were impeccable and charming. In the most profound sense this human being had succeeded, for it was impossible to believe that, had he to live his life again, he would live it very differently.

Such a type of man is, of course, to be found in nearly every country; but the type flourishes with a unique profusion and perfection in the United States; and in its more prominent specimens the distinguishing idiosyncrasy of the average American successful man of business is magnified for our easier inspection. The rough, broad difference between the American and the European business man is that the latter is anxious to leave his work, while the former is anxious to get to it. The attitude of the American business man toward his business is pre-eminently the attitude of an artist. You may say that he loves money. So do we all—artists particularly. No stock-broker's private journal could be more full of dollars than Balzac's intimate correspondence is full of francs. But whereas the ordinary artist loves money chiefly because it represents luxury, the American business man loves it chiefly because it is the sole proof of success in his endeavor. He loves his business. It is not his toil, but his hobby, passion, vice, monomania—any vituperative epithet you like to bestow on it! He does not look forward to living in the evening; he lives most intensely when he is in the midst of his organization. His instincts are best appeased by the hourly excitements of a good, scrimmaging commercial day. He needs these excitements as some natures need alcohol. He cannot do without them.

On no other hypothesis can the unrivaled ingenuity and splendor and ruthlessness of American business undertakings be satisfactorily explained. They surpass the European, simply because they are never out of the thoughts of their directors, because they are adored with a fine frenzy. And for the same reason they are decked forth in magnificence. Would a man enrich his office with rare woods and stuffs and marbles if it were not a temple? Would he bestow graces on the environment if while he was in it the one idea at the back of his head was the anticipation of leaving it? Watch American business men together, and if you are a European you will clearly perceive that they are devotees. They are open with one another, as intimates are. Jealousy and secretiveness are much rarer among them

417

than in Europe. They show off their respective organizations with pride and with candor. They admire one another enormously. Hear one of them say enthusiastically of another: "It was a great idea he had—connecting his New York and his Philadelphia places by wireless—a great idea!" They call one another by their Christian names, fondly. They are capable of wonderful friendships in business. They are cemented by one religion—and it is not golf. For them the journey "home" is often not the evening journey, but the morning journey. Call this a hard saying if you choose: it is true. Could a man be happy long away from a hobby so entrancing, a toy so intricate and marvelous, a setting so splendid? Is it strange that, absorbed in that wondrous satisfying hobby, he should make love with the nonchalance of an animal? At which point I seem to have come dangerously near to the topic of the singular position of the American woman, about which everybody is talking.

41

Persisting Ideals

Woodrow Wilson (1856–1924) was elected President of the United States on November 5, 1912, only the second Democrat to serve in the White House since the Civil War. His campaign speeches against William Howard Taft and Theodore Roosevelt revealed his anxiety over the power certain "interests" had attained in American life and his desire to restore the meaningful competition and sense of participation that the previous decades of industrial concentration had helped erode.

A student of American history and government, from his graduate days at Johns Hopkins and his teaching at Wesleyan and Princeton, Wilson used the public forum as a means of inspiring men to share his version of the possibilities of democracy. His first inaugural, coming on the eve of dramatic reforms in the nation's financial structure, summed up with a religious intensity his assessment of the meaning of American life, and the wrongs that needed righting. As a statement of purposes and a declaration of mission, it stands in a long line of eloquent American testaments, going back, perhaps, to John Winthrop's famous exhortation on board the *Arbella* in 1630.

THE FIRST INAUGURAL
Woodrow Wilson

My Fellow Citizens:

There has been a change of government. It began two years ago, when the House of Representatives became Democratic by a decisive majority. It has now been completed. The Senate about to assemble will also be Democratic. The offices of President and Vice-President have been put into the hands of Democrats. What does the change mean? That is the question that is uppermost in our minds to-day. That is the question I am going to try to answer, in order, if I may, to interpret the occasion.

It means much more then the mere success of a party. The success of a party means little except when the Nation is using that party for a large and definite purpose. No one can mistake the purpose for which the Nation now seeks to use

From *Inaugural Addresses of the Presidents of the United States*, U.S. 82nd Congress, 2nd Session, House Document 540 (1952), 189–192.

the Democratic Party. It seeks to use it to interpret a change in its own plans and point of view. Some old things with which we had grown familiar, and which had begun to creep into the very habit of our thought and of our lives, have altered their aspect as we have latterly looked critically upon them, with fresh, awakened eyes; have dropped their disguises and shown themselves alien and sinister. Some new things, as we look frankly upon them, willing to comprehend their real character, have come to assume the aspect of things long believed in and familiar, stuff of our own convictions. We have been refreshed by a new insight into our own life.

We see that in many things that life is very great. It is incomparably great in its material aspects, in its body of wealth, in the diversity and sweep of its energy, in the industries which have been conceived and built up by the genius of individual men and the limitless enterprise of groups of men. It is great, also, very great, in its moral force.

Nowhere else in the world have noble men and women exhibited in more striking forms the beauty and the energy of sympathy and helpfulness and counsel in their efforts to rectify wrong, alleviate suffering, and set the weak in the way of strength and hope. We have built up, moreover, a great system of government, which has stood through a long age as in many respects a model for those who seek to set liberty upon foundations that will endure against fortuitous change, against storm and accident. Our life contains every great thing, and contains it in rich abundance.

But the evil has come with the good, and much fine gold has been corroded. With riches has come inexcusable waste. We have squandered a great part of what we might have used, and have not stopped to conserve the exceeding bounty of nature, without which our genius for enterprise would have been worthless and impotent, scorning to be careful, shamefully prodigal as well as admirably efficient. We have been proud of our industrial achievements, but we have not hitherto stopped thoughtfully enough to count the human cost, the cost of lives snuffed out, of energies overtaxed and broken, the fearful physical and spiritual cost to the men and women and children upon whom the dead weight and burden of it all has fallen pitilessly the years through. The groans and agony of it all had not yet reached our ears, the solemn, moving undertone of our life, coming up out of the mines and factories and out of every home where the struggle had its intimate and familiar seat. With the great Government went many deep secret things which we too long delayed to look into and scrutinize with candid, fearless eyes. The great Government we loved has too often been made use of for private and selfish purposes, and those who used it had forgotten the people.

At last a vision has been vouchsafed us of our life as a whole. We see the bad with the good, the debased and decadent with the sound and vital. With this vision we approach new affairs. Our duty is to cleanse, to reconsider, to restore, to correct the evil without impairing the good, to purify and humanize every process of our common life without weakening or sentimentalizing it. There has been something crude and heartless and unfeeling in our haste to succeed and be great. Our thought has been "Let every man look out for himself, let every generation look out for itself," while we reared giant machinery which made it impossible that any but those who stood at the levers of control should have a chance to look out for themselves. We had not forgotten our morals. We remembered well enough that we had set up a policy which was meant to serve the humblest as well as the most powerful, with an eye single to the standards of justice and fair play, and remembered it with pride. But we were very heedless and in a great hurry to be great.

We have come now to the sober second thought. The scales of heedlessness have fallen from our eyes. We have made up our minds to square every process of our national life again with the standards we so proudly set up at the beginning and have always carried at our hearts. Our work is a work of restoration.

We have itemized with some degree of particularity the things that ought to be altered and here are some of the chief items: A tariff which cuts us off from our proper part in the commerce of the world, violates the just principles of taxation, and makes the Government a facile instrument in the hands of private interests; a banking and currency system based upon the necessity of the Government to sell its bonds fifty years ago and perfectly adapted to concentrating cash and restricting credits; an industrial system which, take it on all its sides, financial as well as administrative, holds capital in leading strings, restricts the liberties and limits the opportunities of labor, and exploits without renewing or conserving the natural resources of the country; a body of agriculatural activities never yet given the efficiency of great business undertakings or served as it should be through the instrumentality of science taken directly to the farm, or afforded the facilities of credit best suited to its practical needs; water-courses undeveloped, waste places unreclaimed, forests untended, fast disappearing without plan or prospect of renewal, unregarded waste heaps at every mine. We have studied as perhaps no other nation has the most effective means of production, but we have not studied cost or economy as we should either as organizers of industry, as statesmen, or as individuals.

Nor have we studied and perfected the means by which government may be put at the service of humanity, in safeguarding the health of the Nation, the health of its men and its women and its children, as well as their rights in the struggle for existence. This is no sentimental duty. The firm basis of government is justice, not pity. These are matters of justice. There can be no equality or opportunity, the first essential of justice in the body politic, if men and women and children be not shielded in their lives, their very vitality, from the consequences of great industrial and social processes which they can not alter, control, or singly cope with. Society must see to it that it does not itself crush or weaken or damage its own constituent parts. The first duty of law is to keep sound the society it serves. Sanitary laws, pure food laws, and laws determining conditions of labor which individuals are powerless to determine for themselves are intimate parts of the very business of justice and legal efficiency.

These are some of the things we ought to do, and not leave the others undone, the old-fashioned, never-to-be-neglected, fundamental safeguarding of property and of individual right. This is the high enterprise of the new day: To lift everything that concerns our life as a Nation to the light that shines from the hearthfire of every man's conscience and vision of the right. It is inconceivable that we should do this as partisans; it is inconceivable we should do it in ignorance of the facts as they are or in blind haste. We shall restore, not destroy. We shall deal with our economic system as it is and as it may be modified, not as it might be if we had a clean sheet of paper to write upon; and step by step we shall make it what it should be, in the spirit of those who question their own wisdom and seek counsel and knowledge, not shallow self-satisfaction or the excitement of excursions whither they can not tell. Justice, and only justice, shall alway be our motto.

And yet it will be no cool process of mere science. The Nation has been deeply stirred, stirred by a solemn passion, stirred by the knowledge of wrong, of ideals lost, of government too often debauched and made an instrument of evil. The feelings with which we face this new age of right and opportunity sweep across our heartstrings like some air out of God's own presence, where justice and mercy are reconciled and the judge and the brother are one. We know our task to be no mere task of politics but a task which shall search us through and through, whether we be able to understand our time and the need of our people, whether we be indeed their spokesmen and interpreters, whether we have the pure heart to comprehend and the rectified will to choose our high course of action.

This is not a day of triumph; it is a day of dedication. Here muster, not the forces of party, but the forces of humanity. Men's hearts wait upon us; men's lives hang in the balance; men's hopes call upon us to say what we will do. Who shall live up to the great trust? Who dares fail to try? I summon all honest men, all patriotic, all forward-looking men, to my side. God helping me, I will not fail them, if they will but counsel and sustain me!

42

Over There

With high-minded slogans, Americans entered World War I, on their way to make the world safe for democracy. But the crusade had to be organized—men were to be trained, shipped abroad, supplied, put into units, deployed on a European front, and coordinated in battle with the Allies. Yet Americans had little military experience on which to draw. The Spanish-American War had been too brief and against too weak an enemy to teach the nation much. Yet despite their inexperience, Americans made quick progress, and their effort in World War I was remarkable for its effectiveness and efficiency. The troops fought bravely. They were well trained and well supplied.

The letters between General of the Army John J. Pershing and Woodrow Wilson's Secretary of War, Newton D. Baker, reveal some of the dimensions and details of this accomplishment. Pershing was a critical figure, a general who could not only fight, but who could organize. Graduating from West Point in 1886 at the age of twenty-six, Pershing had no military experience until the Spanish-American War. He served first as a captain in the army, and subsequently was an officer in the Philippine Occupation Army. He also led an unsuccessful expedition in 1916 against the Mexican outlaw Pancho Villa. In 1917 Pershing took command of the American forces and helped to put together a modern, organized, and efficient army.

EXPERIENCES IN THE WORLD WAR
John J. Pershing

**1   General John J. Pershing
to Newton D. Baker, June 18, 1918**

My Dear Mr. Secretary:

I wish to take up a subject of very great importance. That is the burning one of getting troops over here and forming an army as rapidly as possible. I think it is imperative that our whole program for the next ten or twelve months be reconstructed. The Department's estimate of 91,000 men per month after August is

From *My Experiences in the World War* (New York, 1931), II: 107–108, 110–113, 181–191, with permission of the Estate of General Pershing.

not nearly as much as we must do. Mr. Secretary, I cannot emphasize this point too forcibly. We should have at least three million men in France by next April ready for the spring and summer campaign. To achieve this will involve the shipment of 250,000 men per month for the eight months ending April 1st. This is the smallest program that we should contemplate. The situation among our Allies is such that unless we can end the war next year we are likely to be left practically alone in the fight. If further serious reverses come to us this year it is going to be very difficult even to hold France in the war.

The morale of both the French and British troops is not what it should be. The presence of our troops has braced them up very much but their staying powers are doubtful. Our 2d and 3d Divisions actually stopped the Germans. The French were not equal to it. I fear that I must put some of our regiments into the weaker French divisions, temporarily, to give them courage.

After checking the German offensive, we must be prepared to strike as soon as possible. The German divisions are growing weaker and their manpower is running low. The German people would be inclined to make peace if they felt a few very heavy blows. We should be ready to give them. On the other hand, if we do not hasten, and the war is allowed to drag along during next year and the year after, we shall run a very great risk that Germany will recuperate by conscripting manpower from the Western Provinces of Russia. The British and French Governments are alarmed about this, as you know, and I consider it a real danger.

Then, we must bear in mind the effect of a long war upon our own people. The idea seems prevalent at home that the war is going to be finished within a year and our people are wrought up and wish to see a big effort at once. But if we do not make ourselves strong enough on this front to assume the offensive and push the war to a finish, there is going to be criticism and dissatisfaction at home and a general letting down of our war spirit. Moreover, by using a large force and ending the war we shall avoid the large losses that have so dreadfully depleted our Allies. Let us take every advantage of the high tide of enthusiasm and win the war.

I think that with proper representations as to the necessity for shipping, the British would do all they could to assist us. In fact, Sir Graeme Thomson said he thought the British would be able to continue the recent shipping schedule indefinitely. On our side, we should demand a greater amount of American tonnage than has hitherto been allotted to the army from the sum total of our available shipping, which is constantly increasing. Our shipping advisers here say that several hundred thousand tons can be added to the army allotment by proper paring.

As to the preparation of this new army, may I not beg of you to consider a draft of 2,000,000 men by December 1st? My recent cable asking that 1,500,000 be called out should now be increased to 2,000,000. They should be called out, beginning now, at the rate of 400,000 per month for the next five months. We should not again be without trained men as we find ourselves now. Every possible means should be exhausted to train, clothe, and equip this force by the end of the year. These are strong words and the force looks large, but we are face to face with the most serious situation that has ever confronted a nation, and it must be met at any sacrifice and without any delay.

I think we must bring women into our factories, transforming the whole country into an organization to push the war. The British could help on clothing. As to munitions, it matters little whether we have a particular kind of artillery; if we cannot get the French, we should take the British. The same can be said of small arms and personal equipment. If our ordnance cannot furnish them, the French and British have them. So in equipment and armament, there should be no delay.

I am having a detailed study made of the supply and shipping questions involved, especially as to the amount of supplies that can be obtained in Europe. The pooling program will soon be in operation and I think we shall be able to obtain a greater amount of supplies here than we had anticipated. Spain is practically a virgin field for us which is as yet undeveloped and which, with diplomatic handling, should yield much more than she has hitherto yielded. I shall look into this further.

The question of accommodations for our troops may have to be considered. If that stands in the way, then I am in favor of asking Congress to permit the billeting of troops. The French people are standing for it even by the forces of two foreign nations, why should not we at home be willing to billet our own troops among our own people?

As to handling everything that must be sent over under this program, I stand ready now, without waiting for detailed study, to say that we can do it. The supply question will be less difficult as the pooling and the feeding of our troops by the Allies develop. The great port of Marseille is largely unused and will handle much additional tonnage. Our port construction and port facilities are progressing, the railroads are getting better and storage is becoming easier because the French are finding more and more room. The horse question will also probably be worked out here. So that there need be no hesitation in adopting the plan. We should do all that is humanly possible to carry it out.

There is nothing so dreadfully important as winning this war and every possible resource should be made immediately available. Mr. Secretary, the question is so vital to our country, and the necessity of winning the war is so great, that there is no limit to which we should not go to carry out the plan I have outlined for the next ten months, and we must be prepared to carry it on still further after that at the same rate or maybe faster.

I have outlined the plan as the least we should count upon to insure success, and I hope, with your strong support, that the President will approve it.

2 General John J. Pershing to Newton D. Baker, June 21, 1918

My Dear Mr. Secretary:

The present state of the war under the continued German offensive makes it necessary to consider at once the largest possible military program for the United States. The morale of the French Government and of the High Command is believed to be good but it is certain that the morale of the lower grades of the French Army is distinctly poor. Both the French and British people are extremely tired of the war and their troops are reflecting this attitude in their frequent inability to meet successfully the German attacks. It is the American soldiers now in France upon whom they rely. It is the moral as well as material aid given by the American soldier that is making the continuation of the war possible. Only the continual arrival of American troops and their judicious employment can restore the morale of our Allies and give them courage. The above represents the views of the Allied Military leaders as told me in person by General Foch himself, and I believe it is also the view of the civil leaders. We must start immediately on our plans for the future and be ready to strike this fall in order to tide us over till spring, when we should have a big army ready. The war can be brought to a successful conclusion next year if we only go at it now. From a purely military point of view it is essential that we make this effort, especially for the reasons above stated and on account of the grave possibility that the enemy will obtain supplies and men from Russia before next year.

To meet the demands imposed by the above plan our minimum effort should be based on sending to France prior to May, 1919, a total force, including that already here, of 66 divisions (or better, if possible) together with the necessary corps and army troops, service of supply troops, and replacements. This plan would give an available force of about 3,000,000 soldiers for the summer campaign of 1919, and if this force were maintained, would in conjunction with our Allies give us every hope of concluding the war in 1919.

3   Newton D. Baker
to General John J. Pershing, July 6, 1918

My Dear General Pershing:

I have your letter of June 18, which reached me promptly. I have been studying with more than ordinary care and interest the dispatches of the past week or two with reference to the enlargement of our military effort and program. When your cablegram suggesting a 60-division program came I immediately set about the necessary inquiries to discover just how far it fell within the range of industrial possibility. When the 100-division program came it occurred to me that we ought to study the situation with the view of determining the maximum amount we can do. I have the feeling that this war has gone on long enough and if any exertion on our part or any sacrifice can speed its successful termination even by a single day, we should make it. We are therefore now having studies made to show the things necessary to be done for three possible programs, one involving 60, one 80, and the other 100 divisions by the first of July, 1919. As soon as these programs are worked out we will, in consultation with the War Industries Board, determine how far manufacturing facilities already in existence or possible to be created can supply the necessary material, and the assistance we shall have to have in the way of heavy artillery and transportation from the British and French. It will then be possible to take up with those Governments a frank exhibition of the possibilities and to arrange for concerted action among us which will lead to the increase in our effort which you and General Foch recommend. In the meantime, I have asked the British Government to continue the troop ships which they have had in our service during June through July and August, and have told them frankly that we are considering an enlargement of our program which may require for a time at least the uninterrupted service of all the ships which we have been using. If we are able in July and August to match the performance of June, it will mean another half-million men in France, as the June embarkation figures from this country show slightly more than 279,000 men. Our own ships carried during that month something more than 100,000, which is, of course, doing better than our part as we originally calculated it. I think it highly important that neither General Foch nor the British and French Governments should assume our ability to carry out an enlarged program until we ourselves have studied it. There is no disposition on the part of the United States to shrink from any sacrifice or any effort, and yet experience has taught us that great as our capacity is in industry it takes time to build new factories, get the necessary machine tools, and bring together the raw materials for any large increase in industrial output, and I am especially concerned that there should be no disappointment on the part of our Allies. I would very much rather they expect less and receive more, than to expect more and be disappointed in the result. One of the happy effects of the recent accelerated shipment of troops has been that we have out-stripped our promises and, if I judge correctly the effect of this in Europe, it has been most agreeable and heartening.

The Operations Committee of the General Staff is pressing forward the necessary studies. They involve, of course, questions of clothing, small arms, ammunition, transportation, and training. On the latter subject I am beginning to be fairly free from doubts; the troops which we have recently sent you have admittedly been of an uneven quality, chiefly because we have made up deficiencies in divisions about to sail by taking men from other divisions, with consequent disorganization of those divisions from which men were repeatedly taken, and when we got to a place where we could no longer carry out this process, fairly raw men had to be used in order to keep divisions from sailing short. The plan inaugurated by General March of having replacement divisions in this country from which deficiencies could be supplied without robbing other divisions and disorganizing them, seems to me to solve the problem, and the divisions which come to you in August and September will, I am sure, show highly beneficial results from this policy. In the meantime, we have discovered two things about training in this country which apparently nobody knew or thought of before we went into the war; first, that while it may take nine months or a year to train raw recruits into soldiers in peace time, when there is no inspiration from an existing struggle, it takes no such length of time now when the great dramatic battles are being fought and men are eager to qualify themselves to participate in them. We are certainly able to get more training into a man now in three months than would be possible in nine months of peace-time training. And, second, we have learned that to keep men too long in training camps in this country makes them go stale and probably does as much harm by the spirit of impatience and restlessness aroused as it does good by the longer drilling. The men in our training camps are champing at the bit, and this applies not only to the officers, who naturally want their professional opportunity, but to the men as well. Indeed, one of the difficulties in America is to make people content with the lot which keeps them here for any length of time, so impatient are we all, military men and civilians alike, to get to France where the real work is being done. As a consequence of these discoveries, I feel that we will be perfectly safe if we have a million men in training in the United States at all times. That will enable us to feed them out to you at the rate of 250,000 a month and bring that number in by draft at the other end, which will always give us an adequate supply of men who have had as much training as they can profitably secure here in the United States. The finishing touches in any event will have to be given in France, and I think you will find that men who have had four months' training here are pretty nearly ready for use in association with your veteran and experienced troops, and that no prolonged period of European training, for infantry at least, will be found necessary. This makes the problem very simple from the point of view of the draft and the training camps. A number of the camps originally established by us have now been developed for specialized technical uses, but we still have a large number, and I think an adequate number, of camps which can be enlarged without great expense, and there seems little likelihood of our being obliged to resort to the billeting system, although of course we should not hesitate to do it if the need arose.

All accounts which we receive in this country of the conduct of our men are most stimulating and encouraging. Apparently the common opinion is that we have rendered valuable, if not indispensable, service already, in a purely military way, in the great battles. I saw a letter a day or two ago from Mr. Cravath to Mr. Leffingwell, in which he gave the opinion of British and French men of affairs on the subject of the American troops, and it was enthusiastic. I was a little afraid that too enthusiastic comment might create a feeling of resentment on the part of our allies. Their men, of course, have stood these attacks for a long time, and it would only be human if they resented the newcomers getting too much attention at the expense of organizations which are battle-scarred and have had their valor tested in great conflicts; and I have a little feared, too, that if our people here at home were fed too many stories of success they might get the notion that this great task is going to be easy for Americans and be ill-prepared for any reverse, no matter how slight, which might come. For that reason I have exercised a good deal of self-restraint in my own discussion with the newspapermen and in such public addresses as I have made, seeking always to couple up the British and the French with our American soldiers and to make the whole war a matter of common effort, rather than of our own national effort. This has been especially easy because the spirit of America is now very high. The country is thoroughly unified and is waiting only to be shown how it can make further effective sacrifices and efforts. It occurs to me in this connection that it might be wise for you in your communiqués, from time to time, to refer to slight repulses suffered by our men; but of course I do not want our men to be repulsed merely to balance the news.

On the 1st of July I wrote the President that 1,019,000 men had embarked from the United States for France. There had been so much speculation about numbers that it seemed necessary to be frank and tell the facts. The American people are accustomed to demanding the facts and there was some impatience manifested with the Department for its continued policy of silence on this subject. I realized when I made the statement that in all likelihood I should have to discontinue further reference to numbers, at least further specific references. The Germans, French, and British of course make no such announcements, and our allies will not like to have us adopting a different course. There are doubtless good military reasons for not being very generous with information of this kind, which finds its way to the enemy and enables them to make more certain calculations. Still, if the rate of shipments which we have maintained for the last two or three months can be kept up for another six months, I am not very sure that exact news carried to Germany of the arrival of Americans in France might not be helpful to us, rather than harmful. The German Government cannot fail to be impressed by this steady stream of fresh soldiers to the Western front.

The President and I have had several conferences about your situation in France, both of us desiring in every possible way to relieve you of unnecessary burdens, but of course to leave you with all the authority necessary to secure the best results from your forces and to supply all the support and assistance we possibly can. As the American troops in France become more and more numerous and the battle initiative on some parts of the front passes to you, the purely military part of your task will necessarily take more and more of your time, and both the President and I want to feel that the planning and executing of military undertakings has your personal consideration and that your mind is free for that as far as possible. The American people think of you as their "fighting General," and I want them to have that idea more and more brought home to them. For these reasons, it seems to me that if some plan could be devised by which you would be free from any necessity of giving attention to services of supply it would help, and one plan in that direction which suggested itself was to send General Goethals over to take charge of the services of supply, establishing a direct relationship between him and Washington and allowing you to rely upon him just as you would rely upon the supply departments of the War Department if our military operations were being conducted in America, instead of in France. Such a plan would place General Goethals rather in a coördinate than a subordinate relationship to you, but of course it would transfer all of the supply responsibilities from you to him and you could then forget about docks, railroads, storage houses, and all the other vast industrial undertakings to which up to now you have given a good deal of your time and, as you know, we all think with superb success. I would be very glad to know what you think about this suggestion. I realize that France is very far from the United States and that our reliance upon cables makes a very difficult means of communication, so that you may prefer to have the supply system as one of your responsibilities. I would be grateful if you would think the problem over and tell me quite frankly just what you think on the subject. The President and I will consider your reply together, and you may rely upon our being guided only by confidence in your judgment and the deep desire to aid you.

One other aspect of your burdens the President feels can be somewhat lightened by a larger use of General Bliss as diplomatic intermediary. The President is adopting as a definite rule of action an insistence upon Inter-Allied military questions being referred to the Permanent Military Representatives. Our difficulty here has been that the British representative would present something for consideration without the knowledge of the French, or the French without the knowledge of the British, and when we took the matter up for decision we would sometimes find that the other nation felt aggrieved at not being consulted. As each of the Allied Nations is represented at Versailles, the President is now uniformly saying with regard to all Inter-Allied military questions, that their presentation to him should come through the Permanent Military Representatives who, in a way, are a kind of staff for General Foch and undoubtedly maintain such close relations with him as to make any proposition which they consider one upon which his views are ascertained. As the President deals in matters of military diplomacy with General Bliss, it would seem that he could with propriety relieve you of some part of the conferences and consultations which in the early days you were obliged to have with the British War Office and the French War Office, thus simplifying the presentation of Inter-Allied questions to the President.

Mr. Stettinius will leave very shortly for Europe; I enclose you copy of a letter which I have given him, outlining the inquiries which I desire to have him make. You will find him a very considerate man in the matter of demands upon your time, as he is accustomed to dealing with busy men and not prolonging conferences beyond their useful limit.

It seems not unlikely at present that I shall myself come over to Europe in connection with our enlarged military program. If we find that our ability to do the thing depends upon French and British coöperation it will be a good deal simpler to put the whole question up to the British and French Cabinets and get definite agreements of coöperation and concerted action. Cablegrams are of course inconclusive and uncertain, and I constantly find that even letters fail to carry just the spirit in which they are dictated. When I write you, of course I know that our personal relations and knowledge of each other are too cordial and entire to allow any sort of misunderstanding, but I haven't the same acquaintance with the British and French Cabinet officers, and with them the presumptions do not obtain which are always implied in our correspondence. I confess I am somewhat moved to this idea of the necessity for my going by my desire to go; it is a tremendous inspiration to see our forces and to look at the work which you and they have done.

Cordially Yours.

4   General John J. Pershing
to Newton D. Baker, July 28, 1918

My Dear Mr. Secretary:

I have your letter of July 6th and have gone over it very carefully.

I realize that a very large undertaking has been proposed in the 80 to 100 division program, and that to carry it out is going to require very great sacrifices on our part. But, as you say, the war has gone on long enough and should be brought to a close as early as it is possible for us to do it.

The main reason for an extreme effort on our part next year is the stimulating effect that our immediate entry into the war in a large way will have upon our allies. If we should not demonstrate our wish thus to bring the war to a speedy end our allies might not hold on over another year, and we shall need every ounce of fight they have left in them to win, not that we have not the men and the resources at home, but that if left to carry on the war alone, even on French soil, we would soon come to the limit of our ability to bring them over and supply them.

I realize that we shall be put to it to furnish all the equipment, the aviation, the artillery, the ammunition, the tanks, and especially the horses, but if we can win next year it will be worth the supreme effort necessary to provide all these things. I do not, of course, overlook the shipping, nor the very strenuous work necessary at this end to handle the immense quantity of freight that will be required. Our port facilities must be increased, our railroads must be improved, and we must have a large increase in cars and locomotives. These things must come along rapidly from now on. We are preparing estimates for what we shall need and will forward them by cable as soon as finished.

Just now we are passing through a very critical time. When the shipment of infantry and machine guns was increased during May, June and July, of course we had to reduce, or rather postpone, the corresponding troops for our service of the rear, with the result that we now find ourselves shorthanded and unable to handle as quickly as we should like the increase of supplies incident to the great expansion of our combatant forces.

To add to the difficulties there has been a shortage of replacements in men, as we have had to throw all available troops into the lines to stop the German advance. So that we have not even had any troops to spare for work to help out the rear, making it appear that we are unnecessarily falling behind in unloading ships. I have cabled a request for service of the rear troops to be sent at once and hope they will not be delayed. We have a lot to do to catch up and get our ports and lines of communication in shape to meet the heavy demands that are to be made upon them.

On June 23d, when Mr. Clemenceau was at my headquarters for the conference, I had an opportunity to speak about the use of our troops. I told him that they were being wasted and that instead of the Allies being always on the defensive, an American Army should be formed at once to strike an offensive blow and turn the tide of the war. He was very much impressed at such boldness, as he had heard only of our men going into French divisions as platoons or at most as regiments. Soon after that Pétain was called to Paris and I have heard was told my views. Anyway Pétain soon began to take another view.

Our troops have done well for new troops and the part they have taken has encouraged our allies, especially the French, to go in and help put over a counteroffensive. This offensive, between Soissons and Château-Thierry, was planned some time ago, to be undertaken especially in the event of the Germans

431

attempting to push their line south of the Marne; or to the east between the Marne and Reims. I had conferred with General Pétain and had arranged to put the 1st, 2d, and 26th Divisions in the attack north of the Marne, supported by the 4th, while the 3d and 28th were to be used south of the Marne. As it turned out, all these troops were engaged with results you already know. The participation by our troops made this offensive possible and in fact the brunt of it fell to them. Our divisions in this advance completely outstepped the French and had to slow down their speed occasionally for them to catch up.

Two American corps are now organized and on the active front. These are to be organized into the Field Army which will take its place in line under my immediate command on August 10th. We shall occupy a sector north of the Marne and probably replace the 6th French Army. At the same time we shall take over a permanent sector north of Toul and Nancy, where I shall organize a second army at an early date. After that we shall soon have troops enough for a third army. So that before long I shall have to relinquish command of the Field Army and command the group.

I have had to insist very strongly, in the face of determined opposition, to get our troops out of leading strings. You know the French and British have always advanced the idea that we should not form divisions until our men had three or four months with them. We have found, however, that only a short time was necessary to learn all they know, as it is confined to trench warfare almost entirely, and I have insisted on open warfare training. To get this training, it has been necessary to unite our men under our own commanders, which is now being done rapidly.

The additional fact that training with these worn-out French and British troops, if continued, is detrimental, is another reason for haste in forming our own units and conducting our own training. The morale of the Allies is low and association with them has had a bad effect upon our men. To counteract the talk our men have heard, we have had to say to our troops, through their officers, that we had come over to brace up the Allies and help them win and that they must pay no attention to loose remarks along that line by their Allied comrades.

The fact is that our officers and men are far and away superior to the tired Europeans. High officers of the Allies have often dropped derogatory remarks about our poorly trained staff and high commanders, which our men have stood as long as they can. Even Mr. Tardieu said some of these things to me a few days ago. I replied, in rather forcible language, that we had now been patronized as long as we would stand for it, and I wished to hear no more of that sort of nonsense. Orders have now been given by the French that all of our troops in sectors with the French would be placed under our own officers and that American division commanders would be given command of their own sectors. This has come about since my insistence forced the French to agree to the formation of an American Field Army.

At a conference called by General Foch last Wednesday, the 24th instant, plans for assuming the offensive this year were discussed, as well as tentative plans for 1919. This is the first time the American Army has been recognized as a participant, as such, alongside the Allies. I shall give you from time to time an outline of what our plans are, but hope you will soon be here so that I may discuss them with you.

I entirely agree with what you say regarding General Bliss as a diplomatic intermediary. However, very little of my time has been taken up with that sort of thing, except as it concerned questions of troop shipments and their use with British and French. As you know, I have the highest regard for General Bliss and our relations have been the most pleasant. I think he is admirably fitted to represent the President in many of these perplexing diplomatic questions that come up. He has excellent judgment, and is very highly regarded by the Allied official world.

Mr. Stettinius has arrived and we have had several conferences. I am very much delighted to have him here. His presence is going to relieve me entirely of all those difficult questions pertaining to the allocation of materials, and the determination of manufacturing programs and the like. His action will be able to prevent the continuous flow of cablegrams from the Allies to our War Department on all these subjects.

On the subject of General Goethals, I thank you very much for referring this matter to me. Mr. Secretary, our organization here is working well. It is founded upon sound principles. May I not emphasize again the principle of unity of command and responsibility. It has always been my understanding that you believed that full power should be given to the man on the spot and responsible for results. I would say this regardless of the person in command. Our organization here is so bound up with operations, and training, and supply, and transportation of troops, that it would be impossible to make it function if the control of our service of the rear were placed in Washington. Please let us not make the mistake of handicapping our army here by attempting to control these things from Washington, or by introducing any coördinate authority. All matters pertaining to these forces, after their arrival in France, should be under the General Staff here where they are being and can be handled satisfactory.

May I say a word about our training. Our successes here should not be hastily accepted as the basis for conclusions on the possibilities of building up efficient units by intensive training for short periods. Four months should be the minimum for drafts that are to enter as replacements in among old soldiers in organized units. But, it requires a much longer time than that to build units from the ground up. Eight or nine months, or even a year, would be better, so that if we could get all of next year's army in the ranks by November we should be much better prepared in the Spring for the immense task we are preparing for.

May I again express my warm appreciation of your confidence, and say also how gratifying it is to me to enjoy the personal relations that exist between us.

Will you please convey to the President my best compliments and the Army's faith in his leadership.

With very warm regards and sincere good wishes, I am

Very Faithfully.

433

43

The Diplomacy
of Woodrow Wilson

Woodrow Wilson's efforts at the negotiating table in Paris were not as successful as his armies in the field. The Treaty of Versailles was far from perfect. At times secret covenants and imperialism played a larger role than open diplomacy and national self-determination. Still, there had been victories for democratic procedures at Versailles, and some of the new national boundaries were excellent. But most important to Wilson was the provision for a League of Nations. The peace treaty itself might not be perfect, but the League, Wilson believed, would correct deficiencies. Confidently he returned home to defend his work.

The history of his effort in the fall and winter of 1919–1920 is still a subject of controversy. Was Wilson stubborn, refusing to make limited concessions to gain more important ends? Did his moralism and his sudden illness blind him to political realities? And what of his opponents? Was the leading foe of the League, Henry Cabot Lodge, acting from a personal dislike of Wilson? Joseph Tumulty, Wilson's private secretary, close friend, and adviser, addressed himself to these questions in a volume written in 1921. As one would expect, he gave Wilson the benefit of every doubt; but his account is an inside story with sufficient detail to allow the reader an opportunity to reach his own conclusions.

WOODROW WILSON
AS I KNEW HIM
Joseph Tumulty

The Treaty Fight

Upon his return home from Paris, the President immediately invited, in most cordial fashion, the members of the Senate Foreign Relations Committee to confer with him at the White House. Some of those who received the invitation immediately announced that as a condition precedent to their acceptance they

From *Woodrow Wilson as I Knew Him* (New York: Doubleday, 1921), 422–425, 430–431, 434–435, 438–448, 452–455.

would insist that the conference should not be secret in character and that what would happen there should be disclosed to the public. The President quickly accepted the conditions proposed by the Republican senators and made a statement from the White House that the conditions which the conferees named were highly acceptable to him and that he was willing and anxious to give to the public a stenographic report of everything that transpired. Never before did the President show himself more tactful or more brilliant in repartee. Surrounded by twenty or thirty men, headed by Senator Lodge, who hated him with a bitterness that was intense, the President, with quiet courtesy, parried every blow aimed at him.

No question, no matter how pointed it was, seemed to disturb his serenity. He acted like a lawyer who knew his case from top to bottom, and who had confidence in the great cause he was representing. His cards were frankly laid upon the table and he appeared like a fighting champion, ready to meet all comers. Indeed, this very attitude of frankness, openness, sincerity, and courtesy, one could see from the side-lines, was a cause of discomfort to Senator Lodge and the Republicans grouped about him, and one could also see written upon the faces of the Democratic senators in that little room a look of pride that they had a leader who carried himself so gallantly and who so brilliantly met every onslaught of the enemy. The President anticipated an abrupt adjournment of the conference with a courteous invitation to luncheon. Senator Lodge had just turned to the President and said: "Mr. President, I do not wish to interfere in any way, but the conference has now lasted about three hours and a half, and it is half an hour after the lunch hour." Whereupon, the President said: "Will not you gentlemen take luncheon with me? It will be very delightful."

It was evident that this invitation, so cordially conveyed, broke the ice of formality which up to that time pervaded the meeting, and like boys out of school, forgetting the great affair in which they had all played prominent parts, they made their way to the dining room, the President walking by the side of Senator Lodge. Instead of fisticuffs, as some of the newspaper men had predicted, the lion and the lamb sat down together at the dining table, and for an hour or two the question of the ratification of the Treaty of Versailles was forgotten in the telling of pleasant stories and the play of repartee.

Although, at this conference of August 19, 1919, the President had frankly opened his mind and heart to the enemies of the Treaty, the opposition instead of moderating seemed to grow more intense and passionate. The President had done everything humanly possible to soften the opposition of the Republicans, but, alas, the information brought to him from the Hill by his Democratic friends only confirmed the opinion that the opposition to the Treaty was growing and could not be overcome by personal contact of any kind between the President and members of the Foreign Relations Committee.

It is plain now, and will become plainer as the years elapse, that the Republican opposition to the League was primarily partisan politics and a rooted personal dislike of the chief proponent of the League, Mr. Wilson. His reëlection in 1916, the first reëlection of an incumbent Democratic President since Andrew Jackson, had greatly disturbed the Republican leaders. The prestige of the Republican party was threatened by this Democratic leader. His reception in Europe added to their distress. For the sake of the sacred cause of Republicanism, this menace of Democratic leadership must be destroyed, even though in destroying it the leaders should swallow their own words and reverse their own former positions on world adjustment.

An attempt was made by enemies of the President to give the impression to the country that an association of nations was one of the "fool ideas" of Woodrow Wilson; that in making it part of his Fourteen Points, he was giving free rein to his idealism.

The storm centre of the whole fight against the League was the opposition personally conducted by Senator Lodge and others of the Republican party against the now famous Article X. The basis of the whole Republican opposition was their fear that America would have to bear some responsibility in the affairs of the world, while the strength of Woodrow Wilson's position was his faith that out of the war, with all its blood and tears, would come this great consummation.

It was the President's idea that we should go into the League and bear our responsibilities; that we should enter it as gentlemen, scorning privilege. He did not wish us to sneak in and enjoy its advantages and shirk its responsibilities, but he wanted America to enter boldly and not as a hypocrite.

With reference to the argument made by Senator Lodge against our going into the League, saying that it would be a surrender of American sovereignty and a loss of her freedom, the President often asked the question on his Western trip: How can a nation preserve its freedom except through concerted action? We surrender part of our freedom in order to save the rest of it. Discussing this matter one day, he said: "One cannot have an omelet without breaking eggs. By joining the League of Nations, a nation loses, not its individual freedom, but its selfish isolation. The only freedom it loses is the freedom to do wrong. Robinson Crusoe was free to shoot in any direction on his island until Friday came. Then there was one direction in which he could not shoot. His freedom ended where Friday's rights began."

There would have been no Federal Union to-day if the individual states that went to make up the Federal Union were not willing to surrender the powers they exercised, to surrender their freedom as it were.

Opponents of the League tried to convey the impression that under Article X we should be obliged to send our boys across the sea and that in that event America's voice would not be the determining voice.

Lloyd George answered this argument in a crushing way, when he said:

> We cannot, unless we abandon the whole basis of the League of Nations, disinterest ourselves in an attack upon the existence of a nation which is a member of that league and whose life is in jeopardy. That covenant, as I understand it, does not contemplate, necessarily, military action in support of the imperilled nation. It contemplates economic pressure; it contemplates support for the struggling people; and when it is said that if you give any support at all to Poland it involves a great war, with conscription and with all the mechanism of war with which we have been so familiar in the last few years, that is inconsistent with the whole theory of the covenant into which we have entered.

Tentative plans for a Western trip began to be formed in the White House because of the urgent insistence from Democratic friends on the Hill that nothing could win the fight for the League of Nations except a direct appeal to the country by the President in person.

Admiral Grayson, the President's physician and consistent friend, who knew his condition and the various physical crises through which he had passed here and on the other side, from some of which he had not yet recovered, stood firm in his resolve that the President should not go West, even intimating to me that the President's life might pay the forfeit if his advice were disregarded. Indeed, it needed not the trained eye of a physician to see that the man whom the senators were now advising to make a "swing around the circle" was on the verge of a nervous breakdown. More than once since his return from the Peace Conference I had urged him to take a needed rest; to get away from the turmoil of Washington and recuperate; but he spurned this advice and resolved to go through to the end.

No argument of ours could draw him away from his duties, which now involved not only the fight for the ratification of the Treaty, but the threatened railway strike, with its attendant evils to the country, and added administrative burdens growing out of the partisanship fight which was being waged in Congress for the ostensible purpose of reducing the high cost of living.

One day, after Democratic senators had been urging the Western trip, I took leave to say to the President that, in his condition, disastrous consequences might result if he should follow their advice. But he dismissed my solicitude, saying in a weary way: "I know that I am at the end of my tether, but my friends on the Hill say that the trip is necessary to save the Treaty, and I am willing to make whatever personal sacrifice is required, for if the Treaty should be defeated, God only knows what would happen to the world as a result of it. In the presence of the great tragedy which now faces the world, no decent man can count his own personal fortunes in the reckoning. Even though, in my condition, it might mean the giving up of my life, I will gladly make the sacrifice to save the Treaty."

He spoke like a soldier who was ready to make the supreme sacrifice to save the cause that lay closest to his heart.

As I looked at the President while he was talking, in my imagination I made a comparison between the man, Woodrow Wilson, who now stood before me and the man I had met many years before in New Jersey. In those days he was a vigorous, agile, slender man, active and alert, his hair but slightly streaked with gray. Now, as he stood before me discussing the necessity for the Western trip, he was an old man, grown grayer and grayer, but grimmer and grimmer in his determination, like an old warrior, to fight to the end.

When it became evident that the tide of public opinion was setting against the League, the President finally decided upon the Western trip as the only means of bringing home to the people the unparalleled world situation.

At the Executive offices we at once set in motion preparations for the Western trip. One itinerary after another was prepared, but upon examining it the President would find that it was not extensive enough and would suspect that it was made by those of us—like Grayson and myself—who were solicitious for his health, and he would cast them aside. All the itineraries provided for a week of rest in the Grand Canyon of the Colorado, but when a brief vacation was intimated to him, he was obdurate in his refusal to include even a day of relaxation, saying to me, that "the people would never forgive me if I took a rest on a trip such as the one I contemplate taking. This is a business trip, pure and simple, and the itinerary must not include rest of any kind." He insisted that there be no suggestion of a pleasure trip attaching to a journey which he regarded as a mission.

As I now look back upon this journey and its disastrous effects upon the President's health, I believe that if he had only consented to include a rest period in our arrangements, he might not have broken down at Pueblo.

Never have I seen the President look so weary as on the night we left Washington for our swing into the West. When we were about to board our special train, the President turned to me and said: "I am in a nice fix. I am scheduled between now and the 28th of September to make in the neighbourhood of a hundred speeches to various bodies, stretching all the way from Ohio to the coast, and yet the pressure of other affairs upon me at the White House has been so great that I have not had a single minute to prepare my speeches. I do not know how I shall get the time, for during the past few weeks I have been suffering from daily headaches; but perhaps to-night's rest will make me fit for the work of to-morrow."

No weariness or brain-fag, however, was apparent in the speech at Columbus, Ohio. To those of us who sat on the platform, including the newspaper group who accompanied the President, this speech with its beautiful phrasing and its effective delivery seemed to have been carefully prepared.

Day after day, for nearly a month, there were speeches of a similar kind, growing more intense in their emotion with each day. Shortly after we left Tacoma, Washington, the fatigue of the trip began to write itself in the President's face. He suffered from violent headaches each day, but his speeches never betrayed his illness.

In those troublous days and until the very end of our Western trip the President would not permit the slightest variation from our daily programme. Nor did he ever permit the constant headaches, which would have put an ordinary man out of sorts, to work unkindly upon the members of his immediate party, which included Mrs. Wilson, Doctor Grayson, and myself. He would appear regularly at each meal, partaking of it only slightly, always gracious, always good-natured and smiling, responding to every call from the outside for speeches—calls that came from early morning until late at night—from the plain people grouped about every station and watering place through which we passed. Even under the most adverse physical conditions he was always kind, gentle, and considerate to those about him.

I have often wished, as the criticisms of the Pullman smoking car, the cloak room, and the counting house were carried to me, picturing the President's coldness, his aloofness and exclusiveness, that the critics could for a moment have seen the heart and great good-nature of the man giving expression to themselves on this critical journey. If they could have peeped through the curtain of our dining room, at one of the evening meals, for instance, they would have been ashamed of their misrepresentations of this kind, patient, considerate, human-hearted man.

438

It was on the Western trip, about September 12th, while the President, with every ounce of his energy, was attempting to put across the League of Nations, that Mr. William C. Bullitt was disclosing to the Committee on Foreign Relations at a public hearing the facts of a conference between Secretary Lansing and himself, in which Mr. Bullitt declared that Mr. Lansing had severely criticized the League of Nations.

The press representatives aboard the train called Mr. Bullitt's testimony to the President's attention. He made no comment, but it was plain from his attitude that he was incensed and distressed beyond measure. Here he was in the heart of the West, advancing the cause so dear to his heart, steadily making gains against what appeared to be insurmountable odds, and now his intimate associate, Mr. Lansing, was engaged in sniping and attacking him from behind.

On September 16th, Mr. Lansing telegraphed the following message to the President:

On May 17th, Bullitt resigned by letter giving his reasons with which you are familiar. I replied by letter on the 18th without any comment on his reasons. Bullitt on the 19th asked to see me to say good-bye and I saw him. He elaborated on the reasons for his resignation and said that he could not conscientiously give countenance to a treaty which was based on injustice. I told him that I would say nothing against his resigning since he put it on conscientious grounds, and that I recognized that certain features of the Treaty were bad, as I presumed most everyone did, but that was probably unavoidable in view of conflicting claims and that nothing ought to be done to prevent the speedy restoration of peace by signing the Treaty. Bullitt then discussed the numerous European commissions provided for by the Treaty on which the United States was to be represented. I told him that I was disturbed by this fact because I was afraid the Senate and possibly the people, if they understood this, would refuse ratification, and that anything which was an obstacle to ratification was unfortunate because we ought to have peace as soon as possible.

When the President received this explanation from Mr. Lansing, he sent for me to visit with him in his compartment. At the time I arrived he was seated in his little study, engaged in preparing his speech for the night's meeting. Turning to me, with a deep show of feeling, he said: "Read that, and tell me what you think of a man who was my associate on the other side and who confidentially expressed himself to an outsider in such a fashion? Were I in Washington I would at once demand his resignation! That kind of disloyalty must not be permitted to go unchallenged for a single minute. The testimony of Bullitt is a confirmation of the suspicions I have had with reference to this individual. I found the same attitude of mind on the part of Lansing on the other side. I could find his trail everywhere I went, but they were only suspicions and it would not be fair for me to act upon them. But here in his own statement is a verification at last of everything I have suspected. Think of it! This from a man who I raised from the level of a subordinate to the great office of Secretary of State of the United States. My God! I did not think it was possible for Lansing to act in this way. When we were in Paris I found that Lansing and others were constantly giving out statements that did not agree with my viewpoint. When I had arranged a settlement, there would appear from some source I could not locate unofficial statements telling the correspondents

439

not to take things too seriously; that a compromise would be made, and this news, or rather news of this kind, was harmful to the settlement I had already obtained and quite naturally gave the Conference the impression that Lansing and his kind were speaking for me, and then the French would say that I was bluffing."

I am convinced that only the President's illness a few days later prevented an immediate demand on his part for the resignation of Mr. Lansing.

Uncomplainingly the President applied himself to the difficult tasks of the Western trip. While the first meeting at Columbus was a disappointment as to attendance, as we approached the West the crowds grew in numbers and the enthusiasm became boundless. The idea of the League spread and spread as we neared the coast. Contrary to the impression in the East, the President's trip West was a veritable triumph for him and was so successful that we had planned, upon the completion of the Western trip, to invade the enemy's country, Senator Lodge's own territory, the New England States, and particularly Massachusetts. This was our plan, fully developed and arranged, when about four o'clock in the morning of September 26, 1919, Doctor Grayson knocked at the door of my sleeping compartment and told me to dress quickly, that the President was seriously ill. As we walked toward the President's car, the Doctor told me in a few words of the President's trouble and said that he greatly feared it might end fatally if we should attempt to continue the trip and that it was his duty to inform the President that by all means the trip must be cancelled; but that he did not feel free to suggest it to the President without having my coöperation and support. When we arrived at the President's drawing room I found him fully dressed and seated in his chair. With great difficulty he was able to articulate. His face was pale and wan. One side of it had fallen, and his condition was indeed pitiful to behold. Quickly I reached the same conclusion as that of Doctor Grayson, as to the necessity for the immediate cancellation of the trip, for to continue it, in my opinion, meant death to the President. Looking at me, with great tears running down his face, he said: "My dear boy, this has never happened to me before. I felt it coming on yesterday. I do not know what to do." He then pleaded with us not to cut short the trip. Turning to both of us, he said: "Don't you see that if you cancel this trip, Senator Lodge and his friends will say that I am a quitter and that the Western trip was a failure, and the Treaty will be lost." Reaching over to him, I took both of his hands and said: "What difference, my dear Governor, does it make what they say? Nobody in the world believes you are a quitter, but it is your life that we must now consider. We must cancel the trip, and I am sure that when the people learn of your condition there will be no misunderstanding." He then tried to move over nearer to me to continue his argument against the cancellation of the trip; but he found he was unable to do so. His left arm and leg refused to function. I then realized that the President's whole left side was paralyzed. Looking at me he said: "I want to show them that I can still fight and that I am not afraid. Just postpone the trip for twenty-four hours and I will be all right."

But Doctor Grayson and I resolved not to take any risk, and an immediate statement was made to the inquiring newspaper men that the Western trip was off.

Never was the President more gentle or tender than on that morning. Suffering the greatest pain, paralyzed on his left side, he was still fighting desperately for the thing that was so close to his heart—a vindication of the things for which he had so gallantly fought on the other side. Grim old warrior that he was, he was ready to fight to the death for the League of Nations.

During the illness of the President his political enemies sought to convey the impression that he was incapacitated for the duties of his office. As one who came in daily contact with him I knew how baseless were these insinuations. As a matter of fact, there was not a whole week during his entire illness that he was not in touch with every matter upon which he was called to act and upon which he was asked to render judgment.

That there was no real devotion on the part of Mr. Lansing for the President is shown by the following incident.

A few days after the President returned from the West and lay seriously ill at the White House, with physicians and nurses gathered about his bed, Mr. Lansing sought a private audience with me in the Cabinet Room. He informed me that he had called diplomatically to suggest that in view of the incapacity of the President we should arrange to call in the Vice-President to act in his stead as soon as possible, reading to me from a book which he had brought from the State Department, which I afterward learned was "Jefferson's Manual," the following clause of the United States Constitution:

> In case of the removal of the President from office, or his death, resignation, or inability to discharge the powers and duties of the said office, the same shall devolve upon the Vice-President.

Upon reading this, I coldly turned to Mr. Lansing and said: "Mr. Lansing, the Constitution is not a dead letter with the White House. I have read the Constitution and do not find myself in need of any tutoring at your hands of the provision you have just read." When I asked Mr. Lansing the question as to who should certify to the disability of the President, he intimated that that would be a job for either Doctor Grayson or myself. I immediately grasped the full significance of what he intimated and said: "You may rest assured that while Woodrow Wilson is lying in the White House on the broad of his back I will not be a party to ousting him. He has been too kind, too loyal, and too wonderful to me to receive such treatment at my hands." Just as I uttered this statement Doctor Grayson appeared in the Cabinet Room and I turned to him and said: "And I am sure that Doctor Grayson will never certify to his disability. Will you, Grayson?" Doctor Grayson left no doubt in Mr. Lansing's mind that he would not do as Mr. Lansing suggested. I then notified Mr. Lansing that if anybody outside of the White House circle attempted to certify to the President's disability, that Grayson and I would stand together and repudiate it. I added that if the President were in a condition to know of this episode he would, in my opinion, take decisive measures. That ended the interview.

It is unnecessary to say that no further attempt was made by Mr. Lansing to institute ouster proceedings against his chief.

I never attempted to ascertain what finally influenced the action of the President peremptorily to demand the resignation of Mr. Lansing. My own judgment is that the demand came as the culmination of repeated acts of what the President considered disloyalty on Mr. Lansing's part.

When I received from the President's stenographer the letter to Mr. Lansing, intimating that his resignation would not be a disagreeable thing to the President, I conferred with the President at once and argued with him that in the present state of public opinion it was the wrong time to do the right thing. At the time the President was seated in his invalid chair on the White House portico. Although physically weak, he was mentally active and alert. Quickly he took hold of my phrase and said, with a show of the old fire that I had seen on so many occasions: "Tumulty, it is never the wrong time to spike disloyalty. When Lansing sought to oust me, I was upon my back. I am on my feet now and I will not have disloyalty about me."

When the announcement of Lansing's resignation was made, the flood-gates of fury broke about the President; but he was serene throughout it all. When I called at the White House on the following Sunday, I found him calmly seated in his bathroom with his coloured valet engaged in the not arduous task of cutting his hair. Looking at me with a smile in his eye, he said: "Well, Tumulty, have I any friends left?" "Very few, Governor," I said. Whereupon he replied: "Of course, it will be another two days' wonder. But in a few days what the country considers an indiscretion on my part in getting rid of Lansing will be forgotten, but when the sober, second thought of the country begins to assert itself, what will stand out will be the disloyalty of Lansing to me."

Reservations

On June 25, 1919, I received from President Wilson the following cabled message:

> My clear conviction is that the adoption of the treaty by the Senate with reservations will put the United States as clearly out of the concert of nations as a rejection. We ought either to go in or stay out. To stay out would be fatal to the influence and even to the commercial prospects of the United States, and to go in would give her a leading place in the affairs of the world. Reservations would either mean nothing or postpone the conclusion of peace, so far as America is concerned, until every other principal nation concerned in the treaty had found out by negotiation what the reservations practically meant and whether they could associate themselves with the United States on the terms of the reservations or not.
> *Woodrow Wilson*

The President consistently held to the principle involved in this statement. To his mind the reservations offered by Senator Lodge constituted a virtual nullification on the part of the United States of a treaty which was a contract, and which should be amended through free discussion among all the contracting parties. He did not argue or assume that the Covenant was a perfected document, but he believed that, like our American Constitution, it should be adopted and subsequently submitted to necessary amendment through the constitutional processes of debate. He was unalterably opposed to having the United States put in the position of seeking exemptions and special privileges under an agreement which he believed was in the interest of the entire world, including our own country. Furthermore, he believed that the advocacy for reservations in the Senate proceeded from partisan motives and that in so far as there was a strong popular opinion in the country in favour of reservations it proceeded from the same sources from which had come the pro-German propaganda. Before the war pro-German agitation had sought to keep us out of the conflict, and after the war it sought to separate us in interest and purpose from other governments with which we were associated.

By his opposition to reservations the President was seeking to prevent Germany from taking through diplomacy what she had been unable to get by her armies.

The President was so confident of the essential rightness of the League and the Covenant and of the inherent right-mindedness of the American people, that he could not believe that the people would sanction either rejection or emasculation of the Treaty if they could be made to see the issue in all the sincerity of its motives and purposes, if partisan attack could be met with plain truth-speaking. It was to present the case of the people in what he considered its true light that he undertook the Western tour, and it was while thus engaged that his health broke. Had he kept well and been able to lead in person the struggle for ratification, he might have won, as he had previously by his determination and conviction broken down stubborn opposition to the Federal Reserve system.

So strong was his faith in his cause and the people that even after he fell ill he could not believe that ratification would fail. What his enemies called stubbornness was his firm faith in the righteousness of the treaty and in the reasonableness of the proposition that the time to make amendments was not prior to the adoption of the Treaty and by one nation, but after all the nations had agreed and had met together for sober, unpartisan consideration of alterations in the interest of all the contracting parties and the peace and welfare of the world.

Even when he lay seriously ill, he insisted upon being taken in his invalid chair along the White House portico to the window of my outer office each day during the controversy in the Senate over the Treaty. There day after day in the coldest possible weather I conferred with him and discussed every phase of the fight on the Hill. He would sit in his chair, wrapped in blankets, and though hardly able, because of his physical condition, to discuss these matters with me, he evidenced in every way a tremendous interest in everything that was happening in the Capitol that had to do with the Treaty. Although I was warned by Doctor Grayson and Mrs. Wilson not to alarm him unduly by bringing pessimistic reports, I sought, in the most delicate and tactful way I could, to bring the atmosphere of the Hill to him. Whenever there was an indication of the slightest rise in the tide for the League of Nations a smile would pass over the President's face, and weak and broken though he was, he evidenced his great pleasure at the news. Time and time again during the critical days of the Treaty fight the President would appear outside my office, seated in the old wheel chair, and make inquiry regarding the progress of the Treaty fight on Capitol Hill.

One of the peculiar things about the illness from which the President suffered was the deep emotion which would stir him when word was brought to him that this senator or that senator on the Hill had said some kind thing about him or had gone to his defense when some political enemy was engaged in bitterly assailing his attitude in the Treaty fight. Never would there come from him any censure or bitter criticism of those who were opposing him in the fight. For Senator Borah, the leader of the opposition, he had high respect, and felt he was actuated only by sincere motives.

I recall how deeply depressed he was when word was carried to him that the defeat of the Treaty was inevitable. On this day he was looking more weary than at any time during his illness. After I had read to him a memorandum that I had prepared, containing a report on the situation in the Senate, I drew away from his wheel chair and said to him: "Governor, you are looking very well to-day." He shook his head in a pathetic way and said: "I am very well for a man who awaits disaster," and bowing his head he gave way to the deep emotion he felt.

A few days later I called to notify him of the defeat of the Treaty. His only comment was, "They have shamed us in the eyes of the world." Endeavouring to keep my good-nature steady in the midst of a trying situation, I smiled and said: "But, Governor, only the Senate has defeated you. The People will vindicate your course. You may rely upon that." "Ah, but our enemies have poisoned the wells of public opinion," he said. "They have made the people believe that the League of Nations is a great Juggernaut, the object of which is to bring war and not peace to the world. If I only could have remained well long enough to have convinced the people that the League of Nations was their real hope, their last chance, perhaps, to save civilization!"

44

Selling the Ford

The 1920s was the decade of the automobile. During these years, the automobile spread through urban and rural counties, putting America on wheels. The Ford system of mass production became a model of organization. By virtue of the needs of the automobile, the production and use of steel and other commodities climbed, stimulating economic growth. The social effects of the automobile are harder to measure, but the feeble remains of a system of chaperons soon died, as the young came to enjoy new mobility and freedom. The auto also gave mobility and freedom to the farmers, bringing them closer to urban centers for their purchases and sales and for entertainment and companionship. At the same time, city people were able to live at even greater distances from their places of work, at the price, of course, of commuting daily in an automobile.

Yet for all their popularity, cars had to be sold day in and day out. An industry established and run on a mass-production system depended on its markets for survival; the economies of large-scale purchases and production needed a high and constant volume of sales in order to bring in profits. Thus, the agent selling the automobiles, located at a key point in the process, often felt the heavy hand of the company on him. In 1927, a reporter for *Harper's Magazine,* Jesse Rainsford Sprague, interviewed a Midwestern Ford dealer, and his "Confession" tells the story, somewhat one-sidedly to be sure, of how the industry went about insuring the continuing sale of its products.

THE CONFESSIONS
OF A FORD DEALER

The former Ford dealer said:

Things have changed a lot around here since 1912, when I bought out the man who had the Ford agency and paid him inventory price for his stock, plus a bonus of five hundred dollars for good-will. A dealer didn't have to hustle so hard then to

From "The Confessions of a Ford Dealer," by Jesse Rainsford Sprague, *Harper's Magazine,* June, 1927, 26–31, 34–35. Copyright © 1927, by Harper's Magazine, Inc. Reprinted from the June, 1927 issue of Harper's Magazine by Special Permission.

make both ends meet. You kept a few cars on your floor and when you needed more you bought them. You were your own boss. There weren't any iron-clad rules laid down for you saying how you had to run your business.

Sometimes I wonder if Mr. Ford knows how things have changed. I have just finished reading his book, and in one place he says: "Business grows big by public demand. But it never gets bigger than the demand. It cannot control or force the demand."

Understand me, I think Mr. Ford is a wonderful man. They say he is worth a billion dollars; and no one can make that much money unless he has plenty of brains. Still and all, when Mr. Ford says business cannot control or force the demand I can't quite think he means it. Or maybe it's his little joke. You *can* force demand if you ride people hard enough. And, believe me, you have only to get on the inside of a Ford agency to learn how.

Take my own case, for instance. Like I say, when I first took the agency I was my own boss like any other business man, selling as many cars as I could and buying more when I needed them. I didn't have to make many sales on installments, because people who wanted cars usually saved up in advance and had the cash in hand when they got ready to buy. Occasionally some man that I knew would want a little time, in which case I just charged it the same as if it was a bill of dry goods or groceries, and when the account fell due he paid me. There was no such thing then as putting a mortgage on the car and taking it away from him if he didn't pay up. If I didn't believe a man was honest I simply didn't give him credit.

I did a pretty good business this way and by 1916 was selling an average of about ten cars a month. Then one day a representative of the Company came to see me. I'll call him by the name of Benson, though that was not his real name. In fact wherever I mention a man's name in giving my experiences I shall call him something different because some of them probably would not like to be identified. Well, anyway, this man that I call Benson came into my place at the time I speak of and said ten cars a month was not enough for a dealer like me to sell. It seems the Company had made a survey of my territory and decided that the sales possibilities were much greater. Benson said my quota had been fixed at twenty cars a month, and from then on that number would be shipped me.

Naturally, I got a little hot under the collar at this kind of a proposition, and I told Benson where he could get off at. I said I was doing all the business that could be done and I intended to buy only the cars that I needed. The Company could ship me as many as they wanted to, but I would pay for what I could sell, and no more.

Benson was pretty hard boiled. He said there was no need of my getting mad at him because he was only doing what he had been ordered to do, and I could take my choice. Either I could buy twenty cars a month or the Company would find another agent. There were plenty of live wires who would jump at the chance.

Of course I knew this last was true. I had got to making a little money during the four years I was Ford agent, and there are always fellows who will go into a thing when someone else has done the hard sledding. My wife had got used to living pretty well and, beside that, my boy was fixing to go away to college. I knew there would be an awful roar at home if I gave up a sure thing and started over again at something else. Still, I couldn't see how I could possibly sell twenty cars a month in my territory. There were only about nine thousand people in the town, and possibly that many more on the farms. Most of them were poor folks. It wasn't, I told Benson, like an Eastern manufacturing community where there are a lot of moneyed people and a big bunch of well-paid mechanics who can afford to have their own cars.

Benson only laughed and said that didn't make any difference. There was a certain population in my territory that called for a certain number of sales, and the Company would show me how to do business. All I had to do was to follow instructions.

Well, I finally decided to take a chance on twenty cars a month rather than lose the agency. I had read a lot of nice things about Mr. Ford in the newspapers and I felt sure he wouldn't ask me to do anything he wouldn't be willing to do himself. Benson said he was glad I looked at things in a businesslike way and promised me plenty of assistance in moving my twenty cars a month. He called it "breaking down sales resistance."

I guess I should explain that out West here an ordinary Ford dealer doesn't do business direct from the factory in Detroit, but works under a general agency. The agency that I worked under was located in the city about a hundred and fifty miles from here, and I suppose the manager there took his orders from the factory. During the fourteen years I was in business there were eight different managers, and some of them rode us local agents pretty hard. I always thought I wouldn't have so many troubles if I could have done business direct with Mr. Ford, but I can realize how busy a big man like him must be, and I guess it is necessary for him to leave things pretty much in the hands of his managers that way. A few times when I thought they were riding me too hard I wrote in to the factory and complained about certain things, but I never got any answer. My letters were sent on to the branch manager, and of course that got me in bad with him. I found that if I wanted to hold my agency I had better do what I was told. Out of the eight managers six were transferred to other branches and two threw up their jobs to go into other lines of business. I met one of these fellows after he had quit and asked him why there were so many changes. He said he guessed it was because the Company believed a man had a tendency to get too friendly with the local agents if he stayed too long in one territory, and to see things too much from the agent's viewpoint. Personally, he said he quit the Company's service altogether because he couldn't stand the pace.

Maybe it was true that a branch manager would get to see things too much from the local agents' standpoint if he stayed too long, but it never seemed that way in my own case. Shortly after I agreed to take my twenty cars a month the War came on, and it was not a case of how many cars I could sell, but of how many I could get. Every day people came in wanting to buy new Fords and, as I never had any stock of cars on hand, all I could do was to take their deposit and set down their names, promising each one that he should have his car according to his number on the waiting list. Then what should develop but a lot of bootleggers in Fords! These fellows would come in, or send someone else in, make a deposit, and get their names on the waiting list. Then when one of their cars came they would pay the balance due, drive it around the corner and sell it for fifty dollars' profit. Sometimes they could even sell their place on the waiting list for that much. Seeing what was going on, I thought I might as well make some of the easy money myself. I entered some fake names on my waiting list and sold myself two or three cars that I sent out on the street and sold over again for a bonus. It was like getting money from home, but it didn't last long. How the Company detectives found out about it I don't know, but one day I got word from the branch manager in the city saying he knew what I was doing and if I wanted to hold my agency I would have to quit it. I guess a lot of local agents were doing the same thing I was, because I understand the order came direct from Detroit. I guess Mr. Ford was right and we had no business to bootleg his product that way. Everything I read in the papers about him is one hundred per cent favorable. Just the same, I thought at the time he might as well let us agents who were making money for him get the extra profit instead of its going to the bootleggers.

Certainly I could have used some of that easy money later on. Of course business kept up fine during the War and for nearly two years afterward, and I made enough money to move out of my rented quarters and put up a nice brick building for my show room, garage, etc. But I sure got it in the neck when the slump of 1920 came on. If anyone wants to know what hard times are he ought to try to do business in a Western farming community during a panic. Almost overnight half of our sheep men went bankrupt when wool dropped from sixty cents a pound to twenty cents, and hardly any buyers at that price. The potato growers couldn't get enough for their stuff to pay freight to the Chicago market, and most of them let their crop rot in the ground. Of our four banks in town two went into the hands of receivers and the other two had to call in every possible loan in order to save their own necks. A lot of our Main Street retailers fell into the hands of their creditors that year, too.

I was in about as bad a fix as anyone else. By then I had agreed to take thirty Fords a month, which was a pretty heavy job to get away with in good times, to say nothing of the sort of a situation we were going through. These cars came in each month, regular as clock work, and I had stretched my credit at the bank about as far as it would go in paying for them as they arrived. The bank kept hounding me all the time to cut down my loan, which I couldn't do with my expenses running on all the time and hardly any business going on. From September to January that year I sold exactly four cars.

Pretty bad? I'll say it was. But the worst was yet to come. Altogether I had more than one hundred and forty new cars on hand, besides a lot of trade-ins, and no immediate prospect of selling any. Then all of a sudden came notice that a shipment of fifteen Fords was on the way to me, and that I would be expected to pay for them on arrival. I thought there must be some mistake, and got the branch manager in the city on the long distance. He was a pretty hard-boiled egg named Blassingham.

"What's the meaning of these fifteen cars that are being shipped me?" I asked. "I've already taken my quota for the month."

"It don't mean anything," Blassingham answered, "except that you're going to buy fifteen extra cars this month."

I tried to explain to him that I was in no position to get hold of the cash for such a purchase, and even if I was I wanted to know the whys and wherefores.

"You know as much about it as I do," he snapped. "Those are the orders, and my advice to you is to pay for those cars when they arrive."

Of course I sensed the reason later on, when it came out in the newspapers about Mr. Ford's little tilt with the money sharks down in New York, how they tried to get a hold on his business and how he fooled them by getting the cash without their help and then told them to go chase themselves.

If you ask me, I'd say Mr. Ford is an absolute humdinger when it comes to handling a lot of crooks who are bent on feathering their own nests off other people. At the moment, however, I was too busy with personal problems to think much about the battles of Big Business. Like I say, my credit at the bank was used up, and the bank had no money to loan, anyhow. I was taking in enough cash to pay my mechanics in the garage, but I had to stand off the office help Saturday nights with part of their wages and ask them to wait on me for the balance. I couldn't sleep much for worrying, and I guess my wife worried as much as I did because at three and four o'clock in the morning she would ask me if I had been to sleep yet and when I would say no, she would say she hadn't either.

I had fully made up my mind I was going on the rock pile when just a couple of days before the extra shipment of Fords was due to arrive I had an unexpected stroke of luck. There was a sheep man named Flanagan I knew who had made a trip out west to Salt Lake City just before the market broke and closed out his entire holdings for something like a hundred thousand dollars in cash, which he put into Liberty Bonds. He had a Ford that he ran around in sometimes, and one day when he drove up to the garage I happened to think about his money and asked him how he would like to come in with me as a silent partner. To make a long story short, he became interested in the proposition and bought a third interest. Of course I had to sell him his share for a lot less than it was worth, but it saved my scalp.

There was kind of a funny sequel to this deal, and I don't know yet whether my taking a moneyed partner had anything to do with it, or whether it would have happened anyway. We took the fifteen extra Fords all right when they arrived and thought everything was settled, but a few days later Blassingham came down from the city and told me fifteen more were about to be shipped to our town. It seems these were extra cars that were intended for some dealers in little nearby villages but they were absolutely flat broke and unable to pay for them. Blassingham didn't actually tell me I had to buy these cars, but from his conversation I knew it would be wise for me to do so if I expected to stay in the automobile business.

449

I went to my silent partner, Flanagan, and told him he would have to put up a few thousand dollars more. He made an awful roar and said he would see Mr. Ford in Hades before he would pay for any more new cars when we already had nearly a hundred and fifty on hand. I explained that Mr. Ford had nothing to do with it, that it was the branch manager, Blassingham, who was riding us; but Flanagan, mad as a hornet, asked me who in hell I supposed gave Blassingham *his* orders. He made me give him my agency contract and took it to a lawyer. Pretty soon he came back, a good deal milder than when he went away, and said he guessed we had better buy those fifteen extra cars, though if he had known what he was getting into he wouldn't have been so quick to invest his money in the Ford game.

Of course, the trouble with Flanagan was that he had been a sheep man all his life and didn't understand big business. Still, I couldn't blame him for getting still madder at what happened next. Counting our trade-ins, we had about a hundred and eighty cars in stock, which was a pretty heavy load to carry with business like it was; but I told him we would come out all right because Ford cars were just as staple as wheat or sugar and we would eventually get our profit on them. But shortly afterward the Company announced a reduction in price in order to stimulate sales. Altogether we ran behind about thirteen thousand dollars between January and July that year.

I am willing to confess that we rode the public a little ourselves while we were getting rid of our big surplus of cars. There are always some people that you can sell anything to if you hammer them hard enough. We had a salesman named Nichols who was a humdinger at running down prospects, and one day he told me he had a fellow on the string with a couple of hundred dollars who would buy a car if we would give him a little extra time on the balance. This prospect was a young fellow that had come out West on account of his health and was trying to make a living for his family as an expert accountant. Just at that time the referee in bankruptcy was doing most of the accounting business around town, and I knew the young fellow wasn't getting on at all. He had about as much use for a car as a jack rabbit. I told Nichols this, but you know how plausible these go-getter salesmen are; he told me it wasn't our business whether the young fellow had any use for a Ford or not; the main thing was he had two hundred dollars in cash.

Well, we went ahead and made the sale, but we never got any more payments. The young fellow took to his bed just after that, and the church people had to look out for him and his family until he died. In the final showdown it turned out that the two-hundred dollar equity in the car was everything they had on earth, and by the time we replevined it and sold it as a trade-in there wasn't anything at all. I gave twenty dollars toward his funeral expenses. I know this sounds pretty tough; but when it's a case of your own scalp or some other fellow's you can't afford to be too particular.

By 1922 things had picked up a little in my territory, though the farmers hadn't entirely recovered from the 1920 setback and our town population had shrunk considerably on account of scarcity of work. It was pretty hard under these conditions to sell my quota of thirty cars a month, but the branch manager in the city held me to it. By this time Blassingham had been transferred, but another man named Cosgrove took his place who rode me harder than Blassingham had done. Like I say, he held me to my quota of Fords though I had fewer people to sell to; and not only that, but he also told me I would have to buy fifteen tractors every year besides. That wasn't all, either. Eventually I was saddled with two Lincoln cars a year and also supposed to take a certain number of subscriptions for a magazine called the *Dearborn Independent* that is owned by Mr. Ford and has a page every week entitled "Mr. Ford's Page." I guess even the best of us like to see our names in print.

I say I was required to do all these things, but there was in reality a little leeway. I learned on the quiet that Cosgrove would not take away my agency if I fell down a little on the fifteen tractors and two Lincolns. But on the thirty Fords a month there was no alibi allowed, and the same thing applied to the *Dearborn Independent*. This last gave me a lot of trouble.

About the most nagging thing to me were the visits of the expert salesmen who came around every so often to show us how to sell cars. It seemed to me that so long as I was taking my quota every month I ought to be the best judge of how and who to sell. There was one expert I specially remember by the name of Burke. Among other things I had to do was to keep a card file of people in the territory who had not bought cars, and usually on these cards we wrote items like "says maybe will be in market this fall," or "not ready to buy yet." Burke was always raising Cain because we didn't make people give more explicit reasons for not buying. I remember once he laid me out because a card said only "Can't sell him." The man was a poor devil of a renter seven or eight miles out of town who never had enough cash ahead to buy a wheelbarrow, but Burke insisted that one of my salesmen go out there with him to try and land a sale. When they got there a couple of the children were down with whooping cough and a hailstorm had laid out his bean crop, but Burke came back and told me he would expect me to put over a Ford on the fellow before he came on his next trip.

The thing that made me quit the Ford game was the campaign they put on for farm machinery. Understand, I was in sympathy with it too, because I knew Mr. Ford was trying to make things easier for the farmers—like he says, help them do their whole year's work in twenty days. Still and all, I didn't feel I wanted to go broke even in a good cause.

The first thing I knew of Mr. Ford's plans was on a Saturday afternoon when I got a long-distance call from the city saying the branch manager was coming out next day and for me to be in my office at eleven o'clock. I usually go to church Sunday mornings, and besides I always understood Mr. Ford was against Sunday work; but an order is an order and I wasn't taking any chances on getting in bad with the branch manager. In our town there are laws on Sabbath observance, but if a business man wants to work a little no one bothers him just so he keeps the shades down.

451

The branch manager was a new man by the name of Biggs, and he told me that from then on I would be required to carry a line of farm machinery suitable to go with the Ford tractors. As I remember it, there were no ifs or ands; I understood it to be an order, and I knew what Biggs could do to me if I didn't obey orders. Anyhow I thought it might be a good thing to help move the tractors, which were always harder to sell than Ford cars. I asked Biggs if he wanted me to sign a contract and he said no, that wouldn't be necessary in this case, but when the salesman came along it would be indicated to me what I should buy.

Biggs left that afternoon to see the dealers in some small towns farther up the line, and some time later the machinery man called. I never did quite understand Mr. Ford's arrangements with the machinery manufacturers. The salesman who called on me represented a big jobbing house in the city, and apparently there was no connection between this jobbing house and the branch manager's office; but there must have been some kind of a working agreement because the salesman had my assortment of stuff all lined up for me and all I had to do was to sign the order. Altogether it amounted to about seven thousand dollars' worth. There were seeders, 12-inch plows, etc., all sorts of implements to be hauled by the Ford tractors.

Well, so far as our section of the country was concerned, the farm machinery campaign was a pretty bad flop. In the first place, it was hard to convince the farmers that they ought to buy their machines from the Ford dealers instead of from regular implement merchants. Naturally the implement merchants were down on us for trying to take away their trade, and knocked Ford cars every time they had a chance. Then it was found that 12-inch plows weren't suitable for our territory, and some of the other machines proved too heavy for the Ford tractor. Biggs sent out a lot of demonstrators and high-powered salesmen to help us move the stuff, but none of us could make a go of the line and after a while so many squawks came from the dealers that Biggs called a meeting to hear complaints. As I was the biggest agent in that part of the state the meeting was held in my office and the smaller dealers came there.

Biggs called the meeting to order and asked the different ones to air their complaints. Believe me, there were a plenty. One fellow would tell his troubles with the farm machinery line, and then another, and then half a dozen would be on their feet at once, blaming Biggs, and the Ford Motor Company, and the farm machinery company, and pretty near everyone else, for their griefs. In the midst of it Biggs hopped to his feet and pounded the table.

"If any man here can show a scratch of the pen," he yelled, "to prove he bought his farm machinery at the orders of the Ford Motor Company, I dare him to get up and say so!"

Of course no one could show a scratch of the pen because there wasn't any. Biggs hadn't made any of us sign a contract for our farm machinery. He had just *told* us to buy it, and we took it to be an order from headquarters.

I sold out my business as soon after that as I could find a buyer. I was afraid after Mr. Ford got through helping the farmers he might decide to help out the Hottentots or someone, and I didn't feel like I could afford to assist him. The fellow I sold my business to wouldn't take the farm machinery stock at any price. Since then I have been peddling it wherever I could, but it's a hard game. I sold one machine that cost me $800 for $300, and took the farmer's notes for it, spread out over three years, without interest.

I am sure Mr. Ford can't know about all these things, because if he did he couldn't have written in his book this grand sentiment:

"The principle of the service of business to the people has gone far in the United States and it will spread through and remake the world."

45

The Klan in Mississippi

A darker side of American life in the 1920s revealed itself in immigration restriction, Prohibition, discrimination against ethnic and racial minorities, and, most dramatically, in the Ku Klux Klan. The optimism that led a nation to call for Europe's wretched masses seemed to be replaced with the fears of a hooded man who mumbled magical phrases, burned crosses, and denounced the immigrant at every opportunity.

The KKK had a slow beginning in the years before World War I; but in the 1920s, with leaders capable of effective promotion, it grew popular not only in the South but in the Midwest, not only in small towns but in cities like Chicago as well. The object of its hatred and fear was more often the Catholic than the Negro—the black, after all, was usually kept well in hand by Southern whites. The Catholic, entering business and politics, and often enjoying success, posed a graver threat to the Klan mentality. Its response, at times, was physical coercion, flogging, riding out of town, occasionally murder. More often the Klan used verbal intimidation and carried its program into politics. It enjoyed much success in the 1920s, but ultimately the public's good sense and decency, combined with the Klan's corruption and greed, ended its power.

The account below by William Percy describes the Klan's abortive efforts to take power in a small Southern town. But even where unsuccessful, the Klan, as Percy's reminiscenses make clear, was a serious danger and a threat to community life.

LANTERNS
ON THE LEVEE
William A. Percy

The years following the war were a time of confusion not only to ex-soldiers but to all Americans. The tension of high endeavor and unselfish effort snapped, and Americans went "ornery." In the South the most vital matter became the price of cotton, in the North the price of commodities. Idealism was followed by the grossest materialism, which continues to be the order of the day.

From pp. 229–238 of *Lanterns on the Levee*, by William A. Percy. Copyright 1941 by Alfred A. Knopf, Inc. Reprinted by permission of the publisher.

Our town of about ten thousand population was no better or worse, I imagine, than other little Southern towns. My townsfolk had got along pretty well together—we knew each other so well and had suffered so much together. But we hadn't suffered a common disaster, one that was local and our very own, like a flood or a yellow-fever epidemic, since the flood of 1913, and that had failed as a binder because it didn't flood the town. Unbeknownst, strangers had drifted in since the war—from the hills, from the North, from all sorts of odd places where they hadn't succeeded or hadn't been wanted. We had changed our country attractively for them. Malaria had been about stamped out; electric fans and ice had lessened the terror of our intolerable summer heat; we had good roads and drainage and schools, and our lands were the most fertile in the world. We had made the Delta a good place in which to live by our determination and our ability to endure hardships, and now other folks were attracted by the result of our efforts. The town was changing, but so insidiously that the old-timers could feel but could not analyze the change. The newcomers weren't foreigners or Jews, they were an alien breed of Anglo-Saxon.

Although I was always traveling to strange places, I loved Greenville and never wanted any other place for home. Returning to it was the most exciting part of a trip. You could find friendly idlers round the post-office steps pretending they were waiting for the mail. You could take a coke any time of day with someone full of important news. There'd be amiable people running in and out of the house, without knocking, for tennis or golf or bridge or poker or to join you at a meal or just to talk. It was a lovable town.

I suppose the trait that distinguished it from neighboring towns was a certain laxity in church matters. We didn't regard drunkenness and lechery, Sabbath-breaking and gambling as more than poor judgment or poor taste. What we were slow to forgive was hardness of heart and all unkindness. Perhaps we were overstocked with sinners and pariahs and publicans, but they kept the churches in their places and preserved the tradition of sprightliness. Of course we had church folk, plenty of them—Episcopalians, not numerous but up-stage, whose forebears came from Virginia, Kentucky, or South Carolina; Catholics from Italy or Ireland or New Orleans; Methodists, indigenous and prolific; Baptists, who loved Methodists less but Catholics least, swarms of them; Presbyterians, not directly from Geneva or Edinburgh, but aged in the wood, fairly mellow considering they were predestined; and Jews too much like natives even to be overly prosperous. There were bickerings and fights during election time, but day in and day out we were pretty cozy and neighborly, and nobody cared what to hell was the other fellow's route to heaven. There was no embattled aristocracy, for the descendants of the old-timers were already a rather seedy remnant, and there was no wealth. White folks and colored folks—that's what we were—and some of us were nice and some weren't.

I never thought of Masons. Most of my friends wore aprons at funerals and fezzes (over vine leaves) at knightly convocations. Even Père had been a Mason, to the scandal of the Church and the curtailment of his last rites, but he took it easy. I thought Masonry a good thing for those who liked that sort of thing.

455

We had read in the newspapers that over in Atlanta some fraud was claiming to have revived the old Ku Klux Klan which during reconstruction days had played so desperate but on the whole so helpful a part in keeping the peace and preventing mob violence. This Atlanta monstrosity was not even a bastard of the old organization which General Forrest had headed and disbanded. This thing obviously was a money-making scheme without ideals or ideas. We were amused and uninterested. Even in Forrest's day the Klan had never been permitted to enter our county. It couldn't happen here. But reports of the Atlanta organization's misdeeds—masked night parades to terrorize the Negro, threatening letters, forcible closing of dance-halls and dives, whippings, kidnappings, violent brutalities—crowded the headlines. As citizens of the South we were ashamed; as citizens of Greenville we were not apprenhensive.

Then in the spring of 1922 a "Colonel" Camp was advertised to speak in our courthouse for the purpose of forming a branch of the Klan in Greenville. Thoroughly aroused, we debated whether to permit the speech in the courthouse or to answer it there. We couldn't learn who had invited him to speak or who had given him permission to use the courthouse, but evidently some of our own people were already Klansmen—fifth-column tactic before there was a Hitler. Our best citizens, those who thought for the common good, met in Father's office and agreed almost unanimously that the Colonel should be answered and by Father.

The Klan organizer made an artful speech to a tense crowd that packed every cranny of the room; and every man was armed. Who killed Garfield? A Catholic. Who asssinated President McKinley? A Catholic. Who had recently bought a huge tract of land opposite West Point and another overlooking Washington? The Pope. Convents were brothels, the confessional a place of seduction, the basement of every Catholic church an arsenal. The Pope was about to seize the government. To the rescue, Klansmen! These were statements which any trained mind recognized as lies, but which no man without weeks of ridiculous research could disprove. It was an example of Nazi propaganda before there were Nazis. The very enormity and insolence of the lie carried conviction to the simple and the credulous. The Colonel was listened to with courtesy.

To his surprise, Father answered him: he had never been answered before. I have never heard a speech that was so exciting and so much fun. The crowd rocked and cheered. Father's ridicule was amusing but bitter; and as he continued, it became more bitter, until it wasn't funny, it was terrifying. And the Colonel was terrified: he expected to be torn limb from limb by the mob. I don't blame him. At the close of Father's speech the crowd went quite mad, surging about, shouting and cheering, and thoroughly dangerous. A resolution was passed condemning the Klan. Colonel Camp scuttled out of a side door, appealing to a passing deputy for protection. The deputy, an Irish Catholic and the kindliest of men (out of *Henry IV*), escorted him ceremoniously to his hotel.

It was a triumphant meeting, but for the next two years our town was disintegrated by a bloodless, cruel warfare, more bitter and unforgiving than anything I encountered at the front. In the trenches soldiers felt sorry for one another, whether friend or enemy. In Father's senatorial fight, we were surrounded by ferocious stupidity rather than by hatred. But in the Klan fight the very spirit of hatred materialized before our eyes. It was the ugliest thing I have ever beheld. You didn't linger on the post-office steps or drink cokes with random companions: too many faces were hard and set, too many eyes were baleful and venomous. You couldn't go a block without learning by a glance that someone hated you.

The Klan did not stand for, but against. It stood against Catholics, Jews, Negroes, foreigners, and sin. In our town it chose Catholics as the object of its chief persecution. Catholic employees were fired, Catholic businessmen were boycotted, Catholic office-holders opposed. At first this seemed strange to me, because our Catholics were a small and obscure minority, but I came to learn with astonishment that of all the things hated in the South, more hated than the Jew or the Negro or sin itself, is Rome. The evangelical sects and Rome—as different and un-comprehending of each other as youth and old age! One seems never to have glimpsed the sorrowful pageant of the race and the other, profoundly disillusioned, profoundly compassionate, sees only the pageant. One has the enthusiasm and ignorance of the pioneer, the other the despair of the sage. One's a cheer-leader, the other an old sad-eyed family doctor from Samaria. We discovered that the Klan had its genesis, as far as our community was involved, in the Masonic Temple. The state head of that fraternal organization, a well-meaning old simpleton, had been preaching anti-Catholicism for years when conferring Masonic degrees. He joined the Klan early and induced other Masonic leaders to follow his example. These composed the Klan leadership in our county, though they were aided by a few politicians who knew better but who craved the Klan vote. It was a pretty leadership—fanatics and scalawag politicians. But not all Masons or all the godly were so misguided. The opposition to the Klan at home was led by a Protestant committee (and every denomination was represented in its ranks), who fought fearlessly, intelligently, and unceasingly this evil which they considered as unchristian as it was un-American. Father was not only head of the Protestant anti-Klan committee but of the anti-Klan forces in the South. He spoke as far north as Chicago and published probably the first article on the Klan in any distinguished magazine. It was reprinted from the *Atlantic Monthly* and distributed over the whole country. He felt the Klan was the sort of public evil good citizens could not ignore. Not to fight it was ineffectual and craven.

It's hard to conceive of the mumbo-jumbo ritual of the Klan and its half-wit principles—only less absurd than the Nazi principles of Aryan superiority and lebensraum—as worthy of an adult mind's attention. But when your living, your self-respect, and your life are threatened, you don't laugh at that which threatens. If you have either sense or courage you fight it. We fought, and it was high time someone did.

The Klan's increasing atrocities culminated in the brutal murders at Mer Rouge, where Skipwith was Cyclops. Mer Rouge is across the river from us, on the Louisiana side. It is very near and the murders were very ghastly. The Klan loathed and feared Father more than any other man in the South. For months I never let him out of my sight and of course we both went armed. Never before nor since have our doors been shut and locked at night.

One Sunday night of torrential rain when Father, Aunt Lady, and I sat in the library and Mother was ill upstairs I answered a knock at the door. It was early and I opened the door without apprehension. A dark, heavy-set man with two days' growth of beard and a soft-brimmed black hat stood there, drenched to the skin. He asked for Father and I, to his obvious surprise, invited him in. He wouldn't put down his hat, but held it in front of him. I didn't like his looks, so while Father talked to him I played the piano softly in the adjoining room and listened. The man's story was that he came from near our plantation, his car had run out of gas a few miles from town, he'd left his sister in the car and walked to town, he couldn't find a service station open, and would Father help him? Father, all sympathy, started phoning. The stranger seemed neither interested nor appreciative. I watched him with mounting suspicision. Father's efforts to find a service station open having failed, he said: "My car is here. We might run out and get your sister—I suppose you can drive my car?" The stranger brightened and observed he could drive any make of car. The two of them were still near the phone when Father's three bridge cronies came stamping in, laughing and shaking out the rain. As they came toward Father, the stranger brushed past them and had reached the door when I overtook him. "Say, what's the matter with you?" I asked. "Wait a minute and some of us will get you fixed up." He mumbled: "Got to take a leak," walked into the rain, and disappeared.

We waited for him, but we did not see him again for two years. Then he was in jail charged with a string of robberies. When he saw I recognized him, he grinned sourly and remarked: "Old Skip nearly put that one over." He refused to enlarge on this statement, which presumably referred to Skipwith, Cyclops of Mer Rouge. We found from the neighbors that the night of his visit to us he had arrived in a car with another man and parked across the street from our house.

It looked too much like an attempt at kidnapping and murder for me to feel easy. I went to the office of the local Cyclops. He was an inoffensive little man, a great Mason, and partial to anti-Catholic tirades. I said: "I want to let you know one thing: if anything happens to my Father or to any of our friends you will be killed. We won't hunt for the guilty party. So far as we are concerned the guilty party will be you."

There were no atrocities, no whippings, no threatening letters, no masked parades in our town. The local Klan bent all of its efforts toward electing one of its members sheriff. If they could have the law-enforcement machinery under their control, they could then flout the law and perpetrate such outrages as appealed to them. Our fight became a political fight to prevent the election of the Klan's choice for sheriff. The whole town was involved and the excitement was at fever heat. What appalled and terrified us most was the mendacity of Klan members. You never knew if the man you were talking to was a Klansman and a spy. Like German parachute jumpers, they appeared disguised as friends. For the Klan advised its members to lie about their affiliation with the order, about anything that concerned another Klansman's welfare, and about anything pertaining to the Klan—and its members took the advice. The most poisonous thing the Klan did to our town was to rob its citizens of their faith and trust in one another. Everyone was under suspicion: from Klansmen you could expect neither frankness nor truth nor honor, and you couldn't tell who was a Klansman. If they were elected judges and law-enforcement officers, we would be cornered into servility or assassination.

Our candidate for sheriff was George B. Alexander, a powerful, square-bearded, Kentucky aristocrat drawn by Holbein. He was one of those people who are always right by no discernible mental process. His fearlessness, warm-heartedness, and sheer character made him a person you liked to be with and for. He was Father's favorite hunting companion and friend.

On election night the town was beside itself with excitement. Crowds filled the streets outside the voting booths to hear the counting of the ballots as it progressed. Everyone realized the race was close and whoever won would win by the narrowest of margins. The whole population was in the street, milling, apprehensive, silent. When the count began, Father went home and started a bridge game. I waited at the polls. About nine o'clock a sweating individual with his collar unbuttoned and his wide red face smeared with tears rushed out on the steps and bellowed: "We've won, we've won! Alexander's elected! God damn the Klan!" Pandemonium broke loose. Men yelled and screamed and hugged one another. Our town was saved, we had whipped the Klan and were safe. I ran home with the news and Father's bridge game broke up in a stillness of thanksgiving that was almost religious.

Mother was away. Being a Frenchwoman, she had been neither hysterical nor sentimental during the months and months of tension and danger. But none of us knew what she went through silently and it was then her health began to fail.

While we were talking about the victory, a tremendous uproar came to us from the street. We rushed out on the gallery. From curb to curb the street was filled with a mad marching crowd carrying torches and singing. They swarmed down the street and into our yard. It was a victory celebration. Father made a speech, everybody made a speech, nobody listened and everybody cheered. Klansmen had taken to cover, but the rest of the town was there, seething over the yard and onto the gallery. They cut Mr. Alexander's necktie to bits for souvenirs. And still they cheered and swarmed.

Father, nonplussed, turned to Adah and me and laughed: "They don't seem to have any idea of going home and I haven't a drop of whisky in the house—at least, I'm not going to waste my *good* liquor on them." Adah and Charlie dashed off in their car and returned with four kegs. Father called to the crowd: "Come on in, boys," and into the house they poured. That was a party never to be forgotten.

459

46

Calvin Coolidge in the White House

National political life in the 1920s, to such Presidents as Warren Harding and Calvin Coolidge, was a straightforward and uncomplicated matter, only demanding an occasional adjustment of the rudder to keep the ship going smoothly on its course. In perspective, however, it is evident that inaction and complacency were hardly justified by existing economic and social conditions. In the economy, agriculture, for example, was in serious difficulty. Having overexpanded to satisfy the American and European demand generated by World War I, farmers were caught in a situation of rising costs and declining markets. Other sectors of the economy also needed assistance, and so did much of the unskilled part of the labor force. Moreover, as events would make all too clear, business was in dire need of regulation; when left to itself, it showed little restraint or a sense of the national welfare. Yet the nation's political leaders perceived little of this—and they talked even less about it.

What happened to the inquiring, critical spirit of the Progressive era? What replaced its outlook in the 1920s? The attitudes and actions of Calvin Coolidge as set down in his *Autobiography* may shed some light on these questions. For the President recorded here in simple language his guiding assumptions; and, to a surprising degree, they coincided with the sentiments of many of his fellow Americans.

THE PRESIDENT'S AUTOBIOGRAPHY

It is a very old saying that you never can tell what you can do until you try. The more I see of life the more I am convinced of the wisdom of that observation.

Surprisingly few men are lacking in capacity, but they fail because they are lacking in application. Either they never learn how to work, or, having learned, they are too indolent to apply themselves with the seriousness and the attention that is necessary to solve important problems.

Reprinted with permission of John Coolidge from Calvin Coolidge, *Autobiography* (New York, 1931), 171–177, 182–185, 188–190, 200–204, 222–232, 234–235.

Any reward that is worth having only comes to the industrious. The success which is made in any walk of life is measured almost exactly by the amount of hard work that is put into it.

It has undoubtedly been the lot of every native boy of the United States to be told that he will some day be President. Nearly every young man who happens to be elected a member of his state legislature is pointed to by his friends and his local newspaper as on the way to the White House.

My own experience in this respect did not differ from that of others. But I never took such suggestions seriously, as I was convinced in my own mind that I was not qualified to fill the exalted office of President.

I had not changed this opinion after the November elections of 1919, when I was chosen Governor of Massachusetts for a second term by a majority which had only been exceeded in 1896.

When I began to be seriously mentioned by some of my friends at that time as the Republican candidate for President, it became apparent that there were many others who shared the same opinion as to my fitness which I had so long entertained.

But the coming national convention, acting in accordance with an unchangeable determination, took my destiny into its own hands and nominated me for Vice-President.

Had I been chosen for the first place, I could have accepted it only with a great deal of trepidation, but when the events of August, 1923, bestowed upon me the Presidential office, I felt at once that power had been given me to administer it. This was not any feeling of exclusiveness. While I felt qualified to serve, I was also well aware that there were many others who were better qualified. It would be my province to get the benefit of their opinions and advice. It is a great advantage to a President, and a major source of safety to the country, for him to know that he is not a great man. When a man begins to feel that he is the only one who can lead in this republic, he is guilty of treason to the spirit of our institutions.

On the night of August 2, 1923, I was awakened by my father coming up the stairs calling my name. I noticed that his voice trembled. As the only times I had ever observed that before were when death had visited our family, I knew that something of the gravest nature had occurred.

His emotion was partly due to the knowledge that a man whom he had met and liked was gone, partly to the feeling that must possess all of our citizens when the life of their President is taken from them.

But he must have been moved also by the thought of the many sacrifices he had made to place me where I was, the twenty-five-mile drives in storms and in zero weather over our mountain roads to carry me to the academy and all the tenderness and care he had lavished upon me in the thirty-eight years since the death of my mother in the hope that I might sometime rise to a position of importance, which he now saw realized.

He had been the first to address me as President of the United States. It was the culmination of the lifelong desire of a father for the success of his son.

461

He placed in my hands an official report and told me that President Harding had just passed away. My wife and I at once dressed.

Before leaving the room I knelt down and, with the same prayer with which I have since approached the altar of the church, asked God to bless the American people and give me power to serve them.

The oath was taken in what we always called the sitting room by the light of the kerosene lamp, which was the most modern form of lighting that had then reached the neighborhood. The Bible which had belonged to my mother lay on the table at my hand. It was not officially used, as it is not the practice in Vermont or Massachusetts to use a Bible in connection with the administration of an oath.

Where succession to the highest office in the land is by inheritance or appointment, no doubt there have been kings who have participated in the induction of their sons into their office, but in republics where the succession comes by an election I do not know of any other case in history where a father has administered to his son the qualifying oath of office which made him the chief magistrate of a nation. It seemed a simple and natural thing to do at the time, but I can now realize something of the dramatic force of the event.

My fundamental idea of both private and public business came first from my father. He had the strong New England trait of great repugnance at seeing anything wasted. He was a generous and charitable man, but he regarded waste as a moral wrong.

Wealth comes from industry and from the hard experience of human toil. To dissipate it in waste and extravagance is disloyalty to humanity. This is by no means a doctrine of parsimony. Both men and nations should live in accordance with their means and devote their substance not only to productive industry, but to the creation of the various forms of beauty and the pursuit of culture which give adornments to the art of life.

When I became President it was perfectly apparent that the key by which the way could be opened to national progress was constructive economy. Only by the use of that policy could the high rates of taxation, which were retarding our development and prosperity, be diminished, and the enormous burden of our public debt be reduced.

Without impairing the efficient operation of all the functions of the government, I have steadily and without ceasing pressed on in that direction. This policy has encouraged enterprise, made possible the highest rate of wages which has ever existed, returned large profits, brought to the homes of the people the greatest economic benefits they ever enjoyed, and given to the country as a whole an unexampled era of prosperity. This well-being of my country has given me the chief satisfaction of my administration.

While there have been newspapers which supported me, of course there have been others which opposed me, but they have usually been fair. I shall always consider it the highest tribute to my administration that the opposition have based so little of their criticism on what I have really said and done.

I have often said that there was no cause for feeling disturbed at being misrepresented in the press. It would be only when they began to say things detrimental to me which were true that I should feel alarm.

Perhaps one of the reasons I have been a target for so little abuse is because I have tried to refrain from abusing other people.

The words of the President have an enormous weight and ought not to be used indiscriminately.

It would be exceedingly easy to set the country all by the ears and foment hatreds and jealousies, which, by destroying faith and confidence, would help nobody and harm everybody. The end would be the destruction of all progress.

While every one knows that evils exist, there is yet sufficient good in the people to supply material for most of the comment that needs to be made.

The only way I know to drive out evil from the country is by the constructive method of filling it with good. The country is better off tranquilly considering its blessings and merits, and earnestly striving to secure more of them, than it would be in nursing hostile bitterness about its deficiencies and faults.

There is only one form of political strategy in which I have any confidence, and that is to try to do the right thing and sometimes be able to succeed.

Many people at once began to speak about nominating me to lead my party in the next campaign. I did not take any position in relation to their efforts. Unless the nomination came to me in a natural way, rather than as the result of an artificial campaign, I did not feel it would be of any value.

The people ought to make their choice on a great question of that kind without the influence that could be exerted by a President in office.

After the favorable reception which was given to my Message, I stated at the Gridiron Dinner that I should be willing to be a candidate. The convention nominated me the next June by a vote which was practically unanimous.

With the exception of the occasion of my notification, I did not attend any partisan meetings or make any purely political speeches during the campaign. I spoke several times at the dedication of a monument, the observance of the anniversary of an historic event, at a meeting of some commercial body, or before some religious gathering. The campaign was magnificently managed by William M. Butler and as it progressed the final result became more and more apparent.

My own participation was delayed by the death of my son Calvin, which occurred on the seventh of July. He was a boy of much promise, proficient in his studies, with a scholarly mind, who had just turned sixteen.

He had a remarkable insight into things.

The day I became President he had just started to work in a tobacco field When one of his fellow laborers said to him, "If my father was President I would not work in a tobacco field," Calvin replied, "If my father were your father, you would."

After he was gone some one sent us a letter he had written about the same time to a young man who had congratulated him on being the first boy in the land. To this he had replied that he had done nothing, and so did not merit the title, which should go to "some boy who had distinguished himself through his own actions."

We do not know what might have happened to him under other circumstances, but if I had not been President he would not have raised a blister on his toe, which resulted in blood poisoning, playing lawn tennis in the South Grounds.

In his suffering he was asking me to make him well. I could not.

When he went the power and the glory of the Presidency went with him.

The ways of Providence are often beyond our understanding. It seemed to me that the world had need of the work that it was probable he could do.

I do not know why such a price was exacted for occupying the White House.

Every day of the Presidential life is crowded with activities. When people not accustomed to Washington came to the office, or when I met them on some special occasion, they often remarked that it seemed to be my busy day, to which my stock reply came to be that all days were busy and there was little difference among them. It was my custom to be out of bed about six-thirty, except in the darkest mornings of winter. One of the doormen at the White House was an excellent barber, but I always preferred to shave myself with old-fashioned razors, which I knew how to keep in good condition. It was my intention to take a short walk before breakfast, which Mrs. Coolidge and I ate together in our rooms. For me there was fruit and about one-half cup of coffee, with a home-made cereal made from boiling together two parts of unground wheat with one part of rye. To this was added a roll and a strip of bacon, which went mostly to our dogs.

Soon after eight found me dictating in the White House library in preparation for some public utterance. This would go on for more than an hour, after which I began to receive callers at the office. Most of these came by appointment, but in addition to the average of six to eight who were listed there would be as many more from my Cabinet and the Congress, to whom I was always accessible. Each one came to me with a different problem requiring my decision, which was usually made at once. About twelve-fifteen those began to be brought in who were to be somewhat formally presented. At twelve-thirty the doors were opened, and a long line passed by who wished merely to shake hands with the President. One one occasion I shook hands with nineteen hundred in thirty-four minutes, which is probably my record. Instead of a burden, it was a pleasure and a relief to meet people in that way and listen to their greeting, which was often a bendiction. It was at this same hour that the numerous groups assembled in the South Grounds, where I joined them for the photographs used for news purposes and permanent mementoes of their White House visit.

Lunch came at one o'clock, at which we usually had guests. It made an opportunity for giving our friends a little more attention than could be extended through a mere handshake. About an hour was devoted to rest before returning to the office, where the afternoon was reserved for attention to the immense number of documents which pass over the desk of the President. These were all cleaned up each day. Before dinner another walk was in order, followed by exercises on some of the vibrating machines kept in my room. We gathered at the dinner table at seven o'clock and within three-quarters of an hour work would be resumed with my stenographer to continue until about ten o'clock.

At ten-thirty on Tuesdays and Fridays the Cabinet meetings were held. These were always very informal. Each member was asked if he had any problem he wished to lay before the President. When I first attended with President Harding at the beginning of a new administration these were rather numerous. Later, they decreased, as each member felt better able to solve his own problems. After entire freedom of discussion, but always without a vote of any kind, I was accustomed to announce what the decision should be. There never ought to be and never were marked differences of opinion in my Cabinet. As their duties were not to advise each other, but to advise the President, they could not disagree among themselves. I rarely failed to accept their recommendations. Sometimes they wished for larger appropriations than the state of the Treasury warranted, but they all cooperated most sincerely in the policy of economy and were content with such funds as I could assign to them.

The Congress has sometimes been a sore trial to Presidents. I did not find it so in my case. Among them were men of wonderful ability and veteran experience. I think they made their decisions with an honest purpose to serve their country. The membership of the Senate changed very much by reason of those who sacrificed themselves for public duty. Of all public officials with whom I have ever been acquainted, the work of a Senator of the United States is by far the most laborious. About twenty of them died during the eight years I was in Washington.

Sometimes it would seem for a day that either the House or the Senate had taken some unwise action, but if it was not corrected on the floor where it occurred it was usually remedied in the other chamber. I always found the members of both parties willing to confer with me and disposed to treat my recommendations fairly. Most of the differences could be adjusted by personal discussion. Sometimes I made an appeal direct to the country by stating my position at the newspaper conferences. I adopted that course in relation to the Mississippi Flood Control Bill. As it passed the Senate it appeared to be much too extravagant in its rule of damages and its proposed remedy. The press began a vigorous discussion of the subject, which caused the House greatly to modify the bill, and in conference a measure that was entirely fair and moderate was adopted. On other occasions I appealed to the country more privately, enlisting the influence of labor and trade organizations upon the Congress in behalf of some measures in which I was interested. That was done in the case of the tax bill of 1928. As it passed the House, the reductions were so large that the revenue necessary to meet the public expenses would not have been furnished. By quietly making this known to the Senate, and enlisting support for that position among their constituents, it was possible to secure such modification of the measure that it could be adopted without greatly endangering the revenue.

But a President cannot, with success, constantly appeal to the country. After a time he will get no response. The people have their own affairs to look after and can not give much attention to what the Congress is doing. If he takes a position, and stands by it, ultimately it will be adopted. Most of the policies set out in my first Annual Message have become law, but it took several years to get action on some of them.

One of the most perplexing and at the same time most important functions of

465

the President is the making of appointments. In some few cases he acts alone, but usually they are made with the advice and consent of the Senate. It is the practice to consult Senators of his own party before making an appointment from their state. In choosing persons for service over the whole or any considerable portion of a single state, it is customary to rely almost entirely on the party Senators from that state for recommendations. It is not possible to find men who are perfect. Selection always has to be limited to human beings, whatever choice is made. It is therefore always possible to point out defects. The supposition that no one should be appointed who has had experience in the field which he is to supervise is extremely detrimental to the public service. An Interstate Commerce Commissioner is much better qualified, if he knows something about transportation. A Federal Trade Commissioner can render much better service if he has had a legal practice which extended into large business transactions. The assertion of those who contend that persons accepting a government appointment would betray their trust in favor of former associates can be understood only on the supposition that those who make it feel that their own tenure of public office is for the purpose of benefiting themselves and their friends.

Every one knows that where the treasure is, there will the heart be also. When a man has invested his personal interest and reputation in the conduct of a public office, if he goes wrong it will not be because of former relations, but because he is a bad man. The same interests that reached him would reach any bad man, irrespective of former life history. What we need in appointive positions is men of knowledge and experience who have sufficient character to resist temptations. If that standard is maintained, we need not be concerned about their former activities. If it is not maintained, all the restrictions of their past employment that can be conceived will be of no avail.

The more experience I have had in making appointments, the more I am convinced that attempts to put limitations on the appointing power are a mistake. It should be possible to choose a well qualified person wherever he can be found. When restrictions are placed on residence, occupation, or profession, it almost always happens that some one is found who is universally admitted to be the best qualified, but who is eliminated by the artificial specifications. So long as the Senate has the power to reject nominations, there is little danger that a President would abuse his authority if he were given the largest possible freedom in his choices. The public service would be improved if all vacancies were filled by simply appointing the best ability and character that can be found. That is what is done in private business. The adoption of any other course handicaps the government in all its operations.

In determining upon all his actions, however, the President has to remember that he is dealing with two different minds. One is the mind of the country, largely intent upon its own personal affairs, and, while not greatly interested in the government, yet desirous of seeing it conducted in an orderly and dignified manner for the advancement of the public welfare. Those who compose this mind wish to have the country prosperous and are opposed to unjust taxation and public extravagance. At the same time they have a patriotic pride which moves them with so great a desire to see things well done that they are willing to pay for it. They gladly contribute their money to place the United States in the lead. In general, they represent the public opinion of the land.

But they are unorganized, formless, and inarticulate. Against a compact and well drilled minority they do not appear to be very effective. They are nevertheless the great power in our government. I have constantly appealed to them and have seldom failed in enlisting their support. They are the court of last resort and their decisions are final.

They are, however, the indirect rather than the direct power. The immediate authority with which the President has to deal is vested in the political mind. In order to get things done he has to work through that agency. Some of our Presidents have appeared to lack comprehension of the political mind. Although I have been associated with it for many years, I always found difficulty in understanding it. It is a strange mixture of vanity and timidity, of an obsequious attitude at one time and a delusion of grandeur at another time, of the most selfish preferment combined with the most sacrificing patriotism. The political mind is the product of men in public life who have been twice spoiled. They have been spoiled with praise and they have been spoiled with abuse. With them nothing is natural, everything is artificial. A few rare souls escape these influences and maintain a vision and a judgment that are unimpaired. They are a great comfort to every President and a great service to their country. But they are not sufficient in number so that the public business can be transacted like a private business.

It is because in their hours of timidity the Congress becomes subservient to the importunities of organized minorities that the President comes more and more to stand as the champion of the rights of the whole country. Organizing such minorities has come to be a well-recognized industry at Washington. They are oftentimes led by persons of great ability, who display much skill in bringing their influences to bear on the Congress. They have ways of securing newspaper publicity, deluging Senators and Representatives with petitions and overwhelming them with imprecations that are oftentimes decisive in securing the passage of bills. While much of this legislation is not entirely bad, almost all of it is excessively expensive. If it were not for the rules of the House and the veto power of the President, within two years these activities would double the cost of the government.

Under our system the President is not only the head of the government, but is also the head of his party. The last twenty years have witnessed a decline in party spirit and a distinct weakening in party loyalty. While an independent attitude on the part of the citizen is not without a certain public advantage, yet it is necessary under our form of government to have political parties. Unless some one is a partisan, no one can be an independent. The Congress is organized entirely in accordance with party policy. The parties appeal to the voters in behalf of their platforms. The people make their choice on those issues. Unless those who are elected on the same party platform associate themselves together to carry out its provisions, the election becomes a mockery. The independent voter who has joined with others in placing a party nominee in office finds his efforts were all in vain, if the person he helps elect refuses or neglects to keep the platform pledges of his party.

Many occasions arise in the Congress when party lines are very properly disregarded, but if there is to be a reasonable government proceeding in accordance with the express mandate of the people, and not merely at the whim of those who happen to be victorious at the polls, on all the larger and important issues there must be party solidarity. It is the business of the President as party leader to do the best he can to see that the declared party platform purposes are translated into legislative and administrative action. Oftentimes I secured support from those without my party and had opposition from those within my party, in attempting to keep my platform pledges.

Such a condition is entirely anomalous. It leaves the President as the sole repository of party responsibility. But it is one of the reasons that the Presidential office has grown in popular estimation and favor, while the Congress has declined. The country feels that the President is willing to assume responsibility, while his party in the Congress is not. I have never felt it was my duty to attempt to coerce Senators or Representatives, or to take reprisals. The people sent them to Washington. I felt I had discharged my duty when I had done the best I could with them. In this way I avoided almost entirely a personal opposition, which I think was of more value to the country than to attempt to prevail through arousing personal fear.

Under our system it ought to be remembered that the power to initiate policies has to be centralized somewhere. Unless the party leaders exercising it can depend on loyalty and organization support, the party in which it is reposed will become entirely ineffective. A party which is ineffective will soon be discarded. If a party is to endure as a serviceable instrument of government for the country, it must possess and display a healthy spirit of party loyalty. Such a manifestation in the Congress would do more than anything else to rehabilitate it in the esteem and confidence of the country.

All of these trials and encouragements come to each President. It is impossible to explain them. Even after passing through the Presidential office, it still remains a great mystery. Why one person is selected for it and many others are rejected can not be told. Why people respond as they do to its influence seems to be beyond inquiry. Any man who has been placed in the White House can not feel that it is the result of his own exertions or his own merit. Some power outside and beyond him becomes manifest through him. As he contemplates the workings of his office, he comes to realize with an increasing sense of humility that he is but an instrument in the hands of God.

PART SIX

The World in Conflict, 1929–1968

In 1929 the bubble burst. The stock market, which seemed to Americans of the golden era destined to spiral ever upward, suddenly collapsed. Respected leaders insisted that the economy was fundamentally sound and was only undergoing healthy readjustment, but stock prices continued to plunge downward and wiped out hundreds of thousands of investors. By January 1933 the typical stock sold for only one-fifth of its value on the eve of the October 1929 panic.

Only a modest fraction of the American population actually owned securities, but reverberations of the crisis were felt in every home. Decisions made on Wall Street determined the level of production and employment in the entire economy, and disaster there meant trouble everywhere. Wages plummeted, unemployment shot upward, production fell, prices dropped. In less than four years wages and farm income were halved and unemployment had tripled. One-quarter of the labor force was out of work, and only one-fourth of the jobless were covered by existing public or private relief programs. Municipal garbage dumps, accordingly, swarmed with hungry people; in Philadelphia a family was found subsisting on a diet of dandelions.

The Depression, and the failure of the Hoover administration to arrest its course, provoked a massive political upheaval. Franklin D. Roosevelt, swept into the Presidency in 1932, pledged to bring "a New Deal" to the American people. The extent to which he succeeded is still being debated by historians, but there can be no debate about the political achievement of the New Deal. It forged a new political coalition that brought an end to more than three decades of Republican ascendancy in national politics, and made the Democratic party the majority party in the United States for a generation to come. Prior to the New Deal, farmers outside the South and Negroes leaned strongly to the Republicans, and there was significant GOP strength in the ranks of organized labor and recent immigrant groups. John L. Lewis and many other AF of L leaders threw their support to the Republicans in the 1920s; Fiorello LaGuardia was a Republican. Bitter memories of the Depression and personal attachment to the charismatic FDR brought many of these elements into the Democratic camp and kept them there.

The shock of the economic collapse weakened traditional American assumptions about rugged individualism. "Success is not gained by leaning upon government to solve all the problems before us," declared Hoover in 1931. "That way leads to enervation of will and destruction of character." This belief was repudiated by a large majority of the electorate in 1932, and there followed a wave of new public programs to stimulate, regulate, and reform the sagging economy. The banking system was rearranged; the stock market was subjected to a variety of new restraints; industrial prices and wages were regulated; labor was assisted in the struggle to win recognition and the right of collective bargaining; farmers and homeowners burdened by debt were granted credit; federal relief, public works, and unemployment insurance programs eased the difficulties of the jobless. Some of the hastily planned New Deal efforts proved ineffective, and some were declared unconstitutional by the conservative Supreme Court. But the principle of federal responsibility for the economic welfare of every citizen was securely established.

A measure of recovery had been attained by 1935, and the administration was forced to make some difficult political choices. Until that year there had been a program to benefit virtually every interest, and the President had support throughout the society. By 1935 the honeymoon was over. There were complaints from the left, not so much from the tiny Socialist and Communist sects as from Senator Huey Long, Father Coughlin, and Dr. Francis Townsend, who insisted that the ordinary American was still prey to economic insecurity and that some sharing of wealth was required. A secret poll conducted by the Democratic National Committee in 1935 indicated that such discontent might draw enough votes to cost FDR the election in 1936. At the same time, the Republican opposition and business leaders began to argue that the New Deal had already gone too far. These pressures induced Roosevelt to launch a somewhat more radical "second New Deal." The Wealth Tax Act of 1935 provided a graduated income tax; though its schedules were only mildly progressive, some saw in it the beginnings of a "soak the rich" tax policy. The Wagner-Connery Labor Relations bill of the same year put the federal government more squarely behind the cause of organized labor than ever before, and enabled organizers of the newly formed CIO to exhort the unorganized "FDR wants you to join the union." A federally financed social-security system, providing old-age pensions, aid to dependent children, and unemployment insurance marked the beginnings of the modern American welfare state.

None of these reforms overcame the economic stagnation that plagued the United States in the Depression era, nor did the administration's cautious experiments with pump-priming and deficit financing. John Maynard Keynes had not fully outlined his theory of how fiscal policy could be used to combat business fluctuations until 1936, and even after that New Dealers left the federal budget unbalanced only when they were unable to do otherwise. A sharp cut in federal spending in 1937 provoked another downturn. Unemployment levels shot upward and remained high until rising military expenditures took up the slack toward the end of the decade.

Despite the efforts of New Deal reformers, there remained millions of desperately poor people in America. Few New Deal measures reached to the very bottom of the social order. Conservative political pressures led to the exclusion of many of the disadvantaged from much of the new social legislation. The share of the national income going to the bottom fifth of the population did not increase significantly during the New Deal years. The concentration of wealth in the hands of the very rich diminished modestly by some measures, but the gains went to groups in the middle brackets. It took the tight full employment of the booming World War II economy to lift up the very poor, and then the improvement was modest and short-lived.

American intellectuals of the Depression years were coming to think in increasingly collectivist terms and were more inclined to view society as a struggle between economic interests and classes. Some mechanically applied Marxist ideas to the analysis of American capitalism but more interesting and independent social criticism came from the pens of theologian Reinhold Niebuhr, sociologists Robert and Helen Lynd, and lawyer Thurman Arnold. Economist Paul Douglas, later a distinguished United States Senator from Illinois, spoke for many of these when he wrote in 1933: "Along with the Rooseveltian program must go . . . the organization of those who are at present weak, and who need to acquire that which the world respects, namely, power. Unless these things are done, we are likely to find the permanent benefits of Rooseveltian liberalism to be as illusory as were those of the Wilsonian Era."

By this criterion the New Deal was at best a moderate success. The most significant shift in power relations in American society that it produced, or helped to produce, was the spread of industrial unionism in the mass production industries, automobiles, steel, and rubber, in the latter half of the decade. The semiskilled operatives at Ford Motors, U.S. Steel, and Goodyear's had no place in the American Federation of Labor, which by this time had shed all pretension to any objectives more visionary than better wages for the elite of skilled craftsmen within it. Aided by the National Labor Relations Board, the investigations of the LaFollette Committee, the sympathy of liberal public officials like Governor Frank Murphy of Michigan, and the tactic of well-planned sit-down strikes, the CIO won a series of dramatic victories and gave millions of previously powerless men some control over their wages and working conditions. The new CIO unions became a

471

key source of Democratic strength, and a strong liberal influence on the national scene.

Observers who saw the thrust of labor organization as a challenge to American capitalism and the beginnings of class warfare, however, were mistaken. If manual laborers were more inclined to vote Democratic than their bosses, the class polarization of American parties was never as sharp as in many European countries, nor was the Demorcratic party comparable to European labor, Social-Democratic, or Communist organizations. The first efforts by social scientists like A. W. Jones to study the nature of the American class structure revealed a class-stratified society, but they also showed that few Americans on the lower rungs of the class ladder felt that the entire system was unfair and in need of radical alteration. This was not surprising, for even in the tight Depression years the social system retained considerable fluidity. Large numbers of Americans had experienced social mobility above the level of their father's occupations and their own first jobs. The closing of the "golden door" to European immigrants in the 1920s had cut off a classic source of fluidity, but the continued influx of rural people, especially from the South, had much the same effect. The Depression slowed the process of social circulation somewhat, and inspired class resentments, but during World War II it reached normal levels again. American workers were sufficiently class-conscious to join unions, to vote heavily Democratic, and to insist that the government intervene in the workings of the private enterprise system when it failed to function efficiently; they were not, however, disposed to think that the concentration of great wealth and economic power in private hands was fundamentally inequitable. However inadequate and incomplete the New Deal was, it did enough to prevent that.

Problems of foreign affairs did not intrude much into the American consciousness in the early Depression years. The isolationist mood was dominant, symbolized by neutrality legislation that forbade shipments to belligerents in time of war, outlawed travel by American nationals on belligerent vessels, and prevented the granting of commercial credits to warring parties. All this was intended to prevent the entanglements that had led us into what many citizens regarded as a tragically mistaken world war two decades earlier. The coming to power of Fascist regimes in Italy, Germany, and Spain, however, and of a military clique in Japan, disturbed Americans and eroded isolationist assumptions. Many felt moral outrage at the domestic brutalities of the totalitarian regimes, for instance, Hitler's persecution of the Jews. Some were concerned as well about the aggressively nationalist and expansionist foreign policies of Germany, Italy, and Japan, either out of the conviction that the Axis countries would ultimately seek to conquer America as well, or because such expansion challenged the influence and power of the United States and her allies in Europe and the underdeveloped world. Few Americans were sympathetic to the internal policies of the totalitarian powers, but there was deep and bitter division over the dangers of Fascist expansionism. Many believed that whatever happened across the seas, "fortress America," was safe. There was, in addition, serious questioning of the premise that the existing international status quo was a just one, and of the corollary that the demands of the dissatisfied

472

"have-not" powers were so unjustified that we should risk war to deny them. The isolationist "America First" movement was consequently a potent force in national politics, and both FDR and his Republican opponent in 1940 were forced to pledge that no American troops would be sent overseas. These policy disagreements came to a sudden end in December 1941, when the Japanese attack at Pearl Harbor united the American public in opposition to the Axis powers, but the troubling questions that had been raised about America's role in the world would soon recur.

The deadly mushroom clouds that rose over Hiroshima and Nagasaki in August 1945 brought World War II to a close and opened an era in which every inhabitant of the planet lived under the threat of nuclear destruction. A World War III was by no means impossible, but it was evident that World War IV would have to be fought with clubs, if indeed there were humans alive to fight it at all.

In 1945 two giant powers stood over the ruins of a war-torn world. The United States was the richest country in the world; it had suffered fewer casualties than any other of the leading belligerents, and it was sole possessor of the most deadly weapon mankind had ever devised. Its wartime ally, the Soviet Union, had suffered far more from the war, and as yet it had no nuclear arsenal, but Russian troops had pushed the Nazi invaders out of eastern Europe and were in de facto control of virtually all of eastern Europe and half of Germany. Stalin, Roosevelt, and Churchill had made tentative agreement about the shape of the postwar world in wartime conferences at Teheran and Yalta, but the apparent consensus was superficial and ambiguous. The Russians sought firm guarantees of friendly regimes in the territories they had conquered, and heavy reparations from Germany, both to bolster the damaged Soviet economy and to prevent still another German attack upon Russia in the future. The United States was hesitant about conceding eastern Europe as a Soviet sphere of influence, and extracted from Stalin a vague promise that free elections be held in the captured areas.

The peace soon revealed that the Soviet conception of a "free" election was far removed from that of the United States and Roosevelt's successor, Harry Truman, emboldened by America's nuclear monopoly, initiated a "get tough" policy. From the American point of view, this was intended to liberate eastern Europe; from the Russian perspective it was an effort to deprive the USSR of the security she had won through bloody battles against the Germans and to draw eastern Europe into the American sphere of influence that already extended over western Europe. The Cold War had begun.

The United States soon committed itself to the containment policy, the rationale for which was outlined by foreign service officer George F. Kennan in a famous article in 1947. Kennan's assumption that Russian fears of the West were based solely on the internal stresses of its totalitarian regime rather than on the long record of anti-Communist behavior by the Western powers since 1917, and his conclusion that toughness accordingly was invariably more successful than accommodation may have been doubtful. Kennan himself was later to see greater possibilities for compromise and conciliation with the Soviet Union, and to argue that American reliance upon military threats was excessive; but amidst the pervasive fear of the Red menace that swept through the United States in the early postwar years and sparked by the career of Senator Joseph McCarthy, such questions were swept aside. A bipartisan consensus on the main elements of cold-war foreign policy emerged; disagreement and debate stopped at the water's edge. The dismal failure of Henry Wallace's campaign for the Presidency in 1948 was in part due to Wallace's innocence about the Communist Party's dominating influence in his Progressive Party, but in any event the public mood at the time was entirely unreceptive to pleas for a less militantly anti-Communist foreign policy.

In Europe containment was carried out via the Marshall Plan, providing economic assistance to restore war-devastated economies, the North Atlantic Treaty Organization, and the ultimate threat of nuclear retaliation should NATO forces prove unable to repel Soviet attack. There were no further Russian gains in Europe, evidence either that the policy had been successful, or that it had been based on a misreading of Soviet intentions. The Russians, however, remained in control over the satellite regimes behind the Iron Curtain. President Dwight Eisenhower and his Secretary of State John Foster Dulles spoke of liberating the captive people of eastern Europe and rolling back the Iron Curtain, but by then the USSR possessed a nuclear striking force. The test of American willingness to risk total war came in 1956, when a popular uprising temporarily established an independent government in Hungary. Russian troops quickly moved in to crush the revolution, and America dared not intervene. The threat of total nuclear war loomed ominously on later occasions, notably in the Cuban missile crisis of 1962, but in each instance the uneasy balance of terror was preserved in the end. A nuclear test ban treaty with the Russians later slackened the pace of the arms race slightly, but there was no progress toward actual disarmament. The peace of the world still depended on the caution and restraint of men in the Kremlin and the White House, and recurrent crises continued to put dangerous strains on this delicate equilibrium.

The locus of American-Soviet conflict shifted increasingly from Europe toward the less developed and less stable "third world." Here the task of containing Communism and preserving the integrity of "the free world" was far more difficult. Revolutionary ferment was rising in many parts of the globe. In many cases it was being directed against oppressive landlord or military regimes. At times it seemed that the United States government equated "free" with "pro-American," and that it was determined to preserve in power, through military and economic aid and even American troops, governments that would follow its lead, however undemocratic their character. Though the Soviet Union, and after its establishment in 1949 Communist China, generally looked with favor upon the attempts to overturn these regimes, actual Communists were rarely dominant in the rebel groups. Instead there was a medley of disaffected men of a wide variety of political leanings. Some Americans were incapable of making these distinctions, but more sophisticated defenders of American policy argued that whatever the composition of the revolutionary movement, a situation of revolutionary turmoil was one in which actual Communists were likely to triumph in the long run, and this justified propping up weak pro-American governments as lesser evils.

The difficulties of serving as self-appointed policeman imposing order in the underdeveloped world were not immediately apparent in the first venture of this kind—President Truman's 1947 decision to assist the Greek government to suppress a guerrilla uprising there. The revolutionary forces had considerable popular support, but the government had sufficient strength to put them down with few American troops. Twenty years later, reflecting on the military dictatorship reigning in Greece and the modest easing of totalitarian controls in Communist but neutral Yugoslavia, some observers were wondering how much Greece had been benefited by being saved for the free world, but in 1947 the answer seemed easy to most Americans. The Korean War, too, appeared self-evidently necessary, for it involved a blatant military invasion of one state by another. The public divided only over the question of whether the war was to be fought as a limited war within Korea or whether the United States should run the risk of attacking China.

In subsequent years there were other instances of overt or covert American intervention to prevent or undo political changes regarded as dangerous—in Guatemala in 1954, Lebanon in 1958, Cuba in 1961, and the Dominican Republic in 1965; but not until the Vietnam War was there deep popular revulsion against the fundamentals of cold-war foreign policy, and the beginnings of a searching national debate over America's role in the world. Many Americans viewed the attempt of the National Liberation Front to topple the pro-United States regime as essentially an indigenous popular uprising, albeit one aided and encouraged by Communist North Vietnam; they also believed that America was inflicting fearful casualties on helpless peasants in both sections of the country in a tragically mistaken effort to preserve American prestige and power in Southeast Asia, regardless of the cost in lives. Many others, however, took the administration's position that this was a classic, if somewhat more subtle, instance of aggression against a duly constituted state, and that a peaceful world could be preserved only through resolute action to demonstrate that aggression does not pay. By 1968 there were faint signs that a settlement might be reached in Vietnam, but whether there would be other Vietnams in the future seemed destined to be a central issue in American politics for years to come.

In the years of uneasy peace and intermittent limited war that made up the cold-war years, the American economy performed at a generally high level. There were modest recessions in the late 1940s and the late 1950s, but the major depression many feared following the close of the world war did not materialize then or later. The built-in economic stabilizers developed during the New Deal, and a new sophistication about the functioning of a modern economy, symbolized by the creation of the President's Council of Economic Advisors in 1946, were part of the explanation. The extent of sustained prosperity could not be determined so long as the arms race with the Soviet Union and our extensive military commitments around the world kept the economy on a partial wartime basis. In any event, the gross national product moved steadily upward, and it seemed as though America had become an "affluent society," in which poverty had virtually disappeared and every group had been able to develop "countervailing power" to obtain its fair share.

In the 1960s, however, such optimism about the workings of the economy was weakened, and there was a new wave of public concern about poverty. The Kennedy administration had begun planning a new attack on the problem shortly before the President's assassination, and his successor launched a national War on Poverty in 1964. It had become evident that low-income groups were receiving roughly the same small portion of the national wealth they had been receiving thirty years before. Few Americans were poor by the standards of other societies, or of the American past, but a substantial minority of citizens were living in conditions that had begun to seem intolerable.

This was particularly true of Negroes, who remained impoverished far out of proportion to their representation in the population. The postwar years saw dramatic progress in the Negro's struggle to win a place in American society—the integration of the armed forces, the Supreme Court's striking down of racially segregated schools in 1954, the elimination of segregated public facilities, the beginnings toward protection of voting rights in areas where blacks had been deprived of them. Federal legislation, passed during the Presidency of Lyndon Johnson, climaxed the drive to assure American Negroes of the elementary civil rights long denied them. These gains brought not contentment, but new awareness of problems beyond the purview of traditional civil-rights measures. Negroes living in liberal Northern states like New York had been free of formal segregation for many years without winning economic and social advances as impressive as those of earlier migrants to the urban world. As increasing numbers of blacks concentrated in Northern cities, and the South itself began to evolve toward the Northern pattern of race relations, it began to appear that genuine integration in housing, education, and jobs would continue to elude the mass of Negroes for decades to come, and that other strategies for group advance were required. The riots that erupted in the cities reflected the frustration induced by this disturbing discovery. The slogan "black power" was becoming ever more fashionable, at least among articulate Negroes, but this loose concept embraced everything from internal guerrilla warfare in pursuit of a separate black state to efforts to create a class of responsible Negro businessmen along the lines suggested by Booker T. Washington at the turn of the century. What black power might mean in practice, and what the response of white society would be remained to be seen. A Presidential commission of moderate leaders warned that "white racism" was a dominant fact of American life, and that the United States was rapidly becoming two societies. Some thought this overly pessimistic, but it was difficult to deny that the crisis in black and white was the most painful and challenging domestic problem on the horizon.

47

From the Jazz Age
to the Thirties

In his essay "The Literary Consequences of the Crash," Edmund Wilson sketches the intellectual climate of the 1920s and suggests some of the influences that drove American intellectuals to the left after the collapse in 1929. Wilson, perhaps America's most distinguished literary critic in this century, was on the staff of the *New Republic* throughout the period discussed in this essay. In 1932 he was one of several dozen prominent American writers to sign the manifesto "Culture and the Crisis," an endorsement of the Communist Party's candidates in the elections of that year. His generalizations about the alienation of the intellectuals apply more to writers and artists than to intellectuals of other types—historians and social scientists, for example. The latter felt less of a revulsion against the material achievements of American civilization, and were inclined to believe that the spread of science and technology would foster social progress. Both groups, however, were drawn together by the crash and stimulated to consider plans for the radical reconstruction of American society. The candidates running on the Socialist or Communist tickets never seriously threatened the political dominance of the two major parties, but pressure from disaffected intellectuals was an important influence upon the New Deal.

THE LITERARY CONSEQUENCES
OF THE CRASH
Edmund Wilson

Even before the stock market crash of October, 1929, a kind of nervous dissatisfaction and apprehension had begun to manifest itself in American intellectual life. The liberating movement of the twenties had by that time accomplished its work of discrediting the gentility and Puritanism of the later nineteenth century; the orgy of spending of the Boom was becoming more and more grotesque, and the Jazz Age was ending in hysteria. The principal points of

Reprinted with permission of the author from *The Shores of Light* (New York: Farrar, Straus, and Company, Inc., 1952), 492–499.

view of this period I tried, after the crash, to sum up in an article of March 23, 1932:

The attitudes of the decade that followed the war, before the depression set in, already seem a long way off:

The attitude of the Menckenian gentleman, ironic, beer-loving and "civilized," living principally on the satisfaction of feeling superior to the broker and enjoying the debauchment of American life as a burlesque show or three-ring circus; the attitude of old-American-stock smugness, with its drawing aloof from the rabble in the name of old Uncle Gilead Pilcher who was Governor of Connecticut or Grandfather Timothy Merrymount who was killed in the Civil War—though the parvenus kept crashing the gate so fast, while the prosperity boom was on, that it was becoming harder and harder to get one's aloofness properly recognized; the liberal attitude that American capitalism was going to show a new wonder to the world by gradually and comfortably socializing itself and that we should just have to respect it in the meantime, taking a great interest in Dwight W. Morrow and Owen D. Young; the attitude of trying to get a kick out of the sheer size and energy of American enterprises, irrespective of what they were aiming at; the attitude of proudly withdrawing and cultivating a refined sensibility or of losing oneself completely in abstruse intellectual pursuits—scholastic philosophy, symbolic logic or metaphysical physics; the attitude of letting oneself be carried along by the mad hilarity and heartbreak of jazz, living only for the excitement of the evening; the attitude of keeping one's mind and morals impregnably disinfected with the feeble fascism-classicism of humanism.

I have in one mood or another myself felt some sympathy with all of these different attitudes—with the single exception of humanism; and they have all, no doubt, had their validity for certain people, for special situations. Yet today they all look rather queer: they are no use in our present predicament, and we can see how superficial they were. We can see now that they all represented attempts on the part of the more thoughtful Americans to reconcile themselves to a world dominated by salesmen and brokers—and that they all involved compromises with the salesman and the broker. Mencken and Nathan laughed at the broker, but they justified the system which produced him and they got along with him very well, provided he enjoyed George Moore and had pretensions to a taste in liquor; the jazz-age romantics spent the broker's money as speedily and wildly as possible and tried to laugh off the office and the factory with boyish and girlish jokes; the old-American-stockers sniffed at him, but though they salved their consciences thus, they were usually glad to get in on any of his good things that were going; the liberals, who had been vaguely unhappy, later became vaguely resigned and could never bring themselves to the point of serious quarrelling with him; the poets and philosophers hid from him—and the physicists grew more and more mystical in the laboratories subsidized mainly by the profits from industrial investments; the humanists, in volume after volume, endeavored by sheer hollow thunder to induce people to find in the stock exchange the harmony and dignity of the Parthenon.

I did not include in this catalogue a cult that was spreading in New York and that had converts in and around the *New Republic:* that of the Russo-Greek charlatan Gurdjieff, who undertook to renovate the personalities of discontented well-to-do persons. He combined making his clients uncomfortable in various gratuitous ways—such as waking them up in the middle of the night and training them to perform grotesque dances—with reducing them to a condition of complete docility, in which they would hold, at a signal, any position, however awkward, that they happened to be in at the moment, They were promised, if they proved themselves worthy of it, an ultimate initiation into the mysteries of an esoteric doctrine. Gurdjieff's apostle in the United States was the English ex-journalist A. R. Orage, a funereal and to me a distasteful person, who drilled his pupils, not in dancing, but in a kind of dialectic and who acquired at one time a considerable influence over the mind of Herbert Croly, whose inhibited personality and unsatisfied religious instincts laid him open to the lures of a cult that pretended to liberate the mind and to put one in touch with some higher power. But Croly was a fastidious man, and in the long run he found Orage grating. I was myself the object of several attempts to recruit me to the Orage group, but the only interchange of influence that took place between Orage and me consisted of my once persuading him to go to the National Winter Garden; when I next saw him, he told me with a severity that suggested a sense of outrage that he had not enjoyed it at all. Gurdjieff, however, whom I never met, had apparently a rogue's sense of humor. A young man in the office, a bishop's son who had lost his faith and was groping for something to take its place, told me of the banquets of roast sheep or goat, served in great pots in the Caucasian style and eaten with the fingers, to which Gurdjieff would invite his disciples and at which he would have read aloud to them a book he had written called *A Criticism of the Life of Man: Beëlzebub's Tale to His Grandson*. "It sounds as if it had been written," said this neophyte, "just on purpose to bore you to death. Everybody listens in silence, but every now and then Gurdjieff will suddenly burst out laughing—just roaring—nobody knows about what."

I did not read *Beëlzebub's Tale*, but I did read *Das Kapital*. Not that I want to compare the two works, but there *was* a certain similarity in the way in which people then approached them; and I was surprised to find that an apparently social evening that would turn out to be a conspiracy to involve one in some Communist organization resembled a dinner I had once attended at which I was chilled to discover that the springes of Orage had been laid for me—and these both recalled to me an earlier occasion on which a literary conversation, in the rooms of the proselytizing rector of the Episcopal Church at Princeton, had been prodded by amusing remarks in the direction of the Christian faith. People did want faiths and churches badly, and though I am good at resisting churches, I caught a wave from the impulsion of the Marxist faith.

The stock market crash was to count for us almost like a rending of the earth in preparation for the Day of Judgment. In my articles of the months just before it, I had often urged writers to acquaint themselves with "the realities of our contemporary life," to apply themselves to "the study of contemporary reality," etc. I myself had not exercised enough insight to realize that American "prosperity" was an inflation that was due to burst. I had, however, become aware that we liberals of the *New Republic* were not taking certain recent happenings so seriously as we should. The execution of Sacco and Vanzetti in August, 1927, had made liberals lose their bearings. During the months while the case was working up to its climax, Herbert Croly had been away in Honolulu attending a conference called by the Institute of Pacific Relations. When he returned, I was surprised to learn that he did not entirely approve of the way in which we had handled the case. Croly's method of commenting on current events was impersonal and very abstract; and, in his absence, we had given way to the impulse to print certain articles which were certainly, for the *New Republic*, unusually concrete and militant. I first became aware of a serious divergence between my own point of view and Croly's when I was talking with him one day about a leader called *A Nation of Foreigners* that I wrote for the paper in October. He did approve of this editorial, but for reasons that put me in a false position. My article had dealt with the futility of attempting to identify "Americanism" with the interests and ideas of the Anglo-Saxon element in the United States, pointing out that, in this case, the Irish, who had been snubbed by the Anglo-Saxon Bostonians, had combined with them in the most wolfish way to persecute the immigrant Italians; and I discovered that Croly was pleased at my treating the subject from this angle rather than from that of class animosities. This class aspect he wanted to deny; it was one of the assumptions of his political thinking—I had not then read *The Promise of American Life*—that the class struggle should not, and in its true form did not, occur in the United States.

I had been running the literary department, and this was my first excursion on the political side of the paper, which Croly had kept strictly in line with his own very definite ideas. Sometime in the later months of 1928, he had the first of several strokes, and was never able again to perform his full functions as editor-in-chief. When he died in May, 1930, the paper was carried on by the editors as a group, with no one in Croly's position, and we had—rather difficult with men of conflicting opinions and temperaments, with nobody to make final decisions—to work out a policy of our own. I had been troubled by another incident that took place in the autumn of 1929. The bitter and violent Gastonia strike of the textile workers in North Carolina had been going on ever since spring. It was the first major labor battle conducted by a Communist union. Sixteen union members, including three women, were being tried for the murder of a chief of police, who had invaded without a warrant the tent-colony in which the strikers had been living; and the death penalty was being asked for all of them except the women. Feeling on both sides had been roused to the point of ferocity—we were not then familiar with the Communists' habit of manufacturing martyrs—and, after the execution of Sacco and Vanzetti, one was apprehensive of another judicial lynching. John Dos Passos and Mary Heaton Vorse both asked the *New Republic* to send them to report on Gastonia, but both were thought to be too far to the Left to be reliable from our point of view. "The liberals," Dos Passos said to me, "are all so neurotic about Communists!" This was perfectly true; and the pressure on us to do something about Gastonia had at the time almost no effect. The young man who had been hooked by Orage—who had had no experience of labor disputes—was going down to a fashionable wedding at Asheville, not far from Gastonia, and he was asked to drop in at the seat of trouble. When he came back, this young man reported that there was nothing of interest going on. I do not know whom he could have talked to. He had been in Gastonia on the very day, September 14, when the hostilities were coming to a climax. In an attempt to prevent a union meeting, an armed mob had fired on unarmed strikers and had killed a woman named Ella May

Wiggins, a widow with five children, who had written songs for the strikers and was extremely popular among them. Her death gave the Communists a battle-cry and the strikers an unforgettable grievance. It was obvious that the *New Republic*, which was supposed to cover labor sympathetically, was falling down on this part of its program.

The next month the slump began, and, as conditions grew worse and worse and President Hoover, unable to grasp what had happened, made no effort to deal with the breakdown, a darkness seemed to descend. Yet, to the writers and artists of my generation who had grown up in the Big Business era and had always resented its barbarism, its crowding-out of everything they cared about, these years were not depressing but stimulating. One couldn't help being exhilarated at the sudden unexpected collapse of that stupid gigantic fraud. It gave us a new sense of freedom; and it gave us a new sense of power to find ourselves still carrying on while the bankers, for a change, were taking a beating. With a businessman's president in the White House, who kept telling us, when he told us anything, that the system was perfectly sound, who sent General Douglas MacArthur to burn the camp of the unemployed war veterans who had come to appeal to Washington, we wondered about the survival of republican American institutions; and we became more and more impressed by the achievements of the Soviet Union, which could boast that its industrial and financial problems were carefully studied by the government, and that it was able to avert such crises. We overdid both these tendencies; but the slump was like a flood or an earthquake, and it was long before many things righted themselves.

48

A Christian Marxist Critique of Liberal Rationalism

The tradition of preaching the "social gospel," of relating religion to the burning social issues of the day, began in late nineteenth-century America. Reinhold Niebuhr, a brilliant young minister and theologian, gave it new relevance in the 1930s, when he blended Christian pessimism about human rationality and Marxist notions of class self-interest into a potent attack upon many of the assumptions of American culture. In books like *Moral Man and Immoral Society* (1932) and in numerous essays for religious and political journals like that reprinted here, Niebuhr called attention to glaring social injustice and argued that it was an integral, not an accidental, feature of capitalist civilization. His judgments that "capitalism is dying" and "liberalism in politics is a spent force" proved mistaken, but it is revealing of the depth of the crisis of American society in the early Depression years that they were widely shared by responsible thinkers.

AFTER CAPITALISM—WHAT?
Reinhold Niebuhr

The following analysis of American social and political conditions is written on the assumption that capitalism is dying and with the conviction that it ought to die. It is dying because it is a contracting economy which is unable to support the necessities of an industrial system that requires mass production for its maintenance, and because it disturbs the relations of an international economic system with the anarchy of nationalistic politics. It ought to die because it is unable to make the wealth created by modern technology available to all who participate in the productive process on terms of justice.

The conviction that capitalism is dying and that it ought to die gives us no clue to the method of its passing. Will it perish in another world war? Or in the collapse of the credit structure through which it manipulates its various functions? Will it, perhaps, give way to a new social order created by the political power of those who have been disinherited by it? Or will it be destroyed by a revolution? These questions are difficult to answer for any portion of Western civilization, and they

From "After Capitalism—What?", *The World Tomorrow*, March 1, 1933, 203–205. Reprinted by permission of Reinhold Niebuhr.

are particularly puzzling when directed to the American scene. We may believe that the basic forces moving in modern industrial society are roughly similar in all nations. Yet we cannot evade the fact that various nations reveal a wide variety of unique social and economic characteristics and that our own nation is particularly unique in some of the aspects of its political and economic life. Our wealth has been greater than that of any modern nation, the ideals of a pioneer democracy have retarded the formation of definite classes, the frontier spirit belongs to so recent a past that its individualism is not yet dissipated, and the complete preoccupation of the nation with its engineering task to the exclusion of political and social problems makes us singularly incompetent as a people in the field of politics. All these factors, and some others which might be mentioned, warn the prophet to be circumspect in applying generalizations derived from European conditions to our situation. It is therefore advisable to divide our problem of analysis by considering first those aspects of the situation about which generalizations equally applicable to Europe and America can be made; the uniquely American aspects may then be seen in clearer light.

The most generally applicable judgment which can be made is that capitalism will not reform itself from within. There is nothing in history to support the thesis that a dominant class ever yields its position or privileges in society because its rule has been convicted of ineptness or injustices. Those who still regard this as possible are rationalists and moralists who have only a slight understanding of the stubborn inertia and blindness of collective egoism.

Politically this judgment implies that liberalism in politics is a spent force. In so far as liberalism is based upon confidence in the ability and willingness of rational and moral individuals to change the basis of society, it has suffered disillusion in every modern nation. As the social struggle becomes more sharply defined, the confused liberals drift reluctantly into the camp of reaction and the minority of clear-sighted intellectuals and idealists are forced either to espouse the cause of radicalism or to escape to the bleachers and become disinterested observers. The liberal middle ground has been almost completely wiped out in Germany. It is held today only by the Catholic party, a unique phenomenon in Western politics. In England only the free-trade liberals who managed to extricate themselves from the Tory embrace and the quite lonely and slightly pathetic Mr. Lloyd George stand in the liberal position. The English liberals who interpreted their position as a championship of the community of consumers against warring camps of producers have had to learn that the stakes which men have in the productive process outweigh their interests as consumers. Mr. Roosevelt's effort at, or pretension to, liberalizing the Democratic Party may be regarded as a belated American effort to do what Europe has proved to be impossible. Equally futile will be the efforts of liberals who stand to the left of Mr. Roosevelt and who hope to organize a party which will give the feverish American patient pills of diluted socialism coated with liberalism, in the hope that his aversion to bitter pills will thus be circumvented.

All this does not mean that intellectual and moral idealism are futile. They are needed to bring decency and fairness into any system of society; for no basic reorganization of society will ever guarantee the preservation of humaneness if good men do not preserve it. Furthermore, the intelligence of a dominant group will determine in what measure it will yield in time under pressure or to what degree it will defend its entrenched positions so uncompromisingly that an orderly retreat becomes impossible and a disorderly rout envelops the whole of society in chaos. That ought to be high enough stake for those of us to play for who are engaged in the task of education and moral suasion among the privileged. If such conclusions seems unduly cynical they will seem so only because the moral idealists of the past century, both religious and rational, have been unduly sentimental in their estimates of human nature. Perhaps it will be permitted the writer to add, by way of parenthesis, that he has been greatly instructed by the number of letters which have come to him in late months complaining that a religious radical ought not to give up his faith in human nature so completely lest he betray thereby his lack of faith in the divine. Classical religion has always spoken rather unequivocally of the deprivity of human nature, a conclusion at which it arrived by looking at human nature from the perspective of the divine. It is one of the strange phenomena of our culture that an optimistic estimate of human nature has been made the basis of theistic theologies.

Next to the futility of liberalism we may set down the inevitability of fascism as a practical certainty in every Western nation. A disintegrating social system will try to save itself by closing ranks and eliminating the anarchy within itself. It will thus undoubtedly be able to perpetuate itself for several decades. It will not finally succeed because it will have no way of curing the two basic defects of capitalism, inequality of consumption and international anarchy. It will probably succeed longer in Italy and Germany than in America, because fascism in those countries derives its strength from a combination of the military and capitalistic castes. The military caste has a greater interest in avoiding revolution than in preserving the privileges of the capitalists. It may therefore be counted upon to circumscribe these privileges more rigorously than will be the case in America, where such a caste does not exist and where military men lack social prestige. A von Schleicher can always be counted on to build a more stable fascism than a "committee of public safety" consisting of Owen Youngs, et al., to whom the fascist task will undoubtedly be entrusted in America.

The certainty that dominant social groups which now control society will not easily yield and that their rule is nevertheless doomed raises interesting problems of strategy for those who desire a new social order. In America these problems are complicated by the fact that there is no real proletarian class in this country. All but the most disinherited workers still belong to the middle class, and they will not be united in a strong political party of their own for some years to come. Distressing social experience will finally produce radical convictions among them, but experience without education and an adequate political philosophy will merely result in sporadic violence. We are literally in the midst of a disintegrating economic empire with no receiver in bankruptcy in sight to assume responsibility for the defunct institution. All this probably means that capitalism has many a decade to run in this country, particularly if it should find momentary relief from present difficulties through some inflationary movement. The sooner a strong political labor movement, expressing itself in socialist terms develops, the greater is the probability of achieving essential change without undue violence or social chaos.

One of the difficulties of the situation is that America may have to go through a period of purely parliamentary socialism even after Europe has proved that a socialism which makes a fetish of parliamentarism will not be able to press through to its goal. Though we will probably have to go through the experience of parliamentarism, we may be able to qualify our faith in it sufficiently to be pragmatic and experimental in the choice of our radical techniques. To disavow pure parliamentarism does not mean to espouse revolution. Any modern industrial civilization has a natural and justified instinctive avoidance of revolution. It rightly fears that revolution may result in suicide for the whole civilization. When European nations are unable to achieve a bare Socialist majority in their legislative bodies, it is hardly probable that in America we will ever have such a preponderance of Socialist conviction that Socialist amendments to the constitution could be enacted. But revolution is equally unthinkable. There is no possibility of a purely revolutionary movement establishing order on this continent without years of internecine strife. For this reason it is important that parliamentary socialism seek to enact as much of its program as possible within the present constitutional framework during the next decades, without hoping, however, that socialism itself can be established in this manner. The final struggle between socialism and fascism will probably be a long and drawn-out conflict in which it is possible that fascism will finally capitulate without a military or revolutionary venture being initiated against it. It will capitulate simply because the inexorable logic of history plus the determined opposition of the labor group will finally destroy it. The final transfer of power may come through the use of a general strike or some similar technique.

Prediction at long range may seem idle and useless. But it is important to recognize that neither the parliamentary nor the revolutionary course offers modern society an easy way to the mastery of a technological civilization. If this is the case, it becomes very important to develop such forms of resistance and mass coercion as will disturb the intricacies of an industrial civilization as little as possible, and as will perserve the temper of mutual respect within the area of social conflict. Political realists have become cynical about moral and religious idealism in politics chiefly because so frequently it is expressed in terms of confusion which hide the basic facts of the social struggle. Once the realities of this struggle are freely admitted, there is every possibility of introducing very important ethical elements into the struggle in the way, for instance, that Gandhi introduces them in India.

The inability of religious and intellectual idealists to gauge properly the course of historical events results from their constant over-estimate of idealistic and unselfish factors in political life. They think that an entire nation can be educated toward a new social ideal when all the testimony of history proves that new societies are born out of social struggle, in which the positions of the various social groups are determined by their economic interests.

Those who wish to participate in such a struggle creatively, to help history toward a goal of justice and to eliminate as much confusion, chaos and conflict in the attainment of the goal as possible, will accomplish this result only if they do not permit their own comparative emancipation from the determining and conditioning economic factors to obscure the fact that these factors are generally determining. No amount of education or religious idealism will ever persuade a social class to espouse a cause or seek a goal which is counter to its economic interest. Social intelligence can have a part in guiding social impulse only if it does not commit the error of assuming that intelligence has destroyed and sublimated impulse to such a degree that impulse is no longer potent. This is the real issue between liberalism and political realism. The liberal is an idealist who imagines that his particular type of education or his special kind of religious idealism will accomplish what history has never before revealed: the complete sublimation of the natural impulse of a social group.

Dominant groups will always have the impulse to hold on to their power as long as possible. In the interest of a progressive justice they must be dislodged, and this will be done least painfully and with least confusion if the social group which has the future in its hands becomes conscious of its destiny as soon as possible, is disciplined and self-confident in the knowledge of it destiny and gradually acquires all the heights of prestige and power in society which it is possible to acquire without a struggle. When the inevitable struggle comes (for all contests of power must finally issue in a crisis) there is always the possibility that the old will capitulate and the new assume social direction without internecine conflict. That is why an adequate political realism will ultimately make for more peace in society than a liberalism which does not read the facts of human nature and human history right, and which is betrayed by these errors into erroneous historical calculations which prolong the death agonies of the old order and postpone the coming of the new.

It may be important to say in conclusion that educational and religious idealists shrink from the conclusions to which a realistic analysis of history forces the careful student, partly because they live in the false hope that the impulses of nature in man can be sublimated by mind and conscience to a larger degree than is actually possible, and partly because their own personal idealism shrinks from the "brutalities" of the social struggle which a realistic theory envisages. But this idealism is full of confusion. It does not recognize that everyone but the ascetic is a participant in the brutalities of the social struggle now. The only question of importance is on what side of the struggle they are. Think of all the kind souls who stand in horror of a social conflict who are at this moment benefiting from, and living comfortable lives at the expense of, a social system which condemns 13 million men to misery and semi-starvation. Failure to recognize this covert brutality of the social struggle is probably the greatest weakness of middle-class liberals, and it lends a note of hypocrisy and self-deception to every moral pretension which seeks to eliminate violence in the social struggle.

The relation of the sensitive conscience to the brutal realities of man's collective behavior will always create its own problem—a problem in the solution of which orthodox religion has frequently been more shrewd than liberalism because it did not over-estimate the virtue of human society, but rather recognized the "sinful" character of man's collective life. This problem has its own difficulties, and they ought not to be confused with the problem of achieving an adequate social and political strategy for the attainment of a just society or for the attainment of a higher approximation of justice than a decadent capitalism grants.

49

The Philosophy
of the New Deal

To find a clear, coherent philosophy in the New Deal or in the mind of the leader, Franklin D. Roosevelt, who presided over the country in the New Deal years is exceptionally difficult. The twistings and turnings, the ambiguities and uncertainties, the pragmatic drifting that characterized New Deal policy allow many divergent interpretations; but there was something new about the New Deal: there were assumptions about the character of America's problems and the proper role of government that FDR did not share with his predecessor. The most important and vigorous statement of these assumptions appeared in Roosevelt's 1932 campaign address before San Francisco's Commonwealth Club.

COMMONWEALTH CLUB ADDRESS
Franklin D. Roosevelt

I count it a privilege to be invited to address the Commonwealth Club. It has stood in the life of this city and state, and it is perhaps accurate to add, the nation, as a group of citizen leaders interested in fundamental problems of government, and chiefly concerned with achievement of progress in government through non-partisan means. The privilege of addressing you, therefore, in the heat of a political campaign, is great. I want to respond to your courtesy in terms consistent with your policy.

I want to speak not of politics but of government. I want to speak not of parties, but of universal principles. They are not political, except in that larger sense in which a great American once expressed a definition of politics, that nothing in all of human life is foreign to the science of politics.

The issue of government has always been whether individual men and women will have to serve some system of government or economics, or whether a system of government and economics exists to serve individual men and women. This question has persistently dominated the discussion of government for many generations. On questions relating to these things men have differed, and for time immemorial it is probable that honest men will continue to differ.

The final word belongs to no man; yet we can still believe in chance and in progress. Democracy, as a dear old friend of mine in Indiana, Meredith Nicholson, has called it, is a quest, a never-ending seeking for better things, and in the seeking for these things and the striving for them, there are many roads to follow. But, if we map the course of these roads, we find that there are only two general directions.

When we look about us, we are likely to forget how hard people have worked to win the privilege of government. The growth of the national governments of Europe was a struggle for the development of a centralized force in the nation, strong enough to impose peace upon ruling barons. In many instances the victory of the central government, the creation of a strong central government, was a haven of refuge to the individual. The people preferred the master far away to the exploitation and cruelty of the smaller master near at hand.

But the creators of national government were perforce ruthless men. They were often cruel in their methods, but they did strive steadily toward something that society needed and very much wanted, a strong central state, able to keep the peace, to stamp out civil war, to put the unruly nobleman in his place, and to permit the bulk of individuals to live safely. The man of ruthless force had his place in developing a pioneer country, just as he did in fixing the power of the central government in the development of nations. Society paid him well for his services and its development. When the development among the nations of Europe, however, had been completed, ambition and ruthlessness, having served its term, tended to overstep its mark.

There came a growing feeling that government was conducted for the benefit of a few who thrived unduly at the expense of all. The people sought a balancing—a limiting force. There came gradually, through town council, trade guilds, national parliaments, by constitution and by popular participation and control, limitations on arbitrary power.

Another factor that tended to limit the power of those who ruled, was the rise of the ethical conception that a ruler bore a responsibility for the welfare of his subjects.

The American colonies were born in this struggle. The American Revolution was a turning point in it. After the revolution the struggle continued and shaped itself in the public life of the country. There were those who because they had seen the confusion which attended the years of war for American independence surrendered to the belief that popular government was essentially dangerous and essentially unworkable. They were honest people, my friends, and we cannot deny that their experience had warranted some measure of fear. The most brilliant, honest and able exponent of this point of view was Hamilton. He was too impatient of slow-moving methods. Fundamentally he believed that the safety of the republic lay in the autocratic strength of its government, that the destiny of individuals was to serve that government, and that fundamentally a great and strong group of central institutions, guided by a small group of able and public spirited citizens could best direct all government.

But Mr. Jefferson, in the summer of 1776, after drafting the Declaration of

489

Independence turned his mind to the same problem and took a different view. He did not deceive himself with outward forms. Government to him was a means to an end, not an end in itself; it might be either a refuge and a help or a threat and a danger, depending on the circumstances. We find him carefully analyzing the society for which he was to organize a government. "We have no paupers. The great mass of our population is of laborers, our rich who cannot live without labor, either manual or professional, being few and of moderate wealth. Most of the laboring class possess property, cultivate their own lands, have families and from the demand for their labor, are enabled to exact from the rich and the competent such prices as enable them to feed abundantly, clothe above mere decency, to labor moderately and raise their families."

These people, he considered, had two sets of rights, those of "personal competency" and those involved in acquiring and possessing property. By "personal competency" he meant the right of free thinking, freedom of forming and expressing opinions, and freedom of personal living each man according to his own lights. To insure the first set of rights, a government must so order its functions as not to interfere with the individual. But even Jefferson realized that the exercise of the property rights might so interfere with the rights of the individual that the government, without whose assistance the property rights could not exist, must intervene, not to destroy individualism but to protect it.

You are familiar with the great political duel which followed; and how Hamilton, and his friends, building towards a dominant centralized power were at length defeated in the great election of 1800, by Mr. Jefferson's party. Out of that duel came the two parties, Republican and Democratic, as we know them today.

So began, in American political life, the new day, the day of the individual against the system, the day in which individualism was made the great watchword of American life. The happiest of economic conditions made that day long and splendid. On the Western frontier, land was substantially free. No one, who did not shirk the task of earning a living, was entirely without opportunity to do so. Depressions could, and did, come and go; but they could not alter the fundamental fact that most of the people lived partly by selling their labor and partly by extracting their livelihood from the soil, so that starvation and dislocation were practically impossible. At the very worst there was always the possibility of climbing into a covered wagon and moving west where the untilled prairies afforded a haven for men to whom the East did not provide a place. So great were our natural resources that we could offer this relief not only to our own people, but to the distressed of all the world; we could invite immigration from Europe, and welcome it with open arms. Traditionally, when a depression came a new section of land was opened in the West; and even our temporary misfortune served our manifest destiny.

It was in the middle of the 19th century that a new force was released and a new dream created. The force was what is called the industrial revolution, the advance of steam and machinery and the rise of the forerunners of the modern industrial plant. The dream was the dream of an economic machine, able to raise the standard of living for everyone; to bring luxury within the reach of the humblest; to annihilate distance by steam power and later by electricity, and to release everyone from the drudgery of the heaviest manual toil. It was to be expected that this would necessarily affect government. Heretofore, government had merely been called upon to produce conditions within which people could live happily, labor peacefully, and rest secure. Now it was called upon to aid in the consummation of this new dream. There was, however, a shadow over the dream. To be made real, it required use of the talents of men of tremendous will, and tremendous ambition, since by no other force could the problems of financing and engineering and new developments be brought to a consummation.

So manifest were the advantages of the machine age, however, that the United States fearlessly, cheerfully, and, I think, rightly, accepted the bitter with the sweet. It was thought that no price was too high to pay for the advantages which we could draw from a finished industrial system. The history of the last half century is accordingly in large measure a history of a group of financial Titans, whose methods were not scrutinized with too much care, and who were honored in proportion as they produced the results, irrespective of the means they used. The financiers who pushed the railroads to the Pacific were always ruthless, often wasteful, and frequently corrupt; but they did build railroads, and we have them today. It has been estimated that the American investor paid for the American railway system more than three times over in the process; but despite this fact the net advantage was to the United States. As long as we had free land; as long as population was growing by leaps and bounds; as long as our industrial plants were insufficient to supply our own needs, society chose to give the ambitious man free play and unlimited reward provided only that he produced the economic plant so much desired.

During this period of expansion, there was equal opportunity for all and the business of government was not to interfere but to assist in the development of industry. This was done at the request of business men themselves. The tariff was originally imposed for the purpose of "fostering our infant industry", a phrase I think the older among you will remember as a political issue not so long ago. The railroads were subsidized, sometimes by grants of money, oftener by grants of land; some of the most valuable oil lands in the United States were granted to assist the financing of the railroad which pushed through the Southwest. A nascent merchant marine was assisted by grants of money, or by mail subsidies, so that our steam shipping might ply the seven seas. Some of my friends tell me that they do not want the Government in business. With this I agree but I wonder whether they realize the implications of the past. For while it has been American doctrine that the government must not go into business in competition with private enterprises, still it has been traditional particularly in Republican administrations for business urgently to ask the government to put at private disposal all kinds of government assistance. The same man who tells you that he does not want to see the government interfere in business—and he means it, and has plenty of good reasons for saying so—is the first to go to Washington and ask the government for a prohibitory tariff on his product. When things get just bad enough—as they did two years ago—he will go with equal speed to the United States government and ask for a loan; and the Reconstruction Finance Corporation is the outcome of it. Each group has sought protection from the government for its own special interests, without realizing that the function of government must be to favor no small group at the expense of its duty to protect the rights of personal freedom and of private property of all its citizens.

In retrospect we can now see that the turn of the tide came with the turn of the century. We were reaching our last frontier; there was no more free land and our industrial combinations had become great uncontrolled and irresponsible units of power within the state. Clear-sighted men saw with fear the danger that opportunity would no longer be equal; that the growing corporation, like the feudal baron of old, might threaten the economic freedom of individuals to earn a living. In that hour, our antitrust laws were born. The cry was raised against the great corporations. Theodore Roosevelt, the first great Republican progressive, fought a Presidential campaign on the issue of "trust busting" and talked freely about malefactors of great wealth. If the government had a policy it was rather to turn the clock back, to destroy the large combinations and to return to the time when every man owned his individual small business.

This was impossible; Theodore Roosevelt, abandoning the idea of "trust busting", was forced to work out a difference between "good" trusts and "bad" trusts. The Supreme Court set forth the famous "rule of reason" by which it seems to have meant that a concentration of industrial power was permissible if the method by which it got its power, and the use it made of that power, was reasonable.

Woodrow Wilson, elected in 1912, saw the situation more clearly. Where Jefferson had feared the encroachment of political power on the lives of individuals, Wilson knew that the new power was financial. He saw, in the highly centralized economic system, the despot of the twentieth century, on whom great masses of individuals relied for their safety and their livelihood, and whose irresponsibility and greed (if it were not controlled) would reduce them to starvation and penury. The concentration of financial power had not proceeded so far in 1912 as it has today; but it had grown far enough for Mr. Wilson to realize fully its implications. It is interesting, now, to read his speeches. What is called "radical" today (and I have reason to know whereof I speak) is mild compared to the campaign of Mr. Wilson. "No man can deny", he said, "that the lines of endeavor have more and more narrowed and stiffened; no man who knows anything about the development of industry in this country can have failed to observe that the larger kinds of credit are more and more difficult to obtain unless you obtain them upon terms of uniting your efforts with those who already control the industry of the country, and nobody can fail to observe that every man who tries to set himself up in competition with any process of manufacture which has taken place under the control of large combinations of capital will presently find himself either squeezed out or obliged to sell and allow himself to be absorbed." Had there been no World War—had Mr.

Wilson been able to devote eight years to domestic instead of to international affairs—we might have had a wholly different situation at the present time. However, the then distant roar of European cannon, growing ever louder, forced him to abandon the study of this issue. The problem he saw so clearly is left with us as a legacy; and no one of us on either side of the political controversy can deny that it is a matter of grave concern to the government.

A glance at the situation today only too clearly indicates that equality of opportunity as we have known it no longer exists. Our industrial plant is built; the problem just now is whether under existing conditions it is not overbuilt. Our last frontier has long since been reached, and there is practically no more free land. More than half of our people do not live on the farms or on lands and cannot derive a living by cultivating their own property. There is no safety valve in the form of a Western prairie to which those thrown out of work by the Eastern economic machines can go for a new start. We are not able to invite the immigration from Europe to share our endless plenty. We are now providing a drab living for our own people.

Our system of constantly rising tariffs has at last reacted against us to the point of closing our Canadian frontier on the north, our European markets on the east, many of our Latin American markets to the south, and a goodly proportion of our Pacific markets on the west, through the retaliatory tariffs of those countries. It has forced many of our great industrial institutions who exported their surplus production to such countries, to establish plants in such countries, within the tariff walls. This has resulted in the reduction of the operation of their American plants, and opportunity for employment.

Just as freedom to farm has ceased, so also the opportunity in business has narrowed. It still is true that men can start small enterprises, trusting to native shrewdness and ability to keep abreast of competitors; but area after area has been preempted altogether by the great corporations, and even in the fields which still have no great concerns, the small man starts under a handicap. The unfeeling statistics of the past three decades show that the independent business man is running a losing race. Perhaps he is forced to the wall; perhaps he cannot command credit; perhaps he is "squeezed out," in Mr. Wilson's words, by highly organized corporate competitors, as your corner grocery man can tell you. Recently a careful study was made of the concentration of business in the United States. It showed that our economic life was dominated by some six hundred odd corporations who controlled two-thirds of American industry. Ten million small business men divided the other third. More striking still, it appeared that if the process of concentration goes on at the same rate, at the end of another century we shall have all American industry controlled by a dozen corporations, and run by perhaps a hundred men. Put plainly, we are steering a steady course toward economic oligarchy, if we are not there already.

Clearly, all this calls for a re-appraisal of values. A mere builder of more industrial plants, a creator of more railroad systems, an organizer of more corporations, is as likely to be a danger as a help. The day of the great promoter or

493

the financial Titan, to whom we granted anything if only he would build, or develop, is over. Our task now is not discovery or exploitation of natural resources, or necessarily producing more goods. It is the soberer, less dramatic business of administering resources and plants already in hand, of seeking to reestablish foreign markets for our surplus production, of meeting the problem of underconsumption, of adjusting production to consumption, of distributing wealth and products more equitably, of adapting existing economic organizations to the service of the people. The day of enlightened administration has come.

Just as in older times the central government was first a haven of refuge, and then a threat, so now in a closer economic system the central and ambitious financial unit is no longer a servant of national desire, but a danger. I would draw the parallel one step farther. We did not think because national government had become a threat in the 18th century that therefore we should abandon the principle of national government. Nor today should we abandon the principle of strong economic units called corporations, merely because their power is susceptible of easy abuse. In other times we dealt with the problem of an unduly ambitious central government by modifying it gradually into a constitutional democratic government. So today we are modifying and controlling our economic units.

As I see it, the task of government in its relation to business is to assist the development of an economic declaration of rights, an economic constitutional order. This is the common task of statesman and business man. It is the minimum requirement of a more permanently safe order of things.

Every man has a right to life; and this means that he has also a right to make a comfortable living. He may by sloth or crime decline to exercise that right; but it may not be denied him. We have no actual famine or dearth; our industrial and agricultural mechanism can produce enough and to spare. Our government formal and informal, political and economic, owes to every one an avenue to possess himself of a portion of that plenty sufficient for his needs, through his own work.

Every man has a right to his own property; which means a right to be assured, to the fullest extent attainable, in the safety of his savings. By no other means can men carry the burdens of those parts of life which, in the nature of things, afford no chance of labor; childhood, sickness, old age. In all thought of property, this right is paramount; all other property rights must yield to it. If, in accord with this principle, we must restrict the operations of the speculator, the manipulator, even the financier, I believe we must accept the restriction as needful, not to hamper individualism but to protect it.

These two requirements must be satisfied, in the main, by the individuals who claim and hold control of the great industrial and financial combinations which dominate so large a part of our industrial life. They have undertaken to be, not business men, but princes—princes of property. I am not prepared to say that the system which produces them is wrong. I am very clear that they must fearlessly and competently assume the responsibility which goes with the power. So many enlightened business men know this that the statement would be little more than a platitude, were it not for an added implication.

This implication is, briefly, that the responsible heads of finance and industry instead of acting each for himself, must work together to achieve the common end. They must, where necessary, sacrifice this or that private advantage; and in reciprocal self-denial must seek a general advantage. It is here that formal government—political government, if you choose, comes in. Whenever in the pursuit of this objective the lone wolf, the unethical competitor, the reckless promoter, the Ishmael or Insull whose hand is against every man's, declines to join in achieving an end recognized as being for the public welfare, and threatens to drag the industry back to a state of anarchy, the government may properly be asked to apply restraint. Likewise, should the group ever use its collective power contrary to the public welfare, the government must be swift to enter and protect the public interest.

The government should assume the function of economic regulation only as a last resort, to be tried only when private initiative, inspired by high responsibility, with such assistance and balance as government can give, has finally failed. As yet there has been no final failure, because there has been no attempt; and I decline to assume that this nation is unable to meet the situation.

The final term of the high contract was for liberty and the pursuit of happiness. We have learnt a great deal of both in the past century. We know that individual liberty and individual happiness mean nothing unless both are ordered in the sense that one man's meat is not another man's poison. We know that the old "rights of personal competency"—the right to read, to think, to speak, to choose and live a mode of life, must be respected at all hazards. We know that liberty to do anything which deprives others of those elemental rights is outside the protection of any compact; and that government in this regard is the maintenance of a balance, within which every individual may have a place if he will take it; in which every individual may find safety if he wishes it; in which every individual may attain such power as his ability permits, consistent with his assuming the accompanying responsibility.

Faith in America, faith in our tradition of personal responsibility, faith in our institutions, faith in ourselves demands that we recognize the new terms of the old social contact. We shall fulfill them, as we fulfilled the obligation of the apparent Utopia which Jefferson imagined for us in 1776, and which Jefferson, Roosevelt and Wilson sought to bring to realization. We must do so, lest a rising tide of misery engendered by our common failure, engulf us all. But failure is not an American habit; and in the strength of great hope we must all shoulder our common load.

50

Labor on the March

At the outset of the Depression the American labor movement was smaller and weaker than the labor movement of most other advanced societies. Organization was largely confined to the skilled crafts; the millions of semiskilled operatives in such mass production industries as steel, automobiles, and rubber were without effective voice. One of the most dramatic developments of the decade was the breaking away of the newly formed Congress of Industrial Organizations, the CIO, from the craft-dominated American Federation of Labor, and its phenomenal successes in winning the support of previously unorganized workers against the bitter and sometimes brutal resistance of great corporations. The journalist Edward Levinson provides a spirited and sympathetic narrative of a decisive battle between GM and the fledgling United Automobile Workers, a battle won by the workers via the new tactic of the sit-down strike, in which strikers refused to concede that the plants in which they worked were private property from which they could be expelled at the whim of the employer. This seemed to many Americans a violation of a sacred principle, but the strikes succeeded and helped to establish a new and competing principle: that workers are entitled to collective bargaining and that the power of a corporation over its property is not absolute. In many previous labor conflicts in the American past the government had interpreted the law narrowly and had employed force to break strikes. Its refusal to do so in this struggle marked a new stage in the definition of human rights and property rights.

LABOR ON THE MARCH
Edward Levinson

The strike of General Motors workers in January and February of 1937 was the most significant industrial battle since labor's defeat at Homestead. It held in its hands the future of the C.I.O. and the new labor movement which was soon to sweep millions of American breadwinners into its ranks. It aroused bitterness equal

Reprinted with permission from *Labor on the March* (New York: University Books, 1938), 149–168.

to that which accompanied the brief heyday of the Knights of Labor. It was more than a strike. It was a momentous struggle between the aroused forces of labor and the third largest corporation in the country, typifying years of unchallenged anti-unionism. It involved seizure of industrial plants worth more than $50,000,000 and the failure of the owners, vigilantes, courts, police, and military to recapture them.

Automobiles and steel-manufacturing form the backbone of American capitalism, and in the realm of autos General Motors was second to none in financial importance and in the 250,000 workers it employed. Its control lay in the hands of the Du Ponts and J. P. Morgan. The Corporation recovered strikingly from the depression years. Its net profit in 1934 was $167,000,000, while 1936 brought a profit of $227,940,000. Its average wage to its workers in 1935 was $1,150, which meant that many workers received far less. The auto workers were not comforted at all to know that the Corporation paid Alfred P. Sloan its president, $374,505 in 1935, vice-president William F. Knudsen $325,868, and a total of $3,779,730 to seventeen top officials. General Motors employees felt the speed-up more keenly than low wages. Belt-line production and the conveyor system were based on speed, and in the quest for ever-quicker, uninterrupted production the limbs and eyes and strength of the workers were geared to meet the pace of the machines. The workers had to meet competition between corporations, between plants and even sections of plants. Foremen, driven to bring up production, in turn drove the workers under them. The mere twist of a dial determined the speed of the line, and those workers who could not meet it faced the scrapheap. Automobile manufacturing yearly consigned men who had given their best years to the horror of being "old" at forty years or less. Over and over again, the strikers of 1937 summarized their chief complaints.

"We don't want to be driven," they said; and "We don't want to be spied on."

The espionage activities financed and promoted by General Motors sought several general objectives: to keep men from evading the demands of the speeded belt-line; to keep their unions, when they joined them, weak and ineffective; and eventually to destroy the unions. Without union grievance committees to speak up for them, many workers conspired in simple manner to keep down production. Word would pass through a section of a plant: "Only ten crank-shafts to be turned this hour; let's not burn ourselves up." To workers deprived of recognized spokesmen this was one way out of an intolerable situation. Here the work of the plant stool pigeon came in. General Motors accumulated weekly sheafs of reports on workers who had joined to keep down production. These "ears" also reported friendly references to unionism. It became so that no man could tell whether his neighbor was a friend or a company spy. In the ranks of the unionists, the General Motors espionage system had another function: to ferret out the leaders, to turn them in for discharge or discrimination and to watch the "outside agitators," i.e., the organizers. The La Follette committee which investigated violations of labor and civil rights discovered that General Motors spent $994,855 on private detective services from January 1, 1934, to July 31, 1936. As the probe got under way, most of the files of the company were stripped of spy reports. Knudsen sought to explain

497

the use of Pinkerton men and detectives of the Railway Audit and Inspection Company as the maintenance of a force to police and protect G.M.'s vast properties. But that did not explain how shadowing Adolph Germer, spies' attendance at picnics of Fisher Body employees, and spy reports on the reading habits of employees contributed to protection of its properties.

The strike which General Motors reaped from these practices had an inconspicuous start in the Fisher Body plant at Atlanta, Georgia. Four men who appeared in the plant with U.A.W. buttons on their workshirts were fired. A strike followed on November 18, 1936. The Atlanta unionists wanted the walkout extended to other plants, but the union and C.I.O. strategists felt such a move would be premature. A month later, the Kansas City Fisher Body plant discharged a unionist for an infraction of what was felt to be an unimportant, constantly violated rule. The response to the C.I.O. organizing campaign had meanwhile become so great, that Lewis and the auto union leaders on December 21st wired Knudsen, asking for a collective bargaining conference. They took as the text of their request, an address in which the corporation's executive head had said that "collective bargaining should take place before a shut-down, rather than after." General Motors replied that the respective plant managers should be approached with grievances that came within their jurisdictions. The U.A.W. locals thereupon handed in contract forms to the plant heads, and met with universal rebuffs. There appeared to be no alternative to spreading the walkout.

The efficiency of the specialized production units of the General Motors system proved its fatal weakness in the strike. Simple strategy indicated to the auto-union leaders that with the key plants tied up, production would inevitably be brought to a halt throughout the entire system. The principal organizing efforts had therefore been directed at the key plants, and these were now brought to a standstill. The Cleveland Fisher Body plant stamped turret tops for General Motors models. Organized under the leadership of Vice-president Mortimer, its workers had one of the strongest of the U.A.W. locals. On December 28th, all of the 7,000 Cleveland workers went on strike, more than a thousand remaining in the plant. The Cleveland and local promptly announced that any settlement of its grievances would have to be part of a settlement for the entire General Motors system.

Flint was next in the line of the union's attack. In Fisher Body No. 1 plant were important dies, which, if removed to a less strong union center, might become the instruments for breaking the strike. On the evening of December 30th the night-shift men at Fisher No. 1 saw the dies being loaded on to trucks, bound for Grand Rapids and Pontiac. The events of that memorable day in Flint's history are detailed in the "Song of the Fisher Body No. One Strikers," a homespun parody to the music of "The Martins and the Coys," which soon became the epic song of the great strike. As the song told the story:

> Now this strike it started one bright Wednesday evening
>> When they loaded up a box car full of dies.
> When the union boys they stopped them,
>> And the railroad workers backed them,
> The officials in the office were surprised.

CHORUS
These 4,000 union boys
Oh, they sure made lots of noise.
They decided then and there to shut down tight.
In the office they got snooty,
So we started picket duty,
Now the Fisher Body shop is on a strike.

Now they really started out to strike in earnest.
They took possession of the gates and buildings too.
They placed a guard in either clock-house,
Just to keep the non-union men out,
And they took the keys and locked the gates up too.

Closing of the Cleveland and Flint plants would have been enough to paralyze General Motors' sixty-five automotive plants, but the union in fifteen other units were too restive to await shut-downs by order of the Corporation. Sit-down strikers ensconsed themselves in the Fleetwood and Cadillac plants in Detroit, in Fisher Body No. 2. Flint, and in the Guide Lamp factory at Anderson, Indiana. The Cleveland local, strong enough to keep the plant closed without a sit-down, called its members out within a week after they had ceased working. In the last weeks of the strike the Chevrolet motor assembly plant at Flint also was occupied by the strikers. Strikes of the traditional type were called in Janesville, Wisconsin; Norwood, Atlanta, St. Louis, Kansas City, and Toledo, Ohio. A shortage of glass, brought about by a strategically timed strike of C.I.O. glass workers, closed several other plants. By January 11, 112,800 of the Corporation's 150,000 production workers were idle. Before the strike ended the total rose to 140,000.

A detailed statement of the union's grievances was forwarded to the Corporation on January 4th. It requested an immediate conference to discuss eight demands: signing of a national agreement; abolition of piece work and fixing of day rates of pay; a thirty-hour week, six-hour day, and time-and-a-half for overtime; minimum rates of pay; reinstatement of men discharged for union activities; a seniority system to govern employment and reemployment after slack periods; recognition of the U.A.W. as the sole bargaining agency of all G.M. employees; and regulation of the speed of the belt-line and other machinery by union plant committees and the management. This appeal, like the union's previous requests, was turned down, and the conflict became a belligerent endurance test. An effort by General Motors to create a united front of all automobile manufacturers broke down when the Ford Motor Company refused to coöperate. *Steel*, the trade journal of the iron-and-steel industry, reported on January 18th that the Automobile Chamber of Commerce had sponsored a meeting at which such a plan was broached. General Motors proposed that all companies cease operations. *Steel* reported the Ford management feared such a move would precipitate a national panic, responsibility for which would be placed at the doors of the auto industry.

During the second week in January, Governor Frank Murphy vigorously took over the task of peacemaker. Elected to office in the Roosevelt landslide of the

499

previous November, he had received the endorsement of the auto union and the entire Michigan labor movement. The difficulties which Governor Murphy encountered were enlarged by the sit-down strikes. General Motors insisted that the sit-downs constituted illegal seizure of its property and refused to confer with the union until the sitters were withdrawn. The strike leaders and the C.I.O., on the other hand, declared they had no faith in the verbal promises of General Motors and would not order their men out of the plants until assurances of sincere collective bargaining efforts were given in writing and surrounded by conditions which would make resumption of operations impossible until collective bargaining conferences had been concluded. In this stand, the U.A.W. leaders had their backs stiffened by Lewis.

After days and nights of effort, Governor Murphy on January 15th announced that a truce had been arranged under which bargaining conferences might proceed. The union agreed to evacuate all the plants its members were holding; the corporation promised that negotiations would start at once on the union's eight-point memorandum of January 4th. This represented a substantial gain for the union, since the corporation had insisted that many of the eight points were not subjects for a general conference. The negotiations were to continue "until a satisfactory settlement of all issues shall be effected, if possible." In no event were the negotiations to be terminated in less than fifteen days. The corporation, meanwhile, was not to remove any dies, tools, machinery, material or equipment from any of the plants on strike, nor to endeavor to resume operations.

Hundreds of workers carrying blankets, radios, accordions paraded out of the Fleetwood and Cadillac plants on Saturday afternoon, January 17th. At the same time, the Guide Lamp sitters gave over the Anderson factory. The spirit of the strikers was high with the confidence that they had won important concessions. The Flint plants were to be surrendered the following day.

Flint held the key to peace as well as to the strength of the strike. The Cadillac, Fleetwood, and Guide Lamp plants had no great strategic importance, but the Flint Fisher Body No. 1 plant, which sprawled over half a mile, was an ace in the auto strikers' hands. Much of the bitterness of the battle was concentrated in Flint, where the C.I.O. and General Motors, respectively, despatched their specialists in striking and strike-breaking. The entire city of 163,000 men, women, and children was dependent on the local General Motors plants for its existence. More than 50,000 Flint workers toiled in Chevrolet and Buick plants, as well as in Fisher Body factories. Several times in the course of the six weeks' strike Flint was on the verge of serious violence. Early in the strike, the Flint Alliance came into existence. Chairmanned by George E. Boysen, a former General Motors' paymaster and owner of a spark-plug factory, the Alliance set itself up as the true voice of the Flint citizenry and its General Motors' employees. To translate this voice into propaganda and organization, Floyd E. Williamson, a New York promoter-publicity man, was imported. The Alliance attack varied from righteous appeals to civic pride, through Williamson's denunciation of outside agitators, to threats of violence against the strikers. Its financing has not been revealed to this date, but Boysen made no secret of its dependence on the business interests of the city. Before the strike had ended, the Alliance was publicly reprimanded by Governor Murphy as would-be instigators of violence.

The tense atmosphere of the city boiled over but once into bloodshed, in what has become known as "The Battle of the Running Bulls." "Fisher 2," two miles away and across the city from "Fisher 1," had been held by sit-down strikers since the day their fellow-unionists had "locked the gates" of their plant. During the afternoon of January 11th, while Governor Murphy was laboring for a basis on which the plants would be evacuated and negotiations set in motion, the heat in Fisher 2 was shut off. The need to protect plant equipment, including its water system, had hitherto led the corporation to maintain the heating supply without interruption. A few hours later, the Flint police surrounded the entrance and announced there would be no further shipments of food. A ladder placed to a window by strikers was immediately torn down. Dinner time on a cold day came with the police still at their stations. The strikers faced an effort to freeze and starve them out of the plant. The Fisher 2 sitters, captained by William (Red) Mundale, a union rank-and-filer, had been considered one of the weak links in the strike. The shutting off of heat and food for them, the union felt, would be followed by similar efforts at Fisher 1.

A union sound truck pulled up at Fisher 2 in the early evening. Scores of strikers soon surrounded it. Victor Reuther, U.A.W. organizer, was at the microphone. The police were asked to permit delivery of food. The voice inside the car, carried to the strikers in and out of the plant, as well as to the police, first made pleas of labor solidarity to the officers. These failing, more belligerent appeals were uttered. Shortly before seven P.M., pickets rushed the door, swept the police aside, and moved coffee and bread into the plant. Two hours later, fifty policemen, almost half of Flint's entire force, attacked the pickets at the doors with clubs, driving some inside the building and attempting to scatter the others. A policeman shattered the glass pane in the door, poked a tear gas gun through the crevice and fired it. The gassed strikers inside fell back, and the battle was on. The police poured buckshot into the pickets and through the windows of the plant. Tear gas discharges alternated with the crack of the guns. The strikers fought back with sticks, metal pipes, nuts and bolts, soda-pop bottles, coffee-mugs, and a continuous rain of two-pound steel automobile door hinges. Throughout the three hours of fighting which followed a group of stalwart strikers surrounded the automobile with the loud speaker and resisted efforts to dismantle it. First one strike leader, then another, took the microphone, directing the strategy of the battle, cheering on the strikers and shouting pleas and threats at the police. "We wanted peace. General Motors chose war. Give it to them," the voice would shout.

Sheriff Thomas Wolcott drove his sedan into the battle zone. Before many minutes, strikers turned it on its side, its headlights still glaring and lighting up a wide path strewn with broken glass, rocks, and door hinges. Before the battle had ended, three other police cars had been captured. The police reformed for a new attack at midnight, but at a shouted signal from the car the nozzle of a rubber hose appeared at the door of the plant, and the strikers turned a powerful stream of cold water on their attackers. The Flint police retreated under the barrage of water and

501

door hinges. They ran fifty yards to a bridge that approached the plant gate; then they went fifty yards more to the far end of the bridge. The fighting was over.

The strikers' guard continued their vigil through the wintry night while the strident battle cries from the plant and the car gave way to labor songs and cheers of victory. Fourteen strikers were removed to the hospital with bullet wounds, but by dawn the strikers were unchallenged in their possession of the plant. "Solidarity Forever" and cheers for the C.I.O. from tired voices pierced the cold morning air as determined bands of men and women, huddled around two street fires, guarded against a possible new attack on their fellow strikers in the plant. "The Battle of the Running Bulls" proved to be the only effort forcibly to remove sit-down strikers from General Motors plants.

The battle brought 1,500 Michigan national guardsmen to Flint, but Governor Murphy refused to yield to demands of the Flint Alliance and local authorities that the troops be employed to dislodge the sit-down strikers. Instead, the Governor ordered the corporation to make no further efforts to halt the food supplies. While Boysen bitterly denounced him, Murphy summoned union and corporation heads to meet him in the state Capitol at Lansing. There he worked out the truce of January 15th which brought the sitters out of the Detroit and Anderson factories.

The Flint strikers were to evacuate their plants on Sunday, the 17th, and negotiations, under the terms of the Lansing truce, were to start the following day. Sunday morning, the auto union leaders learned of an exchange of telegrams between Boysen and Knudsen. The chairman of the Flint Alliance, assaying the rôle of unionist, wired the General Motors' executive asking for a conference in behalf of G.M. workers said to be members of the Alliance. The request was written to challenge the growing confidence of the auto union that it might win sole bargaining rights in the negotiations. Knudsen's reply sought to assure Boysen that no such rights would be granted. He agreed to meet with Boysen and asserted, "we stand ready always to discuss with your group or any group of our employees any questions without prejudice to anyone." The strike leaders now charged a "double-cross." The telegrams were not to have been made public until Sunday evening, after the Flint strikers had given up the plants. It was only by accident that a reporter learned of Boysen's wire on Sunday morning. He had then sought Robert Travis's comment and the entire auto union knew within a few hours that the Flint Alliance had been promised a collective bargaining conference.

The national and Flint strike leaders, after acquainting Lewis of the development, declared that General Motors had presumed to rule out the union's demand for sole recognition before negotiations had even started. Sole recognition was, in fact, one of the eight points which were to have been debated at the parleys. The truce had been violated, the strike leaders announced. To the Flint incident they added charges that in Anderson local police had dispersed a picket line and demolished picket shanties, and that in Detroit some employees of the Cadillac plant had received instructions to return to work. Knudsen denied all three charges, but the Flint strikers reinforced their makeshift "fortifications" of the plants. The negotiations of the following day consisted of Knudsen's handing Brophy, Martin, Mortimer, and other U.A.W. officials a refusal to meet until the plants were evacuated. A few days later, G.M. promised not to confer with the Flint Alliance until U.A.W. negotiations had ended, but the union responded that it no longer had the slightest faith in the corporation's words. It insisted on an agreement before evacuation.

With the breakdown of the Lansing truce, Governor Murphy turned to Washington for assistance. In the national capital General Motors was impatient for word from Secretary of Labor Frances Perkins that the sit-downs were illegal; and the C.I.O. was as vigorously seeking intercession of the federal government in behalf of recognition of the auto union. Miss Perkins persuaded Sloan and Knudsen to meet with her. She was making slight progress when the conference recessed. Meanwhile, Lewis had told a full complement of the Washington newspapermen that labor was expecting Presidential support for its crucial struggle.

"For six months during the Presidential campaign," said Lewis, "the economic royalists represented by General Motors and the Du Ponts contributed their money and used their energy to drive this Administration from power. The Administration asked labor for help to repel this attack and labor gave it. The same economic royalists now have their fangs in labor. The workers of this country expect the Administration to help the strikers in every reasonable way."

Scanning a newspaper as he left Miss Perkins' office, Sloan read Lewis' pointed remarks, which included also a reiteration of his refusal to urge evacuation of the plants pending a settlement of basic union demands. The General Motors' president seized upon the statement and announced that it made further peace efforts futile. Pressed by interviewers, Sloan said he particularly resented Lewis' references to the President. That evening Sloan left the capital for New York.

At a White House interview, the next day, President Roosevelt indirectly but deliberately rebuked the C.I.O. leader for his plea that the Administration aid the strikers. Unperturbed, Lewis said that Miss Perkins' only success with Sloan was to have him meet with her in the Department of Labor Building, instead of secretly in the recesses of the plutocratic Metropolitan Club, where a first conference betwen the Secretary of Labor and the G.M. president had been held. The press, largely unfriendly to Lewis and the auto strikers, made much of the Presidential rebuke. A few days later the President spanked Sloan, evening things up but bringing a settlement of the strike no nearer. Miss Perkins had invited both Lewis and Sloan to meet with her. Lewis agreed, but Sloan declined, and President Roosevelt declared that the automobile magnate had made a "very unfortunate decision." A few days later Sloan returned to the city for a second meeting with the Secretary of Labor. When the conference ended, Miss Perkins was under the impression that a basis for ending the strike had been found. "Sloan had promised to have the corporation attend another peace conference in Lansing," said Miss Perkins. Later he called to say it was "all off."

"He ran out on me," said the troubled Secretary of Labor, providing avid headline-writers with ready-made text.

The central stage of the strike had meanwhile shifted back to Flint, where General Motors for the second time turned to the courts for aid in recapturing its plants. The first court proceeding had reacted in the strikers' favor when it was revealed that Judge Edward D. Black, Genesee County's most venerable jurist, was the owner of G.M. stock worth $150,000 at the time he ordered the strikers to vacate the factories. The embarrassing publicity attendant on the revelation made Black's order a dead letter. The sitters laughed and jeered when Sheriff Wolcott read them the text.

On January 29th the corporation went before Circuit Judge Paul V. Gadola. The corporation told the court that the occupation of the two Fisher Body plants was maintained by force and violence as part of a conspiracy by Martin, Mortimer, and all other international officers of the union, Bud Simons and Red Mundale, leaders of the sitters in the Fisher Body plants, and Travis and Roy Reuther, U.A.W. organizers, to cripple the business of the corporation. This had been accomplished by the "continuous trespass" of the sit-down strikers, by the refusal of the strikers to permit G.M. executives access to the plants, and by the "clubs, sticks, and other weapons" of the strikers, it was alleged. Almost coincidental with the application for an injunction came a brutal physical attack on several auto union and C.I.O. organizers. Six organizers were driven by a mob from Bay City, Michigan, to Saginaw, both of them G.M. centers. Some were slugged and all were piled into a taxi which was forced to drive to Flint, thirty miles away, with a caravan of vigilantes behind them. As the unionists' car reached the outskirts of Flint, one of the pursuing automobiles forced the taxi to crash into a telegraph pole. Anthony Federoff, organizer for the C.I.O. and a Pennsylvania miner, had his scalp torn away; three others also had to be taken to the hospital with bad injuries. Ring-leaders of the mob were identified as G.M. foremen, but none were apprehended in the investigation which Saginaw, Flint, and county authorities set in motion. The incident served to heighten the tenseness of an already jittery city.

Argument on the corporation's plea for an injunction took place before Judge Gadola on February 2nd. It dragged through the day as Pressman, Maurice Sugar, and Larry S. Davidow, U.A.W. lawyers, insisted that the corporation was violating the National Labor Relations Act, and thus came into the court with unclean hands. The guilt of trespass was denied, while the General Motors' lawyers insisted the sitters had violated every tenet of the law by seizing property which was not their own. Meanwhile, more potent affairs were transpiring outside the crowded courtroom.

The huge Chevrolet works in Flint had been operating a few days a week, stocking up a reserve of parts. Since no cars could be completed, the strikers had no objections to this work and urged their members to take advantage of the opportunity to earn a few dollars. Unionists employed at Chevrolet soon complained, however, that they had been unjustly fired. Strike-leader Travis requested a conference with the plant management. A meeting was promised, then postponed as more union men were sent home. Demands for a sit-down strike in Chevrolet began to be heard. The strike leaders weighed the possibilities of success of a sit-down, which in this case would mean capturing a plant. It would be a difficult task. The troops were still in the city and the strikers' ranks had scores of informers among them. Nevertheless, the strike strategists felt it would be a worthwhile effort. The strike was not more than a month old. Capture of another huge plant would enthuse all the strikers and set at rest reports that their spirit was weakening. It might have a salutary effect on negotiations for a settlement which finally appeared to be getting under way in Detroit. There was also the consideration that it would be a practical demonstration, in the midst of the court proceedings, of the strikers' contempt for judge-made law and injunctions.

With the increase of discharges at Chevrolet, U.A.W. members insisted that they be allowed to make a counter attack. Travis, Hapgood, and the other leaders agreed. The problem of how to plan and then take over a large plant worth millions of dollars without betraying the preparations to G.M. spies required consummate strategy. Travis, Hapgood, and Kermit Johnson, "Chevvy" union leader, were equal to it. Of the several buildings which made up the Flint Chevrolet works, Plant No. 4, the motor-assembly division, was the most important. Should the Fisher 1 strikers be ousted, possession of Chevvy 4 would still prevent a single shiny Chevrolet from rolling out of any G.M. factory in the world. The Chevrolet workers insisted Plant 4 was the ideal place to sit down. The strike leaders knew this to be true, but since the project had been discussed by a large committee, they felt it necessary to keep the details a secret until the plan was ready for execution. Travis and Hapgood proposed that Chevrolet 9, a ball-bearing plant, was the one to be taken. The strikers set up a derisive howl. Ball-bearings could be gotten here, there, and everywhere, they said. It would do no good to take Chevvy 9, they argued hotly, sometimes with contempt for the ignorance of the outside organizers who presumed to tell G.M. workers that a ball-bearing plant was more important than a motor-assembly plant. The strike leaders stood their ground and their authority prevailed. Then came the problem of selecting a spy-proof committee which could be trusted with the truth, since their services would be needed at Chevvy 4. Each prospective committeeman was interviewed separately so that no striker knew what others had been considered for the task. Those appointed to the committee were ordered not to talk; those suspected and rejected were secretly and impressively told to proceed to Fisher 1, more than a mile away from Chevvy 4, on the afternoon of the projected plant capture.

Monday afternoon, several thousand strikers were in and near Pengelly Hall, the old three-story brick-and-wood structure which housed the union headquarters. By a prearranged plan word came to the strikers that some of their number were being attacked outside of Chevvy 9. Led by Hapgood, Roy Reuther, and an inevitable sound-truck, the strikers proceeded to Plant 9, arriving at 3:30 P.M. at the change of the shifts. Inside the ball-bearing plant, a group of unionists set up a shout for a sit-down strike. Warned by the false reports of informers, the plant management was fully prepared. The strikers in Chevvy 9, not one of the strongest union plants, staged a valiant battle for half an hour, many of them sustaining severe beatings from G.M. plant police, Flint detectives and other burly men who had been installed in the factory. Tear gas was thrown by company guards and police. Outside, several score members of the union's Emergency Brigade, made up exclusively of women and daughters of the strikers, smashed all windows within reach to permit air into the plant. Surrounded by hundreds of strikers, Hapgood

505

was at the microphone of the sound-truck, keeping alive the impression that the striker's interest was concentrated at Chevvy 9.

Shortly after four o'clock, a union messenger brought Hapgood word that the occupation of Chevvy 4 had been accomplished peacefully and completely. The strike leader called upon the strikers to disperse, an order promptly obeyed. He then joined the sitters in Plant 4, located several hundred yards from Plant 9. The strategy had worked, completing one of the most audacious bits of strike strategy the country had ever seen. Some 400 Chevvy 4 strikers, joined by a few score from near-by Chevvy 6, had taken the motor-assembly plant with no more difficulty than a few harsh words to amazed foremen. Within a few minutes union guards had been placed at the doors and gates and patrol committees organized to guard against surprise attacks. The sitters blossomed into expert barricade-builders. Steel-plant trucks weighing several hundred pounds were piled on each other in front of entrances and windows until they reached from floor to ceiling. By morning of February 2nd, national guardsmen patrolled the plant, but Chevy 4 strikers, perched on the roof, were serenading Fisher 2 strikers, heroes of the "Battle of the Running Bulls," with "Solidarity Forever." And from the roof and windows of Fisher 2, across and fifty yards down the street, husky voices shouted the union song back. Below, in the street, khaki-clad troops with bayoneted rifles walked to and fro, while machine-guns were focused on the captive plants.

For an entire day, soldiers' bayonets barred delivery of food to the men in Chevvy 4 plant and Fisher 2, which had been included in the militarized zone. Pressure was again exerted on Governor Murphy to use the troops to clear the plants. Among some national guard officers plans to attack were being suggested. Some proposed simply to shoot the strikers out; another hoped to project vomiting gas through the ventilating systems. The intelligence division furnished the press with a lurid tale of 500 "loyal" Chevrolet employees being held as hostages by the strikers. The plans and military propaganda came to nothing, however, as Murphy's abhorrence and fear of violence continued to dominate his efforts. Again General Motors looked to the courts. On the day following the capture of Chevvy 4, Judge Gadola signed an order directing the men to leave the Fisher body plants under pain of imprisonment for conempt and of having a fine of $15,000,000—the estimated value of the plants—levied against them. Sheriff Wolcott proceeded to Plant 2 to read the order. A few strikers came to the door, dropped a steel barrier they had erected, and listened to the labored reading of the legal edict. At Fisher 1, the strikers permitted the sheriff to enter and stood about him in the cafeteria, gibing and assuming poses of mock seriousness while the recital was repeated. The order gave the strikers until three o'clock of the afternoon of February 3 to leave the factories.

The sit-down strikers called meetings in their plants on the evening before the ominous deadline. Seated on boxes, cans of paint, and kegs of nails, determined men in gray shirts, overalls, and work pants, all with loved ones at home, discussed a problem which they knew held life or death for some of them. The entire nation watched, fearing the bloodiest of industrial battles. It was obvious that only an army of sheriff's deputies and militiamen could enforce the court's ruling. In Fisher

2, surrounded by troops who barred all civilians from approaching, the sitters could not take counsel with their outside leaders. Nevertheless, the discussion in both plants was brief and arrived at unanimous conclusions. The decisions were conveyed to Governor Murphy in two telegrams.

"We the workers in the plant," said the message sent by the strikers in Fisher 1, "are completely unarmed, and to send in the military, armed thugs and armed deputies . . . will mean a bloody massacre of the workers.

"We have carried on a stay-in strike over a month in order to make General Motors Corporation obey the law and engage in collective bargaining. . . . Unarmed as we are, the introduction of the militia, sheriffs, or police with murderous weapons will mean a blood bath of unarmed workers. . . . We have decided to stay in the plant. We have no illusions about the sacrifices which this decision will entail. We fully expect that if a violent effort is made to oust us many of us will be killed, and we take this means of making it known to our wives, to our children, to the people of the state of Michigan and the country that if this result follows from the attempt to reject us, you are the one who must be held responsible for our deaths."

The temperature was again near zero in Flint the next day, but the vision of thousands of strikers battling armed deputies and possibly the militia was colder still. There was a spirit of a zero hour before an army's charge into enemy territory. Hysteria, mixed with eager anticipation, was evident in some quarters. Into the early hours of the morning plant executives, Flint Alliance leaders, and Flint police heads drank potent liquor in the exclusive Town Club at the Durant Hotel. Boisterously, they sang the songs of the strikers, giving them raucous, mocking accents. In the plants the strikers sat silently at their radios and card games. Wooden clubs and blackjacks produced with belt-line technique and speed hung at their waists.

Early morning of the ominous day, the roads to Flint were filled with strikers from near-by cities, some many miles away. Thousands of workers, many women among them, came with squared jaws to take their places on a picket line around Fisher 1. By noon delegations of workers had arrived in battered and new cars and trucks from Detroit, Lansing, Toledo, and Pontiac. Akron sent rubber workers, shock troops of the C.I.O. Walter Reuther came at the head of 500 strong from the West Side of Detroit. The Dodge workers from Detroit also arrived in disciplined phalanxes. Kelsey-Hayes Wheel unionists waved aloft a banner, "Kelsey-Hayes workers never forget their friends." As three o'clock approached, a long train of almost 5,000 workers, two abreast, circled the lawn that fronted the approach to Fisher 1. An American flag led the procession, then came members of the women's Emergency Brigades, their red and green berets the only color spots in a grim assembly. Men and women carried clubs and stout sticks; several had crowbars, stove pokers, and lengths of pipe. A few had knocked the base off clothes-trees, and carried the poles, with metal hangers, on their shoulders. Like the Minute Men of '76 and as fully determined that their cause was righteous, they had seized whatever weapon lay at hand and rushed off to do battle. The constantly arriving auto-loads of workers soon blocked the street, and strikers, aided by sound-trucks, took over direction of traffic. Not a policeman was in sight. At the windows of the plant were the sit-down strikers, their number augmented from the usual 400 to almost 2,000. Strips of cheesecloth hung round their necks, ready for use as some slight protection against tear gas. Windows were barricaded by steel plate, pierced with holes for the nozzles of hoses which lay on the floors nearby. A street valve that controlled the plant's water supply had been enclosed by a new wooden picket shanty. A special detail of strikers guarded the shanty. Inside were drums of gasoline, fuel for a protective wall of fire should an effort be made to capture the valve and cut off the plant's water system.

The zero hour at Fisher 2 and Chevvy 4 was far different. Here there were no crowds of cheering comrades, only a dreary, deserted broad street dotted with soldiers carrying muskets in a ceaseless patrol. The strikers at the windows of the plants displayed no outward reaction to the machine guns and 37-milimeter howitzers poised in the gutters. For hours as the afternoon fraught with tragedy wore on, the Chevvy and Fisher strikers chanted back and forth, "Solidarity Forever, For the Union Makes Us Strong."

Thus the deadline passed, Governor Murphy, in Detroit, where he had finally prevailed upon Knudsen to meet with Lewis, wired Sheriff Wolcott that he was to take no action. The sheriff, more than eager to comply, thereupon became a legal authority and asserted Judge Gadola's order was directed at the strikers alone and did not yet call upon him for enforcement. Boysen and local General Motors' attorneys raged at both the sheriff and the Governor. Meanwhile, the strikers' battle lines turned into celebrating. The sit-down strikers' band in Fisher 1 played hill-billy airs, and before many minutes the pickets, men and women, were square-dancing on the hard-frozen lawns. Flint's day of fear ended in hilarious, nervous joy for the strikers.

Two days later, Judge Gadola, refusing to postpone action any longer, ordered Sheriff Wolcott to arrest all officials and leaders of the auto union, and every striker in the Fisher Body plants. The sheriff, refusing to swear in new deputies, declared he did not have a sufficient force to make the arrests and asked Governor Murphy for the assistance of militiamen. Murphy noted the request, postponed a decision, and resumed his efforts to effect a settlement.

The end of the General Motors strike came on February 11th. A request from President Roosevelt that the corporation meet with spokesmen of the strikers brought about a conference on February 4th, Knudsen stating that the wish of the President left no alternative but compliance. The conference met in Detroit, with Governor Murphy in the rôle of peacemaker. For a week he shuttled back and forth between Lewis, Pressman, Martin and Mortimer, and Knudsen, John Thomas Smith, and G. Donaldson Brown, the corporation negotiators. Most of the time the two groups did not meet together; frequently they were on the verge of a complete break. At one point, Knudsen insisted that the talks would go no further until the plants were evacuated. "You have an injunction which disposes of that issue," Lewis replied. The chief issue was the insistence of Lewis that the auto union be given exclusive recognition. As the possibilities of forcible eviction of the Flint strikers dwindled, the resistance of G.M. weakened.

The settlement which Governor Murphy finally announced included a written pledge by the corporation that it would not, without the Governor's consent, for a period of six months recognize or deal with any other employee spokesman than the United Automobile Workers in the seventeen plants closed by strikes. In all other G.M. automotive plants, the union was to be recognized as the agent of its members. There was to be no discrimination against union members, and all strikers were to be rehired regardless of their union membership or strike activities. Union members were to be permitted to discuss the union with other workers during lunch and rest hours in the plant. Injunction and contempt proceedings against the Flint sit-down strikers were to be dropped. Negotiations were to start at once looking toward a signed contract on those of the eight original union demands which were not disposed of.

The agreement constituted a monumental advance for unionism in the automobile industry. The mere fact of General Motors signing a contract with a union would in itself have been an historic victory. The exclusive recognition accorded the U.A.W. in seventeen plants, however, was the outstanding union gain. The plants affected were those which held within their grasp the entire G.M. system. The prestige of the union was enhanced in all union plants, and as Lewis had foreseen, led to enrollment in the union of a great majority of all G.M.'s production workers. The pledge of no discrimination against union men might have been a mere pious declaration were it not for the lifting of restrictions on the right to talk about the union and the right to wear union buttons on plant property. The right to talk during one's lunch hour and to wear the insignia of one's organization seems an obvious enough privilege in a free country but the auto workers had never enjoyed it. These were more than academic gains. They effectively ended the spy system, for every man could now talk freely and proclaim openly his union affiliation without fear of reprisal. The agreement to reëmploy all strikers was a reversal of G.M.'s determination that all the sit-down strikers had been fired. Coincidental with the signing of the agreement, General Motors announced a general wage increase of five per cent. This was fixed in the auto workers' minds as a by-product of the strike.

There was good ground for the night-long celebrations which filled Flint and the auto workers' halls in Cleveland, Detroit, Toledo, and other G.M. centers. The auto workers had won a great victory for themselves, and for the Committee for Industrial Organization they had created the psychology of success and the enthusiasm which were needed to raise a great campaign to the dimensions of a crusade.

51

Class Consciousness
in an Industrial City

The preceding selection well conveys a sense of the social ferment of the 1930s, but Levinson and many other observers were inclined to exaggerate the extent to which American workingmen had become alienated from the capitalist system. Many were disrespectful of *particular* propertied interests when these seemed to conflict with their own welfare, but outside of intellectual circles there was little generalized antagonism toward an economy dominated by large corporations and wealthy individuals. A useful antidote to the view that class consciousness and class hatreds were acute in the New Deal era is Alfred Winslow Jones' pioneering study, *Life, Liberty and Property*. In 1938–1939 Jones went to Akron, Ohio, a city that had experienced violent labor conflicts in its rubber plants shortly before. If class antagonisms and the polarization of attitudes concerning public policy were sharp anywhere in the United States they were so in Akron; however, Jones' careful analysis of the relationship between class position and attitudes toward corporate property, based on interviews in which men were asked to respond to six stories involving conflicts between property rights and other values, revealed that even in Akron the trend toward cleavage was weak and the pull of what Jones calls "the central morality" strong. On the scale referred to in the selection, a score of 32 represented the choice of property rights over all other values in each of the stories: a score of 0 represented the complete subordination of property to other values.

LIFE, LIBERTY AND PROPERTY
Alfred W. Jones

The investigator is bound to approach with considerable trepidation the drawing of conclusions from a type of study that has never before been attempted. There are not many generalizations that can be fully supported by the data from a single study. It needs, therefore, to be pointed out that the following statements are in varying degrees borne out by the evidence gathered in Akron, and that they range from those that we regard as well-substantiated by the data to those that can be advanced only tentatively, as hypotheses, pending further investigation.

1. The attitude toward corporate property of industrial executives and business leaders, corresponds closely to their economic position.

The leaders of industry in Akron have prospered under the auspices of the corporate form of organization. They have advanced themselves to managerial positions of power and prestige and have acquired wealth in the form of corporate securities. It would have been a handicap to them, to say the least, if they had turned aside to show sympathy for the other side in any of the conflict situations in which they found themselves. This applies, of course, to the struggle they have had with each other as well as to the conflicts as in our stories—in which the general rights of corporate property were involved. The leaders of economic life in Akron are in the main line of American business with its tradition of self-reliance and ruthless, competitive acquisitiveness.

At first glance, there might be reason to expect a difference of interests and therefore of attitude between management and the absentee stockholders. In *The Modern Corporation and Private Property,* Berle and Means have demonstrated that a cleavage of interests exists between "control" and stockholders. The "pure" property rights of the stockholders do not correspond exactly to the rights of the managers of industry either in so far as the latter have their own interests, or in so far as they represent the "control," although the rights of both management and "control" derive traditionally from ownership. If managers were concerned wholly with the technical problems of production, we might expect from them a lower regard for corporate property rights than from the stockholders. In practice we could not, in Akron, isolate the three groups, stockholders, "control," and management. Even if we could have done so, it is doubtful whether our interview method would have uncovered any differences in attitudes between them.

Management is forced to be concerned with many considerations other than the problems of production. Managers are almost always wealthy men and stockholders themselves, and all three groups obviously derive benefits from the corporate form of wealth, whatever quarrels they may have with each other.

So it is not surprising that the scores of the eighteen Akron business leaders whom we interviewed tend to pile up at the 32 end of our scale.

2. Attitude toward corporate property corresponds to economic position fairly closely among the workers—especially those organized along industrial lines, *i.e.*, in the C.I.O., but less clearly than among the business leaders.

The worker derives no such special benefit from the existence of corporate property as does the manager of industry. On the contrary, "labor" is popularly supposed to, and does actually, confront "capital" on a variety of issues such as we have described in our stories, and it is conceivable that the working man would invariably set himself against the property rights of corporations wherever they come into conflict with the rights of interests of workers or poor people. We might expect that the economic position at least of manual workers would cause them to take a position exactly opposed to that of the leaders of industry.

There is a tendency for the scores of the 193 C.I.O. rubber workers in Akron to pile up at the lower end of our scale. But whereas ten out of eighteen, or 56.3 per cent, of the business leaders scored in the four highest places, no more than seventy-five out of 193 C.I.O. rubber workers, or 38.9 per cent, scored in the four lowest places.

Turning to other workers, the difference is even more marked. Random samples were taken of rubber workers who are not members of the C.I.O. (some of whom may be members of the Employee Associations); members of the A.F. of L. (mostly from the building trades); W.P.A. manual workers.

We can get a composite picture of the manual workers of Akron by taking the above groups along with the C.I.O. members.

No more than 28 per cent scored in the 0-3 class.

If we may say that the four highest scores represent at least the immediate economic interests of the business leaders, and the four lowest scores at least the immediate economic interests of the workers in Akron, then it is clear that the former show attitudes more in accordance with their interests. A majority (56 per cent) of our small sample of business executives scored in the 29-32 class. Only 28 per cent of the workers scored in the 0-3 class.

3. The middle groups, taken as a whole, show a greater tendency to divergence in their attitude toward corporate property than either the business leaders or the workers, with a predominant tendency to a moderate attitude, but with many individuals drawn toward the extremes. Other than immediately economic interests seem to play a considerable part in the divergence.

By middle groups we mean those whose position in industry is considered to be intermediate between that of the top management and the manual workers: or, if outside of big industry, those independent merchants and producers whose status and wealth is intermediate. Thus we should include both the new and old middle classes, along with the lower-salaried employees, some of whom may not be so well paid as many manual workers. Such a category would admit all such groups as technicians, white collar workers, salespeople, professionals (with certain exceptions), small storekeepers, independent producers, etc.

The best composite result that we can get is by throwing together the scores of the five middle groups that we studied in Akron—24 chemists, 97 female office workers, 40 teachers, 26 ministers, and 52 small merchants.

We saw above that these groups are not as bunched in the middle as our small sample of farmers. It is an easy conclusion that life in the city has exerted a pull upon them and has subjected some in each group to the influence of extreme ideas about corporate property. This is true both of those that are connected with big industry and of those independent of it.

5. Even in Akron, with almost everything in its background making for cleavage, the trend toward conformity with the compromising position seems to be stronger than the trend toward cleavage.

In a placid farm community, to which only echoes of industrial conflict penetrate, we might expect that the opinions of the middle people (who would be the bulk of the community) would pile up in the middle of the range—perhaps in a manner even more marked than was the case with our farmers to whose ears the shouts of the Akron battles come rather clearly. Or even in an industrial city where the issues between capital and labor have been peacefully worked out—either because unions have never appeared or because the employers have easily accommodated themselves to unionism—we might look for a marked middle-of-the-road tendency among the bulk of the middle people. We might then further expect that this would have an influence on the attitudes of the workers, drawing a great number of them in toward the central area. On the whole, then, the tendency toward conformity would be great and the tendency toward cleavage so slight that the end lines might even disappear entirely.

Akron, on the other hand, was the first city in this country (and, for that matter, in the world) in which large-scale sitdown strikes were deliberately used by the workers. Akron was the first city of any importance in which the C.I.O. succeeded in setting up a new industrial union. Nor was this done with the complacent non-interference of the big companies. Not only was the help of the Federal government called for, but also a series of militant strikes took place. In the fierceness of the industrial struggle of recent years, Akron is an extreme case among American cities, along with such others as Minneapolis, Toledo, and San Francisco. Akron is a one-industry town, and the theory can be advanced and defended that extreme points of view and attitudes build up more readily and quickly the more homogeneous the population. Not only is social interaction in Akron heightened because all have in common an interest in the rubber industry, but there is also, owing to the preponderance of "American" stock, an unusual absence of ethnic heterogeneity. Furthermore, if extreme attitudes develop out of suffering, we might expect to find them in the city that had been earlier keyed to such high expectations and had then been so hard hit by the depression. Finally, Akron is to an extraordinary degree an industrial city. According to the 1940 census it is the thirty-eighth city in the country in population, and according to Department of Commerce figures it is the twelfth in the country in value of manufactured goods. Akron is not a city of wealthy and middle class consumers—making for culture (in the narrow sense) and for the presence of a multitude of small service businesses. It is rather a city of producers with a minimum of the cushioning effect provided by administration, consumption, and leisure for education and the arts. Therefore, if anywhere, we might expect to find in Akron a city in which a great degree of polarization in economic attitudes had taken place, the middle groups having deserted their traditional middle position and therefore providing no point of attraction either for workers or capitalists.

Instead we find that the population of Akron yields a random sample of its citizens 76 per cent of whose scores fall within the central tendency rather than within the area piled up at the ends, and over half of whose scores are between 6 and 18.

6. No distinction is made between the property rights of corporations and of individuals, but rather between the rights of the wealthy, the "big interests," the banks etc., on the other hand, and the small property holders on the other. For many decades the Supreme Court has interpreted the due process clause of

the Fourteenth Amendment (". . . nor shall any state deprive any person of life, liberty, or property, without due process of law") in such a way as to uphold firmly the legal fiction that corporations are persons. In a dissenting opinion that stands by itself, Justice Black said, "The words 'life' and 'liberty' do not apply to corporations. . . . However, the decisions of this court which the majority follows hold that corporations are included in this clause insofar as the word 'property' is concerned." In the same opinion he said, "I do not believe the word 'person' in the Fourteenth Amendment includes corporations. . . . I believe this court should overrule previous decisions which interpreted the Fourteenth Amendment to include corporations."

Clearly, a man is related in one way to the farm soil that he has worked and cherished, or to any product of toil, "with which he hath mixed his labour" and thereby made it part of himself (whether it is intended for further production or immediate consumption); and in another way to a gigantic factory that he may never have seen and whose ownership he shares with thousands of others. It is equally clear that the emotional impact on the common man of these two relationships must be vastly different. Simple private property—the right of a man to his farm, his tools, his dwelling place—is valued only lower than the even more basic personal rights—life and liberty. If a way in which these personal rights might be secured could be clearly and cogently shown, and if such a way should happen to infringe that vast complex of prerogatives and control that we call corporate property (without violating the basic personal security of the owners) there is every reason to believe that corporate property rights would crack up and fall apart, and those parts that demonstrably stand in the way of the general welfare would disappear.

But no such persuasive demonstration has been given, and, in the meantime, Justice Black's is a lone voice. At least as far as Akron is concerned, its common people show merely a tendency rather vaguely and blindly to project over to the companies and their owners the property rights that they readily accord to private persons in general. To be sure, this is one of the tentative conclusions from our work for which there is no statistical evidence, since we asked no direct questions allowing a differentiation between corporate property and private property in general. But it is based on negative evidence in the remarks made by the respondents, and on the general impression received by the investigators. Many of the persons interviewed were quick to see that each of our stories was concerned with a conflict between property rights and "human" rights, and even more mentioned "bank" and "companies" in such a way as to make clear that their opinions would be different if the property of humble individuals were involved. The blurring and confusion of the people of the central area derives plainly from the attribution to corporations of property rights, and then the two-way pull— toward the protection of property and toward human welfare. Our society has in the past protected both tolerably well, and the people of the central area somehow uneasily think it should continue to do so.

On the other hand, if the persuasive demonstration should ever be provided, it is more than possible that Justice Black, who would like to see the corporation lose its character as a person, would find an echo among the people, and then corporate property would lose its character as private property.

7.a. The persons whose scores fall in the central area make marked concessions to corporate property.

Something more than half (155) of the 303 scores in the random sample are clustered between the scores 6 and 18, inclusive. These 155 scores are the most closely grouped of any of the central area, and, if we leave out of account the zeros, they are the most closely grouped in the entire range. Of the 155, a majority (55 per cent) disapprove of the action of the farmer's neighbors in helping him to get rid of his obligation to the bank. An even larger majority (61 per cent) are in favor of having the stockholders of the given company get at least part of the net profits. (The card giving the stockholders everything was put in first place by 12 per cent and the compromise card—stockholders and employees—by 49 per cent.)

7.b. The persons whose scores fall in the central area accept violations of corporate property in the interest of human welfare and the alleviation of suffering, such as to suggest that they would accept changes curtailing—even sharply—the rights of corporate property.

8. The group with the highest regard for corporate property (most top business executives and some others) is not likely to gain (or regain) political and social leadership and a broad popular following if it bases its statements and actions on the sentiments and attitudes it manifested in our study.

"This is not a moral question, but a matter of sheer business. The company owes nothing to the workers or to the town. Its only obligation is to make money for the stockholders. If the management considers morals in this case, the stockholders ought to vote for a change in management." This was not an exceptional statement to hear from the industrial leaders in Akron. It corresponded to their scores, as did also, in a way, their hatred of the New Deal and almost all of its works. The difference between a score of 32 and one of 8 corresponds to the difference between such a statement and the following: "I used to think differently —I wouldn't be so willing now to let things take their course, and have people suffer. If a way can be found to prevent all this misery it ought to be put into effect—and I don't hardly see why big companies and rich people should be allowed to stand in the way."

A recent survey shows that Federal provision for all the needy having no other means of subsistence is now a desire of a considerable majority of the American people, and the assertion is made that this function of the Federal government was not accepted before the New Deal. In earlier times when things went relatively well there was little reason why the majority of people in the middle groups, and even a majority of workers, should not allow the big business man to speak for them. But our study shows that in Akron he is still speaking an old language that does not now meet the emotional needs of very many beside those of his own kind.

9. The central morality exerts a powerful pull upon the attitudes of the workers.

The leaders of industry sit secure and confident in the stronghold of their opinions—at least to all outward appearances. They feel that the law fortifies them in their ideas, as do the traditions of the system that has elevated them. If they are in fact frightened, we may venture that it is because they are not really sure that they know what to do to bring back the confidence of others in them. They have learned, however, since the early days of the Roosevelt administration to work off their anxiety in the form of anger against the New Deal. In any case they enjoy a sort of ideological autonomy.

So do the middle groups, in spite of the conflicting pulls upon them and in spite of the fact they are troubled and confused. In fact the middle groups have perhaps an advantage over the capitalists in that they are not only willing to make concessions to the traditional claims of property, but also to the claims of humanitarianism which are likewise deeply rooted in our culture. Humanitarianism, of course, can lie dormant during good times. Even in times of general suffering, if there is no way to implement it, it will not add to the self-confidence of the groups that entertain it. That confidence has, in a measure, been provided by the New Deal, which made its appeal to the "people" and which provided a hope (a powerful hope for a time, and still a hope, though a weaker one) that its values could be realized. We have seen what an influence this hope had in Akron on most of the population and particularly on the workers.

It is significant that the staunchest supporters of the New Deal have been the workers, both organized and unorganized, in spite of the fact that it has shown no inclination to abolish the rights of corporate property. We have seen also that without the help of the Federal administration, and, probably, without the good will of the middle groups in Akron, the rubber workers would not have been able to organize. It is also important that workers in Akron (and elsewhere) have shown themselves willing to give up the sitdown strike as a weapon, in spite of its effectiveness, because it offended the middle groups. The evidence gathered in the present study indicates further how little ideological independence the workers possess, even on the subject and in a community where we might expect it to be the greatest.

Of course our study does not prove conclusively anything concerning the future. But the Akron data would seem to strengthen the further contention that the conforming, central morality or ideology of our society bears on the workers so heavily as to make it unlikely that they can shake it off as long as the conditions that have created and perpetuated it persist.

10. The group with the lowest regard for corporate property (some industrially organized workers, fewer other workers, and still fewer others) would find it possible to gain social and political leadership and a broad popular following only under extraordinary circumstances, if at all.

This statement, like (7) above and the two following, is in the nature of a speculation concerning the future and is, of course, merely hinted at by our data, rather than fully supported. Furthermore, the influences of the country as a whole upon any city are such that a statement of this sort is meaningless when applied to Akron alone. It ought, therefore, to be prefaced—"If the rest of the country were like Akron." As we have seen, the rest of the country is not like Akron, and this statement could be much more easily supported for the country as a whole than for Akron.

For the lowest scoring group to gain leadership there would almost certainly have to be (1) a united labor movement and (2) the fairly complete organization of the unorganized. (3) This would have to come about under a labor leadership with no regard for corporate property, and yet be achieved through statements and actions acceptable to the central tendency. (4) A competent leadership, political and economic, would have to be developed along with a workable and plausible program, ahead of what would probably also be called for, namely (5) such an economic breakdown as to demoralize the other groups.

We have seen in the scores of the workers (even many of the C.I.O.), in their remarks, and in the actual behavior of the labor unions in Akron, ample evidence of dependence on the ideas and values that are commonly associated with the middle groups. So much is this the case that it is hard to conceive of a unified labor movement and then the drawing in of those as yet unorganized unless this were to be brought about through statements and actions that would be approved of by the "central tendency." This would not be a barrier to organization, to be sure, since what we heard in Akron indicates amply that the central tendency is not opposed to unions nor even to their militant action where that seems to be called for by the intransigence of the employers. But even the first condition—the early settlement of labor's internal problems such as would permit the emergence of a strong and unified labor movement—has not yet taken place.

For it to come about under the necessary circumstances seems still more unlikely, and for the remaining conditions making for the leadership of the lowest scoring group to be fulfilled seems very improbable.

11. Economic and social action that satisfied the people whose scores fall in the central area could also satisfy the preponderant number of workers of all categories.

It is fairly safe speculation that the central mode in our distribution has been shifted toward the zero end of the scale by the events of the 1930's. It is likely that in earlier, more prosperous times the middle groups had a higher regard for corporate property and the complex of authority established around it. It is possible that this higher regard would have been represented by a sharper peak and one perhaps located above the middle of the range.

At present, however, the peak comes at 8, which is only one-third of the distance from zero that it is from 32. There can be little doubt but that it will be easier for the middle groups and workers (in so far as they are represented in the central tendency) to come together even with the lowest scoring group than with those that scored the highest.

The central morality is humanitarian and approves of acts in the interest of human welfare and alleviation of suffering even if they entail the infringement of corporate property. It approves of trade unions, and would like to see a well-led, unified, strong labor movement, but one that refrained from violence. The central morality is not pacifist, however, and would even approve of violence if there were wrongdoers that it thinks could be met in no other way. In all of these particulars it could completely satisfy the workers, with the exception of those few that have taken the point of view of the employers.

We believe that the considerations just mentioned are paramount with the workers. If they are met the workers would go along with the people of the central area in their desire to make some concessions to the rights of corporate property.

12. There exists widespread anxiety and doubt, which will persist and even grow, not merely if conditions become worse, but if they remain as they are. Further consequences are unpredictable, but it is not likely that the rights of corporate property will be strengthened.

Our stories reflect the times and put particular emphasis on the hardship and insecurity to which a considerable proportion of our population is subject. It is therefore only natural that they should have brought out in the respondents, as their remarks showed, feelings of pessimism and apprehension. It was equally clear that very few think they know what ought to be done, or have faith that anyone else is in possession of a program capable of meeting the country's present needs.

52

The Doctrine of Containment

George F. Kennan wrote this essay on "The Sources of Soviet Conduct" and published it in the magazine *Foreign Affairs* under the pen name "Mr. X" in 1947, while serving in the United States Department of State. It quickly became the classic statement of the rationale for the policy of containment adopted by the Truman administration and followed by subsequent administrations as well. Kennan did not recommend an aggressive military assault upon the Soviet Union, but rather "the adroit and vigilant application of counter-force at a series of constantly shifting geographical and political points, corresponding to the shifts and maneuvers of Soviet policy"; and he was later to complain that America had relied too heavily upon military threats as a technique of containment. The fundamental premise of his essay, however, was that expansion was integral to the Soviet system, the inevitable consequence of the inner dynamics of totalitarian rule, and that nothing but the threat of superior force could prevent it. The USSR was like "a persistent toy automobile wound up and headed in a given direction, stopping only when it meets some unanswerable force." If that premise was correct, it was difficult to dissent from the main outlines of postwar American foreign policy.

THE SOURCES
OF SOVIET CONDUCT
George F. Kennan

I

The political personality of Soviet power as we know it today is the product of ideology and circumstances: ideology inherited by the present Soviet leaders from the movement in which they had their political origin, and circumstances of the power which they now have exercised for nearly three decades in Russia. There can be few tasks of psychological analysis more difficult than to try to trace the interaction of those two forces and the relative role of each in the determination of official Soviet conduct. Yet the attempt must be made if that conduct is to be understood and effectively countered.

It is difficult to summarize the set of ideological concepts with which the Soviet leaders came into power. Marxian ideology, in its Russian-Communist projection, has always been in process of subtle evolution. The materials on which it bases itself are extensive and complex. But the outstanding features of Communist thought as it existed in 1916 may perhaps be summarized as follows: (*a*) that the central factor in the life of man, the fact which determines the character of public life and the "physiognomy of society," is the system by which material goods are produced and exchanged; (*b*) that the capitalist system of production is a nefarious one which inevitably leads to the exploitation of the working class by the capital-owning class and is incapable of developing adequately the economic resources of society or of distributing fairly the material goods produced by human labor; (*c*) that capitalism contains the seeds of its own destruction and must, in view of the inability of the capital-owning class to adjust itself to economic change, result eventually and inescapably in a revolutionary transfer of power to the working class; and (*d*) that imperialism, the final phase of capitalism, leads directly to war and revolution.

The rest may be outlined in Lenin's own words: "Unevenness of economic and political development is the inflexible law of capitalism. It follows from this that the victory of Socialism may come originally in a few capitalist countries or even in a single capitalist country. The victorious proletariat of that country, having expropriated the capitalists and having organized Socialist production at home, would rise against the remaining capitalist world, drawing to itself in the process the oppressed classes of other countries." It must be noted that there was no assumption that capitalism would perish without proletarian revolution. A final push was needed from a revolutionary proletariat movement in order to tip over the tottering structure. But it was regarded as inevitable that sooner or later that push be given.

For fifty years prior to the outbreak of the Revolution, this pattern of thought had exercised great fascination for the members of the Russian revolutionary movement. Frustrated, discontented, hopeless of finding self-expression—or too impatient to seek it—in the confining limits of the Tsarist political system, yet lacking wide popular support for their choice of bloody revolution as a means of social betterment, these revolutionists found in Marxist theory a highly convenient rationalization for their own instinctive desires. It afforded pseudo-scientific justification for their impatience, for their categoric denial of all value in the Tsarist system, for their yearning for power and revenge and for their inclination to cut corners in the pursuit of it. It is therefore no wonder that they had come to believe implicitly in the truth and soundness of the Marxian-Leninist teachings, so congenial to their own impulses and emotions. Their sincerity need not be impugned. This is a phenomenon as old as human nature itself. It has never been more aptly described than by Edward Gibbon, who wrote in *The Decline and Fall of the Roman Empire:* "From enthusiasm to imposture the step is perilous and slippery; the demon of Socrates affords a memorable instance how a wise man may deceive himself; how a good man may deceive others, how the conscience may slumber in a mixed and middle state between self-illusion and voluntary fraud." And it was with this set of conceptions that the members of the Bolshevik Party entered into power.

Now it must be noted that through all the years of preparation for revolution, the attention of these men, as indeed of Marx himself, had been centered less on the future form which Socialism would take than on the necessary overthrow of rival power which, in their view, had to precede the introduction of Socialism. Their views, therefore, on the positive program to be put into effect, once power was attained, were for the most part nebulous, visionary and impractical. Beyond the nationalization of industry and the expropriation of large private capital holdings, there was no agreed program. The treatment of the peasantry, which according to the Marxist formulation was not of the proletariat, had always been a vague sport in the pattern of Communist thought; and it remained an object of controversy and vacillation for the first ten years of Communist power.

The circumstances of the immediate post-Revolution period—the existence in Russia of civil war and foreign intervention, together with the obvious fact that the Communists represented only a tiny minority of the Russian people—made the establishment of dictatorial power a necessity. The experiment with "war Communism" and the abrupt attempt to eliminate private production and trade had unfortunate economic consequences and caused further bitterness against the new revolutionary regime. While the temporary relaxation of the effort to communize Russia, represented by the New Economic Policy, alleviated some of this economic distress and thereby served its purpose, it also made it evident that the "capitalistic sector of society" was still prepared to profit at once from any relaxation of governmental pressure, and would, if permitted to continue to exist, always constitute a powerful opposing element to the Soviet regime and a serious rival for influence in the country. Somewhat the same situation prevailed with respect to the individual peasant who, in his own small way, was also a private producer.

Lenin, had he lived, might have proved a great enough man to reconcile these conflicting forces to the ultimate benefit of Russian society, though this is questionable. But be that as it may, Stalin, and those whom he led in the struggle for succession to Lenin's position of leadership, were not the men to tolerate rival political forces in the sphere of power which they coveted. Their sense of insecurity was too great. Their particular brand of fanaticism, unmodified by any of the Anglo-Saxon traditions of compromise, was too fierce and too jealous to envisage any permanent sharing of power. From the Russian-Asiatic world out of which they had emerged they carried with them a skepticism as to the possibilities of permanent and peaceful coexistence of rival forces. Easily persuaded of their own doctrinaire "rightness," they insisted on the submission or destruction of all competing power. Outside of the Communist Party, Russian society was to have no rigidity. There were to be no forms of collective human activity or association which would not be dominated by the Party. No other force in Russian society was to be permitted to achieve vitality or integrity. Only the Party was to have structure. All else was to be an amorphous mass.

And within the Party the same principle was to apply. The mass of Party members might go through the motions of election, deliberation, decision and action; but in these motions they were to be animated not by their own individual wills but by the awesome breath of the Party leadership and the overbrooding presence of "the world."

Let it be stressed again that subjectively these men probably did not seek absolutism for its own sake. They doubtless believed—and found it easy to believe—that they alone knew what was good for society and that they would accomplish that good once their power was secure and unchallengeable. But in seeking that security of their own rule they were prepared to recognize no restrictions, either of God or man, on the character of their methods. And until such time as that security might be achieved, they placed far down on their scale of operational priorities the comforts and happiness of the peoples entrusted to their care.

Now the outstanding circumstance concerning the Soviet regime is that down to the present day this process of political consolidation has never been completed and the men in the Kremlin have continued to be predominantly absorbed with the struggle to secure and make absolute the power which they seized in November 1917. They have endeavored to secure it primarily against forces at home, within Soviet society itself. But they have also endeavored to secure it against the outside world. For ideology, as we have seen, taught them that the outside world was hostile and that it was their duty eventually to overthrow the political forces beyond their borders. The powerful hands of Russian history and tradition reached up to sustain them in this feeling. Finally, their own aggressive intransigence with respect to the outside world began to find its own reaction; and they were soon forced, to use another Gibbonesque phrase, "to chastise the contumacy" which they themselves had provoked. It is an undeniable privilege of every man to prove himself right in the thesis that the world is his enemy; for if he reiterates it frequently enough and makes it the background of his conduct he is bound eventually to be right.

Now it lies in the nature of the mental world of the Soviet leaders, as well as in the character of their ideology, that no opposition to them can be officially recognized as having any merit or justification whatsoever. Such opposition can flow, in theory, only from the hostile and incorrigible forces of dying capitalism. As long as remnants of capitalism were officially recognized as existing in Russia, it was possible to place on them, as an internal element, part of the blame for the maintenance of a dictatorial form of society. But as these remnants were liquidated, little by little, this justification fell away; and when it was indicated officially that they had been finally destroyed, it disappeared altogether. And this fact created one of the most basic of the compulsions which came to act upon the Soviet regime: since capitalism no longer existed in Russia and since it could not be admitted that there could be serious or widespread opposition to the Kremlin springing spontaneously from the liberated masses under its authority, it became necessary to justify the retention of the dictatorship by stressing the menace of capitalism abroad.

This began at an early date. In 1924, Stalin specifically defended the retention of the "organs of suppression," meaning, among others, the army and the secret police, on the ground that "as long as there is a capitalist encirclement there will be danger of intervention with all the consequences that flow from that danger." In accordance with that theory, and from that time on, all internal opposition forces in Russia have consistently been portrayed as the agents of foreign forces of reaction antagonistic to Soviet power.

By the same token, tremendous emphasis has been placed on the original Communist thesis of a basic antagonism between the capitalist and Socialist worlds. It is clear, from many indications, that this emphasis is not founded in reality. The real facts concerning it have been confused by the existence abroad of genuine resentment provoked by Soviet philosophy and tactics and occasionally by the existence of great centers of military power, notably the Nazi regime in Germany and the Japanese government of the late 1930's, which did indeed have aggressive designs against the Soviet Union. But there is ample evidence that the stress laid in Moscow on the menace confronting Soviet society from the world outside its borders is founded not in the realities of foreign antagonism but in the necessity of explaining away the maintenance of dictatorial authority at home.

Now the maintenance of this pattern of Soviet power, namely, the pursuit of unlimited authority domestically, accompanied by the cultivation of the semi-myth of implacable foreign hostility, has gone far to shape the actual machinery of Soviet power as we know it today. Internal organs of administration which did not serve this purpose withered on the vine. Organs which did serve this purpose became vastly swollen. The security of Soviet power came to rest on the iron discipline of the Party, on the severity and ubiquity of the secret police, and on the uncompromising economic monopolism of the state. The "organs of suppression," in which the Soviet leaders had sought security from rival forces, became in large measure the masters of those whom they were designed to serve. Today the major part of the structure of Soviet power is comfitted to the perfection of the dictatorship and to the maintenance of the concept of Russia as in a state of siege, with the enemy lowering beyond the walls. And the millions of human beings who form that part of the structure of power must defend at all costs this concept of Russia's position, for without it they are themselves superfluous.

As things stand today, the rulers can no longer dream of parting with these organs of suppression. The quest for absolute power, pursued now for nearly three decades with a ruthlessness unparalleled (in scope at least) in modern times, has again produced internally, as it did externally, its own reaction. The excesses of the police apparatus have fanned the potential opposition to the regime into something far greater and more dangerous than it could have been before those excesses began.

But least of all can the rulers dispense with the fiction by which the maintenance of dictatorial power has been defended. For this fiction has been canonized in Soviet philosophy by the excesses already committed in its name; and it is now anchored in the Soviet structure of thought by bonds far greater than those of mere ideology.

523

II

So much for the historical background. What does it spell in terms of the political personality of Soviet power as we know it today?

Of the original ideology, nothing has been officially junked. Belief is maintained in the basic badness of capitalism, in the inevitability of its destruction, in the obligation of the proletariat to assist in that destruction and to take power into its own hands. But stress has come to be laid primarily on those concepts which relate most specifically to the Soviet regime itself: to its position as the sole truly Socialist regime in a dark and misguided world, and to the relationships of power within it.

The first of these concepts is that of the innate antagonism between capitalism and Socialism. We have seen how deeply that concept has become imbedded in foundations of Soviet power. It has profound implications for Russia's conduct as a member of international society. It means that there can never be on Moscow's side any sincere assumption of a community of aims between the Soviet Union and powers which are regarded as capitalism. It must invariably be assumed in Moscow that the aims of the capitalist world are antagonistic to the Soviet regime and, therefore, to the interests of the peoples it controls. If the Soviet government occasionally sets its signature to documents which would indicate the contrary, this is to be regarded as a tactical maneuver permissible in dealing with the enemy (who is without honor) and should be taken in the spirit of *caveat emptor*. Basically, the antagonism remains. It is postulated. And from it flow many of the phenomena which we find disturbing in the Kremlin's conduct of foreign policy: the secretiveness, the lack of frankness, the duplicity, the war suspiciousness, and the basic unfriendliness of purpose. These phenomena are there to stay, for the foreseeable future. There can be variations of degree and of emphasis. When there is something the Russians want from us, one or the other of these features of their policy may be thrust temporarily into the background; and when that happens there will always be Americans who will leap forward with gleeful announcements that "the Russians have changed," and some who will even try to take credit for having brought about such "changes." But we should not be misled by tactical maneuvers. These characteristics of Soviet policy, like the postulate from which they flow, are basic to the internal nature of Soviet power, and will be with us, whether in the foreground or the background, until the internal nature of Soviet power is changed.

This means that we are going to continue for a long time to find the Russians difficult to deal with. It does not mean that they should be considered as embarked upon a do-or-die program to overthrow our society by a given date. The theory of the inevitability of the eventual fall of capitalism has the fortunate connotation that there is no hurry about it. The forces of progress can take their time in preparing the final *coup de grâce*. Meanwhile, what is vital is that the "Socialist father-land"—that oasis of power which has been already won for Socialism in the person of the Soviet Union—should be cherished and defended by all good Communists at home and abroad, its fortunes promoted, its enemies badgered and confounded. The promotion of premature, "adventuristic" revolutionary projects abroad which might embarrass Soviet power in any way would be an inexcusable, even a counter-revolutionary act. The cause of Socialism is the support and promotion of Soviet power, as defined in Moscow.

This brings us to the second of the concepts important to contemporary Soviet outlook. That is the infallibility of the Kremlin. The Soviet concept of power, which permits no focal points of organization outside the Party itself, requires that the Party leadership remain in theory the sole repository of truth. For if truth were to be found elsewhere, there would be justification for its expression in organized activity. But it is precisely that which the Kremlin cannot and will not permit.

The leadership of the Communist Party is therefore always right and has been always right ever since in 1929 Stalin formalized his personal power by announcing that decisions of the Politburo were being taken unanimously.

On the principle of infallibility there rests the iron discipline of the Communist Party. In fact, the two concepts are mutually self-supporting. Perfect discipline requires recognition of infallibility. Infallibility requires the observance of discipline. And the two together go far to determine the behaviorism of the entire Soviet apparatus of power. But their effect cannot be understood unless a third factor be taken into account: namely, the fact that the leadership is at liberty to put forward for tactical purposes any particular thesis which it finds useful to the cause at any particular moment and to require the faithful and unquestioning acceptance of that thesis by the members of the movement as a whole. This means that truth is not a constant but is actually created, for all intents and purposes, by the Soviet leaders themselves. It may vary from week to week, from month to month. It is nothing absolute and immutable—nothing which flows from objective reality. It is only the most recent manifestation of the wisdom of those in whom the ultimate wisdom is supposed to reside, because they represent the logic of history. The accumulative effect of these factors is to give to the whole subordinate apparatus of Soviet power an unshakeable stubbornness and steadfastness in its orientation. This orientation can be changed at will by the Kremlin but by no other power. Once a given party line has been laid down on a given issue of current policy, the whole Soviet governmental machine, including the mechanism of diplomacy, moves inexorably along the prescribed path, like a persistent toy automobile wound up and headed in a given direction, stopping only when it meets with some unanswerable force. The individuals who are the components of this machine are unamenable to argument or reason which comes to them from outside sources. Their whole training has taught them to mistrust and discount the glib persuasiveness of the outside world. Like the white dog before the phonograph, they hear only the "master's voice." And if they are to be called off from the purposes last dictated to them, it is the master who must call them off. Thus the foreign representative cannot hope that his words will make any impression on them. The most that he can hope is that they will be transmitted to those at the top, who are capable of changing the party line. But even those are not likely to be swayed by any normal logic in the words of the bourgeois representative. Since there can be no appeal to common purposes, there can be no appeal to common mental approaches. For this reason, facts speak louder than words to the ears of the Kremlin; and words carry the greatest weight when they have the ring of reflecting, or being backed up by, facts of unchallengeable validity.

But we have seen that the Kremlin is under no ideological compulsion to accomplish its purposes in a hurry. Like the Church, it is dealing in ideological concepts which are of long-term validity, and it can afford to be patient. It has no right to risk the existing achievements of the revolution for the sake of vain baubles of the future. The very teachings of Lenin himself require great caution and flexibility in the pursuit of Communist purposes. Again, these precepts are fortified by the lessons of Russian history: of centuries of obscure battles between nomadic forces over the stretches of a vast unfortified plain. Here caution, circumspection, flexibility and deception are the valuable qualities; and their value finds natural appreciation in the Russian or the oriental mind. Thus the Kremlin has no compunction about retreating in the face of superior force. And being under the compulsion of no timetable, it does not get panicky under the necessity for such retreat. Its political action is a fluid stream which moves constantly, wherever it is permitted to move, toward a given goal. Its main concern is to make sure that it has filled every nook and cranny available to it in the basin of world power. But if it finds unassailable barriers in its path, it accepts these philosophically and accommodates itself to them. The main thing is that there should always be pressure, increasing constant pressure, toward the desired goal. There is no trace of any feeling in Soviet psychology that that goal must be reached at any given time.

These considerations make Soviet diplomacy at once easier and more difficult to deal with than the diplomacy of individual aggressive leaders like Napoleon and Hitler. On the one hand it is more sensitive to contrary force, more ready to yield on individual sectors of the diplomatic front when that force is felt to be too strong, and thus more rational in the logic and rhetoric of power. On the other hand it cannot be easily defeated or discouraged by a single victory on the part of its opponents. And the patient persistence by which it is animated means that it can be effectively countered not by sporadic acts which represent the momentary whims of democratic opinion but only by intelligent long-range policies on the part of Russia's adversaries—policies no less steady in their purpose, and no less variegated and resourceful in their application, than those of the Soviet Union itself.

In these circumstances it is clear that the main element of any United States policy toward the Soviet Union must be that of a long-term, patient but firm and vigilant containment of Russian expansive tendencies. It is important to note, however, that such a policy has nothing to do with outward histrionics: with threats, or blustering or superfluous gestures of outward "toughness." While the Kremlin is basically flexible in its reaction to political realities, it is by no means unamenable to considerations of prestige. Like almost any other government, it can be placed by tactless and threatening gestures in a position where it cannot afford to yield even though this might be dictated by its sense of realism. The Russian leaders are keen judges of human psychology, and as such they are highly conscious that loss of temper and of self-control is never a source of strength in political affairs. They are quick to exploit such evidences of weakness. For these reasons, it is a *sine qua non* of successful dealing with Russia that the foreign government in question should remain at all times cool and collected and that its demands on Russian policy should be put forward in such a manner as to leave the way open for compliance not too detrimental to Russian prestige.

III

In the light of the above, it will be clearly seen that the Soviet pressure against the free institutions of the Western world is something that can be contained by the adroit and vigilant application of counter-force at a series of constantly shifting geographical and political points, corresponding to the shifts and maneuvers of Soviet policy, but which cannot be charmed or talked out of existence. The Russians look forward to a duel of infinite duration, and they see that already they have scored great successes. It must be borne in mind that there was a time when the Communist Party represented far more of a minority in the sphere of Russian national life than Soviet power today represents in the world community.

But if ideology convinces the rulers of Russia that truth is on their side and that they can therefore afford to wait, those of us on whom that ideology has no claim are free to examine objectively the validity of that premise. The Soviet thesis not only implies complete lack of control by the West over its own economic destiny, it likewise assumes Russian unity, discipline and patience over an infinite period. Let us bring this apocalyptic vision down to earth, and suppose that the Western world finds the strength and resourcefulness to contain Soviet power over a period of ten to fifteen years. What does that spell for Russia itself?

The Soviet leaders, taking advantage of the contributions of modern technique to the arts of despotism, have solved the question of obedience within the confines of their power. Few challenge their authority; and even those who do are unable to make that challenge valid as against the organs of suppression of the state.

The Kremlin has also proved able to accomplish its purpose of building up in Russia, regardless of the interests of the inhabitants, an industrial foundation of heavy metallurgy, which is, to be sure, not yet complete but which is nevertheless continuing to grow and is approaching those of the other major industrial countries. All of this, however, both the maintenance of internal political security and the building of heavy industry, has been carried out at a terrible cost in human life and in human hopes and energies. It has necessitated the use of forced labor on a scale unprecedented in modern times under conditions of peace. It has involved the neglect or abuse of other phases of Soviet economic life, particularly agriculture, consumers' goods production, housing and transportation.

To all that, the war has added its tremendous toll of destruction, death and human exhaustion. In consequence of this, we have in Russia today a population which is physically and spiritually tired. The mass of the people are disillusioned, skeptical and no longer as accessible as they once were to the magical attraction which Soviet power still radiates to its followers abroad. The avidity with which people seized upon the slightest respite accorded to the Church for tactical reasons during the war was eloquent testimony to the fact that their capacity for faith and devotion found little expression in the purposes of the regime.

527

In these circumstances, there are limits to the physical and nervous strength of people themselves. These limits are absolute ones, and are binding even for the cruelest dictatorship, because beyond them people cannot be driven. The forced labor camps and the other agencies of constraint provide temporary means of compelling people to work longer hours than their own volition or mere economic pressure would dictate; but if people survive them at all they become old before their time and must be considered as human casualties to the demands of dictatorship. In either case their best powers are no longer available to society and can no longer be enlisted in the service of the state.

Here only the younger generation can help. The younger generation, despite all vicissitudes and sufferings, is numerous and vigorous; and the Russians are a talented people. But it still remains to be seen what will be the effects on mature performance of the abnormal emotional strains of childhood which Soviet dictatorship created and which were enormously increased by the war. Such things as normal security and placidity of home environment have practically ceased to exist in the Soviet Union outside of the most remote farms and villages. And observers are not yet sure whether that is not going to leave its mark on the over-all capacity of the generation now coming into maturity.

In addition to this, we have the fact that Soviet economic development, while it can list certain formidable achievements, has been precariously spotty and uneven. Russian Communists who speak of the "uneven development of capitalism" should blush at the contemplation of their own national economy. Here certain branches of economic life, such as the metallurgical and machine industries, have been pushed out of all proportion to other sectors of economy. Here is a nation striving to become in a short period one of the great industrial nations of the world while it still has no highway network worthy of the name and only a relatively primitive network of railways. Much has been done to increase efficiency of labor and to teach primitive peasants something about the operation of machines. But maintenance is still a crying deficiency of all Soviet economy. Construction is hasty and poor in quality. Depreciation must be enormous. And in vast sectors of economic life it has not yet been possible to instill into labor anything like that general culture of production and technical self-respect which characterizes the skilled worker of the West.

It is difficult to see how these deficiencies can be corrected at an early date by a tired and dispirited population working largely under the shadow of fear and compulsion. And as long as they are not overcome, Russia will remain economically a vulnerable, and in a certain sense an impotent, nation, capable of exporting its enthusiasms and of radiating the strange charm of its primitive political vitality but unable to back up those articles of export by the real evidences of material power and prosperity.

Meanwhile, a great uncertainty hangs over the political life of the Soviet Union. That is the uncertainty involved in the transfer of power from one individual or group of individuals to others.

This is, of course, outstandingly the problem of the personal position of Stalin.

We must remember that his succession to Lenin's pinnacle of preeminence in the Communist movement was the only such transfer of individual authority which the Soviet Union has experienced. That transfer took twelve years to consolidate. It cost the lives of millions of people and shook the state to its foundations, the attendant tremors were felt all through the international revolutionary movement, to the disadvantage of the Kremlin itself.

It is always possible that another transfer of preeminent power may take place quietly and inconspicuously, with no repercussions anywhere. But again, it is possible that the questions involved may unleash, to use some of Lenin's words, one of those "incredibily swift transitions" from "delicate deceit" to "wild violence" which characterize Russian history, and may shake Soviet power to its foundations.

But this is not only a question of Stalin himself. There has been, since 1938, a dangerous congealment of political life in the higher circles of Soviet power. The All-Union Party Congress, in theory the supreme body of the Party, is supposed to meet not less often than once in three years. It will soon be eight full years since its last meeting. During this period membership in the Party has numerically doubled. Party mortality during the war was enormous, and today well over half of the Party members are persons who have entered since the last Party congress was held. Meanwhile, the same small group of men has carried on at the top through an amazing series of national vicissitudes. Surely there is some reason why the experiences of the war brought basic political changes to every one of the great governments of the West. Surely the causes of that phenomenon are basic enough to be present somewhere in the obscurity of Soviet political life, as well. And yet no recognition has been given to these causes in Russia.

It must be surmised from this that even within so highly disciplined an organization as the Communist Party there must be a growing divergence in age, outlook and interest between the great mass of Party members, only so recently recruited into the movement, and the little self-perpetuating clique of men at the top, whom most of these Party members have never met, with whom they have never conversed, and with whom they can have no political intimacy.

Who can say whether, in these circumstances, the eventual rejuvenation of the higher spheres of authority (which can only be a matter of time) can take place smoothly and peacefully, or whether rivals in the quest for higher power will not eventually reach down into these politically immature and inexperienced masses in order to find support for their respective claims. If this were ever to happen, strange consequences could flow for the Communist Party: for the membership at large has been exercised only in the practices of iron discipline and obedience and not in the arts of compromise and accommodation. And if disunity were ever to seize and paralyze the Party, the chaos and weakness of Russian society would be revealed in forms beyond description. For we have seen that Soviet power is only a crust concealing an amorphous mass of human beings among whom no independent organizational structure is tolerated. In Russia there is not even such a thing as local government. The present generation of Russians have never known spontaneity of collective action. If, consequently, anything were ever to occur to disrupt

529

the unity and efficacy of the Party as a political instrument, Soviet Russia might be changed overnight from one of the strongest to one of the weakest and most pitiable of national societies.

Thus the future of Soviet power may not be by any means as secure as Russian capacity for self-delusion would make it appear to the men in the Kremlin. That they can keep power themselves, they have demonstrated. That they can quietly and easily turn it over to others remains to be proved. Meanwhile, the hardships of their rule and the vicissitudes of international life have taken a heavy toll of the strength and hopes of the great people on whom their power rests. It is curious to note that the ideological power of Soviet authority is strongest today in areas beyond the frontiers of Russia, beyond the reach of its police power. This phenomenon brings to mind a comparison used by Thomas Mann in his great novel *Buddenbrooks*. Observing that human institutions often show the greatest outward brilliance at a moment when inner decay is in reality farthest advanced, he compared the Buddenbrook family, in the days of its greatest glamour to one of these stars whose light shines most brightly on this world when in reality it has long since ceased to exist. And who can say with assurance that the strong light still cast by the Kremlin on the dissatisfied peoples of the Western world is not the powerful afterglow of a constellation which is in actuality on the wane? This cannot be proved. And it cannot be disproved. But the possibility remains (and in the opinion of this writer it is a strong one) that Soviet power, like the capitalist world of its conception, bears within it the seeds of its own decay, and that the sprouting of these seeds is well advanced.

IV

It is clear that the United States cannot expect in the foreseeable future to enjoy political intimacy with the Soviet regime. It must continue to regard the Soviet Union as a rival, not a partner, in the political arena. It must continue to expect that Soviet policies will reflect no abstract love of peace and stability, no real faith in the possibility of a permanent happy coexistence of the Socialist and capitalist worlds, but rather a cautious, persistent pressure toward the disruption and weakening of all rival influence and rival power.

Balanced against this are the facts that Russia, as opposed to the Western world in general, is still by far the weaker party, that Soviet policy is highly flexible, and that Soviet society may well contain deficiencies which will eventually weaken its own total potential. This would of itself warrant the United States entering with reasonable confidence upon a policy of firm containment, designed to confront the Russians with unalterable counter-force at every point where they show signs of encroaching upon the interests of a peaceful and stable world.

But in actuality the possibilities for American policy are by no means limited to holding the line and hoping for the best. It is entirely possible for the United States to influence by its actions the internal developments, both within Russia and throughout the international Communist movement, by which Russian policy is largely determined. This is not only a question of the modest measure of informational activity which this government can conduct in the Soviet Union and elsewhere, although that, too, is important. It is rather a question of the degree to which the United States can create among the peoples of the world generally the impression of a country which knows what it wants, which is coping successfully with the problems of its internal life and with the responsibilities of a World Power, and which has a spiritual vitality capable of holding its own among the major ideological currents of the time. To the extent that such an impression can be created and maintained, the aims of Russian Communism must appear sterile and quixotic, the hopes and enthusiasm of Moscow's supporters must wane, and added strain must be imposed on the Kremlin's foreign policies. For the palsied decrepitude of the capitalist world is the keystone of Communist philosophy. Even the failure of the United States to experience the early economic depression which the ravens of the Red Square have been predicting with such complacent confidence since hostilities ceased would have deep and important repercussions throughout the Communist world.

By the same token, exhibitions of indecision, disunity and internal disintegration within this country have an exhilarating effect on the whole Communist movement. At each evidence of these tendencies, a thrill of hope and excitement goes through the Communist world; a new jauntiness can be noted in the Moscow trade; new groups of foreign supporters climb on to what they can only view as the band wagon of international politics; and Russian pressure increases all along the line in international affairs.

It would be an exaggeration to say that American behavior unassisted and alone could exercise a power of life and death over the Communist movement and bring about the early fall of Soviet power in Russia. But the United States has it in its power to increase enormously the strains under which Soviet policy must operate, to force upon the Kremlin a far greater degree of moderation and circumspection than it has had to observe in recent years, and in this way to promote tendencies which must eventually find their outlet in either the break-up or the gradual mellowing of Soviet power. For no mystical, Messianic movement—and particularly not that of the Kremlin—can face frustration indefinitely without eventually adjusting itself in one way or another to the logic of that state of affairs.

Thus the decision will really fall in large measure in this country itself. The issue of Soviet-American relations is in essence a test of the over-all worth of the United States as a nation among nations. To avoid destruction the United States need only measure up to its own best traditions and prove itself worthy of preservation as a great nation.

Surely, there was never a fairer test of national quality than this. In the light of these circumstances, the thoughtful observer of Russian-American relations will find no cause for complaint in the Kremlin's challenge to American society. He will rather experience a certain gratitude to a Providence which, by providing the American people with this implacable challenge, has made their entire security as a nation dependent on their pulling themselves together and accepting the responsibilities of moral and political leadership that history plainly intended them to bear.

53

McCarthyism
and the Intellectuals

Shock at the post-World War II expansion of the Soviet Union and frustration at the inability of even the most powerful country in the world to control the course of events led many Americans to search within their own society for subversives whose misdeeds could explain our impotence. In 1950 the obscure junior Senator from Wisconsin, Joseph R. McCarthy, claimed that he had a list of fifty-seven Communists employed by the United States Department of State, declared that the Roosevelt and Truman years had been "twenty years of treason," and began a brilliantly successful career as a demagogue and character assassin. Though uncomfortable about McCarthy's inability to distinguish between dissent and disloyalty, many liberal intellectuals did not condemn him flatly, partly because they believed the country had been blind to a serious internal subversive threat, partly for the reasons critic Harold Rosenberg pungently analyzes here.

COUCH LIBERALISM
AND THE GUILTY PAST
Harold Rosenberg

I

What is remarkable about the manufacture of myths in the twentieth century is that it takes place under the noses of living witnesses of the actual events and, in fact, cannot dispense with their collaboration.

Everyone is familiar with the Communist method of transforming the past; the formula for the production of historical fictions is no longer any more secret than for the atom bomb. Through a series of public confessions a new collective Character is created, retrospectively responsible for the way things happened. The Trotskyite Assassin or the Titoist Agent of Imperialism who emerges from the judicial vaudeville changes events after they have taken place. But to accomplish this, former builders of the future must agree to destroy their personal pasts in order to substitute the one offered them by the political police. At their trials, the condemned Communists are still making history—only this time backwards.

Reprinted with permission of the author from *The Tradition of the New* (New York, 1959), 221–240.

In the United States, too, recent history is being re-made. If Russia has purloined our nuclear know-how, we have evened the score by mastering her technique of psychological fission and fusion. To be able to dissolve segments of time is at least as important in modern politico-military struggle as the capacity to devastate areas of space. It is now definitely in our power to alter at will the contents of the past twenty years.

Since under our free system the government undertakes enterprises only when private initiatives fail, our official investment in mythology has so far been a limited one. Save for occasional contributions by Congress and the Attorney General's office, most of the work of changing American history has been carried on by volunteers; although various Republican Party leaders have indicated their bafflement at their Administration's refusal to use to the hilt a weapon which has been proved so effective. A single full-scale blast and the years 1932–1952 could have been turned into the desert of "twenty years of treason."

Modern history-changing needs the help of persons prepared to make a gift of their own pasts to the new one under construction. Confession is a species of autobiography; but in the political confession the "I" of the confessor is not the genuine interest of either the accused or his prosecutor. The photo of the final verdict is not of a collection of individuals but of a single "we." The Enemy is *one*—the effect of a composite of self-accusations, each of which, through fitting into the rest, exceeds the specific guilt assumed by the accused.

The reason for this overlapping was made clear by Radek in his last plea, after indicating in his testimony that he was the Fermi of psyche splitting. "There are in the country," he explained, "semi-Trotskyites, one-eighth Trotskyites and . . . people who from liberalism . . . gave us help." The guilty "we" being fashioned at his trial had to cover all of these. Vishinsky's counter-revolutionary Mad Dog had to resemble equally the desperado with the bomb, the ideologically skeptical professor, the gossipy and all-but-innocent clerk. A problem of intersecting planes and contrasting hues and light values. In the end, the Adversary had to have the face of almost anybody.

Precisely in these wider radiations of his guilt lies the reward of the confessor. An act at once individual and collective, his confession, besides giving effective vent to his resentment against those both less and more guilty than he, becomes the means by which he rejoins society. His opposition to the regime, no matter if it consisted only of an occasional doubt, isolated him through having the tonality of his individual conscience; especially if he was *not* part of an organized conspiracy his hidden criticism burdened him with the full weight of subversion. To whom could he communicate its exact nuance? Did not his friends, his wife, his children, exist in the façade of common agreement? His arrest had been but the physical confirmation of his removal from society.

In being forced to accuse himself the distracted dissident is given a chance for uniformity. Models of guilt are placed before him; he is invited to make full use of them in portraying himself. His confession will not only bestow upon him solidarity with other confessing culprits, it will supply him with a community definition. Out of the solitude of his dungeon he marches in an ensemble of comrades into the full tableau of pre-fabricated history. That the scene is a hoax matters less than that he is no longer alone and has a role to play.

In America the part of the repentant history maker has been played by the ex-radical intellectuals, some, former Communists, others, liberals and rebels who could no longer find any substance but anti-Communism in their earlier dissent. Which category they had belonged to made little difference once the confessions began. In accordance with the recipe for recasting history, all threw themselves into the same melting pot, were changed into the same Person and assumed the identical guilt. Looking backwards, paying dues to the Party or following its line were only deeper shadings of criticizing capitalism, questioning the motives of certain of America's foreign policies or making distinctions between Red and White totalitarianism.

II

Though confessing in America lacked the fatal finale of Iron Curtain confessions, it was not without its difficulties. The very absence of the bludgeon created special problems. It is possible that without the inspiration of the Russian originals, as an earlier generation was inspired by the Moscow Art Theatre, the entire effort would have failed. Far from being goaded to their parts by police agents hidden in the wings, the American guilty had to all but force their way on to the stage. Chambers himself, that witness of witnesses (one almost slips into calling him The Supreme Witness), came close to breaking under the ordeal of gaining the notice of people whose vital interests he was determined to defend. In time, we know, the barriers went down and whoever had a story to tell found a campfire waiting.

Still, the fact that one had possessed a radical bent did not of itself make him the star of a Congressional hearing nor supply him with a list of interesting names. Some leading confessors have probably never even been interviewed by the FBI. When the appetite of the ex-radicals for at least a spear-carrying assignment exceeded their stock of misdeeds, they were compelled to draw upon a psychological reserve of guilt, the confession of dangerous frames of mind to which "we the intellectuals" are prone—what had been called in totalitarian courts *moral responsibility* for sabotage or assassination performed by strangers. Obviously, the exposure of such data was as urgently needed as of dates and places when packages of film were passed. How else than through "our" instruction could a cop or a congressman understand and guard against the obscure mental processes of an Oppenheimer? Yet the sales resistance of the dumb outsiders to these more refined services could never be quite overcome.

Since there was no one effectively to extract confessions—even the threats of McCarthy fell far short of propelling the ultimate self-doubt that was the specialty of Russian interrogation—the potential confessor had to supply his own heckling. In the United States psychoanalysis assumed the function of the secret police. If Americans spoke in order to escape from a dungeon, it was from the dungeons of their own selves. Yet hasn't the Russian prosecutor since *Crime and Punishment* been rather easily recognizable as the personification of an inner voice? Despite the handicap of the Bill of Rights, our fugitive radicals succeeded admirably in making themselves victims; their example of Do-It-Yourself initiative ought to convince Khrushchev that prisons and torture are obsolete and that the cellars of the Lubianka may as well be refitted as a game room.

The final result was that a neo-liberal became available to admit the justice of any accusation, no matter how ridiculous. Since Oppenheimer gave money to aid the Spanish Loyalists, it mattered not that at the height of Russian-American cooperation he unequivocally rejected the approaches of Communist agents; "we," including Oppenheimer, may as well own up that we are unreliable types and deserve to be fired, regardless of actual service to the country. When McCarthy attempted to bully James Wechsler and spread his invented history into the headlines, the confessing liberal showed his objectivity by conceding that "we" never tendered names to the FBI unless we were forced to and are, consequently, "McCarthyites of the Left," in fighting distortion with distortion. Guilty ex-radicalism has even evolved of its Freudian researches a a new GUILT BY RHETORIC, consisting of a contaminating passion for certain words and phrases. "How desperately," exclaims a characteristic document, "they [the guilty liberals] wish in each case that the Hiss, the Lattimore *who speaks their language* might be telling the truth." The important step here beyond mere Guilt By Association is that to be incriminated it is no longer necessary to know Hiss or Lattimore personally.

The quotation above regarding complicity through language with persons with whom we may violently disagree is from Leslie Fiedler's *An End to Innocence,* a collection of "essays on culture and politics," recently published by Beacon Press. This book is as representative of what I hereby christen Couch Liberalism as anything one may hope to find. Most of the pieces in it have appeared during the past five years in the leading organs of this sect: *Commentary, Encounter, Partisan Review*; and its meditations on the evils "we" have wrought are headed by a passage from that St. John of the Couch, Whittaker Chambers, to the effect that History will get you if you don't get it first.

Half of Fiedler's book is devoted to an essay apiece on the Hiss Case, the Rosenberg Case and McCarthy, in each of which it turns out that whoever suffered deserved what he got for not confessing and that we intellectuals with our "shorthand" that the people cannot understand are deeply implicated; the rest of the book consists of literary essays with a strong discovery-of-the-true-America motif.

When I first read some of these political articles, together with pieces like them by other writers, I must confess (it's contagious) that I did not grasp what was happening. These slippery arguments that directed themselves against persons who had already been punished by law, that complained about "our" over-fussiness on the subject of civil rights, that while believing McCarthy was a crook placed under suspicion those who called him one, seemed to me simply odd. I could not grasp especially why these messages appeared under the name of liberalism. I, too, believed that Hiss was guilty, but so had the jury, he was in jail—so why these profound evocations of his perfidy and of Chambers's ordeal and triumph by a "liberal?" Or why a "liberal" indictment of Lattimore to supplement that of the

535

Attorney General's office? Or an assault on people who, conceding the guilt of the Rosenbergs, opposed their electrocution? It was only after I had noticed that these ideas were appearing in concert that I recognized that a collective person was in the process of formation which named itself "liberal" out of the same default of historical truth that caused the Communist sympathizers to cling to this title.

Fiedler's essays blend the new fake-liberal anti-Communist with that of the old fake-liberal fellow traveler to produce a "liberal" who shares the guilt for Stalin's crimes through the fact alone of having held liberal or radical opinions, *even anti-Communist ones!* For Fiedler *all* liberals are contaminated by the past, if by nothing else than through having spoken the code language of intellectuals.

Fertilized by left-wing sophistication and by Freud, Fiedler's essays are confessions on another plane than autobiography. He has no facts to relate—one does not learn that he ever did anything in politics. The guilt he assumes is that of an essence; he confesses for the guilty "we" without an "I." His theorizing about American politics derives from a vision of wrestling stereotypes, Right and Left wing, in which the collective Left sinks under a bad conscience. As one of our new volunteer cultural ambassadors "explaining us" to the Europeans, Fiedler must have done as much as anyone to confirm the belief that everybody in America lives on a billboard.

III

An End to Innocence adds perhaps the final dimension to penitence. Fiedler's line is: We have been guilty of being innocent. Only by confessing will we terminate our culpability. In a rhetoric in which the kettles predominate, Fiedler laments Alger Hiss's refusal to confess as a defeat for all of "us." Hiss "failed all liberals, all who had, in some sense and at some time shared his illusions (and who that calls himself a liberal is exempt?), all who demanded of him that he speak aloud a common recognition of complicity. And yet . . . at the bottom of their hearts, they did not finally want him to admit anything, but preferred the chance he gave them to say: He is, we are, innocent." Hiss's drama of Hush Or Tell could have cleansed us all had but its protagonist acknowledged his "mistake."

Whom Fiedler is here describing, except possibly repentant Communists who haven't confessed yet, I defy anyone to specify. His "all liberals" is a made-up character with an attributed past. To his question "Who is exempt?" I raise my right hand and reply that I never shared anything with Mr. Hiss, including automobiles or apartments; certainly not illusions, if my impression is correct that he was a typical government Communist or top-echelon fellow traveler. I shall have a few words to say about these "innocents" later. Here I insist that it was Chambers who shared with Hiss, not "all liberals"; Chambers who was never a liberal, who in his book gives no hint of having ever criticized the Communist Party in his radical days from a libertarian position and who after he broke with Communism became something quite different from a liberal. Fiedler's "common recognition of complicity" is simply slander, ex-Communist style. Had Hiss testified according to his suggestion he would have deserved another five years.

Perhaps from the point of view of the Department of Justice or of Couch Liberalism Hiss made a "mistake" by not confessing as Chambers did. But from the point of view of liberals and independent radicals the activities of the Chambers-Hisses when they were Communists were never "mistakes." Communists on this level belonged to the Party's apparatus of intimidation and bribery. Their respectability did not conflict with their support of Communist treachery and violence against non-Party Leftists or radical democrats throughout the world. On the contrary, boycotting, informing against or condemning to the executioner socialists, anarchists, Trotskyites, POUMists, strengthened their patriotic disguise. Nor did confession ever purge these agents of power of their passion to browbeat critics of their historical mission. The same people who as Communists persecuted free opinion continued to do so with the same vehemence after they had turned themselves inside out and become organizers of anti-radical penance. Conversion alters the world in which a man acts; it does not change his character. Before he confessed the GPU chief Yagoda executed countless dissenters; by his confession he dragged down unnumbered others. The first law of the spurious "we" is its malice.

How could we intellectuals, asks Fiedler, have been so wrong about Communism, as against its lowbrow enemies? And if so wrong about the issue of the age might we not be equally wrong about everything else? Ought we not therefore abandon our intellectuals' ghetto and take our place in the citizens' non-intellectual America? In a word, the end of innocence is a guilty return, as with the Moscow defendants, to the defined community—the address of "responsibility" is not the library, the study or the café but Main Street.

"The unpalatable truth we have been discovering is that the buffoons and bullies, those who *knew* really nothing about the Soviet Union at all, were right—stupidly right, if you will, accidentally right, right for the wrong reasons, but damnably right. This most continuing liberals, as well as ex-Communists and former fellow travelers, are prepared to grant in the face of the slave labor and oppression and police terror in the Soviet Union; but yet they, who have erred out of generosity and open-mindedness (!), cannot feel even yet on the same side as Velde or McCarthy or Nixon or Mundt."

It takes devotion to compile so gross a statement. Under the radiations of the fused "we," facts have grown bulbous, lost their outlines, finally dissolved. Nothing is left but a conflict of opinions. I will leave to Fiedler the explanation of how a man can be "right" without knowing anything about his subject. One recalls Lenin's incognito discussions with peasants who *knew* as against the damnably wrong intellectuals; their knowledge remains one of the mysteries of Bolshevik dialectic. Fiedler, however, cannot avail himself of Lenin's epistemology. His demand for self-surrender and intellectual abdication has nothing behind it but the will to move to the right side.

In this project Fiedler is aided by his approach, which consists of a literary critcism of events; actually, of their journalistic caricatures. Instead of political ideas, Fiedler relies upon "a sensibility trained by the newer critical methods." Through symbolist elaboration Kenneth Burke used to find endless sociological and psychological clues in a cigarette ad. Fiedler's method is to place facing each other the popular and fellow-traveler stereotypes of Hiss, Chambers, McCarthy; getting in between he lets his "sensibility" quiver with their possible meanings. For him the contrasting "myths" of Left-wing and public opinion have a wonderfully complex existence. But reality, the Soviet Union, for example, as the most baffling social, political and historical fact of our civilization, is so bare of literary suggestion, so obvious, that it may be left to the judgment of those who know nothing.

The effect of Fiedler's application of his sensibility to the public showcases of criminals, liars and corpses is that the history of the past two decades appears ultimately as a two-character melodrama. One character speaks in refined tones and idealistic abstractions in favor of the CIO, the New Deal, Socialism, defense of the Soviet Union, the dangers of Fascism—the other mutters "Dirty Reds!" Number Two wins the argument by throwing Number One in the clink. Let me reemphasize that the loser is not the *Communist* "liberal"—besides being "innocent" he has become also "generous and open-minded." But in return for these compliments to the fakers, fools and position-seekers of yesterday, all intellectuals are urged to crawl under the cloak of a spiritualized Hiss who would capitulate to the club wielder who was "right."

IV

Fiedler's "Afterthoughts on the Rosenbergs" appeared originally in *Encounter,* the international magazine published in London by the Congress for Cultural Freedom. His thesis is "that there were two Rosenberg cases," the actual case and the legendary one concocted by the Communists. Naturally, Fiedler is not interested in the "first," or actual, case. His meat is the legendary one that placed before the world the fiction of a pair of persecuted innocents. The Rosenbergs themselves, Fiedler contends, believed in their fictional counterpart so completely that they neither had any conscious guilt for having stolen the atom secrets nor any cause which they could openly champion. Thus they died as neither heroes nor martyrs—more important, they were not even human. A couple of Red cardboard cutouts were burned; there was nobody to feel sorry for, and the liberals who protested the electrocution were dupes. Just the same, Fiedler argues, it was an error to kill them, since America could have won a moral victory over Communism by sparing them. By acting as if there were a core of personal reality inside these self-made nothings we could have appeared before the world as champions of humanity.

In this scholasticist apologia, shuffling between psychological speculation and the author's insulting pose of moral conscience—for what but apology could induce the exile from humanity of a pair of corpses—Fiedler supplies a model of how to becloud historical events and the issues arising therefrom. After reading his article, I wrote a letter to *Encounter* pointing out its distortions. Although I was a contributor, my letter was not published. In its sense of Cold War "responsibility." Couch Liberalism had learned to mimic the toughness of Red Front liberalism with its why-rock-the-boat cynicism. I suggest that in doing so they have been laying the ground for future confessions.

I reproduce below excerpts from my letter to *Encounter*. If my remarks are somewhat milder than they would be today, it is because in 1953 I still naively believed I was criticising the idiosyncrasies of an individual mind rather than of the spokesman of a trend.

Fiedler . . . was shrewd to deal with Stalinism (is this still the right word?) in terms of its bad poetry. The characteristic of our time is that corn can be killing.

The Rosenberg case was the absolutely deadly mixture of American corn and Moscow mash. That in this incredibly shallow farce the Rosenbergs were playing for their lives was, of course, pathetic. This pathos Fiedler brought out very well.

I cannot, however, accept the explanation that the execution represented merely a negative failing on the part of the United States, the absence of a higher humanity, resulting from "political innocence," a "lack of moral imagination" and a "certain incapacity to really believe in Communists as people."

Fiedler is gumming up the issue with misplaced profoundity . . . He is talking about psychology, morality and "myth," when we are confronted primarily with a question of injustice, the injustice of applying the death penalty in this case. What shocked liberal opinion was the objective factor of the disproportion between the crime as charged, and for which the defendants were convicted, and the death penalty. There was, and is, something hideous and unbelievable about transporting the act from the loose atmosphere of the time in which it was committed, when RESTRICTED DOCUMENTS used to lie around like leaves, to the tense one of the 1950s. When the act was committed no one was that serious . . . Granted that the Rosenbergs were justly convicted, and I don't question that any more than any other liberal, they did not seem to deserve the electric chair. (This question of timing was implicit in Justice Douglas' desire to review which law applied.)

Sure, it was easier to perpetrate this injustice because Communists de-humanize themselves . . . But Sacco and Vanzetti, with whom Fiedler contrasts the Rosenbergs, weren't saved by their innocence or their human reality. Massachusetts did not experience them as "people" either. The fact is that no defendant is a "person"— nor ought to be. The law defines a man by his act. Justice requires only that he shall not be made to personify an act that he did not perform; and that the punishment shall not be cruel and inhuman and shall fit the crime.

The psychological question regarding the inability of many people (including myself) to feel sympathy for the Rosenbergs as individuals . . . would never have arisen had it not been for the disproportion I have mentioned between the crime, in its specific quality as an act, and the penalty. Because of this disproportion the government itself, the press, the whole "official" U.S., had to be the first to resort to psychology and the "moral imagination," that is, to unreality . . . This monster-making, which took place before the Communists countered with their own milksop Frankenstein, is something quite different from "political innocence" or an "incapacity to accept Communists as human beings."

In denying the appeal for clemency, President Eisenhower devoted his statement entirely, as I recall, to overcoming the disproportion between the crime and the legal penalty and to justifying the death sentence . . . by holding these two feeble tools responsible for starting the Korean War and for the potential death of millions of Americans, in opposition to the statements of atomic scientists that the Rosenbergs could not possibly have transmitted, by the means alleged, information worth a good goddamn . . .

The scandal of the Rosenberg Case would not exist if, as Fiedler contends, the United States had simply failed in the opportunity to save the defendants from their own masquerade as patriotic Americans. The scandals exists, not because of lack of humanity, but because of human-all-too-human passions not properly restrained by law but on the contrary making use of law. Instead of preserving the objectivity and *abstractness* of law, the government took up the slack in the law by creating its own fictional person, that of the fiendishly efficient underground incendiary capable of setting whole continents on fire. This caricature, which caused every act of the defendants to take on a enormous magnitude, was needed to enable the court to render a brutal decision and the officialdom and the press to justify it. The dramatic imagination, *with its power of creating the person it judges,* supplemented the law and replaced the creature with the creation. This is demonism, not just an absence of Christian charity.

Fiedler is exactly wrong. It seemed to him there was too little humanity in the Case, instead of too much, because he looked at this affair as if it were a stage performance and compared the Rosenbergs as bad actors to Sacco and Vanzetti as genuine personalities . . . I think it is gruesome and a bit cowardly to drag out the corpses of Communists in order to show that there are no dead bodies here but self-constructed dummies incapable of bleeding. If the Communist executes not men but devils and animals that is his basic crime. If we in turn take over this process and forget about justice because we are dealing with "made" people, we are making our own contribution to the nightmare of the twentieth century.

V

To impede the process of turning American intellectual history of our own lifetime into a comic-strip encounter between a cock-eyed egghead and a right-thinking goon, I beg leave to cite a few data.

1. Whatever its weakness in understanding Communist power and techniques, liberalism was in no sense responsible for Communist vileness. It is false to say that a belief too naive in freedom, equality, individuality, induced adherence to the band, with its underband of party bosses, spies and masterminds. The liberal sentiment for radical equality and freedom was, in fact, the single intellectual mooring that held against the powerful drag of the totalitarian "we," supported by the offer of a heroic part, social scheming and material reward. Moreover, the sentiment of freedom alone *presented Marxism itself in its living intellectual form, that is, as a problem.* One of the few serious discussions concerning the Bolshevik conception of ends and means was begun by John Dewey around the time he went to Mexico to sit on the commission of inquiry before which Trotsky crushed the Moscow Trials and permanently damaged the revolutionary pretensions of international Communism (no, it was not Fiedler's buffoons who did that). The totalitarian liberals were too "responsible" to let the fate of an individual get in the way of the prestige of the USSR "just when we are fighting fascism." Like the Couch Liberals they were also too "responsible" to take thinking seriously.

2. The intellectuals and fellow travelers who remained with Communism through the execution of the old Bolsheviks, the extermination of POUMists and anarchists in Spain, the Stalin-Hitler Pact, the fight of the Communist International against French and British resistance to the Nazis, the partition of Poland, all of which took place in public and behind no curtain of any kind, were not innocent, to

say nothing of "generous and open-minded." They were, as a type, middle-class careerists, closed both to argument and evidence, impatient with thought, psychopaths of their "radical" conformity. The "idealism" of this sodden group of Philistines, distinguished from the rest of their species by their more up-to-date smugness and systematic malice, can be emphasized only by one who ignores its function in hiding from themselves the cynicism which hardened their minds against any human plea or valid idea embarrassing to the Party. Feeling themselves on The Stage of History, they were prepared to execute the particular atrocities assigned to them, while keeping one eye on a post in the future International Power, the other on the present Good Spot in the government, the university, Hollywood, publishing. Most of their assignments were *intellectual* crimes, the concoction of arguments and boycotts to cover up acts of the Party anywhere. One recalls, for instance, the international libel let loose against André Gide when he published his account of his trip to the USSR.

All criticism by any one but the "buffoons" was met with the stare of the social climber or busy man of affairs. During the Spanish Civil War, Left professors and party-givers identified themselves with Malraux and Hemingway as ruthless franc-tireurs of the International. Without an appreciation of slapstick in both its absurdity and cruelty, it is impossible to recall these "innocents" accurately. A leadership mania centering on a dream of the power that would fall into their hands after a new Ten Days That Shook The World staged under their direction transformed these sorry bourgeois into sleep-walking social highwaymen. Undoubtedly, there were individual sympathizers whom this image does not fit, professionals too busy to look beyond the Communist explanation of events. But these innocents, if it be innocent to be made a tool through phrases and flattery, were in a minority. The Communist intellectual, *as a distinct figure* produced by the movement, was innocent in one sense only: the *non sui juris* of pathology. He had been taken over completely by a false or assumed "we"—which is the basis of mystification in our century. But the spurious "we" is also the basis of modern terrorism. If the Communist intellectuals were merely "mistaken" so were the *gauleiters*. And the Couch Liberals, with their repentant "we," are bringing more innocents of this stamp into the world.

3. The most significant falsification of the ex-Communist confessional is the suppression of the account of the struggle that raged on the Left during the epoch of Communist influence in America. This omission in itself would be almost enough to prove that Couch Liberalism is a Communist Party spirit that has changed its spots.

Like their master in Moscow, the Communist intellectuals in America detested above all, not capitalism nor even fascism, to both of which the switching Party line taught them to accommodate themselves—their one hatred which knew no amelioration was that toward the independent radical intellectual. New ideas, modern art and literature, non-conformity in taste, behavior, morals, inevitably produced in them a venomous recoil; to the antipathy officially demanded by the Party toward its foes on the Left, the sordid leftish mass willingly added its own spite toward the outsiders who undermined their revolutionary conceit, especially in the days when the Party had traded in revolution for Defense Of The USSR. Soft to the point of servility to its foes on the Right, the Stalinist front never varied in its violence against those who struck in any form against its vanguard hijacking.

Instead of Communists, fellow travelers, liberals and radicals in one lump, the reality of the period lay in its battles. Nor were the attacks all from one side. I have before me a manifesto of the "League for Cultural Freedom and Socialism," published in the *Partisan Review* in Summer, 1939. Signed by 34 writers, it denounces the "so-called cultural organizations under control of the CP" as "the most active forces of reaction among advanced intellectual circles in the United States. Pretending to represent progressive opinion, these bodies are in effect but apologists for the Kremlin dictatorship. They outlaw all dissenting opinion from the Left, they poison the intellectual atmosphere with slander." At the time this statement was issued Fiedler's bullies were more concerned with what they could sweat out of a Federal road-building contract than with the truth about the USSR. That some who signed it have, shrinking from the word "socialism" in the title, today adapted their past to the Couch Liberal distortion, does not alter the fact that such demands of the Left upon the intellectual conscience cost the Communist Party dear each time it swung at the end of the tail of the Moscow bureaucracy. Granted that no permanent victory could have been won by intellectual means alone, the FBI, the courts and Committees have not assured that victory either. Let the Cold War give way to an era of East-West trade and collaboration, and Russian caviar and contracts, citations and free trips, will begin to count their ideological votes. Yet as a major intellectual current in the United States Communism had been rather decisively defeated long before a single ex-Communist had voided his memory from the witness stand.

The Communist who "passed" from Red to Ex is himself, very often, the product of this criticism. Is Fiedler, in his idolization of Chambers, simple-minded enough to believe the Witness' yarn that it was the light of God glowing through his offspring's ear and not an argument drummed in his own by his anti-Communist radical friends that first revealed to him what was wrong with Communism? The new Good Citizen cannot change his ancestry by forgetting his disreputable father.

The Confession Era in the United States is about over. It is hard to imagine anyone adding facts likely to prove useful to the government's prophylaxis. Beyond the facts, each repentant Communist or radical has contributed his bit of himself to the collective protagonist of subversion and vanished into the common life.

The attempt to change past history has probably failed, largely because of the two-party system and the common sense and boredom of the public. Mystification has been quarantined in the quarters where it originated: the colony of the ex-radical intelligentsia.

An End to Innocence is already out of date. Its political and social morale belong to the days of McCarthy's putsch, when yesterday's vanguard saw itself blinking in the footlights with a pistol at its head. The moment this physical threat vanished the posture was bound to appear ludicrous.

54

Voices from the City

One of the most important developments altering the character of American life in the second third of the twentieth century was the rise of scientific public-opinion polling. Public opinion, as measured by a questionnaire administered to a sample of respondents, was used to determine the dimensions of a new cake of soap, the style of a political candidate, and even of the course of public policy in some instances. The historian of this era, therefore, had to consider the poll an important source of evidence. The standard questionnaire, however, was ill-equipped to measure the full depth, complexity, and intensity of popular feeling. An alternative complementary method of feeling the public pulse is represented in the following selections from Studs Terkel's *Division Street: America*. Armed with a tape recorder. Terkel walked the streets of Chicago, and talked with seventy residents about their lives, their hopes, and their feelings about what was happening to their society. We cannot be sure of the representativeness of the four voices that speak here, or even of the full group of seventy. Terkel "played hunches" in selecting his cast of characters, instead of following systematic procedures that would permit scientific generalizations about the population of Chicago as a whole. But these interviews deepen our understanding of American life in the mid-1960s.

DIVISION STREET: AMERICA
Studs Terkel

Tom Kearney, 53

An apartment in a high-rise complex on the Near Side of the city, adjacent to Michael Reese Hospital. A well-thumbed copy of Gunnar Myrdal's An American Dilemma *was on the coffee table.*

I've been a policeman for twenty-three hard years. . . .

I worked as a patrolman and a detective. Then I was promoted to a detective sergeant and from there I went to the traffic division. So I've covered all bases so far.

From pp. 79–88, 135–139, 159–165, 285–289 of *Division Street: America*, by Studs Terkel. © Copyright 1967 by Studs Terkel. Reprinted by permission of Pantheon Books, a division of Random House, Inc.

Sometimes you're disenchanted, you're disillusioned, you're cynical. When people attempt to offer a bribe. I know I've been negligent in my duty because I should have arrested the person. At the same time, that's universal, everywhere. I turn it down. I told him, you know, "No harm trying. But I just don't go that way." (Laughs sadly.) It's a corrupt society. . . .

I was born in Chicago, my father was born in Chicago, and my grandfather was born here. His father came to America to dig the Sag Canal. They were promised they could have farmland where they could grow anything. In the winter, they'd dig the canal. Unfortunately, it was all rocks. So they wound up with a rock farm.

There's something you gotta understand about the Irish Catholics in Chicago. Until recently, being a policeman was a wonderful thing. 'Cause he had a steady job and he knew he was gonna get a pension and they seemed to think it was better than being a truck driver, although a truck driver earns far more than a policeman today.

Someone had to be police, you know? They sacrificed anything. They just knew that so-and-so in the family would be. It was another step out of the mud. You figured at least you'd have some security. They felt they no longer worked with their hands. They weren't laborers any more.

If the Depression hadn't come along, my father would have been able to do more educational-wise for us. He couldn't provide. There was no money for two years. At that time, the firemen and policemen weren't paid. My father was a fireman for forty years. They were the only ones who didn't get their back pay. Whoever could work and earn anything at all . . . that's what kept us going.

I recall the hunger marches. I remember the police at that time, they had mounted police. I had a job at Madison and Canal, and they were marching, trying to get into the Downtown area, from the west to the east. The police charged them. Whether they were right or wrong, I didn't know then. I was too much concerned with my own self. 'Cause things were rather brutal and you expected that, you know.

I remember at Blue Island and Ashland—there's a lumber company there now—that was a big transient camp. I remember the food lines. I also remember getting off the Elevated and men waiting in line for the newspaper. If you were through reading it, they'd take it. They had a little code among themselves. What they used them for was probably to sleep on. . . .

There's no colored there [Bridgeport]. A mixture of white—different ethnic groups: Polish, Slavic, Irish, Italian, anything and everything. A few Jewish families. In the old days, it was all Irish. The streets, the names were Irish. The street my grandmother lived on was named after one of my father's sisters who died very young.

We moved farther south, to Roseland. My father was assigned there. It was a community begun by people who had left Pullman. They had rebelled against the company by moving out. If you worked for him you had to live in one of his Company houses. You bought from the Company store. If profits fell below a certain level, wages were cut. The rents weren't lowered, the rents remained the same. Now, of course, there's nothing much over there.

My father was one of the radicals. Even though he had status, you know, being a fireman and the fact he got a pension, he used to say, "Why should I get a pension when the fellow next door doesn't get one?" He was a good Irish Catholic, so he wasn't a Commie, but at the same time he used to say, "You know, maybe they got something over there that we should know about, because they keep on talking about how bad it is over there."

My family wasn't devout. Certain things my mother, of course, insisted upon. On Good Fridays, you had to sit in a chair in the kitchen. In those days they didn't have any foam rubber seats. It was hard wood. And you had to sit there till about five minutes to twelve. Don't laugh and don't talk. You sat for three hours. She had some of an idea that it helped you spiritually. But I don't think we were deeply religious.

I find myself at odds with the Church at various times. I knew the nuns taught me some things that weren't true. At the same time, I realized they themselves didn't know whether they were true or not. They were simple women, you know. You say you'd rather have your son go to a public school because he's gonna have to get along with those people and he might as well start young. The same as going to school with the colored. You're going to have to get along with them. They're here, so you might as well go to school with them and get along with them.

HOW DO YOU FEEL ABOUT YOUNG NUNS AND PRIESTS
TAKING PART IN STREET DEMONSTRATIONS?

They have every right to do so, although not to violate the law. I'm not saying that because I'm a policeman, but simply because having been in parochial school all my life, all I ever heard was: "Don't do anything wrong." Respect for authority.

Today things are changing. If one married outside the religion I remember this: "Oooh, tear out all my hair. I can't face my friends, we gotta move." Oooh, terrible, terrible. And what happened? I have five brothers and one sister. Of the brothers, one is a bachelor. The rest of us married Protestants. My sister married a Protestant. My older brother had two daughters. They raised one a Catholic and one a Protestant. The girl raised a Catholic married a Protestant and the one raised a Protestant married a Catholic. Today, for convenience's sake, my brother and his wife go to the Catholic Church. She hasn't been converted, but just goes for convenience's sake. It isn't any big deal any more.

It's changing rapidly. Look at the city. Of course, everyone resists change, good or bad. Even if it's good for them, they resist it. Take the color situation today. The whites, they're only fighting a rear-guard action. The walls are coming down, that's all. The tragedy is that the program of the colored is still negative. There's no reason to lead a march or sit in the streets any more, as I see it. Because they've won, there's no question about it. They've got to find a way to have the whites accept them.

Unfortunately, the colored man came to the industrial North just too late. He came after there were so few jobs to begin with. The Caucasian immigrants came with nothing but their hands and they worked in steel mills and maybe they were snapping cinders, which is one of the most difficult jobs and the lowest paid. They watched another fellow do a job and they learned his job and climbed up. Well, the colored man didn't have that opportunity after the wave of migration from the South. There were so few labor jobs that he could start out from and learn how to get up. The machine took care of that. They didn't need him any more. One man can do the work of ten today.

WHAT DO YOU THINK THE OBJECTIVE OF THE COLORED IS?

The same as mine, the same as mine. Everything best for him and his family that he can possibly have. I can see where they'd want to move away from a completely colored neighborhood and integrate. I can understand that. He also understands that his family is gonna have to live with whites and if he doesn't live with the whites he can't understand them either. The colored man says: "Well, you don't know us." Naturally we don't. They don't know the white either.

I think people are intelligent enough to accept integration. We've done one thing, it's a bad thing, but I can't think of anything better. The quota. It's bad because you have to exclude someone sometimes, but the whites wouldn't have any fear of being overwhelmed. And the colored wouldn't have any fear that the white would run. This high-rise complex I live in now works on a quota. It's highly controlled.

Most of urban renewal is bad in a sense. People were displaced. Yet it had to be done. Where we're sitting now was one of the foulest slums in America. It was worse than Calcutta, believe me. I've been in here as a police officer on many occasions. Right across the street, they had a fence to protect the institution there. It must have been eighteen feet in the air, with barbed wire.

Actually it's not really integrated now because there's no community life here at all. You don't know the fella next door usually. Your wife may meet them or something like that, but you yourself come and go, that's all. There's no way for people to know one another. You at least vote together, you know, at election time. Well, each building is its own precinct. So people just go in and out. There isn't any standing outside like you do normally at an election. There's no church in the immediate vicinity. Most people, they have to go several blocks to an known place. And these complexes have very few children. An adult population, more or less concerned with their own problems. When we first moved in here, I thought I'd go insane, being cooped in and actually nowhere to go, because the neighborhood is sterile. It's not a neighborhood at all.

People don't want to become involved. Most people have had some dealings with court, like traffic courts. People have sat for long periods of time, waiting for their case to be called. In criminal court, they've found themselves returning there and then continuances being granted after continuances. This man, he loses his day's pay from work. If it's a woman, she becomes frightened, that they might retaliate in some way. The fear. Like many cabdrivers that don't report a robbery, 'cause normally they might not have eight or ten dollars when he's held up. He won't report it because he'd lose a day's work if they finally apprehended the offender and the loss is a loss.

This fear of involvement. I wondered why there were so few colored in the crowd greeting the astronauts yesterday. Most of the fellows said, "They don't care if anybody went to the moon. They don't have any feeling about it." I said, I don't think that's true. We were briefed to search for colored people who might be a threat, you know. It was the week of demonstrations. The average colored person is just like you and I. If there was a great crowd some place and there was a threat to all people wearing blue shirts, you certainly wouldn't go down there in a blue shirt.

DO YOU HAVE ANY COLORED FRIENDS?

Oh yes. Yes. (Pause.) I *say* colored friends and I *think* colored friends . . . but actually I really don't know.

YOU DON'T KNOW WHAT THEY THINK OF YOU?

Not really. I can understand that. Because if I were colored, I'd be bitter, too. I *think* I'd try to control myself, try to be rational about it. I remember one night, a colored schoolteacher I know, we're at a party, an interracial party, very nice. She forgot the potency of martinis and I sitting talking to her and suddenly she looked at me very hard and said, "You're my Caucasian enemy." Very indignantly. Of course, I realized, you know . . . I mean, she just didn't realize how potent a martini was. So you really don't know.

Some guys that I know, colored, we talk and discuss the family and how things are going, and how their wives are and things like that, but I don't think I know. (Pause.) I don't think I know.

My son, a twenty-two-year-old boy, who's been going to college, I really don't think I know *him*. I think he knows me better than I know him. That's one thing he really doesn't like. I think he'd like it the other way around. The younger generation doesn't think too highly of us. They think we made a mess of things, which we did. We seem to lead disorganized lives. Most of us dislike the work we're doing. Most of us are anxious to go someplace else, thinking we could leave our troubles behind. They love us, our sons and daughters. But at the same time, they don't think we did things correctly. They're critical of us. They discuss things far more intelligently than we do. They think for themselves.

One day he brought up a charming little blond girl, not overly dressed, but not ragged or beatnik type. She was going down South to teach in one of the Freedom schools. Very much enthused about it. And she seemed to have a good idea why she was doing it. I mean she wasn't looking for publicity or anything like that. She really thought she should be doing this. And then again, he met a colored girl, a beautiful creature, who also had a brilliant mind, you know, straight-A student, one of those types. And she had absolutely no interest in civil rights. None. couldn't mean less to her, although she identifies with the colored people. She makes no attempt to pass, 'cause she could very easily. And then he has a friend whose sister and mother are both active in the civil-rights movement. The sister was arrested twice in the last week.

547

DID YOU HAVE TO ARREST HER?

No, I . . . (Laughs.) It woulda really been funny, you know. I asked her, "Now what is this about police brutality?" And she said, the way some policeman talk, you know, and then I suppose holler at them at some degree or another, I mean to keep them in control and get them in the wagon or something. But I said, "What happened to you?" I mean, the voice means nothing, I mean, I holler at people, too, you know—stand back, or something. Well, she said, "When the policeman arrested me, he said, 'Now come along, honey, step up in the wagon.' " (Laughs.) That was police brutality.

. . . So the difference in them, more freedom. You never say, "Go to your room, I want to talk to your mother." When I was a boy, when they had company, I was always excluded. Today, even when our son was young, he sat in on conversation and he learned to judge and evaluate things. In my home, when my father was there, he got the paper. When he was through with it, you got it. That's all. Sometimes he didn't get through with it until you were in bed. About the only thing that was discarded was the comics on Sunday. They didn't think you were interested in other things.

I was surprised to see what these young people were thinking. Civil rights. Some couldn't care less. Others were militant. Then others like himself approved of what was going on but didn't participate. They had some very good ideas about it. Some of the most controversial things, Vietnam, Cuba.

They began wondering. Of course they have more time. You and I have to make a living. But their level of conversation is much higher than the adults' level today. I think we tend to be more humorous, even if we force it, probably because of age and years of work. I find myself in a group, visiting, where there's very little conversation of any depth. Did you hear the latest Polish joke? or things like that. Or talk about some play or movie. You know, there's no . . .

But these young people really have a feeling. They trade views. I find they seldom argue in a—in disagreement. They give and take, back and forth, but they don't stand on their points. They want to know the other person. They seem to accept other people more easily than we did.

The only thing is there's a great many pressures on them. The fear of the draft is always there. It's stupid, they feel. It doesn't accomplish a thing, and why do it. They don't seem—outside of this one girl who was arrested twice in one week for sitting in the streets—they don't seem to have any great drive. I mean, it's a problem. Everything is so complex.

They see all our values changing. Just as we see the city changing, with the expressways and with the high-rise living, which I never thought I'd live or could possibly afford.

YOU'RE TWO YEARS AWAY FROM RETIREMENT.
DO YOU LOOK FORWARD TO IT?

Not particularly. I do in one way. I'd like to take up something else if I can. Be able to enter—this sounds sort of corny—more of a community life, in a smaller community where you participated more, you know. *In doing something.*

I myself haven't done everything a man should do. Some guy once said the four things a man had to do: he had to be in love, he had to get married, he had to have children, and he had to fight a war. So you accomplish these things, and I did. Now there's the Bomb. As far as I'm concerned, I'd hold on as long as I could. I don't think this is as serious with the older generation, this fear, as it is with the young. They believe here's a possibility of working your way out of this intelligently and we don't seem to work toward that end. We're constantly in turmoil. That's the older generation. After you're fifty, it's all the way down, no speed limits. That's it, you've had it. I mean you have nothing left.

A policeman starts out young and very impressionable, and you see people at their worst, naturally. You don't go into the better homes, because they have fewer problems, or they keep them under control. Sure, a man and wife argue, but usually it's on a quiet level. In the poorer classes of homes, frustrations are great, pressures are tremendous. They turn on the TV set and they have these give-away programs and someone's winning thousands of dollars. Or if they're watching a play of some kind, everything's beautiful and lovely. They watch this and they don't have any of it and they can't get any of it. Then when an argument breaks out, the closest one to 'em, he's gonna get it. We were taught, you know, if my mother and father argued, my mother went around shutting down the windows and the doors because they didn't want the neighbors to hear 'em. But they deliberately open the doors and open the windows, screaming and hollering, and it's a release from their emotions. So when they have an argument, it's a good argument and it necessitates the police coming to quiet it down. Naturally, the impression of a young police officer is that they aren't really people, you know, get rid of them.

I've often worked with policemen who became very angry when we'd arrest a narcotic addict, a burglar. And then have to notify the parents. This one police officer, he used to get insane, he'd be so mad. Why couldn't you do something with your son? One day I finally said to him, "What would you do if your son came home and said he was a junkie?" He wouldn't know what to do. He wouldn't know why his son did it. The son would know, but he wouldn't. You understand?

Mike Kostelnik, 36

His home is on the Far Northwest Side of the city, bordering the suburb Norridge. An area primarily of one-family dwellings of a new middle class.

He is a window washer, earning $160 a week. He has worked eighteen years for the same contractor. He has a wife and two children, a boy and a girl.

I'm losing a very good neighbor. He's a fireman, captain, and he's retiring. As a matter of fact, he's leaving today. So before I went to work this morning, I even had to say goodbye to him and his wife. They had one boy, but he's gone now. He's married, you know. So he decided to retire, a man fifty-some years old. He's doing very well. Shelby, Michigan. When you're owning individual property you have a community feeling. Everyone's more interested because they have more at stake. And when you come outside, I mean, there's Joe Blow or whatever his name is, he's doing a concrete job. Well, the thing to do is go over and give him a hand. I've got a neighbor across the way, well, he can't do heights, so I cut his trees. So the next time the guy comes over my house, he's gonna do my plumbing.

We had our street paved where we were living. Now everybody had to do this, because you wanted the block to look right, you know. And if you didn't—'cause a couple were real slow at it—all the rest of the people looked at them: "Hey, when are you going to get yours?" A month or two and you see the guy's not doing it, so you, well, you sort of look it over every time you go by. You give the guy a subtle hint that this should be done. You know. "Lookit, uh, why should you leave it this way? You like the area? That's why you moved here. You like the area? Keep it up." I mean, why should you go into an area that you pick and then right away let the weeds grow, you know? Why should I be a nonconformist? You have to conform to society.

What makes people scared of the colored race is they're scared of deteriorating property. Now if these people just go ahead and show that they're intelligent enough . . . And there are a lot of wonderful people. I've done work for colored lawyers, educated people, and you couldn't find a better group of people. These people don't like their own type, they don't like their own people in their own race. Now there must be a reason for it. I have quite a few Negro friends. I've discussed this basic thing with them. I know a parking-lot fella here. I've met a lot of wonderful Negro people, don't get me wrong. It's never a question of color, it's the way a lot of them live.

So why should anybody tell me, the property I'm sweating for right now and I'm working every day and sweating for . . . why should I be told who to sell it? Where are *my* civil rights? There's the twister. Why should I be told what I sweated for and earned—this is against the constitution actually—how I should dispose of it? Don't you think that's wrong? I don't want to infringe on any man's freedom. But I also don't want mine infringed on.

SUPPOSE A NEIGHBOR LEFT
AND SOLD HIS HOUSE TO A NEGRO?

I would not run. But I tell you one thing, he better keep up his property, because then I'd get disturbed. I'd be one of the first guys on the phone and keep on calling City Hall and telling them: "Here's your man now, let's see how he keeps up his property." 'Cause I bought my property and I want my property value to be up. I'm taking care of mine and so are all my neighbors. Now if this gentleman conforms to this type of situation, there's no restriction. Of course, his moral code I would watch out for, too. . . .

Maybe I've gotten in contact with some poor ones, but the few of them have left me with a very poor idea. It seems the biggest thing to do is to live with two, three women. Well, maybe I'm a little old-fashioned, but I've been married to the same woman for sixteen years and I'm pretty happy with her.

Now, I'm just a window washer, okay, I'm just a bum window washer, some people would say. But I'll tell you one thing, when I walk away from a building, I like it to look like it's been done. Follow me? It might be a simple thing to other people, but when it's done, it's done. I mean I can go up and take a look at this glass and say, great. And then I don't have to take back seat from my boss. I do my work. No brown-nosing, no nothing: "If I'm not doing it for you, I'll do it for another man. I stayed here for eighteen years because you wanted me and I enjoyed being here. But I don't have to kowtow to you." And this is the point of pleasure. If you're willing to do your job, everybody wants you.

Window cleaners, like I told you, they're independent people. And they love challenges. They'll match against each other to see how much speed they have. Now I'm getting a little out of the stage, but when I was a little younger man, I used to enjoy it. When I was eighteen or nineteen, My God, the worst thing that could be told about you was he could beat you. You were the Johnny-on-the-spot, man, you went and moved. To show him that you were as good as him, if not better. Personal pride in work. This we're losing in window cleaning. And when we used to race like this, against each other, any streak on the window, that window was discounted. These were the challenges, this is what made your job interesting. A different group of men, they were big, burly men, rough, big drinkers, and all this . . . but they had a feeling about it, they took pride in their work. Today, a lot of it's gone.

It's a new age. Automation's the big thing. People who're really getting hurt are the office people, as of now. Factory workers was hurt before, now it's got to the office field. You know I heard this—they said something Henry Ford said to Martin Luther . . . no, it wasn't Martin Luther . . .

THOMAS EDISON?

No, no, the big union man. Walter Reuther, that's it. He took him through the plant. I heard this story somehow, it hit me pretty good. He said, "I like that machine there," he says. "It does the work of six men." "And yet," as an added remark, he tells him, he says, "it doesn't have to pay union dues." And Martin Luther told him, he says, "Yeah, it's a good part. But you tell me how many cars that machine will buy. You can produce all you want, but you have to have a market for it. And if you don't have a market for it, you're not gonna sell your products." So . . .

They can work a man, heat, cold, snow. You want a job, you want to earn a living, you go in, go do it. You know these machines have to have a 72 temperature. So they talk about a working man fighting for better working conditions. Here's a machine, just don't work, has nobody to support. It doesn't have to work. It just sits there, unless you give it the proper working conditions, it just don't work. . . .

My kids are gonna have a better education than me. When my boy hits a certain age, when he's qualified to be a window washer, which I hope is another two years, he'll be working with me in the summer months, picking up about a thousand dollars for the summer months. He's hoping to get a scholarship through football.

He told the boys he didn't want to have any part of smoking, because it kills his wind, and he intended to play football. These are things that make a man feel good. He doesn't have to impress anybody. His size impresses, you know what I mean?

551

He doesn't have to make like a bully. Nobody picks on him, because anybody in his age bracket doesn't want no part of him.

Today he's got a beautiful arm on him. I like strength myself. I'm one of these individuals that enjoys a good Indian rassle or a handshake, or stuff like that. If it's a nice bout or challenge. I enjoy it. My son, I guess he gets it from me. We've been doing this—God, since he's about ten years old. Now he's got an arm on him, he could take a grown man, at fourteen, you know. And this is the fun of it.

I've got an insurance policy, this will guarantee his education, the one I couldn't get. This will make him a better man. And this isn't done overnight. My dad was a laborer all his life. He came from Poland. We used to speak it in the home. I read and write it. My dad never owned a home. My dad never owned a car. I own all this. And this is true, generation after generation.

Yet, these kids today . . . I've got four nephews in the teaching profession. One, he's six feet two, but at times he's a little scared. He says a fifteen-, sixteen-year-old with a switchblade sort of scares you.

A regular school, not only colored. Maybe a Puerto Rican kid might do this or another white kid. We're talking about people. What did it do to these kids? When I was a kid, I came from an awful rough neighborhood. You don't like someone, man, you matched up against him with your fists. If he whipped you, you knew him better next time. But this idea of switchblades and knives and what have you, it scares a man.

And these kids come from good homes. What is a good home? If you don't spend your time with those kids . . . no, I'm trying my best. For all I know, maybe next year, or two years from now, my son might change and become one of these big bullies. Right now, he's a wonderful kid. Who knows what happens to a kid? Who knows what happens to anything?

Helen Peters, "slightly past forty"

A middle-class area in the city. Two-flats and three-flats are being suddenly surrounded by high-rises. It is near the lake.

> *She came to Chicago in the early Forties from a farm near Pontiac, about a hundred miles southwest of Chicago. "Most people leave. The town isn't progressive."*

> *She does market research a couple of days a week, thus a second car has become necessary for the family. One of her discoveries on the job: "The more successful a man is—and you can tell by going into his office how successful he is—the more anxious he is to help you."*

> *She is active in the PTA, a neighborhood bowling league, and numerous fund-raising activities. She keeps house for her husband and two children. Her eldest daughter is married and has "two babies."*

We have right on this street almost every class. I shouldn't say class because we don't live in a nation of classes. But we have janitors living on the street, we have doctors, we have businessmen, CPA's.

Take janitors, for instance. The ones we have contact with and happen to know are very class-conscious. And it's not because people make them feel that way. It's something . . . they have come from a family of janitors, they feel they have to prove themselves, that they are as good as the next person. One of our mutual friends calls this the janitor syndrome. (Laughs.) They are constantly trying to prove that they are as good as someone else. Well, that isn't necessary. Just because he cleans boilers or carries garbage, he's making an honest dollar.

My husband, as he says, is a Jack-of-all-trades. He's assistant to the president of a corporation right now. He's primarily interested in over-all management. He's very machine-conscious. He's a sort of systems-and-procedures man. It expedites things. I mean, he's a firm believer, do it the best way possible, the fastest. And he—blowing my own horn—is a very smart man.

I think when your children are small, a woman's place is definitely in the home. But once they're partially grown a woman is foolish if she sits around and stagnates. I think you become unhappy.

I know many women who have become bridge bums, they've become alcoholics, or they are doing clubwork which they do not enjoy. Because it's the thing to do. There are women who play bridge every afternoon. They also play bridge every night. Their whole life, their whole outlet, is bridge. And I feel that if these women don't have bridge, they would be hitting the bottle quite hard. In fact, there are a lot of so called bridge players that are very heavy drinkers. And some of them take dope, too.

Also in PTA, there are women there are in their sixties that are still in the PTA. Their grandchildren must be out of PTA. I feel sorry for them. Their life must be so empty that their only outlet is PTA, and they are to be pitied.

. . . The kids . . . I wonder if they're getting the proper education. I went to a country school, out in the country where a teacher taught all eight grades. I learned the eight parts of speech when I was in grammar school. I could still give them if I had to. Most kids in school now don't know there are eight parts. They do not teach grammar as such.

You know, nouns, verbs, prepositions, and so forth. But the kids are not taught to diagram sentences, that is no longer considered necessary. I don't know, they just aren't taught. If they write a composition, if it's correct, it's strictly an accident. Not by thought, word, or deed, shall we say? It's a subject I think should be brought back. We hear all children say, "I don't got any"—and, mine included, until I could strangle them.

My boy is sixteen, he likes to go out. I trust him. I know he won't go out and steal or break into a car, what do you call it? Mug somebody? But maybe he's going to be the one who gets mugged. I don't know all his friends. You can't possibly know. Most of them have been to the house. But you can't keep them in the house all the time. So I'm one of those worrying mothers who stands in the window and watches (laughs) for them to come home, and if they're five minutes after curfew, yell, "If you're picked up by the police, you can stay there all night."

And especially with an eleven-year-old girl, you worry about some mentally deranged people. I'm not neurotic about it. But if they come home later than they should, then I'm always, shall we say, a little upset.

I love Chicago, contacting people, talking to people. Despite the violence. If I go out late in the car, and I can't park right out here on the street, I jump out and run in the house and get Cliff and say, "Come on." (Laughs.)

. . . I would think it was all right if a Negro family moved next door to me. If he moved on this street to begin with, he's going to have to have a job that supports himself and his family in order to pay the rent around here. Rents on this particular street are not excessively high, but they are not low. On the next street, there is a colored woman living, did you know? She is married to a white man, she came to the PTA the other day, and I'm very sorry to say there were only three of us who talked to her. We invited her to join our bowling league, and as you know, asked her to please come again. She is very nice. She is a very pretty Negro woman.

In Pontiac, we knew one Negro man down there. He was a junkman and came out and I imagine he made as good a living as anyone else. Buying and selling junk. Probably better than most people, during the Depression. (Laughs.) But somehow or other, well, there was an incident when I was a child. A colored man shot a white man, and they put a curfew on the colored people. They had to be off the streets at six o'clock. Whenever this man came, we weren't exactly afraid of him, because we knew he was Les Summerville, he was the junkman. But he was different. If he was at our house collecting junk over the noon hour, call it dinner hour on all farms, Les was asked to come in and eat with us, and he ate with us at the table. And I can remember as a child that the insides of his hands were white, which amazed us when we were small. That the insides of his hands should be so white and the backs of his hands so dark.

We have a neighborhood school policy. I believe in the neighborhood school policy. I also believe in open housing. I think a man should be able to live in the neighborhood of his choosing, where he can afford to pay the rent. Like they say, water will seek its own level.

But I think these demonstrations are horrible. I don't think they prove a thing. I don't know how much patience I could have if I were a policeman, with these people laying down in the streets. When they are asked to move, they will not move. The demonstration in what was that place, the so-called ghetto in the West Coast? Watts. I think that was the most disgraceful thing that ever happened in any country. I think the National Guard were within their rights, if they just mowed them down wholesale with machine guns.

I think somebody has come in and stirred these people up. I know they are not brilliant people, they are easily led, they're poorly educated. A lot of them are from the South where they really have been forced down. They really don't have rights in the South, but I think here, I mean, everyone has the opportunity to go to school, he has the opportunity to go to college if he chooses. I'm sure if they want to work and earn a living that they can.

I think it's highly possible that there's a communist influence here, that if you don't have it, go out and take it. It is your right, which these people did by looting and taking things out of stores, that that man was walking away with a couch on his back. (Laughs.) It's horrible even to think, but I really couldn't have blamed those troopers if they had . . . because they were being shot at by snipers.

About that march in the South . . . this woman that was killed from Michigan. I think that's awful that the Ku Klux Klan, we know they're a violent group, but to shoot people in the dark, it's not . . . it sounds trite to say, it's not nice. She felt, from what I read in the paper, that she was helping those poor people. Each one has his own compulsions and drives, and maybe she felt it was her moral obligation, maybe she had a feeling of religion about it. I don't know. But she did have a home and five children, and I don't feel she had a place down there.

DO YOU AND YOUR HUSBAND TALK POLITICS MUCH?

We have mixed politics in our family, and the name of Roosevelt can almost turn my husband purple. I think he's the greatest president, or what have you, that ever lived. Of course, I think Truman is too. And I like Johnson. We are not solid Democrats or Republicans. We both vote a split ticket. But primarily he's a Republican and I'm a Democrat, and we have friendly arguments. We also have, shall I call them discussions?—like what year did Baumholtz play for the Cubs, and I'm up in the middle of the night looking up references to find out. (Laughs.)

At parties, Vietnam always makes a good topic of conversation. I think it has to be cleaned up. It just cannot continue and continue. And even though my son-in-law is going to have to go—by the first of the year I know he will have to go—he's in the Strategic Air Command, and SAC is stationed on Guam, where they take off, these big planes, B-52's. They're going to have to get more men in there and just clean it up. War can't go on forever and ever and ever, and you get sick when you think, gee, Cliffy is only sixteen, in two years he's going to have to register. And he's going to be seventeen pretty soon. And you think: Holy smoke, I would hate to have to see him . . . I lived through that Second World War, it was horrible; the Korean War was horrible. But now your own kids are coming up into it again.

I don't think they will come to a truce. They're going to have to clean out all the guerillas, and something has to be done. It's too much a drain on our young men, too much of a dollar drain. We have to get enough boys in there to bring things to a sudden halt somewhere along the line.

WE'RE TOLD THAT H-BOMBS TODAY CAN DESTROY THE WORLD.
DOES IT EVER BOTHER YOU?

Yes, because in August of this year we went to South Dakota. We were lucky enough to tour Ellsworth Air Force Base. We saw these terrific bombers, these tremendous B-52's. We went through the bomber. It amazed us, all the equipment that is in this plane. The plane is so loaded down, if I'm not mistaken it can carry only two bombs. This multimillion-dollar thing. Then we drove up the country of South Dakota. We saw these, they're called silos. They're the missiles, I think they're called. They're out in the middle of wheat fields. Evidently at a moment's notice a button can be pushed and these things will be shot off.

It makes you feel, oh, aren't we lucky to have such an organization as SAC And then you see these young kids, these eighteen-year-olds, and they're responsi-

555

ble for your safety. But they are put through rigid training. So you feel, gee, aren't we lucky? That we have this.

You feel so insignificant when you see this tremendous B-52 plane, with eight engines, four on each wing. And the wingspan of the plane we were under. We went out and saw the launching, and they take off on their practices within fifteen seconds of each other, and if you think that isn't a sight! To see these tremendous big planes come at you. The first plane you can see, the second one, in the fifteen-second time that it takes, is completely blacked out because of this jet take-off from those eight engines. You see it come up out of this black mess, and when the third plane comes up, it is wavering because of the air current. But they all get off and they're gone, but you're so glad that they're for our side.

YOU FEEL SO INSIGNIFICANT, YOU SAID?

Yes, I wonder if we'll ever come to a time that will be like the Dark Ages again . . . it's highly possible. And I don't think I can do one lousy, miserable thing. Look how crazy Hitler was. We could get another man like that. We don't know the Russians. Red China, probably. Or one of those little grubby hungry countries that are playing both sides against the middle: "If you don't do this, we'll go over here."

SO THE INDIVIDUAL FEELS HELPLESS?

I think there are a lot of people in very prominent, important places that can cause an awful lot of trouble for the whole world. I think these Vietnam protesters ought to be taken home and whipped with a strap. (Laughs.) Really I do. I honestly do. These boys are over there for something they believe in, and these smart-aleck upstarts, because we have freedom of speech, are allowed to go and more or less demoralize people that are over there. They're doing our country an awful lot of harm. This gives us a black eye in the eyes of the world.

I think that some people are professional dissenters. They take the opposite point of view whether they believe it or not, just for the sake of argument. There are those who dissent because they are looking for the overthrow of our government. (Almost whispers.) They infiltrate all our organizations, even the PTA.

YOU FEEL THAT?

It's a known fact.

COMMUNISTS, YOU'RE TALKING ABOUT NOW?

Yes, and Birchers. I think Birchers are an obnoxious lot. I came in contact with one on our trip to the West. He cannot come out openly against or for anything, so he's a fence rider, he's not a member. But I tell you he's the biggest John Birch leaner I have ever seen. I think that the John Birch Society flourishes in small communities where people have no outlet. This is a town of only nine hundred people. If someone comes in with any highfalutin ideas and all these people that don't get anywhere . . . every day they're out working in town in the little post offices or courthouses, you know, that probably has four rooms . . . they think this is marvelous. Why, he's right. I think they are easily led because they have not come in contact with the world.

Yes, I'd like to see a peaceful world. I mean, a world without war, the terrors of war and the abject poverty that comes from war. There'd have to be a meeting of the minds. It brings Kennedy to mind: his meeting with Khrushchev, where these two men of two great nations grew to respect each other. They knew they couldn't walk on each other. Do unto others as you would have others do unto you.

Maybe I've grown to appreciate more things. I think we all grow as we grow into more understanding people. You learn to be more tolerant of your fellow man.

Gene Willis, Revisited

Now he is one of the owners of another tavern on the Near North Side; his clientele, the same sort of "swingers" who patronized the place where he had worked as a bartender.

You make your own break the best way you can. If I had to shovel streets for some guy for ten years and finally I can move up and own the sidewalk, I mean that's the break you take. I have many more things I want to do. I hope to get in real estate and buy some more things. But this takes time and I'm just a young guy anyways. Buy a couple of apartment buildings and let 'em pay . . . just like anything else. As soon as I can. It costs me a lot to live. I'm not a millionaire but I'd rather go first class and go out once a week than go out and spend forty cents a night and sit around and worry about having a good time. Find a good-lookin' chick, a few bucks in your pocket, and you can go many ways. I'm a high roller.

A high roller is after I've had a couple of drinks. If I walk into a bar and I see three guys and they're with ten people, I buy everybody a drink. I always leave a deuce or three bucks tip because I been in the business. Always paid my way. That's a high roller. I can't see a guy that worries about a nickle or a dime, because then he's in trouble.

I have a nice apartment that runs into a lotta dough. Very high-rise, seventeenth floor, overlooking the whole thing. My average day? After I kick my girl out . . . I get up at ten o'clock, breakfast, shower, the whole bit. Then we get a golf game going and we play in the afternoon. Then I cry for an hour while I have a drink, while I count all the money I lost. Grab a date about five o'clock for a drink or so. Dinner. Then I go to work. About nine now. I'm through at four. Whatever's happening, of course, you never know what's happening around Near North. You always try to grab something, so you never know what you're doing.

My philosophy is that I have only one life to live, and it's enough the way I'm doing. I don't have room for anything else.

A ginger man, he recounts his early life and some picaresque experiences. Father, a burlesque comic, alcoholic. Mother, several bad-luck marriages. All-state basketball player out East. "We used to get CARE packages from Europe, sort of that kind of family, that's how poor we were." Coast to coast, after the army. Bellhop, fired for 'pushing booze, pushing broads." Bartender at posh joints and those less so; pocket-

557

ing about $125 a week on the side; shilled at a Las Vegas casino; swung all the way on a Diner's card left by some drunk at a bar; running up $600 hotel bill, friend stuck with it, but getting away with "towels, peppermills, dishes, glasses, the whole bit." Arrived in Chicago a year ago.

DO YOU EVER FEEL GUILTY ABOUT THIS STUFF?

About what stuff?

YOU KNOW, WHEN YOU . . .

No, shit, no. I believe the world is based on gettin' a little bit of the pie, everything's hunky-dory. But as soon as you're not gettin' it, the first thing you say is, "Why aren't I in that?" And of course it's not right. But show me a person that's not makin' a few bucks on the side, goddam it. I believe that everybody, if they make a little bit more, get a little greedier, and they want a little bit more. There are a certain amount of straight arrows, they don't know any better. But they got a lotta dough or they don't care. But give like a guy that come up and he's up there by cutting a few fences, he's not gonna stop cuttin' fences. It's too late for him to stop cuttin' fences. When you cut a fence, you have to involve somebody else usually. So everybody's always helping somebody, one way or the other. Most guys I know would do anything for a buck. (Laughs.)

Like Vietnam. People think the reason whoever are gettin' their ass shot off, we love the other guy. I don't know anybody who want to get his ass shot off because he loves somebody else. It's not that way. The pressure is on us from the guy with the big buck. We have a lot of money invested. You have to go that way. With more power, you make more money. The Russians want the same thing. How does it change? Take the guy that sells peanuts. He's trying to make more peanuts, that's all. Or take the guy with more dough that's selling gold bars, it's the same.

Chicago is the only area of a big city that I've ever been, like in the Near North where I know everybody. They're all good people. A lotta bullshit goes on there, but you have to pass on it. I have a brother I brought back with me. He's bartending. He's a nice kid, but he's got so much shit that it's unbelievable. He's just a dreamer. He never had anything, you know. He bought a T-Bird, so he can impress the girls. He tells 'em he owns planes, yachts, and all this sort of stuff. Fantasy. A terrible dreamer. I don't mind it, but when I'm talkin' to a broad, I don't want him to lie.

SUPPOSE ONE OF YOUR BARTENDERS
DID WHAT YOU DID?

Impossible. You don't swing in the area, because you don't work in this area again if you do. The difference is in L.A., you can go anywhere and get a job with no reference. There are thousands of bars in L.A. and it's so spread out. Here a guy who swings wouldn't go anywhere. You can't get away with anything here.

But I don't bother anybody and I don't like anybody to bother me. If I were walkin' down the street and they were robbin' a bank, the guy would walk out and say, "Hi, Gene, how are you?" And if I knew him or didn't know him, I'd say, "Hi, how are you?" And as long as he didn't step on my foot while I was walkin' by the bank, let him do what he wants to do. It's none of my goddam business. I could care less. (Indignantly.) Nothin' bothers me more than people that are tryin' all the time to say, "Oh, did you see what he did over there?" It's none of your business, he's not bothering you. If nobody hurt me, let them do what they want to do. I'm glad they're gettin' away with it. If they can get away with it, all the more power to 'em, that's their business. If I were a police officer, then of course that's my problem. I'm pleasant, get along, courteous.

I'll tell you what I want in life. I'd like to have a nice home in Evanston, on the lake. I'd like to have a ranch in Mexico, where I could retire a couple of months. I'd like to have a girl with a lot of qualities: intelligence, good-looking, which is tough to find, a little common sense, which could be very important. With high ideals, which you don't find around here. Morals. Broads around here, Christ, they screw you one night and they wanna screw someone else the next night, and they could care less. And they lie to you. I got all the broads I can handle now.

I'd like to find somebody that could be a companion. Some girl that you have to bend and sway. The way I am now, I could care less with the girls I meet. I'd like a girl you can discuss things, you can do things together, the important things. Respect and faith. Respect is the most important. You can't do anything in this life without respect for the other person. Once you lose respect for anybody, you can't go anywhere. If I find the right girl, I'll marry her tomorrow.

WHAT KIND OF PEOPLE WOULD YOU
LIKE YOUR KIDS TO BE?

Just like me. I want' em to work like I have. I want 'em to be open-minded like I am. I want them to be respectful and respect myself because I demand respect. If you don't respect me, I don't want you because I don't need you. I want the kids to have a good education which I never got. And I want a very close-knit family, because the close-knit family is the whole thing.

I like people. If you know somebody, you can give him an even break, and if you don't know him, you screw him. When I wake up in the morning, there's only one person thinking about me and that's me. If I were God, I couldn't say anything else that's different, because where else could you go? Everybody's human. You have to change the human being to change the world. The world is beautiful in itself, terrain-wise and etcetera. Everybody has greed, lust, and wants power, so you can't do it differently. As long as there's man, then that's it.

55

Crisis in Black and White

In August 1966, a year after the Watts Riot, a subcommittee of the United States Senate, chaired by Senator Abraham Ribicoff, held hearings on "The Federal Role in Urban Problems." By this time the racial crisis shaking American society was becoming widely recognized. "Urban problems" and "the urban crisis" had become synonyms for the racial crisis. The Ribicoff Committee asked three Negroes to testify about conditions in the ghettoes of New York City. Claude Brown, a young law student, had recently published his sensational autobiography, *Manchild in the Promised Land*. Arthur Dunmeyer was his boyhood friend, who had never escaped the life both had lived as youths; at this time, aged 30, Dunmeyer had spent roughly half of his life in jail. Ralph Ellison, who offered a somewhat different perspective in his testimony, is the author of *The Invisible Man*, one of the finest American novels published since World War II.

RIBICOFF HEARINGS: FEDERAL ROLE IN URBAN PROBLEMS

Ribicoff: How old were you when you had your first child?

Dunmeyer: Fifteen.

Ribicoff: You were 15. And how old was your daughter when she had her first child?

Dunmeyer: Twelve.

Ribicoff: So your first child was born at 15 and your daughter's child was born when she was 12.

Dunmeyer: That is right.

Ribicoff: Is this a common situation where you live?

Dunmeyer: Very much so. As I said before, it is our way of life. We have but so many ways to express ourselves, and when you are a kid you have the expressions that want to come out, and this is the closest thing that you can get as a solvent. You know you have a girl, you have a mother, you have a friend, or you have somebody away from the crowd, and you can express yourself sexually because you do know all of the facts about sex long before society thinks you know or says you know. This is a normal thing.

Brown: I would like to say something here. Our society is always condemning

From the Ribicoff Committee hearings, as reprinted in *The New Leader*, September 26, 1966.

the high rate of illegitimacy in Negro ghettos, and it always seems so ridiculous to me to give any group of people so little means with which to cope with the dictates, the moral dictates of the society and expect them to live up to them. The Negroes' views on sex and the whites' views on sex are so completely diverse that the two will almost never get together. As has been said, never shall the twain meet, because Negroes don't have the money, they don't have the education.

The parents didn't have the education to send children to private schools, to give them the proper supervision. Both parents had to work. When I was say about nine years old, both of my parents had to work to make $50 a week—you know, eight hours a day. This is why at the age of six I was left out on the street to be brought up by the criminal elements, prostitutes, the hustlers, the pimps, the stick-up artists, the dope dealers, the fences and this sort of thing. I had to learn about sex because like—and this was at the age of six—everybody else was doing it, you know. It was the biggest. This was the most we had. We had no money to—well, TVs weren't even out at that time, but many of us couldn't afford radios. We had no money to go to any camps. Our parents weren't interested. They were from the South.

I am telling you, we were the progeny of the Southern generation that had migrated to the North during the 30s, the late 30s, early 40s, during the decade following the Depression. Anyway, it is like these people, they hadn't the slightest awareness of what the urban ghetto was all about, and they were ill-equipped to cope with it. They knew nothing about taking kids to Ys, to day nurseries and camps and this sort of thing, and so we were out on the streets learning about sex at five and six. We knew at five and six that, well, it was a nice thing. It was good. By the time we were 13 we knew it was a great anodyne, you know, before you got to heroin.

Ribicoff: What is the impact on the Negores who come from the South, the rural South, to the slums of New York? What do you find happens to them physically, emotionally, mentally, morally? What do you find happens when they have to make the change? Your parents came and you were born here, or you [Dunmeyer] were just a child in arms, and now you are older than you observe this. What happens?

Brown: Once they get there and become disillusioned, once they can see the streets aren't paved with gold and no great economic opportunities exist for them, they become pressured, you know. Many of the fathers who brought the families, they can't take the pressure any more, the economic pressure. How can you support a family of five kids on $65 a week. So they just leave. A father just ups one day and leaves, maybe becoming an alcoholic. Maybe he just goes out one night because he is so depressed about having missed a day's pay. During the week he was sick. He couldn't help it. And he wasn't in the union. And this depression leads to a sort of touchiness I will say, to become more mundane, so that in a bar a person can step on his foot and he or the person gets his throat cut. Somebody is dead. The other is in jail. He is going to the electric chair. It won't happen in New York today since they have abolished capital punishment. But this was one of the reactions.

Many take out their frustrations on their kids. They beat the hell out of them. My father used to beat me to death nearly everyday. But, still they take it out on their wives. They beat their wives. It is just frustration that they feel.

The wives will say—well, they lose respect for their husbands. The husbands can't really support their families. There are many affairs, you know. Like Mama—I am using the word generally—is screwing the butcher for an extra piece of meat. Pardon the term. Mama is having sexual relationships with the butcher for an extra piece of pork chop for the kids. She wants to see them well fed—this sort of thing.

Or maybe the numbers runner on the corner digs Mama or something. She has got a couple of kids. He can give her $25 a week. The most her husband can make is say $60 a week, and it isn't enough, and the $25 helps because she wants her kids to have the things that TV says they should have.

You know, these are many of the reactions. And then there is the shooting. The guy comes home. He is trying. He is trying. He comes home. He hears about his wife and he goes out one day and picks up a gun. He says, "Oh, Lord, I have tried so hard. It is just not for me. It is my lot to always be a day late and a dollar short. But this guy has been making it with my woman and he has got to die. This is an affront to my masculinity." So he goes out and kills him. Then he is in jail. His family is on welfare or he is in the electric chair. These are emotional and physical reactions.

Dunmeyer: I would like to bring this up also. In some cases this is the way you get your drug dealers and prostitutes and numbers runners. You get people that come here and it is not that they are disillusioned. They see that these things are the only way they can compete in the society, the only way to get some sort of status. The realize that there aren't any real doors open to them, and they can't go back south. There is nothing to go back to. This is understood; this is why they came.

The only thing to do is to get something going to benefit themselves, and in their minds this is not a criminal thing. It is a way to live, a way to have enough to keep your wife from going to bed with the butcher. It is a way to keep from killing the butcher. You kill him in small ways, by taking him off, by holding him up, by seeing that he don't hang out in the neighborhood after the store is closed. It is cheating. It is stealing. These things are just a way of life.

Brown: I would like to make an interjection at this point, just to avoid any misconstruing of what has been said. You know, there are many solid citizens in Harlem, the nice old people who get up and go to church every Sunday and pray for their sons. They hope he won't go out and get caught on none of that old dope. They work hard every day for $50 a week, you know, like for Mrs. Goldberg in the book.

These people believe in the game that has been run down, the con game of American society, equal opportunity and all that, and that everybody is supposed to be a solid citizen, like my friend here. You know, work hard every day. To most of the younger generation all this is a myth. But even to these people, the good solid citizens, the Christians, the church-going people who want to live righteously, something like numbers is an economic institution in Harlem. It is not a crime to them, and they will go to war for it.

You would have a riot if everybody hit the numbers or something and the police came and wanted to make a bust—to arrest the guy who pays off for the numbers. These women who go to church every Sunday, and scrub floors every day during the week, would jump on top of the police. They would have to call out the entire precinct, you know, to calm this thing down. Even with the solid citizens, it is like they know they must have some kind of a dream. The only way they can possibly make it is one day maybe they will hit a number. So, if you take the numbers away from them you take away their dream. They know they are not going to be able to make it off their $50 a week.

Dunmeyer: Our people happen to be the minority, they are in the ghettos, so this is where all the limelight is focused and because of this we are considered people with problems, people who have something wrong with them. But, believe it or not, I would never think of going on the roof and jumping off. I would never think of going on the roof and taking a rifle and shooting five or six people for no reason at all. But I might think of having some children, not thinking of if the woman is married to me or not, because I want to have children, not thinking it is right or wrong. This is because I want to have children, you see. But I would never do a lot of things that I see the accepted standards allow and make excuses for it.

These things never come across my mind. I wouldn't steal just to be stealing. I'd steal for a purpose, if I stole. It means something to me, but perhaps not to you or any other person who is always asking why do we steal, who do we steal. They are not even thinking of what I stole. They are not thinking that I stole an orange because I was hungry, see, whereas another person may steal $10,000 and not be hungry. I might steal just an orange, but I am considered a criminal for two reasons—because I was caught, and because society says to steal is wrong, you see.

As I said before, it is not a matter of race. It is a matter of the upper class and the lower class, those who have and those who haven't got.

Kennedy: If you were in charge of the Establishment, whether it is the economic or the political or whatever it might be, whether it is state, city or Federal, if you had control over that, what would you do in the situation—whether it is Harlem, Bedford Stuyvesant, Watts, or whatever it might be?

Dunmeyer: First of all, I would find the numbers runners in the neighborhood, and all the dope pushers in the neighborhood who are doing this because, like I said, this is a way of life, but who have something more to offer in the way of intelligence. They know how to get around the police. These people I could use to my advantage. They might know how to get around another problem by using the same ideas, and I would use these people. And I wouldn't come out of this neighborhood until these people themselves felt that they were human again, not until I felt it, because unless I was living there, unless I was a part of this thing—you see, I couldn't sit behind a desk and do it. I would have to know what was going on inside and out.

And I would employ each person that I take on in any capacity and use him to the extent of what he can offer himself, not what the books say is right. I couldn't sit down and write any laws, any mandates for anyone to follow. I would have to feel out the block itself. I would have to feel out the people themselves.

You can walk three blocks in any direction in Harlem, or in the Bedford Stuyvesant section, and you will find a whole different world, class of people. For instance, I live in a block where the people are together and they don't even know it themselves. They have this gregarious thing going for them and they don't realize it. In the next block the people all have big fine cars, and they have their own homes, and there is no noise. The police are always walking up and down the streets protecting them. These people don't even know each other. These people don't even know each other and they are the ones who are played up to by the politicians when it is time to vote.

These are the people that are considered people. But the people that really are people are the ones who are suffering together, and they have something already together. Just to suffer makes them together, and this is what you have to look at. You have to go into a neighborhood or a block and look at it for that block, that neighborhood, those people. You can't say, well, all the black people all over the world, all the black people all over the country, all the ghettos are the same. All the ghettos are different. This is a name you put on it.

Ellison: I would like to suggest here that there is a basic difference between what has happened in the South, to the Southern Negro, and what has happened to people living in such slums as Harlem. At Tuskegee, for instance, in Macon County, Alabama, where I attended school, I knew exactly where I could go and where I could not go. The contempt which was held for me by whites was obvious in the most casual interracial contacts.

I got to know Alabama and North Georgia fairly well, because I was playing trumpet in a jazz orchestra. We played in the various country clubs, and for dances for both whites and Negroes, and we got to know the country people, the white people most antagonistic to my race, and there was a certain sense of security about knowing their ways. They were very interested—some of them—in provoking me to violence so that they could destroy me. And my struggle was to keep from being provoked, to keep my eye on my own goals. I was not there to hold a contest of violence with white people. I was there to get an education and go on to the North and become a composer of symphonies.

Now, I think that my experience, the discipline which I acquired, sums up a certain aspect of Southern Negro character. We have been disciplined for over 300 years not to be provoked. We have been disciplined for over 300 years to define the nature of the reality of society and the human predicament for ourselves. We have been disciplined to accept our *own* sense of life regardless of what those antagonistic to us thought about us.

Now, this makes for the most complex personalities among those so disciplined and it makes for a certain split, a certain ambivalence within the Negro American's conception of the United States. But of one thing I am certain: We were hopeful. We made the sacrifices necessary for survival. We tried to educate our children—as we still do—and we lived as we could live and had to live, because we had great hopes and great confidence in the promises of American democracy.

We Negroes have long memories. We know what went on before 1865 and after 1876. And if you think about it, there is hardly a Negro of my generation who can't touch a grandparent or two and be right back in slavery—it has been that recent. So, we have within our very lives and our memories a sense of the reality of slavery and what had been promised by Emancipation. So that by 1954, when the civil rights bills began to be passed, when the law of the land began to change, we were able to transform our old discipline, our fortitude before physical provocation and casual brutalization, into an agency to help ourselves achieve the freedom which was now guaranteed by the law. To walk through hostile groups of people now became a *political* instrumentality, and it has worked. And even little children, little Negro children, have been disciplined to confront the new possibilities unflinchingly. And this courage is not something found overnight, but is part of a heritage of over 300 years.

In the North, Southern tradition breaks down. You get to Harlem. You have expected a great deal of freedom that does not exist. Or when it does exist you haven't been taught how to achieve it. Too often, you don't have the education or experience necessary to go into many of the jobs and places which attract you and which others take for granted, and you find yourself frustrated. Thus when the civil rights laws began to be passed, they did not have the same impact within the Northern slums because we had certain of the rights which were symbols at least of what Southern Negroes had not had.

I think that the shock is apt to be sustained by the second generation of Southern Negroes. At least during the 30s and 40s and 50s this was true. The adult who came usually found some way of bettering himself. Even though he didn't get the good job that he expected, there was a greater freedom of movement about the cities.

With the children of such people, you had a different situation, because they could see what is possible within the big city. They could see the wonderful possibilities offered by the city to define one's own individuality, to amplify one's talent, to find a place for one's self.

But for many, many Negroes, this proved impossible. They came to the North with poor schooling. Very often their parents had no schooling, and thus two strikes were against them. This makes for a great deal of frustration.

Now, on the other hand, these are American children, and Americans are taught to be restless, to be mobile, to be daring. Our myths teach this, our cartoons teach us this, our athletic sports teach us this. The whole society is geared to making the individual restless, to making him test himself against the possibilities around him. He gets this from the motion pictures. He gets it from the television cameras, He gets it from every avenue of life, and Negroes are as much subjected to it as anybody else.

So you see little Negro Batmen flying around Harlem just as you see little white Batmen flying around Sutton Place. It is in the blood. But while the white child who is taken with these fantasies has many opportunities for working them into real

565

life situations, too often the Negro child is unable to so do. This leads the Negro child who identifies with the heroes and outlaws of fantasy to feel frustrated and to feel that society has designated him the outlaw, for he is treated as one. Thus his sense of being outside the law is not simply a matter of fantasy, it is a reality based on the incontrovertible fact of race. This makes for frustration and resentment. And it makes for something else, it makes for a very cynical and sometimes sharp perspective on the difference between our stated ideals and the way in which we actually live. The Negro slum child knows the difference between a dishonest policeman and an honest one because he can go around and see the numbers men paying off the police. He observes what is in the policeman's eyes when he is being ordered around.

56

Vietnam and the American Will to Power

The long and indecisive war in Vietnam provoked larger doubts about the general outlines of American foreign policy of the cold war era. Perhaps the most eloquent and influential critical statement on this issue was the essay "The Responsibility of Intellectuals" written by Noam Chomsky, an outstanding linguist from the Massachusetts Institute of Technology. The advent of the nuclear age had brought many members of the intellectual community into close relationships with political and military decision-makers; the expertise of social as well as physical scientists played an increasing role in the operations of government. This seemed entirely appropriate to those who accepted the premises upon which American foreign policy was based and believed in the essential righteousness of American actions in the world arena. The events of the Kennedy and especially the Johnson years, however, were deeply disillusioning to some who came to share Chomsky's revulsion against American policies in the underdeveloped areas of the world and his distrust of the academic "experts" who devised or at least rationalized those policies.

THE RESPONSIBILITY OF INTELLECTUALS
Noam Chomsky

Twenty years ago, Dwight Macdonald published a series of articles in *Politics* on the responsibilities of peoples, and specifically, the responsibility of intellectuals. I read them as an undergraduate, in the years just after the war, and had occasion to read them again a few months ago. They seem to me to have lost none of their power or persuasiveness. Macdonald is concerned with the question of war guilt. He asks the question: To what extent were the German or Japanese people responsible for the atrocities committed by their governments? And, quite properly, he turns the question back to us: To what extent are the British or American people responsible for the vicious terror bombings of civilians, perfected as a technique of warfare by the Western democracies and reaching their culmination in

Reprinted in abridged form from the *New York Review of Books*, February 23, 1967, with the permission of the author. Copyright © 1967 by Noam Chomsky.

Hiroshima and Nagasaki, surely among the most unspeakable crimes in history? To an undergraduate in 1945–1946—to anyone whose political and moral consciousness had been formed by the horrors of the 1930s, by the war in Ethiopia, the Russian purge, the "China Incident," the Spanish Civil War, the Nazi atrocities, the Western reaction to these events and, in part, complicity in them—these questions had particular significance and poignancy.

With respect to the responsibility of intellectuals, there are still other, equally disturbing questions. Intellectuals are in a position to expose the lies of governments, to analyze actions according to their causes and motives and often hidden intentions. In the Western world, at least, they have the power that comes from political liberty, from access to information and freedom of expression. For a privileged minority. Western democracy provides the leisure, the facilities, and the training to seek the truth lying hidden behind the veil of distortion and misrepresentation, ideology and class interest, through which the events of current history are presented to us. The responsibilities of intellectuals, then, are much deeper than what Macdonald calls the "responsibility of peoples," given the unique privileges that intellectuals enjoy.

The issues that Macdonald raised are as pertinent today as they were twenty years ago. We can hardly avoid asking ourselves to what extent the American people bear responsibility for the savage American assault on a largely helpless rural population in Vietnam, still another atrocity in what Asians see as the "Vasco da Gama era" of world history. As for those of us who stood by in silence and apathy as this catastrophe slowly took shape over the past dozen years, on what page of history do we find our proper place? Only the most insensible can escape these questions. I want to return to them, later on, after a few scattered remarks about the responsibility of intellectuals and how, in practice, they go about meeting this responsibility in the mid-1960s.

It is the responsibility of intellectuals to speak the truth and to expose lies. This, at least, may seem enough of a truism to pass without comment. Not so, however. For the modern intellectual, it is not at all obvious. Thus we have Martin Heidegger writing, in a pro-Hitler declaration of 1933, that "truth is the revelation of that which makes a people certain, clear, and strong in its action and knowledge"; it is only this kind of "truth" that one has a responsibility to speak. Americans tend to be more forthright. When Arthur Schlesinger was asked by the *New York Times*, in November 1965, to explain the contradiction between his published account of the Bay of Pigs incident and the story he had given the press at the time of the attack, he simply remarked that he had lied; and a few days later, he went on to compliment the *Times* for also having suppressed information on the planned invasion, in "the national interest," as this was defined by the group of arrogant and deluded men of whom Schlesinger gives such a flattering portrait in his recent account of the Kennedy administration. It is of no particular interest that one man is quite happy to lie in behalf of a cause which he knows to be unjust; but it is significant that such events provoke so little response in the intellectual community—no feeling, for example, that there is something strange in the offer of a major chair in humanities to a historian who feels it to be his duty to persuade the world that an American-sponsored invasion of a nearby country is nothing of the sort. And what of the incredible sequence of lies on the part of our government and its spokesmen concerning such matters as negotiations in Vietnam? The facts are known to all who care to know. The press, foreign and domestic, has presented documentation to refute each falsehood as it appears. But the power of the government propaganda apparatus is such that the citizen who does not undertake a research project on the subject can hardly hope to confront government pronouncements with fact.

The deceit and distortion surrounding the American invasion of Vietnam is by now so familiar that it has lost its power to shock. It is therefore well to recall that although new levels of cynicism are constantly being reached, their clear antecedents were accepted at home with quiet toleration. It is a useful exercise to compare government statements at the time of the invasion of Guatemala in 1954 with Eisenhower's admission—to be more accurate, his boast—a decade later that American planes were sent "to help the invaders." Nor is it only in moments of crisis that duplicity is considered perfectly in order. "New Frontiersmen," for example, have scarcely distinguished themselves by a passionate concern for historical accuracy, even when they are not being called upon to provide a "propaganda cover" for ongoing actions. For example, Arthur Schlesinger describes the bombing of North Vietnam and the massive escalation of military commitment in early 1965 as based on a "perfectly rational argument": "so long as the Vietcong thought they were going to win the war, they obviously would not be interested in any kind of negotiated settlement." The date is important. Had the statement been made six months earlier, one could attribute it to ignorance. But this statement appeared after months of front-page news reports detailing the UN, North Vietnamese, and Soviet initiatives that preceded the February 1965 escalation and that, in fact, continued for several weeks after the bombing began, after months of soul-searching by Washington correspondents who were trying desperately to find some mitigating circumstances for the startling deception that had been revealed (Chalmers Roberts, for example, wrote with unconscious irony that late February 1965 "hardly seemed to Washington to be a propitious moment for negotiations [since] Mr. Johnson . . . had just ordered the first bombing of North Vietnam in an effort to bring Hanoi to a conference table where bargaining chips on both sides would be more closely matched"). Coming at this moment, Schlesinger's statement is less an example of deceit than of contempt—contempt for an audience that can be expected to tolerate such behavior with silence, if not approval.

To turn to someone closer to the actual formation and implementation of policy, consider some of the reflections of Walt Rostow, a man who, according to Schlesinger, brought a "spacious historical view" to the conduct of foreign affairs in the Kennedy administration. According to his analysis, the guerrilla warfare in Indochina in 1946 was launched by Stalin, and Hanoi initiated the guerrilla war against South Vietnam in 1958. Similarly, the Communist planners probed the "free world spectrum of defense" in Northern Azerbaijan and Greece (where Stalin "supported substantial guerrilla warfare") operating from plans carefully laid in 1945. And in Central Europe, the Soviet Union was not "prepared to accept a solution which would remove the dangerous tensions from Central Europe at the risk of even slowly staged corrosion of communism in East Germany."

It is interesting to compare these observations with studies by scholars actually concerned with historical events. The remark about Stalin's initiating the first Vietnamese war in 1946 does not even merit refutation. As to Hanoi's purported initiative of 1958, the situation is more clouded. But even government sources concede that in 1959 Hanoi received the first direct reports of what Diem referred to as his own Algerian war and that only after this did they lay their plans to involve themselves in this struggle. In fact, in December 1958 Hanoi made another of its many attempts—rebuffed once again by Saigon and the United States—to establish diplomatic and commercial relations with the Saigon government on the basis of the status quo. Rostow offers no evidence of Stalin's support for the Greek guerrillas; in fact, though the historical record is far from clear, it seems that Stalin was by no means pleased with the adventurism of the Greek guerrillas, who, from his point of view, were upsetting the satisfactory postwar imperialist settlement.

Rostow's remarks about Germany are more interesting still. He does not see fit to mention, for example, the Russian notes of March—April 1952, which proposed unification of Germany under internationally supervised elections, with withdrawal of all troops within a year, *if* there was a guarantee that a reunified Germany would not be permitted to join a Western military alliance. And he has also momentarily forgotten his own characterization of the strategy of the Truman and Eisenhower administrations: "to avoid any serious negotiation with the Soviet Union until the West could confront Moscow with German rearmament within an organized European framework, as a *fait accompli*"—to be sure, in defiance of the Potsdam agreements.

But most interesting of all is Rostow's reference to Iran. The facts are that there was a Russian attempt to impose by force a pro-Soviet government in Northern Azerbaijan that would grant the Soviet Union access to Iranian oil. This was rebuffed by superior Anglo-American force in 1946, at which point the more powerful imperialism obtained full rights to Iranian oil for itself, with the installation of a pro-Western government. We recall what happened when, for a brief period in the early 1950s, the only Iranian government with something of a popular base experimented with the curious idea that Iranian oil should belong to the Iranians. What is interesting, however, is the description of Northern Azerbaijan as part of "the free world spectrum of defense." It is pointless, by now, to comment on the debasement of the phrase "free world." But by what law of nature does Iran, with its resources, fall within Western dominion? The bland assumption that it does is most revealing of deep-seated attitudes toward the conduct of foreign affairs.

In addition to this growing lack of concern for truth, we find, in recent statements, a real or feigned naiveté with regard to American actions that reaches startling proportions. For example, Arthur Schlesinger has recently characterized our Vietnamese policies of 1954 as "part of our general program of international goodwill." Unless intended as irony, this remark shows either a colossal cynicism or an inability, on a scale that defies comment, to comprehend elementary phenomena of contemporary history. Similarly, what is one to make of the testimony of Thomas Schelling before the House Foreign Affairs Committee, January 27, 1966, in which he discusses the two great dangers if all Asia "goes Communist"? First, this would exclude "the United States and what we call Western civilization from a large part of the world that is poor and colored and potentially hostile." Second, "a country like the United States probably cannot maintain self-confidence if just about the greatest thing it ever attempted, namely to create the basis for decency and prosperity and democratic government in the underdeveloped world, had to be acknowledged as a failure or as an attempt that we wouldn't try again." It surpasses belief that a person with even minimal acquaintance with the record of American foreign policy could produce such statements.

It surpasses belief, that is, unless we look at the matter from a more historical point of view, and place such statements in the context of the hypocritical moralism of the past; for example, of Woodrow Wilson, who was going to teach the Latin Americans the art of good government, and who wrote (1902) that it is "our peculiar duty" to teach colonial peoples "order and self-control . . . [and] . . . the drill and habit of law and obedience." Or of the missionaries of the 1840's who described the hideous and degrading opium wars as "the result of a great design of Providence to make the wickedness of men subserve his purposes of mercy toward China, in breaking through her wall of exclusion, and bringing the empire into more immediate contact with western and Christian nations." Or, to approach the present, of A. A. Berle, who, in commenting on the Dominican intervention, has the impertinence to attribute the problems of the Caribbean countries to imperialism—*Russian* imperialism.

As a final example of this failure of skepticism, consider the remarks of Henry Kissinger in concluding his presentation in a Harvard-Oxford television debate on American Vietnam policies. He observed, rather sadly, that what disturbs him most is that others question not our judgment but our motives—a remarkable comment on the part of one whose professional concern is political analysis, that is, analysis of the actions of governments in terms of motives that are unexpressed in official propaganda and perhaps only dimly perceived by those whose acts they govern. No one would be disturbed by an analysis of the political behavior of Russians, French, or Tanzanians, questioning their motives and interpreting their actions in terms of long-range interests, perhaps well concealed behind official rhetoric. But it is an article of faith that American motives are pure and not subject to analysis. Although it is nothing new in American intellectual history—or, for that matter, in the general history of imperialist apologia—this innocence becomes increasingly distasteful as the power it serves grows more dominant in world affairs and more capable, therefore, of the unconstrained viciousness that the mass media present to us each day. We are hardly the first power in history to combine material interests, great technological capacity, and an utter disregard for the suffering and misery of the lower orders. The long tradition of naiveté and self-righteousness that disfigures our intellectual history, however, must serve as a warning to the Third World, if such a warning is needed, as to how our protestations of sincerity and benign intent are to be interpreted.

571

The basic assumptions of the "New Frontiersmen" should be pondered carefully by those who look forward to the involvement of academic intellectuals in politics. For example, I have referred to Arthur Schlesinger's objections to the Bay of Pigs invasion, but the reference was imprecise. True, he felt that it was a "terrible idea," but "not because the notion of sponsoring an exile attempt to overthrow Castro seemed intolerable in itself." Such a reaction would be the merest sentimentality, unthinkable to a tough-minded realist. The difficulty, rather, was that it seemed unlikely that the deception could succeed. The operation, in his view, was ill-conceived but not otherwise objectionable. In a similar vein, Schlesinger quotes with approval Kennedy's "realistic" assessment of the situation resulting from Trujillo's assassination: "There are three possibilities in descending order of preference: a decent democratic regime, a continuation of the Trujillo regime or a Castro regime. We ought to aim at the first, but we really can't renounce the second until we are sure that we can avoid the third." The reason why the third possibility is so intolerable is explained a few pages later: "Communist success in Latin America would deal a much harder blow to the power and influence of the United States." Of course, we can never really be sure of avoiding the third possibility; therefore, in practice, we will always settle for the second, as we are now doing in Brazil and Argentina, for example.

Or consider Walt Rostow's views on American policy in Asia. The basis on which we must build this policy is that "we are openly threatened and we feel menaced by Communist China." To prove that we are menaced is of course unnecessary, and the matter receives no attention; it is enough that we feel menaced. Our policy must be based on our national heritage and our national interests. Our national heritage is briefly outlined in the following terms: "Throughout the nineteenth century, in good conscience Americans could devote themselves to the extension of both their principles and their power on this continent," making use of "the somewhat elastic concept of the Monroe doctrine" and, of course, extending "the American interest to Alaska and the mid-Pacific island. . . . Both our insistence on unconditional surrender and the idea of post-war occupation . . . represented the formulation of American security interests in Europe and Asia." So much for our heritage. As to our interests, the matter is equally simple. Fundamental is our "profound interest that societies abroad develop and strengthen those elements in their respective cultures that elevate and protect the dignity of the individual against the state." At the same time, we must counter the "ideological threat," namely "the possibility that the Chinese Communists can prove to Asians by progress in China that Communist methods are better and faster than democratic methods." Nothing is said about those people in Asian cultures to whom our "conception of the proper relation of the individual to the state" may not be the uniquely important value, people who might, for example, be concerned with preserving the "dignity of the individual" against concentrations of foreign or domestic capital, or against semifeudal structures (such as Trujillo-type dictatorships) introduced or kept in power by American arms. All of this is flavored with allusions to "our religious and ethical value systems" and to our "diffuse and complex concepts" which are to the Asian mind "so much more difficult to grasp" than Marxist dogma, and are so "disturbing to some Asians" because of "their very lack of dogmatism."

Such intellectual contributions as these suggest the need for a correction to De Gaulle's remark, in his *Memoirs*, about the American "will to power, cloaking itself in idealism." By now, this will to power is not so much cloaked in idealism as it is drowned in fatuity. And academic intellectuals have made their unique contribution to this sorry picture.

Let us, however, return to the war in Vietnam and the response that it has aroused among American intellectuals. A striking feature of the recent debate on Southeast Asian policy has been the distinction that is commonly drawn between "responsible criticism," on the one hand, and "sentimental," or "emotional," or "hysterical" criticism, on the other. There is much to be learned from a careful study of the terms in which this distinction is drawn. The "hysterical critics" are to be identified, apparently, by their irrational refusal to accept one fundamental political axiom, namely, that the United States has the right to extend its power and control without limit, insofar as is feasible. Responsible criticism does not challenge this assumption, but argues, rather, that we probably can't "get away with it" at this particular time and place.

A distinction of this sort seems to be what Irving Kristol has in mind, for example, in his analysis of the protest over Vietnam policy, in *Encounter,* August 1965. He contrasts the responsible critics, such as Walter Lippmann, the *New York Times*, and Senator Fulbright, with the "teach-in movement." "Unlike the university protesters," he maintains, "Mr. Lippmann engages in no presumptuous suppositions as to 'what the Vietnamese people really want'—he obviously doesn't much care—or in legalistic exegesis as to whether, or to what extent, there is 'aggression' or 'revolution' in South Vietnam. His is a *realpolitik* point of view; and he will apparently even contemplate the possibility of a *nuclear* war against China in extreme circumstances." This is commendable, and contrasts favorably, for Kristol, with the talk of the "unreasonable, ideological types" in the teach-in movement, who often seem to be motivated by such absurdities as "simple, virtuous 'anti-imperialism,'" who deliver "harangues on 'the power structure,'" and who even sometimes stoop so low as to read "articles and reports from the foreign press on the American presence in Vietnam." Furthermore, these nasty types are often psychologists, mathematicians, chemists, or philosophers (just as, incidentally, those most vocal in protest in the Soviet Union are generally physicists, literary intellectuals, and others remote from the exercise of power), rather than people with Washington contacts, who, of course, realize that "had they a new, good idea about Vietnam, they would get a prompt and respectful hearing" in Washington.

I am not interested here in whether Kristol's characterization of protest and dissent is accurate, but rather in the assumptions that it expresses with respect to such questions as these: Is the purity of American motives a matter that is beyond discussion, or that is irrelevant to discussion? Should decisions be left to "experts" with Washington contacts—that is, even if we assume that they command the necessary knowledge and principles to make the "best" decision, will they invariably do so? And, a logically prior question, is "expertise" applicable—that is, is there a body of theory and of relevant information, not in the public domain, that can be applied to the analysis of foreign policy or that demonstrates the correctness of present actions in some way that the psychologists, mathematicians, chemists, and philosophers are incapable of comprehending? Although Kristol does not examine these questions directly, his attitudes presuppose answers, answers which are wrong in all cases. American aggressiveness, however it may be masked in pious rhetoric, is a dominant force in world affairs and must be analyzed in terms of its causes and motives. There is no body of theory or significant body of relevant information, beyond the comprehension of the layman, which makes policy immune from criticism. To the extent that "expert knowledge" is applied to world affairs, it is surely appropriate—for a person of any integrity, quite necessary—to question its quality and the goals that it serves. These facts seem too obvious to require extended discussion.

A corrective to Kristol's curious belief in the administration's openness to new thinking about Vietnam is provided by McGeorge Bundy in a recent article. As Bundy correctly observes, "on the main stage . . . the argument on Viet Nam turns on tactics, not fundamentals," although, he adds, "there are wild men in the wings." On stage center are, of course, the President (who in his recent trip to Asia had just "magisterially reaffirmed" our interest "in the progress of the people across the Pacific") and his advisers, who deserve "the understanding support of those who want restraint." It is these men who deserve the credit for the fact that "the bombing of the North has been the most accurate and the most restrained in modern warfare"—a solicitude which will be appreciated by the inhabitants, or former inhabitants, of Nam Dinh and Phu Ly and Vinh. It is these men, too, who deserve the credit for what was reported by Malcolm Browne as long ago as May 1965: "In the South, huge sectors of the nation have been declared 'free bombing zones,' in which anything that moves is a legitimate target. Tens of thousands of tons of bombs, rockets, napalm and cannon fire are poured into these vast areas each week. If only by the laws of chance, bloodshed is believed to be heavy in these raids."

Fortunately for the developing countries, Bundy assures us, "American democracy has no enduring taste for imperialism," and "taken as a whole, the stock of American experience, understanding, sympathy and simple knowledge is now much the most impressive in the world." It is true that "four-fifths of all the foreign investing in the world is now done by Americans" and that "the most admired plans and policies . . . are no better than their demonstrable relation to the American interest"—just as it is true, so we read in the same issue of *Foreign Affairs*, that the plans for armed action against Cuba were put into motion a few weeks after Mikoyan visited Havana, "invading what had so long been an almost exclusively American sphere of influence." Unfortunately, such facts as these are often taken by unsophisticated Asian intellectuals as indicating a "taste for imperialism." For example, a number of Indians have expressed their "near exasperation" at the fact that "we have done everything we can to attract foreign capital for fertilizer plants, but the American and the other Western private companies know we are over a barrel, so they demand stringent terms which we just cannot meet," while "Washington . . . doggedly insists that deals be made in the private sector with private enterprise." But this reaction, no doubt, simply reveals once again how the Asian mind fails to comprehend the "diffuse and complex concepts" of Western thought.

It may be useful to study carefully the "new, good ideas about Vietnam" that are receiving a "prompt and respectful hearing" in Washington these days. The United States Government Printing Office is an endless source of insight into the moral and intellectual level of this expert advice. In its publications one can read, for example, the testimony of Professor David N. Rowe, Director of Graduate Studies in International Relations at Yale University, before the House Committee on Foreign Affairs. Professor Rowe proposes that the United States buy all surplus Canadian and Australian wheat, so that there will be mass starvation in China. These are his words: "Mind you, I am not talking about this as a weapon against the Chinese people. It will be. But that is only incidental. The weapon will be a weapon against the Government because the internal stability of that country cannot be sustained by an unfriendly Government in the face of general starvation." Professor Rowe will have none of the sentimental moralism that might lead one to compare this suggestion with, say, the *Ostpolitik* of Hitler's Germany. Nor does he fear the impact of such policies on other Asian nations, for example Japan. He assures us, from his "very long acquaintance with Japanese questions," that "the Japanese above all are people who respect power and determination." Hence "they will not be so much alarmed by American policy in Vietnam that takes off from a position of power and intends to seek a solution based upon the imposition of our power upon local people that we are in opposition to." What would disturb the Japanese is "a policy of indecision, a policy of refusal to face up to the problems [in China and Vietnam] and to meet our responsibilities there in a positive way," such as the way just cited. A conviction that we were "unwilling to use the power that they know we have" might "alarm the Japanese people very intensely and shake the degree of their friendly relations with us." In fact, a full use of American power would be particularly reassuring to the Japanese, because they have had a demonstration "of the tremendous power in action of the United States . . . because they have felt our power directly." This is surely a prime example of the healthy "*realpolitik* point of view" that Irving Kristol so much admires.

Having settled the issue of the political irrelevance of the protest movement, Kristol turns to the question of what motivates it—more generally, what has made students and junior faculty "go left," as he sees it, amid general prosperity and under liberal, Welfare State administrations. This, he notes, "is a riddle to which no sociologist has as yet come up with an answer." Since these young people are well-off, have good futures, etc., their protest must be irrational. It must be the result of boredom, of too much security, or something of this sort.

Other possibilities come to mind. It might be, for example, that as honest men the students and junior faculty are attempting to find out the truth for themselves rather than ceding the responsibility to "experts" or to government; and it might be that they react with indignation to what they discover. These possibilities Kristol does not reject. They are simply unthinkable, unworthy of consideration. More

575

accurately, these possibilities are inexpressible; the categories in which they are formulated (honesty, indignation) simply do not exist for the tough-minded social scientist.

In this implicit disparagement of traditional intellectual values, Kristol reflects attitudes that are fairly widespread in academic circles. I do not doubt that these attitudes are in part a consequence of the desperate attempt of the social and behavioral sciences to imitate the surface features of sciences that really have significant intellectual content. But they have other sources as well. Anyone can be a moral individual, concerned with human rights and problems; but only a college professor, a trained expert, can solve technical problems by "sophisticated" methods. Ergo, it is only problems of the latter sort that are important or real. Responsible, nonideological experts will give advice on tactical questions; irresponsible "ideological types" will "harangue" about principle and trouble themselves over moral issues and human rights, or over the traditional problems of man and society, concerning which "social and behavioral science" have nothing to offer beyond trivialities. Obviously, these emotional, ideological types are irrational, since, being well-off and having power in their grasp, they shouldn't worry about such matters.

When we consider the responsibility of intellectuals, our basic concern must be their role in the creation and analysis of ideology. And, in fact, Kristol's contrast between the unreasonable ideological types and the responsible experts is formulated in terms that immediately bring to mind Daniel Bell's interesting and influential essay on the "end of ideology," an essay which is as important for what it leaves unsaid as for its actual content. Bell presents and discusses the Marxist analysis of ideology as a mask for class interest, in particular, quoting Marx's well-known description of the belief of the bourgeoisie "that the *special* conditions of its emancipation are the *general* conditions through which alone modern society can be saved and the class struggle avoided." He then argues that the age of ideology is ended, supplanted, at least in the West, by a general agreement that each issue must be settled on its own individual terms, within the framework of a welfare state in which, presumably, experts in the conduct of public affairs will have a prominent role. Bell is quite careful, however, to characterize the precise sense of "ideology" in which "ideologies are exhausted." He is referring only to ideology as "the conversion of ideas into social levers," to ideology as "a set of beliefs, infused with passion, . . . [which] . . . seeks to transform the whole of a way of life." The crucial words are "transform" and "convert into social levers." Intellectuals in the West, he argues, have lost interest in converting ideas into social levers for the radical transformation of society. Now that we have achieved the pluralistic society of the Welfare State, they see no further need for a radical transformation of society; we may tinker with our way of life here and there, but it would be wrong to try to modify it in any significant way. With this consensus of intellectuals, ideology is dead.

There are several striking facts about Bell's essay. First, he does not point out the extent to which this consensus of the intellectuals is self-serving. He does not relate his observation that, by and large, intellectuals have lost interest in "transforming the whole of a way of life" to the fact that they play an increasingly prominent role in running the Welfare State; he does not relate their general satisfaction with the Welfare State to the fact that, as he observes elsewhere, "America has become an affluent society, offering place . . . and prestige . . . to the onetime radicals." Secondly, he offers no serious argument to show that intellectuals are somehow "right" or "objectively justified" in reaching the consensus to which he alludes, with its rejection of the notion that society should be transformed. Indeed, although Bell is fairly sharp about the empty rhetoric of the "New Left," he seems to have a quite utopian faith that technical experts will be able to come to grips with the few problems that still remain; for example, the fact that labor is treated as a commodity, and the problems of "alienation."

It seems fairly obvious that the classical problems are very much with us; one might plausibly argue that they have even been enhanced in severity and scale. For example, the classical paradox of poverty in the midst of plenty is now an ever increasing problem on an international scale. Whereas one might conceive, at least in principle, of a solution within national boundaries, a sensible idea as to how to transform international society in such a way as to cope with the vast and perhaps increasing human misery is hardly likely to develop within the framework of the intellectual consensus that Bell describes.

A good case can be made for the conclusion that there is indeed something of a consensus among intellectuals who have already achieved power and affluence, or who sense that they can achieve them by "accepting society" as it is and promoting the values that are "being honored" in this society. And it is also true that this consensus is most noticeable among the scholar-experts who are replacing the free-floating intellectuals of the past. In the university, these scholar-experts construct a "value-free technology" for the solution of technical problems that arise in contemporary society, taking a "responsible stance" towards these problems, in the sense noted earlier. This consensus among the responsible scholar-experts is the domestic analogue to that proposed, in the international arena, by those who justify the application of American power in Asia, whatever the human cost, on the grounds that it is necessary to contain the "expansion of China" (an "expansion" which is, to be sure, hypothetical for the time being)—to translate from State Department Newspeak, on the grounds that it is essential to reverse the Asian nationalist revolutions, or at least to prevent them from spreading. The analogy becomes clear when we look carefully at the ways in which this proposal is formulated. With his usual lucidity, Churchill outlined the general position in a remark to his colleague of the moment, Joseph Stalin, at Teheran in 1943: ". . . the government of the world must be entrusted to satisfied nations, who wished nothing more for themselves than what they had. If the world-government were in the hand of hungry nations, there would always be danger. But none of us had any reason to seek for anything more. The peace would be kept by peoples who lived in their own way and were not ambitious. Our power placed us above the rest. We were like rich men dwelling at peace within their habitations."

For a translation of Churchill's biblical rhetoric into the jargon of contemporary social science, one may turn to the testimony of Charles Wolf, Senior Economist of the RAND Corporation, at the congressional committee hearings cited earlier:

> I am dubious that China's fears of encirclement are going to be abated, eased, relaxed in the long-term future. But I would hope that what we do in Southeast Asia would help to develop within the Chinese body politic more of a realism and willingness to live with this fear than to indulge it by support for liberation movements, which admittedly depend on a great deal more than external support . . . the operational question for American foreign-policy is not whether that fear can be eliminated or substantially alleviated, but whether China can be faced with a structure of incentives, of penalties and rewards, of inducements that will make it willing to live with this fear.

In short, we are prepared to live peaceably within our—to be sure, rather extensive—habitations. And quite naturally, we are offended by the undignified noises from the servants' quarters. If, let us say, a peasant-based revolutionary movement tries to achieve independence from foreign domination or to overthrow semifeudal structures supported by foreign powers, or if the Chinese irrationally refuse to respond properly to the schedule of reinforcement that we have prepared for them, if they object to being encircled by the benign and peace-loving "rich men" who control the territories on their borders as a natural right, then, evidently, we must respond to this belligerence with appropriate force.

It is this mentality that explains the frankness with which the United States government and its academic apologists defend the American refusal to permit a political settlement in Vietnam at a local level, a settlement based on the actual distribution of political forces. Even government experts freely admit that the NLF is the only "truly mass-based political party in South Vietnam"; that the NLF had "made a conscious and massive effort to extend political participation, even if it was manipulated, on the local level so as to involve the people in a self-contained, self-supporting revolution"; and that this effort had been so successful that no political groups, "with the possible exception of the Buddhists, thought themselves equal in size and power to risk entering into a coalition, fearing that if they did the whale would swallow the minnow." Moreover, they concede that until the introduction of overwhelming American force, the NLF had insisted that the struggle "should be fought out at the political level and that the use of massed military might was in itself illegitimate. . . . The battleground was to be the minds and loyalties of the rural Vietnamese, the weapons were to be ideas"; and correspondingly, that until mid-1964, aid from Hanoi "was largely confined to two areas—doctrinal know-how and leadership personnel." Captured NLF documents contrast the enemy's "military superiority" with their own "political superiority," thus fully confirming the analysis of American military spokesmen who define our problem as how, "with considerable armed force but little political power, [to] contain an adversary who has enormous political force but only modest military power."

Similarly, the most striking outcome of both the Honolulu conference in February and the Manila conference in October was the frank admission by high officials of the Saigon government that "they could not survive a 'peaceful settlement' that left the Vietcong *political* structure in place even if the Vietcong guerilla units were disbanded," that "they are not able to compete *politically* with the Vietnamese Communists." Officials in Washington understand the situation very well. Thus Secretary Rusk has pointed out that "if the Vietcong come to the conference table as full partners they will, in a sense, have been victorious in the very aims that South Vietnam and the United States are pledged to prevent" (January 28, 1966). Similarly, Max Frankel reported from Washington: "Compromise has had no appeal here because the Administration concluded long ago that the non-Communist forces of South Vietnam could not long survive in a Saigon coalition with Communists. It is for that reason—and not because of an excessively rigid sense of protocol—that Washington has steadfastly refused to deal with the Vietcong or recognize them as an independent political force."

In short, we will—magnanimously—permit Vietcong representatives to attend negotiations only if they will agree to identify themselves as agents of a foreign power and thus forfeit the right to participate in a coalition government, a right which they have now been demanding for a half-dozen years. We know well that in any representative coalition, our chosen delegates could not last a day without the support of American arms. Therefore, we must increase American force and resist meaningful negotiations, until the day when a client government can exert both military and political control over its own population—a day which may never dawn, for as William Bundy has pointed out, we could never be sure of the security of a Southeast Asia "from which the Western presence was effectively withdrawn." Thus if we were to "negotiate in the direction of solutions that are put under the label of neutralization," this would amount to capitulation to the Communists. According to this reasoning, then, South Vietnam must remain, permanently, an American military base.

All of this is of course reasonable, so long as we accept the fundamental political axiom that the United States, with its traditional concern for the rights of the weak and downtrodden, and with its unique insight into the proper mode of development for backward countries, must have the courage and the persistence to impose its will by force until such time as other nations are prepared to accept these truths—or simply to abandon hope.

If it is the responsibility of the intellectual to insist upon the truth, it is also his duty to see events in their historical perspective. Thus one must applaud the insistence of the Secretary of State on the importance of historical analogies, the Munich analogy, for example. As Munich showed, a powerful and aggressive nation with a fanatic belief in its manifest destiny will regard each victory, each extension of its power and authority, as a prelude to the next step. The matter was very well put by Adlai Stevenson, when he spoke of "the old, old route whereby expansive powers push at more and more doors, believing they will open, until, at the ultimate door, resistance is unavoidable and major war breaks out." Herein lies the danger of appeasement, as the Chinese tirelessly point out to the Soviet Union, which they claim is playing Chamberlain to our Hitler in Vietnam. Of course, the aggressiveness of liberal imperialism is not that of Nazi Germany, though the distinction may seem rather academic to a Vietnamese peasant who is being gassed or incinerated. We do not want to occupy Asia; we merely wish, to return to Mr. Wolf, "to help the Asian countries progress toward economic modernization, as relatively 'open' and stable societies, to which our access, as a country and as individual citizens, is free and comfortable." The formulation is appropriate. Recent history shows that it makes little difference to us what form of government a country has as long as it remains an "open society," in our peculiar sense of this term—a society, that is, that remains open to American economic penetration or political control. If it is necessary to approach genocide in Vietnam to achieve this objective, then this is the price we must pay in defense of freedom and the rights of man.

Quite often, the statements of sincere and devoted technical experts give surprising insight into the intellectual attitudes that lie in the background of the latest savagery. Consider, for example, the following comment by economist Richard Lindholm, in 1959, expressing his frustration over the failure of economic development in "free Vietnam": "the use of American aid is determined by how the Vietnamese use their incomes and their savings. The fact that a large portion of the Vietnamese imports financed with American aid are either consumer goods or raw materials used rather directly to meet consumer demands is an indication that the Vietnamese people desire these goods, for they have shown their desire by their willingness to use their piasters to purchase them."

In short, the Vietnamese *people* desire Buicks and air conditioners, rather than sugar-refining equipment or road-building machinery, as they have shown by their behavior in a free market. And however much we may deplore their free choice, we must allow the people to have their way. Of course, there are also those two-legged beasts of burden that one stumbles on in the countryside, but as any graduate student of political science can explain, they are not part of a responsible modernizing elite, and therefore have only a superficial biological resemblance to the human race.

In no small measure, it is attitudes like this that lie behind the butchery in Vietnam, and we had better face up to them with candor, or we will find our government leading us towards a "final solution" in Vietnam, and in the many Vietnams that inevitably lie ahead.

Let me finally return to Macdonald and the responsibility of intellectuals. Macdonald quotes an interview with a death-camp paymaster who bursts into tears when told that the Russians would hang him. "Why should they? What have I done?" he asked. Macdonald concludes: "Only those who are willing to resist authority themselves when it conflicts too intolerably with their personal moral code, only they have the right to condemn the death-camp paymaster." The question "What have I done?" is one that we may well ask ourselves, as we read, each day, of fresh atrocities in Vietnam—as we create, or mouth, or tolerate the deceptions that will be used to justify the next defense of freedom.

Index of Documents